THE ROUTLEDGE HISTORY HANDBOOK OF CENTRAL AND EASTERN EUROPE IN THE TWENTIETH CENTURY

Violence analyzes both the violence exerted on the societies of Central and Eastern Europe during the twentieth century by belligerent powers and authoritarian and/or totalitarian regimes and armed conflicts between ethnic, social and national groups, as well as the interaction between these two phenomena.

Throughout the twentieth century, Central and Eastern Europe was hit particularly hard by war, violence and repression, with armed conflicts in the Balkans at the start and end of the period and two world wars in between. In the shadow of these full-scale wars, ethnic, social and national conflicts were intensified, found new forms and were violently played out. The interwar period witnessed the emergence of authoritarian states who enforced their claim to power through continued violence against political opponents, stigmatized ethnic, national and social groups, and were themselves fought with subversive or terrorist techniques. This volume focuses specifically on physical violence: war and civil war, ethnic cleansing, systematic starvation policies, deportations and expulsions, forced labour and prison camps, persecution by state security – such as intensive surveillance, which had an enormous impact on the lives of those it affected – and other forms of government oppression and militant resistance. Geographically, it considers the western regions of Belarus and Ukraine as sites of extreme violence that had a noticeable impact on neighbouring Central and Eastern European countries as well.

The concluding volume in a four-volume set on Central and Eastern Europe in the twentieth century, it is the go-to resource for those interested in violence in this complex region.

Jochen Böhler is acting Chair of Eastern European History at the University of Jena, Germany.

Włodzimierz Borodziej was Professor of History at Warsaw University, Poland.

Joachim von Puttkamer is Professor of Eastern European History at Jena University, Germany and Co-Director of the Imre Kertész Kolleg.

The Imre Kertész Kolleg at the Friedrich Schiller University in Jena is an institute for the advanced study of the history of Eastern Europe in the twentieth century.

The Kolleg was founded in October 2010 as the ninth Käte Hamburger Kolleg of the German Federal Ministry for Education and Research (BMBF). The directors of the Kolleg are Professor Joachim von Puttkamer and Dr Michal Kopeček. Professor Włodzimierz Borodziej was the Kolleg's co-director from 2010 to 2016 and was chairman of its advisory board until 2021.

SPONSORED BY THE

THE ROUTLEDGE TWENTIETH CENTURY HISTORY HANDBOOKS

The Routledge History Handbook of Central and Eastern Europe in the Twentieth Century
Volume 1: Challenges of Modernity
Edited by Włodzimierz Borodziej, Stanislav Holubec and Joachim von Puttkamer

The Routledge History Handbook of Central and Eastern Europe in the Twentieth Century
Volume 2: Statehood
Edited by Włodzimierz Borodziej, Sabina Ferhadbegović and Joachim von Puttkamer

The Routledge History Handbook of Central and Eastern Europe in the Twentieth Century
Volume 3: Intellectual Horizons
Edited by Włodzimierz Borodziej, Ferenc Laczó and Joachim von Puttkamer

The Routledge History Handbook of Central and Eastern Europe in the Twentieth Century
Volume 4: Violence
Edited by Jochen Böhler, Włodzimierz Borodziej and Joachim von Puttkamer

For more information about this series, please visit: https://www.routledge.com/The-Routledge-Twentieth-Century-History-Handbooks/book-series/RHHC20.

THE ROUTLEDGE HISTORY HANDBOOK OF CENTRAL AND EASTERN EUROPE IN THE TWENTIETH CENTURY

Volume 4: Violence

Edited by
Jochen Böhler, Włodzimierz Borodziej
and Joachim von Puttkamer

LONDON AND NEW YORK

First published 2022
by Routledge
2 Park Square, Milton Park, Abingdon, Oxon OX14 4RN

and by Routledge
605 Third Avenue, New York, NY 10158

Routledge is an imprint of the Taylor & Francis Group, an informa business

© 2022 selection and editorial matter, Jochen Böhler, Włodzimierz Borodziej and Joachim von Puttkamer; individual chapters, the contributors

The right of Jochen Böhler, Włodzimierz Borodziej and Joachim von Puttkamer to be identified as the authors of the editorial material, and of the authors for their individual chapters, has been asserted in accordance with sections 77 and 78 of the Copyright, Designs and Patents Act 1988.

All rights reserved. No part of this book may be reprinted or reproduced or utilised in any form or by any electronic, mechanical, or other means, now known or hereafter invented, including photocopying and recording, or in any information storage or retrieval system, without permission in writing from the publishers.

Trademark notice: Product or corporate names may be trademarks or registered trademarks, and are used only for identification and explanation without intent to infringe.

Cover image: November 1918: Soldiers and citizens of Lviv on the main square, courtesy National Digital Archive, Poland

British Library Cataloguing-in-Publication Data
A catalogue record for this book is available from the British Library

Library of Congress Cataloging-in-Publication Data
Names: Borodziej, Włodzimierz, editor. | Ferhadbegović, Sabina, editor. | Puttkamer, Joachim von, editor.
Title: The Routledge history handbook of Central and Eastern Europe in the twentieth century / edited by Włodzimierz Borodziej, Sabina Ferhadbegović and Joachim von Puttkamer.
Other titles: Central and Eastern Europe in the twentieth century
Description: New York : Routledge, 2019- | Series: Routledge twentieth century history handbooks | Volume 1 title information from publisher's website. | Includes bibliographical references and index. | Contents: [Volume 1. The Challenges of Modernity] -- Volume 2. Statehood --
Identifiers: LCCN 2019049033 (print) | LCCN 2019049034 (ebook) | ISBN 9781138301665 (hardback) | ISBN 9780367822118 (ebook)
Subjects: LCSH: Europe, Central--Politics and government--1989- | Europe, Eastern--Politics and government--1989- | Post-communism--Europe, Central--History--20th century. | Post-communism--Europe, Eastern--History--20th century.
Classification: LCC DAW1051 .R68 2019 (print) | LCC DAW1051 (ebook) | DDC 943.009/04--dc23
LC record available at https://lccn.loc.gov/2019049033
LC ebook record available at https://lccn.loc.gov/2019049034

ISBN: 978-1-138-30167-2 (hbk)
ISBN: 978-0-367-51864-6 (pbk)
ISBN: 978-1-003-05551-8 (ebk)

DOI: 10.4324/9781003055518

Typeset in Bembo
by SPi Technologies India Pvt Ltd (Straive)

CONTENTS

Series introduction	vi
Włodzimierz Borodziej and Joachim von Puttkamer	
Acknowledgements	viii
List of maps	ix
List of abbreviations	x
List of contributors	xiii
Volume introduction: violence	xv
Jochen Böhler, Włodzimierz Borodziej and Joachim von Puttkamer	

1	The Balkan Wars: patterns of violence in the Balkans leading up to the First World War Mark Biondich	1
2	The war in the East, 1914–16 Włodzimierz Borodziej	30
3	The radicalization of violence and Intermarium's interwar Jochen Böhler	70
4	Mass violence and its immediate aftermath in Central and Eastern Europe during the Second World War, 1939–47 Alexander Korb and Dieter Pohl	122
5	State socialism: violence, oppression and surveillance Włodzimierz Borodziej and Dragoș Petrescu	194
6	The violent dissolution of Yugoslavia, 1989–2001 Mark Biondich	280
Index		320

SERIES INTRODUCTION

Włodzimierz Borodziej and Joachim von Puttkamer

What were the central twentieth-century experiences for Eastern European societies? Depending on whom you ask and depending on which country their thoughts intuitively drift towards, the answer is likely to be quite different. The answer could refer to significant dates, such as the 1939 Molotov-Ribbentrop Pact, the 1956 Hungarian uprising, the Prague Spring of 1968 or the year of Solidarity in 1980–81. It could also revolve around the experiences in various countries – the Stalinist deportations left deep scars in the Baltic states, as did the wars of the 1990s in former Yugoslavia. The thoughts of a Western European are likely to jump to 1989 and the collapse of communist rule – perhaps also to the disappointed (or at least unlikely) prospects of a unified Europe. Hopefully, he or she might learn something from this volume.

As that Western European will discover, there were particular as well as shared experiences. The volumes presented here focus on both, grouped around what the editors regard as central, overarching themes. To emphasize the experience of *Violence* (vol. 4) is just as obvious as prioritizing the manifold *Challenges of Modernity* (vol. 1) of a region that has often been described – and perceived by its own inhabitants – as the periphery of Europe. The need to address the transformation of *Statehood* (vol. 2) over the course of the century may initially seem less apparent, but it allows for an elucidation of profound changes and phenomena that are otherwise obscured in a discussion of the emergence and emancipation of modern nation-states. *Intellectual Horizons* (vol. 3) reflects the wealth of self-descriptions and self-localizations in and about the region.

What do these volumes offer the reader? Not an encyclopaedia of Central, Eastern and Southeastern Europe in the long twentieth century, but a series of essays written from different perspectives and life experiences. The authors live in Bulgaria, Germany, Canada, Austria, Poland, Romania, Serbia, Czechia, Hungary and the United States. They belong to different generations and milieus and often have vastly different conceptions of historiography and the writing of history. Therein lies – according to the editors – the appeal of these volumes.

The shared goal of these contributions is to tell the story of *the suburbs of Europe* in the twentieth century; to tell how the story unfolded, how it was perceived within this region and how it can be interpreted today.

Series introduction

The authors were not given any methodological parameters to follow. Some contributions may seem conservative or even old-fashioned; others argue in the spirit of what, in many universities today, is considered mainstream. None of the authors, however, crosses the boundary beyond which they see traditional sources as nothing more than merely conceptual obstacles. If the present volumes provide a new impetus for a collective reflection on Eastern Europe, both in teaching and in research, then much will have been gained.

ACKNOWLEDGEMENTS

A comprehensive volume such as this one is always a highly collaborative undertaking. The editors wish to thank Thomas Lampert, who translated the chapter on the First World War into English, and Peter Palm, who provided the much-needed maps. Special regards go to Daniela Gruber and Dr Raphael Utz, who once again helped to get the project over all the administrative hurdles. Tila de Almeida Mendonça, Anna Bundt, Barborá Fischerova and Laird McNeal provided the geographical index. Zoe Thomson from Routledge has guided us through the publication process of all four volumes of our four-volume series. We are particularly grateful for the funding that we received from the German Federal Ministry of Education and Research to establish the Imre Kertész Kolleg, without which this volume and the entire series would have been unthinkable. Finally, special thanks go once again to Jaime Elizabeth Hyatt, our experienced language editor, for all her diligence and patience with the authors and editors alike.

Although he was part of the editing process through the completion of the manuscript, Włodzimierz Borodziej sadly passed away in July 2021 before this volume reached its final phase of publication. He considered the entire four-volume series to be his intellectual legacy; this volume, to which he contributed two major chapters, was particularly close to his heart.

MAPS

Map 1.1	The Balkans after the Second Balkan War	19
Map 2.1	The Eastern Front, 1914–18	40
Map 3.1	Central and Eastern Europe, 1918–1939	105
Map 4.1	Central and Eastern Europe, 1941–42	124
Map 4.2	Southeastern Europe, 1941	125
Map 5.1	Eastern Europe, 1945–89	257
Map 6.1	Yugoslavia, 1989–2001	291

ABBREVIATIONS

ABiH – Armija Republike Bosne i Hercegovine/Army of the Republic of Bosnia and Herzegovina
BANU – Bǎlgarski Zemedelski Naroden Sǎjuz/Bulgarian Agrarian National Union
BCP – Balgarska Komunisticheska Partiya/Bulgarian Communist Party
BStU – Bundesbeauftragter für die Stasi-Unterlagen/Federal Commissioner for the Stasi Files
BTI – Bertelsmann Stiftung's international Transformation Index
CC – Central Committee
CEE – Central and Eastern Europe
CIA – Central Intelligence Committee
Cominform – Communist Information Bureau
Comintern – Communist International
CPCz – Komunistická strana Československa/Communist Party of Czechoslovakia
CPSU – Kommunisticheskaya partiya Sovetskogo Soyuza/Communist Party of the Soviet Union
CSSR – Československá socialistická republika/Czechoslovak Socialist Republic
CUP – İttihad ve Terakki Cemiyeti/Committee of Union and Progress
DS – Darzhavna Sigurnost/State Security of Bulgaria
EAM – Ethnikó Apeleftherotikó Métopo/National Liberation Front
EC – European Community
EDES – Ethnikós Dimokratikós Ellinikós Sýndesmos/National Republican Greek League
ELAS – Ellinikós Laikós Apelevtherotikós Stratós/Greek People's Liberation Army
EU – European Union
GDR – German Democratic Republic
GUPVI – Glavnoye upravleniye po delam voyennoplennykh i internirovannykh/Main Administration for Affairs of Prisoners of War and Internees
HDZ – Hrvatska demokratska zajednica/Croatian Democratic Union
HDZ BiH – Hrvatska demokratska zajednica Bosne i Hercegovine/Croatian Democratic Union of Bosnia-Herzegovina
HVO – Hrvatsko vijeće obrane/Croatian Defence Council
ICTY – International Criminal Tribunal for the former Yugoslavia

List of abbreviations

IDC – Istraživačko dokumentacioni centar Sarajevo/Research and Documentation Centre Sarajevo
IFOR – Implementation Force
IMRO – Vnatrešna Makedonska Revolucionerna Organizacija/Internal Macedonian Revolutionary Organization
IRMCT – International Residual Mechanism for Criminal Tribunals
JNA – Jugoslovenska narodna armija/Yugoslav People's Army
JSO – Jedinica za specijalne operacije/Special Operations Unit of the Serbian State Security Service
KDS – Komitet za durzhavno sigurnost/Committee for State Security
KGB – Komitet Gosudarstvennoy Bezopasnosti/Committee for State Security
KLA – Ushtria Çlirimtare e Kosovës (UCK)/Kosovo Liberation Army
KOR – Komitet Obrony Robotników/Workers' Defence Committee
KOS – Kontraobavještajna služba/Counterintelligence Service of the JNA
KPD – Kommunistische Partei Deutschlands/Communist Party of Germany
LAF – Lietuvių Aktyvistų Frontas/Lithuanian Activist Front
LCC – Savez komunista Hrvatske/League of Communists of Croatia
LCY – Savez komunista Jugoslavije/League of Communists of Yugoslavia
LDK – Lidhja Demokratike e Kosovës/Democratic League of Kosovo
MAVC – Makedono-odrinsko opalchenie/Macedonian Adrianople Volunteer Corps
MBP – Ministerstwo Bezpieczeństwa Publicznego/Ministry of Public Security
MGB – Ministerstvo Gosudarstvennoy Bezopasnosti SSSR/Ministry of State Security
MKS – Międzyzakładowy Komitet Strajkowy/Inter-Factory Strike Committee
MNB – Ministerstvo národní bezpečnosti/Ministry of National Security
MSW – Ministerstwo Spraw Wewnętrznych/Ministry of Internal Affairs
MUP RH – Ministarstvo unutarnjih poslova Republike Hrvatske/Ministry of the Interior of the Republic of Croatia
MV – Ministerstvo vnitra/Ministry of Internal Affairs
MVD – Ministerstvo Vnutrennykh Del/Ministry of the Interior
NATO – North Atlantic Treaty Organization
NCO – Non-commissioned Officer
NDH – Nezavisna Država Hrvatska/Independent State of Croatia
NKVD – Narodnyi Komissariat Vnutrennykh Del/People's Commissariat for Internal Affairs
NLA – Ushtria Çlirimtare Kombëtare/Albanian National Liberation Army
NOV – Narodnooslobodilačka Vojska/National Liberation Army
NPP – The Kozloduy Nuclear Power Plant
OSCE – Organization for Security and Cooperation in Europe
OSO – Osoboye soveshchanie pri NKVD/Special Council of the NKVD
OSS – US Office of Strategic Services
OUN – Orhanizatsiya Ukrayins'kykh Natsionalistiv/Organization of Ukrainian Nationalists
POW – prisoner of war
PPU – The Plastic People of the Universe
PUWP – Polska Zjednoczona Partia Robotnicza/Polish United Workers' Party
RCP – Partidul Comunist Român/Romanian Communist Party
RFE – Radio Free Europe
RFE/RL – Radio Free Europe/Radio Liberty

List of abbreviations

ROPCiO – Ruch Obrony Praw Człowieka i Obywatela/Movement for Defence of Human and Civic Rights
RS MUP – Republika Srpska Ministarstvo unutrašnjih poslova/Bosnian Serb Ministry of the Interior
RSK – Republika Srpska Krajina/Republic of the Serbian Krajina
RUMNO – Razuznavatelno upravlenie kym Ministerstvoto na narodnata otbrana/ Razuznavatelno Management at the Ministry of National Defence
RYM – Hnutí Revoluční Mládeže/Revolutionary Youth Movement
SD – Sicherheitsdienst/Security Service of the SS
SDA – Stranka demokratske akcije/Party for Democratic Action
SDB – Služba državne bezbednosti/Serbian State Security Service
SDK – Srpski Dobrovoljački Korpus/Serbian Volunteer Corps
SDS – Srpska demokratska stranka/Serbian Democratic Party
SLOMR – Sindicatul Liber al Oamenilor Muncii din România/Free Trade Union of the Working People in Romania
SNB – Sbor národní bezpečnosti/National Security Corps
SRS – Srpska radikalna stranka/Serbian Radical Party
StB – Státní bezpečnost/State Security
SVK – Srpska vojska Krajine/Serb Army of the Krajina
TO – Teritorijalna Odbrana/Territorial Defence
UDBA – Uprava Državne Bezbednosti Armije/State Security Administration of the Army
UDF – Union of Democratic Forces
UM – Unitate Militară/Military Unit
UNMIK – United Nations Mission in Kosovo
UNPROFOR – United Nations Protection Force
UNSC – UN Security Council
UNSCR – UN Security Council Resolution
UPA – Ukrayins'ka Povstans'ka Armiya/Ukrainian Insurgent Army
USSR – Union of Soviet Socialist Republics
VONS – Výbor na Obranu Nespravedlivě Stíhaných/Committee for the Defence of the Unjustly Persecuted
VRS – Vojska Republike Srpske/Army of the Serb Republic
WTO – Warsaw Treaty Organization
ZISPO – Zakłady Metalowe im. Józefa Stalina w Poznaniu/Joseph Stalin Metal Works in Poznań
ZOMO – Zmotoryzowane Odwody Milicji Obywatelskiej/Motorized Reserves of the Citizens' Militia

CONTRIBUTORS

Mark Biondich is an Adjunct Research Professor at the Institute of European, Russian and Eurasian Studies at Carleton University in Ottawa, Canada, where he teaches seminars on the history of twentieth-century Southeastern Europe and the politics of post-communist transitions. He is also a senior security analyst at Public Safety Canada. He is the author of *The Balkans: Revolution, War and Political Violence since 1878* (Oxford UP 2011) and *Stjepan Radić, the Croat Peasant Party, and the Politics of Mass Mobilization, 1904–1928* (Toronto 2000), in addition to several articles on fascism and the Holocaust in the former Yugoslavia and Southeastern Europe. He is currently writing a history of Croatian fascism from 1929 to 1945.

Jochen Böhler is acting Chair of Eastern European History at the University of Jena. He is the author of *Civil War in Central Europe: The Reconstruction of Poland* (Oxford UP 2018) and has recently edited (with Ota Konrád and Rudolf Kučera) *In the Shadow of the Great War: Physical Violence in East-Central Europe, 1917–1923* (Berghahn 2021) and (with Robert Gerwarth) *The Waffen-SS: A European History* (Oxford UP 2017) and (with Włodzimierz Borodziej and Joachim von Puttkamer) *Legacies of Violence: Eastern Europe's First World War* (De Gruyter 2014). He has published widely on the First and Second World Wars, German occupation and Nazi crimes in Central and Eastern Europe.

Włodzimierz Borodziej was Professor of Modern History at Warsaw University. He was Co-Director of the Imre Kertész Kolleg in Jena (2010–16) and was the chairman of the Kolleg's academic advisory board until 2021. His books include *The Warsaw Uprising of 1944* (English translation, Univ. of Wisconsin 2006), a seminal twentieth-century history of Poland (*Geschichte Polens im 20. Jahrhundert*, C.H. Beck 2010) and many key studies of Polish and Polish–German history. The two-volume monograph, which he co-authored with Maciej Górny, *Nasza Wojna: Imperia 1912–1916* (WAB 2014) and *Nasza Wojna: Narody 1917–1923* (WAB 2018) has been published in German as *Der Vergessene Weltkrieg: Europas Osten 1912–1923* (wbg Theiss 2018), in English as *Forgotten Wars: Central and Eastern Europe, 1912–1916* (Cambridge UP 2021) and it offers the most comprehensive account of the First World War in Central and Eastern Europe.

Alexander Korb is Associate Professor of Modern European History at the University of Leicester and member of the Stanley Burton Centre for Holocaust and Genocide Studies. He is the author of *Mass Violence in Western Yugoslavia During the Second World War* (Oxford UP, forthcoming). The book has been published in German (Hamburger Edition 2013) and Italian (Massari 2018). Korb has published widely on popular opinion in Nazi Germany, on the history of journalism in the Third Reich, on collaboration in Southeastern Europe during the Second World War, and in the field of Holocaust and Genocide Studies.

Dragoş Petrescu is Professor (hab.) of Comparative Politics at the University of Bucharest and is the author of *Entangled Revolutions: The Breakdown of the Communist Regimes in East-Central Europe* (Editura Enciclopedica 2014) and *Explaining the Romanian Revolution of 1989: Culture, Structure, and Contingency* (Editura Enciclopedica 2010), and co-editor of *Nation-Building and Contested Identities: Romanian & Hungarian Case Studies* (Regio Books 2001). He has published extensively on political and social change in East-Central Europe, with an emphasis on the regime changes of 1989 and the post-1989 transitions to democracy in the region.

Dieter Pohl is Professor of Contemporary History at the University of Klagenfurt, Austria. He is author of *Nationalsozialistische Verbrechen, 1939–1945* ('The National Socialist Crimes 1939–1945', Klett-Cotta 2022), *Die Herrschaft der Wehrmacht: Deutsche Militärbesatzung und einheimische Bevölkerung in der Sowjetunion 1941–1944* ('The Rule of the Wehrmacht: German Military Occupation and the Native Population in the Soviet Union 1941–1944', Oldenbourg 2008) and co-editor of the 16-volume series, *Die Verfolgung und Ermordung der europäischen Juden durch das nationalsozialistische Deutschland 1933–1945* ('The Persecution and Murder of European Jews by National Socialist Germany 1933–1945', Oldenbourg/De Gruyter 2007–2021). Pohl has published widely on Nazi Germany, its occupation policies and the Holocaust, the history of post-war East Germany and the history of the Soviet Union.

Joachim von Puttkamer is Co-Director of the Imre Kertész Kolleg and Chair of Eastern European History at the Friedrich Schiller University of Jena. He has published widely on the histories of nationalism, state-building and statehood, education and security apparatuses, as well as on cultures of memory and political thought in the region. He is the author of the survey history *Ostmitteleuropa im 19. und 20. Jahrhundert* ('East-Central Europe in the 19th and 20th centuries', Oldenbourg 2010), *1956- (nieco) inne spojrzenie* ('1956: A Somewhat Different Perspective', co-edited with Jerzy Kochanowski, Neriton 2016) and is co-editor of numerous publications including *From Revolution to Uncertainty: The Year 1990 in Central and Eastern Europe* (Routledge 2019) and *Catastrophe and Utopia: Jewish Intellectuals in Central and Eastern Europe in the 1930s and 1940s* (De Gruyter 2017).

VOLUME INTRODUCTION: VIOLENCE

Jochen Böhler, Włodzimierz Borodziej and Joachim von Puttkamer

Throughout the twentieth century, Central and Eastern Europe were hit particularly hard with war, violence and repression. The Balkan Wars in 1912/13 and again in the 1990s have been characterized as marking the beginning and the end of the twentieth century, respectively. In between, the region witnessed two World Wars, Nazi occupation and communist dictatorships, all of which exerted influence on the conflict-ridden history of the region. In the shadow of the full-scale wars that came to dominate that history, ethnic, social and national conflicts intensified and were violently played out in new forms across these 'shatterzones of empires'.[1] Since the beginning of the First World War, the conventional pattern of interstate wars dissolved into complex civil wars. The interwar period in Central and Eastern Europe witnessed the emergence of authoritarian states of either 'rightist' or 'leftist' orientations. To enforce their claim to power, these states used persistent violence against political opponents and enemies, stigmatized ethnic, national and social groups, and were themselves fought against by way of subversive or terrorist techniques.

Since the publication of Timothy Snyder's seminal book *Bloodlands* in 2010, much attention has been drawn to the region between Germany and Russia during the totalitarian age, spanning from collectivization in the 1930s to the brutal occupation policies of the Nazi and Soviet regimes during the Second World War.[2] For many Western readers, the mass murder that took place east of Auschwitz (erected within the borders of the German Reich) was a novelty. By focusing on the genocidal policies of the two totalitarian regimes that frame Central and Eastern Europe on the one hand, and the experience of the local population on the other, Snyder has written an empathic history of our region of interest in the age of extremes, the scope of which has reached far beyond academic circles.

This volume does not aim to revise this picture, but rather to complement it and broaden its scope in both spatial and temporal terms. Instead of framing the region as the 'bloodlands' of the twentieth century, which runs the risk of highlighting genocide and victimhood as its dominant features, this volume analyzes the violence exerted on the societies of Central and Eastern Europe, including Southeastern Europe, during the twentieth century. It places particular emphasis on the interaction between ethnic conflicts on the one hand, and occupation powers, authoritarian regimes and totalizing dictatorships on the other in order to give a more nuanced

---

1   Omer Bartov and Eric D. Weitz, eds, *Shatterzone of Empires: Coexistence and Violence in the German, Habsburg, Russian, and Ottoman Borderlands* (Bloomington, IN: Indiana University Press, 2013).

2   Timothy Snyder, *Bloodlands: Europe Between Hitler and Stalin* (London: Random House, 2010).

understanding, not only of their interplay amongst the spiralling violence, but also in addressing its legacies. To keep a study of this magnitude manageable, its scope has been limited to the phenomenon of *physical* violence. As such, we primarily focus on war and civil war, ethnic cleansing, systematic starvation policies, deportations and expulsions, the use of forced labour and prison camps as well as government oppression and militant resistance. This study also examines persecution by State Security forces, which – like intensive surveillance – affected the lives of those who were persecuted in very significant ways. Some of the key questions of this volume, therefore, are which forms of violence were 'imported', and what potential for violence already existed in the region? Which place does violence hold in the region's cultures? Is it considered a legitimate technique, as part of the political culture? Behind such a broad survey also lies the implicit question, to what extent has Eastern Europe experienced a general shift in social attitudes towards violence, as Richard Bessel has vehemently argued in the case of the democratic West?[3]

Violence did not occur evenly throughout Central and Eastern Europe. Geographically, the western regions of Belarus and Ukraine are included here, since they belonged to the Polish Republic during the interwar period and since they became sites of extreme violence during both World Wars. Since war in twentieth-century Central and Eastern Europe started and ended in the Balkans, the first and last chapter of this volume are dedicated to Yugoslavia's violent prologue and epilogue. However, these chapters by no means argue for a kind of 'Balkan mentality' (whatever that might be) that would have made the region especially prone to atrocities and interethnic violence. As a matter of fact, it is the major aim of this volume to do away with such prejudices that Central and Eastern Europe often face. Violence is not a disposition engraved in the DNA or the minds of certain peoples or nations, passed on from generation to generation. Rather, distinct forms of violence evolve in distinct historical situations, and the forms of physical violence presented in this volume are not a specific Eastern-European experience. As other authors have shown, the rise of the modern nation state came with the price of political purges and ethnic cleansing;[4] but before such phenomenon hit Eastern Europe in the twentieth century, it swept through Western Europe in the nineteenth.[5]

The contributions to this volume summarize our current knowledge of the region and make a plea for differentiation: although contemporary international observers have claimed that violence in the Balkans in 1912/13 was in most cases fratricidal – a result of the region's alleged backwardness and the 'barbarity' of its inhabitants – generally speaking, the perpetrators were either regular soldiers or paramilitaries that came from outside the region. At the Eastern Front of the First World War, non-military violence was exceptional and exerted not by the locals, but by soldiers of the imperial armies who were the occupying forces.[6] Interethnic violence in the threshold period 1917–1923 was not only witnessed in the lands between Germany and Russia, but in Ireland, the early Weimar Republic and the Soviet Union as well. The 1920s and 1930s

---

3 Richard Bessel, *Violence: A Modern Obsession* (London: Simon & Schuster a CBS Company, 2015).
4 Norman M. Naimark, *Fires of Hatred: Ethnic Cleansing in Twentieth-Century Europe* (Cambridge, MA: Harvard University Press, 2001); Michael Mann, *The Dark Side of Democracy: Explaining Ethnic Cleansing* (Cambridge: Cambridge University Press, 2005); Philipp Ther, *The Dark Side of Nation-States: Ethnic Cleansing in Modern Europe* (New York: Berghahn Books, 2014); John Connelly, *From Peoples into Nations: A History of Eastern Europe* (Princeton, NJ: Princeton University Press, 2020).
5 Mark Levene, *The Rise of the West and the Coming of Genocide* (London: I.B. Tauris, 2005).
6 Włodzimierz Borodziej and Maciej Górny, *Forgotten Wars: Central and Eastern Europe, 1912–1916* (Cambridge: Cambridge University Press, 2021).

in Central and Eastern Europe were neither a 'golden age' (as is the prevailing narrative in many successor states today), nor were they a theatre of incessant, deadly interethnic violence – the only civil war of this period renownedly unfolded in far-away Spain. During the Second World War, the region witnessed the most extreme forms of ethnic cleansing and political persecution, but, as the Croatian, Hungarian and Romanian cases show, such forms of violence in the region were not solely enacted through the genocidal regimes in Berlin and Moscow. During the following decades, Central and Eastern Europe found itself behind the Iron Curtain, but a closer look shows that the experience of violence and surveillance was a phenomenon that was not only imported to socialist satellite states from the Soviet Union but was also instigated and implemented by local institutions and personnel. The interethnic violence of the Yugoslav wars was no reflexive backslide into the time before the First World War, but rather a process deliberately set in motion and instrumentalized by political elites to achieve their respective goals in times of systemic regime change.

By unearthing the mechanisms underlying physical violence in Central and Eastern Europe in the past century, this volume aims to historicize and contextualize such mechanisms within the framework of a history of the entire continent during the 'age of extremes'.[7]

---

7 Eric John Hobsbawm, *Age of Extremes: The Short Twentieth Century, 1914–1991* (London: Abacus, 1995).

1
THE BALKAN WARS
Patterns of violence in the Balkans leading up to the First World War

Mark Biondich

What we conceive of today as the modern Balkans were born in the period between the Treaties of Berlin and Lausanne, that is, between 1878 and 1923, as a post-imperial space with distinctive ethno-cultural and religious attributes. The Berlin agreement had conferred independence on the nascent Balkan nationalizing states, while the Lausanne settlement confirmed the victory of the nationality principle, which is to say that the homogeneous nation state won out over other possible types of polity. The road from Berlin to Lausanne was littered with millions of casualties. Between 1878 and 1912, millions of Balkan Muslims emigrated or were forced from the region. When one adds up those who were killed or expelled between the Balkan Wars (1912–13) and Greco-Turkish War (1919–22), the number of Balkan-Muslim casualties may have exceeded three million. By 1923, fewer than one million Muslims remained in the Balkans.[1] If one adds Greek and other Christian casualties from the Greco–Turkish War, in addition to Bulgarian, Romanian and Serb casualties in the decade before Lausanne, the number of victims (dead, wounded and refugees) may exceed six million. The multi-ethnic mosaic that was the Ottoman Balkans was torn asunder by the ideology of nationalism and modern patterns of warfare.

This chapter seeks to contextualize the violence of the Balkan Wars within the framework of the evolution of the modern nation state in the Balkans and its endeavours to assert a monopoly on the legitimate use of violence. In doing so, it explores patterns in the evolution of the political violence in the region which culminated with the Balkan Wars (1912–13). It seeks to address both the sources and the forms of violence experienced by the region in this period while examining its immediate and lasting impact on these societies. A central aspect of the problem of violence in the contested borderlands of the Balkans of this period is the relationship between nascent nationalizing states, paramilitaries and identity. One of the noteworthy features of the violence in contested zones such as antebellum Macedonia (1903–12) is its novelty; the conflict over Macedonia represented the first instance of modern

---

1 Mark Mazower, *The Balkans: A Short History* (New York: Random House, 2002), xxxvii–xxxviii; Justin McCarthy, *The Ottoman Peoples and the End of Empire* (London: Arnold, 2001), 149–62.

political violence between Orthodox peoples in the region. The importance of this fact should not be underestimated, as violence was in many respects crucial to the completion of the nation-building process in the Balkans. In the earlier Balkan revolutionary wars, between 1804 and 1876, Muslims had been the primary victims of nationalist violence. For large segments of the Christian rural population, religion remained a far more formative reality than nationality. The violence perpetrated by Orthodox Christian peoples against one another in Macedonia served to assert the primacy of national loyalties over religious identities by compelling the still nationally unconscious Slavophone Macedonian peasantry to declare itself for one of the Balkan national causes. This was no simple task – the peasantry obdurately refused to identify with these causes – but irregular warfare between fellow Orthodox Christians gradually shattered a common identity rooted in Orthodoxy in favour of the state-sponsored national identities. In actual fact, the process was more complex and depended on a range of considerations that often had little to do with the national orientations of local communities. What made the Balkan borderlands so problematic in general – and in particular, the contested zones of Macedonia and Kosovo – was their ethno-cultural heterogeneity. This made policies of national homogenization and ideologies of irredenta problematic in the Balkan context; citizenship was subordinated to the dominant nation everywhere while the weakness of 'civil society' exacerbated this problem. Over the course of time, the prevailing discourse of nationhood became institutionalized by the native intelligentsias and political elites, and by the first decade of the twentieth century the attempts of the Balkan states to achieve national homogenization produced intense interstate rivalries, leading eventually to violence, discriminatory practices against national minorities and forced population exchanges.

Modernization and the roots of populism in the Balkans

In the period between 1878 and 1914, the newly independent Balkan states – Greece, Serbia, Romania and Montenegro, with autonomous Bulgaria – attempted to make the leap towards modernity. The region's political and intellectual elites were, with few exceptions, deeply impressed with the achievements of Europe, which was their paragon of modernity and 'progress'. These elites practically equated modernization with 'Europeanization', that is, with the advance of technology, the growth of industry and commerce, urbanization, the establishment of efficient, centralized state power and the institutional trappings of parliamentary democracy. During these decades, the Balkans witnessed the growth of towns, ambitious public works projects, the creation of communication networks, and the commercialization of national economies, in addition to the spread of education and literacy. By 1914, the region remained overwhelmingly rural, with numerically insignificant and socially marginal proletariats and bourgeoisies, although urbanization, the advent of modern technologies and the establishment of modern bureaucratic states had nonetheless already begun to undermine traditional rural society. The role of the state in promoting development was pronounced, as government revenues were invested in the expansion of state administrations, modern militaries including gendarmeries and industry. This entailed growing government indebtedness, eventually leading to greater foreign control over national economies and a concomitant dependence on European capital markets. While it may be true that the Balkans had, by 1914, experienced only the beginnings of industrialization and an uneven pattern of development, it is undeniable that the path to modernity had been entered upon.

In most Balkan states, the political elites were an outgrowth of the national liberation struggles of the nineteenth century that relied on the state for social status and power. The highly centralized state apparatuses and politicized bureaucracies that governed these states proved to be attractive instruments for social advancement. The Balkan state was thus seen by many in the region as the only agent capable of mobilizing the necessary resources needed to pursue social and economic reform and the concomitant tasks of state-building and national integration; the state alone possessed the power needed to mobilize resources, carry out modernizing reform and safeguard the national interest.[2] In this context, political power in the Balkan states was not wielded by liberalizing bourgeois elites but by intelligentsias and politicized bureaucracies. They were determined to adapt their societies to the organizational patterns of the European state. State-building was integral to the modernist project, and as such, resulted in highly centralized Balkan states with relatively large administrations. The emergence of bureaucratic ruling elites had a powerful impact on political culture, as existing social realities reinforced the vertical exercise of political authority.

The growth and expansion of the Balkan state after 1878 was accompanied, as elsewhere in Europe, by new demands on the citizenry. In a region where the peasantry comprised a majority of the population, state-building naturally entailed coercing peasants into supporting modernization. While the progress that was achieved from the last two decades of the nineteenth century onwards was financed by foreigners and high taxation, it was necessarily borne by the Balkan peasant who was compelled to conform to nascent state structures in the name of modernity. Although the condition of the Balkan peasant varied considerably from one country to the next, by the turn of the twentieth century, the typical peasant remained quite poor. Modernization and the penetration of the market into the Balkan countryside wrought significant changes to traditional rural life, leading to significant – if ephemeral – resistance. The Timok Rebellion (1883) of Serbia, during which Serb peasants attacked local officialdom and briefly neutralized state authority, is emblematic of popular resistance to the costs of state-building in the Balkans. That same year the so-called 'national movement' occurred in Croatia, which was largely motivated by difficult, rural economic circumstances and a substantial increase in taxation resulting from the growth of a semi-autonomous Croatian state apparatus within the Austro-Hungarian monarchy after 1868. Across the late nineteenth-century Balkans, the new bureaucratic state collected taxes in the form of currency, forcing peasants into the market and increasing their need for credit. The peasants' struggle against exploitation quickly became a clash against the city, where the modernizing state bureaucracy had replaced the native gentry (or Ottoman officialdom) as a veritable new scourge. Even in autonomous Bulgaria, where rural conditions were generally more favourable than elsewhere in the region, the situation of the peasants deteriorated rapidly after autonomy was achieved in 1878 and, as a result, the countryside harboured a deepening resentment against the town and nascent state bureaucracy.

By the turn of the twentieth century, parliamentary regimes existed in much of the Balkans and were based on relatively liberal constitutional systems by the standards of the time. In practice, however, these regimes restricted popular participation. The modernizing Balkan states were controlled by oligarchs or professional politicians, even while maintaining some pluralism through legislative assemblies, which were in most cases, with the exception of Romania, Montenegro and the Habsburg Monarchy's South Slav lands (Bosnia-Herzegovina, Croatia and Dalmatia), theoretically elected through universal manhood suffrage. These restrictive parliamentary governments were reformed to varying degrees only after military coups in Serbia (1903) and Greece (1909) or following the First World War, as was the case in Bulgaria,

---

2 On the relationship between war and state formation, see Siniša Malešević, 'Did Wars Make Nation-States in the Balkans? Nationalisms, Wars and States in the 19th and early 20th Century South East Europe', *Journal of Historical Sociology* 25, no. 3 (2012): 299–330.

Romania, Croatia and the other Balkan provinces of the former Habsburg monarchy, which joined with Serbia and Montenegro in December 1918 to form the Kingdom of Serbs, Croats and Slovenes ('Yugoslavia'). In short, the nature of modernization in the Balkans inevitably led to growing social crevices and disenchantment, but it did confirm the steady ascendancy of the modern state over traditional society.

The Balkan state and monopolies of violence

Max Weber's description of the state as the sole claimant to the monopoly of the legitimate use of force within a defined political territory remains the foundation of our understanding of state capacity. State actors that monopolize violence – be it the military and gendarmerie, the police or their legitimate auxiliaries – are supposed to serve as the primary organizations through which the legal monopoly of violence is maintained. Much of the literature on political violence in the nineteenth and early twentieth-century Balkans has emphasized the importance of the region's cultural and historical patterns to explain the inability of the Balkan states to establish – let alone enforce – a monopoly of violence. Wolfgang Höpken has argued that in the Balkans a clear state monopoly of violence was not firmly established by 1912, 'and a borderline between society and the military was never clearly drawn'.[3] However, as Ariel Ahram has recently observed, viewed in an historical context, few states have ever fully attained Weber's ideal-type and in several circumstances have either actively or passively collaborated with a range of armed actors that remained outside their formal bureaucratic structures.[4] These 'paramilitary' entities have taken a variety of forms; in some cases they have been closely linked to the state from their very inception, and in other cases, they have emerged autonomously, but were eventually co-opted by the state. In the discussions about Balkan political violence, these state-sponsored militias and paramilitaries are often identified as the primary perpetrators of violence against civilian populations.[5]

The widespread existence of brigandage in the Ottoman Empire in the eighteenth and early nineteenth centuries reflected the decentralized nature of the Ottoman state, which created conditions conducive to the rise of armed non-state actors that challenged the Ottoman state's monopoly of violence through irregular warfare. These actors supported themselves or supplemented their compensation through the plundering and extortion of local inhabitants, although the Ottoman state occasionally availed itself of these forces when it required additional manpower to quell internal unrest.[6] The phenomenon of irregular armed bands persisted in several of the Ottoman Empire's Balkan successor states. Known variously as *hajduks* or *haiduts* (among the South Slavs), *klephts* (among the Greeks), *haiduci* (among the Romanians), and *kaçaks* (among the Albanians), the brigand came to symbolize, depending on one's perspective, either the struggle against oppression (in the Balkan context, this usually meant 'the Ottoman Turk') or

---

3 Wolfgang Höpken, 'Performing Violence: Soldiers, Paramilitaries and Civilians in the Twentieth Century Balkan Wars', in *No Man's Land of Violence: Extreme Wars in the 20th Century*, eds Alf Lüdtke and Bernd Weisbrod (Gottingen: Wallstein Verlag, 2006), 247.
4 Ariel I. Ahram, 'The Role of State-Sponsored Militias in Genocide', *Terrorism and Political Violence* 26, no. 1 (2014): 1–16.
5 Cathie Carmichael, *Ethnic Cleansing in the Balkans: Nationalism and the Destruction of Tradition* (New York: Routledge, 2002).
6 See Fikret Adanir, 'Semi-Autonomous Provincial Forces in the Balkans and Anatolia', in *The Cambridge History of Turkey: The Later Ottoman Empire, 1603–1839*, ed. Suraiya Faroqhi (Cambridge: Cambridge University Press, 2006), 157–85.

simply criminality and lawlessness. In Balkan nationalist historiography, the bandit has generally served as an important trope: he was first and foremost a national hero who struggled for the liberty of his people. But the continued existence of banditry raised critical issues of how the newly formed and modernizing Balkan nation states were to deal with rural lawlessness and private power. The 1870 incident in Greece, known as 'the Dilessi Murders', which involved the killing of English travellers by Greek brigands, provoked scathing commentary throughout Europe on the inability of Greece to become a 'civilized', modern state. Thereafter, the Greek state set about to eradicate the phenomenon while brigandage was increasingly represented in nationalist discourse as an 'epidemic' transmitted to Greece from the Ottoman Empire. By the turn of the century, the larger Balkan states (Bulgaria, Greece and Serbia) had essentially eradicated brigandage as an autonomous social phenomenon. The one important exception was the Ottoman Empire, which for a variety of reasons failed to exercise a monopoly of legitimate force in its remaining Balkan territories. This created ample room for the Balkan nation states and the Macedonian and Albanian national movements to contest Ottoman authority, turning the Ottoman Balkans into a zone of violence between the late 1890s and 1914.

The prevalence of irregulars throughout the nineteenth century had more to do with the teething troubles of modernization than the region's cultural traits as such. In Greece, Serbia and Bulgaria, the irregular contingents that had fought in the national revolutionary wars were, in most cases, demobilized and returned to their villages soon after peace was restored. For example, the Greek kingdom possessed, at the time of its creation, a professional army of 3,500 soldiers, mainly German and Swiss mercenaries, who were deployed to maintain internal order as much as to secure the new state's frontiers. Within a decade, the Greek Army and gendarmerie had grown to 7,000 men, divided equally between Greeks and foreign mercenaries, representing approximately one soldier per 100 Greek citizens. The military absorbed more than half the annual state budget.[7] The Greek revolutionaries, who at the time numbered perhaps 5,000 irregulars, were disbanded by the Greek authorities. This proved to be complicated, as many of the irregulars could not return to their villages because their lands were still under Ottoman rule. Without regular pay and being accustomed to living off the land, they formed an incipient threat to social stability in the new state. Many took up brigandage inside Greece or in adjacent Ottoman territories such as Crete, Thessaly, Thrace, Macedonia and Epirus.[8] The Greek military, on the other hand, began to take shape only after the Congress of Berlin; rigorous military training and conscription were established by the mid-1880s, leading to a standing army of 25,000. Following the humiliating Greek defeat in the 1897 war against the Ottoman Empire, the Greek military underwent considerable reform with a reserve system providing for the military's wartime expansion to at least 60,000.[9]

However, the Greek state had, beginning with the Crimean War (1854–56), utilized irregulars to stir revolt among Greek irredenta, drawing on refugees who had settled in Greece from Macedonia and Thessaly. During the Crimean War, Greek nationalists sent thousands of irregulars across the border to Epirus and Thessaly to support the rebels. This was repeated in Crete and Thessaly in 1866–67, and again during the Eastern Crisis (1875–78), as hundreds of Greek officers and soldiers joined the rebels in Ottoman Macedonia, Thessaly and Crete. By the late nineteenth century, a pattern had emerged in Greece whereby irregular bands were formed

---

7 Charles Jelavich and Barbara Jelavich, *The Establishment of the Balkan National States, 1804–1920* (Seattle, WA: University of Washington Press, 1977), 72.
8 Ibid.
9 Ibid., 176.

from among nationalist circles and refugee ranks; these irregulars proved to be the sole medium through which the Greek authorities could reach their irredenta.[10]

Similar patterns were discernible in Serbia and Bulgaria. The modern Serbian army began to take shape under Mihailo Obrenović in the 1860s as a people's militia, but a formal military was only created in the 1880s following Serbia's independence, and all able-bodied males between the ages of 20 and 50 were subject to military service. Although still ill-equipped and poorly trained at the time, as early as the 1860s, the Serbian militia was able to field 90,000 soldiers from a population of 1.1 million.[11] Following disastrous defeats against the Ottoman Empire (1875–76) and Bulgaria (1885), when it again utilized irregulars, the Serbian military underwent significant and rapid modernization under European tutelage. Similarly, in autonomous Bulgaria after 1879, all able-bodied males were compelled to perform military service for two years. Between 1879 and 1911, the share of the Bulgarian budget devoted to military expenditures fell from 40.6 per cent to 21.7 per cent, but the army, created in 1888, accounted for the single largest share of the budget as Sofia worked rapidly to establish modern armed forces.[12] Bulgaria's military was widely regarded by the turn of the century as the best in the region. In 1910, a Bulgarian general proclaimed that 'we have become the most militaristic state in the world – putting over 350,000 men into the field'.[13] This was boastful, but it nevertheless speaks to the immense strides made since 1878, as the emphasis in both Serbia and Bulgaria was on the development of European-trained professional militaries utilizing the latest military technologies. Consequently, when considering the question of political violence in the Balkans, the importance of banditry as a legacy of the Ottoman era needs to be qualified. By the turn of the twentieth century, brigandage as an independent phenomenon had largely disappeared within the independent Balkan nation states and persisted principally as a means to conceal what was, in effect, state-sponsored violence in the Ottoman Balkans.

By the late nineteenth century, militaries had become an enormous expense for the nascent Balkan nation states and commanded a significant share of limited financial and economic resources. These militaries were comparatively large, in relation to the size of the population and available resources, but their elevated status in Balkan society stemmed from the new states' emphasis on irredenta. By the turn of the twentieth century, there was widespread recognition among Balkan political elites that strong armies were needed to accomplish national unification. These elites also realized that the problem of irredenta would be resolved through the armed action of modern states and militaries rather than by paramilitary units or guerrilla bands. This realization only reinforced the need to allocate ever greater resources for the construction of effective, modern militaries. Admittedly, most European military observers continued to

---

10 On the states' use of brigands for nationalist causes, see John S. Koliopoulos, *Brigands with a Cause: Brigandage and Irredentism in Modern Greece 1821–1912* (Oxford: Clarendon Press, 1987), 215–36.

11 Jelavich, *The Establishment of the Balkan National States*, 65.

12 On Bulgaria and the military, see Veselin Ianchev, *Armiia, obshtestven red i vŭtreshna sigurnost. bŭlgarskiiat opit, 1878–1912* [The army, social order and internal security: the Bulgarian experience, 1878–1912] (V. Tŭrnovo: IF-94, 2006). On the Serbian military, see Života Djordjević, *Srpska narodna vojska: studija o uredjenju narodne vojske Srbije 1861–1864* [The Serbian national army: a study of the organization of the national army of Serbia, 1861–1864] (Belgrade: Narodna knjiga, 1984); and Milić Milićević, *Reforma vojske Srbije, 1897–1900* [The reform of the Serbian army, 1897–1900] (Belgrade: Vojnoizdavački zavod, 2002).

13 Cited in Keith Brown, '"Wiping out the Bulgar Race": Hatred, Duty and National Self-Fashioning in the Second Balkan War', in *Shatterzone of Empires: Coexistence and Violence in the German, Habsburg, Russian and Ottoman Borderlands*, eds Omer Bartov and Eric D. Weitz (Bloomington, IN: Indiana University Press, 2013), 299.

underrate the quality and professionalism of Balkan military forces. Commenting on the Greek military's capabilities at the time, one British official in 1910 remarked: 'if there is war [between Greece and Ottoman Turkey] we shall probably see that the only thing Greek officers can do besides talking is to run away'.[14] His assessment was undoubtedly shaped by Greece's pitiful performance against the Ottoman Empire in 1897, but he misjudged the strides that had been made since then. Two years later, during the Balkan Wars, Greece mobilized 125,000 troops, excluding additional reservists, which was well beyond the expectations of most contemporary observers. Bulgaria would eventually mobilize nearly 600,000 regulars and reservists and Serbia another 255,000.[15] The 'Balkan League' fielded and sustained a substantial number of troops in light of the fact that the combined population of the four Balkan allies was barely 10 million. Their superiority in numbers and Western technology (modern artillery, aerial reconnaissance, wireless telegraphy, ships) dictated a disastrous outcome during 1912–13 for the Ottoman Empire, which for the first time confronted modern Balkan armies rather than motley brigands and insurgents.

Bandits and paramilitaries: the Macedonian conflict

Where banditry (that is, irregular or paramilitary forces) still possessed an important role for the Balkan nation state was in its mobilization and utilization beyond state frontiers, in contested zones such as Ottoman Macedonia between the 1890s and 1912. The relatively slow evolution of professional militaries after 1878 was paralleled by the indirect violence sponsored by nationalist organizations, volunteer and veterans' groups financed by the Balkan states. The Serbian and Bulgarian detachments (or, *chetas*) and the Greek detachments (*andartes*) that began operating in Macedonia in the 1890s adopted the habits and dress of the bandit, in order to conceal what was essentially state-sponsored violence. Ottoman Macedonia consequently became a flashpoint of conflict beginning in the 1890s. The contest waged in Macedonia between the Balkan states on the one hand, and the native Macedonian national movement on the other, was primarily over the loyalty and identity of the region's Orthodox Christian population. The Balkan states provided funds and personnel, supported and promoted competing nationalizing institutions such as schools, relief agencies, churches, cultural institutions and armed volunteers that promoted the identities of the competing nation states. Nationalist propaganda was disseminated by the Bulgarian Cyril and Methodius Committee (1884), the Serbian Saint Sava Society (1886), and the Greek National Society (1894). Denying the existence of a Macedonian Slav nationality, these organizations based their claims on a combination of ethnographic, cultural and historical proofs. All three claimed to have a plurality in Macedonia, although the politics of statistics revealed enormous anomalies. Cultural propaganda was followed by the activities of militant societies, particularly after 1897, which dispatched irregulars to Macedonia under the guise of brigandage. Supporting these groups were the Balkan consuls in Macedonia, who provided money, weapons and diplomatic protection.[16] These irregular detachments were for the most part led by Greek, Bulgarian and Serb officers who believed that they would

---

14 Cited in Zisis Fotakis, *Greek naval strategy and policy, 1910–1919* (New York: Routledge, 2005), 42.
15 Richard C. Hall, *The Balkan Wars, 1912–1913: Prelude to the First World War* (New York: Routledge, 2002), 16–18; Edward J. Erickson, *Defeat in Detail: The Ottoman Army in the Balkans, 1912–1913* (London: Praeger Publishers, 2003), 70.
16 Gül Tokay, 'A Reassessment of the Macedonian Question, 1878–1908', in *War and Diplomacy: The Russo-Turkish War of 1877–1878 and the Treaty of Berlin*, eds M. Hakan Yavuz with Peter Sluglett (Salt Lake City, UT: The University of Utah Press, 2008), 253–66.

find compatriots of the same tongue who would greet them as liberators. The reality they confronted proved to be quite different and far more complex.[17]

These armed detachments not only contested Ottoman authority in the region but also the IMRO (Internal Macedonian Revolutionary Organization), which had taken up the political struggle for Macedonian autonomy. Founded in 1893 by a group of Macedonian intellectuals, IMRO called for Macedonia's political autonomy under the slogan 'Macedonia for the Macedonians', which was to be achieved in the Balkan revolutionary tradition, as the nucleus of a future Balkan confederation. In late 1894 a rival organization known as the Supreme Committee (*Vrhovists*) was formed in Sofia, largely as an instrument of the Bulgarian ruling elite. By the late 1890s, IMRO had organized regional committees in Macedonia and launched a campaign of political violence; clashes between IMRO detachments (*chetas*) and the Ottoman gendarmerie became commonplace. IMRO's insurgency became a war of attrition against the Ottoman state. Between 1896 and 1903, IMRO detachments employed guerrilla operations against select targets in order to prevent extensive, punitive reprisals. Their targets included Ottoman installations, troops, other irregulars or individuals, thereby ostensibly promoting the group's credentials as 'guardians' of the people. IMRO had virtually established a state within a state, to the point of collecting taxes in some areas to support its activities. Violence against civilians occurred on both sides – and was perpetrated by irregulars sponsored by the neighbouring states – but prior to 1903 the violence was rarely indiscriminate.

The Ilinden Uprising (1903) was the most significant incidence of political violence to occur in Ottoman Macedonia during the decades preceding the Balkan Wars. Despite its massive scale, involving more than 15,000 Orthodox Christian irregulars and likely twice that number of Ottoman regular and irregular troops, the insurrection failed in part because the majority of the Orthodox Christian population avoided direct participation. IMRO detachments augmented their units by recruiting Orthodox Christian peasants, often by threat and playing on their fears of inevitable reprisals.[18] Duncan Perry has estimated that less than one per cent of Ottoman Macedonia's Orthodox population participated in the insurrection.[19] IMRO violence was designed to stir mass support for the liberation cause by fomenting inter-communal tension, with the expectation of Ottoman repression, and to incite international opprobrium. The Ottoman response entailed various tactics in the countryside, including collective punishment by regular and irregular forces, but was constrained by European intervention. In the event, more than 100 Macedonian villages were destroyed, and there were 5,000 fatalities recorded on all sides. IMRO never recovered from the uprising's suppression, resorting thereafter to more systematic forms of terrorism. Violence was directed at civilians, as a form of intimidation to deter collaboration either with the authorities or detachments from the neighbouring states. Irregular warfare in this context had a 'signalling' character, used primarily by both sides to shape the population's political behaviour. In short, political violence served as an essential resource and possessed a strategic importance; it was seldom gratuitous and almost always calculated. What gave the violence in Macedonia its seemingly pernicious character, at least to contemporary European observers, was the absence of structures of authority which

---

17 On the role of violence in shaping identity, see Dimitris Livanios, '"Conquering the Souls": Nationalism and Greek Guerrilla Warfare in Ottoman Macedonia, 1904–1908', *Byzantine and Modern Greek Studies* 23 (1999): 195–221.
18 See Duncan M. Perry, *The Politics of Terror: The Macedonian Liberation Movements, 1893–1903* (Durham, NC: Duke University Press, 1988), 110–35.
19 Ibid., 153–4.

might have otherwise served to constrain ('civilize') fighting in the first place and minimize civilian victimization. As an irregular civil war, the very nature of the conflict in Macedonia – with legitimate authorities and competing armed insurgents contesting the former and each other – made for a complex and fluid environment where frontlines were absent and where it was increasingly difficult to distinguish between civilian and combatant.

By the early twentieth century, Macedonia had become a zone of insurgency and political violence where IMRO contested detachments sponsored by Bulgaria, Serbia and Greece on the one hand, and the Ottoman authorities on the other. The abortive Ilinden Uprising prompted, as its plotters had hoped, European intervention. Austria-Hungary and Russia imposed the Mürzsteg Agreement (October 1903), a reformist agenda which dictated that European officials would supervise the local Ottoman gendarmerie and civilian administration; the underlying premise behind the programme was that the Ottoman state had failed to maintain security on its territory and to provide unbiased treatment of its Orthodox Christian subjects. As such, the Mürzsteg Agreement dictated a restructuring of the Ottoman gendarmerie in Macedonia; Orthodox Christians were to provide the rank-and-file in Christian-majority districts, under the command of European officers. Ironically, the Mürzsteg Agreement resulted in an increase in political violence in Macedonia, as the Balkan states concluded that more unrest would only further undermine Ottoman authority and incite greater foreign intervention.[20] For instance, the Ottoman census in Macedonia, recorded in 1904, caused another bout of paramilitary activity as Balkan state-sponsored bands worked persistently to convince the local Orthodox Christian peasantry of its 'Greek', 'Bulgarian' or 'Serbian' identity.[21] These irregular bands, and the Balkan states that sponsored them, operated under the assumption that the European Great Powers would dictate any future territorial settlement in the Ottoman Balkans; the need to win the ethnic allegiance of the Orthodox Christian population of Macedonia was thus paramount.

Between 1904 and 1908, Serbian and Bulgarian *chetas* and Greek *andartes* entered the contest for Macedonia, clashing with the remaining IMRO detachments and Ottoman officialdom. One estimate of the number of casualties in Macedonia between 1903 and 1908 places the figure at 8,000, of whom 3,500 were irregulars.[22] This violence would continue until external circumstances – i.e. the Young Turk Revolution (1908), the fall of Sultan Abdülhamid II (1909), and the Bosnian Annexation Crisis (1908–09) – brought the insurgencies to an end. Ottoman Macedonia thus presented a complex set of problems. The Ottoman leadership failed to implement meaningful reform, while the majority of Orthodox Christians in the Ottoman Balkans no longer believed that reform would provide either meaningful or lasting solutions to their problems. The Balkan states had no long-term interest in Ottoman stability and instead

---

20 For example, see the argument in İpek K. Yosmaoğlu, *Blood Ties: Religion, Violence and the Politics of Nationhood in Ottoman Macedonia, 1878–1908* (Ithaca, NY: Cornell University Press, 2013), 30–3.

21 According to the *millet* system, the Ottoman authorities registered their population based on religion rather than nationality. In Ottoman Macedonia, they recognized only two Orthodox churches: the Ecumenical Patriarchate and the Bulgarian Exarchate. Hence, Greek irregulars sponsored churches that were loyal to the Ecumenical Patriarch; their local followers were thus termed 'patriarchists'. The Bulgarian irregulars and Macedonian autonomists supported the Bulgarian Orthodox Church, the Exarchate, and hence their local adherents were known as 'exarchists'. According to the special survey conducted by the Ottoman authorities after the Ilinden Uprising, the Bulgarian Orthodox Church outnumbered the Greek Church by 796,000 to 307,000. See Stanford Jay Shaw and Ezel Kural Shaw, *History of the Ottoman Empire and Modern Turkey: Reform, Revolution, and Republic – The Rise of Modern Turkey 1808–1975* (Cambridge: Cambridge University Press, 1977), 208.

22 Yosmaoğlu, *Blood Ties*, 32.

promoted political violence when it suited their interests. The confluence of failed Ottoman reform, Balkan state rivalry, and European Great Power competition meant that revolution and violence would remain driving forces in Macedonia and indeed in the Balkans in the antebellum period.

Determining the local population's attitude towards and role in the violence of this period is not a modest task, but recent studies have emphasized both the relative stability of communal relations in the face of extensive pressure, and the role of outside actors in perpetrating much of the violence. To be sure, maintaining confessional and interethnic harmony in the aftermath of the Ilinden Uprising was problematic; violence between neighbours was likely present to some degree. The principal purveyors of violence, however, were members of irregular armed bands supported by the Balkan states on the one hand and the Ottoman forces (regular and irregular) on the other. A considerable number of the Balkan irregular units were composed of men from outside Macedonia, although some certainly originated from within the region. Among the Bulgarian-backed Vrhovists and the Greek irregulars, the number of outsiders was significant. Stefan Sotiris Papaioannou has shown that among the 385 *andartes* killed in Macedonia between 1904 and 1908, 136 (or 35.3 per cent) came from Crete. Similarly, the proportion of *andarte* commanders who originated outside of Ottoman Macedonia was even higher; 45 of 70 commanders killed in Ottoman Macedonia between 1904 and 1908 were from outside Macedonia.[23] What is more, these paramilitary units were composed of volunteers who were socially distinct from the peasant population among which they operated. They were typically of urban origin or members of certain professional groups (especially teachers), even if they themselves were only one generation removed from the village, as often was the case.

What is noteworthy here is that these irregulars, whether Bulgarian or Greek, often stood apart from the social and even ethnic fabric of the peasant communities in which they perpetrated their violence.[24] As Papaioannou has shown in his discussion of the 1905 massacre of 79 'Bulgarian' villagers in Zagorichani (today, Vasiliada, Greece) by Greek irregulars, the village was in fact ecclesiastically 'mixed' (the peasants supported both the Greek and Bulgarian churches) although its inhabitants were in fact all Slavophones. The Greek detachment targeted prominent 'Exarchists' – supporters of the Bulgarian Orthodox Church – but killed both 'Greeks' and 'Bulgarians' as they found it difficult to distinguish between the two in an exclusively Slavophone community.[25] The Zagorichani massacre is but one illustration of the way in which violence was visited by outsiders against the region's autochthonous residents in the name of the nationalist cause. A Greek military officer who led a guerrilla unit in Macedonia observed that violence – what he termed 'the persuasion of the gun' – ultimately determined whether a village community opted for a Greek or Bulgarian identity.[26] These irregular paramilitary units were hardly representative of the local Orthodox Christian community among which they operated, and their violence is hardly a reliable indicator or reflection of the state of communal relations. Nevertheless, they played an enormous role in escalating the violence in the region, and often operated on agendas of personal greed that occasionally superseded any directives they had from the states that had dispatched them to the field. The paramilitary violence in

---

23 Stefan Sotiris Papaioannou, 'Balkan Wars Between the Lines: Violence and Civilians in Macedonia, 1912–1918', PhD diss., University of Maryland, 2012.
24 Papaioannou, 'Balkan Wars Between the Lines', 62–4.
25 Ibid., 60–2.
26 Dimitris Livanios, '"Conquering the Souls": Nationalism and Greek Guerrilla Warfare in Ottoman Macedonia, 1904–1908', *Byzantine and Modern Greek Studies* 23 (1999): 195–221, here 197.

Macedonia suggests that, notwithstanding the objectives of regional governments, the specific agendas of non-state actors may have had an impact on determining the targets, timing and forms of violence. That the Christian population often feared these irregular bands seems abundantly clear. By 1908, both Slavophone and Greek-speaking communities in Macedonia were petitioning the Ottoman authorities with complaints about the extortionist practices of several of these irregulars, including those of their co-religionists.[27] In short, the paramilitary bands that operated in Macedonia further destabilized the Ottoman Balkans and undermined the Ottoman state's already precarious monopoly of force. The Ottoman state was simply incapable of controlling the actions of these paramilitary groups, which were too numerous and often indistinguishable from the local Orthodox Christian population.

This was demonstrated again in the adjacent Albanian lands, which were in open revolt against the Ottoman Empire between 1909 and 1912. At the Congress of Berlin, the European Great Powers began awarding Albanian-populated territories to the newly independent Balkan states. It was within this context, in June 1878, that the first political manifestation of a modern Albanian national movement appeared in the form of the 'League of Prizren'. Convened as an assembly of 'all Albanian lands', the League had demanded several reforms, in particular the creation of a unified Albanian administrative district within the Ottoman Empire, encompassing the Albanian-populated provinces (*vilayets*) of İşkodra (today, Shkodër), Kosova (today, Kosovo), Monastir (today, Bitola) and Yenya (Janina, located in modern Greece; today, Ioannina). The League openly turned against the Ottoman state and Sultan Abdülhamid II, and they were suppressed by Ottoman troops in April 1881. From that point on, the role of the European powers – notably, the Habsburg Monarchy and Italy – became more pronounced in Albanian affairs.

Despite the setbacks of 1878–81, Albanian national elites attempted to work with the Ottoman authorities. Moreover, several Albanians were involved in the Young Turk movement and its political wing, the CUP (Committee of Union and Progress), believing that constitutionalism would address the concerns of the empire's minorities. However, 'Ottomanism', as practiced by the Young Turks after their 1908 revolution, entailed modernizing the empire: this involved the centralization of authority in Constantinople, and the suppression of all nationalisms that undermined their unitarist conceptions of empire. Resistance to Young Turk centralization resulted in the Albanian revolts of 1909–10, centred on Kosovo and Western Macedonia. Ottoman reprisals were harsh and only brought new support to the insurgency. Although Ottoman forces had retaken most of the towns in Albanian-populated regions by mid-1910, and reasserted imperial authority with reprisals against the insurgents and the civilian population, Ottoman authority was limited to the towns and lowland areas. Despite Sultan Mehmed V's (r. 1909–18) visit to Pristina in June 1911, and his declaration of an amnesty for insurgents, a new Albanian revolt occurred in 1912 which led to the capture of Skopje, the administrative centre of the Kosovo vilayet. Ottoman reverses in Libya during the Tripolitanian War (1911–12) convinced Albanian rebels to press their claims. The revolt only ended in September 1912 when the Ottoman authorities granted the insurgents' demand for a broad administrative autonomy, namely, the formation of an autonomous Albanian administration centred on the four Albanian-populated vilayets. The following month, however, the First Balkan War began and much of the newly autonomous Albania was occupied by Serbian, Montenegrin and Greek armies.

---

27 Papaioannou, 'Balkan Wars Between the Lines', 65–6.

The Balkan Wars, 1912–13: wartime violence

The Balkan Wars (October 1912–August 1913) took an immense toll on the region.[28] The casualties suffered by the combatants not only attest to the scale of the violence, but also to the region's poor infrastructure and lack of medical capabilities. All of the combatants suffered significant combat losses, but infectious diseases took an even greater toll. The Ottoman military suffered approximately 100,000 to 120,000 deaths and 100,000 casualties. Among those who died in Ottoman ranks, a majority (approximately 75,000) probably died of epidemic diseases. According to an official Greek military history of the Balkan Wars, Greece suffered 2,373 combat deaths, 9,295 wounded and 1,558 dead of disease. The official figure on Bulgarian military losses was 53,825 dead and wounded, while Serbia and Montenegro together suffered nearly 40,000 dead and 58,000 wounded.[29] Casualties among non-combatants are difficult to determine conclusively, but the victimization of civilians was widespread; they were killed, tortured, raped and forced from their homes and regions. It has been estimated that as much as 15 per cent of the Orthodox Christian population living in Ottoman Macedonia was displaced as a result of the Balkan Wars.[30] It was the region's Muslim communities, however, who were the primary targets of Balkan military and paramilitary violence. At least 177,000 Muslims emigrated to the Ottoman Empire, most of them forced to flee as a result of armed conflict.

On 30 May 1913, the Great Powers imposed the Treaty of London on the combatants. Within two months however, on the night of 29–30 June 1913, the Bulgarian military, which had done the bulk of the fighting against the Ottoman army and now believed that its erstwhile allies were attempting to satisfy their own ambitions at Bulgaria's expense, launched a surprise attack on Serbian and Greek positions in Macedonia, initiating the Second Balkan War. The assault proved disastrous for Bulgaria. The fighting ended by 31 July and was formally concluded on 10 August 1913 with the Treaty of Bucharest between Serbia, Greece, Romania, Montenegro and Bulgaria.

Between October 1912 and August 1913, the political geography of the Balkan Peninsula was significantly redrawn; the new political frontiers would last for decades, with the minor exception of the Bulgarian territories on the Aegean which were ceded to Greece in 1919. The Balkan Wars also put an end to Ottoman rule in the Balkans. The empire lost 83 per cent of its land and 69 per cent of its population in Europe. By contrast, the Balkan states experienced enormous gains. Serbia's population swelled from an estimated 2.9 million to 4.5 million (an

---

28 It is not my intention here to chronicle the military and diplomatic developments surrounding the Balkan Wars. These issues, alongside the crimes perpetrated against civilians and the implications of the wars, have been covered by several authors. In addition to the two works cited in note 15 (by Hall and Erickson), see Andre Gerolymatos, *The Balkan Wars: Conquest, Revolution and Retribution from the Ottoman Era to the Twentieth Century and Beyond* (New York: Basic Books, 2002); Nicholas Murray, *The Rocky Road to the Great War: The Evolution of Trench Warfare to 1914* (Dulles, VA: Potomac Books, 2013), 171–210; and Valery Kolev and Christina Koulouri, eds, *The Balkan Wars* (Thessaloniki: CDRSEE, 2005).

29 On the estimated losses of the various combatants, see Erickson, *Defeat in Detail*, Table 10.5, 329; Hall, *The Balkan Wars 1912–1913*, 16, 108 and 136; and Army History Directorate, *A concise history of the Balkan Wars, 1912–1913* (Athens: Hellenic Army General Staff, 1998), 287. On Ottoman casualties, see Hikmet Özdemir, *The Ottoman Army, 1914–1918: Disease and Death on the Battlefield* (Salt Lake City, UT: The University of Utah Press, 2008), 16–26; and Oya Dağlar Macar, 'Epidemic Diseases on the Thracian Front of the Ottoman Empire during the Balkan Wars', in *War and Nationalism: The Balkan Wars, 1912–1913, and Their Sociopolitical Implications*, eds M. Hakan Yavuz and Isa Blumi (Salt Lake City, UT: The University of Utah Press, 2013), 272–94.

30 Papaioannou, 'Balkan Wars between The Lines', 7–8.

increase of 55 per cent) and its territory increased by 81 per cent. The corresponding percentage gains in population and territory for Greece and Montenegro were equally dramatic: 67.6 and 63.6 per cent; and 100 and 61.2 per cent, respectively. In the Bulgarian case, these gains were far more modest.[31] The new frontiers were subsequently ratified in a series of separate treaties between the Ottoman Empire and Bulgaria (29 September 1913), Serbia (14 November 1913), and Greece (14 March 1914). These treaties were supposed to regulate the status of Ottoman-owned property and of the remaining Muslim minorities in the Balkan states, who were given four years to decide if they wished to remain under Christian rule or to emigrate. If they opted to leave, they were theoretically permitted to sell their property and transfer their assets to the Ottoman Empire. Those who chose to remain were promised civil equality and political rights, with the freedom to practise their religion and culture. These provisions were never implemented, in part because the First World War created a new and radically distinct set of circumstances.

Several Western contemporaries and later observers attributed the widespread brutality directed against civilians during the Balkan Wars to the region's backwardness or cultural specifics. They typically expressed great shock at the nature of the violence. The International Commission on the Balkan Wars of the Carnegie Endowment for International Peace claimed that the violence revealed a specific inclination among the region's peoples towards 'barbarity'; it alleged that the violence was often perpetrated by neighbours against neighbours, 'a local circumstance which has its root in Balkan history'.[32] These peoples were allegedly driven by 'the old hatreds and resentments'.[33] A German lieutenant, who witnessed the Balkan Wars as a correspondent, blamed the extraordinary brutality on the 'semi-culture' of the region.[34] Notwithstanding the existence of fratricidal conflict in some areas, the crimes against civilians were perpetrated in the vast majority of cases either by soldiers of regular Balkan (or Ottoman) military units or hardened irregulars who worked in tandem with military units. In places like Macedonia, Thrace and Kosovo, which witnessed the brunt of the violence, the perpetrators (whether regulars or irregulars) were quite often from outside these regions and perpetrated violence against communities they believed were hostile to their respective national causes or states.

Recent scholarship has emphasized the point that it is the modernity of the violence that is one of the most striking hallmarks of the Balkan Wars. The wars prefigured twentieth-century warfare, combining attributes of modern technology (wireless telegraphy, aerial reconnaissance), national liberation and war on the enemy's culture and civilian population. The ideology of integral nationalism was combined with the revolution in fire power and communications with lethal consequences, drawing in, as Alan Kramer has noted, 'ever broader swathes of society as victims – and as perpetrators'.[35] The widely reported atrocities were neither a discrete phenomenon nor a mere by-product of the fighting, but part of the longer term project of nation- and state-building, and they served as a prelude to the far greater carnage that befell Europe in 1914.[36] The Balkan Wars were the Ottoman state's first 'total war', while the Balkan

---

31 McCarthy, *The Ottoman Peoples and the End of Empire*, 151.
32 Carnegie Endowment for International Peace, *Report of the International Commission to Inquire into the Causes and Conduct of the Balkan Wars* (Washington, DC: 1914), 148.
33 Ibid.
34 Cited in Höpken, 'Performing Violence', 224.
35 Alan Kramer, *Dynamic of Destruction: Culture and Mass Killing in the First World War* (Oxford: Oxford University Press, 2007), 140.
36 Ibid., 136.

states mobilized more than half a million men to prosecute their collective war effort.[37] Soldiers and civilians alike suffered the appalling effects of modern warfare, but without the infrastructure of modern medicine.[38] Hence, while Habsburg medical officers noted the appalling injuries caused by French-manufactured Serbian artillery, they also observed that the Bulgarian military lacked the equipment to combat lice or the bandages needed to treat the wounded. Outbreaks of cholera and malaria were reported across the entire Balkan theatre.[39]

The violence perpetrated by the belligerents was widespread and systematic. As Serbian troops moved into Kosovo and Macedonia in October 1912, they proceeded to wipe out entire Albanian villages. In the environs of Kumanovo, on the Serbian-Ottoman border, entire Albanian villages were razed to the ground. This picture was repeated the whole way to Skopje. In their liberated territories, the Serbian authorities treated the population harshly, directing most of the violence at Muslims generally, and Albanians specifically. Of Prizren's thirty-two mosques, only two were being used for worship by 1914. Edith Durham witnessed the war around Shkodër during the Montenegrin siege, travelling through destroyed villages and aiding those Albanian peasants who had been expelled or had fled. She noted, 'The most piteous thing of all was that few of the unhappy victims had any idea why this ruin had fallen upon them'.[40] Durham observed that the perpetrators 'all gloried in their bestiality and related in detail their nose-cutting exploits'.[41] The International Commission on the Balkan Wars detailed an extensive list of atrocities on all sides. Reporting on conditions in territories in predominantly Albanian-populated areas now under Serbian and Montenegrin control, it found 'whole villages reduced to ashes, unarmed and innocent populations massacred en masse, incredible acts of violence, pillage and brutality of every kind'. The Commission understood these methods as part of official policy, 'with a view to the entire transformation of the ethnic character of regions inhabited exclusively by Albanians'.[42] Its report concluded that 'all the Balkan races have grown up amid Turkish models of warfare', and that 'the extreme barbarity of some episodes was a local circumstance which has its root in Balkan history'.[43] Quite often, once regular military units moved through an area, law and order fell to irregular units to protect the rear; these units often did as they pleased.[44]

The MAVC (Macedonian–Adrianople Volunteer Corps) serves as a case in point of the paramilitary phenomenon in the Balkan Wars. MAVC was an independent military unit of 18,870 men organized in early October 1912 by the Bulgarian army. Although officially proclaimed to be a unit of Ottoman Balkan 'volunteers', in fact it consisted of a core group of IMRO irregulars co-opted by the Bulgarian military. According to the Bulgarian military directive establishing the MAVC, its ostensible mission was to collect information on the Ottoman armies in the Balkans, but it was also expected to conduct sabotage behind enemy lines by destroying bridges, weapons depots, railways and telegraph lines. With respect to the treatment of the civilian population, the MAVC was ordered to afford protection to the

---

37 Ginio Eyal, 'Mobilizing the Ottoman Nation during the Balkan Wars (1912–1913): Awakening from the Ottoman Dream', *War in History* 12 (2005): 156–77.
38 Özdemir, *The Ottoman Army*, 16–26.
39 Kramer, *Dynamic of Destruction*, 135–6.
40 M. Edith Durham, *The Struggle for Scutari (Turk, Slav, and Albanian)* (London: E. Arnold, 1914), 296.
41 Ibid., 236.
42 Carnegie, *Report of the International Commission*, 151.
43 Ibid., 108.
44 Höpken, 'Performing Violence', 234–5.

'Bulgarian population' but not instructed specifically on conduct towards non-Bulgarians. While MAVC battalions, fighting alongside the Bulgarian armed forces, took part in direct combat operations against Ottoman troops, several units engaged in the persecution of non-combatants.[45] During the First World War, the MAVC was dissolved and formed the nucleus of the 11th Macedonian–Adrianople Infantry Division of the Bulgarian armed forces. The example of the MAVC demonstrates how Balkan states were able, for the most part successfully, to co-opt and utilize paramilitaries in pursuit of their state objectives.

When the Bulgarian military captured Adrianople (today, Edirne) in late March 1913, their violence was directed at combatants and civilians alike: Muslim, Orthodox Christian (Greek, Armenian) and Jew.[46] The British vice-consul in Macedonia, H.E.W. Young, reported extensively on Bulgarian atrocities against civilians in Sérres, Cavalla and Xanthi, despite the fact that the authorities had surrendered to the Bulgarians without a fight.[47] The Muslim village of Ada, which had a population of 1,900 locals and 200 refugees, was reportedly attacked, according to Ottoman sources, by Bulgarian brigands and local Greek villagers; the village was plundered, women were raped and most of the community was murdered. Fewer than 100 survived the massacre.[48] Retreating Ottoman forces in Thrace exacted their own revenge in several villages. In one case, 600 Greek men, women and children were massacred ostensibly by local Muslims 'with every conceivable circumstance of barbarity'.[49] During the Second Balkan War, as the erstwhile allies wrestled for control of Macedonia, dehumanizing propaganda incited brutal forms of violence; Greek war posters in Athens and Thessaloniki (Salonika) depicted a Greek soldier gouging out the eyes of a Bulgarian.[50] A Greek officer wrote to his wife at the start of the Second Balkan War of the unimaginable picture of destruction: 'Everywhere we go we come across desolation and misery'. There was 'always a burning village in sight'. He was unmoved by the plight of the Bulgarians, however, whom he described as 'scoundrels' and 'monsters'.[51] Indeed, Balkan military officers generally appeared to have little regard for civilian casualties and the treatment of civilians by their own troops. One Greek soldier justified Greek atrocities 'as a measure of security and prudence'.[52] Military officers appeared to rationalize outrages against 'hostile' non-combatants as legitimate, and quite often believed they were an appropriate reaction to either real or rumoured crimes perpetrated by enemy combatants against their own troops and civilians. Military officers also possessed a strong preoccupation with 'honour' to the exclusion of other concerns. This entailed not only safeguarding one's own honour but also humiliating and dishonouring the enemy, which led to a range of abuses against prisoners-of-war and non-combatants alike.[53]

---

45 Tetsuya Sahara, 'Paramilitaries in the Balkan Wars: The Case of Macedonian Adrianople Volunteers', in Yavuz and Blumi, *War and Nationalism*, 399.
46 Carnegie, *Report of the International Commission*, 327. On the violence in Thrace, including the process of exclusion and discriminatory practices initiated subsequently by the Ottoman Empire in their new western borderlands, see Eyal Ginio, 'Paving the Way for Ethnic Cleansing: Eastern Thrace during the Balkan Wars (1912–1913) and their Aftermath', in Bartov and Weitz, *Shatterzone of Empires*, 283–97.
47 Gerolymatos, *The Balkan Wars*, 240.
48 Ginio, 'Paving the Way for Ethnic Cleansing', 290–1.
49 Carnegie, *Report of the International Commission*, 79 and 131.
50 Ibid., 97.
51 Cited Kolev and Koulouri (eds.), *The Balkan Wars*, 82.
52 Cited in Papaioannou, 'Balkan Wars Between the Lines', 187.
53 Ibid., 188–90.

As occupation regimes and rudimentary administrations were established, various pressures were exerted on the population to conform to the new nation states. Orthodox priests were employed to 'persuade' survivors to convert. Vice-consul Young reported an incident of forced conversion of Bulgarian-speaking Pomaks by a group of Bulgarian Orthodox clergy who were accompanied by irregular troops. When Young complained to the Bulgarian authorities, he was told that these 'fanatical' Muslims had signed a petition requesting conversion.[54] The Carnegie International Commission concluded that the Exarchate, with the support of the military and civilian authorities, conducted the policy 'systematically' and on a massive scale, through violence and intimidation.[55] The British consul in Monastir (today, Bitola) reported a similar phenomenon. In this case, the Serbian authorities compelled the remaining Macedonian and Bulgarian intelligentsia and villagers to sign a declaration of loyalty to their new king and to swear that, since their forefathers had allegedly been Serbs, they were merely asserting their patrimony by declaring themselves 'Serbs' in the present.[56] As the Serbian administration was extended to Macedonia, the Serbian Orthodox Church replaced the Bulgarian Exarchate as the dominant nationalizing institution, which entailed the cultural assimilation of the non-Serb Orthodox population of the region. The Bulgarian and Greek churches performed the same function in their respective territories.

Since the Balkan states conceived of the First Balkan War as a war of national liberation, they were committed to the removal of potentially hostile populations through ethnic cleansing. This was achieved by various means, including murder, intimidation and expulsion. The actions of all the Balkan combatants were additionally driven by the trepidation that an intervention by the European Great Powers would dictate a settlement at variance with their own plans, as had occurred in the past; expelling Muslims and others from their occupation zones served to strengthen their diplomatic claims. These fears were buttressed by the fact that the peace negotiations, which began in London on 3 December 1912 and were concluded in May 1913, were dual track: the European Great Powers deliberated separately from the parties who were local to the conflict and eventually dictated peace terms to the latter. This only fuelled the destruction on the ground and the expulsion of civilians from some regions. While Muslim civilians of diverse nationality were the primary victims of this campaign, during the Second Balkan War the violence became internecine as Bulgarians turned on Greeks and Serbs, and vice versa.

The enormous scale of violence visited upon the populations of Macedonia, Kosovo and Thrace during the wars left a bitter legacy. Despite a significant exodus of Muslims and the displacement of Orthodox Christians, the Balkan states now possessed significant minority populations; they ceased being, as Serbia and Greece had been prior to the Balkan Wars, relatively homogeneous nation states. The ruling political elites of these states were unaccustomed to governing multi-ethnic societies. Moreover, as the Second Balkan War had been the first modern armed conflict between Balkan Orthodox nation states, with a high level of popular mobilization, nationalist rhetoric and killing on an unprecedented scale, it could be said to mark the final victory of secular nationalism and the modern nation state in the Balkans.

---

54 Gerolymatos, *The Balkan Wars*, 241. On the practice of forced conversions during the Balkan Wars, see McCarthy, *The Ottoman Peoples and the End of Empire*, 93–4.
55 Kolev and Koulouri, *The Balkan Wars*, 77.
56 Gerolymatos, *The Balkan Wars*, 241.

As such, the strains that came to the forefront in Balkan society after the conflicts of 1912–13 were associated more than ever with national identity.[57]

The territories conquered (or 'liberated') during the Balkan Wars – namely, Kosovo, Macedonia and Thrace – barely possessed administrations that could be easily co-opted or seamlessly absorbed into the Balkan states. Bulgaria, Greece and Serbia had to extend their administrative systems, militaries, gendarmeries and police forces to the new territories. Circumstances dictated that irregular forces would continue to thrive in such an environment, partly because they were beyond the full control of these states but also because they were de facto extensions of these states, which lacked formal administrative capacities in these territories. In some cases, irregular detachments continued to exist as substitute administrators, exercising coercive force to buttress still relatively weak bureaucratic systems. In the case of Macedonia, what was exceptional about 'Balkan violence' in the relatively short period between the end of the Balkan Wars and the start of the First World War was the relative weakness of regional states, which allowed non-state actors occasionally to usurp state authority in order to exercise coercive force within their own borders.[58] Paramilitary groups continued to exact violence against civilians, although admittedly on a lesser scale. Equally problematic was the increase in criminality across the region, which was likely a function of a weak administration and corrupt officials.[59]

Notwithstanding the administrative weaknesses of the Balkan states in their newly conquered territories, after the Balkan Wars these states worked assiduously to ensure the political loyalty of their citizens. The first concentrated efforts were made towards systematic national homogenization, including assimilation and expulsion.[60] The Balkan states began to adopt new bureaucratic methods of thwarting perceived threats to their authority from minority groups. Limited population transfers were also discussed and enacted in 1913. Bulgaria and the Ottoman Empire signed a separate protocol on population exchange and associated property settlement to the peace agreement they concluded on 29 September 1913, which codified the earlier movement of 20,000 Orthodox Christian and Muslim families to Bulgaria and the Ottoman Empire, respectively. The protocol served as a model for subsequent population exchanges, although the 1913 agreement called only for 'voluntary' exchanges.[61] In 1914 the Greek and Ottoman authorities initiated similar but abortive discussions premised on a 'voluntary' exchange of populations.[62] These negotiations revealed a willingness on the part of regional political elites to consider bureaucratic measures of population regulation, as they increasingly came to view minority groups as threats to state consolidation. It should be noted, however, that exclusionary policies were not applied uniformly against all minorities. Such policies were shaped by strategic considerations and a state's foreign policy objectives. As Harris Mylonas has shown in his study of Greek policy towards minorities in Western Macedonia,

---

57 For a detailed study of the Balkan states after the wars, see Katrin Boeckh, *Von den Balkankriegen zum Ersten Weltkrieg: Kleinstaatenpolitik und ethnische Selbstbestimmung auf dem Balkan* (München: Oldenbourg, 1996), 117–18.
58 Papaioannou, 'Balkan Wars between the Lines', 226.
59 Ibid., 227–30.
60 Boeckh, *Von den Balkankriegen*, 200–1.
61 Stephen P. Ladas, *The Exchange of Minorities: Bulgaria, Greece and Turkey* (New York: The Macmillan Company, 1932), 10–23; and, Bruce Clark, *Twice a Stranger: The Mass Expulsions that Forged Modern Greece and Turkey* (London: Granta, 2006), 53.
62 Yannis G. Mourelos, 'The 1914 Persecutions and the First Attempt at an Exchange of Minorities between Greece and Turkey', *Balkan Studies* 26, no. 2 (1985): 389–431.

Greece's relations with neighbouring states impacted decisively how Athens treated its new minorities. The Slavophone population was widely suspected of harbouring Bulgarophile sympathies and was perceived to be a threat, and as a result, was targeted with intense assimilationist measures. On the other hand, the Vlach population was never regarded as a serious threat and was accommodated.[63] It was primarily Balkan Muslims, predominantly from Macedonia and Thrace, who continued to leave for the Ottoman Empire, with nearly 140,000 doing so between 1914 and 1917.[64]

In the immediate aftermath of the Balkan Wars, local governments also began to deport some persons from among their new minority populations, both internally and across international borders. Greek and Bulgarian officials practiced deportations from 1913 to 1914. In the Greek case, a December 1913 law broadened the scope of possible reasons for 'administrative deportation' to include political criteria. The banishment of ethnically suspect residents still largely occurred on an individual basis, however.[65] Population exchanges and deportations in during 1913–14 indicate that the notion of employing bureaucratically planned coercion to achieve a cartography of homogenization had occurred to Balkan officials prior to the beginning of the First World War. What is equally important to note, as Erin Jenne's study of the post-1918 Balkan population transfers has demonstrated, is that state interests invariably superseded those of local communities. Jenne concludes that, despite the de facto compulsory nature of these population exchanges, many of those involved would later attempt to return to their original homes. It was the state's priorities rather than local ethnic animosities that determined the course of ethnic relations and the recourse to coercive policies and violence.[66]

This is an argument convincingly put forth also by Theodora Dragostinova in her recent study of the fate of Bulgaria's Greek minority, which examines how, during the final transition from empire to nation states in the Balkans, both states and peoples approached the subject of national belonging. Her study treats nationality not as a fixed category that repeatedly engendered conflict, but as a complex process that was continually being redefined. As tensions between Bulgaria and Greece intensified at the turn of the twentieth century, the Ilinden Uprising led to an influx of Macedonian Slav refugees to Bulgaria which in turn led to attacks against the Greek minority throughout Bulgaria. While the majority remained in Bulgaria, more than 20,000 Greeks fled their homes and were welcomed in Greece, where the authorities offered them expropriated Muslim property in Thessaly. Disillusioned with their putative Greek homeland, roughly one-quarter returned to Bulgaria. Considering the reluctance of most ethnic Greeks to abandon Bulgaria and the disillusionment of those who did, Dragostinova suggests that their loyalty was not tied either to the Bulgarian or Greek nation state as such, but rather to their native places and narrowly conceived 'homeland'. Dragostinova thus questions the popular basis of 'ethnic un-mixing'; national identities were still mutable, and ethnically distinct communities in the borderland had managed to sustain a significant degree of solidarity.

---

63 Harris Mylonas, 'Assimilation and its Alternatives: Caveats in the Study of Nation-Building Policies', in *Rethinking Violence: States and Non-State Actors in Conflict*, eds Erica Chenoweth and Adria Lawrence (Cambridge, MA: MIT Press, 2010), 83–116.

64 Although precise figures are difficult to determine, it is estimated that in the years between 1912 and 1920, i.e. between the Balkan Wars and the Greek-Turkish War, approximately 413,000 Muslims left the Balkans for Ottoman territory. See Kolev and Koulouri, *The Balkan Wars*, 120, table 17.

65 Papaioannou, 'Balkan Wars between the Lines', 239–44.

66 Erin K. Jenne, 'Ethnic Partition under the League of Nations: The Cases of Population Exchanges in the Interwar Balkans', in Chenoweth and Lawrence, *Rethinking Violence*, 117–40.

This interpretation should also inform our understanding of the level of popular support for and participation in violence: if local communities sustained a substantial measure of solidarity, it is unlikely that they participated eagerly in the violence that characterized the Balkan Wars. The Greek minority in Bulgaria survived the Balkan Wars and the First World War, only to be swept up by the post-1918 population exchanges crafted under international supervision.[67]

Map 1.1 The Balkans after the Second Balkan War

---

67 Theodora Dragostinova, *Between Two Motherlands: Nationality and Emigration among the Greeks of Bulgaria, 1900–1949* (Ithaca, NY: Cornell University Press, 2011). The determined repression of minority culture in Macedonia ultimately helped to forge identities in Greece and Bulgaria. See Anastasia Karakasidou, *Fields of Wheat, Hills of Blood: Passages to Nationhood in Greek Macedonia, 1870–1990* (Chicago, IL: The University of Chicago Press, 1997). The Balkan experience also suggests wars are generally important catalysts of state formation albeit not necessarily the formation of nations. Siniša Malesevic, 'Did Wars Make Nation-States in the Balkans? Nationalisms, Wars and States in the 19th and early 20th Century South East Europe', *Journal of Historical Sociology* 25, no. 3 (September 2012): 299–330.

Dragostinova's study, like those of Jenne and others, shows that ordinary people, when faced with the prodigious capabilities of the modern nation state, often had little recourse other than acquiescence; they still possessed at that time an ambivalent attitude towards state-sponsored nationalist programmes.

The First World War and its aftermath, 1914–23

The Balkan Wars were without a doubt remarkably violent, yet they lacked the institutionalized and planned mass murder of non-combatants that came to characterize later European conflicts.[68] The Balkan Wars were wars of movement rather than attrition and, as such, were characterized by hurriedly shifting front lines; the violence was contained to a few comparatively short periods (October-November 1912, March-April 1913 and July 1913). Partly because of the rapidly shifting dynamics on the ground, some of the violence directed against civilians was undoubtedly extemporaneous although the perpetrators likely understood that their victims were 'legitimate' targets. Regular military units and their irregular auxiliaries made hasty judgements about local civilian populations; when they deemed local populations to be of doubtful loyalty and a potential threat (which they often did in the case of Muslims, regardless of their nationality), they frequently proceeded to destroy their homes or entire villages, and civilians were often killed. Some of the violence may have been selectively perpetrated, to intimidate the civilian population into submission or flight. Nonetheless, the Balkan Wars arguably represented a trend towards more radicalized 'ethnic' warfare.[69]

The First World War only intensified some of these tendencies, as it would prove to be an important watershed for the bureaucratization of violence against civilians in Europe.[70] This was equally true of the Balkans, although the region was only precipitously drawn into the European conflict between 1914 and 1917. Patterns of warfare in the Balkans in the early phases of the First World War remained relatively unchanged from the Balkan Wars, but this changed as the conflict became a war of attrition. By 1916, much of the region was under direct Great Power occupation: Serbia, Montenegro, the nascent Albanian state and part of Romania were occupied by the Central Powers, while neutral Greece experienced an acrimonious fissure between the monarchy and the Liberal Party over the issue of neutrality. This schism resulted in the actual division of the state between October 1916 and June 1917 into two hostile entities. A Provisional Government based at Thessaloniki (Salonika), supported by Entente troops, called for Greece's participation in the war while the royal government in Athens remained neutral until King Constantine's forced abdication under Entente pressure in June 1917. The exigencies of war led the wartime alliances and their Balkan allies to adopt novel solutions in addressing the problem of seemingly unreliable populations. The Greek and Bulgarian authorities asserted greater state control over raw materials, scarce industrial goods and people; they eventually imposed controls and ordered the deportation of civilians, as they came to see some communities as prospective liabilities that might undermine the war effort. As in the rest of Europe, so

---

68 Höpken, 'Performing Violence', 240.
69 Ibid., 248.
70 On the First World War, see Włodzimierz Borodziej, 'Der Krieg im Osten, 1914–1916', 1–53. See also Richard C. Hall, 'Bulgaria, Romania and Greece', in *The Origins of World War I*, eds Richard F. Hamilton and Holger H. Herwig (Cambridge: Cambridge University Press, 2003), 389–413. On Serbia and the war, see Andrej Mitrović, *Serbia's Great War, 1914–1918* (West Lafayette, IN: Purdue University Press, 2007). On Greece and the politics of the First World War, see George B. Leon, *Greece and the Great Powers, 1914–1917* (Thessaloniki: Institute for Balkan Studies, 1974).

too in the Balkans, the First World War saw the imposition of state controls and the bureaucratization of violence.[71] Furthermore, in those occupation zones affected by irregular warfare, as in Serbia and Montenegro during the period 1916–17, anti-partisan warfare invariably entailed the victimization of large numbers of non-combatants, either through reprisal executions, mass internment or displacement. Mass deportations were ordered for categories of civilians deemed suspect, sometimes to labour camps under harsh conditions, as well as large-scale evacuations of civilians from the front, in both cases wreaking massive social and economic havoc.

In this sense, there were some significant discontinuities between the political violence of the antebellum period (1904–13) and the First World War. The difference was primarily in the state treatment of civilian populations and planned population movements: Balkan states introduced labour camps and intensified forms of bureaucratically organized violence, as the belligerents increasingly treated non-combatants in or near combat zones as potential liabilities. In autumn 1915, following their landing at Thessaloniki and subsequent push northwards to assist the retreating Serbian army, Entente forces caused thousands of civilians to flee northward. In December 1915, Bulgarian forces repelled the Entente offensive; the German High Command's refusal to permit the Bulgarian army's advance into Greece, in pursuit of the retreating Anglo-French troops, allowed the Entente forces to maintain themselves along a front north of Thessaloniki.[72] The Macedonian Front endured until the last months of the war. After the frontline had stabilized in December 1915 and became more static in 1916, and as Macedonian refugees returned to their devastated villages now behind Bulgarian lines, the regional Bulgarian commander warned his superiors of the spectre of infectious disease and starvation. The Bulgarian Chief of Staff sanctioned his proposal to 'evacuate' the population – numbering in the tens of thousands – to the interior. The male population was deployed as labour around Štip, then Skopje and finally near Sofia, where they were used as factory labour. Although the population's nationality had little to do with its removal, the incident demonstrated the transition to a more bureaucratic approach by regional states and their militaries in dealing with civilian populations.[73] In 1919, an Inter-Allied Commission concluded that the Bulgarian authorities had deported 42,000 civilians from their occupation zone in Macedonia, of whom 12,000 reportedly died in exile.[74] These figures are likely too high although at least 28,000 were 'evacuated' from the area by the Bulgarian authorities, while thousands died of starvation or inhumane treatment.[75]

As the war dragged on, however, civilian loyalties were increasingly questioned, and a range of coercive measures were adopted. The French army in control of western Greek Macedonia ordered the disarmament of the local population in March 1917; those who were found to be in possession of weapons could be executed by firing squad. In this case, French commanders feared subversion by local supporters of the Greek monarchy, which sought to maintain Greece's neutrality. Even seemingly innocuous complaints about the behaviour of Entente forces could

---

71 Papaioannou, 'Balkan Wars Between the Lines', 284–6.
72 In spring 1916, now with German military support, Bulgarian troops advanced into northern Greece, and between May and September, occupied positions northeast of Thessaloniki, including Seres, Drama and Kavala.
73 Papaioannou, 'Between the Lines', 283–6.
74 Ibid., 291.
75 See Tassos Kostopoulos, 'How the North was won: Épuration ethnique, échange des populations et politique de colonisation dans la Macédoine grecque', *European Journal of Turkish Studies* 12 (2011), http://ejts.revues.org/4437 (accessed 3 January 2021).

lead to imprisonment. After Greece entered the war on the side of the Entente, the authorities expanded the criteria under which persons could be deported internally.[76]

Where civilians eventually resisted military occupation, as in Serbia, reprisals by the Austro-Hungarian and Bulgarian authorities were commonplace and quite often deliberately harsh to increase their deterrent effect. The Bulgarian occupation authorities adopted increasingly harsh measures in occupied Macedonia and in eastern Serbia (Morava Military Inspectorate), which they occupied in late 1915. Both the Austro-Hungarian and Bulgarian militaries were confronted by armed resistance in 1916–17, primarily in Serbia and Montenegro, culminating in the Toplica Uprising (February–March 1917). Irregular warfare was critical both to the insurgency, which employed guerrilla tactics and regular military commands staging counter-insurgency operations, as they relied on paramilitary detachments. The nature of these operations being what they were, few distinctions were drawn between armed combatants and civilians, resulting in growing abuses against the latter. During the suppression of the Toplica Uprising, which began in the Bulgarian occupation zone but expanded to the Austro-Hungarian zone, as many as 20,000 insurgents and civilians may have been killed.[77] When coupled with the occupation authorities' greater exploitation of the local economy, the living conditions of the local population deteriorated to subsistence levels. The scale of the violence is testified to by the wartime losses. Jonathan Gumz's study of the Austro-Hungarian occupation of Serbia emphasizes the Habsburg military's rejection of modern definitions of war,[78] but also details the mass detentions, summary executions and shooting of hostages which resulted in the deaths of thousands.[79] Of the nearly 450,000 Habsburg troops deployed to Serbia during the war, 273,000 casualties were suffered, while Serbian losses were proportionally significantly larger: 300,000 civilians and 250,000 soldiers.[80] Whether in terms of reprisals against civilians or the increasingly bureaucratic measures used to relocate non-combatants, the First World War marked a departure for the region. Admittedly, the First World War severely tested the Balkan states' monopoly of violence, but this had as much to do with the nature of the conflict and the fact that several states either ceased to exist during the war, were strained by outside interventions or shattered because of existing political cleavages. This was especially the case in the latter stages of the First World War when, under the impact of the Russian Revolutions and American entry, the conflict became more overtly ideological in nature.

---

76 Papaioannou, 'Between the Lines', 247, 290.
77 On the Toplica Uprising, see Mitrović, *Serbia's Great War*, 245–77; Jonathan Gumz, *The Resurrection and Collapse of Empire in Habsburg Serbia, 1914–1918* (Cambridge: Cambridge UP, 2009), 195–230; and Božica Mladenović, ed., *Toplički ustanak 1917 godine* [The Toplica Uprising of 1917] (Belgrade: Vojnoistorijski institute, 1997). The Swiss criminologist Rodolphe Archibald Reiss was commissioned by the Serbian authorities to compile information related to violations of the customs of wars by the Central Powers. See Rodolphe Archibald Reiss, *The Kingdom of Serbia: Infringements of the Rules and Laws of War Committed by the Austro-Bulgaro-Germans* (London: George Allen & Unwin, 1919). On occupation policies and the victimization of civilians in Serbia and Macedonia, see also Benjamin Lieberman, *Terrible Fate: Ethnic Cleansing in the Making of Modern Europe* (Chicago, IL: Ivan R. Dee, 2006), 80–7.
78 Gumz, *The Resurrection and Collapse of Empire*, 141.
79 Ibid., 58.
80 Kramer, *Dynamic of Destruction*, 143. The post-war Yugoslav authorities erected more than 200 memorials and monuments to commemorate the Balkan Wars and the First World War. See Melissa Bokovoy, 'Scattered Graves, Ordered Cemeteries: Commemorating Serbia's Wars of National Liberation, 1912–1918', in *Staging the Past: The Politics of Commemoration in Habsburg Central Europe, 1848 to the Present*, eds Nancy Wingfield and Maria Bucur (West Lafayette, IN: Purdue University Press, 2001), 236–54.

The last days of the First World War were accompanied by significant internal disruption and violence, which ensured that peace would not be restored until well after 1918.[81] By late 1918, as shortages of food and other materials affected towns and the military alike, the state of affairs in Bulgaria, which had been at war almost continuously since 1912, deteriorated rapidly. An Entente offensive on the Macedonian front, launched on 14 September 1918, overwhelmed Bulgarian forces at Dobro Pole. Although some units continued to resist, the Bulgarian military effort collapsed and by 25 September, Entente forces had crossed into Bulgaria proper. As disaffected Bulgarian soldiers streamed back towards Sofia, a group of rebels, eventually numbering 30,000, proclaimed a republic in Radomir on 27 September.[82] On 30 September, a hurriedly assembled force including military cadets and German troops, defeated the insurgents. On 4 October, Tsar Ferdinand abdicated and fled to Germany. The Radomir Rebellion had threatened the government in Sofia and forced it to sign an armistice on 29 September. Although it had been suppressed, it was a portent of the dramatic (and occasionally violent) changes that would rack the country between 1919 and 1923.

In the South Slav territories of the Austro-Hungarian monarchy, specifically in Croatia-Slavonia, the last months of the First World War witnessed widespread rural disturbances directed at the authorities and city folk in general.[83] These were gradually quashed by late 1918 with the arrival of the Serbian army and the proclamation of the Kingdom of Serbs, Croats and Slovenes. On 5 December 1918, a minor revolt of Croat soldiers of the former Austro-Hungarian Army occurred in Zagreb, but it was quickly neutralized; some of its ringleaders relocated to Hungary, from where they worked for Croatian independence and eventually, after 1929, joined forces with the Ustasha movement. The Serbian army, now acting as the de facto military force of the new Yugoslav state, expanded by July 1919 to nearly 450,000 men as it enforced the authority of the new political regime.[84] Unification was contested early on across the new state, however. In Montenegro, the Podgorica Assembly was the representative political body of the Montenegrin people from November 1918 until December 1919. Two dominant political factions were represented in it: the so-called 'Whites', who favoured unconditional unification with Serbia and other South Slavs in a Yugoslav state; and the 'Greens', who initially supported a confederation of states and remained loyal to the Petrović dynasty and King Nikola I. In January 1919, the Greens, with some Italian support, launched an insurrection against unification; it was suppressed but continued in limited form until 1926.[85] Across the new

---

81 On these post-war conflicts, see Robert Gerwarth, *The Vanquished: Why the First World War Failed to End, 1917–1923* (London: Allen Lane, 2016); and Aviel Roshwald, *Ethnic Nationalism and the Fall of Empires: Central Europe, Russia, and the Middle East, 1914–1923* (New York: Routledge, 2001), 156–97.

82 Richard C. Hall, *Balkan Breakthrough: The Battle of Dobro Pole 1918* (Bloomington, IN: Indiana University Press, 2010), 154.

83 See Ivo Banac, '"Emperor Karl has become a Comitadji": The Croatian Disturbances of Autumn 1918', *Slavonic and Eastern European Review* 70, no. 2 (April 1992): 284–305; and John Paul Newman, 'Post-imperial and Post-war Violence in the South Slav Lands, 1917–1923', *Contemporary European History* 19, no. 3 (2010): 249–65. See John Paul Newman, 'The Origins, Attributes, and Legacies of Paramilitary Violence in the Balkans', in *War in Peace: Paramilitary Violence in Europe after the Great War*, eds Robert Gerwarth and John Horne (Oxford: Oxford University Press, 2012).

84 John Paul Newman, *Yugoslavia in the Shadow of War Veterans and the Limits of State Building, 1903–1945* (Cambridge: Cambridge University Press, 2015), 42–3.

85 On the question of unification and violence in Montenegro after 1918, see Srdja Pavlović, *Balkan Anschluss: The Annexation of Montenegro and the Creation of a Common South Slavic State* (West Lafayette, IN: Purdue University Press, 2008).

Yugoslav state, resistance to the new regime – primarily from disaffected minorities (Albanians, Macedonians) – ensured the persistence of violence into the early 1920s.

The last and perhaps most consequential conflict in the region was the Greek–Turkish War (1919–22), fought in Anatolia between Greece, which sought to realize the goal of an Hellenic empire on both sides of the Aegean Sea, and the nascent Turkish national movement, which resisted the partitioning of the Ottoman Empire. Beginning in November 1918, the Entente occupied the Ottoman capital of Istanbul while France and Italy occupied Southeastern and Southwestern Anatolia, respectively. In August 1920, the Ottoman government signed the Treaty of Sèvres which sanctioned the formation of Entente-controlled zones of influence and occupation in Anatolia. The treaty also authorized the formation of an independent Armenia, and Anglo–French mandates in Palestine, Iraq and the Levant. The Treaty of Sèvres was never ratified, however, as the Turkish national resistance under Mustafa Kemal rejected it. While the Ottoman Sultanate in Istanbul was basically controlled by the occupying Entente forces, the Turkish nationalist government in Ankara failed to comply with the partition of Ottoman territory. The Greco–Turkish War began with the Greek occupation of Smyrna (today, İzmir) in May 1919 and would end there in August 1922, under catastrophic circumstances. In January 1921, the Greek Army, despite shortages of equipment and lengthy, vulnerable supply lines, launched an offensive deep into central Anatolia. Although repelled in April, the Greek Army renewed its attack in July and advanced towards Ankara until its defeat at Sakarya (August–September 1921). The Turkish revolutionaries' military successes of 1921–22, culminating in the August 1922 Great Fire of Smyrna and their capture of the town early the following month, effectively ended the war, resulted in the collapse of Greek nationalist dreams and the destruction of the Greek communities of Anatolia.[86] The conflict was formally resolved by the Treaty of Lausanne, which was concluded on 24 July 1923 and was in effect the final treaty concluding the First World War; Western military forces evacuated Istanbul by early October 1923. The treaty forced Greece to return to Turkey several territories it had occupied since 1919 and, most meaningfully, the two parties agreed to a state-organized and internationally sanctioned exchange of populations which profoundly changed the ethnic and cultural composition of the region.[87] As a result of the Lausanne settlement, 1.2 million Ottoman citizens of Greek Orthodox faith (many of them non-Greeks) and 400,000 Muslims were exchanged by Turkey and Greece. Addressing the Lausanne peace conference in December 1922, Fridtjof Nansen, the League of Nations' High Commissioner for Refugees, remarked that 'to unmix the populations of the Near East will tend to secure [the] true pacification of the Near East'.[88]

---

86 On the war, see Sean McMeeking, *The Ottoman Endgame: War, Revolution, and the Making of the Modern Middle, 1908–1923* (New York: Penguin Press, 2015), 448–96; and Michael Llewellyn Smith, *Ionian Vision: Greece in Asia Minor, 1919–1922* (Ann Arbor, MI: The University of Michigan Press, 1973, revised 1998).

87 On the population exchange, see Clark, *Twice a Stranger*; Renée Hirschon, *Crossing the Aegean: An Appraisal of the 1923 Compulsory Population Exchange between Greece and Turkey* (London: Berghahn, 2003). On the integration of the refugee population in Aegean Macedonia and the interplay with the Macedonian Slav issue, see Karakasidou, *Fields of Wheat, Hills of Blood*. According to the Greek census of May 1928, the country had 1,221,849 registered refugees from among a total population of 6.2 million inhabitants. From among this refugee population, 1,069,957 had arrived in Greece since August 1922. The census data are discussed in Kostopoulos, 'How the North was won'.

88 Cited in McMeeking, *The Ottoman Endgame*, 483.

Conclusions

Because of a sequence of wars between October 1912 and July 1923 – the Balkan Wars (1912 and 1913), the First World War (1914–18) and a series of post-war conflicts (1918–23) – the Balkans were transformed in many fundamental respects and were quite dissimilar from antebellum Southeastern Europe.[89] The most obvious difference was reflected in political geography; the end of empire saw the emergence of new states, such as Albania and the Kingdom of Serbs, Croats and Slovenes ('Yugoslavia'). Equally dramatic was the demographic catastrophe. Serbia had approximately 320,000 men under arms in late July 1914 after its initial mobilization, of whom perhaps 250,000 were battle ready.[90] By mid-1915, it had already suffered more than 69,000 combat deaths.[91] At the time of mobilization in late September 1915, the Bulgarian army had 8,900 officers and 522,395 NCOs (non-commissioned officers) and soldiers organized in three divisions. Bulgarian troop strength peaked in September 1918 at 878,000 troops, with 697,000 in the military.[92] Romania's army stood at more than 600,000, albeit poorly trained and equipped, while Greece mobilized, within one year of officially entering the war, 300,000 troops to support the Entente.[93] The four core Balkan states – Serbia, Bulgaria, Greece and Romania – probably suffered more than 1.8 million combined civilian and military casualties, from among a combined population of 22 million. In Greece and Bulgaria, casualty figures may have exceeded 3 per cent of the population, while in Romania and Serbia they may have exceeded 9 and 16 per cent, respectively. When one adds to the demographic losses the experiences of occupation and exploitation, and the loss of economic production for approximately a decade, it is not difficult to understand the impact on local populations, popular culture and the national psyche.

The First World War and the Bolshevik Revolution had a radicalizing effect on the region's socially dominant countryside and its peasant masses, who formed the bulk of wartime military conscripts. By 1918, the combined effect of war and revolution was exhaustion coupled with a tide of social and political radicalism which seemed to foreshadow the victory of the region's previously marginalized democratic Left, such as the Agrarians and Social Democrats, and the newly constituted Communists. Social disturbances became widespread across much of the region. Communist parties were formed everywhere except Albania between late 1918 and early 1921; in Bulgaria and Yugoslavia they emerged as major parties in the immediate post-war period. Similarly, in both countries Agrarian parties either held power – as was the case with Aleksandŭr Stamboliiski's BANU (Bulgarian Agrarian National Union), from October 1919 to June 1923 – or emerged as principal advocates of reform. The ascent of the Left was illustrative of the loss of faith in pre-war political elites, the rise of social revolutionary tendencies and the adoption of universal manhood suffrage after 1918. The First World War had changed the relationship between state and society in multiple ways. States

---

89 See Chapter 3 in this volume by Jochen Böhler, 'The radicalization of violence and Intermarium's interwar'. For an earlier treatment, see Jochen Böhler, 'Enduring Violence: The Postwar Struggles in East-Central Europe, 1917–21', *Journal of Contemporary History* 50, no. 1 (2015): 58–77.
90 James Lyon, *Serbia and the Balkan Front, 1914: The Outbreak of the Great War* (London: Bloomsbury Academic, 2015), 501. See also Dušan Babac, *The Serbian Army in the Great War, 1914–1918* (Solihull: Helion and Company, 2015).
91 Mitrovic, *Serbia's Great War*, 102.
92 Hall, *Balkan Breakthrough*, 41–2.
93 George B. Leontaritis, *Greece and the First World War: From Neutrality to Intervention, 1917–1918* (New York: East European Monographs, 1990), 61–7, 149–79.

had adopted unprecedented wartime regulations of their citizens' lives and hardened cultures of violence emerged over these years.

In the event, the democratic Left and the Communists were gradually suppressed everywhere as traditional elites employed repressive measures and violence against ideological and ethnic opponents, which certainly reflected changes in political culture. Quite often, these elites employed irregular forces to quell disturbances, suppress dissent or even to overthrow democratically elected governments. Communist parties were banned and violently suppressed in Yugoslavia (1921) and in Bulgaria and Romania (1924), and much later in Albania (1928) and Greece (1936). In Bulgaria, the 1923 coup led to the overthrow of the BANU government and the murder of Stamboliiski. In 1924, the democratic revolution in Albania that was sponsored by Bishop Fan Noli ended in a military coup led Ahmed Zogu and armed supporters sponsored by Yugoslavia.[94] Defeat in Anatolia during 1922–23 produced the National Schism in Greece and, among other things, repeated military interventions in Greek politics over 1923–24. A decade of violence between 1912 and 1923 contributed to a perceptible change in political cultures: violence was no longer exceptional but was widely regarded – by regimes and political groups on the extreme Left and Right – as integral to the achievement of national and/or ideological ends. At the same time, traditional conservative elites now asserted their prerogatives over minorities, social groups and ideological opponents, prepared more than ever to resort to repression.

By 1923–24 the political system of every Balkan state had been decided upon. All five interwar Balkan states were highly centralized nationalizing states that attempted with varying degrees of success to homogenize their societies and even to negate their multicultural character. They were built around core nations construed along ethnolinguistic lines which not only laid claim to ownership of their respective polities but attempted to enforce nationalization in politics, culture and in socio-economic life. As the interwar period advanced, most states codified discriminatory practices against minorities, whether Jews, Muslims (e.g. Turks and Pomaks in Bulgaria, Albanians in Yugoslavia), Roma or others. At the same time, political violence was wielded by irredentist groups against established states for control of disputed territories. There were several Balkan zones of contestation – some of these were on the region's peripheries (Istria/Dalmatia, Transylvania and Bessarabia), but the core zones were the same as between 1878 and 1912, namely, Macedonia, Kosovo and Bosnia-Herzegovina. IMRO employed violence against the interwar Yugoslav and Greek states in Vardar and Aegean Macedonia, respectively, where harsh nationalizing policies had been adopted to assimilate the indigenous Macedonian population. Similarly, until 1924, Albanian nationalists and *kaçaks* ('outlaws', irregulars) contested Serbian rule in Kosovo and attempted to capitalize on a marginalized population which was denied legitimate channels to express its identity and political preferences.[95] Montenegrin separatists ('Greens') contested Yugoslav unification through irregular warfare between 1919 and 1926, as did Italian paramilitaries under Gabriele

---

94 See Robert C. Austin, *Founding a Balkan State: Albania's Experiment with Democracy, 1920–1925* (Toronto: University of Toronto Press, 2012).

95 The movement was led by Bajram Curi and Hasan Pristina, but it faced harsh reprisals in Yugoslavia and failed to generate widespread support from the Albanian establishment. After the death of Azem Bejta, the movement was weakened significantly. On the kaçak movement in Kosovo, see Dragi Malinković, 'Kačački pokret na Kosovu i Metohiji 1918–1924' [The Kaçak movement in Kosovo and Metohija, 1918–1924], *Novopazarski zbornik* 25 (2001): 231–57; and D. Malinković, 'Kačački pokret na Kosovu i Metohiji 1922–1924' [The Kaçak movement in Kosovo and Metohija, 1922–24], *Baština* 15 (2003): 89–102.

D'Annunzio who occupied Fiume (today, Rijeka) in September 1919. Armed resistance to new state structures and their frontiers created internal instability.[96] Irredentist violence in turn contributed to intensified political repression.

In the decade between 1912 and 1923, the Balkans was ensnared in a dynamic of imperial collapse and nationalist struggle. Although much of the violence of this period took the form of irregular warfare, what intensified the scale of the violence was the growing power of the state which was only further amplified as a consequence of these wars. The decade after 1912 contributed to the gradual yet appreciable militarization of state bureaucracies – not only the growth in importance of military establishments, but the rhetoric of violence as part of national renewal. While the Balkan militaries had already emerged in the late nineteenth century as significant actors, after 1923 their roles were enhanced. This was demonstrated in the rise of military dictatorships in Bulgaria (1934–35), Greece (1936), and Romania (1940), as putative solutions to domestic political crises. In Yugoslavia, the centralist, Serbian-dominated regime relied increasingly on veteran associations and paramilitary societies to promote its goals and to assert its authority, particularly in the period of the royal dictatorship after 1929. Across the board, the rhetoric of violence became increasingly prominent in political discourse although this tendency was also powerfully influenced by the rise of fascism and the radical right in interwar Europe. The instability, trauma and violence of 1912–23 contributed to a perceptible change in the region's political culture, as political groups on the extreme Left and Right saw violence as integral to the achievement of national or ideological ends.

This transformation would have been unimaginable without the rise of the modernizing nation state, whatever its limitations in the Balkans at the time, the ideology of integral nationalism and the transformative traumas of the Balkan Wars and First World War. Although they struggled to establish monopolies of violence in the decades immediately before the Balkan Wars, notwithstanding enduring weaknesses they had made great strides in their collective efforts. In the decades prior to the Balkan Wars, the region's states largely succeeded in co-opting and institutionalizing irregular violence within their own military and administrative structures. Because of the Balkan Wars and the First World War, civilian populations in the region now understood that these states were prepared and, in most cases, able to adopt a range of coercive measures against them if it served the purpose of state consolidation and the defence of its new political frontiers. The adoption of some of these coercive measures had seemed unimaginable two decades earlier. The First World War had also radicalized mentalities across Europe and, measured in terms of the scale of political violence visited upon non-combatants, arguably witnessed the integration of the Balkans into Europe.

Further reading

Army History Directorate. *A Concise History of the Balkan Wars, 1912–1913* (Athens: Hellenic Army General Staff, 1998).

Austin, Robert C. *Founding a Balkan State: Albania's Experiment with Democracy, 1920–1925* (Toronto: University of Toronto Press, 2012).

Babac, Dušan. *The Serbian Army in the Great War, 1914–1918* (Solihull: Helion and Company, 2015).

---

96 It is worth noting, however, that once these irredentist groups were neutralized by the states which harboured them – by Ahmed Zogu in Albania (1925) and the dictatorship in Bulgaria (1934) – they became relatively marginal phenomena. This again demonstrated a truism of modern Balkan violence: it was typically wielded and controlled by the state when it served the fulfilment of elite objectives.

Bartov, Omer, and Eric D. Weitz, eds. *Shatterzone of Empires: Coexistence and Violence in the German, Habsburg, Russian and Ottoman Borderlands* (Bloomington, IN: Indiana University Press, 2013).

Carnegie Endowment for International Peace. *Report of the International Commission to Inquire into the Causes and Conduct of the Balkan Wars* (Washington, DC: 1914).

Carmichael, Cathie, *Ethnic Cleansing in the Balkans: Nationalism and the Destruction of Tradition* (New York: Routledge, 2002).

Chenoweth, Erica, and Adria Lawrence, eds. *Rethinking Violence: States and Non-State Actors in Conflict* (Cambridge, MA: MIT Press, 2010).

Clark, Bruce. *Twice a Stranger: The Mass Expulsions that Forged Modern Greece and Turkey* (London: Granta, 2006).

Dragostinova, Theodora. *Between Two Motherlands: Nationality and Emigration among the Greeks of Bulgaria, 1900–1949* (Ithaca, NY: Cornell University Press, 2011).

Durham, M. Edith. *The Struggle for Scutari (Turk, Slav, and Albanian)* (London: E. Arnold, 1914).

Erickson, Edward J. *Defeat in Detail: The Ottoman Army in the Balkans, 1912–1913* (London: Praeger Publishers, 2003).

Faroqhi, Suraiya, ed. *The Cambridge History of Turkey: The Later Ottoman Empire, 1603–1839* (Cambridge: Cambridge University Press, 2006).

Fotakis, Zisis. *Greek Naval Strategy and Policy, 1910–1919* (New York: Routledge, 2005).

Gerolymatos, Andre. *The Balkan Wars: Conquest, Revolution and Retribution from the Ottoman Era to the Twentieth Century and Beyond* (New York: Basic Books, 2002).

Gerwarth, Robert, and John Horne, eds. *War in Peace: Paramilitary Violence in Europe after the Great War* (Oxford: Oxford University Press, 2012).

Gerwarth, Robert. *The Vanquished: Why the First World War Failed to End, 1917–1923* (London: Allen Lane, 2016).

Gumz, Jonathan. *The Resurrection and Collapse of Empire in Habsburg Serbia, 1914–1918* (Cambridge: Cambridge UP, 2009).

Hall, Richard C. *Balkan Breakthrough: The Battle of Dobro Pole 1918* (Bloomington, IN: Indiana University Press, 2010).

Hall, Richard C. *The Balkan Wars, 1912–1913: Prelude to the First World War* (New York: Routledge, 2002).

Hamilton, Richard F., and Holger H. Herwig, eds. *The Origins of World War I* (Cambridge: Cambridge University Press, 2003).

Hirschon, Renée. *Crossing the Aegean: An Appraisal of the 1923 Compulsory Population Exchange Between Greece and Turkey* (London: Berghahn, 2003).

Jelavich, Charles and Barbara Jelavich. *The Establishment of the Balkan National States, 1804–1920* (Seattle, WA: University of Washington Press, 1977).

Karakasidou, Anastasia. *Fields of Wheat, Hills of Blood: Passages to Nationhood in Greek Macedonia, 1870–1990* (Chicago, IL: The University of Chicago Press, 1997).

Kolev, Valery, and Christina Koulouri, eds. *The Balkan Wars* (Thessaloniki: CDRSEE, 2005).

Koliopoulos, John S. *Brigands with a Cause: Brigandage and Irredentism in Modern Greece 1821–1912* (Oxford: Clarendon Press, 1987).

Kramer, Alan. *Dynamic of Destruction: Culture and Mass Killing in the First World War* (Oxford: Oxford University Press, 2007).

Ladas, Stephen P. *The Exchange of Minorities: Bulgaria, Greece and Turkey* (New York: The Macmillan Company, 1932).

Leon, George B. *Greece and the Great Powers, 1914–1917* (Thessaloniki: Institute for Balkan Studies, 1974).

Leontaritis, George B. *Greece and the First World War: From Neutrality to Intervention, 1917–1918* (New York: East European Monographs, 1990).

Lieberman, Benjamin. *Terrible Fate: Ethnic Cleansing in the Making of Modern Europe* (Chicago, IL: Ivan R. Dee, 2006).

Lüdtke, Alf, and Bernd Weisbrod, eds. *No Man's Land of Violence: Extreme Wars in the 20th Century* (Gottingen: Wallstein Verlag, 2006).

Lyon, James. *Serbia and the Balkan Front, 1914: The Outbreak of the Great War* (London: Bloomsbury Academic, 2015).

Mazower, Mark. *The Balkans: A Short History* (New York: Random House, 2002).

McCarthy, Justin. *The Ottoman Peoples and the End of Empire* (London: Arnold, 2001).

McMeeking, Sean. *The Ottoman Endgame: War, Revolution, and the Making of the Modern Middle, 1908–1923* (New York: Penguin Press, 2015).

Mitrović, Andrej. *Serbia's Great War, 1914–1918* (West Lafayette, IN: Purdue University Press, 2007).
Murray, Nicholas. *The Rocky Road to the Great War: The Evolution of Trench Warfare to 1914* (Dulles, VA: Potomac Books, 2013).
Newman, John Paul. *Yugoslavia in the Shadow of War Veterans and the Limits of State Building, 1903–1945* (Cambridge: Cambridge University Press, 2015).
Özdemir, Hikmet. *The Ottoman Army, 1914–1918: Disease and Death on the Battlefield* (Salt Lake City, UT: The University of Utah Press, 2008).
Pavlović, Srdja. *Balkan Anschluss: The Annexation of Montenegro and the Creation of a Common South Slavic State* (West Lafayette, IN: Purdue University Press, 2008).
Perry, Duncan M. *The Politics of Terror: The Macedonian Liberation Movements, 1893–1903* (Durham, NC: Duke University Press, 1988).
Reiss, Rodolphe Archibald. *The Kingdom of Serbia: Infringements of the Rules and Laws of War Committed by the Austro-Bulgaro-Germans* (London: George Allen & Unwin, 1919).
Roshwald, Aviel. *Ethnic Nationalism and the Fall of Empires: Central Europe, Russia, and the Middle East, 1914–1923* (New York: Routledge, 2001).
Shaw, Stanford Jay, and Ezel Kural Shaw. *History of the Ottoman Empire and Modern Turkey: Reform, Revolution, and Republic – The Rise of Modern Turkey 1808–1975* (Cambridge: Cambridge University Press, 1977).
Smith, Michael Llewellyn. *Ionian Vision: Greece in Asia Minor, 1919–1922* (Ann Arbor, MI: The University of Michigan Press, 1973, revised 1998).
Stefan Sotiris Papaioannou, 'Balkan Wars Between the Lines: Violence and Civilians in Macedonia, 1912–1918', PhD diss., University of Maryland, 2012.
Wingfield, Nancy, and Maria Bucur, eds. *Staging the Past: The Politics of Commemoration in Habsburg Central Europe, 1848 to the Present* (West Lafayette, IN: Purdue University Press, 2001).
Yavuz, Hakan ed., with Peter Sluglett. *War and Diplomacy: The Russo-Turkish War of 1877–1878 and the Treaty of Berlin* (Salt Lake City, UT: The University of Utah Press, 2008).
Yavuz, M. Hakan, and Isa Blumi, eds. *War and Nationalism: The Balkan Wars, 1912–1913, and Their Sociopolitical Implications* (Salt Lake City, UT: The University of Utah Press, 2013).
Yosmaoğlu, İpek K. *Blood Ties: Religion, Violence and the Politics of Nationhood in Ottoman Macedonia, 1878–1908* (Ithaca, NY: Cornell University Press, 2013).

2
THE WAR IN THE EAST, 1914–16

Włodzimierz Borodziej

Experiences of violence

The experience of the Balkan Wars in 1912 and 1913 remained regional. In Germany and in the Habsburg monarchy in 1914, war was remembered primarily by an inactive, elderly generation or had become part of the cultural memory. Besides a statistically irrelevant minority of soldiers who had participated in recent German colonial expeditions, only an older minority in Germany could recall the events of 1870 or 1866, just as an older minority in Austria–Hungary remembered those of 1866, 1859 or even 1848. Russian experiences of violence were significantly more recent: the war with Japan in 1904–05, and especially the subsequent revolution of 1905–07, still served as vivid reference points in Russian social thinking.

The First Russian Revolution is interesting in this context for two reasons. Although forgotten today, this revolution was the first experience of armed struggle for an entire generation of Poles and Balts (although hardly so for Belarusians and Ukrainians), one in which the vast majority of the population did not participate actively, but which nevertheless established new horizons, demonstrating that it was possible to force concessions from the state and the propertied classes. The issues at stake were often the same throughout the tsarist empire in 1905–07: labour protection, wage increases, freedom of assembly, and finally, socially motivated democratization. For this reason, the individual protest waves in the Russian and western parts of the tsarist empire mutually affected and reinforced each other. Martial law, the mass death of protesting workers and peasants, and the executions of protest leaders were experiences shared throughout the empire.

Both sides, moreover, had proved to be vulnerable: property owners and officials, but also police and even the army had been forced to retreat at times. These temporary victories over authorities would have been inconceivable without substantial violence on the part of revolutionaries. There was an additional dimension in the western parts of the tsarist empire: from 1905 to 1907, Poles, Balts and Jews fought simultaneously for social and national emancipation. From this perspective, Poles fought for secession from the tsarist empire or for autonomy within it. Rebelling Estonians and especially Latvians fought against the Russian police and military but focused primarily on large German landowners; Jews fought for political emancipation and equality. This made them the enemies of all those Poles and Balts who were not part of the revolutionary left. Authorities, in turn, supported and protected property: Jewish, Polish and German factory owners in the Kingdom of Poland, the unpopular large Polish landowners in the Lithuanian governorates and their German counterparts in the Baltic provinces who had also been unsuccessfully opposed for decades.¹ More than occasionally, authorities supported all those groups – irrespective of their nationality – that regarded the revolution especially as a vehicle of Jewish emancipation.

Between 1905 and 1907, thousands of people died in the western part of the Russian empire; tens of thousands were wounded, arrested, sentenced and banned; and hundreds of thousands of Russian soldiers were deployed. The situation eased in 1907, and the consequences of the revolution were negotiated in election campaigns, in the Duma itself and particularly among the inner circles of power in St. Petersburg. The experience of the First Russian Revolution played almost no role prior to 1917: in both the literal and the figurative sense the fronts ran along fundamentally different lines, and neither the dimensions nor the forms violence were comparable. Nevertheless, several constellations of the First Russian Revolution returned to Central and Eastern Europe after the second and third revolutions.

The fear of violence and its most extreme form – war – existed in the region as well as elsewhere. Most socialists were opposed to the war, although at the crucial moment almost all of them capitulated, and not only here. Relatively elite circles not associated with Marxism also rejected the war. The best-known current was classical humanitarian pacifism as embodied by Bertha von Suttner, née Countess Kinsky, winner of the Nobel Peace Prize in 1905. Her most important book, *Die Waffen nieder!* ('Lay down your arms!') was published in 1889: it was a bestseller in German-speaking lands and was translated into many languages. The novel recounts the story of a woman who in the midst of nineteenth-century, civilized Europe loses the people closest to her through wars and their consequences. Suttner continued her work for peace by participating in international peace conferences, including The Hague Peace Conference of 1899. The most famous female pacifist (not only) of her own era, Suttner was able to evoke at least as much interest in the issue as Tsar Nicholas II, the initiator of the peace conference.

Jan (Ivan, Jean de, Johann von) Gotlib Bloch, a wealthy Warsaw businessman and another participant of the Hague conference, approached the issue of war from a different perspective. In a multi-volume work published in Polish in the 1890s and translated in excerpts into several languages in 1898–99,² Bloch examined the fear of war from a sober, scholarly perspective. Bloch argued that the potential return to violence between nations posed a basic threat to the achievements of the past decades and in long-winded excursus traced this back to immensely increased destructive capacities. Like many other residents of the region, Bloch lived in a pulsating, rapidly growing metropolis; the old fortifications in Warsaw had been razed to the ground. As in other Central European metropolises, however, new fortifications had recently been built, which were not only obsolete by the time of their completion, but they also impeded the territorial expansion of the city.³ The futility of the arms race was palpable in Warsaw, as it was in other large cities.

Bloch lived in a country that, like most other nations, had introduced compulsory military service. He was one of the few people at the time who could see that a war between the great powers would result in casualties far exceeding the likely deaths of hundreds of thousands of

---

1 Alexander V. Prusin, *The Lands Between: Conflicts in the East European Borderlands, 1870–1992* (Oxford: Oxford University Press, 2010), 32–6. 'Out of two thousand estates burned in the empire, 460 (almost 25%) perished in Latvia and 120 in Estonia', 34.
2 Jan Bloch, *The Future of War in Its Technical, Economic and Political Relations*, trans. R. C. Long, 6 vols. (Boston, MA: Gine, 1899).
3 The Warsaw Fortress had been abandoned in 1909; work on its restoration began in 1913. During the 1890s, Bloch believed that Warsaw was a part of the Russian fortification ring along the Weichsel River, which caused him serious concern.

young men in a few major battles – which would have been bad enough in itself. Over the course of 3,000 pages, Bloch described 'future war' as a catastrophe for all participants. He argued that the development of military technology would turn the battlefield into a slaughtering house in which one modern industrialized state would be not able to defeat another because each side could use previously unimagined capacities of extermination and manpower in the next – ostensibly final – battle. A modern war, in other words, could not be won militarily. At the same time, mobilizing the economy and the population would be paid for through borrowing, which would result in the financial ruin of every economy. Through these theses, Bloch became the best-known spokesman of a small minority in civil society around the turn of the century that regarded modern warfare as a catastrophe for all participating nations because the cost of victory stood in no reasonable relation to a potential success and because the probability of such a victory was extremely low. Contemporary military theorists summarily rejected these fears. They knew better, they had to know better, since Bloch's prophecy fundamentally called into question not only the competency and soundness of the military, but ultimately its very justification for existence.[4]

Enthusiasm for war?

When war broke out almost 15 years later, these discussions had long been forgotten. One indication of their limited effect can be found in the iconic images from August 1914, in which huge crowds of people demonstrated in cities (not only) throughout the German Reich in favour of the war. The fact that the demonstrators were presumably only a minority is of secondary importance here. A more interesting question is whether there was a comparable enthusiasm for war in the East.

Opinions diverge on this question. There are examples that affirm it as well as those that refute it. In the South, where nation states predominated, as well as in the North, in the region predominated by the three empires, the mood was complex in retrospect. In the North, there was evidently some hope of a resounding victory that would resolve all of the social and national tensions between and especially within the great imperial powers. The spontaneous substantial support for the war, however, should not necessarily be traced back to the same emotions that the authorities had sought to incite in capital cities with the decision to take up arms. In the German-dominated parts of multi-language metropolises, imperial patriotism turned almost immediately into pan-German slogans, which at times were also aimed at least indirectly at local neighbours. On the other side, precisely where Germans or German-Austrians lived next to Slavs, the latter's relative lack of enthusiasm was especially conspicuous. After pan-German slogans and songs dominated the streets of Prague for a few days, the governor requested people refrain from further public demonstrations.[5] This did not mean that Slavs refused to fight for

---

4 For example, see Alan Kramer, *Dynamic of Destruction: Culture and Mass Killing in the First World War* (Oxford: Oxford University Press, 2007), 77–8; John Whiteclay Chambers II, 'The American Debate over Modern War, 1871–1914', in *Anticipating Total War: The German and American Experiences, 1871–1914*, eds Manfred Boemke, Roger Chickering and Stig Förster (Cambridge: Cambridge University Press 1999), 241–80, here 259–61. The ultimate consequences of Bloch's book are addressed most clearly in Michael Welch, 'The Centenary of the British Publication of Jean de Bloch's *Is War Now Impossible?* (1899–1999)', *War in History* 7 (2000): 273–94.

5 Jan Galandauer, 'Kriegsbegeisterung in Prag', in *Magister noster: Sborník statí věnovaných in memoriam prof. PhDr. Janu Havránkovi, CSc*, ed. Michal Svatoš (Prague: Karolinum, 2005), 327–33; Jan Havránek, 'Politische Repression und Versorgungsengpässe in den böhmischen Ländern 1914 bis 1918', in *Der Erste Weltkrieg und die Beziehungen zwischen Tschechen, Slowaken und Deutschen*, eds Hans Mommsen, Dušan Kovács and Jirí Malír (Essen: Klartext, 2001), 47–66, here 47–9.

emperor and king: as has been correctly pointed out, the estimated 1.4 million Czechs and Slovaks drafted by 1918 loyally participated in the mobilization of 1914, albeit with 'muted' imperial patriotism.[6] Despite all the subsequent legends about a concrete desire for freedom or secession among Czechs as early as 1914, troops of other nationalities felt quite comfortable in Bohemia:

> [The Austro–Hungarian] IV Army command reported of its journey through Bohemia in August 1914 that 'the behaviour of the populace, of all nationalities, was the best conceivable throughout our journey. Patriotic feeling was everywhere in evidence and at the larger stations the troops were given bread, tea, cigarettes etc. by women of all classes'.[7]

The Poles in Posen remained even more conspicuously in the background than the Czechs in Prague. In Lemberg (or, Lviv), where there were hardly any Germans, the usual processions and church services continued; Poles, Ukrainians and Jews professed their solidarity with the monarchy. The vast majority of political activists and the general population supported the war against the 'Russian threat' for which the dual state seemed to offer more effective protection than any conceivable national political entity.[8] This by no means resolved the problem that the war inevitably raised: people in several borderlands were aware that in the coming war, Poles, Ukrainians, Jews, Romanians and Serbs would fight on both sides of the front, which from the beginning would necessarily mute any enthusiasm for war – despite the loyalty to one's 'own' monarchy. Reality exceeded the worst fears: the first Austro–Hungarian units that were to invade Serbia contained up to 25 per cent Serbs and up to 50 per cent Croats.[9]

The scepticism bordering on fear was also nourished by other sources. A Warsaw journalist wrote expressively and cryptically that the world was facing 'something huge, something terrible in its horror, but nevertheless something unavoidable like a necessity'. Lamenting the unforeseeable risks for every family in Central Europe, the author noted alertly that although the battle had not yet begun, mobilization had already brought with it a 'violent, unexpected suspension of life': 'Modern industrialism has so complicated the economic side of human existence, so tied everything together that the entire world is immediately derailed and finds itself on the eve of an unprecedented economic catastrophe'.[10] Nevertheless, mobilization proceeded smoothly on both sides of the emerging Eastern front.

In the summer of 1914, almost 4 million men were drafted without greater delays in the Russian empire. As on the opposing side, there were demonstrations and processions, religious services and pledges of allegiance in the large cities, irrespective of their ethnic compositions.

---

6 Natali Stegmann, '"Geburt" und "Wiederrichtung" der Tschechoslowakei: Das Legionärsparadigma am Ende des Ersten und des Zweiten Weltkriegs', in *Die Weltkriege als symbolische Bezugspunkte: Polen, die Tschechoslowakei und Deutschland nach dem Ersten und Zweiten Weltkrieg*, ed. Natali Stegmann (Prague: Masarykuv ústav a Archiv AV CR, 2009), 71–90, here 72.
7 Norman Stone, *The Eastern Front 1914–1917* (New York: Charles Scribner's Sons, 1975), 126.
8 For an overview of the pro-Habsburg attitudes of Poles, Jews and Ukrainians in Galicia, see Jerzy Z. Pająk, *Od autonomii do niepodległości. Kształtowanie się postaw politycznych i narodowych społeczeństwa Galicji w warunkach Wielkiej Wojny 1914–1918* [From autonomy to independence: Shaping the political and national attitudes of the Galician society during the Great War of 1914–1918] (Kielce: Wydawn. Uniwersytetu Jana Kochanowskiego, 2012), 55–62, 70–2, 75–80.
9 Andrej Mitrovic, *Serbia's Great War, 1914–1918* (London: Hurst, 2007), 67.
10 Z.[dzisław] Dębicki, 'Wojna!', *Tygodnik Illustrowany* 32 (8 August 1914), 11.

But here as well, appearances could be deceiving: almost simultaneous to his Bohemian colleague, the governor of Livonia forbade the continuation of patriotic street demonstrations on 7 August because they had been misused by the Social Democratic Party for its own purposes.[11] In many locations, usually in towns and villages, there were confrontations between recruits and police with no political background or potential for development as a rule, but they frequently accompanied by alcohol consumption based on tradition and occasion – the marching out of young men.[12] In the most western part of the tsarist empire, that is, the Vistula Land, where political protests would have seemed most likely, mobilization proceeded smoothly. And when Russian troops – including Cossacks (who had been hated even before the revolution of 1905) – advanced to the front, they were bid farewell in the Warsaw city centre as defenders against the German threat, and were showered with flowers, candy and cigars. This apparently spontaneous demonstration of sympathy was carried out not by the small Russian minority but was improvised by Warsaw Poles.

The numerous, often contradictory images of enthusiasm and rejection cannot be reduced to equations. They remain part of the final impressions of an empire that entered the war without being able to offer its multi-ethnic society – divided politically, socially and religiously – any integrative identification figure comparable to a nation state. The issue was not fundamentally different in the Habsburg monarchy, except that Russia lacked any comparable tradition of local communities protesting the conscription of sons and husbands.

In both Vienna and St. Petersburg, the belief that the respective monarchy could hope for the loyalty of its subjects irrespective of ethnic and religious differences appears to have predominated throughout, since the monarchy protected them from the self-proclaimed danger from the East or, as the case may be, the West. This imperial loyalty did in fact exist on both sides, as previously mentioned, but local elites had hoped it would be greater. The divided nations promised themselves that a victory by 'their' empire and the subsequent redrawing of the political map would lead to unification with their countrymen beyond existing borders. Minorities that lived completely in one empire such as Latvians or Czechs hoped for liberalization or, optimally, for autonomy. From the perspective of authorities in Vienna, Budapest or St. Petersburg, these two expectations tied to victory had little appeal as programmes of national emancipation. Even the most pleasing prospect – a resounding defeat of the enemy – would mean territorial gains, which were hardly desirable since they would exacerbate internal ethnic problems, as would the liberalization of domestic relations (promised by all sides), which would necessarily place new emphasis on national and social issues.

The nation states constituted a different world. All of the Balkan states had suffered significant losses in 1912–13. None of them could economically afford a new war. Their populations also feared war. Elites were divided as to what was the best solution: neutrality, joining up with the Central Powers, or an alliance with the Entente Powers.[13] The Austro–Hungarian ambassador in Athens said after one of the domestic crises that placed Greece before the same

---

11 Alfred von Hedenström, *Rigaer Kriegschronik 1914–1917* (Riga: E. Bruhns, 1922), 5.
12 Joshua A. Sanborn, *Drafting the Russian Nation: Military Conscription, Total War, and Mass Politics* (De Kalb, IL: Northern Illinois University Press, 2003), 29–31; see also Aaron B. Retish, *Russia's Peasants in Revolution and Civil War: Citizenship, Identity, and the Creation of the Soviet State, 1914–1922* (Cambridge: Cambridge University Press, 2008), 27–8.
13 'Elsewhere in the Balkans [i.e. outside of Turkey], the mood in 1914 was generally sombre and the wave of popular enthusiasm for war seen in Paris, London, and Berlin was almost entirely absent'. See Mark Biondich, *The Balkans: Revolution, War and Political Violence since 1878* (Oxford: Oxford University Press, 2011), 88.

ordeal: the country is 'indeed pro-Entente, but not eager for war'.[14] His colleagues in Bucharest or Sofia could have written the same lines; 'Entente' and 'Central Powers' were as completely interchangeable here as two figures of thought with unpredictable future prospects.

Only in Serbia were matters different from the outset. The kingdom had virtually no choice but to reject the Austro–Hungarian ultimatum and prepare for a defensive war, for which it lacked the material resources. Nevertheless, this decision was supported by at least part of the population in Belgrade. There was short-lived enthusiasm for a war that was reinforced by attacks on Serbs in the neighbouring provinces of the Habsburg monarchy (which, in turn, gave rise to the demonstrations of loyalty by local southern Slavs to 'their' state).[15] Paradoxically, the local socialists in Belgrade were one of the few political parties of the Socialist International (the others being the Russian Bolsheviks, Mensheviks and Trudoviks) to remain faithful to their basic anti-war principle by voting against war loans in parliament.[16]

The situation was different in neighbouring Bulgaria, the first country to go to war completely voluntarily. In Sofia, the authorities longed for an opportunity to revenge their defeat in the Second Balkan War. Nevertheless, the opposition insisted on maintaining neutrality. Resistance to an alliance with the Central Powers was eliminated only with the arrest of opposition leaders. When Bulgaria declared war on Serbia one week later, on 14 October 1915, no real enthusiasm arose. The new war was more feared than celebrated.[17]

In Bucharest as well, there was no reason for euphoria in the summer of 1914. Domestic disputes continued for another two years, and it remained unclear on which side of the world war the country would enter. The option of neutrality also existed. When Romania attacked the Habsburg monarchy in late 1916, and they achieved temporary military success in Transylvania, despite significant scepticism by many intellectuals and politicians, the sense of jubilation in Bucharest appears to have been great – and yet, the celebrations evaporated within days.[18] A little more than three months later, following the rapid defeat of the Romanian armed forces and the king's flight to Iasi, General Field Marshal August von Mackensen was outraged by the friendly reception from Bucharest residents:

> I am really scandalized by this enthusiasm, since we were celebrated by the same mob that had called for war against us. … One could accept something like this at most in an allied country, but in an enemy country it is downright repulsive.[19]

---

14 Lothar Höbelt, 'Der Balkan und die Strategie der Entente', in *Der Erste Weltkrieg auf dem Balkan: Perspektiven der Forschung*, ed. Jürgen Angelow (Berlin: be.bra, 2011), 57–73, here 59.
15 Daniela Schanes, *Serbien im Ersten Weltkrieg: Feind- und Kriegsdarstellungen in österreichisch-ungarischen, deutschen und serbischen Selbstzeugnissen* (Frankfurt a.M.: Peter Lang, 2011), 138–40, 143–4. For a detailed account of the anti-Serbian reprisals in the Habsburg hinterland, see Mitrovic, *Serbia's Great War*, 74–8.
16 Biondich, *The Balkans*, 84.
17 Björn Opfer, *Im Schatten des Krieges: Besatzung oder Anschluss – Befreiung oder Unterdrückung? Eine komparative Untersuchung über die bulgarische Herrschaft in Vardar-Makedonien 1915–1918 und 1941–1944* (Münster: LIT, 2005), 57, 63, 109–10.
18 Ioan Scurtu, 'August 1916: Starea de spirit a românilor' [August 1916: the mood of the Romanians], *Dosarele Istoriei* 11 (2006): 13–19; idem, *Istoria românilor în timpul celor patru regi (1866–1947)* [The history of the Romanians during the four kings (1866–1947)], vol. 2: *Ferdinand I* (Bucharest: Editura Enciclopedica, 2001). I am grateful to Viorel Achim for pointing out these studies to me and for the translation.
19 Cited in Raymund Netzhammer, *Bischof in Rumänien: Im Spannungsfeld zwischen Staat und Vatikan*, vol. I (München: Südostdeutsches Kulturwerk, 1995), 698, entry from 16 December 1916.

The field marshal correctly understood that residents of the Romanian capital would have greeted the return of a victorious King Ferdinand with similar enthusiasm; but what he did not at all comprehend was that many of the residents saw no reason to mourn an evidently failed elite that, after two years of intense discussions, had unnecessarily made such a completely wrong-headed decision.

Eastern Europe was drawn into the war in 1914. The empires that sent their people into battle had no war objectives in the traditional sense. There were no contested provinces; the issue, rather, was maintaining a balance of power in Europe and preserving their own position as a great power, defending themselves against an enemy who ostensibly wanted to call both of these issues into question, and removing an occasional minor thorn from their sides. In contrast, the nation states of Southeastern Europe (aside from Serbia, which was an exception from the beginning) made the sovereign decision to go to war in the hope of profiting from it. However, there was by no means extensive enthusiasm for war among their own populations. The respective decisions were the work of the elite or that part of the elite that was at the time most assertive or most skilful in terms of tactics and arguments. Nothing had been predetermined by history, emotion, national traditions or even a passion for killing.

Enemy images

Since *The Last Days of Mankind* (1915–22) by Karl Kraus,[20] we have been convinced that Austro–Hungarian troops, especially in the southeast, were driven by a hatred and contempt for humanity and that a specific *esprit de corps* and factual legal impunity in dealing with the local population made them into mass murderers. Before we turn to both alleged and actual war crimes, however, two longer excurses are necessary: the first covers traditional enemy images and the second covers the new enemy images that arose during the world war.

The stereotypes that Germans and Austrians had about the Balkans, which can be traced in part back to previous centuries and decades, were affirmed by the 1903 Serbian regicide and its aftermath as well as by the wars of 1912–13. The ostensibly 'Oriental' traits of 'Balkan peoples' developed into the insult of being 'Asian' – which was used primarily to characterize Turks, Albanians and Bulgarians – and being 'Balkan' (or *balkanisch* in German), which had similarly negative connotations. These terms were supposed to imply backwardness and contentiousness, squalor and malice, cruelty and superstition, unpredictability and corruptibility, aggressiveness and mendacity. Their opposite, of course, was 'Europe', in whose name both Germany and Austria–Hungary were leading a war against culturally and, especially, morally inferior enemies in the southeast.[21] The perfidious qualities were not only attributed to the enemies of the Central Powers (especially the 'traitorous' Romanians) but even to their own allies: friend or foe was not especially important here from moral–cultural perspectives. The Chief of the Great German General Staff, Helmuth von Moltke, summarized this relationship to the entire 'Balkans' when he made the following recommendation to his

---

20 Karl Kraus, *The Last Days of Mankind: The Complete Text*, trans. Fred Bridgham and Edward Timms (New Haven, CT: Yale University Press, 2015).
21 See Mechthild Golczewski, *Der Balkan in deutschen und österreichischen Reise- und Erlebnisberichten 1912–1918* (Wiesbaden: Franz Steiner, 1981), especially 64–7. Similar ascriptions can be found in Schanes, *Serbien im Ersten Weltkrieg*.

Austro–Hungarian counterpart in August 1914: 'Let the Bulgarians loose against the Serbs and let the pack beat each other to death'.[22]

It remains unclear, however, to what extent enemy images actually translated into violence. For example, there are no known German or Habsburg war crimes in Romania, which was especially hated by the two. North of the Eastern front, the Central Powers fought against a barbaric, despotic and ridiculed tsarist empire, which was simultaneously one of the traditional great powers and enjoyed an imperial status incomparable to the Balkan monarchies. While notions of Polish, Latvian and Ukrainian inferiority did influence the patrimonial attitude of the German military, the focus in the occupied – up to this point, western Russian – territories was not on crime and punishment (as in Serbia), but rather on convincing Poles, Balts and Ukrainians to join the fight against Russia or enter into a junior partnership with the German Reich. This consideration for future allies in a German-dominated Central Europe proved to be significantly more effective than notions about enemies and *Kulturträgertum*. The question of enemy images of the other warring powers also appears rather irrelevant. The section below titled 'War Crimes' will examine the behaviour of the Russian army in the parts of East Prussia and Galicia that were briefly occupied, an example that offers little evidence that stereotypes were in fact implemented as actions and attitudes. The Bulgarian occupation was particularly hated in the southeast, which was certainly tied to the anti-Serbian, anti-Greek and anti-Romanian resentments held by the Bulgarian elites. These resentments were not necessarily new but were reinforced in 1913, although they were likely more forcibly articulated in 1915.

Jews, as always, constituted a special case. The rise of anti-Semitism in the Habsburg monarchy has been tied to the approximately 300,000 Jews who fled westwards from Galicia and Bukovina in 1914. Eastern European Jews (*Ostjuden*) were regarded as symbols of filthiness, disease and repellent foreignness wherever they arrived, not only by local authorities and the Christian population, but also by the Jews already living there who had in part become established and had simply adapted to the city; the latter were awkwardly reminded of their own origins and were somewhat ashamed of their compatriots, but they also felt obliged to help them. The Jewish community in Prague had significant difficulty dealing with a relatively small group of refugees.[23] A much larger number of Jews from Galicia and Bukovina (up to an estimated 100,000) found temporary refuge in Vienna. It was not because of the numbers, however, that the aversion to Jews increased tremendously in both cities.[24] In 1917, there were local pogroms in several parts of Cisleithania, including Bohemia and Moravia as well as Galicia, and these even increased in 1918, although they did not (as a rule) result in deaths.[25]

---

22 Cited in Opfer, *Im Schatten des Krieges*, 143. On the constantly tense German-Bulgarian relationship during the 'brotherhood-in-arms' period, see for example, ibid., 140–5; Stefan Minkov, 'Der Status der Nord-Dobrudscha im Kontext des deutsch-bulgarischen Verhältnisses im Ersten Weltkrieg', in Angelow, *Der Erste Weltkrieg auf dem Balkan*, 241–55.

23 Martin Welling, *'Von Haß so eng umkreist': Der Erste Weltkrieg aus der Sicht der Prager Juden* (Frankfurt a.M.: Peter Lang, 2003), 122, 125–6, 150–1.

24 Welling, *'Von Haß so eng umkreist'*, 162–3, 169–72.

25 Peter Heumos, '"Kartoffeln her oder es gibt eine Revolution": Hungerkrawalle, Streiks und Massenproteste in den böhmischen Ländern 1914–1918', in Mommsen, Kovács, and Malír, *Der Erste Weltkrieg*, 255–86, here 265–6. On the Kingdom of Poland, see Konrad Zieliński, *Żydzi Lubelszczyzny 1914–1918* [Jews of the Lublin Region 1914–1918] (Lublin: Lubelskie Tow. Naukowe, 1999); idem, *Stosunki polsko-żydowskie na ziemiach Królestwa Polskiego w czasie pierwszej wojny światowej* [Polish-Jewish relations in the territory of the Kingdom of Poland during the First World War] (Lublin: Wydawnictwo Uniwersytetu Marii Curie-Skłodowskiej, 2005).

The presence of the refugees who were regarded as repulsive or even dangerous (which subsequently caused a readiness in urban residents of the hinterland to resort to violence) was one of several catalysts for anti-Jewish attitudes and actions. As is well known, anti-Semitism increased everywhere, from Great Britain to Germany and the Habsburg monarchy, all the way to Russia. 'Coffee house Jews' (as they were called in the cities of the Dual Monarchy and elsewhere) were regarded everywhere as war profiteers. In a complex, dynamic process that was at once transnational and independent of political systems, they were accused of the same offences almost everywhere: ostensibly not serving on the front, and also being the actual benefactors of the crisis in the hinterland as well as the occupied territories – that is, independent of their citizenship. The obsession with espionage spread along the Eastern front, perhaps even more powerfully than in the West; and again, Jews, who were supposedly notoriously disloyal, assumed the central role irrespective of the country. Only in Russia have historians surmised conscious pre-war policies of social degradation and repression,[26] which – even if the hypothesis is correct – were not necessarily the decisive reason for the spread of ideas about 'Jewish spies'. In any case, the unlimited powers of the tsarist military in the enormous 'war zone', which soon extended from the Baltic Sea to Bukovina, legitimated anti-Jewish practices locally and impeded any access by the judiciary. Moreover, the consequences of these policies were underestimated not only for Jews, but for all ethnicities along the old western border of the tsarist empire: In 1914, 'a total of eight men in the *Stavka* [Russian general staff] (including orderlies) were supposed to administer an area larger than the entire state territory of each of the European powers with which Russia was at war'.[27]

Among German occupiers, there were two competing perceptions regarding Jews. The first was their initially positive surprise at encountering a group of people far to the east of the German Reich, whose wealthiest members evidently clung to German culture. This perception was gradually eclipsed by the fear that Jewish masses were carriers of filth and disease, something that appeared as threatening to soldiers and officers as it was to the residents of Vienna and Prague.

All of them – authorities such as the army, occupation officials and civil servants in the hinterland – shared a basic attitude: Jews were simply the easiest people to exploit and blackmail. Examples in Eastern Galicia and Bukovina are too numerous to cite here,[28] and corresponding examples can also be found in other regions. For example, in Riga in late 1915, one witness noted the rapid spread of 'penalties for insufficient window coverings', which he had already identified as a new source of revenue for the police.

> The punishment for this is on a sliding scale according to ethnicity. Jews have to pay 100 to 200 roubles or are sentenced to a month in prison. For Germans, the punishment is half of this, for Latvians and Russians, one-third of the Jewish amount.[29]

---

26 Prusin, *The Lands Between*, 36, 47.

27 On this, see Jochen Böhler, 'Generals and Warlords, Revolutionaries and Nation-State Builders: The First World War and its Aftermath in Central and Eastern Europe', in *Legacies of Violence: Eastern Europe's First World War*, eds Jochen Böhler, Włodzimierz Borodziej and Joachim von Puttkamer (München: Oldenbourg, 2014), 51–66, here 54–7. The citation has been taken from Daniel William Graf, 'The Reign of the Generals: Military Government in Western Russia, 1914–1915', PhD diss., University of Nebraska-Lincoln (1972).

28 A veritable treasure trove can be found in a report by Dr Bernard Hauser – a secondary school teacher and rabbi in Lemberg – presented to the interior ministry in Vienna about the period of Russian occupation. See Pająk, *Od autonomii*, passim.

29 Hedenström, *Rigaer Kriegschronik*, 76, 86.

This 'ethnic sliding scale' for punishments certainly represented the gentlest manifestation of anti-Semitism evident in everyday life on the Eastern front.

The backdrop for this everywhere was traditional Christian anti-Judaism, reformulated in modernity as the general suspicion of a Jewish world conspiracy and bolstered more recently through an alliance between Marxist Jews and similar thinking groups. New elements were adopted, beginning in 1914: in virtually all of the territories occupied by German-speaking troops, Jews were the preferred transaction partners of the occupiers; in the hinterland, they were seen as the beneficiaries of the general scarcity and as freeloaders who received refugee assistance and simultaneously profited from the black market. They were also frequently accused of denunciation.[30] Thousands of caricatures, newspaper commentaries and other materials printed in the modern era depicted images in which readers could identify both themselves and the cause of their misery: on the one hand, the Jews, who were clever, rich and always, at any price, successful; and on the other, the poor, exploited Christians.

Nevertheless, anti-Jewish excesses were still frowned upon, despite their increasing frequency. Following the withdrawal of Russian occupiers from Galicia in 1915, the issues of war damage, destruction, robbery, the debasement of Jews and pogroms predominated in the local press. Evidently the hostility of 'Russians' or 'Cossacks' to Jews was still considered convincing proof of the backwardness of the tsarist empire. This, however, did not prevent local Christians from regarding Jews as the main cause of their own suffering.

The experience of the front

The two fronts that existed in the East until late 1915 differed significantly. The Russian front alone was twice as long as the Western front,[31] initially spanning from East Prussia over the Kingdom of Poland (west of the Weichsel in the north, and east of the river in the south) to Eastern Galicia and Bukovina. Three great powers fought here, although, despite all the propaganda, none of them contested the others' right to exist.

The Serbian front was 900 kilometres long. The Austro–Hungarian army invaded the 'country of assassins' with the claims of a colonial power intent on subduing local hordes gone wild. This 'punitive expedition' immediately turned into a disaster. The enemy had been hopelessly underestimated in Vienna. Between the summer of 1914 and the summer of 1915 there was mobile warfare on the Russian front, with large armies travelling hundreds of kilometres for relatively brief battles (spanning days rather than weeks), inflicting heavy losses on the enemy (who also frequently engaged in offensive attacks) and suffering them as well. The front ultimately moved very little as a result of singular major events, with two significant exceptions: the Austro–Hungarian defeat in the autumn of 1914 and the collapse of the Russian army over the spring and summer of the following year. In Serbia, troops moved within smaller spaces, with the front line changing little until October 1915. The Austro–Hungarian offensives failed repeatedly due to determined resistance by an underestimated enemy. There was classical mobile warfare in Romania beginning in August 1916: within a little more than

---

30 For example, after the Russian withdraw from Galicia in 1915, Jews were said to have filed charges with the Honved against eleven Ukrainian neighbours in one village – 'unblemished farmers' who were promptly hung; see Hannes Leidinger, '"Der Einzug des Galgens und des Mordes:" Die parlamentarischen Stellungnahmen polnischer und ruthenischer Reichsratsabgeordneter', *Zeitgeschichte* 33, no. 5 (2006): 235–60, here 244.

31 Hew Strachan, *The First World War* (London: Simon and Schuster, 2003), 133.

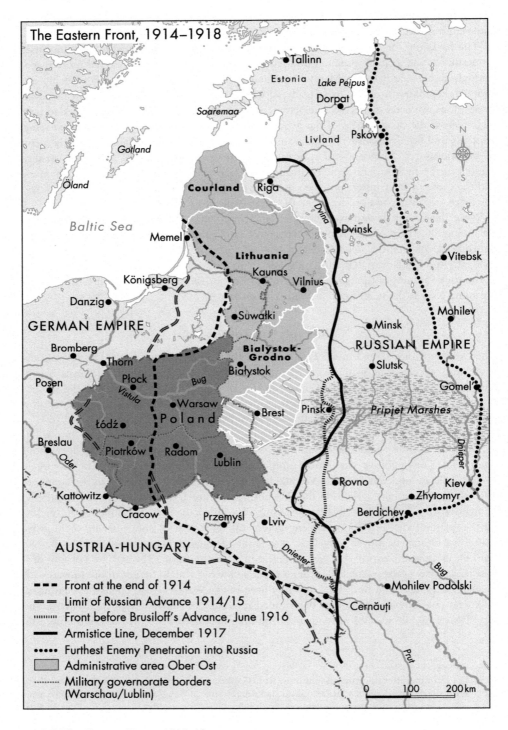

Map 2.1 The Eastern Front, 1914–18

three months, the invading Romanians advanced to Transylvania but were soon pushed back into their own country and forced to retreat to the north-eastern remainder of it, where, with Russian assistance, they were finally able to establish and maintain a stable front against troops of the Central Powers.

How many millions of men who fought on the Eastern front will probably always be a contested issue. According to a daring estimate by Maria Bucur (which correctly underscores the erroneous magnitude of current estimates but is not entirely credible in its own details), a total of about 33 million men fought on the fronts in the East, a greater number than on the Western front. With around 6 million dead, casualties in the East were about twice as high as in the West, proportionally highest in Serbia (37 per cent), the Ottoman Empire (27 per cent), Romania (26 per cent), and Bulgaria (23 per cent).[32]

Bucur's estimate stands in shocking contrast to the usual image of the First World War, in which the trenches in the West and the Battles of Verdun and Somme predominate. The industrialized mass butchery of men, however, was similar on the fronts in the East, beginning with the 12 Battles of the Isonzo in 1915–17, which were part of the Italian front, but continued into Slovenia. Hundreds of thousands of Austrians, Hungarians, Slavs and Romanians fought and died there; tens of thousands of Russian prisoners of war worked and died immediately behind the front lines. Other battles on the Eastern front – the manoeuvre warfare in 1914, the massacre in the Carpathian Mountains in early 1915, the Gorlice–Tarnów Offensive in the spring of that year, and the Brusilov offensive in the following year – did not have fewer dead and wounded than the battles on the Western front, and the number of prisoners in the East was significantly higher.

Nevertheless, there are good reasons to doubt that either the total number of soldiers deployed, or the overall death count, was higher in the East than in the West. But even if the number of soldiers on non-Western battlegrounds may have been less than the totals in the West and in Italy combined, and even if casualties may have been comparable rather than twice as high, Bucur's estimates highlight an undervaluation of the 'unknown front' that has continued from the beginning of the war, up to the present day. In terms of both the number of participants and the endangerment to life and health, the wars on the Eastern fronts were by no means less murderous.

The Battles of Przasnysz, familiar only to a small circle of specialists, can serve as an example here. The town of Przasnysz is located a little more than 100 kilometres to the north of Warsaw, close to the southern border of East Prussia. Hundreds of thousands of Germans and Russians fought here three different times: in November and December of 1914 and then in February and July of the following year. Each of the battles lasted for weeks; the city was conquered numerous times, lost, and then retaken. In the final battle alone, the Germans had more than 16,000 dead and wounded, the Russians, almost 40,000. The total number of casualties and prisoners in the three battles must have far exceeded 100,000. Seventy per cent of the city was destroyed and on average eighty per cent of the surrounding villages.[33]

During the third Battle of Przasnysz, the German offensive proportionally concentrated more artillery on the breakthrough section than at the only well-known battle of the Eastern front in 1915 – that is, Gorlice – which took place two months earlier. The Russians were unable to offer much resistance, as they continued to suffer from an ammunition shortage.

---

32 Maria Bucur, *Heroes and Victims: Remembering War in Twentieth-Century Romania* (Bloomington, IN: Indiana University Press 2010), 51.

33 Apart from local amateur historians, no one has yet dealt with this theatre of war.

The generals of the tsarist regime knew by this time that it was impossible to survive this war without artillery shells in amounts that had been inconceivable in 1914. Russian experts estimated that 400 rounds of heavy artillery or 25,000 rounds of light artillery were needed to tear a 50-metre hole in Germany's position secured threefold with barbed wire.[34] However, it was not until a year later that the munitions industry was able to catch up with demand. While in the first two years of the war Austria–Hungary had had an apparently significant, almost sevenfold increase in the production of shells (from 300,000 to 2,000,000 per month), Russian industry produced about fifty times more in 1916 than it had in 1914 (from 666,000 to over 33,000,000).[35] During the Brusilov offensive in 1915, the Russians smothered the enemy with artillery fire, just as the latter had done to them previously.

The greatest massacre occurred not only because of the extensive use of the most modern killing methods on the Eastern front. An Austrian mountain brigade commander on the Serbian front noted in November 1914 with the beginning of winter:

> For a week already the troops have had no bread, but an abundance of meat, no tobacco and no shoes. … Everything is snowed in and the ground has frozen; our troops are so exhausted that they can no longer function properly. … The situation is awful. Everything is drowning in filth; when you leave your room, you see only misery, bloody casualties, exhausted horses, animal cadavers, tattered soldiers encrusted in filth. How long can this continue?[36]

In the following months it was, if possible, even worse on the Eastern front. The breakthrough at Gorlice in May 1915 occurred after a winter in which Austro–Hungarian and Russian troops had faced off in the Carpathian Mountains. 'The entire day strange looking platoons march past our hut along the street in the driving snow,' wrote German officer Henry Graf Kessler on 1 February 1915. From inside his warm hut, Kessler noted:

> Beasts of burden with loads covered in heavy snow, ox-carts (fifty to a hundred of them in succession), sleds with munitions or food, Austrian infantry who can barely trudge forward; or in the other direction troops of dull looking Russian prisoners, with snowflakes falling on them like fate. You sit as if you were at the movies and watch the Carpathian passage.[37]

Very few people on both sides of the front had this luxury. Both the Russian and the Austro–Hungarian armies were exhausted, undersupplied and unprepared in every respect for winter in the sparsely populated mountains. Since the beginning of the fighting, food and especially warmth had been scarce. Despite the bitter cold, Austro–Hungarian troops engaged in offensives, in which not only the supply chain, but even the simplest weapons failed. No heavy

---

34 Timothy C. Dowling, *The Brusilov Offensive* (Bloomington, IN: Indiana University Press, 2008), 42.
35 Max Stephan Schulze, 'Austria–Hungary's Economy in World War I', in *The Economics of World War I*, eds Stephen Broadberry and Mark Harrison (Cambridge: Cambridge University Press, 2005), 77–111, here 88; Peter Gatrell, 'Poor Russia, Poor show: Mobilising a Backward Economy for War, 1914–1917', in Broadberry and Harrison, *The Economics of World War I*, 235–75, here 242.
36 Cited in Schanes, *Serbien im Ersten Weltkrieg*, 117.
37 Cited in Jens Flemming, Klaus Saul and Peter-Christian Witt, eds, *Lebenswelten im Ausnahmezustand: Die Deutschen, der Alltag und der Krieg, 1914–1918* (Frankfurt a.M.: Peter Lang, 2011), 59.

artillery fire was needed here; weeks of hardship, exertion, cold and hunger sufficed. The Austro–Hungarian Second Army reported on 14 March – neither the cold nor the fighting was over at this point in time – that it had lost 40,000 of its 95,000 men, 6,000 in battle, the rest through disease and frostbite.[38]

> Every day hundreds froze to death; the wounded who could not drag themselves off were bound to die.... Some 800,000 men are said to have disappeared from the army's strength during the Carpathian operation – three-quarters of them from sickness.[39]

The number was presumably closer to 600,000, but statistically an Austro–Hungarian soldier in the mountains had a life expectancy of five or six weeks,[40] and matters on the Russian side were not much different.

During the first year of the war, armies in both the West and the East were unprepared for mass-scale illness. This was unavoidable in the Carpathians during the winter, since it was extremely difficult to transport weakened, fevering, half-starved and half-frozen soldiers to the next sick bay on the limited railway lines or on streets covered with ice and snow. Given the enormous number of patients, a bed in a sick bay or even in a hospital was no guarantee for survival.

When, in May, the Central Powers' offensive forced the enemy to abandon its Carpathian position, the Germans were astonished by how shallow the Russian trenches were in comparison to the Western front. They soon learned that this was due less to sloth of the Russians than to a terrain different than that of Flanders and France. 'The trenches were not what one generally thinks of as a trench', one German artillery lieutenant noted on the Macedonian front. 'Given the hard bedrock and the scarcity of explosives most of the trenches were only 25–30 centimetres deep. Stones had been piled up as a rampart in the direction of the enemy'.[41] Engaging in static warfare in the mountains during the winter required almost inhuman fortitude from the soldiers. Another German officer, transferred to a Bulgarian unit, repeated – unknowingly and precisely – the descriptions of the Russian–Habsburg Carpathian front in the winter of 1914–15:

> People jammed between the rocks, frozen, without supplies, the fear of incoming artillery fire on their faces. No funk hole, no trench, nothing. Between them unburied corpses. The soldiers with weapons so filthy they could not be fired, without any discipline, merely a heap of human misery.[42]

The number of people killed, wounded and captured on the Eastern fronts becomes comprehensible if we take into account the millions of soldiers who fought and their use of modern weapons, the initially insufficient medical care everywhere, and the fact – only recently recognized – that mobile warfare results in particularly heavy losses.

---

38 Wolfdieter Bihl, *Der Erste Weltkrieg: Chronik—Daten—Fakten* (Vienna: Böhlau, 2010), 111.
39 Stone, *Eastern Front*, 114.
40 Lothar Höbelt, 'Österreich-Ungarns Nordfront 1914/1915', *Die vergessene Front: Der Osten 1914/15 – Ereignis, Wirkung, Nachwirkung*, ed. Gerhard P. Groß (Paderborn: Schöningh, 2006), 87–119, here 101. Höbelt estimates that the losses were as high as 600,000 and emphasizes that never before and never again did they reach this number.
41 Cited in Opfer, *Im Schatten des Krieges*, 67.
42 Cited in Ibid., 68.

The Russian army had lost 2.3 million soldiers by the end of 1915,[43] 1.4 million of them in the catastrophe between May and August 1915 (with half of them taken prisoner).[44] Austria–Hungary had lost 1.1 million soldiers by January 1915, and a further 2 million were killed, wounded and captured in the following year.[45] The smallest countries had the greatest losses proportionally: in September 1915, the Serbian army still had over 420,000 soldiers, around two-thirds of whom would be lost by the end of the year.[46] Losses among the Austro–Hungarian troops on this front were similar (over 270,000 of 450,000). The difference here lay in the relationship between the losses and the total potential: the approximately 150,000 Serbs who ultimately reached Corfu and Bizerte were all that remained of the over 700,000 soldiers mobilized in a country with only 4.5 million inhabitants.

Casualties also remained high in 1916. During their victorious attacks in the initial month of the Brusilov offensive, the Russians lost almost 600,000 soldiers and officers, the majority of them in the first week of July, when the resistance of the Central Powers consolidated.[47] Half of these casualties were deaths. Over the course of the summer the number rose to almost 2 million, again half of them deaths, which affected the battle morale of even previously elite troops.[48] On the other side, the Austro–Hungarian 4th Army lost two-thirds of its troops in the first four days of the Russian offensive.[49] In the three summer months, during which the Russians were able to push the Central Powers back about 50 kilometres in the middle section of the front and about 125 kilometres in the southern section, there were around 1.5 million dead and wounded as well as 400,000 prisoners of war, primarily from the Habsburg monarchy.[50]

Spurred on in part by Russian successes in the North, Romania risked an attack on Transylvania in August 1916 and lost significantly more than half of its army in a little over three months (from late August to early December, when Bucharest surrendered): 73,000 dead and wounded, 147,000 captured, and 90,000 missing.[51]

Casualties in the officer corps were dramatic: in the first year of the war both the Habsburg monarchy and tsarist empire lost the majority of their younger commanders.[52] Russia began the war with 80,000 mobilized officers. By 1915, four-fifths of them had been lost; in the following year, casualties consisted of a further 26,000 dead, wounded, missing and captured.[53]

---

43 Gerhard P. Groß, 'Im Schatten des Westens', in Groß, *Die vergessene Front*, 49–64, here 62.
44 Strachan, *The First World War*, 140.
45 Dowling, *The Brusilov Offensive*, 167.
46 Strachan, *The First World War*, 154.
47 Disproportionally in attacks on the Germans. When in mid-June, that is, at the high point of a successful offensive, the Russians attacked the Germans with a five-fold superiority, they lost 7,000 men, while German casualties were 150. See Dowling, *The Brusilov Offensive*, 92–3.
48 Ibid., 101, 111, 160, 162.
49 Ibid., 168 (different figures on p. 103: over 100,000 men, in other words, 57% casualties for the 4th Army during the initial weeks).
50 Ibid., 163.
51 According to Bihl, *Der Erste Weltkrieg*, 145, the Romanian army had over 560,000 men in the late summer of 1916; Dowling, *The Brusilov Offensive*, 159.
52 On the Serbian front alone, the Habsburg monarchy lost two-thirds of its officers. See M. Christian Ortner, 'Die Feldzüge gegen Serbien in den Jahren 1914 und 1915', in Angelow, *Der Erste Weltkrieg*, 123–42, here 135–6.
53 Dietrich Beyrau and Pavel P. Shcherbinin, 'Alles für die Front: Russland im Krieg 1914–1922', in *Durchhalten! Krieg und Gesellschaft im Vergleich 1914–1918*, eds Arnd Bauerkämper and Elise Julien (Göttingen: Vandenhoeck & Ruprecht, 2010), 151–77, here 157.

Troops on both sides of the front were affected by the omnipresence of danger, death, fear, injury and disease. Nothing was predetermined by this, neither social nor national revolutions. In contrast, it was occasionally assumed even at the time that the return to a post-war normality would be even more difficult for the combatants than for the vast majority of the population who had known the brutality of the front only through newspapers, letters, stories and (most rarely) their own direct experience. A historian and propagandist noted the following about the combat readiness of the best Italian troops in 1917: 'All this is very good for the war, but for the peace? Alas, I can imagine already what these men will do who no longer know the value of human life'.[54] The *arditi* were the elite. Others had little or even no desire at all to kill. Very few came home undamaged.

Hinterland

One surprising dimension of the history of the cities and villages behind their own lines is that the majority of them seem to have suffered just as much as those cities and villages that were occupied. As was the case with occupation, the individual fates of these locations differed greatly.

The civilian population in Serbia probably had highest casualties proportionally, although these were not due to acts of violence. In late 1914 and in the first months of 1915, epidemics swept across the initially victorious, but nevertheless exhausted country, causing up to 100,000 deaths in a population of 4.5 million. Nowhere in the North were there numbers comparable to this prior to 1918.

Along the Russian front, almost all the large cities from Königsberg to Cracow became hinterland directly behind the front for several months. This brought radical changes to the life of the entire population: curfews and mass unemployment; radical restrictions on freedom of assembly, movement and communication; requisitioning of public buildings for military purposes and refugee accommodation; the omnipresence of uniformed soldiers; the filling of hospitals and schools with the wounded; the prohibition of alcohol and shortly thereafter an alarming increase in prostitution, along with a scarcity of food and coal; as well as coupons and ration cards that did nothing to alleviate the growing lines in front of shops everywhere. The differences in this new life can be illustrated with many examples. We limit ourselves here to the apparently harmless case of securing emergency accommodation for refugees: what did it mean for Königsberg and its 250,000 residents that during the first weeks of the war, emergency accommodation was established in the city for up to 50,000 refugees? Königsberg was fortunate that the actual number of refugees never approached this upper estimate.[55] The smaller city of Vilna, in contrast, where similar measures had not been taken prophylactically, was forced to take in approximately 50,000 refugees as early as 1915.[56]

Previously unknown tension and brutality emerged in the hinterland not only due to the struggle for provisions related to unemployment and the feeding and housing of refugees. In established households, discord developed which easily turned into conflicts between 'masters' and servants, conflicts which often ended in the denunciation of one by the other. As one

---

54 Cited in Kramer, *Dynamic of Destruction*, 129.
55 Fritz Gause, *Die Geschichte der Stadt Königsberg in Preußen*, vol. III: *Vom Ersten Weltkrieg bis zum Untergang Königsbergs*, second, expanded edition (Köln: Böhlau, 1996), 4.
56 Christian Westerhoff, *Zwangsarbeit im Ersten Weltkrieg: Deutsche Arbeitskräftepolitik im besetzten Polen und Litauen 1914–1918* (Paderborn: Schöningh, 2012), 71.

contemporary noted, 'Spying blossomed into a side job'.⁵⁷ It is impossible to determine whether accusations of alleged disloyalty or even treason were made more frequently for national or for social reasons, or the extent to which denunciations were motivated by personal slights and revenge. They were, in any case, a plague.

From the perspective of urban residents, the most important war experiences were not the threat of death by bullet or grenade, but rather those of scarcity, alarming material need and the destruction of all previous customs and certainties. In Lodz, Königsberg, Cracow, Warsaw and (beginning in the fall of 1915) Riga, residents did hear artillery fire and see tens of thousands of refugees, wounded soldiers and prisoners of war, but they were not shot at themselves, to say nothing of facing the direct threat of urban warfare. Occasionally the previous defenders of cities blew up strategically important objects such as bridges, but left the rest of the city largely unscathed. The exceptions were Cernăuți – where power had changed hands eight times by November 1918 with corresponding casualties – and Belgrade. Cernăuți had been a border city in the eighteenth and nineteenth centuries and thus potentially a front city. It came under artillery fire numerous times in 1914 and 1915, causing the destruction of hundreds of buildings and the flight of tens of thousands of people. Bucharest and Riga, which were bombed by zeppelins in 1916, fared much better. The Russians did significantly more damage with their scorched-earth policy in the summer of 1915, an issue that will be addressed separately below.

The war was experienced very differently in the countryside along the front. While large cities without fortifications did not become theatres of war, this was not the case for towns and villages. Smaller inhabited areas located at or near battles could easily be destroyed. Exactly how many hundreds or thousands of towns and villages along the Eastern front suffered this fate has probably never been calculated.

The vast majority of the hinterland, however, remained untouched. There are many indications that significantly less change occurred in the countryside – as long as it was not near the front – than in the city. The most important distinction from peacetime was the absence of young men, with all the consequences this had on the rural household. Fear for one's son, husband or father was a part of everyday life, as was the altered position of wives and mothers, who were now responsible not only for the family, but also for the farm. Another change was thoroughly positive from the perspective of farmers: 'Today the farmer is the lord. ... We've never had it so good as we do now during the war', boasted a farmer in a Bohemian wine-bar, as she took out a baked chicken and a slice of white bread.⁵⁸

The revenue from the black market compensated for the losses that arose from sinking production, at least on the larger farms everywhere. Joseph Held has argued that clear indications of dissatisfaction in Hungarian villages were widespread only in 1917 and that a 'facade of normality' was even maintained everywhere until 1918.⁵⁹ Heiko Haumann and, following him, Igor' Narskij have come to similar conclusions in regard to Russia in 1917: even in the year of

---

57 Hedenström, *Rigaer Kriegschronik*, 21; Hedenström provides many examples of denunciation. See also Maureen Healy, *Vienna and the Fall of the Habsburg Empire* (Cambridge: Cambridge University Press 2004), passim. The subject has rarely been discussed in other studies, evidently because scholars did not examine or were unable to examine the relevant archival material. The idea that this phenomenon was limited to Riga and Vienna is untenable.

58 Cited in Rudolf Kučera, *Rationed Life: Science, Everyday Life, and Working-Class Politics in the Bohemian Lands, 1914–1918* (New York: Berghahn Books, 2016), 29.

59 Joseph Held, 'Culture in Hungary during World War I', in *European Culture in the Great War: The Arts, Entertainment, and Propaganda, 1914–1918*, eds Aviel Roshwald and Richard Stites (Cambridge: Cambridge University Press, 1999), 176–92, here 177–81.

the revolutions, everyday life – marriages, harvests, work in the public or private sector, as well as personal fortune and misfortune – remained 'much more important than all the events that were beyond their lifeworld'.[60] Outside of revolutionary Russia, the relative peace in the villages of the hinterland held until the end of the war.

We can presume, in general, that the population in the hinterland – farmers and agricultural workers constituted a special group due to their privileged access to food – experienced great change, uncertainty and were subjected to a number of restrictions; for a long time, they met these conditions without resorting to violence – war-related crime, notwithstanding. Despite the resentment and tension unfolding around social and national issues, it appears that the potential for violence incited by war simply did not exist until 1917.

During the course of the war, authorities were increasingly unable to govern the hinterland. The fact that civilians there did not become violent for at least two or even three years does not mean, however, that they simply resigned themselves to their fate. They found other ways to deal with the hardships, adapting to, circumventing, violating or simply ignoring the flood of new decrees, restrictions and regulations. Using the example of Vienna, Maureen Healy has shown that although – or rather because – the state intervened in the life of its citizens in unprecedented ways, it failed completely:

> The provisioning crisis resembled a dance in which the rule-making authorities, unable to secure adequate supplies, lagged one step behind the rule-breaking population, which resorted to illegal means to find them… '[G]overning' became an exercise in wringing hands and issuing empty decrees.

Officials 'issued innumerable laws, decrees, and local ordinances', which 'governed the selling, buying, or using of essential goods: there were twenty-four laws concerning flour, twenty-three on bread, fourteen on milk, thirteen on sugar and eight on alcohol'.[61] Far away from Vienna, directly on the Baltic Sea, an ironic German observer noted the success of similar efforts by Russian authorities in their own hinterland, citing two examples:

> The Livonian governor used street posters to declare that the price of sugar had been set at nineteen kopecks a pound and that merchants who charged higher prices would be subject to fines of up to 3,000 roubles. As a result of this decree, the price of sugar rose from 80 kopecks to 1 rouble 50 kopecks.[62]

In another example, the sardonic witness summarized the activities of a Russian police officer over the course of a year:

> He arrested over 1,000 prostitutes, ferreted out hundreds of brothels and distilleries, collected more than 10,000 protocols about alcohol trade and overindulgence, and had to concede at the end of the year that life in Riga had never been as immoral as in 1916.[63]

---

60 Igor' Narskij, 'Zehn Phänomene, die Russland 1917 erschütterten', in *Schlüsseljahre: Zentrale Konstellationen der mittel- und osteuropäischen Geschichte: Festschrift für Helmut Altrichter zum 65. Geburtstag*, eds Matthias Stadelmann and Lilia Antipow (Stuttgart: Steiner, 2011), 255–72, here 256.
61 Healy, *Vienna*, 10, 64.
62 Hedenström, *Rigaer Kriegschronik*, 110.
63 Ibid., 118.

Authorities in the hinterland everywhere faced challenges similar to those of the Russian police officer. The censor had to read through millions of letters. The quantity of the materials alone presented a huge challenge, which was increased exponentially by multi-lingual populations and multi-lingual prisoners of war, since correspondence in more than 20 languages had to be monitored. In 1917–18, the German censor in Riga simplified this task by having post offices initially accept only letters written in the German language; months later postcards in Russian were permitted, and only at the end of the war were letters in Polish, Estonian, Latvian and Russian also accepted.[64] In what Robert Musil referred to as 'Kakania' (or, Austria–Hungary), censor authorities ostensibly allowed 27 languages.[65] This may not have actually been the case; the impossibility of governing the hinterland according to regulations would also be sufficiently illustrated by a censor authority that had to process the millions of letters 'merely' in the dozen languages customary in the Dual Monarchy.

Given the growing economic and social tension – which the state could, for the most part, barely control, much less resolve – ethnic tensions were initially quite modest. In Vienna, there were complaints about the Hungarians who had stopped delivering provisions to Cisleithania, but frustration was aimed at least as much at compatriots in Lower Austria. The Czech farmer cited above at the wine-bar boasted to her own countrymen as well. Latvians and Lithuanians remained loyal to the Tsar, as did Slovakians to the king in Budapest. Ethnic problems exploded only after the Russian Revolutions.

The one exception – aside from the above-mentioned case of the Jews – were the German Balts in Russia, whose rights were systematically undermined, although their sons fought and died as officers and soldiers in the Russian army; the ethnicization of living conditions was palpable. The situation was more complex for Poles, Ukrainians and Czechs, some of whom remained loyal to the Habsburgs and some of whom hoped for a Russian victory. Supporters of these respective options in Galicia resolved the problem primarily by flight: when the Russian army advanced, the one group fled to the western part of the monarchy; and when Austro–Hungarian troops returned, the other group retreated with the Russians.

The Bohemian lands were far removed from the front and the area behind the front; the option of flight or travel to a foreign country was available only to a few sympathizers of Russia or the entente. From the beginning of the war to the end of 1915, there were several waves of arrests in Bohemia and Moravia, in which pro-Russian politicians (including members of parliament) and journalists were arrested. The best-known case was Karel Kramář, the popular leader of the Young Czech Party, who was arrested in May 1915 and sentenced to death for high treason in June of the following year. The sentence was suspended, and Kramář was ultimately released in May 1917. The significance of this case should not be overestimated. While it did not exactly strengthen the battle morale of Czech soldiers, the idea – widespread even among historians today – that they defected en masse to the enemy as early as 1915 is simply incorrect.[66]

---

64 V. Marcilger, *Riga: Die Postgeschichte bis 1919* (Heide: Sengbusch, 1987), 14-I-4-6, 14-I-16-19. The text of a telegram (up to fifteen words), 'must be dictated to a police official, who writes them down and collects a fee of 1.50 marks'.

65 Schanes, *Serbien im Ersten Weltkrieg*, 251.

66 For details, see Richard Lein, *Pflichterfüllung oder Hochverrat? Die tschechischen Soldaten Österreich-Ungarns im Ersten Weltkrieg* (Vienna: Lit, 2011).

Prisoners of war

The Eastern fronts had the greatest number of prisoners of war. Of the approximately 9 million POWs (prisoners of war) in the entire First World War, 5 million were taken there, and by 1917, of the 2.4 million captured soldiers of the Central Powers, around 90 per cent were members of the Austro–Hungarian forces; 170,000 were Germans and the remainder came from the Ottoman Empire and Bulgaria.[67] At least 2.8 million Russian soldiers were interned in the POW camps of the Central Powers at some point during the war,[68] and this was the highest proportion of all the armies. 'The "Great War" was not the war of soldiers', it has been said of Russia. No army had so many deserters and captured soldiers as the Tsar's.[69]

Being captured brought with it new dangers to one's life and wellbeing. We still do not know the exact numbers, but a mortality rate of an estimated 20 per cent seems realistic for Habsburg and German prisoners in Russia, while for Romanians it was closer to 30 per cent.[70] In Serbia, again an exception, almost half of the men taken prisoner in 1914 died within the first six months. The mass deaths were the result of epidemics that occurred in Serbia during the initial months of 1915 and that resulted in hundreds of thousands of deaths among the civilian population, as mentioned above. The chances of survival for the approximately 70,000 POWs were even worse, with some 30,000 of them dying. 'Only' one-eighth of the approximately 250,000 Serbian soldiers died: this indicates that victims of the epidemics were numerous even among those best provided for in society, but it also makes clear the discrimination against the POWs.[71] Starvation, frostbite, typhus and cholera were only some of the serious dangers there. In late 1915, when the defensive war had been lost and the army began its retreat over the mountains to Albania, Serbian troops took with them those POWs still alive. The Serbs later designated this winter march as their 'Golgotha': the number of Serbs who died must have been at least in the high tens of thousands. Of the approximately 40,000 POWs, 40 per cent are said to have died within a few weeks. The remaining 24,000 were loaded exhausted and sick onto Italian and French ships, where at least 2,000 of them died of cholera within a few days; a further 5,000 died from the disease after being unloaded on Asinara Island.[72] The Italians who met the survivors of the death march at the Albanian coast were astonished at the condition of the captured officers, who were the first arrivals and whom the Serbs had treated as decently as possible:

> Almost all of them had no shoes, but bare, swollen feet, which some of them had wrapped in muddy, blood-drenched rags. What must have been uniforms earlier now looked like a collection of torn, dirty tatters that barely covered their nakedness.

---

67 Reinhard Nachtigal, 'Die Kriegsgefangenen-Verluste an der Ostfront: Eine Übersicht zur Statistik und zu Problemen der Heimatfront 1914/15', in Groß, *Die vergessene Front*, 201–15.
68 Ibid., 202–3. Only Georg Wurzer in, *Die Kriegsgefangenen der Mittelmächte in Russland im Ersten Weltkrieg* (Göttingen: Vandenhoeck & Ruprecht, 2006), cites the suspiciously exact figures from Soviet Russian calculations of 3,395,105 soldiers and 14,328 officers (14% in German captivity and almost 57% in Austro-Hungarian captivity).
69 Beyrau and Shcherbinin, 'Alles für die Front', in Bauerkämper and Julien, *Durchhalten!*, 156.
70 Kramer, *Dynamic of Destruction*, 65. Similar estimates in Peter Hoeres, 'Die Slawen: Perzeptionen des Kriegsgegners bei den Mittelmächten. Selbst- und Feindbild', in *Die vergessene Front*, ed. Groß, 179–200; here 199; Nachtigal, 'Die Kriegsgefangenen-Verluste', ibid., 201–15.
71 Mitrovic, *Serbia's Great War*, 83, 111.
72 Luca Gorgolini, *Kriegsgefangenschaft auf Asinara: Österreichisch-ungarische Soldaten des Ersten Weltkriegs in italienischem Gewahrsam* (Innsbruck: Wagner, 2012).

The brief description of the second group of soldiers arriving as POWs was not much different: 'barefoot, starved, half-naked, injured, and sick', a 'silent procession of living skeletons. ... A column of shadows that touched the ground in steady rhythm, in deathly silence, not making a sound.' When the Serbian soldiers arrived shortly thereafter, the Italian general noticed that the 'drama' was 'not unlike the arrival of the Austrian prisoners': 'Almost all of them had no shoes, having replaced them with rags taken from blankets. With torn clothes, covered with insects, suffering from diseases, they dragged themselves laboriously forward.'[73]

The Italians had little sympathy either for their allies, the Serbs or for the Austro–Hungarian POWs. Their quite credible statements verify that these Austro–Hungarian POWs in Serbia were victims of what is presumably the greatest known war crime on the Eastern front. Nevertheless, the reports also show that the Serbian military cannot be accused of having had genocidal intentions – they simply accepted that a large number of their prisoners would die, not all that different than with their own civilians and soldiers.

The distinction between the Serbian military and other administrations responsible for POWs consisted of, at times, the desire to prevent impending mass death amongst the prisoners, and at other times, consisted of the possibility to prevent such large-scale death altogether. During the same month in which epidemics decimated Austro–Hungarian POWs in Serbia – March of 1915 – typhus broke out among Russian POWs in German camps. Despite German efforts, around 6 per cent of the Russian prisoners died, although 'mortality rates were much higher for the German medical and nursing personnel'.[74] The epidemic, however, was brought under control.

Compulsory labour by POWs, permissible according to international law, is a different issue. As early as the summer of 1915, 70 per cent of POWs transported to Germany and Austria–Hungary were used in the so-called 'war deployment', often in agriculture. Did they really complain about this? Most of them had been agricultural labourers or farmers at home; access to food was certainly greater both during the harvest and afterwards than it was in the prisoner-of-war camps. The question remains an open one and must be answered case by case according to specific working conditions. Uniformly bad, in contrast, are the recollections of tens of thousands of German and Habsburg soldiers who worked under the most severe conditions on the construction of the Kirov railway to the Arctic Ocean from 1915 to 1917.[75]

War crimes

The Hague Convention of 1907 defined the legality of killing during war. Much was now explicitly forbidden, for example, killing the wounded, POWs or otherwise unarmed people; the populations of occupied territories were also protected. Most states that participated in the First World War had ratified the convention with its treaties and declaration. Nevertheless, in the first months of the war, there were already accusations that the great powers had violated the convention on a massive scale on the eastern battlefields. Whenever these accusations have been examined more closely, investigators have encountered a historiographical desert. Phantoms, however, continue to float above this desert, figures and images from war propaganda, often

---

73 Cited in ibid., 72–3, 77. On the treatment of the officers, which was apparently decent in the beginning, see also Schanes, *Serbien im Ersten Weltkrieg*, 209–12.
74 Paul Julian Weindling, *Epidemics and Genocide in Eastern Europe 1890–1945* (Oxford: Oxford University Press, 2000), 79–80.
75 Nachtigal, 'Die Kriegsgefangenen-Verluste', in Groß, *Die vergessene Front*, 211, 214.

presumably products of rumours and information blockades, which have almost never withstood closer examination; nevertheless, these phantoms continue now and again to haunt historiography.

During and immediately after the Russian invasion of East Prussia, there were rumours in Berlin about 'decapitated heads, burned children, and raped women', which fit perfectly with the notion that in north-eastern Germany, the Occident was being defended against barbarian hordes. Somewhat later, the figure of 101 civilian victims was calculated for the German side, which, given the four weeks of continuous fighting, made little impression. Only after the war did this figure increase sixteenfold.[76]

Two additional, almost contemporaneous cases have been relatively well established and can be traced back to the fear of *franc-tireurs* that was rampant among German and Habsburg troops. Kalisz (Kalisch), a city east of the German-Russian border with a population of 65,000, was occupied without resistance during the first days of the war. Soon thereafter, a series of incidents took place that are difficult to reconstruct. It is very probable that German patrols accidentally shot at each other. In response, hostages were taken and ostensibly suspicious civilians were executed; the historic city centre (where occupation rule had not been threatened the entire time) was then destroyed by German artillery. Over the course of these events, which lasted for several days, about 250 city residents were killed in the shootings, executions and artillery fire. At the time, parallels were already being drawn to Louvain. In contrast to the Western front, however, there do not appear to have been any comparable massacres behind the north-eastern front over the subsequent two years.

The idea that civilians (including women) could pull out hidden weapons at any time and 'perfidiously' ambush the invaders was even more widespread on the Serbian front than in the North.[77] In the Serbian city of Šabac (ca. 14,000 residents), Austro–Hungarian troops believed they had been attacked by *franc-tireurs* (almost at the same time that Germans believed they were attacked in Kalisz) and, as a reprisal, they killed between several dozen and 200 civilians. Here as well, an exact reconstruction is difficult, although the incidents were investigated during the course of a court trial in Vienna in 1920. In contrast to Kalisz, the killings in Šabac were not an isolated case, as there were several crimes of this kind in the cities and villages of Serbia, which raises the suspicion that Austro–Hungarian troops on this front consciously sought to terrorize the population and also allowed themselves to be guided by hatred, which can be explained especially through the specific relationship between the Austro–Hungarian monarchy and Serbia in the immediate past.[78] Serbia, at times mentioned in the same breath as Montenegro, was also the only political state on all of the Eastern fronts that opponents wanted to destroy (as reflected in the popular phrase '*Serbien muss sterbien*' ['Serbia must die' in German, but with the word 'die' (*sterben*) misspelled so that it rhymes with 'Serbia']).[79]

In discussions about Austro–Hungarian war crimes in the southeast, it is frequently argued that only the so-called first contingent of the Serbian army wore uniforms, that the second

---

76 Strachan, *The First World War*, 128.
77 Jonathan E. Gumz, *The Resurrection and the Collapse of Empire in Habsburg Serbia, 1914–1918* (Cambridge: Cambridge University Press, 2009), 36–43, 46–51.
78 Anton Holzer, 'Mit allen Mitteln', *Die Presse*, 20 September 2008. See also Daniel Marc Segesser, 'Kriegsverbrechen auf dem Balkan und in Anatolien während der Balkankriege und des Ersten Weltkriegs', in Angelow, *Der Erste Weltkrieg*, 193–209, here 200–3. Segesser considers the first aspect alone to be significant.
79 See for example Kramer, *Dynamic of Destruction*, 88–90.

was at best only partially uniformed, while the third wore only civilian clothing, which is why Austro–Hungarian troops viewed combat with units of the second and third contingents as perfidious and illegal attacks by civilians and why they responded to them so ruthlessly. This argument is apparently correct. Regardless of whether it actually contributed significantly to the murders, we can almost certainly rely on the calculations by Jonathan Gumz and Mark Biondich, who realistically estimate that there were between 3,500 and 4,000 victims of Austro–Hungarian reprisals in the few weeks prior to the retreat in December 1914.[80]

The Bulgarian occupation regime had the worst reputation in terms of war crimes. Evidently, members of the Serbian intelligentsia who remained in Macedonia frequently 'went to Sofia', which meant they were kidnapped by a Bulgarian patrol and executed at the nearest remote location.[81] It is difficult to estimate the magnitude of this and similar practices, since we do not have reliable data, but only reports and rumours circulated by contemporaries. Biondich speaks very cautiously of 2,000 'persons allegedly executed for resisting the new regime'.[82]

The issue of violence against civilians in Eastern Galicia in 1914–15 is even more complex and has also not been investigated thoroughly. Austro–Hungarian troops took revenge on ostensible or actual pro-Moscow Ruthenians during their retreat in the late summer of 1914, although the reprisals also affected people without pro-Russian sympathies. There were sporadic executions, but the core of the reprisals consisted of transporting up to 10,000 Ukrainians to the soon infamous Thalerhof concentration camp near Graz and to less well-known camps.[83] Suspects were also executed in the summer and the fall, a measure that can be traced back especially to the panic and bewilderment of Austro–Hungarian troops faced with an increasingly apparent defeat in the battle for Galicia. 'Suspects', ordered the fortifications command of Przemyśl on 2 October 1914 (after several defeats), 'are to be put down immediately regardless of where they are found, even without something they can be accused of at that moment'.[84]

The Russian occupying forces could hardly be guided by anti-Slavic resentment. Their weaknesses – which, from the perspective of the civilian population, were expressed especially in an incomprehensible and incalculable brutality – consisted mainly in their incompetence and lack of authority as well in their notorious corruption. The cultural war against the Ukrainians was also a factor: the Russians not only opposed Ruthenian nationalists, but also disbanded their institutions, deported their leaders (including the Greek-Catholic archbishop of Lemberg) and suppressed the 'minor Russian dialect'. Even officially sponsored pro-Moscow Ruthenians felt humiliated and ignored by the Russians. It goes without saying that the Russification of

---

80 Gumz, *Resurrection*, 53–8, here 58; Biondich, *The Balkans*, 86.
81 Opfer, *Im Schatten des Krieges*, 116; Oliver Stein, '"Wer das nicht mitgemacht hat, glaubt es nicht": Erfahrungen deutscher Offiziere mit den bulgarischen Verbündeten 1915–1918', in Angelow, *Der Erste Weltkrieg*, 271–87, here 278, which confirms that the Bulgarian measures against the Serbian and Romanian civilian populations were interpreted by the Germans as confirmation of all the prejudices they had about their own ally.
82 Biondich, *The Balkans*, 86.
83 Pająk, *Od autonomii*, 84–8. This figure may be exaggerated, but it does reflect the magnitude. It is regarded as certain that there were at least 6,000 inmates in Thalerhof alone and that the mortality rate was almost one-third, especially due to epidemics in 1914/15.
84 Several similar or identical orders of the fortifications command of Przemyśl are cited by Hannes Leidinger, 'Eskalation der Gawalt', in *Habsburgs schmutziger Krieg: Ermittlungen zur österreichisch-ungarischen Kriegsführung 1914–1918*, eds Hannes Leidinger, Verena Moritz, Karin Moser and Wolfram Dornik (Vienna: Residenz Verlag 2014), 51–91, here 81–2.

the public sphere and the school system met with little approval from the Poles, who had been predominant until then.[85]

Jews were most severely affected. The elimination of national Ukrainian elites and organizations was an official goal of Russian policies. The suppression of Poles was inhibited by consideration of the 'Polish question' as well as the necessity of maintaining order and supplies with the help of existing institutions. In the case of the Jews, neither objectives nor other rational calculus is evident. They were beaten and robbed; after the invasion of Russian troops, Jewish houses were apparently burned down more frequently than Christian ones; people were raped and there was widespread extortion.[86] The magnitude of this non-coordinated violence – which arose spontaneously and usually disappeared shortly thereafter – is difficult, if not impossible, to reconstruct. Some of it should be attributed to war propaganda, as the stereotype of Cossacks pillaging Jews fit perfectly with the propaganda of defending the Occident against Asia. Nevertheless, no sources contest the fact that Jews fared worse than any other group under Russian occupation.

Austria–Hungary returned to its own state territory in the spring of 1915. Even today, the extent of Austro–Hungarian reprisals against ostensibly traitorous Poles and Ukrainians after the reoccupation remains unclear. In any case, the reconquering of the northeast Crown land was no longer regarded as a liberation by the local population. The Honvéd was seen as a special plague, in contrast to units from the Alpine and Danube lands.

Two years later, in the re-opened Reichsrat in Vienna, Polish, Ukrainian and South Slavic members of parliament repeatedly complained sharply about marauding soldiers and described the mass executions and hangings of their compatriots. They spoke of 30,000 victims in Galicia ('…others say there were twice as many',[87] Polish socialist Ignacy Daszyński stated in parliament) and another 30,000 in Serbia. These figures were subsequently adopted in the scholarly literature,[88] but have never been confirmed in any way: there is evidence for a total of 620 civilian victims of Austro–Hungarian reprisals in Galicia, however, for 1914 and 1915 combined. Even if we supplement this figure with a significantly greater number of unreported victims, the resulting estimate of several thousand deaths would be far less than the five-digit figure claimed by Polish and Ukrainian members of parliament in the Reichsrat in 1917. We also know that both the emperor and the army high command had already taken a stand against the 'abuses' of their own troops in September 1914.[89] The Austro–Hungarian interior ministry had intervened at the time in Styria (due to the persecution of Slovenians) and then in Galicia in April 1915, with remarkably clear-sighted words: a draconian and potentially incompetent

---

85 Pająk, *Od autonomii*, 97–110, 124–7. Here Pająk describes several measures taken by Russian authorities to supress 'minor Russian' (i.e. 'Ukrainian') activities.
86 See especially Alexander V. Prusin, *Nationalizing a Borderland: War, Ethnicity, and Anti-Jewish Violence in East Galicia, 1914–1920* (Tuscaloosa, AL: University of Alabama Press, 2005), Part I. Pająk, *Od autonomii*, especially 136–43, also points to several cases of Christian neighbours participating in the theft of Jewish property.
87 Leidinger, 'Der Einzug des Galgen', 245.
88 See for example Anton Holzer, *Die andere Front: Fotografie und Propaganda im Ersten Weltkrieg* (Darmstadt: Primus, 2007), 254–5; idem, *Das Lächeln der Henker* (Darmstadt: Primus, 2008), 74–6.
89 Leidinger, 'Der Einzug des Galgen', 242–7. The Ukrainian emergency motion of 5 June 1917, states tellingly: 'Thousands of men, women and children were hanged or executed according to martial law or simply on the spot; in the most fortunate cases, they were arrested and deported' (ibid., 245).

judiciary would violate not only human rights, but also the interests of the state, in whose name executions were carried out.[90]

As a final point, let us turn to the issue of hostages. Throughout occupation rule, occupying powers everywhere took hostages from the functional elite as a security measure. This strategy was completely different than hostage taking in the Second World War. The detentions behind the Eastern front during the First World War were a legally permissible measure that did not, at least in the best-known cases, end in the death of the hostages, but rather in their release after several months of arrest. In Romania, the army took members of the Central Powers as hostages on its retreat to the northeast. Beginning in December, the Germans began to take Romanian hostages, especially respected citizens of the region. In the negotiations, which were supposed to lead to an exchange of both hostage groups, the Germans tellingly threatened to turn 'their' hostages over to the Bulgarians. The approximately 6,000 Germans, Austrians, Hungarians and Romanians were finally released after the ceasefire in December 1917.[91]

In Serbia, matters were more brutal in this regard as well. Austrian authorities interned thousands of Serbs during the campaign in the fall of 1915, and a second major wave of arrests followed a year later. In late 1916, 70,000 Serbs were detained. Simply being 'capable of bearing arms' was sufficient grounds for arrest; the target here was the intelligentsia of the country, whom authorities wanted to eliminate once and for all.[92] Conditions in at least several camps must have been among the worst in all of Europe during the war.[93]

A final wave of arrests followed in February and March 1917 in response to the so-called 'Toplica Uprising'. Hostages were taken quite randomly in Belgrade: 'Everyone who was considered suspicious was interned'. The situation did, however, not escalate after this. Despite the fears of the occupying power, the uprising remained local, and authorities were now responsible for feeding more detainees and hostages who were also unable to show up for work. All hostages taken in the first months who were deemed not 'politically suspicious' were then released in the summer of 1917, since especially farmers and specialists such as physicians were urgently needed.[94]

Flight, evacuation and deportation

Before the territory located in the Riga–Lodz–Cernăuți triangle became occupied territory in the summer of 1915 (and a few months later, Serbia as well), there was an unprecedented uprooting of people in the areas behind both Eastern fronts. This began with the flight of an estimated 1,300,000 people from Galicia and Bukovina in the summer and fall of 1914. They

---

90 On Serbia, see Mitrovic, *Serbia's Great War*, 66; On Galicia, see Leidinger, 'Der Einzug des Galgens', 248: 'It is an elementary duty of humanity, but also the highest interest of the state and legal order to reduce as much as possible the danger coefficients of irreparable injustice'.
91 Lisa Mayerhofer, *Zwischen Freund und Feind – deutsche Besatzung in Rumänien 1916–1918* (München: Meidenbauer 2010), 99.
92 Gumz, *Resurrection*, 90, 97–8.
93 Matthew Stibbe, 'Civilian Internment and Civilian Internees in Europe, 1914–1920', *Immigrants & Minorities* 26, nos. 1–2 (March–July 2008): 49–81, here 63: 'Yet the harshest treatment of all was reserved for Bosnian Serbs and for subjects of the pre-war Kingdom of Serbia arrested and imprisoned by Habsburg and Bulgarian troops during and after the invasions of 1914 and 1915'. Josef Redlich has described this as 'a systematic policy of extermination', quoted in Mark Mazower, *The Balkans: From the End of Byzantium to the Present Day* (London: Phoenix, 2003), 119.
94 Tamara Scheer, 'Manifestation österreichisch-ungarischer Besatzungsmacht in Belgrad (1916–1918)', in Angelow, *Der Erste Weltkrieg*, 211–39, here 226.

fled to Cisleithania, with approximately one-quarter of them finding more or less emergency asylum in Vienna and Lower Austria.[95] We cannot speak here of direct violence, but rather of a condition between fear and situational force since the vast majority did not flee from actual compulsory measures by the Russians, but apparently from a tremendous sense of fear that they would be subject to such measures if they remained. Since 1882, Russia had had, even among its neighbours, a fearful reputation as the land of pogroms. The flight of one-eighth of the population (including around 75 per cent Christians) suggests that the image could be universalized: a state that tolerated or even supported violence against part of its own population in times of peace incited substantial fear that it would act similarly towards civilians as an occupying power.

In terms of magnitude the mass flight from Galicia and Bukovina exceeded the exodus of Serbs one year later, although the latter was incomparably bloodier (see pages 49–50, 'Prisoners of war', in the present chapter). No one knows how many tens of thousands of soldiers and civilians fleeing with them died in the 'Serbian Golgotha'. We cannot speak of situational force in the Serbian case because it was the decision of a sovereign government after a lost battle to expose its soldiers to what was, even at first glance, an extremely risky undertaking. The civilians went into the mountains voluntarily. A war crime was committed, however, against the POWs who were forced to take part in the retreat.

Another mass migration was connected to a shortage of labourers in the German Reich. Around 300,000 people, primarily agricultural labourers from so-called 'Russian Poland', were not allowed to return to their homeland after the war broke out. From 1915 to 1917, 160,000 to 200,000 people in the General Governorate are said to have been recruited for work in the German Reich – which can also be explained only in part through situational force (i.e. unemployment).[96]

The largest forced uprooting can be traced back to Russian scorched-earth policies in the spring and summer of 1915. First businesses and then people were transported eastward: at least 300,000 Lithuanians, 250,000 Latvians, 500,000 Jews, and 750,000 Poles,[97] as well as over 100,000 Germans. This forced evacuation was clearly different than the flight from Galicia and Bukovina as well as the Serbian retreat. It was solely the result of Russian efforts to leave the enemy as few resources as possible, human and otherwise. Nevertheless, like the previously mentioned incidents, this was not a case of ethnic cleansing since there was no attempt to remove a population group from a particular territory (whether from its own territory, a claimed territory or a recently occupied territory), but rather the temporary evacuation of a territory that had just fallen into the hands of the enemy. This applies even to the forced evacuation of Germans, who were particularly hated at the time, but who were not expropriated during the course of these scorched-earth tactics.[98]

---

95 On the figures for refugees in Cisleithania in 1915, see Pająk, *Od autonomii*, 90.
96 Westerhoff, *Zwangsarbeit*, 113–4, 260. At least, officially registered unemployment fell to less than half by March 1916. Westerhoff estimates that during the entire war 200,000 to 240,000 residents of the General Governorate of Warsaw were recruited for work in the German Reich.
97 These are older estimates by Werner Conze, which in the absence of better ones have been adopted by other scholars, including Kramer, *Dynamic of Destruction*, 151.
98 Severin Gawlitta, *Zwischen Einladung und Ausweisung: Deutsche bäuerliche Siedler im Königreich Polen 1815–1915* (Marburg: Herder-Institut, 2009), 292–303, 332. Tens of thousands of Germans also emigrated before the deportations.

The number of refugees and evacuees increased in the following years, especially in Russia (from 3.3 million in late 1915 to over 6 million by the beginning of 1917).[99] Without going into the details, it should be noted that within the borders of the old Russian state, Latvians were the most severely affected group proportionally at around 50 per cent: Courland alone lost about two-thirds of its population (future Lithuania did lose some of its population and future Estonia significantly less).[100] 'An empty land', one journalist commented; 'Empty already in peace and even emptier now'.[101] The future capital city Riga also lost two-thirds of its 500,000 residents even before the German invasion in September 1917.[102] The consequences of such a demographic revolution were evident in every domain: in the proud Baltic metropolises, furnished apartments were rented at no charge in the late fall of 1915; occupants simply had to commit to heating the apartments in the coming winter.[103]

A similar depopulation can be documented on the Romanian front, which was established in 1916. The inhabitants of Dobruja, however, were not evacuated by force, but rather fled the feared Bulgarians in large numbers in the fall. Almost two-thirds of the population left the country (only 82,000 remained of 235,000). The provincial capital Constanța was almost empty, with 7,000 residents instead of 34,000.[104] In the entire Kingdom of Romania, one-fifth of the more than 4 million citizens fled.

Only in the front city of Belgrade was the situation worse than in Constanța: when Austro-Hungarian troops took Belgrade for the second time in October 1915, only 7,000 to 12,000 people remained of the city's approximately 90,000 residents. Under occupation, both old and new residents returned to the city, and several months later, 48,000 people lived in Belgrade again, a little more than half of the population compared to the beginning of the war.[105]

The uprooting of millions of people – in many places combined more with the fear of violence than with actual force – was the most significant alternative to life under occupation, which an even greater number of people experienced during the war.

Occupation

With few exceptions, the population of an occupied country regards the occupation as a serious evil. Foreign rule usually brings material disadvantages, undermines established certainties and restricts civil rights; it also often involves humiliation – and less frequently – direct, physical threat. From 1914 to 1917 as well, occupation meant change, at times dramatic and at times

---

99 Peter Gatrell, *A Whole Empire Walking: Refugees in Russia during World War I* (Bloomington, IN: Indiana University Press: 2005), 3.
100 Sigmar Stopinski, *Das Baltikum im Patt der Mächte: Zur Entstehung Estlands, Lettlands und Litauens im Gefolge des Ersten Weltkriegs* (Berlin: Berliner Wissenschafts-Verlag, 1997), 141–2. In a little more than a year, by September 1915, the population of Courland fell from 812,000 to 245,000. Detlef Henning, 'Der ethnische Wandel in Estland und Lettland', in *Der ethnische Wandel im Baltikum zwischen 1850–1930*, ed. Heinrich Wittram (Lüneburg: Carl-Schirren-Gesellschaft, 2005), 7–21, here 13–14.
101 Cited in Westerhoff, *Zwangsarbeit*, 71.
102 Mark R. Hatlie, 'Riga und der Erste Weltkrieg: Eine Exkursion', *Nordost-Archiv NF* XVII (2008): 13–33, here 18–9, 24–5; idem, 'Bevölkerungsverschiebungen in Riga während des Welt- und Bürgerkrieges 1914–1919', in Wittram, *Der ethnische Wandel*, 53–80, here 66.
103 Hedenström, *Rigaer Kriegschronik* (29 November 1915), 84.
104 Mayerhofer, *Zwischen Freund und Feind*, 39–41, 59.
105 Jovana Lazic Knezevic, 'The Austro-Hungarian occupation of Belgrade during the First World War: Battles at the home front', PhD diss., Yale University (2006), 14–5, 28.

only gradual; it did not, however, provoke visions of decline within the affected societies, which learned to live with the new situation as best as they could. This was the case, first of all, because no occupying power pursued genocidal aims or engaged in ethnic cleansing. Second, the populations themselves showed no willingness to engage in counter-violence: during the first years of the war, no combat readiness was evident among civilians, organized or otherwise. Third, there is no evidence of extensive, ethnically motivated violence against neighbours – Ukrainians did not, for instance, settle scores with Poles in Galicia, nor did Christian residents attack their Jewish neighbours along the Northern front (which does not, however, mean that they did not participate in the plundering). And fourth, although the occupiers did offer advantages to their political supporters, they remained primarily interested in maintaining order and exploiting resources, rather than in exacerbating ethnic and social tensions.

Several larger cities were already occupied by the enemy in the first year of the war – Belgrade temporarily, Lemberg for several months, Lodz, Warsaw, and somewhat later, Vilna until the end of the war. Belgrade definitively became occupied territory in late 1915, Bucharest a year later, and Riga in September 1917. Occupation was characterized everywhere by hardships and restrictions, although the new powers did offer positive incentives for local supporters, which were intended to promote the pacification of the new hinterlands as well as economic utilization or exploitation. These basic objectives often collided. The new rulers proceeded on a case-by-case basis, with individual administrative branches and offices frequently pursuing thoroughly contradictory goals.

The occupiers punished criminal acts, especially those affecting their own members (soldiers and officials), with fines or prison sentences. Newspapers included reports of these crimes. Only rarely were civilians sentenced to death.[106] As a rule, criminals were sent to prison; increasingly, these were economic criminals who had (more consciously than unconsciously) violated the enormous flood of new restrictions, prohibitions and regulations. The harshest penalties were usually for espionage, although even today it is unclear whether this suspicion was justified or merely a result of the general and impending omnipresent hysteria among both officials and the local population.

There were several occupying powers along the fronts in the East. The smallest of them was Bulgaria, which occupied Macedonia/Thrace and Dobruja. Although comparative studies are lacking, Bulgarian occupation rule was probably perceived as a particular affront. Surprisingly, the great power Russia played almost no role as an occupier. Except in Bukovina, where fighting lasted until 1917 and where establishing a stable occupation administration was condemned to failure due to the constantly changing – and continually approaching – front line, the tsarist empire occupied only Eastern Galicia and a part of Western Galicia and only during the approximately ten months between September 1914 and May–July 1915. When Russia occupied the eastern districts of Galicia for a second time in 1916 following the Brusilov offensive, the military was able prevent a renewal of the regulatory policies from 1914 to 1915: the high command of the Southwest front wanted no additional turmoil, which national-political, religious or other kinds of experiments would have promoted.[107]

Austro–Hungarian occupation policies offered more substance. From late 1915 until the end of the war, the monarchy occupied the southern parts of the kingdoms of Poland and

---

106 Scheer, 'Manifestation' in Angelow, *Der Erste Weltkrieg*, 218, points out that many of the death sentences were not carried out.
107 Pająk, *Od autonomii*, 167–9.

Serbia – 400,000 square kilometres containing 20 million people.[108] The basic traits of Austro–Hungarian occupation rule will be examined below in connection with, or in contrast to, the policies of its more powerful ally, Germany.

The German Reich was by far the largest and most important occupying power in the East. It occupied the western part of the Kingdom of Poland in December 1914, the entire northwest of the country including Warsaw in the summer of 1915, and several previously western Russian governorates in the late summer, where the Ober Ost area was established. In the final months of 1916, primarily German troops established a new occupation territory encompassing about 80 per cent of Romania. In the fall of the following year, Germany conquered a significant part of the southern Baltic Sea coast including Riga. In March and April 1918, German troops occupied the entire area west of the line from St. Petersburg to Rostov-on-Don; that is, Estonia, Belarus and Ukraine.

Recent research suggests that most of the standard judgements about Austro–Hungarian and German occupation are exaggerated or implausible. The 60,000 men forcibly conscripted in 1917 can serve here as a paradigmatic example: in virtually all books and articles about Ober Ost, the treatment of these men is presented as exemplary of the ruthlessness of German occupation policies.[109] For the men affected and their families, conscription to compulsory labour can justifiably be viewed as an improper hardship, especially since working and living conditions were frequently bad or even very bad. However, if the goal of an occupying power is the ruthless exploitation of the local workforce, we must ask ourselves whether 60,000 forced labourers in a total population of over two million people during the third year of occupation is evidence of the weakness of the occupying forces and not of their success and unbending will? This example also points to a significant lacuna in the scholarly research regarding the discrepancy between the war games, regulations and the registration mania of the occupier on the one hand, and the counterstrategies of the occupied population, on the other.

Bogislav Tilka, a somewhat unusual German soldier (who published a book about his experiences in the First World War under the name Gerhard Velburg[110]), arrived in occupied Romania as a private. His diary provides a vivid description of his superiors' high-flying plans, which repeatedly proved impossible to implement on the ground: 'All over the desk there are decrees upon decrees, orders upon orders, and in the file cabinets form upon forms', he noted in 1917.

> 'It must be reported immediately', 'It must be reported every three days', 'The counting must be made most precisely', and 'Is strictly prohibited', have been written repeatedly in the decrees and orders. And all the things that are supposed to be counted! Every newborn calf, every hatched egg, every goose and every curd cheese.

The legal bases were contained in the *Official Army Gazette*, the *Official Gazette of the Army Group Mackensen* and the *Official Gazette of the Military Administration in Romania*, which provided instructions for everything, including the 'collection of coffee grounds', 'travel luggage

---

108 See for example, Tamara Scheer, *Zwischen Front und Heimat: Österreich-Ungarns Militärverwaltungen im Ersten Weltkrieg* (Frankfurt a.M.: Peter Lang, 2009); Gumz, *Resurrection*, 9.
109 For example in Kramer, *Dynamic of Destruction*, 47. More precise numbers can be found in Westerhoff, *Zwangsarbeit*, 218–9, who points out that the figure 60,000 refers only to the so-called work crews within the military administration of Lithuania (ca. two million people) and that several thousand members of civilian work battalions should added to this.
110 Tilka/Velburg subsequently made his career as a legal scholar in Jena, Thuringia.

for officers', and 'forbidden clothing for soldiers'. 'Truly', Tilka sighed, 'if the war could be won by decrees, we would have already won it long ago'.[111]

The occupiers may have done a lot of imaging, dreaming and planning, but in reality, they were dealing with individuals and communities who were at least as quick-thinking as themselves and instinctively elusive; they were always considering their own advantage or how to survive with as little damage as possible and counteracting the German's (or, *Kulturträger*) regulatory rage, even where the latter felt completely superior. A few people such as Tilka/Velberg were aware that the situation on the ground was at times completely different than what was apparent from the general's desk, or that every new decree that left the administrative office might produce the opposite of what was intended. Tilka/Velburg had already experienced this in 1917. When he arrived in Bucharest after the invasion of German troops in December 1916, he had enjoyed the cheap and abundant food that was no longer available in Germany. He described the visit to a famous pastry shop in Bucharest as follows: 'Our group also really dug in, since German thoroughness would lead one to presume that decrees about restrictions on the consumption of fat and sugar will soon be pinned onto these walls as well'.[112]

Tilka/Velburg's presumption proved to be correct. During the first year of the German occupation, the supply situation remained satisfactory or even good (especially in the countryside), but in the second year, things became more like his homeland in Thuringia than Romania during the first phase of German occupation. What had happened? The answer is provided by more recent works on German and Austro–Hungarian occupation.

The objectives of German-speaking occupying forces were the same everywhere: whether in Courland or in Serbia, in Poland or in Romania, local resources were to be extracted in order to improve supply in the homeland. Given the economic structure of the occupied territories, this meant first and foremost agricultural products, lumber in the North,[113] as well as occasional industrial resources (Romanian petroleum or coal in the Dabrowa Basin). The extent to which labour recruitment could provide relief in the hinterland remained an open question. The second objective was the self-sufficiency of the troops stationed in the occupied territory who were supposed to be fed locally. Third, were the needs of the population in the occupied territory – the occupiers wanted to avoid hunger-related epidemics and social unrest that would only result in new problems for them.

While this latter objective in fact remained of tertiary importance, satisfying the needs of the troops on location evidently replaced supplying the hinterland as the main objective everywhere. Jonathan Gumz has argued that in Serbia this shift in emphasis can be explained by the arrogance of the military, which considered itself the embodiment of the 'true' monarchy and thus regarded the civilian population of Cisleithania as a subordinate priority, to whom the armed forces owed little. A similar interpretation can be drawn from the files of Ober Ost, which, according to Vejas Liulevicius, also sought to establish a kind of ideal state, which under these circumstances could be erected only by the military stationed on the ground. These motives were lacking in occupied Poland, where the German and the Habsburg military governorates had no such ambitions, as well as in Romania, which was simply an occupied land.

---

111 Gerhard Velburg, *Rumänische Etappe: Der Weltkrieg, wie ich ihn sah* (Minden: Köhler, 1930), passim, citation on 109, 177.
112 Cited in Mayerhofer, *Zwischen Freund und Feind*, 227.
113 On the special case of Białowieża in the west of Ober Ost, where the occupiers apparently came quite close to achieving their main objective through an enormous expenditure of means, infrastructure measures and force, see Westerhoff, *Zwangsarbeit*, 168–77.

Nevertheless, the results of extracting resources to improve supply in the hinterland remained similar throughout: during the entire war (in other words, for four harvests), the General Governorate of Warsaw supplied less than one per cent of the potatoes that were harvested in Germany during the especially bad year of 1916; the Austro–Hungarian military governorate in Lublin (43,000 square kilometres of solidly agrarian areas with 3.5 million inhabitants) increased the grain production of the monarchy around 0.5 per cent; in the Ukraine in 1918, the actual grain exported was only 10 per cent of the expected amount.[114] Larger amounts of grain, food and livestock were supplied only by Romania in 1916–17 and by Serbia in 1917–18.

Irrespective of whether local military administrations actually sought to establish 'separate' and 'better' states outside of the homeland, there were also significantly more banal reasons for the failure of this strategy to the transfer of food from the occupied territory to the hinterland. Many foods such as fruits and vegetables were unsuited or suited only to a limited degree for transregional transport, and trains were also lacking. Over the course of a learning process that was regionally limited in each case, a mixture of state control (which ultimately meant every possible kind of regulation) and a more-or-less free market economy developed everywhere. In many places, the occupiers learned quite quickly that as a rule, compulsion was less effective than incentives, especially for farmers. They paid for products, and wherever money increasingly lost its value, they coaxed with in-kind bonuses.[115] Austro–Hungarian authorities implemented this strategy impressively in Serbia in 1917, when they paid cash for shipments, which then even exceeded expectations and planning figures.[116]

The most thoroughly investigated case is that of Romania, for which the Tilka/Velburg diary cited above provides an inestimable corrective to extant official documents. In Romania, contexts and nuances come to light that appear to be applicable, at least as an approach, to other occupied territories examined here.

The Germans occupied territories in the east and southeast that were largely foreign to them. This was less so the case for Austria–Hungary, as its authorities in Serbia and southern Congress Poland had, at least theoretically, linguistic and cultural competencies that Germany could only dream of in Lithuania and Romania.[117] The German Reich attempted to survey, register and regulate the occupied territory in the sense of a modern state so that the burdens could be distributed accordingly. While this objective proved difficult even in distinguishing between men and women, determining national affiliation confronted the Germans with what seemed to them an incomprehensible confusion of traditional identities that could not fit into the modern categories of national politics. In Lithuania and Belarus, many people identified themselves as 'locals', as 'Christians', and occasionally – somewhat more precisely – as 'Catholics'. Who was 'Lithuanian', 'Polish', 'White Russian', or 'Great Russian' – there was a wide variety of opinions about this, and even the astonished census takers noted that this was not always

---

114 Stefan Lehnstaedt, 'Fluctuating between "Utilisation" and Exploitation', in *Legacies of Violence: Eastern Europe's First World War*, eds Jochen Böhler, Włodzimierz Borodziej and Joachim von Puttkamer (München: Oldenbourg, 2014), 89–112, here 102, 107, 109–111.

115 In addition to numerous examples in Mayerhofer, see also Stephan Lehnstaedt, 'Das Militärgouvernement Lublin im Ersten Weltkrieg: Die 'Nutzbarmachung' Polens durch Österreich-Ungarn', *Zeitschrift für Ostmitteleuropa-Forschung* 61, no. 1 (2012): 1–26, here 20.

116 For more detail on this, see Gumz, *Resurrection*, chapter 4 ('Food as Salvation'), 142–92.

117 Lehnstaedt, 'Militärgouvernement Lublin', 6, points out, however, that the senior positions in the military administration as well as in the *Gendarmerie* were filled by non-Poles, who, according to the foreign ministry in Vienna in 1916, were a 'well-organized clique…. The behaviour of this clique is capricious, but always dictated by the greatest mistrust toward Poles'.

an intentional 'deception' on the part of the respondents. The dividing lines even ran through families. A report cited by Vejas Liulevicius from the Lithuanian town of Mariampol – the name itself would have posed an enigmatic riddle to the German occupiers – touched the core of the issue: the responsible authorities there identified several families whose names evidently derived from the vocational designation 'smith': one named Schmidt, another Kowalski and a third, Kusnjetzow. The official noted:

> We discover, with a sense of distress, that all three have distanced themselves from their national identity. Because … Mr Schmidt, who on top of everything carries the [German] given name Heinrich, professes himself an incarnate nationalist Pole, Mr Kowalski as a thorough Russian and the apparently Muscovite Mr Kusnjetzow as a genuine German. And the situation is no better with the confessional identity of the three: the Pole Schmidt is Roman Catholic, the Russian with the Polish name of Kowalski is Orthodox, while Mr Kusnjetzow, in spite of his Russian name, belong the Evangelical community.[118]

In its unambiguousness, the story reads more like pure fiction than tendentious reportage. The resourceful official actually spared his superiors: if he had included 'locals' or Lithuanians, the issue would have been even more confusing. His goal remained clear, irrespective of the actual truth of this all too beautiful situation: the census proved impossible to carry out on the ground because the local data did not fit into the official parameters. An ellipse cannot be drawn as a rectangle.

The traditional local elite functioned as mediator between the German occupation administration – numerically sparse and overburdened in every respect – and the rural population that was supposed to especially provide food and labour. In Romania, this spanned from the secretary of state in Bucharest to local mayors and village elders. The surveying enterprise (and the exploitation enterprise behind it) did not fail because senior Romanian officials did everything they could to protect their country; the Bucharest elite had too little power for this. Rather, the entire enterprise proved to be ineffective at the lowest levels, where a few German soldiers who neither spoke the language nor knew the area were confronted with the traditional defensive strategies of a village community. Completely independent of possible patriotic motives, the farmers acted as if they did not understand: the people being questioned claimed to be uncertain about their own family names, and suddenly could not count their own possessions or name their own birthdays; but they did offer the Germans a good supper with a lot of alcohol as a substitute for continuing their arduous task. The farmers instinctively played dumb, complained about their hardships, showed sympathy for the overburdened occupier and offered minor, but real advantages instead of the major ones that were difficult for either side to imagine. This defensive strategy functioned quite well as a rule. Moreover, it was not an attitude specific to Romania, the Balkans or military occupation. In the distant land of Kirghizia in 1916, Russian officials chose not to create their own new-population registers but demanded instead that clan elders provide the names of potential soldiers. Not unexpectedly, the lists brought little clarity: ostensibly, thirty-year-old men fit for service were consistently mixed up with sixty-year-olds and visa-versa. Officials, of course, presumed extensive corruption and were probably correct.[119] Pre-modern rural communities did not worry much about this kind of accusation.

---

118 Cited in Vejas Gabriel Liulevicius, *War Land on the Eastern Front: Culture, National Identity, and German Occupation in World War I* (Cambridge: Cambridge University Press, 2005), 34.
119 Sanborn, *Drafting the Russian Nation*, 35.

Corruption, inefficiency and falling short of their own wishful thinking, however, still produced better results than the ruthless use of force. The Bulgarians adopted such a policy in Vardar Macedonia, confiscating as many agricultural products as possible. The result was a food catastrophe. The first deaths from starvation occurred in early 1917. In 1918, German grain depots had to send breadstuffs to the Bulgarians.[120]

Although the German Ober Ost did not engage in such evidently counterproductive ruthlessness, it did rely significantly more on compulsion than, for instance, the General Governorate in Warsaw. In 1926, a Reichstag report confirmed what those knowledgeable about the practices of the two occupation administrations had known 10 years earlier: the Warsaw model, which was based on the limited participation of local elites, clearly functioned more efficiently: 'Much of what was decreed [by Ober Ost] remained on paper, since there was a dearth of real contact with the lower administrative posts and a complete absence of contact with the local population'.[121]

Theoretically, the occupiers had an easier time in the city. They could expropriate, confiscate and place things under state administration; they could issue ration cards, impose curfews, give privileged treatment to members of the Central Powers, decree meatless days, determine the schedule of streetcars and inspect the mail. In practice, however, the Germans failed almost as completely in the cities as they did in the countryside. Bucharest, with its population of 300,000, was the only metropolis in the Balkans which survived the war and the occupation impoverished, but without experiencing complete existential collapse. Even in June 1917, the official bread rations for Bucharest residents allocated by the German occupiers were higher than those typical in the big cities of the Central Powers.[122] Despite this, the black market flourished in Bucharest. Farmers who had successfully avoided registering their property with the occupying powers were willing to take the risk and supply the black market, especially since the prices in the capital were usually two to five times higher than in the countryside due to German regulatory measures. It was well worth the risk.[123] It was, in particular, the occupiers who paid these high prices, as well as the middle class (who in turn also made money in other domains of the black market.)

In the end, the middle class – the traditional losers in war and occupation – were impoverished everywhere. Nevertheless, they survived and were comparatively healthy and still able to afford many black-market products by selling their household furnishings. The lower classes had to turn to soup kitchens, heated halls and shelters, which were established on a previously unknown scale. Despite this, the number of deaths rose significantly, especially in winter.[124]

Former industrial labourers constituted a significant portion of poor people. Many of them returned to their home villages after factories were closed down, as had been the case in Lodz and Warsaw in 1914. This also occurred under German occupation irrespective of the country: under the new rulers, the manufacturing sector – especially the textile industry – was closed down without any consideration of the fact that people who did not own multiple coats and sweaters in 1914 were soon walking around in rags. Most of the damage had been caused by the loss of export markets and material supplies even before the occupation. The last local businesses

---

120 Opfer, *Im Schatten des Krieges*, 96–101.
121 Cited in Westerhoff, *Zwangsarbeit*, 80.
122 3,080 grams of bread compared to 1,600 grams in Berlin, 1,500 grams in Westphalia, and 1,260 grams in Vienna. Mayerhofer, *Zwischen Freund und Feind*, 222.
123 This entire paragraph draws on ibid., 231.
124 Ibid., 237.

now went bankrupt. German occupiers had no interest in competition, and they were not alone in this regard: Riga, the fifth-largest Russian industrial centre, had already been closed down for all intents and purposes in the first year of war, although the Germans did not occupy the city until the fall of 1917. Unemployment and misery were the results not of politics in the narrower sense of the term, but of the war-related disruption of economic relationships either caused by the occupiers or accepted by them as a result of their own priorities. In Vilna, where the Germans succeeded in making themselves unpopular amongst Poles, Jews and Lithuanians more or less at the same time, the city's population decreased approximately 30 per cent by September 1917. Of the almost 140,000 remaining and newly arrived residents in the city, more than three-quarters of them (110,000) were fed in soup kitchens. The death rate tripled for Jews, who had made up almost half of the population of Vilna before the war, while the number of Jewish births sank to one third of the pre-war period. The death rate doubled for Poles between 1915 and early 1917.[125] Given these conditions, the fact that the German military had at the same time (1915–16) built two standard gauge railway tracks with a total length of more than 200 kilometres – one connecting the southwest of Lithuania by train for the first time, and the other connecting the future capital city Kaunas to Riga – did little to change the attitudes of the inhabitants of Ober Ost.[126] Elsewhere, there was certainly acceptance among the local residents for German infrastructure projects, insofar as these occurred close to where they lived: the Jews in Lodz even complained that the Polish city council was assigning desirable jobs in road construction in the surrounding areas exclusively to Polish volunteers.[127]

The occupiers also proved flexible in several other areas with regard to employment policy. In Romania, German occupiers released a portion of their POWs: tens of thousands of farmers and agricultural labourers were allowed to return to the jobs they held prior to 1916. 'On leave' from the prison camp, they helped to alleviate the shortage of farm workers and also relieved the German prisoner-of-war system while improving relations between the occupiers and the local population. Similar measures were taken in Serbia, where soldiers from the occupying forces, local compulsory conscripts, detainees and prisoners of war all took part in the same work.[128]

Finally, we should not forget that the occupying powers were dependent on local authorities – albeit to varying degrees – especially since they had established a number of these authorities themselves. This was the case not only with regard to the political role of various local organs in establishing a quasi-state (although the German hopes for a future buffer state dependent on the German Reich impeded the use of force and exploitation), but also with regard to everyday life under occupation. When in October 1916, the German administration ordered the Warsaw city council to compile lists of unemployed people who were to be sent to work in Germany, the council twice refused to comply, without being punished for this.

Resistance to the occupier was seldom as blatant and as successful as this. An almost simultaneous example in Vilna was more typical: representatives of the local population here protested against the introduction of universal compulsory labour for men. Occupation authorities

---

125 Theodore R. Weeks, 'Vilnius in World War I, 1914–1920', *Nordost-Archiv* NF XVII (2008): 34–57, here 46–7.
126 Christopher Kopper, 'Der Erste Weltkrieg als Eisenbahnkrieg', in *Neue Wege in ein neues Europa: Geschichte und Verkehr im 20. Jahrhundert*, eds Ralph Roth and Karl Schlögel (Frankfurt a.M.: Campus, 2009), 222–34, here 232.
127 Westerhoff, *Zwangsarbeit*, 132. This complaint, moreover, was successful.
128 Scheer, 'Manifestation', 224.

ignored this protest, and local leaders subsequently called for illegal, but nonetheless successful boycotts and resistance.[129]

These examples in Warsaw and Vilna in the fall of 1916 belong to the rare cases of open resistance in occupied territories. In both instances, subsidiary bodies of the occupiers resisted – in the first case legally, in the second case illegally, but without any hope that this sabotage could be concealed from the occupier. Both subsidiary bodies engaged in civil, unarmed resistance. Despite the experience of revolution a decade earlier, and despite over two years of war, military resistance and political terrorism were not among the conceivable, let alone practicable, options in 1916.

Total war?

Did Russians, Central, Eastern and Southeastern Europeans experience a total war from 1914 to 1916? The answer depends on how this mutable and often misused term is defined. When Roger Chickering attempted this in the late twentieth century, he had a more limited body of literature available than we have today. Nevertheless, the criteria he compiled remain useful as points of orientation.[130]

First of all, a 'total war' is a global event that is unprecedented in terms of intensity and scope. If we apply this criterion to Central and Eastern Europe, we can speak of a total war since even in the summer of 1915 the acts of war and the occupation regimes encompassed the entire area between the eastern provinces of the German Reich (of which only East Prussia was directly involved in the hostilities) and the line from Riga to Cernăuți, the northeast of the Habsburg monarchy, as well as Serbia. Over the course of the following year, the war came to include Montenegro, Albania, for a brief time the eastern part of Transleithania and Romania, as well as Bulgaria as an exclusively warring (that is, not occupied) state. During 1917–18, violence in the form of revolution, civil war and foreign intervention encompassed large parts of European Russia, so that the entire territory between the south-eastern coast of the Baltic Sea, the Adria and the Black Sea were involved in some form of war that frequently included occupation and destruction. It should also be added, however, that within this enormous space, these manifestations of war differed greatly for the people on the ground, for both soldiers and civilians alike; factors include the concentration and intensity of the war, one's immediate personal threat of violence, and the fact that people lived in fear and uncertainty amidst a seemingly endless war. An elderly Hungarian, Slovenian or Slovakian farmer saw neither war nor occupation; during these years the wife of a Jewish artisan in Grodno would have witnessed foreign troops marching through only once and later would have encountered an occupation regime no more threatening than the usual Russian rule.

The people most severely affected were the young men who were drafted in 1914. The less fortunate they were, the more horrible their experiences, until the front stabilized and the risks they faced sank significantly following the Brusilov offensive in the spring and summer of 1916 and the defeat of Romania in the following months. In this case, time was a central factor, for

---

129 Westerhoff, *Zwangsarbeit*, 206–7, 228–9. In this case, the Warsaw city council capitalized on the moment or on the bad timing of the occupation authorities: the dispute occurred in the weeks before the imperial proclamations of 5 November. The General Governor declared the dispute to be resolved on 6 November, as it directly conflicted with the central political plan.
130 Roger Chickering, 'Total War: The Use and Abuse of a Concept', in *Anticipating Total War: The German and American Experiences, 1871–1914*, eds Manfred Boemke, Roger Chickering and Stig Förster (Cambridge: Cambridge University Press, 1999 [2006]), 13–28, here 16.

which – as always – nuances can be identified only through comparison. As Mark Biondich has argued with justification, 'The Balkan Wars were the Ottoman state's first "total war", while the Balkan states mobilized more than half a million men to prosecute their collective war efforts'.[131] The first Balkan War lasted a few months with interruptions; the second, almost exactly one month. Within a short time, total mobilization thus produced results that brought the warring parties back to the negotiating table. The Great War in the East lasted significantly longer. Nevertheless, totality was lacking from 1914 to 1916, since the western part of the Russian empire – the main theatre of the war – ceased to be a mobilization reservoir after the first year. The unfortunate men drafted from these provinces in 1914 had to endure two more years of senseless, fruitless war.

Let us return to Chickering. His second criterion is that the participants of a total war act in ways that exceed the bounds of morality, customary law or martial law because they let themselves be guided by a hatred fuelled by modern ideologies. This second criterion is fulfilled nowhere in Central and Eastern Europe, except for the Russian civil war beginning in 1917. Despite the special case of Serbia (including the war crimes and other violations addressed above) and despite the intention of occupiers to reorganize society in the northeast (as described above by Liulevicius), one cannot prove that any army on the Eastern fronts or any occupying power behind the fronts engaged in a programmatic break with the existing moral ideas and legal orders. This fundamental distinction to the Eastern front and occupation rule during the Second World War renders any further discussion unnecessary. The First World War in the East was a military conflict that was new in every dimension but was nevertheless not a total war.

Third, Chickering examines the extent of mobilization among the civilian population as well as the latter's potential endangerment, which in the case of a total war is at least similar to that of combatants. These are two different criteria. Even the question of incorporating the civilian population into war production cannot be answered unambiguously since it developed differently from state to state and region to region. If, for instance, an occupied region had been subject only to the conscription process of 1914 (as in Ober Ost or the Kingdom of Poland), there were still too many 'unproductive' men – war-related in cities, structurally in the countryside – who were initially recruited or organized for voluntary labour for the occupation regime and later for compulsory labour, both with limited success (see the sub-chapter 'Occupation'). Matters were similar in Romania and in territories where there had been two years of fighting, such as Bukovina, Eastern Galicia and central Belarus, which were located on the front lines and where even the remaining farmers were barely able to work.

Mobilization for the war economy led to rising employment figures, but often coexisted with simultaneous unemployment. In the years before the revolutions of 1917, there was significant growth in several branches of industry in St. Petersburg and Moscow, two of the most important industrial centres of the tsarist empire; armaments production and armament employment increased dramatically. The opposite occurred in Warsaw, Lodz and Riga – the next three largest industrial centres in the tsarist empire – where production sank significantly: only one-fifth of their capacities were used and unemployment rates rose accordingly until

---

131 See Chapter 1 of the present volume, 'The Balkan Wars: patterns of violence in the Balkans leading up to the First World War', 13–14; Ginio Eyal, 'Mobilizing the Ottoman Nation during the Balkan Wars (1912–1913): Awakening from the Ottoman Dream', *War in History* 12 (2005): 156–77.

the end of the war, which (for Warsaw and Lodz) meant especially under German occupation. Thus, we can hardly speak of a state-guided, countrywide mobilization of the male civilian population in the service of war.

We can, in contrast, speak without reservation of a context-dependent, non-state-guided mobilization of women. This resulted from the mobilization of men, which directly affected the social and professional role of women and especially of wives. In both the city and the countryside, there were suddenly many more women than men everywhere. In Belgrade, women had constituted 43 per cent of the population before the war; in 1916, they made up almost two-thirds of city residents.[132] Whether in the hinterland and under occupation rule, the situation must have been similar in many places. Women now assumed new public roles since this was required by the absence of men. Given the agrarian-related population structure of Central, Eastern and Southeastern Europe, women worked most frequently in agriculture: since their husbands were in battle, they had to take over the farm. This often meant they travelled to the city accompanied by their eldest son in order to sell crops and livestock. The fact that they could be seen with growing frequency with cigarettes in their mouths suggests a social transformation in conventions and notions of propriety.

Urban women did not, as a rule, assume the vocations of their own husbands, but rather of other deployed men, working as saleswomen, female conductors and waitresses, staff members of local administration, auxiliary workers for the army, or in whatever jobs became free or arose due to the war. Tens of thousands of women went to work in industry. The participation of women in the steel and machine-building industry in the Pilsen region (where Škoda, the largest arms manufacturer in the monarchy, was located) rose from 2.4 per cent at the beginning of the war to almost 20 per cent by 1916. This substantial increase in a traditionally male-dominated sector was accompanied, on the one hand, by chance privilege: the Austrian War Service Act of 1912 with its draconian regulations against possible worker protests referred solely to men; legislators at the time had been unable to imagine an armaments industry with a significant proportion of women workers. On the other hand, a context-dependent gender equality now developed in industry and elsewhere that – like smoking – virtually amounted to a symbolic erasing of gender differences. After many work-related accidents, women in industry began to wear men's clothing, including trousers (previously worn only by feminists) and as much headgear as possible. Since food rations continued to be limited, secondary sexual characteristics became less and less apparent: dressed in work attire, men and women looked increasingly similar.[133] It is doubtful whether this was the case in the countryside as well since women were not pressed to wear work uniforms there nor did they suffer from malnutrition.

Both types, female farmers and urban working women, were soon part of everyday life, as were the mothers who stood in line in front of shops to get their children through the war. All three types were present in large numbers in the local hinterland as well as in the occupied territories.

By far the numerically smallest group of women (who were nevertheless quite visible) worked in healthcare and social welfare, on innumerable aid and national committees financed by state, local and private sources, providing the enormous amount of poor and sick people a chance at survival. In Galicia alone, during the second year of the war, there were over one hundred such organizations, each of which had between 200 and 900 members in district

---

132 Knezevic, 'The Austro-Hungarian occupation', 152.
133 Kučera, 'Losing Manliness', 8–12.

towns.[134] Despite regional differences, this appears to have been a significant advance for women in both the professional world and the public sphere[135] – although this entire development has been vehemently contested, for instance, for Romania and the entirety of the 'Balkans'.[136]

The next question – that of the endangerment of civilians – can be answered unambiguously. Except in immediate vicinity to the front (of the larger cities, only Belgrade and Cernăuți), civilians were rarely shot at or bombed. In the few months between Romania's entry into the war and the German invasion, residents in Bucharest regarded attacks by the German zeppelins as a high-level threat. While a number of civilians did die in zeppelin attacks, none of the estimates exceeds double digits.

Reprisals against the civilian population affected thousands, not hundreds of thousands or millions. Thus, we cannot speak of a threat comparable to that faced by soldiers on the front. Hunger and disease, which millions of civilians suffered in the hinterland as well as under occupation, are not characteristics of total war.

Finally, Chickering's fourth criterion cannot be meaningfully applied to Eastern Europe: unlimited war objectives that aim at the destruction or extermination of an enemy. While none of the four empires fighting on the Eastern or Southeastern fronts survived the war, their demise cannot be attributed to the exterminatory will of an enemy, but rather to their own mistakes, which revealed and exacerbated internal weaknesses and ultimately allowed them to implode. Nevertheless, two-and-a-half years after the summer of 1914, when the First Russian Revolution erupted, the idea that all of the great powers participating in the war would collapse still appeared to be an absurd idea.

Bibliographical comment

Between 2014 and 2020, a lot has happened in this area of research. Over the course of the past six years, while a number of cities have recognized their respective 100-year anniversaries (from Tannenberg in 1914, to Gorlice in 1915; from Compiègne in 1918 and Versailles in 1919 to Warsaw in 1920), numerous articles and books have been published that do not necessarily impart new knowledge, but rather attempt to integrate into the pan-European memory the facts along the 'Eastern fronts' that were already known in the interwar period. The following bibliographical commentary refers mainly to the 'Eastern-related' English- and German-language literature of the period 1914–16 as an eminently important part of the First World War, situated between classical military, social and cultural history.

In *Der vergessene Weltkrieg* ('The Forgotten World War'), Maciej Górny and I have attempted – perhaps even more so than Mark Biondich does in the present volume – to portray the so-called

---

134 Pająk, *Od autonomii*, 173.
135 This issue has been discussed in the great detail in regard to Russia. See Melissa K. Stockdale, '"My death for the Motherland is Happiness": Women, Patriotism, and Soldiering in Russia's Great War, 1914–1917', *The American Historical Review* 109, no. 1 (February 2004): 78–116, here 84.
136 Bucur, *Heroes and Victims*, 52: 'The celebrated entry of women in factories and the service industries … didn't even become a dream in the Balkans. Russia was one exception in the East', ostensibly due to the greater integration of women in the economy and to better organization prior to 1914. 'Far from experiencing the economic empowerment of their counterparts in the West, most women who lived through the war on the Eastern front merely got by and experienced constant uncertainty. They greeted the end of the war with relief' (p. 53). Women fared the same elsewhere, however, which casts doubt on Bucur's central thesis about the special fate of women in Romania and in the Balkans.

Balkan Wars of 1912–13 not as regional skirmishes between post-Ottoman small states, but as an epilogue to the impending war between world powers: the mobility of the troops being similar to that on the Eastern fronts between 1914 and 1916, and their equipment not much worse.[137] The majority of the fortresses were rather inconsequential in contrast to the railway network, which was a decisive factor in the course of battles everywhere. Occupation, hunger and disease in the hinterland: all these phenomena were repeated in the struggle of the imperial armies on the Russian Western front, as well as in Serbia and Romania.

However, it should be clearly stated that more recent research concentrates much more on the period between 1918 and 1923, in which the 'forgotten wars' after 11 November 1918 are the focus.[138] The comparison with Ireland[139] and the Greek-Turkish war proves to be particularly productive. Robert Gerwarth and John Horne (curators of the exhibition 'A l'Est la Guerre sans fin, 1918–23' in the Musée des Armées in Paris, which opened in the fall of 2018), neither of whom are experts on Eastern Europe, were pioneers here. The fact that the seeds of the largely irregular wars of succession, which were marked by mass migration and national and social upheaval, were planted before the Russian Revolution (whose role justifiably remains the focus of attention) can, however, be demonstrated in various fields. To limit it to two examples: first, Rudolf Kučera approaches his study on industry in the Czech lands from the history of science.[140] For Kučera, the *L'homme Machine* ('man as machine') is no longer a blasphemous thought experiment, but is rather being scientifically remeasured from decades before 1914 according to the most modern standards. After the outbreak of the war, such knowledge provides the authorities with numerous, scientifically plausible indications for the treatment of workers or the management of agricultural shortages. Although the explosion of the exploited did not take place until 1918, it would not be understandable without the history of rationing, rationalization and repression.

On another level, Jörn Leonhard, as the second example, reintegrates the first years of the 'forgotten world war' into the era of the First World War. Since his 'Pandora's Box' is divided into annual chapters (yet within them, Leonhard follows factual questions), there is enough room for social processes, emotional reactions, doubt, fear and frustration – even in the hinterland of the Eastern fronts.[141] Comparative social history thus (hopefully) receives inspiring material for reflection. Not only that; it remains hopeful that humanities research will continue to be as productive as it has been in recent years, even after the celebration of the final 100th anniversary (the Treaty of Lausanne 1923–2023).

Further reading

Biondich, Mark. *The Balkans: Revolution, War and Political Violence since 1878* (Oxford: Oxford University Press, 2011).

---

137 Włodzimierz Borodziej and Maciej Górny, *Der vergessene Weltkrieg: Europas Osten 1912–1923*, vol. 1, *Imperien 1912–1916*, trans. from Polish by Bernhard Hartmann (Darmstadt: wbg, 2018).
138 For recent literature on the topic – mainly articles – see the English translation of *Der vergessene Weltkrieg* as Włodzimierz Borodziej and Maciej Górny, *Forgotten Wars: Central and Eastern Europe, 1912–1916* (Cambridge: Cambridge University Press, 2021).
139 See 'Forum: Das Gedenkjahr 1918/1919 in Europa – Krieg und Frieden, Schlamm und Schlachten, Erinnerung und Forschung; A Discussion with Włodzimierz Borodziej, Maciej Górny, Heather Jones and Jörn Leonhard', *Journal of Modern European History* 18, no. 1 (2020): 3–15.
140 Kučera, *Rationed Life*.
141 Jörn Leonhard, *Pandora's Box: History of the First World War* (Cambridge, MA: Harvard University Press 2018).

Bloch, Jan. *The Future of War in Its Technical, Economic and Political Relations*, trans. R. C. Long, 6 vols. (Boston: Gine, 1899).
Boemke, Manfred, Roger Chickering, and Stig Förster, eds. *Anticipating Total War: The German and American Experiences, 1871–1914* (Cambridge: Cambridge University Press, 1999).
Böhler, Jochen, Włodzimierz Borodziej, and Joachim von Puttkamer, eds. *Legacies of Violence: Eastern Europe's First World War* (München: Oldenbourg, 2014).
Borodziej, Włodzimierz, and Maciej Górny, *Forgotten Wars: Central and Eastern Europe, 1912–1916* (Cambridge: Cambridge University Press, 2021).
Broadberry, Stephen, and Mark Harrison, eds. *The Economics of World War I* (Cambridge: Cambridge University Press, 2005).
Bucur, Maria. *Heroes and Victims: Remembering War in Twentieth-Century Romania* (Bloomington, IN: Indiana University Press 2010).
Dowling, Timothy C. *The Brusilov Offensive* (Bloomington, IN: Indiana University Press, 2008).
Gatrell, Peter. *A Whole Empire Walking: Refugees in Russia during World War I* (Bloomington, IN: Indiana University Press, 2005).
Gumz, Jonathan E. *The Resurrection and the Collapse of Empire in Habsburg Serbia, 1914–1918* (Cambridge: Cambridge University Press, 2009).
Kramer, Alan. *Dynamic of Destruction: Culture and Mass Killing in the First World War* (Oxford: Oxford University Press, 2007).
Kraus, Karl. *The Last Days of Mankind: The Complete Text*, trans. Fred Bridgham and Edward Timms (New Haven, CT: Yale University Press, 2015).
Kučera, Rudolf. *Rationed Life: Science, Everyday Life and Working-Class Politics in the Bohemian Lands, 1914–1918* (New York: Berghahn, 2016).
Leonhard, Jörn. *Pandora's Box: History of the First World War* (Cambridge, MA: Harvard University Press 2018).
Liulevicius, Vejas Gabriel. *War Land on the Eastern Front: Culture, National Identity, and German Occupation in World War I* (Cambridge: Cambridge University Press, 2005).
Mitrovic, Andrej. *Serbia's Great War 1914–1918* (London: Hurst, 2007).
Prusin, Alexander V. *Nationalizing a Borderland: War, Ethnicity, and Anti-Jewish Violence in East Galicia, 1914–1920* (Tuscaloosa, AL: University of Alabama Press, 2005).
Prusin, Alexander V. *The Lands Between: Conflicts in the East European Borderlands, 1870–1992* (Oxford: Oxford University Press, 2010).
Retish, Aaron B. *Russia's Peasants in Revolution and Civil War: Citizenship, Identity, and the Creation of the Soviet State, 1914–1922* (Cambridge: Cambridge University Press, 2008).
Roshwald, Aviel, and Richard Stites, eds. *European Culture in the Great War: The Arts, Entertainment, and Propaganda, 1914–1918* (Cambridge: Cambridge University Press, 1999).
Sanborn, Joshua A. *Drafting the Russian Nation: Military Conscription, Total War, and Mass Politics* (De Kalb, IL: Northern Illinois University Press, 2003).
Stone, Norman. *The Eastern Front 1914–1917* (New York: Charles Scribner's Sons, 1975).
Strachan, Hew. *The First World War* (London: Simon and Schuster, 2003).
Weindling, Paul Julian. *Epidemics and Genocide in Eastern Europe 1890–1945* (Oxford: Oxford University Press, 2000).

3

THE RADICALIZATION OF VIOLENCE AND INTERMARIUM'S INTERWAR

Jochen Böhler

Introduction

The term 'Intermarium' in this chapter's title, which functions as a geographical metaphor for the lands between Germany and Russia that extended from the Baltic Sea in the north to the coast of the Black Sea in the south, certainly needs further explanation. My choice to use this term is deliberately provocative, since, as it is well known, 'Intermarium' (*Międzymorze*) was a Polish interwar conception of a federation of Central and Eastern European nation states – supposed to counterbalance Russian and German preponderance – that never materialized.[1] But if one thumbs through the Polish memorandum 'The Federation of Central Europe', which was drafted in French by Ryszard Sandecki sometime between 1922 and 1926, one grasps the tremendous hope that contemporaries attached to a post-war Central European commonwealth stretching from sea to sea as an alternative to the Great Powers of the East and West: 'To our brothers from Bulgaria, Czechoslovakia, Estonia, Finland, Greece, Hungary, Latvia, Lithuania, Poland, Romania and Yugoslavia. Hail! The gravity of the hour commands us to understand each other and to connect our fates. It's time!'[2]

Ex post, we might smile at the pathos and euphoria of the memorandum. But we should nonetheless be aware that for the contemporaries living in the region between irredentist and expansionist Germany and revolutionary Russia which regarded violence as reason of state, thoughts of a joint economic and security policy were a question of survival. The fragile nation states of 'Intermarium' had just evolved from a carnage of hitherto unknown proportions

---

1 Nevertheless, Marek J. Chodakiewicz, in *Intermarium: The land between the Black and Baltic Seas* (New Brunswick, NJ: Transaction Publishers, 2012) has recently used it for the same purpose, but without any reference to Polish interwar *Międzymorze* concepts. For further Polish conceptions of Central Europe, see Daria Nałęcz, 'The Evolution and Implementation of the Intermarium Strategy in Poland: A Historical Perspective', in *The Intermarium as the Polish-Ukrainian Linchpin of Baltic-Black Sea Cooperation*, ed. Ostap Kushnir (Newcastle upon Tyne: Cambridge Scholars Publishing, 2019), 1–21.
2 Ryszard Sandecki, *La Fédération de l'Europe Centrale: Le Mémoire* (Warsaw: Szerző, 1922–1926), 2.

which left the region devastated and depopulated, with the survivors severely traumatized. And the author of the memorandum made it absolutely clear what he considered to be the alternative, should the mission fail:

> In spite of the terrible trials imposed on the world by the last war, we have no right to delude ourselves, and we must coolly consider the probability of a new conflict, which would certainly be infinitely more terrible than the recent world war.

Consequently, the memorandum foresaw the stationing of multinational armed forces in all federal states: a federation of Central and Eastern Europe would obviate the need for its member states to fight one another; rather, member states would offer one another military aid in securing their external borders.[3]

The failure to build such a strong and solidary federation of the Central European nation states in the interwar period was, without a shadow of a doubt, a contributing factor for their almost effortless dissection and dismantling by Nazi Germany and Soviet Russia during 1938/39 and onwards. The question is not why the seemingly megalomaniacal plans for a 'Middle Europe' were made between the wars, but rather why they were not realized. The Polish desire for a maritime empire was by far not the only draft of a strong Central and Eastern European federation between the World Wars that failed. Other comparable concepts shared its fate, for example, several plans – schemed with French support – for an economic federation of the Danube riparian states were made. Thus, one should always remember that parallel to the often cited quarrels and disputes between the heirs of the European land empires in real politics,[4] there was still room for visions or even attempts to build alliances between equals rather than coalitions with one or more of the stronger neighbours to the east and to the west.[5] The somewhat anachronistic use of the term 'Intermarium' in this chapter's title underlines a certain degree of self-reliance and agency on the part of the states in the region, counterbalancing the common perception of them as mere marionettes of Europe's Great Powers at that time. It is this perspective from inside rather than outside the region that is of interest here.

Hopefully, this explanation might suffice in appeasing the reader of this chapter with its admittedly ironic title, without making the reader forget that in the end, all plans for federal state-building in Central and Eastern Europe in the interwar period failed due to the lack of enthusiasm and devotion amongst its potential members. 'There are at least ten reasons for which the accomplishment of a Danubian confederation is not possible', as the lifelong Czech politician Edvard Beneš put it in the mid-1920s, 'the first is that the states do not want this, the second … shall I continue?'[6] Some years earlier, his political counterpart, Tomáš G. Masaryk, preferred the national to the federal naval dream when at the peace talks in Paris (1919–20), he unsuccessfully promoted exclusive access to the Adriatic for Bohemia.[7] The Polish utopia of an 'Intermarium', as a thread running through the whole interwar period – from Józef Piłsudski to

---

3 Ibid., 3.
4 Mihai Chioveanu, 'A Fragmented World: Cooperation, Conflict and Conquest in Central East Europe', *Studia Politica* 9, no. 1 (2009): 81–104.
5 Małgorzata Morawiec, 'Antiliberale Europäisierung? Autoritäre Europakonzeptionen im Polen der Zwischenkriegszeit', *Zeithistorische Forschungen* 9, no. 3 (2012): 409–27, also available online at http://www.zeithistorische-forschungen.de/3-2012/id=4609 (accessed 10 December 2021).
6 Cited in Chioveanu, 'A Fragmented World', 98.
7 Stefan Troebst, '"Intermarium" und "Vermählung mit dem Meer": Kognitive Karten und Geschichtspolitik in Ostmitteleuropa', *Geschichte und Gesellschaft* 28 (2002): 435–69, here 443.

Józef Beck – under the label of a 'Third Europe', resembled at most a federation of Central and Eastern European states (at least in theory); it was certainly always under the guise of unchallenged Polish supremacy and was directed in part at their Czech neighbour, despised since the Czech seizure of large parts of Cieszyn Silesia which had a considerable Polish-speaking population in 1919.[8] The bottom line is that one is well advised to refrain from mockery here: instead, it might be worthwhile to look closer at the underlying patterns of the dreams and failures of federalism in the region, especially the part that past, present or envisaged forms of violence played in both.

The timeframe covered in this chapter spans a period usually referred to as 'the interwar years'. Let us pause here for a moment and reflect on what this means in the context of this volume's core theme, violence. In this reading, a distinct meaning seems to be attributed to the roughly two decades that separated the Second World War from the First: that of a mere transitional phase between two global conflicts. And within this timeframe, the states of Central and Eastern Europe have often been identified merely as troublesome locations that inherited a significant amount of violence and residual problems from the First World War, which only helped pave the way for the Second World War. The violence and turmoil never having fully ceased in between the wars, has given the impression that these states were unable to overcome the legacies of war and violence in their domestic and foreign policies, the evidence of which can be found in their persecution of national minorities, in the development of authoritarian forms of government and in their harbouring of resentment against their neighbours.[9]

Of course, this master narrative is not pure invention, and therefore this chapter by no means aims to dismantle it. But by changing the focus from an outside perspective to an inside perspective, such a narrative demands differentiation. At least since Marxist theory was declared bankrupt, Historians have been hesitant to take automatisms in their field for granted. The 1920s and 1930s were not a mere sliding board from one World War to the next. In between, there were successful and unsuccessful attempts in Central and Eastern Europe to stem and quell the violence directed both in- and outwards, and there were regional similarities as well as differences; in carving these out, it will be possible to first re-evaluate the role of the states in our region, and second, to discern different forms of violence, their causes and their impact on the indigenous populations in question.

Nevertheless, use of the term 'interwar' is practical and will therefore be used henceforth; not so much because it refers to the two World Wars which it connects, but because it also reverberates a level of paramilitary, societal and state violence characteristic of the period between 1917–18 and 1939, which is not reminiscent of the two decades that preceded the First World War in all of Central and Eastern Europe. To speak of the 'interwar period' does not mean that we are merely lost in transition between the wars: it is much more than that – the period will be treated as a transitional phase that in and of itself is worth studying. It is a period whose beginning is marked by extreme forms of paramilitary violence, accompanied by enthusiasm and high expectations, whereas its end is marked by disappointment, disenchantment and a

---

8 Ibid., 445; Elżbieta Znamierowska-Rakk, 'Sprawa połączenia Bałtyku z Morzem Czarnym i Morzem Egejskim w polityce II Rzeczypospolitej' [The issue of connecting the Baltic Sea with the Black Sea and the Aegean Sea in the policy of the Second Republic of Poland], in *Międzymorze: Polska i kraje Europy Środkowo-Wschodniej; XIX–XX wiek*, ed. Andrzej Ajnenkiel (Warsaw: IH PAN, 1995), 287–98.

9 Zara S. Steiner, *The Lights that Failed: European International History, 1919–1933* (Oxford: Oxford University Press, 2005); Erwin Oberländer, ed., *Autoritäre Regime in Ostmittel- und Südosteuropa, 1919–1944* (Paderborn: F. Schöningh, 2001).

bitterness that would soon turn into disaster. But it is also a period in which, for the first time in history, several independent Central and Eastern European states entered the international scene and became autonomous actors.

Looking more precisely at the interwar years under the heading of 'Violence', this chapter takes these evolving states of Central and Eastern Europe more seriously than one feels has hitherto been the case. This chapter shies away from simplistic answers, like blaming a bunch of allegedly immature and stubborn newcomer-states for a failed European peaceful order because they had shown themselves unable to quell the violence brought about by the First World War and to pacify their populations. Instead, the aim is to look for the deeper reasons behind that failure, analyzing first the years between 1917–18 and 1923 which were not at all tantamount to peace in the region, but rather witnessed an enormous wave of paramilitary violence as a side effect of a Central European Civil War. A second concern of this chapter is to question the notion of a new 'Thirty Years' War' or 'European Civil War' (1914–1945),[10] and more precisely, the notion of a peer-to-peer connection between certain forms of violence – such as interethnic violence – characteristic of the First and Second World Wars.[11] Studies that underline this theory often tend to simply overlook the two decades that separated these two wars and the different forms of violence that accompanied them.[12] Third, this chapter closely examines and compares the causes and implications of the authoritarian turn that all these states witnessed in the late 1920s or early 1930s (including the rise of fascist movements in some of them), as well as the part that such an authoritarian turn played in aggravating their internal and external policies in the decade preceding the Second World War.

Part I: Armed conflicts, 1917–1923

The previous chapter on the First World War dealt mainly with the engagement of regular armies (i.e. the rather conventional warfare in the years 1914–16) and its impact on the soldiers and the civil population of Central and Eastern Europe. Of course, the First World War did not end there, in 1916; but it did not end in 1918 either. With 1917 as a turning point, the gargantuan struggle between the empires dissipated into what at first might look like a loose bundle of isolated armed conflicts, which, given their limited scope and length, historians hesitate to call wars. Indeed, it was rare that only two states were engaged in these conflicts, but they were rather between a confusing number of military and paramilitary units with changing fronts and coalitions. Generally speaking, fully fledged states with clearly defined and settled boundaries, rubber-stamped by the international community, were not the major players at the

---

10 For the establishment of the notions of a 'Thirty Years' War' or a 'European Civil War' in academics, see Enzo Traverso, *Fire and Blood: The European Civil War, 1914–1945* (London: Verso, 2017), 23–30.
11 Hans-Ulrich Wehler, 'Der zweite Dreißigjährige Krieg: Der Erste Weltkrieg als Auftakt und Vorbild für den Zweiten Weltkrieg', *DER SPIEGEL Special: 1914–1945 – Der Zweite Dreißigjährige Krieg* (15 February 2004): 138–43.
12 Mark Levene, 'Frontiers of Genocide: Jews in the Eastern War Zones, 1914–1920 and 1941', in *Minorities in Wartime: National and Racial Groupings in Europe, North America, and Australia During the Two World Wars*, ed. Panikos Panayi (Oxford: Berg, 1993), 83–117; Eva Reder, 'Im Schatten des polnischen Staates: Pogrome 1918–1920 und 1945/46 – Auslöser, Bezugspunkte, Verlauf', *Zeitschrift für Ostmitteleuropaforschung* 60, no. 4 (2011): 571–606; Alexander V. Prusin, 'A "Zone of Violence": The Anti-Jewish Pogroms in Eastern Galicia in 1914–1915 and 1941', in *Shatterzone of Empires: Coexistence and Violence in the German, Habsburg, Russian, and Ottoman Borderlands*, eds Omer Bartov and Eric D. Weitz (Bloomington, IN: Indiana University Press, 2013), 362–77.

beginning of these conflicts in Central and Eastern Europe, but were rather shaped by them. The first argument of this subchapter (which will be elaborated upon further) is that these seemingly unrelated sparks were, in reality, part of a larger fire, i.e. the Central European Civil War that raged west of, often blending into, the Russian Civil War (1917–21), while centring around the emerging Polish Republic as the geographical hub.

The second argument for regarding 1917 as a watershed is that from that point on, a variety of local actors in Central and Eastern Europe started to take their fate into their own hands and fight for their own goals, not only against the receding Great Powers, but also against one another. Since the perspective and experience of the indigenous population is at the very heart of this compendium, this is an important point to make. The immediate post-war period and the interwar years in Central and Eastern Europe are often looked at from the outside and only regarded as a result of the First World War's imperial battles at the Eastern Front, the Russian Revolutions or of the peace negotiations in Paris that were dominated by the Western powers. It is mostly overlooked that in 1917 armed men in the region were creating precedents, in situ, using violent force. Lines drawn on maps alone never establish new state borders, lest they are enforced with significant armed assistance – a resource that the war-worn allies, after the nightmarish experiences of 1914–18, were neither able nor willing to provide.[13] In contrast, the heirs of the European land empires inherited a significant number of weapons left over from the sizeable passage of arms, and along with the weapons came the men that were able to bear them and who had a vital interest in using them. In what follows, the post-war struggles of 1917–23 will be described from a war correspondent's perspective rather than an observer of international policies; this will introduce some of the major agents of violence, without, needless to say, any claim to comprehensiveness.

The third argument is that the forms of violence accompanying the armed conflicts following the Russian Revolutions of 1917 significantly differed from the preceding forms. We have just learned in the previous chapter that in Central and Eastern Europe 'despite the resentment and tension unfolding around social and national issues, ... the potential for violence incited by war simply did not exist until 1917'.[14] In stark contrast, violence from 1917 onwards took a form that was much more typical for civil wars than conventional wars. This is not to say that the First World War of 1914–16 had been fought exclusively according to international conventions, and that no crimes against civilians had been committed then. But from 1917 onwards, our region of interest was plunged into a maelstrom of paramilitary violence which was now the rule rather than the exception. Since the conflicts ran along ethnic, ideological, religious and national lines, the question becomes how such lines predetermined the perpetrators' motivation to draw on violence and to which forms of violence they referred.

Finally, Part I of this chapter will make up for its earlier omission and extend past the local level to include international entanglements. This is advisable because the Central and Eastern European post-war conflicts were as isolated from world policies as from one another. Above all, this applies to the international armed intervention and assistance on the battlefields of the Central European and the Russian Civil War, to the world's opinion on the violence perpetrated in the war's wake, and to the impact the post-conflict settlements had on the future geographical and political shape of Central and Eastern Europe. Including

---

13 For the most recent history of Allied involvement in the post-war struggle, see: Ian Moffat, *The Allied Intervention in Russia, 1918–1920: The Diplomacy of Chaos* (Basingstoke: Palgrave Macmillan, 2015).
14 See Chapter 2, 'The war in the East, 1914–16', 47.

international entanglements will also provide a suitable point of reference for the discussion of the evolvement and fate of an interwar peace order for Central and Eastern Europe which will be elaborated in Part II of this chapter.

In summary, the armed conflicts of 1917–21 examined in Part I significantly shaped both the post-war map and the post-war order of Central and Eastern Europe and its self-determined states (which is the main reason why they are dealt with here and not in Chapter 2 of this volume). The turmoil of the post-war Central European Civil War (1918–21) was rather the violent overture of interwar unrest than the frictionless continuation of conventional warfare; it was rather the labour pains of independent Central and Eastern Europe than the death throes of the Imperial World.

The Central European Civil War, 1918–1921

When did the First World War begin, and when did it end? For the western part of the European continent, this question seems easy to answer, and it is common sense in that hemisphere's historiography that the First World War sewed its wild oats between the confines of the Austrian attack on Serbia in August 1914 and the collapse of the Central Powers' Western Front in November 1918. But if one casts their view to the Eastern war parties and their internal struggles, the situation becomes obscured: does it make sense to simply ignore the Balkan Wars of 1912–13? Most certainly not, as the first chapter of this volume convincingly argues.[15]

Similarly, the fighting in Eastern Europe did not simply end with the armistices of 1918. Yet, the violent sequel to the First World War – the struggle of the newly emerging nation states for territory and national unity all over Central and Eastern Europe – has almost vanished from our memory. Where it has been described, its major and minor conflicts have been treated rather dispersedly, as isolated incidents between two respective nation states 'in-the-making' rather than as coherent parts of the violent establishment of the post-war order in the region.[16] Instead of merely repeating such master narratives – with independence as the teleological result – Part I of this chapter argues for the notion of one 'extended European civil war'[17] the former citizens of the imperial land empires – Austria, Russia and Germany – fought against one another for the establishment of nation states that would be dominated by a single ethnic group. As has been elaborately shown, these 'fires of hatred' which constituted the 'dark side

---

15 See also Dominik Geppert, William Mulligan and Andreas Rose, eds, *The Wars Before the Great War: Conflict and International Politics Before the Outbreak of the First World War* (Cambridge: Cambridge University Press, 2015).

16 For the Polish case, see Adam Zamoyski, *The Battle for the Marchlands: A History of the 1920 Polish–Soviet War* (New York: Columbia University Press, 1981); Mieczysław Pruszyński, *Wojna 1920: Dramat Piłsudskiego* [The war of 1920: Piłsudski's drama] (Warsaw: BGW, 1994); Piotr Łossowski, *Jak Feniks z popiołów: Oswobodzenie ziem polskich spod okupacji w listopadzie 1918 roku* [Like a phoenix from the ashes: The liberation of the Polish lands from occupation in November 1918] (Łowicz: MWSH-P, 1998).

17 'In this light, the violence of the Russian Civil War appears not as something perversely Russian or uniquely Bolshevik, but as the most intense case of a more extended European civil war, extending through the Great War and stretching several years after its formal conclusion.' Peter Holquist, 'Violent Russia, Deadly Marxism? Russia in the Epoch of Violence, 1905–21', *Kritika: Explorations in Russian and Eurasian History* 4, no. 3 (2003): 627–52, here 644–5.

of democracy' were the nemesis of the twentieth century.[18] According to historian Robert Gerwarth, military defeat, revolutionary upheaval and counter-revolutionary reactions towards the end of the First World War turned Central and Eastern Europe into 'a transnational zone of paramilitary violence'.[19]

The postulate of a Central European Civil War following the First World War certainly requires elaboration. As a matter of fact, the trend to see the post-war struggles following the armistices in Central and Eastern Europe as isolated conflicts rather than parts of one phenomenon is predominant in literature, which surely has some justification. Christoph Mick, for example, has argued for a 'variety of wars', including civil wars, state wars, state-building wars, revolutionary wars, aggressive and defensive wars.[20] Arguing instead for one civil war which embraces all different kinds of conflicts does not mean to ignore these variants. But first of all, in terms of violence, the above list is far from complete; to get the whole picture, one would surely have to add sub-war level violence such as warlordism, banditry and pogroms. But the more we divide the larger picture into different pieces of a puzzle, the less we are able to perceive the ubiquitous experience of the military – and above all, paramilitary – violence the civil population of Central and Eastern Europe suffered at the hands of armed men from their own region between 1918 and 1921. Furthermore, both views are not at all exclusive, as Joshua Sanborn argues when writing that 'great wars are almost by definition conglomerations of multiple conflicts that proceeded simultaneously'.[21] If we speak of a Central European Civil War 1918–21 which included various forms of violence and multiple conflicts, this is because we prefer the perspective of those perpetrating and suffering violence to a mere political history of the region in that very period.

Besides, even contemporaries had already realized that the bell for a new era had sounded: 'Thus, after the Great War, arises a new war of nations', noted the chronicles of the Jesuit monastery in Chyrów shortly after the armistices.[22] Similarly, the Polish-Lithuanian politician and lawyer Michał Römer confided in his diary in early 1919:

> The war, finished in autumn, has not died away. Peace and a return to stability appear to be as remote, if not more distant, as in autumn when the war was formally approaching its end. Evicted from the trenches, front lines and from the official and regular struggle of militarized powers, it reached into human societies and

---

18 Norman M. Naimark, *Fires of Hatred: Ethnic Cleansing in Twentieth-Century Europe* (Cambridge, MA: Harvard University Press, 2001); Michael Mann, *The Dark Side of Democracy: Explaining Ethnic Cleansing* (Cambridge: Cambridge University Press, 2005).

19 Robert Gerwarth, 'The Central European Counter-Revolution: Paramilitary Violence in Germany, Austria and Hungary after the Great War', *Past and Present* 200, no. 1 (2008): 175–209, here 177.

20 Christoph Mick, 'Vielerlei Kriege: Osteuropa 1918–1921', in *Formen des Krieges: Von der Antike bis zur Gegenwart*, vol. 37, *Krieg in der Geschichte*, eds Dietrich Beyrau, Michael Hochgeschwender and Dieter Langewiesche (Paderborn: Schöningh, 2007), 311–26, here 311.

21 Joshua A. Sanborn, *Imperial Apocalypse: The Great War and the Destruction of the Russian Empire* (Oxford: Oxford University Press, 2014), 4. Peter Gatrell has grasped this virtual contradiction in an essay titled 'War After the War', and in a subchapter with the same title subsequently speaks of 'Revolutionary Challenges and Civil Wars'. See idem, 'War After the War: Conflicts, 1919–1923', in *A Companion to World War I*, ed. John Horne (Chichester: Wiley-Blackwell, 2010), 558–75, here 558–9.

22 '*Hoc modo post magnum bellum mundanum exorta nova bella nationum*', quoted from 'Fragment kroniki klasztoru i konwiktu oo. Jezuitów w Chyrowie za lata 1918–1919' [A Fragment of the Chronicle of the Jesuit Monastery and Convent in Chyrów for the years 1918–1919], in Józef Wołczański, ed., *Kościół rzymskokatolicki i Polacy w Małopolsce Wschodniej podczas wojny ukraińsko-polskiej 1918–1919: Źródła*, 2 vols. (Cracow: Wydawn. Naukowe Uniw. Papieskiego Jana Pawła II, 2012), 27–79, here 28. Thanks to Maciej Górny for this quote.

transformed itself into a state of permanent chaos, a *bellum omnium contra omnes* [a war of all against all]. Formally, the regular war has stopped, but the catastrophe, of which the war was only the first act, goes on and is far from over. Who knows if it is only in its initial stage?[23]

Almost simultaneously, an American Colonel – less sinister and with a pinch of wicked humour – at the sight of a troop of young boys about fourteen years old marching past in military step through a Czech town, remarked:

> It does not seem as if these people believe that the world's last war has just been finished … You will get very tired of this militarism before you are through with your trip. Chauvinism has become popular everywhere. As far as I can judge, every second day in these new Central European countries is a holiday to celebrate their sudden national independence.[24]

Furthermore, the notion of a Central European Civil War serves to rebalance the prevalence that the Russian Revolutions of 1917 would otherwise have had on our region. Unquestionably, these revolutions constituted a turning point in the East, but their vital political consequences did not immediately reverberate in the lands bordering Russia proper. The revolutions rather heralded the irrevocable decline of the old imperial order, and at best, a vaguely defined better future for the masses of landless peasants and poor workers in Central and Eastern Europe. The most significant immediate geopolitical consequence of the Russian Revolutions – the short-lived German occupation of the better part of all Eastern and Central Europe in the wake of the Treaty of Brest-Litovsk in 1918 – was, of course, not part of the revolutionary scenario. From the Bolshevik point of view, it was a deplorable but unavoidable side effect of having played the pacifist card to win over the masses; a side effect which, to be sure, would be reversed as soon as revolutionary Russia would have the military means to do so.[25] Early on in 1918, the German army was already up to its neck in paramilitary and counter-revolutionary upheavals and thus – analogous to the Red Guard which would later become the Red Army – became one of several players in a civil war which opened up a new era of self-determined agency for the people of Central and Eastern Europe.[26]

As a result, after the retreat of the empires, the battlefields of the Eastern Front turned into a tabula rasa for revolutionary and nationalist state-building, the former being characteristic for Russia and the latter for the territories beyond its Western borders. To say it in the words of the grand Doyen of Europe's transnational history in the twentieth century, Dan Diner, the

---

23 Michał Römer, 'Kulisy misji kowienskiej: Fragment Dziennika: wiosna 1919' [The background of the Kaunas mission: excerpt from a diary, spring 1919], *Arcana* 70–71, nos. 4–5 (2006): 33–81, here 52; English translation found in Piotr Wróbel, 'The Revival of Poland and Paramilitary Violence, 1918–1920', in *Spießer, Patrioten, Revolutionäre: Militärische Mobilisierung und gesellschaftliche Ordnung in der Neuzeit*, eds Rüdiger Bergien and Ralf Pröve (Göttingen: V&R unipress, 2010), 281–303, here 303.
24 Quoted in Artur L. Goodhart, *Poland and the Minority Races* (London: Allen & Unwin, 1920), 13–14.
25 The peace treaty and its enormous impact on the political development in Central and Eastern Europe in 1918 is treated extensively in Borislav Chernev, *Twilight of Empire: The Brest-Litovsk Conference and the Remaking of East-Central Europe, 1917–1918* (Toronto: University of Toronto Press, 2017).
26 Włodzimierz Mędrzecki, *Niemiecka interwencja militarna na Ukrainie w 1918 roku* [The German Military Intervention in Ukraine in 1918] (Warsaw: DiG, 2000); Wolfram Dornik et al., eds, *Die Ukraine: Zwischen Selbstbestimmung und Fremdherrschaft 1917–1922* (Graz: Leykam, 2011).

various situations in which military defeat combined with hunger blockades, social misery, territorial losses, and national humiliations were crucial for both the social rebellions and the ensuing counter-revolutionary reactions… A distinct arc of conflict emerged from this general meshing of military defeat, social revolution, and national battles on the frontier. It spanned Central and East Central Europe, from the Baltic to northern Italy and the Adriatic.[27]

To hammer the argument home: this was not simply a random conglomeration of isolated local conflicts, but rather the new stage of a worldwide conflict; this conflict shifted from a largely conventional war between European land empires into a civil war between their successors, with its epicentre in Central and Eastern Europe[28] and its repercussions noticeable as far away as Paris, Washington, Petrograd or Irkutsk.

The prelude in the Balkans has its counterpart in the post-war struggles that shook Central and Eastern Europe to the early 1920s on the battlefields of the second European war – *omnium contra omnes* – where ethno-political conflicts erupted with a vengeance.[29] After a period during which the war can be described as rather conventional, the demise of Imperial Russia, the retreat of the Central Powers and the battles for one's share of independence between the nascent nation states turned the region into a hotbed of military and paramilitary violence. These conflicts did not evolve organically out of the preceding war years, but rather constituted a clear cut which in its tumultuous consequences left its mark on interwar Europe as a whole and to some extent lay the foundation of a 'future war'.

Agents of violence

The years 1917–1923 mark the period in which the people of Central and Eastern Europe entered the scene of the First World War as independent political actors. Whereas before, only men fit for military service had fought – sometimes hand to hand – within the ranks of the respective imperial armies, at this point, they began to develop their own agenda. Their disengagement with the old order and their fight for a new one was a two-stage process. Firstly, the demise of the Empires would free many of them from bonds that had tied them against their will to the policies of Berlin, Vienna, Moscow or Istanbul, constraining their scope of action – in some cases, for over a century. Secondly, their respective struggles for independence would automatically result in a number of conflicts amongst themselves, and in the end, to either abortive or successful projects of state- and nation-building. Consequently, both developments – the implosion of the old order and the imposition of the new one – resulted in armed clashes of many kinds that shook the region at its periphery as well as in its very centre. In both cases, it was the course of the war's subsequent battles from 1918 onwards that made way for the new movements.

Following the Russian Revolutions of 1917, the imperial strongholds in the region were dismantled one after the other. But revolution was not the prime selection of the nations

---

27 Dan Diner, *Cataclysms: A History of the Twentieth Century from Europe's Edge* (Madison, WI: University of Wisconsin Press, 2008), 63–4.
28 Holquist, 'Violent Russia, Deadly Marxism', 644–5.
29 For paramilitary violence in the Balkans after the First World War, see the end of Chapter 1 in this volume, 'The Balkan Wars: patterns of violence in the Balkans leading up to the First World War' by Mark Biondich, 23–4.

populating the 'lands between' Russia and Germany.[30] With the important exception of Hungary, the few attempts to establish Soviet puppet governments here between 1918 and 1920 – such as the Lithuanian–Belorussian Soviet Socialist Republic (Litbel) or the Soviet Republic of Slovakia – were not only extremely short-lived, but absolutely marginal.[31] None of the new states emerging from the imperial debris followed the Petrograd example.

The attempt to establish a Polish Soviet Socialist Republic under the auspices of a Provisional Polish Revolutionary Committee (a.k.a. Polrevkom) in the summer of 1920 is a particularly good example for the vanity of these early communist experiments outside post-war Russia. The Polrevkom was founded in Moscow in July 1920. It was unofficially headed by Feliks Dzierżyński[32] – the notorious Polish chief of the Soviet Secret Police ('*Cheka*') from 1917 to 1926 – and it operated from an armoured train headed from Smolensk to Białystok. The Polrevkom's reign in north-eastern Poland lasted exactly three weeks and two days. Norman Davies convincingly concludes:

> The failure of the Polrevkom was due to the simple fact that it did not enjoy the respect or confidence of the people it sought to liberate. It operated in the wake of military operations whose destruction and brutality had already alienated the civil population. It operated under the patronage of a Russian army. It operated among people for whom national independence was far clearer than social revolution. It sought to import an ideology entirely alien to the prevailing beliefs and attitudes of the time.[33]

Stefan Żeromski, a Polish writer with sympathies for socialism, who visited Wyszków near Warsaw when it had just been evacuated by the Polrevkom, disillusioned, concluded: 'Having defeated Bolshevism on the battlefield, it must be defeated at the very heart of its ideas. Bolshevism must be replaced with principles that are nobler, fairer, wiser, and more perfect'.[34]

This raises the question as to why the world 'revolution', prophesized by Marx and Engels, ignited Russia but not the better part of Central and Southeastern Europe. Were the idealistic notions of a classless society more appealing to Russians than to, let us say, Latvians, Czechs or Serbs? Eventually, Józef Piłsudski, one of the most powerful players in the struggle for the Central European post-war order (and who, as a youth, had been a revolutionary and socialist

---

30 This geographical denomination of our area of interest seems first to have been used by Alan Palmer, *The Lands Between: A History of East-Central Europe Since the Congress of Vienna* (London: Weidenfeld & Nicolson, 1970), and subsequently gained popularity, such as in e.g. Alexander V. Prusin, *The Lands Between: Conflict in the East European Borderlands, 1870–1992* (Oxford: Oxford University Press, 2010).
31 Jerzy Borzęcki, *The Soviet-Polish Peace of 1921 and the Creation of Interwar Europe* (New Haven, CT: Yale University Press, 2008), 16, 18, 21, 25; Kirsteen D. Croll, 'Polish–Soviet Relations 1919–1921', PhD diss., University of Glasgow, 2009, 134–69; Palmer, *The Lands Between*, 161.
32 Officially, Julian Marchlewski was the head of the Polrevkom.
33 Michał Klimecki, *Sowietyzacja Polski w 1920 roku: Tymczasowy Rewolucyjny Komitet Polski oraz jego instytucje latem i jesienią tegoż roku* [The Sovietization of Poland in 1920: The Provisional Revolutionary Committee of Poland and its institutions in the summer and autumn of that very year] (Toruń: Wydawnictwo Naukowe Uniwersytetu Mikołaja Kopernika, 2016). Furthermore, the PolRevKom is briefly mentioned in Norman Davies, *White Eagle, Red Star: The Polish–Soviet War, 1919–20*, (London: Orbis Books, 1983), 152–59, here 158; Borzęcki, *The Soviet-Polish Peace of 1921*, 92.
34 Stefan Żeromski, *Na probostwie w Wyszkowie* [At the rectory in Wyszków] (London: Polonia Book Fund, 1979), 18.

himself) would, with the help of his troops in the Polish–Soviet War of 1919–20, halt the advance of the Red Army at the gates of Warsaw; he did this virtually without any help from the Western allies, and thus forced Lenin to proceed with the concept of socialism in one country instead.[35]

One probable answer to the conundrum is that in the case of Russia, a war-weary population with its millions of armed men, wanted to get rid of its own outlived government, and so it finally threw in its lot with the revolutionary Bolsheviks. They wanted an end to mass slaughter and the bourgeois alternative, Alexander Kerenski's provisional government, stood for its prolongation. In contrast, the new proto-nationalist governments of the Baltic States, Poland and the Czech Republic emerged while the former war-mongering imperial forces were withdrawing. They could therefore always claim to be fighting for the majority of people in their sphere of influence and only to be securing territory they regarded as genuinely their own, their Eastern frontiers being threatened by the Red Army as the carrier of the revolution. To most people living in the lands between, the beweaponed Bolshevik was a bogeyman, not a knight in shining armour.[36] In 1919, Lithuanian paramilitaries could draw on the help of around 2,000 civilians which voluntarily joined them in the battle against the Bolsheviks.[37] As Włodzimierz Borodziej highlights,

> The historical misfortune of the Bolsheviks was that they approached the potential hot spot of a European revolution from the wrong side: to the west of Warsaw and Lodz there was no industrial centre for miles and miles, just an agricultural province without any communist structures worth mentioning.[38]

This insight did not slip the attention of the contemporaries. In retrospect, Lenin himself admitted that 'in the Red Army the Poles saw enemies, not brothers and liberators. The Poles thought, and acted, not in a social, revolutionary way but as nationalists, as imperialists'.[39] The head of the Litbel Republic, Vincas Mitskevich-Kapsukas, conceded that

> disorderly requisitioning from the local population and its endless compulsory services provoked mistrust, and embittered even those sections of the population who had formerly welcomed the Red Army as their liberators from the hated German occupation and from landlord oppression.[40]

Even the Serbian Social Democratic Committee in Paris, whose members were not totally unsympathetic to the Bolshevik cause, opted unanimously for a federation of Balkan nation states which, although envisaged as a 'fruit of revolutionary activity', had to be founded 'on the basis of respect for the principle of self-determination'.[41] Hungary was the exception of the rule. After all, its revolutionary government had come to power when the country was militarily threatened by literally all its neighbours and a call for help to the Red Army seemed

---

35 Davies, *White Eagle, Red Star*.
36 Chioveanu, 'A Fragmented World', 85.
37 Ēriks Jēkabsons, 'Latvijos ginkluotųjų pajėgų partizanų daliniai 1919 metais' [Partisan Units of the Latvian Armed Forces in 1919], *Acta Historica Universitatis Klaipedensis* 28 (2014): 57–71.
38 Włodzimierz Borodziej, *Geschichte Polens im 20. Jahrhundert* (München: C.H. Beck, 2010), 115.
39 Davies, *White Eagle, Red Star*, 266.
40 Quoted in Borzęcki, *The Soviet-Polish Peace of 1921*, 25.
41 Andrej Mitrović, *Serbia's Great War, 1914–1918* (London: Hurst, 2007), 312.

the last resort. But a devastating defeat in August 1919 put an end to what was by then the only socialist state outside Russia, after not even half a year's existence.[42] Predominantly rural, non-industrialized societies – such as Bulgaria, Romania or Serbia –provided no fertile ground for communist propaganda.[43]

In contrast, and further to the east, the Russian Civil War, which was triggered by the revolutionary upheavals, ravaged on until 1922.[44] After a short intermezzo of German rule, which was the immediate result of the treaty of Brest-Litovsk in 1918, the vast combat zone of this eschatological battle between revolutionary and counter-revolutionary Russian forces occasionally stretched from Siberia to the Baltic, White Russia and Ukraine, thus sometimes also extending into the territory of the neighbouring states that were evolving in the West, bringing their leaders – mostly former tsarist generals – and their troops into contact with the indigenous population. When the February Revolution had weakened the centralized state power, some Russian generals in the field had already decided to act autonomously in hopes of restoring discipline and order on the front, where soldiers' councils were established, and the authority of superiors was questioned. The bid to replace the chaos by military order often served as an attempt to install a military dictatorship.

But the proverbial 'military order' was far from reality when it comes to the antagonizing armies of the Russian Civil War. Here, we can see a clear difference between the times before 1917 and those after. The White 'Volunteer' Army of Anton Denikin, consisting mainly of former tsarist officers and Cossacks, was as small a 'regular' army as the Red Army-in-the-making that forcibly recruited thousands of war-weary peasants.[45] Only towards the end of the Russian Civil War did the latter resemble a professional army that totalled five million men. Facing mass desertion and an appalling lack of professionalism, the Bolshevik revolutionaries had to draw on the pool of ex-tsarist officers that in 1920 comprised of over 70,000 men, more than one third of the overall officer corps.[46]

From 1917 to 1923, the former imperial borderlands were crossed by numerous paramilitary troops, and the Whites and Reds were by no means the only major players on the battlefields. In Ukraine, local warlords – the so-called 'Atamans' – gathered the scattered soldiers and peasants.[47] For the year 1921, about 100 such Ataman armies with an average strength of 500 members

---

42 Rudolf L. Tőkés, *Béla Kun and the Hungarian Soviet Republic: The Origins and Role of the Communist Party of Hungary in the Revolutions of 1918–1919* (Stanford, CA: Hoover Institution Publications, 1967); György Borsányi, *The Life of a Communist Revolutionary, Béla Kun* (Boulder, CO: East European Monographs, 1993); William J. Chase, 'Microhistory and Mass Repression: Politics, Personalities, and Revenge in the Fall of Béla Kun', *Russian Review* 67, no. 3 (2008): 454–83, here 460.

43 Chioveanu, 'A Fragmented World', 85; John P. Newman, 'Post-Imperial and Post-War Violence in the South Slav Lands, 1917–1923', *Contemporary European History* 19, no. 3 (2010): 249–65, here 262–3.

44 It can be – and has been – argued, however, that the period of civil war in Russia started earlier and lasted much longer. See Jonathan D. Smele, *The 'Russian' Civil Wars 1916–1926: Ten Years that Shook the World* (Oxford: Oxford University Press, 2015).

45 Felix Schnell, *Räume des Schreckens: Gewalträume und Gruppenmilitanz in der Ukraine, 1905–1933* (Hamburg: Hamburger Edition, 2012), 246.

46 Francesvo Benvenuti, 'The Red Army', in *Critical Companion to the Russian Revolution, 1914–1921*, eds Edward Acton, Vladimir Cherniaev and William Rosenberg (London: Arnold, 1997), 403–15, here 413; Gatrell, 'War After the War', 569; Orlando Figes, 'The Red Army and Mass Mobilization During the Russian Civil War 1918–1920', *Past and Present*, no. 129 (1990): 168–211.

47 On the warlord phenomenon as such, see Joshua A. Sanborn, 'The Genesis of Russian Warlordism: Violence and Governance during the First World War and the Civil War', *Contemporary European History* 19, no. 3 (2010): 195–213; for an overview, see Vladimir Brovkin, *Behind the Front Lines of*

have been recorded,[48] but the troops led by mighty Atamans like Aleksander Antonov were able to count up to 20,000 men.[49] The Makhno Movement (*Makhnovshchina*) led by the young Ukrainian anarchist Nestor Makhno was another of these strong Ataman armies in Ukraine. In the summer of 1919, his unit had up to 15,000 fighters.[50] Whereas the operation range of Nestor Makhno and his motley crew was rather limited, comparable rural self-defence units were more widespread. Such units were usually made up of war veterans or deserters who came from the area and were supported by local peasants. These units formed spontaneously either against the marauding soldieries or against the local Bolsheviks who were wreaking havoc in the countryside. Apart from in the Ukraine, they could be witnessed in Croatia and Czechoslovakia (as the 'Green' movement, mainly composed of former k.u.k. soldiers) as well as in the north-eastern part of Poland and in the Baltic where they drew their manpower from former soldiers of the Imperial Russian Army. Nevertheless, one would hesitate to classify these 'Green' groups as a coherent movement – unlike their colourful part-time enemies or allies, the 'Whites' and the 'Reds' – since in contrast to the Whites and the Reds, the local Green units were mostly formed under extemporaneous circumstances and lacked central organization and command. However, anti-governmental and anarchic ideologies played a certain roll in almost all of these units, and many fancied the idea of a radical democratic peasant state. Still, given the timely and circumstantial similarity of their occurrence in the belt stretching from the Baltic to the Balkans, it might be justified to regard them as a transnational phenomenon.[51] The irony and

---

the Civil War: Political Parties and Social Movements in Russia, 1918–1922 (Princeton, NJ: Princeton University Press, 1994).
48 Robert Conquest, *The Harvest of Sorrow: Soviet Collectivization and the Terror-Famine* (London: Pimlico, 2002), 41. See Schnell, *Räume des Schreckens*, 261.
49 Gatrell, 'War After the War', 561.
50 Schnell, *Räume des Schreckens*, 298; Mędrzecki, *Niemiecka interwencja militarna na Ukrainie w 1918 roku*, 277–9.
51 See Tibor Hajdu, 'Socialist Revolution in Central Europe, 1917–21'," in *Revolution in History*, eds Roy Porter and Mikuláš Teich (Cambridge: Cambridge University Press, 1987), 101–20. A comprehensive transnational study of the 'Green movement' is a desideratum. For local case studies, see Orlando Figes, *Peasant Russia, Civil War: The Volga Countryside in Revolution, 1917–1921* (Oxford: Clarendon Press, 1989); Oliver H. Radkey, *The Unknown Civil War in Soviet Russia: A Study of the Green Movement in the Tambov Region, 1920–1921* (Stanford, CA: Hoover Institution Press, 1976); idem, *The Agrarian Foes of Bolshevism: Promise and Default of the Russian Socialist Revolutionaries, February to October 1917* (New York: Columbia University Press, 1958); Graeme J. Gill, *Peasants and Government in the Russian Revolution* (London: Palgrave Macmillan, 1979); Schnell, *Räume des Schreckens*; Alexandre Skirda, *Nestor Makhno, Anarchy's Cossack: The Struggle For Free Soviets in the Ukraine 1917–1921* (Oakland, CA: AK Press, 2004); Christopher Gilley, 'The Ukrainian Anti-Bolshevik Risings of Spring and Summer 1919: Intellectual History in a Space of Violence', *Revolutionary Russia* 27, no. 2 (2014): 109–131; Nina Stużyńska, 'Antysowiecka konspiracja i partyzantka Zielonego Dębu na terenie Białorusi w latach 1919–1945' [Anti-Soviet Conspiracy and Partisanship of the Green Oak in Belarus in 1919–1945], in *Europa nieprowincjonalna: Przemiany na ziemiach wschodnich dawnej Rzeczypospolitej (Białoruś, Litwa, Łotwa, Ukraina, wschodnie pogranicze III Rzeczypospolitej Polskiej) w latach 1772–1999*, ed. Krzysztof Jasiewicz (Warsaw: RYTM, 1999), 859–866; Oleg Łatyszonek, 'Zielony Dąb: Przez pięć lat stawiali opór bolszewikom: Dopiero dziś mówi się o nich na Białorusi' [The Green Oak: For five Years They Resisted the Bolsheviks: Only Today They Are Spoken of in Belarus], *UWAŻAM RZE / Special Issue HISTORIA* 13 (2013): 72–5; Tomáš Balkelis, 'From Defence to Revolution: Lithuanian Paramilitary Groups in 1918 and 1919', *Acta Historica Universitatis Klaipedensis* 28 (2014): 43–56; Jakub Beneš, 'The "Green Cadres" and the Collapse of Austria-Hungary in 1918', *Past and Present* 236, no. 1 (2017): 207–41.

tragedy of their prima facie idealistic movement was that they often turned violent themselves: not only against their adversaries, but also against the local populations of remote territories.

Another transnational paramilitary armed force, which, in contrast, was highly mobilized and welded together by a shared radical ideology, was a whole range of anti-Bolshevik units mushrooming in the contact zone of the Central European successor states and revolutionary Russia. Although the Bolsheviks, apart from their troops on horseback, had no power base to speak of outside Russian territory, the spectre of communism mobilized a phalanx of counter-revolutionaries in Central Europe proper.[52] They were mostly composed of war veterans who for a number of reasons refused to put down their weapons and go home, including young men who had been too young to fight on the fronts of the First World War. Instead, they had experienced defeat, deprivation and depression and were thirsty to prove themselves in heroic battle. Their fighting aims, incentives and the means they were willing to use thus deviated significantly from those that had been valid during the times of conventional warfare. Robert Gerwarth writes:

> Together, they formed an ultra-militant masculine subculture that differed from the 'community of the trenches' in its social make-up, its 'liberation' from the constraints of military discipline, and its self-imposed purpose of destroying both the external and internal enemies.[53]

The mobilization of counter-revolutionary forces was not at all limited to those places where the Red Army operated. The Central European states that lost almost everything in the First World War – Hungary, Germany and Austria – especially hosted an amalgam of warriors which would not easily accept defeat, but rather attempt to turn the tide in their favour. Failing that, they at least wanted to continue the fighting during peacetime as a kind of *raison d'être*: 'When they told us that the war was over, we laughed, because we ourselves were the war', noted a veteran of the German 'Freikorps' in 1929, one of the colourful units that made up this protofascist paramilitary subculture.[54]

But in the realm of the emerging Central European nation states, the common enemy sometimes formed even rather improbable brotherhoods in arms. In order to fight the invading Red Army in the Baltic littoral in 1919, the Lithuanian armed forces were joined by German mercenaries, the so-called 'Saxon volunteers'– mainly consisting of soldiers who, some months before, had been regarded as members of an occupational force. As Tomáš Balkelis maintains, this is just one example of how demobilization processes from the First World War blended into remobilization for the post-war struggles with their ever-changing fronts, the most obvious

---

52 Robert Gerwarth and John Horne, 'Bolshevism as Fantasy: Fear of Revolution and Counter-Revolutionary Violence, 1917–1923', in *War in Peace: Paramilitary Violence in Europe After the Great War*, eds Robert Gerwarth and John Horne (Oxford: Oxford University Press, 2012) 40–51.

53 Gerwarth, 'The Central European Counter-Revolution', 207–08; Gerwarth, 'Fighting the Red Beast: Counter-Revolutionary Violence in the Defeated States of Central Europe', in Gerwarth and Horne, *War in Peace*, 52–71; for revolutionary Russia, see Peter Kenez, 'Pogroms and White Ideology in the Russian Civil War', in *Pogroms: Anti-Jewish Violence in Modern Russian History*, eds John D. Klier and Shlomo Lambroza (Cambridge: Cambridge University Press, 2004) 293–313; see also Paul Hanebrink, *A Specter Haunting Europe: The Myth of Judeo-Bolshevism* (Cambridge, MA: Belknap Press, 2018).

54 Gerwarth, 'The Central European Counter-Revolution', 185.

being between nationalist and revolutionary forces.⁵⁵ That these fronts were not clear-cut but rather fuzzy is evidenced by the numerous cases of desertion and defection characteristic for all Central European battlefields from 1918 onwards. The case of the Latvian Riflemen, though, appears to be an extraordinary one: their socialist units became the Praetorian vanguard of the Bolsheviks and the nucleus of the Red Army, whereas their nationalist units formed the core of the Latvian state army.⁵⁶

When the dust clouds of the First World War began to settle, new national armies were forged out of the leftover war material and men. Despite national sagas of mass volunteering and large waves of national enthusiasm nearing hysteria, the setup of these standing armies faced the same enormous difficulties almost everywhere. After sometimes four or even more years of heavy fighting, many war veterans were war-weary and longed to join their families back home, happy that they themselves had survived the mass slaughter. The deprivation brought about by the war on the one hand, and the possibilities of participation and mobilization that the new nation states offered on the other, seemed to call for the determined effort of every individual to construct their post-war life far from the trenches and battlefields. Many of those who decided to continue fighting joined paramilitary units which offered an atmosphere of rampancy and the prospect of swift personal gain. This contrasted sharply with the rigorous discipline and low wages that the imperial armies offered, but which was often copied by their national successors. So, for which of the emerging fighting forces should one opt? A peasant from the Wilna region that had lived all his life under the tsar and fought for him between 1914 and 1917 might have had difficulty in deciding which to choose: should he join the emerging Polish or Lithuanian national armies, or chance his luck with the Russian Bolsheviks? This was an especially difficult choice not knowing which of them in the end would win the fight, as they seemed evenly matched.

Moreover, the new national armies had to overcome almost insuperable obstacles. The weaponed branches of movements which claimed to be unified on the ground with common roots and future goals were, first of all, often no more than preposterously ragged groups of individuals. Their soldiers came from different regions, were from different ethnic and religious backgrounds and spoke different languages, which made the question of the command language a tricky one. Even worse, many of them had been bitterly fighting against one another during the imperial battles and were now suddenly supposed to fight together against former comrades who were mobilized in enemy national armies on the other side of the frontline.

But even before the first shot was fired, the new national governments had to build up both the structure and the staff of their armed forces from scratch. As was the case with the Red Army, they could not do so without the know-how of the imperial military elite, which, since everything had been turned upside down, largely did not come from within the ranks of the titular nation. The elites that were now in power, *after* 1918, had been kept, by and large, at bay from the imperial war academies *before* 1918, rendering higher military careers impossible. To what extent the imperial brass commanding the new armed forces would honestly and wholeheartedly engage in a war now fought for national unity and integrity was an open question

---

55 Tomáš Balkelis, 'Demobilization and Remobilization of German and Lithuanian Paramilitaries after the Great War', *Journal of Contemporary History* 50, no. 1 (2015): 38–57; Tomáš Balkelis, 'Turning Citizens into Soldiers: Baltic Paramilitary Movements after the Great War', in Gerwarth and Horne, *War in Peace*, 126–44.
56 Geoffrey Swain, 'The Disillusioning of the Revolution's Praetorian Guard: The Latvian Riflemen, Summer-Autumn 1918', *Europe-Asia Studies* 51, no. 4 (1999): 667–86.

in 1918 and shortly thereafter. The Commander in Chief and head of the reborn Polish State, Marshal Piłsudski, called a spade a spade when, in retrospect, he wrote that in 1919–20, the 'difficulties the Commander in Chief faced' were that of 'unusual diversity combined with the mutual ignorance of the officer corps … In most cases the commanders lacked confidence in their troops, and very often the troops in their commanders'. Furthermore, he pointed out the catastrophic material situation of the troops, who were first and foremost in need of literally everything, from boots to ammunition.[57]

The Lithuanian example vividly demonstrates the practical obstacles to conjuring up a functioning army out of literally nothing. Its first chief commander was a tsarist general who had to be removed because of his sympathies for the Whites. Furthermore, commands were initially given in Russian. At the turn of 1918–19, they had 150 volunteers, amongst them, 82 tsarist officers. The number was substantially augmented to 3,000 volunteers by the end of January 1919 due to a call that promised the recruits a monthly salary of 100 marks plus support for their families. The call had to be published in four different languages. By February, 4,500 soldiers of the Lithuanian national forces were to face the invasion of a Red Army who outnumbered them by a factor of four[58] and who also featured Lithuanian units among their ranks.

Thus, the era of fratricide was far from over. Polish armed forces were more successful, mobilizing 600,000 soldiers by the end of 1919, but their units formed a similar patchwork and 'shared experiences that made it difficult for the soldiers to be reformed into disciplined members of a large modern army'.[59] The Czech and the Yugoslav national armies faced massive problems with integrating veterans who had both fought with and against the Habsburg troops, conflicts that cast a long shadow far into the interwar period.[60]

This short and incomplete panopticon of military and paramilitary formations commanded by generals and warlords which roamed the area between Soviet Russia and the West might demonstrate that simple dichotomies do not really give us an idea to what happened on the spot. In the grand design, Marc Levene might have a point when he sees 'an essentially Western-sponsored "New Europe" system founded on nationalism, and, on the other, its Bolshevik antithesis' at work here in the period of 1917–1923.[61] But the closer we get, the fuzzier gets the picture, and the cases where seemingly allies turned against each other become more frequent than cases where representatives of the two world ideologies of the time – Western liberal

---

57 Andrzej C. Żak, ed., *Polska generalicja w opiniach Marszałka Piłsudskiego* [Polish generals in the opinion of Marshal Piłsudski] (Warsaw: Centralne Archiwum Wojskowe im. mjr. Bolesława Waligóry, 2012), 13–14.
58 Balkelis, 'Demobilization and Remobilization', 47–9.
59 Piotr Wróbel, 'The Revival of Poland and Paramilitary Violence, 1918–1920', in Bergien and Pröve, *Spießer, Patrioten, Revolutionäre*, 281–303, here 300–01; idem, 'The Seeds of Violence: The Brutalization of an Eastern European Region, 1917–1921', *Journal of Modern European History* 1, no. 1 (2003): 125–49.
60 Martin Zückert, 'National Concepts of Freedom and Government Pacification Policies: The Case of Czechoslovakia in the Transitional Period After 1918', *Contemporary European History* 17, no. 3 (2008): 325–44; Martin Zückert, *Zwischen Nationsidee und staatlicher Realität: Die tschechoslowakische Armee und ihre Nationalitätenpolitik 1918–1938* (München: Oldenbourg, 2006); Katya Kocourek, '"In the Spirit of Brotherhood, United We Remain!" Czechoslovak Legionaries and the Militarist State', in *Sacrifice and Rebirth: The Legacy of the Last Habsburg War*, eds Mark Cornwall and John P. Newman (New York: Berghahn Books, 2016); John P. Newman, 'Silent Liquidation? Croatian Veterans and the Margins of War Memory in Interwar Yugoslavia', in Cornwall and Newman, *Sacrifice and Rebirth*, 197–215.
61 Mark Levene, *Devastation: The European Rimlands 1912–1938* (Oxford: Oxford University Press, 2013), 176.

capitalism against Russian communism – got on each other's throat. At the end, the post-war struggles were not about ideologies. They were about assets and territories. And it is only if we take our agents of violence serious as acting individuals, not as puppets of Paris or Moscow, that we get to a closer understanding of what exactly happened on the ground, and which forms of violence materialized in the wake of the First World War.

Experiences of violence

Before addressing special forms and experiences of violence at the end of the First World War, it seems necessary to shed some light on the prevailing living conditions in our region. Experience is at the heart of the research at hand, and one cannot understand everyday life between 1917 and 1923 in Central and Eastern Europe without recognizing the hardships and deprivations that affected a large majority of the population. The suffering of the locals was not at all limited to physical violence, which, logically, could only materialize where potential perpetrators met potential victims. The devastating consequences of the First World War were much more comprehensive than that. Besides the enormous death toll from the battlefields, there were three deadly waves which also affected civilians: forced displacement, famine and disease. If we speak of the experience of violence in the post-war years, we should always bear in mind that these three waves cost more lives than acts of immediate physical violence. They should be regarded as the indirect consequences of the violence of war and its continuation.

To begin with, the number of casualties of soldiers alone reached new proportions during the First World War. A post-war statistic estimated a total of 13 million fallen troops, half of which came from Central and Eastern Europe (including Austria and Greece). Even still, this was not the climax of the sombre summary. The author of the post-war study concluded:

> it may fairly be estimated that the loss of civilian life due directly to war or to causes induced by war equals, if indeed it does not exceed, that suffered by the armies in the field. In view of the facts cited, such an estimate must be regarded as conservative. And yet this does not take into account the appalling effects, some of them unquestionably permanent, of war, famine, pestilence, and disease on the sufferers who did not die.[62]

The last cited scourges of mankind affected most and foremost Central and Eastern Europe. Serbia was the first victim, with hunger and disease raging the occupied country in 1916 and 1917.[63] Central and Eastern Europe were soon to follow. At the banks of the Volga and at the foothills of the Ural, between one and two million people died of starvation between 1921 and 1922.[64] Between 1919 and 1921, a raging typhus epidemic peaked in Russia (700,000 to 1,200,000 cases), in Poland (219,066 to 231,206) and in Ukraine (591,842),[65] and threatened to proliferate in the West. 'From this vast centre of infection [Russia] the disease is carried westward by an unceasing stream of immigrants. Prisoners returning to their homes, refugees fleeing for safety, crowd the railways', warned a report in August 1920. 'Two million of these

---

62 Ernest L. Bogart, *Direct and Indirect Costs of the Great World War* (New York: Oxford University Press, 1920), statistics on 277, quote on 282.
63 Mitrović, *Serbia's Great War, 1914–1918*, 110–13, 232–5.
64 Bertrand M. Patenaude, *The Big Show in Bololand: The American Relief Expedition to Soviet Russia in the Famine of 1921* (Stanford, CA: Stanford University Press, 2002), 197–8.
65 According to Paul J. Weindling, *Epidemics and Genocide in Eastern Europe 1890–1945* (Oxford: Oxford University Press, 2000), 432–4.

unfortunate persons have passed the Polish Disinfection Stations since the armistice, and doubtless many more have entered Poland without being subject to medical examination'.[66] As the quotation insinuates, a mass of people – both sick and healthy – did not simply stay put in the immediate post-war years. During the war, hundreds of thousands of them had been deported – mainly by Russian troops – and in the post-war years, they sought their way back westwards to their homeland, anxious to see what might await them there. Between May and November 1918, 400,000 fled Russia alone (in the western parts of the region, the number of displaced persons surpassed seven million in 1917).[67] 'By 1925 the total number of Polish citizens who had been repatriated from the Soviet Union stood at 1,265,000, of whom the majority returned to Poland in 1919–22.'[68]

Although it might appear an impossible task, shortly after the war, Earnest L. Bogart even attempted to quantify the property losses of the belligerent countries and their successors. Totalling 7.5 billion USD, the Central and Eastern European states suffered one quarter of the overall estimated property loss.[69] Given their financial and economic inferiority, it is clear that in comparison to the West, these countries were incapable of coping with such loss on their own. Throughout the early post-war years, they were heavily reliant on foreign relief, mainly coming from America.[70] Additionally, if one visualizes the lunar landscapes of the vast battlefields scarred by trenches and wire, one gets a picture of the Central and Eastern European scenery which was awash with new waves of violence after the war's end, in which children could be witnessed playing with human remains.[71]

Whoever thought that the armistices of 1918 would initiate a peaceful and nonviolent era in Europe was utterly mistaken. The new obscurity of politics and power relations produced new agents and victims of violence and left ample space for the abuse of force. 'Some veterans', maintains historian Peter Gatrell,

> believed they had a duty to 'beat the world into new shapes', even if this meant trampling over non-combatants. For this reason, as well as the high stakes created by the virulent ideologies of revolutionary socialism and nationalism, conflict frequently assumed a particularly brutal form, with civilians often numbered among the casualties.[72]

---

66 Letter from Arthur J. Balfour to the members of the League of Nations, 21 August 1920, printed in, Herbert Hoover and Arthur J. Balfour, eds, *Central European Relief* (New York: American Association for International Conciliation, 1921), 117–19, here 117–18.
67 Jochen Böhler, 'Generals and Warlords, Revolutionaries and Nation State Builders: The First World War and its Aftermath in Central and Eastern Europe', in *Legacies of Violence: Eastern Europe's First World War*, eds Jochen Böhler, Wlodzimierz Borodziej and Joachim von Puttkamer (München: Oldenbourg, 2014), 51–66, here 51–4.
68 Nick Baron and Peter Gatrell, 'Population Displacement, State-Building, and Social Identity in the Lands of the Former Russian Empire, 1917–23', *Kritika: Explorations in Russian and Eurasian History* 4 (2003): 51–100, here 64, 76. See also the chapter titled 'Deconstructing and Reconstructing Statehood: The Impact of the World Wars (Part I) – The First World War' in the volume *Statehood* of this series, 117–47.
69 Bogart, *Direct and Indirect Costs of the Great World War*, 287.
70 See also the chapter titled 'Deconstructing and Reconstructing Statehood: The Impact of the World Wars (Part I) – The First World War' in the volume *Statehood* of this series, 117–47.
71 Joice M. NanKivell and Sydney Loch, *The River of a Hundred Ways: Life in the War-Devasted Areas of Eastern Poland* (London: Allen & Unwin, 1924), 85–6.
72 Gatrell, 'War After the War', 559.

In addition, the scarcity of resources that came with the devastation of wartime, pushed men with weapons to use them against easy targets, which they found in abundance. This was especially the case in rural areas which still harboured grain and food, and were, in the meantime, stripped of their able-bodied men (husbands, fathers and sons) who had been called to the colours. The emergence of paramilitary formations produced a double-sided effect which exacerbated the situation: group coherence often depended to a large degree on the common exertion of violence, while the lack of an all-encompassing military jurisdiction guaranteed virtual impunity. Such settings created new forms of violence which sometimes even became a distinctive marker of certain armed units.

Historians of our period have marked three forms of macro-violence which were the attending ills of the two formative state-building projects of the time, the two projects being the ideological confrontation between Bolshevik and anti-Bolshevik units on the one hand, and the ethnic struggle for domination in a future nation state on the other. The three identified forms of macro-violence were: 1) the Red and the White Terrors; 2) the atrocities against the local population in general and against Jews in particular; and 3) projects of engineered ethnic cleansing. Whereas the latter was a distinct feature of the aftermath of the Greco–Turkish War and has already been dealt with elsewhere in this volume,[73] the first two forms of macro-violence occurred largely in the backwater of the Russian Civil War which, according to Peter Holquist, 'was that conjuncture at which many of the practices of violence forged for "normal" war were redirected to the project of the revolutionary transformation of society'. But, as Holquist himself concludes, these violent practices were not limited to the Russian soil, since 'the "revolutionizing" programme of the Bolshevik state bore certain parallels to the "nationalizing" programs of the new states throughout eastern and southern Europe'.[74]

Following the line of argument put forth by Arno Mayer, the specific forms of violence brought by revolution and counter-revolution can not only be traced further west geographically, but also further back in time: in his voluminous monograph, *The Furies*, Mayer compared the Russian Revolution and the ensuing Civil War with the French Revolution and the war in the Vendée. In his reading, revolutionary violence in both historical settings was not an end in itself, but the result of a final battle between the new and the old order, between utopianism and conservatism, fought with a vengeance by both sides amidst a quagmire of civil war and international intervention. Thus, in the western Russian borderlands in the period 1917–1923, Red (revolutionary) Terror and White (counter-revolutionary) Terror were not self-referential: they were retaliative in nature and therefore interdependent and subject to change.[75]

The Russian Civil War is not at the centre of this study, since its territorial extension to northern Russia and Siberia is far beyond our geographical focus. It comes into play at its western fringes where it interfered with the Central European Civil War and its various projects of state-building and peasant revolt against collectivization, which by their very nature were opposed to the Bolshevik revolutionary programme. The fracture zone ran from the Baltic in the north via eastern Poland to Ukraine in the south.

At the turn of 1918, the invading Red Army threatened the existence of the newly founded Estonian, Lithuanian and Latvian national assemblies. Since there were no Baltic national armies

---

73 See Chapter 1, 'The Balkan Wars: patterns of violence in the Balkans leading up to the First World War' by Mark Biondich in the present volume, 23–4.
74 Holquist, 'Violent Russia, Deadly Marxism', 644–5.
75 Arno J. Mayer, *The Furies: Violence and Terror in the French and Russian Revolutions* (Princeton, NJ: Princeton University Press, 2000).

yet to speak of, they had to call in German paramilitary troops (after the armistices, the regular German troops were dissolved and on their way home), which halted the tide of the Red Army in early 1919. But in the long run, the German mercenaries were hardly more welcome than the Bolsheviks. They had been tempted into the region – which harboured a strong German upper class (the *Baltendeutsche*, mainly present in Latvia and Estonia) and a long tradition of German colonization – with the promise of Baltic citizenship and, so they were told, plots of arable land. What resulted was a triangular constellation in which each party – Baltic nationalists, German ultra-conservatives and Russian Bolsheviks – was struggling for dominance in a dog-eat-dog competition: the Germans sometimes fighting with – sometimes against – the Baltic national forces, and the Baltic communists fighting the Baltic nationalists. At the end, both the Germans and the Russians had to withdraw completely from the scene: the former because their central government shied away from any conflict with their Western Allies; the latter because they were driven out of the country by a joint Latvian-Polish military advance in 1920, and in the same year, Bolshevik Russia ratified the peace treaties of Tartu (with Estonia in February) and Riga (with Latvia in August) and thus de jure recognized the Baltic eastern border.[76]

The commander of the Freikorps, Rüdiger von der Goltz, reluctantly resigned from his post only after Allied pressure. His troops were not only comprised of former veterans of the First World War, but contained all sorts of criminal elements from the Reich who had followed the call of the land. The mercenary force killed thousands of Latvians, ravaged the countryside and established a reign of terror with a draconian military jurisdiction which was largely blind to the atrocities committed by the German soldiers. The Red Army exhibited the exact same behaviour. An estimated 10,000 Latvians fell prey to the encroachments, divided equally between the two militias. Both sides were notorious for killing their prisoners.[77]

The main battle between the Bolsheviks and their adversaries occurred on Polish soil and this time without German participation. After the treaty of Brest-Litovsk in 1918, German troops of the *OberOst* ('Supreme Commander of All German Forces in the East') occupied large parts of the former Russian territory. With the defeat at the Western Front, their withdrawal was merely a matter of time, and since they occupied a virtual buffer zone between the Red Army and the emerging Polish national forces, a direct confrontation was inevitable. It began in early 1919 with skirmishes between Polish and Bolshevik troops in a no man's land but soon turned into bloody guerrilla warfare that also heavily affected the civilian population. 'The fighting in the Polish–Soviet War', writes historian Norman Davies,

> was undoubtedly vicious. The Poles frequently shot captured commissars outright. The Soviets shot captured officers and cut the throats of priests and landlords. On occasion, both sides murdered Jews. The atmosphere was somehow ripe for atrocity. The soldier was surrounded by confusion and insecurity. He rarely found himself in a comfortable trench, or in the reassuring company of his regiment. More often he was on his own out in the forest, or standing guard on the edge of a village, never

---

76 Prusin, *The Lands Between*, 77–80; Georg v. Rauch, *The Baltic States: The Years of Independence – Estonia, Latvia, Lithuania, 1917–1940* (Berkeley, CA: University of California Press, 1974), 70–5; Endel Krepp, *The Estonian War of Independence 1918–1920: On the Occasion of the 60th Anniversary from the Treaty of Brest-Litovsk to the Treaty of Peace at Tartu* (Stockholm: Estonian Information Centre, 1980).

77 Mark R. Hatlie, *Riga at War 1914–1919: War and Wartime Experience in a Multi-Ethnic Metropolis* (Marburg: Herder-Institut, 2014), 113–33; Inta Pētersone, ed., *Latvijas Brīvības cīņas, 1918–1920: Enciklopēdija* [Latvian freedom fights: 1918–1920] (Rīga.: Preses Nams, 1999), 26, 36–7.

knowing whether the surprise attack would come from in front or behind, never knowing whether the frontline had moved forward or back. Ambushes and raids bred panic, and invited vengeance. Meetings with the enemy were infrequent but bloodthirsty.[78]

Neither Poles nor Russians could be sure of the support of the locals in the ethnic melting pot of the Polish eastern borderlands (*Kresy*): it was the home of Lithuanians and Belarusians in the north, and Ukrainians in the south, with large Polish, Jewish and German minorities spread throughout. Reliable statistics giving an overview of military and civilian victims of the atrocities in this remote and mainly rural area have not been recorded.

By the summer of 1920, as Polish deputy minister of military affairs Kazimierz Sosnkowski observed, the civil war had taken over traits of 'a regular war of massed forces, where we encounter all the firepower and mechanised aids of the recent World War, a national war'.[79] A Polish-Ukrainian joint offensive had failed near Kiev in April and triggered a Bolshevik invasion of Poland, which at the time of Sosnkowski's remark had brought the Red Army to the outskirts of Warsaw. Its defeat and ejection was little short of a wonder, and thus consequently made its entry into the history books as the 'Miracle at the Vistula'.[80] Peace was made and the Polish-Russian border, secured in March 1921 at Riga, ending all Belarusian and Ukrainian nationalists' dreams of their own nation state.[81]

Thus, the former Polish allies – the Ukrainians – were duped, but that is hardly a surprise. Traditionally, the relationship between these geographical neighbours and rival national movements was more than strained. Indeed, the Polish-Ukrainian War of 1918–19 marked the beginning of the Central European Civil War, lasting until the summer of 1919, with both sides fighting for territory of their envisaged future states. Both sides committed atrocities against civilians.[82] During the following nine months, 10,000 Polish and 15,000 Ukrainian soldiers died in battle,[83] while 20,000 – one-fifth of the 100,000 Ukrainian prisoners of war – fell victim to infectious diseases in the camps of the eventually victorious Polish army.[84]

Since, as I have demonstrated, the northern and eastern borders of Central and Eastern Europe witnessed civil war and waves of violence motivated by conflicts along ideological, national or ethnic lines in the wake of the First World War, it surely does not come as a

---

78 Davies, *White Eagle, Red Star*, 38.
79 Ibid., 190.
80 This mystical labelling already started soon after the events and is still unchallenged today, see e.g. in Peter Hetherington, *Unvanquished: Joseph Pilsudski, Resurrected Poland, and the Struggle for Eastern Europe*, 2nd ed (Houston, TX: Pingora Press, 2012), 425–58.
81 Borzęcki, *The Soviet-Polish Peace of 1921*; Benjamin Conrad, *Umkämpfte Grenzen, umkämpfte Bevölkerung: Die Entstehung der Staatsgrenzen der Zweiten Polnischen Republik 1918–1923* (Stuttgart: Steiner, 2014), 238–51.
82 Julia Eichenberg, 'The Dark Side of Independence: Paramilitary Violence in Ireland and Poland after the First World War', *Contemporary European History* 19, no. 3 (2010): 231–48, here 328. The extent and number of victims still laying in the dark. Ukrainian accusations were published immediately after the events, see Mykhalo Lozynsky and Petro Karmansky, *Krivava Knyha: vol II: Ukraïnska Halychyna pid okupatsiieiu Polshchi v rr. 1919–1920* [The bloody book: vol. II, Ukrainian Galicia under Polish occupation] (Vienna: Zakhidno-Ukraïnska Narodna Republyka, 1921), http://www.archive.org/details/krivavaknyha02lozyuoft (accessed 10 December 2021).
83 Bogdan Musial, 'Die Ukrainepolitik Polens 1918–1922', in *Die Ukraine: Zwischen Selbstbestimmung und Fremdherrschaft 1917–1922*, eds Wolfram Dornik et al. (Graz: Leykam, 2011), 449–63, here 454.
84 Wróbel, 'The Seeds of Violence', 138.

surprise that the western and southern borders are no exception to the rule. In the south, at the beginning of 1919, a local war between Czechoslovakia and Poland over the border region of Cieszyn Silesia was accompanied by atrocities, again from both sides.[85] In the meantime, the First Czechoslovak Republic was shaken by eruptions of socio-ethnic violence against Germans, Jews and Hungarians within the new confines of the state. The heaviest outbreaks occurred in the Slovak part of the country, which bordered Hungary and witnessed a short-lived invasion of the Red Army of Béla Kun's revolutionary government in Budapest. Czech military and paramilitary units harassed the Slovak population in a way that made the Czech writer Josef Holeček comment: 'They invaded Slovakia like Germans did Cameroon or Belgium and raged there in a way that bore sad testimony to their being blind imitators of the Germans ...'.[86]

Speaking of which, in the west, we again encounter the notorious German Freikorps, whose struggle this time was not half anti-Bolshevik / half anti-Baltic, but entirely anti-Polish. The bone of contention was Silesia, a typical borderland with a population which was largely bilingual and featured at best loosely defined ethnic affiliation.[87] Three Polish uprisings between 1919 and 1921 aimed at the annexation of the region to the Polish Second Republic. German Freikorps soldiers engaged in bitter struggles with bands of Polish insurgents. Despite the massive presence of Allied troops, the intensity of violence remained high: between 11 November 1918 and 30 June 1922, the region witnessed an estimated number of 2,824 fatalities.[88] In 1922, the larger western part went to the German state, while the industrial area of East Upper Silesia was allocated to Poland, thus ending the Central European Civil War.

The nation states in the southeast – Hungary, Romania, Bulgaria and Yugoslavia – were not battlegrounds of the Central European Civil War. To be sure, they were not spared the eruption of post-war violence typical for the borderlands between Russia and Germany either, but in their case, no large-scale confrontation with the armed forces of an equally ambitious neighbour state took place. In Hungary, the backdrop was that of internal

---

85 Edward Długajczyk, *Polska konspiracja wojskowa na Śląsku Cieszyńskim w latach 1919–1920* [Polish military conspiracy in Cieszyn Silesia 1919–1920] (Katowice: Wydawn. Uniwersytetu Śląskiego, 2005); Jiří Bílek, *Kyselá těšínská jablíčka: československo-polské konflikty o Těšínsko 1919, 1938, 1945* [Sour Těšín apples: Czechoslovak-Polish conflicts over the Těšín Region 1919, 1938, 1945] (Prague: Nakl. Epocha, 2011).

86 Josef Holeček, *Prvé tříletí československé Republiky* [The first three years of the Czechoslovak Republic] (Prague: československé podniky tiskařské a vydavatelské, 1922); the English translation of the quote is taken from Václav Šmidrkal, '"Dancing on a Volcano": Why the Czech Lands Did not Turn into Bloodlands after 1918', in *The Years of Upheaval, 1914–1924: Europe and Greece*, eds Athanasios Markopoulos and Evanthis Hatzivassiliou (Athens: European Cultural Centre of Deplhi, 2017), 293–317, here 310.

87 Brendan Jeffrey Karch, *Nation and Loyalty in a German-Polish Borderland: Upper Silesia, 1848–1960* (Cambridge: Cambridge University Press, 2018).

88 The unusually accurate estimate of casualties (for our time and region) is owed to the presence of Allied observers in the region. See in general Tim Wilson, *Frontiers of Violence: Conflict and Identity in Ulster and Upper Silesia 1918–1922* (Oxford: Oxford University Press, 2010), 5 (on fatalities), 29 (on Italian and French troop presence). While Wilson extensively describes the cultural, religious, linguistic and political diversity of Upper Silesia in comparison to Ulster, the acts of violence perpetrated by the conflicting parties are not at the centre of his rewarding study. For more on Freikorps engagement at the Polish border see T. Hunt Tooley, 'German Political Violence and the Border Plebiscite in Upper Silesia, 1919–1921', *Central European History* 21, no. 1 (1988): 56–98; idem, *National Identity and Weimar Germany: Upper Silesia and the Eastern Border, 1918–1922* (Lincoln, NE: University of Nebraska Press, 1997).

revolution and counter-revolution. The 'White Guards', the Hungarian counterpart to the German Freikorps, built up ultra-violent environments that served two purposes: first, to prove themselves in battle, and second, to take revenge on and eventually overcome the despised Red Terror. 'We shall see to it', wrote Hungarian officer Miklós Kozma in August 1919 (referring to the 400–500 victims of the short-lived communist regime of Béla Kun), 'that the flame of nationalism leaps high .... We shall punish. Those who for months have committed heinous crimes must receive their punishment'.[89] Since Bolshevism, in the eyes of the counter-revolutionaries, was the result of a 'Jewish conspiracy', their violent acts were directed first and foremost against Jews. In Transdanubia alone, a report from 1922 listed 3,000 Jewish victims of the White Terror. For these paramilitary militias, violence not only had a destructive side, but a constructive side as well, which was building up a brutalized form of group identity, and distinctly separating the perpetrators from the 'civilized' part of society.[90]

The First Republic of Czechoslovakia and the First Hungarian Republic are hybrid cases since they feature forms of violence typical of the theatre of the Central European War without being full-fledged participants. Further to the southeast of Europe, lies a different geographical zone – the Balkans – where paramilitary violence was not a legacy of the First World War but rather had its roots in the nineteenth century.[91] Here, writes John Paul Newman, 'the disintegration of Austria-Hungary and the creation of a large South Slav state in 1918 linked previously separated regions and actors, creating new and expanded "zones of violence"'[92] which were geographically unconnected to the Central European Civil War. These regions are therefore treated separately, although they featured comparable patterns of violent behaviour and experience.

Romania, like Czechoslovakia, took advantage of the tumultuous situation in revolutionary Hungary and invaded the country in 1918–19. But whether this military operation was accompanied by similar patterns of socio-ethnic violence, as in the Czechoslovak case, is still an insufficiently researched area of history – the potential for such violence was surely high, given the ethnic patchwork of the new Hungarian-Romanian border zone.[93] The historical regions and melting pots of Transylvania, Bukovina and Bessarabia, for their part, joined Greater Romania in the year 1918 without turmoil, thus constituting a remarkable exception to what was the order of the day in the rest of Central and Eastern Europe by that time.[94]

---

89 Gerwarth, 'The Central European Counter-Revolution', 194.
90 See Béla Bodo, 'Paramilitary Violence in Hungary after the First World War', *East European Quarterly* 38, no. 2 (2004): 129–73.
91 For the pre-war history of paramilitary violence in the Balkans, see Chapter 1, 'The Balkan Wars: patterns of violence in the Balkans leading up to the First World War' by Mark Biondich in the present volume, 4–11.
92 John P. Newman, 'The Origins, Attributes, and Legacies of Paramilitary Violence in the Balkans', in Gerwarth and Horne, *War in Peace*, 145–63, here 145.
93 There are references to alleged Hungarian atrocities against the Romanian Moți minority in the Romanian interwar press. See Roland Clark, 'Claiming Ethnic Privilege: Aromanian Immigrants and Romanian Fascist Politics', *Contemporary European History* 24, no. 1 (2015): 37–58, here 40.
94 The accession of Transylvania, Bukovina and Bessarabia to Greater Romania was related to the disintegration of the Austro-Hungarian Empire on the one hand, and the threat of revolutionary Russia on the other. In this precarious situation, the non-Romanian minorities in those areas obviously regarded their absorption into a Romanian nation state as the lesser evil. See Keith Hitchins, *A Concise History of Romania* (Cambridge: Cambridge University Press, 2014), 154–6.

With a certain level of justification, the part of the Balkans that remained immediately after the war can be divided into two larger zones of violence: the Adriatic littoral where the newly founded Kingdom of the Serbs, Croats and Slovenes bordered with Italy, and the Southern Balkans with the historical regions of Macedonia and Kosovo that Serbs with proprietary attitude called 'Old Serbia' and 'South Serbia'.[95] Both zones were highly contested, the first between Italy and Yugoslavia, the second between Yugoslavia, Bulgaria and Greece.

Italian forces were stationed in the eastern Adriatic from the end of 1918 until its integration in the Kingdom of Italy as an occupying force. Here, the violent encounters were not between two clearly ethno-nationally defined groups, such as Italians against Croats and Slovenes. Much more so, the agenda was set by the political and ideological attitude of the administrative and military apparatus, which ranged from conservative Italian irredentism to fascism. In their eyes, the enemies were the socialist Italians and Slavs amidst the population, who had to be identified and publicly bullied to ensure the frictionless transition of the highly contested space into Italian state territory. The result was a permanent atmosphere of latent paramilitary violence in everyday life, which was prone to erupt.[96] However, the area did not witness the same waves of large-scale violence (with thousands wounded or dead) as the contested spaces of Central Europe further to the north. Italy and Yugoslavia, both on the winners' side of the First World War belligerents but disunited regarding the future affiliation of the littoral, were not interested in having the delicate situation escalate unduly. The cold war turned hot when, in September 1919, Italian right-wing writer Gabriele D'Annunzio with several hundred mercenaries marched on the Adriatic harbour city of Fiume to prevent it becoming a free state according to the plans of the peacemakers of Paris. He captured the city without a fight from an inter-allied occupation force and managed to head a half anarchist, half proto-fascist city state for a period of 15 months. After Italians and Yugoslavs had attributed Fiume the status of a free state in the Treaty of Rapallo, D'Annunzio and his men, who refused to accept the treaty, were thrown out at gunpoint by the Italian Army in the last week of 1920.[97] But even during this 'Christmas of Blood', the casualties on both sides were so few they were almost neglectable.[98]

Bloodshed and arson were more the trademark of the two arguably strongest paramilitary formations in the post-war Balkans: the Green Cadres, which can be assigned to the Green movements that spread from the Baltic to the Black Sea,[99] and the IMRO (Internal Macedonian Revolutionary Organization). The Green Cadres were bands of tens of thousands deserters and outlaws without a central command, mostly active in the Croatian hinterland, but they were also on Czech and Hungarian territory.[100] The uncontrollable nature of their locally organized paramilitary groups, mostly headed by a charismatic leader, urged the National Council of

---

95 Newman, 'The Origins, Attributes, and Legacies', 152–3.
96 Borut Klabjan, 'Borders in Arms: Physical Violence in the North-Eastern Adriatic, 1918–1920', unpublished paper presented at the international conference 'Beyond Defeat and Victory: Physical Violence and the Reconstitution of East-Central Europe, 1914–1923', organized by the Imre Kertész Kolleg Jena and the Masaryk Institute and Archives of the Czech Academy of Science, Prague, 19 September 2015.
97 Margaret MacMillan, *Paris 1919: Six Months that Changed the World* (New York: Random House, 2003), 294–305.
98 Dominique Kirchner Reill, *The Fiume Crisis: Life in the Wake of the Habsburg Empire* (Cambridge, MA: Harvard University Press, 2020), 1–22.
99 See the subchapter *Agents of violence* above, 82–3.
100 Newman, 'The Origins, Attributes, and Legacies', 155–6; Jakub Beneš, 'The Green Cadres and the Collapse of Austria-Hungary in 1918', *Past and Present* 236, no. 1 (2017): 207–41.

Serbs, Croats and Slovenes to issue a plea to the not-entirely-demobilized k.u.k. soldiers and members of the 'Green Cadres' reading: 'Don't destroy, don't burn down, don't kill, since you are destroying and burning that which is yours, soldiers!'[101]

In the meantime, Yugoslavia and Greece witnessed the rise of a phenomenon which would become crucial for all of (but not only) Central and Eastern Europe at the beginning of the 1920s: terroristic violence at the hands of radicalized minorities in pursuit of their own state, and in the case of Yugoslavia and Greece, it was the IMRO. The IMRO was the 'largest paramilitary force in the Balkans in the post-war period', and in comparison to the Green Cadres, it was a strictly organized terrorist group, fighting for the establishment of a Macedonian body politic, either independent or associated with Sofia. Its operational base being Bulgaria, from 1920 onwards it concentrated its terrorist attacks against uniformed officials and civilians in the Macedonian regions of Greece and, above all, Serbia.[102] As historian Stefan Troebst has pointed out:

> The IMRO fighters (*četniks*) were able to count on a broad support milieu on the ground. Farmers, shepherds, popes, monks, and other so-called 'hiders' (*yatak*) provided logistical and medical assistance, as well as reconnaissance services. This dense network of *yataks* also allowed major IMRO volunteers considerable freedom of movement during their stays, often lasting several months, on Yugoslav territory, which was virtually teeming with regular army units, police, intelligence agencies, and special paramilitary anti-IMRO formations.[103]

Indeed, under such conditions, it is clear that the region came close to a local civil war.

In the end, the activities of the Green Cadres as well as those of the IMRO backfired because they only strengthened the position and influence of the Serbian army in the Kingdom of Serbs, Coats and Slovenes which was far from being internally united. As one Slavonian deputy of the Yugoslav National Council put it:

> The people are in revolt. Total disorganization prevails. Only the army, moreover only the Serbian army, can restore order. The people are burning and destroying. I do not know how we shall feed Dalmatia and Bosnia. The mob is now pillaging the merchants, since all the landed estates have already been destroyed. Private fortunes are destroyed. The Serbian army is the only salvation.[104]

The Central European Civil War of 1918–1921 and the ethno-national conflicts further to the south were all fought with a vengeance. The accompanying experiences of violence were largely comparable. 'To a certain extent, violent attempts to impose an integral national programme onto contested regions in the Balkans shared many of the traits of the violent nationalizing projects of post-1918 paramilitary groups in Austria, Hungary, Germany, Poland,

---

101 Newman, 'Post-Imperial and Post-War Violence in the South Slav Lands, 1917–1923', 254.
102 Newman, 'The Origins, Attributes, and Legacies', 152–5, here 153.
103 Stefan Troebst, 'Nationalismus und Gewalt im Osteuropa der Zwischenkriegszeit: Terroristische Separatismen im Vergleich', *Berliner Jahrbuch für osteuropäische Geschichte* 3, no. 1 (1996): 273–314, here 284–5. For the IMRO before 1914, see Chapter 1 in the present volume, 8–14.
104 Ivo Banač, *The National Question in Yugoslavia: Origins, History, and Politics* (Ithaca, NY: Cornell University Press, 1993), 131. Thanks to Jakub Beneš for referring me to this quote.

and Ukraine'[105] and, to round up the argument, the Baltic. All over this gigantic shatter zone of empires, houses were plundered then set aflame, women were raped, enemies were tortured and their corpses mutilated, and civilians were killed en masse; in short: paramilitary violence replaced military violence, the law of the jungle replaced military law.

Amid this ordeal, political goals often became subsidiary. The only real perceptible fronts ran between the opposing military or paramilitary units, whose members would nevertheless frequently change sides. Since literally all formations that operated remotely from their centre were cut off from any kind of regular supply, they relied heavily on looting; after all, no central state authority was able to control them, and since their leader's authority depended on the leader's ability to maintain a ruthless reign of terror, violence against civilians became an aim in and of itself. Even the Green peasant armies in Ukraine had to use force against other peasants when acting in areas far from home.[106] As historians Robert Gerwarth and John Horne have noted, in civil wars 'much of what might appear to be political, or was indeed claimed to be political by actors at the time, was motivated by pre-existing social tensions or was a by-product of envy, greed or lust'.[107] In a landscape saturated with violence and marked by scarcity as a result of the war years, the reasons for taking up arms, in fact, could also be of a very basic nature, such as organizing food, clothes or shelter in order to survive.

For many uprooted men in the borderlands, the mere struggle for survival was often reason enough to join or stay with armed groups that either never had or quickly lost any political agenda: deserters from the frontlines, men trying to avoid conscription or death by starvation filled their ranks, terrorizing and pillaging the war-torn countryside.[108] The most extreme case was probably the Ukraine, with violence – perpetrated or experienced – as the proverbial sword of Damocles. Here, peasant unrest in 1918 mobilized up to 80,000 men and allegedly affected 10 to 12 per cent (2.5 million) of the agrarian population. By then, the military and paramilitary forces of the puppet government under the Hetman Pavlo Skoropadskyi had gathered about 65,000 men in their ranks. After the Bolshevik seizure of power at the end of the year, an army of between 150,000 and 250,000 Ukrainian soldiers was dissolved, leaving 50,000 men under arms, most of them former supporters of the Hetmanate. The rest decided to go home, where there was the chance to benefit from Bolshevik land reforms.[109] In other words, the region was overflowing with weapons and men that knew how to use them. Furthermore, the causes of violence were not only diverse, but often entangled. Bolsheviks and Nationalists at least pretended to fight for political aims in the first place, while bands of peasants took hold of their former master's estates and sometimes exacted bloody revenge for years of oppression, while interethnic violence was dominant everywhere. In addition to the marauding gangs, nomadic deserters and displaced persons added to a general atmosphere of insecurity.

---

105 Newman, 'The Origins, Attributes, and Legacies', 162.
106 Schnell, *Räume des Schreckens*, 260–1.
107 Robert Gerwarth and John Horne, 'The Great War and Paramilitarism in Europe, 1917–23', *Contemporary European History* 19, no. 3 (2010): 267–73, here 270.
108 Dietrich Beyrau, 'Der Erste Weltkrieg als Bewährungsprobe: Bolschewistische Lernprozesse aus dem "imperialistischen" Krieg', *Journal of Modern European History* 1, no. 1 (2003): 96–124, here 109–10.
109 Georgiy Kasianov, 'Die Ukraine zwischen Revolution, Selbständigkeit und Fremdherrschaft', in *Die Ukraine: Zwischen Selbstbestimmung und Fremdherrschaft 1917–1922*, eds Wolfram Dornik et al. (Graz: Leykam, 2011), 131–79, here 155–63. Skoropadskyi had answered the German occupation force.

Literally all parties engaged in fighting in East-Central Europe killed Jews. As previously noted, the first anti-Jewish measures were implemented by the Tsarist army.[110] 'The Jews', a report from 1915 stated, 'are maybe even more detested than the Germans. Anyway, after the war both elements will be completely expelled from Russia. That's a widespread thought within the army'.[111] More than half a million of the deportees in the first year of the war were Jews.[112] From 1917 onwards, the borderlands witnessed large-scale anti-Semitic violence, including mass killings. In the Ukraine alone, between 1918 and 1920 some 1,500 anti-Jewish pogroms cost the lives of between 50,000 and 200,000 people.[113] The perpetrators were soldiers of the White, Red and Ataman Armies, aided by parts of the local Christian populations.[114]

While outbreaks of anti-Jewish violence – like the anti-Polish and the anti-German violence – had started as coordinated tsarist state policy early on in the war, particularly in the Russian western borderlands, anti-Jewish pogroms had become endemic by 1918–19. Indeed, Jews fell prey to military and paramilitary units, often assisted by raging mobs. This was the case not only in the Ukraine, which was the most extreme, but it was also the case in the whole of Central and Eastern Europe, albeit to a lesser extent. In the Polish *Kresy*, also the heartland, Polish soldiers were the main perpetrators[115]; in the Balkans, the Green Cadres gained a questionable reputation for harassing and sometimes also killing Jews.[116] Jews were also the main victims of the ultra-conservative and fascist phalanx, which, like a crescent facing the east spanned from the Baltics via Germany, Austria and Italy to Hungary, Romania and Croatia. 'The anti-Jewish animus, however', to quote Mark Levene's convincing conclusion, 'clearly transcended the division between military victors and losers and was much more pointedly a transnational phenomenon'.[117] It was the most discernible common form of violence witnessed in the borderlands between Russia and Germany between 1917 and 1921.

The anti-Jewish violence that took place between 1917 and 1921 is surely a topic that, for the regions west of Russia, has not yet been sufficiently quantified and compared transnationally. Nevertheless, it seems questionable whether the study of violence gains insight by singling out specific forms of violence and clinically separating them from other forms that appeared at the same time and place. Literally all the units that engaged in anti-Jewish pogroms engaged in atrocities against other groups of the local population as well, even if they were of

---

110 See Chapter 2 in the present volume, 'The war in the East, 1914–16', 38.
111 Report from Samara in 1915, quoted in Beyrau, 'Der Erste Weltkrieg als Bewährungsprobe', 103.
112 Wróbel, 'The Seeds of Violence', 130.
113 Sanborn, 'The Genesis of Russian Warlordism', 208–9. See also Alexander V. Prusin, *Nationalizing a Borderland: War, Ethnicity, and Anti-Jewish Violence in East Galicia, 1914–1920* (Tuscaloosa, AL: University of Alabama Press, 2005); Frank M. Schuster, '"Für uns ist jeder Krieg ein Unglück": Die Auswirkungen des Ersten Weltkriegs auf die Welt der osteuropäischen Juden', in *Über den Weltkrieg hinaus: Kriegserfahrungen in Ostmitteleuropa 1914–1921*, ed. Joachim Tauber (Lüneburg: Nordost-Institut, 2008), 153–75.
114 Piotr Wróbel, 'The Kaddish Years: Anti-Jewish Violence in East Central Europe, 1918–1921', *Jahrbuch des Simon-Dubnow-Instituts* 4 (2005): 211–36; Mark Levene, 'Frontiers of Genocide', 98–105; Prusin, 'A "Zone of Violence"'.
115 William W. Hagen, *Anti-Jewish Violence in Poland, 1914–1920* (Cambridge, MA: Cambridge University Press, 2018).
116 Jakub Beneš, 'The Green Cadres', 207–41.
117 Levene, *Devastation*, 192.

the same ethnicity.[118] While being aware of the singular significance of anti-Semitic violence in the context of the First World War and its aftermath, especially with the view of the similarities and differences to the extermination of the European Jews in the course of the Second World War, it seems reasonable to see such violence as an extreme case, as a wave of ethno-national violence that inundated Central and Eastern Europe in the aftermath of war and revolution in 1917–1923.

Between the collapse of the empires and their replacement by nation states, the borderlands were arguably the most dangerous tracts of land in Europe in which to live. New state structures emerging from the chaos created by war and revolution needed time to crystallize. Since the armies of the new states were born within this chaos and were often – as we have seen – even part of the problem, the containment of the ubiquitous threat of violence was only achieved at the beginning of the 1920s.

The view from outside

Of course, the Central and Eastern European struggle for the post-war order was keenly watched from the outside. As I elaborated upon earlier, after the failed attempt to carry the revolution to Germany via Poland in the summer of 1920, Bolshevik Russia retreated from the area and instead concentrated on defending its conquests. In the meantime, the Western powers tried to make up their mind about how to react to the revolutionary turn in Russia, a turn which some of them had at first regarded with sympathy as a better alternative to the oppressive tsarist regime. The Western powers' half-hearted decision to send troops to Archangelsk and Siberia in 1918 became bogged down after a few months. The disillusioned soldiers from Canada or the United States felt they did not belong on a continent that had officially entered peace.[119] The allied intervention in northern Russia and Siberia was an expression of cluelessness on their part, a phase of indetermination and desultoriness towards an ally-cum-ideological foe at the war's end, a point which deserves further examination. It was 'part of a historical continuum springing out of the Great War, which witnessed the death of Tsarist Russia and the birth of the Soviet regime'.[120]

Such somnambulant volte-face was not symptomatic only for the Western politicians' position towards Russia. The Bolshevik misjudgement of Central Europe as a field of revolutionary experimentation was mirrored by the West's almost colonial attitude towards the region. Indeed, the multitudinous conflicts that the area witnessed from 1918 onwards led statesmen like Winston Churchill to see Central and Eastern Europe as a kind of colonial 'backyard' of the

---

118 For such different approaches in the case of violence perpetrated by Polish soldiers during the Polish–Soviet war in the *Kresy* compare Jerzy Borzęcki, 'German Anti-Semitism à la Polonaise: A Report on Poznanian Troops' Abuse of Belarusian Jews in 1919', *East European Politics and Societies and Cultures* 26, no. 4 (2012): 693–707; and Łukasz Lewicki, 'Przestępczość w Wojsku Polskim podczas wojny polsko-bolszewickiej' [Crimes of the Polish Army during the Polish-Bolshevik War], http://www.konflikty.pl/historia/1918-1939/przestepczosc-w-wojsku-polskim-podczas-wojny-polsko-bolszewickiej/ (accessed 10 December 2021).
119 Ralph Albertson, *Fighting Without a War: An Account of Military Intervention in North Russia* (New York: Harcourt Brace & Howe, 1920).
120 Moffat, *The Allied Intervention in Russia*, 265. See also Carl J. Richard, *When the United States Invaded Russia: Woodrow Wilson's Siberian Disaster* (Lanham, MD: Rowman & Littlefield Publishers Inc, 2013).

continent. This is best reflected in what he famously said on the night of the armistices: 'The war of the giants has ended; the quarrels of the pygmies have begun.'[121]

Actually, the British Prime Minister's misplaced metaphor poignantly illustrates the Western mixture of indifference and indecisiveness with regard to Central and Eastern European affairs at the time. Take for example the 'Inquiry', a US-American think tank which was built in haste to counsel President Woodrow Wilson prior to and during the peace negotiations in Paris. Charles Seymour, a specialist on elections in Britain who had been assigned to the 'Inquiry' to deal with nationality problems, admitted much later that

> very few regional experts were available. [Robert H.] Lord was a specialist on [sic] Poland. [George L.] Beer had broad knowledge of contemporary as well as historical colonial conditions. [Charles H.] Haskins knew his French history and politics. But [Clive] Day, and [William] Lunt, and I, myself, had not special knowledge of the regions to which we were assigned. [William L.] Westermann as a classical historian was supposed to know about the Near East, but he found a difference between Syrian politics and papyri. We were kept on because [Isaiah] Bowman [a prominent member of the American Geographic Society and one of the leading figures of the 'Inquiry'] liked our reports.[122]

Even still, the Inquiry had some of the most knowledgeable experts on Central and Eastern European affairs at its disposal, however, it would not always handle such affairs prudently. In early 1918, based on Inquiry expertise, US President Wilson, despite his 14 points (which, among other things, had promised self-determination and the re-building of the Polish state), still preferred the principal of Russian territorial integrity to that of national independence in Central Europe. In several Inquiry memoranda, Russian immigrant and Columbia University Professor Vladimir Simkhovitch had called the nationalists active in the area between Germany and Russia, 'fools', 'idiots', 'fanatics' and 'ignoramuses'.[123] Less than half a year later, the US launched their armed intervention in Russia, the very country they had favoured instead of the independent national movements at its western and southern borders.

It is obvious that up until 1919, 'few on the Allied side had given much thought to the future of Central Europe and even less to the Balkans'.[124] Still stuck in a nineteenth-century attitude towards Europe as a concert of power, at the end of the First World War, many Western politicians saw the region itself only as a geostrategic asset, which to a certain extent explains their inconsequence, and they disagreed on the implications: France saw strong Polish, Czech and Yugoslav states as establishing a counterweight to irredentist Germany and a buffer zone against revolutionary Russia. The British favoured Germany as a stronghold in Central Europe and mistrusted the revitalized Poland, especially its National Committee under Roman Dmowski, who issued anti-Semitic slogans in Paris, and its armed forces under Józef Piłsudski, who was carving out the country's eastern borders. The US found themselves in the middle; plus, they were torn between opposing the Bolsheviks and helping the Russian people. 'This was civil war', commented a YMCA secretary on the evacuation of Allied troops from Archangelsk in

---

121 Cited in Davies, *White Eagle, Red Star*, 21.
122 Letter of Charles Seymour to Lawrence E. Gelfland, 7 October 1953, cited in Lawrence E. Gelfand, *The Inquiry: American Preparations for Peace, 1917–1919* (New Haven, CT: Yale University Press, 1963), 314–15.
123 Mieczysław B. Biskupski, 'Re-Creating Central Europe: The United States "Inquiry" into the Future of Poland in 1918', *International History Review* 12, no. 2 (1990): 249–79, here 274.
124 MacMillan, *Paris 1919*, 115.

1919. 'Every man's hand is set against his neighbour. And now as we confess the futility of our intervention and evacuate, the evil harvest is to be reaped'.[125]

Politicians and military leaders in Central and Eastern Europe – depending on their aptitude – would sometimes profit from the West's cocktail of hesitancy and indifference. Military successes – as in the Polish case against Ukraine and Lithuania – could create a fait accompli. But between the Baltic Sea and the Carpathian Mountains, new borders were mostly negotiated in Allied conferences – as was the case with Lithuania, Latvia and Estonia, all of which gained their independence in Paris. Edvard Beneš and Tomáš Masaryk were masters at presenting the Czechoslovak cause, and they got the most out of the peace talks, sometimes arguing by way of ethnicity, sometimes historical rights, sometimes by arguing for the viability of a singular Czech and Slovak state. In the Balkans, the Serbs – who had fought on the Allied side – and the Croats, would present monumental geographical claims for the 'South Slave State' (Yugoslavia) which the West amply granted, hurting and alienating all neighbouring states except Greece. In the end, only the Ukrainians were left, who nobody would listen to: 'I only saw a Ukrainian once', commented the British Prime Minister with bad grace; 'It is the last Ukrainian I have seen, and I am not sure that I want to see any more.'[126]

There is only one case in which news from Central Europe woke the West from its indifference: news about the ongoing anti-Jewish pogroms by Polish troops in eastern Poland, which cost the lives of several hundred Jews in 1918–19, was some of the worst press Poland ever received.[127] At that same time, however, the fact that racism – especially anti-Semitism – was still widespread and socially accepted in the West was deliberately ignored. During the 'Red Summer' of 1919, the US themselves faced race riots in which hundreds of black compared to a handful of white Americans were killed – a point which, incidentally, was widely discussed in Warsaw: 'It has been suggested that a Polish Mission be sent to America to investigate the negro pogroms', noted a member of an American commission investigating Jewish pogroms in eastern Poland.[128] Moreover, the much deadlier anti-Semitic violence in Ukraine, which claimed the lives of more than 50,000 Jews, were neither reported in the Western press at that time, nor have they been sufficiently discussed in relation to the concurrent pogroms in Poland up until today.[129] A significant exception to Western indifference towards Central and Eastern Europe, however, was the field of humanitarian aid. The United States especially outdid themselves by bringing relief to a region facing catastrophe in the wake of the war – with famine raging though the devastated landscapes and epidemics spreading westwards.[130]

All in all, as might have become apparent, a certain Western and Russian colonial attitude and feeling of superiority towards Central and Eastern Europe in the formative years of

---

125 Albertson, *Fighting Without a War*, 120.
126 MacMillan, *Paris 1919*, 226. The Polish and Baltic case ibid., 205–28; the Czech case: 229–42; the Yugoslav case: 109–124. See the subchapter 'War and statehood – occupation and persistence (I)' in my chapter on the First World War in *The Routledge History Handbook of Central and Eastern Europe in the Twentieth Century*, volume II: *Statehood*, 119–26, which admittedly uses the same quote – the quote itself being too fitting not to mention here as well.
127 Neal Pease, '"This Troublesome Question": The United States and the "Polish Pogroms" of 1918–1919', in *Ideology, Politics and Diplomacy in East Central Europe*, ed. Mieczysław B. Biskupski (Rochester, NY: University of Rochester Press, 2003), 58–79.
128 Goodhart, *Poland and the Minority Races*, 108.
129 Prusin, *Nationalizing a Borderland*; idem, *The Lands Between*.
130 See the subchapter 'War and destruction – relief and reconstruction (I)' in my chapter on the First World War in *The Routledge History Handbook of Central and Eastern Europe in the Twentieth Century*, volume II: *Statehood*, 135–9.

1918–1920 often led them to misjudge und underestimate the region's agency. Yet, contemporaries such as British historian Robert William Seton-Watson have already contested this attitude, feeling that it was neither the revolution in the East nor the peace-making in the West, but the ongoing armed conflicts in Central and Eastern Europe that created precedents. Countering Wilson in 1920, he claimed: 'Almost all that is likely to prove permanent in the territorial settlement [of the Paris peace treaties] has been the work of titanic forces beyond the control of the pygmies of Paris'.[131]

Explaining violence in Central and Eastern Europe 1917–1923

The wave of revolutionary and counter-revolutionary, military and paramilitary violence that swept Central and Eastern Europe between 1917 and 1923 demands explanation and interpretation. Put simply, the crucial question is whether violence in these contexts was targeted or arbitrary, organized or spontaneous. Many a historian of the First World War's aftermath has tackled this problem. Therefore, some summary reflections on the underlying reasons of these distinct forms of violence at the beginning of the interwar period and the others we have just presented shall suffice.

The Red Terror and its counterpart, the White Terror, emerged at the very beginning of this period, and they had not ceased by its end. Bolshevik revolutionary violence transformed into collectivization and the Great Terror in Russia, and proto-fascist counter-revolutionary violence transformed into the rise of fascist movements in Central and Southeastern Europe in the 1930s. This transformation process will be dealt with in Part II of this chapter. For the period of 1917–1923, Dietrich Beyrau states that the 'Red Terror' – and I would add here, the White Terror as well – 'had several functions: it allowed redistribution within the parameters of class warfare, permitted "surgical operations" with population and class-oriented political goals, and served as a deterrent to potential enemies'; he is, herein, confirmed by Peter Holquist.[132]

Similar macro-level theories of intentional, state-directed violence can be found with regard to the evolving nation states. Rogers Brubaker's model of the Polish Second Republic as a 'nationalizing state' describes how the core (Polish-catholic) nation tended to build and dominate their state, regarding all means that served their goal as legitimate, including the use of violence and restrictive legislation against ethno-national rivals.[133] Additionally, Joshua Sanborn, by taking the example of the decline of the Russian Empire, has argued that in a process of 'decolonization', new 'state-building' elites engaged in establishing their own polity.[134] It could be argued that another phase has to be added to Sanborn's model, where the de-colonized heirs of vanished empires used the practices of colonial rule themselves to control and subdue other ethnic groups: this is exactly what happened in 1917–1923 in Central and Eastern Europe. From the moment they were formed, the new Central European 'self-styled nation states', for

---

131 Robert W. Seton-Watson, 'J. M. Keynes, The Economic Consequences of the War: (review)', *The New Europe* 13, no. 168 (1920): 363–9, here 363.
132 Dietrich Beyrau, 'Brutalization Revisited: The Case of Russia', *Journal of Contemporary History* 50, no. 1 (2015): 15–37, here 35. Holquist states, 'It was the "new regime" that dictated the course. While all sides in the Russian civil wars extravagantly employed violent practices and coercive measures, the Soviet state's use of violence clearly was both more open-ended and more purposeful', in Holquist, 'Violent Russia, Deadly Marxism', 650–1.
133 Rogers Brubaker, ed., *Nationalism Reframed: Nationhood and the National Question in the New Europe* (Cambridge: Cambridge University Press, 1996).
134 Sanborn, *Imperial Apocalypse*.

the most part, simply acted 'as little empires', a notion that, by the way, did not escape their contemporaries.[135]

These macro-level theories are useful as they offer an initial first overview of the broad lines that violence drew across the map of Europe immediately after the First World War. But to look for the underlying reasons in the ideological predispositions of the major agents of violence or the in overall political situation alone, will not suffice as an explanation. How do we explain mass phenomena such as treason, desertion, denunciation, robbery and the volte-face of entire units that were observed fighting on each of the warring sides of the civil war? And how do we understand why individual civilians as well as entire villages turned criminal and joined in the violence overnight? How does violence fit within rather static models when it became a non-static, transformative social practice which would not only profoundly change the lives of the surviving victims, but also the perpetrators, like this *Freikorps* member, who noted in retrospective:

> None of those who, at the beginning of 1919, on their own, with a few comrades in the endless expanse of the snowy, wintry Baltic country, went through the most dogged and pitiless of all petty wars, got away without a trace of this experience. ... Such a life of war inevitably changes a person, and those changes can only be explained in the rarest of cases.[136]

As we narrow our focus to the level of regions, cities and towns, intentions become blurred, and a number of factors determined by the situation on the ground come into play. Often the perpetrators were not merely following orders, but they were thinking individuals, reacting to local circumstances, acting to their own advantage – rarely to that of their targets' – especially when military discipline was loosened or abandoned. As such, Jörg Baberowski certainly has a point: in his model of 'violent' and 'state-remote spaces' (*Gewalt- und staatsferne Räume*) he enters the danger zone, arguing that 'in the struggle for survival' during the Russian Civil War – and, again, I would add that it was also the case in the Central European Civil War and in the Balkans – 'political goals or programmes that hardly anyone knew or understood anyway lost their significance. For the combatants, the only thing that mattered at some point was to stand their ground and impose their will on others.'[137]

Who, then, settles the score: is it the theorists of targeted violence, or those of pulse-triggered violence? It probably depends on the perspective, and on the level of violent behaviour in question. Violence during revolutionary or civil wars and nation state-building processes often takes place far away from the central decision-making bodies, from local commanders to the men executing it on the ground. Ideology-driven, intentional violence can be traced to the point at which the 'great design' was drafted – whether revolutionary, counter-revolutionary or state-building – and to which its concomitant orders to engage in, or

---

135 Pieter M. Judson, *The Habsburg Empire: A New History* (Cambridge, MA: Harvard University Press, 2016), 451; Oscar Jászi, *The Dissolution of the Habsburg Monarchy* (Chicago, IL: University of Chicago Press, 1966), 453–4.
136 Bernhard Sauer, 'Vom "Mythos eines ewigen Soldatentums": Der Feldzug deutscher Freikorps im Baltikum im Jahre 1919', *Zeitschrift für Geschichtswissenschaft* 43, no. 10 (1995): 869–902, here 869.
137 Jörg Baberowski, 'Verwüstetes Land: Macht und Gewalt in der frühen Sowjetunion', in *Gewalträume: Soziale Ordnungen im Ausnahmezustand*, eds Jörg Baberowski and Gabriele Metzler (Frankfurt a.M.: Campus Verlag, 2012), 169–87, here 172. See also Schnell, *Räume des Schreckens*; Felix Schnell, 'Ukraine 1918: Besatzer und Besetzte im Gewaltraum', in Baberowski and Metzler, *Gewalträume: Soziale Ordnungen im Ausnahmezustand*, 135–68.

contain, violent activity were issued. Situational violence is present where the physical contact between perpetrator and victim is made. Over the past two decades, similar considerations have influenced the field of perpetrator studies in relation to the Second World War,[138] and indeed, it seems beneficial to apply their detailed findings to the period of the aftermath of the First World War in Central and Eastern Europe.

As may have become apparent, a profound difference to the war experience up to 1917 is that from then onwards violence entered civil life not only in exceptional cases, but in many parts of Central and Eastern Europe, it became an everyday experience. Ideologically motivated violence was aimed at the transformation of society as a whole, whereas situational violence could occur wherever armed groups of men marched through a village. Until the formation of stable state structures and their successful enforcement of its monopoly on the use of force, civilian lives were in danger. A fatal amalgam of revolutionary, counter-revolutionary, state-building violence and perpetrator behaviour on the ground gained momentum in the period 1917–1923 and resulted in a deluge of paramilitary violence in which Central and Eastern Europe nearly drowned. How the region finally found its way out of these dark waters is a question which will be addressed in Part II of this chapter. I will close Part I with some general remarks on the experience of violence for the population of Central and Eastern Europe; my intention here is to give the reader something to think about, rather than put forward an entirely new argument.

It is important to note that when speaking of organized agents of violence, I am not speaking for the entire population of the regions either affected or omitted by their activities. The large majority of Central and Eastern European inhabitants did not actively take part in the struggle for the post-war order, either because they did not belong to the male population fit for military service, or because they did not identify with the pursued final goals: that of achieving a class society or nation state. One has to keep in mind that by 1917, vast areas of Central Europe consisted of agricultural land tilled by peasants who, if asked for their nationality or political worldview would probably just shrug their shoulders. These people mostly identified with regional, not national or ideological communal values, and from their perspective, borders did not divide nations, but rather towns, regions and ethnic and religious groups.[139] These frontiers very rarely coincided with the borders that separated the Central and Eastern European states when the fighting subsided.[140] Paradoxically, such incommensurability meant that after the settling of the post-war order, some of the former bystanders became agents of violence as well, fighting a state order that trespassed, restricted or destroyed the world they had formerly known. Being at the mercy of such military and paramilitary units, large parts of the population of Central and Eastern Europe found themselves in a difficult situation for

---

138 Here, I refer to two pioneering books: Christopher R. Browning, *Ordinary Men: Reserve Police Battalion 101 and the Final Solution in Poland* (New York: Harper Collins, 1992); and Daniel J. Goldhagen, *Hitler's Willing Executioners: Ordinary Germans and the Holocaust* (New York: Knopf, 1996). These two seminal books have triggered a plethora of works on the underlying, well-documented conflict between 'functionalists' vs. 'intentionalists', see Richard Bessel, 'Functionalists vs. Intentionalists: The Debate Twenty Years On *or* Whatever Happened to Functionalism and Intentionalism?' *German Studies Review* 26, no. 1 (2003): 15–20.

139 Felix Schnell, 'Die erwartete Nation: Imperien, Bauern und Konjunkturen des Nationalen in der Ukraine (Zarenreich und Sowjetunion)', *Journal of Modern European History* 11, no. 3 (2013): 375–96, here 376.

140 Peter Thaler, 'Fluid Identities in Central European Borderlands', *European History Quarterly* 31, no. 4 (2001): 519–48.

months, sometimes even years. And although their operational range was rather limited, the generals of the White and Red armies, the Atamans and the commanders of the unruly national armies became the masters of life and death within the region. Whereas the conventionally fought First World War had witnessed the encounter of regular armies (although they were sometimes hastily advancing or retreating, showing signs of dissolution and erosion of discipline, or even systematically harassing the local population), its subsequent battles brought a totally new dimension of violence to Central and Eastern Europe: it literally marked every armed man as a possible perpetrator and every defenceless civilian – including women, children and the elderly – as a possible victim of violence. Nevertheless, it is important to keep in mind that on the local level, civilians could turn into agents of violence themselves, with agendas that had nothing to do with the overall political situation.

Recent sociological findings under the banner of macro-violence theory help us understand more about the complicated mechanisms and motives at work in Central Europe between 1917 and 1923. Christopher Read is not alone in claiming that like most civil wars, the Russian Civil War was 'not fought between easily definable and territorially contiguous entities' and 'was not so much along a frontline but was more like a patchwork quilt, red patches here, white patches there, green patches ... scattered around, and many patches which combined the main colours'.[141] As Stathis N. Kalyvas argues in his detailed study 'The Logic of Violence in Civil War', major, overarching ideological conflicts are supplemented on the micro-level by a variety of violent or criminal behaviour which often has little or nothing to do with the greater political setting in which it occurs. The urge to destroy the ideological enemy is accompanied by an urge to survive in, or even profit from, obscure situations. Under these circumstances, violence becomes a currency which can buy survival, freedom and victory, whereas waiving it off means putting oneself at risk. And, indeed, this extends beyond uniformed men:

> There is a tendency to see violence as being externally imposed on unsuspecting and, therefore, innocent civilians .... However, individuals cannot be treated simply as passive, manipulated, or invisible actors; instead, they often manipulate central actors in helping them fight their own conflicts. In short, they must be explicitly incorporated into the theories of civil war in ways that reflect the complexity of their participation.[142]

Equally under-researched for the period and region under consideration here are questions of survival strategies and the long-term consequences of violence, which have previously been addressed in the context of the Russian Civil War. Indeed, in Russia, certainly millions of people died, but millions of others survived because they had

> moved back to the village. Almost all city dwellers had relatives in rural areas and many had land, wives, children in their native village. The village proved itself, as it had many times before in Russian history, to be the national safety net. ... This is not to say the rural population did not suffer, far from it, but they were more likely to survive.[143]

---

141 Christopher Read, *War and Revolution in Russia, 1914–22: The Collapse of Tsarism and the Establishment of Soviet Power* (Basingstoke: Palgrave Macmillan, 2013), 139.
142 Stathis N. Kalyvas, *The Logic of Violence in Civil War* (Cambridge: Cambridge University Press, 2006), 390.
143 Read, *War and Revolution in Russia, 1914–22*, 160–1.

When it comes to the devastating effects of mass violence on individuals and families, a recent study of the Ural region in the post-Russian Civil War period noted a surge in divorce, family abandonment and suicide.[144] Conducting a similar study of Central and Eastern Europe in the aftermath of the First World War seems a worthwhile endeavour.

Part II: Instability and crisis in the post-war order (1923–1939)

The violent process of their materialization notwithstanding, to describe the interwar governments of Central and Eastern Europe as a bunch of hopelessly backward, repressive and quarrelsome regimes (as was too often the case in the past), would draw a distorted picture of the 1920s and 1930s: after all, the new distribution of power had 'freed three times as many people from nationally alien rule as they subjected to such rule'.[145] All newcomers on the international stage began as nation states with parliamentary democracies, thus representing the modern ideal of a balanced ratio between government and participation. Bulgaria, Romania and Hungary endured the war as monarchies, however, during peacetime (with the exception of the latter), they initially allowed a certain degree of parliamentary participation. Furthermore, one should keep in mind that for nearly 20 years, the post-war states of Central and Eastern Europe managed to keep a precarious balance and to avoid major military conflicts between one another or with any other outside neighbours.

That said, what were the underlying mechanisms that caused interwar Central and Eastern European affairs to deteriorate? Here, I point to a seemingly redundant, but unfortunately necessary, statement: the comparative weakness of Central and Eastern European states has been the subject of mockery, especially from Western politicians and historians (and not only in the past), attributing to them a kind of 'eastern mentality' that is allegedly prone to crisis and disorder. But the problems they struggled with from the very moment of their formation (those that they were the least to blame for) were not cultural in nature: they were structural and political; and furthermore, they were imported rather than domestic.

'Latecomer' nation states

Part I of this chapter focused on the violent formation of nation states in the period 1917–1923; but, in order to understand the reason that peace was so fragile in the region after 1923, one has to look further back. It is true that the First World War triggered the downfall of the European land empires and thus finally enabled the emergence of nation states in Central and Eastern Europe. But this was only part of the formation process which began much earlier and is inextricably linked to the history of modern Western Europe. Looking more closely, one realizes that the conflicts Central and Eastern Europe witnessed in the wake of the First World War were not the antithesis to 'Western civilization', but rather they mirrored a process the Western nation states had undergone during the previous century when they first formed. Indeed, only the parameters had dramatically changed.

The concept of the nation state entered the continental scenery at the end of the eighteenth century with the French Revolution, and although such a watershed event is commonly

---

144 Aaron B. Retish, *Russia's Peasants in Revolution and Civil War: Citizenship, Identity, and the Creation of the Soviet State, 1914–1922* (Cambridge: Cambridge University Press, 2008), 259–60.
145 Joseph Rothschild, *East Central Europe Between the Two World Wars* (Seattle, WA: University of Washington Press, 1992), 4.

Radicalization and the interwar period

Map 3.1 Central and Eastern Europe, 1918–1939

regarded as the harbinger of the Enlightenment and a major turning point in Western civilization, its reputation is not spotless. As general François Joseph Westermann, then commander of the French Army of the West, reported in 1794:

> The Vendée is no more … I have buried it in the woods and marshes of Savenay … According to your orders, I have trampled their children beneath our horses' feet; I have massacred their women, so they will no longer give birth to brigands. I do not have a single prisoner to reproach me. I have exterminated them all. The roads are sown with corpses. At Savenay, brigands are arriving all the time claiming to surrender, and we are shooting them non-stop … Mercy is not a revolutionary sentiment.[146]

It is with good reason that historians have compared this outbreak of revolutionary violence and its continuation in the Napoleonic Wars (1803–1815) to the troubles of the Russian Civil War (1917–1921).[147] Although recent historiography has stressed the direct connection between nation-building and violence, it has – with the notable exception of Mark Levene's work – located its origins mainly in Central and Southeastern Europe at the beginning of the twentieth century, and thus widely overlooked its prototype in the West.[148]

Although for decades to come France would remain the only nation state on the continent deserving of the name, the process, once set in motion, was unstoppable. Italy followed suit making its appearance as a nation state in the Italian Wars of Independence (1848–1866). But the national idea also spread east and southeast to the Prussian, Habsburg, Russian and Ottoman empires, slowly but surely modifying them, so that it is difficult to draw a line between their imperial and their national cores. Ambivalence is thus characteristic for this transitional phase, evidence of which is reflected in the terms 'imperial nations' and 'nationalizing empires' which have appeared in recent literature.[149]

The nationalizing process of the empires which ruled Central and Southeastern Europe during the nineteenth century worked in two directions: it integrated the titular nationalities – Germans, Russians and Turks – while antagonizing the respective imperial minorities which harboured their distinct national dreams. Due to the rather organic nature (owing to the relatively long timespan over which it took place), the process advanced steadily, but mostly without bloodshed. Physical violence was not a major part of the experience for the population settled in the lands between the rivers Danube, Oder and Dnieper prior to the First World War. Although aware of the swift changes of the modern world, most people in the region lived their lives undisturbed by brutal state intervention or physical attacks at the hands of their neighbours of different faith, language, political preference or national affiliation. While the empires that owned most of the region lost wars outside the borderlands – Austria against Prussia in 1866, Russia during the Crimean War of 1853–56 – these military defeats made the borderlands themselves an even more important safety zone, which, on the Austrian

---

146 Mark Levene, *The Rise of the West and the Coming of Genocide* (London: I.B. Tauris, 2005), 163–212, here 104. Further publications by Mark Levene which continue this line of thought are the previously cited *Devastation: The European Rimlands 1912–1938* and *Annihilation: The European Rimlands 1939–1953* (Oxford: Oxford University Press, 2013).
147 Mayer, *The Furies*.
148 Brubaker, *Nationalism Reframed*; Naimark, *Fires of Hatred*; Mann, *The Dark Side of Democracy*.
149 For an overview, see Stefan Berger and Alexei Miller, 'Building Nations in and Within Empires: A Reassessment', in *Nationalizing Empires*, eds Stefan Berger and Alexei Miller (Budapest: Central European University Press, 2015), 1–30.

side, led to half-hearted domestic reforms in hopes of appeasing the population, a development that could even be observed after the harsh oppression of domestic resistance. Russian policies were certainly more repressive, yet they were also adjusted so as to not threaten the fragile balance between external rule and internal cooperation at their western borders.[150] But the rising tensions between the autocratic rule of the imperial centres and the awakening of a cultural, national and ethnic self-conception at the periphery constantly heated the region like a giant pressure cooker. From time to time, it blew off steam, as the national uprisings in partition-era Poland (in 1830 and 1863), Bulgaria, Montenegro and Bosnia-Herzegovina (in 1875) and Bulgaria (in 1876) all testify. Nevertheless, the partial independence of Hungary in the Austro-Hungarian Compromise of 1867 and the appearance of Bulgaria, Romania and Serbia as autonomous states – although all monarchically ruled – irreversibly changed the Central and Southeastern European political scenery towards national self-consciousness without invoking the spectre of war.[151]

During the course of the First World War when the iron fists of the empires suddenly opened, and as mass violence swept the region, the overheated pressure cooker finally exploded. The ensuing period of state-formation that emerged in Central and Eastern Europe between 1918 and 1923 was both extremely short *and* extremely violent. This points to the conclusion that state- and nation-building in 'fast forward' mode (as was the case in the wake of the French Revolution) necessitates brutal force in order to make up for a lack of time. The Polish nationalists of the outgoing nineteenth century knew about this connection when they weighed the benefits and odds of revolutionary action against those of negotiation (what they called 'organic work') in the imperial parliaments.

When the fighting subsided, all Central and Eastern European states had to struggle with the legacies of war- and peace-making: millions of their most gifted men had died at (and often on different sides of) the front, and millions more of their civilians had fallen victim to violence, famine and disease; their economy lay in ruins; their imperial administration had evaporated; their lines of communication had been severed by war or new frontiers; their populations not only suddenly featured several official languages, but also currencies, systems of measurement and technical standards (as, for example, differing train track widths). In addition to that, their political elite had been trained in decades of clandestine and opposition work against the imperial centre, not in the application of the two cardinal virtues of democracy: negotiating and compromising. The military elite, for their part, relied on the armed forces as the sole guarantor of their newly achieved independence and freedom – a view widely shared within civil society – and since their new-found freedom came at the cost of violent clashes with their neighbours, there were many scenarios in which use of military force was justified in their eyes.

Thus, the problems faced by the Central and Eastern European states between the wars were only partly homemade. First and foremost, they were predefined by their imperial past and by the global conflict these very empires had unleashed. With the ushering in of a new era in 1918, the states of Central and Eastern Europe were still not totally free in their actions. Due to the victory of the Western powers and the progressing isolation of Bolshevik Russia, sealed by the defeat of the Red Army in the summer of 1920 at the gates of Warsaw, it was beyond question that if they sought international recognition, the newly created states would have to adopt the principal of parliamentary democracy. Whereas this term was unanimously accepted – after

---

150 Prusin, *The Lands Between*, 18–27.
151 Giuseppe Motta, *Less than Nations: Central-Eastern European Minorities after WWI*, 2 vols. (Newcastle upon Tyne: Cambridge Scholars Publishing, 2014), 1: 3–11.

all, to most contemporaries west of Russia, it seemed the better alternative to the Bolshevik spectre – another term was unanimously frowned upon: namely, the 'minority treaties', which became an integral part of all peace settlements in the area.

Interethnic and terrorist violence

The peace treaties signed in the suburbs of Paris in the wake of the First World War have often been criticized, especially for the short-sightedness concerning the heavy burden – i.e. considerable land loss and reparations – they placed on the Berlin and Budapest governments, thus precipitating Germany and Hungary's drift towards the revanchist positions of the extreme right. But the new Central and Eastern European states also harboured other problems that destabilized the interwar order: while ethnic conflict did exist in the pre-war multi-ethnic land empires, as previously mentioned, such conflict led to short outbreaks of unrest from below which were rigorously suppressed from above. The new arrangement of states along boundaries of nationality on the one hand caused a constant antagonism between the titular nation and the various minorities living within these boundaries, and on the other hand, it spurred an irredentist thirst for a reunion with co-nationals living outside these borders. As a result, this created the strong tensions within and between the respective states, characteristic of the interwar period.

The Allies in Paris were aware of this enormous challenge, and as such they insisted on the implementation of minority rights in the post-war states, codified in the peace regulations. But the League of Nations, founded in order to prevent future conflicts of a global scale and to guarantee interstate cooperation, proved rather ineffective in guaranteeing minority rights: first, because it did not deal with those exerting pressure within the region, and second, because its major members – like the former allies Britain, France or the United States – did not sign the minority treaties themselves, although (or rather because) all of them had their own issues with racism and state violence against minorities. Thus, in the eyes of the younger nation states, the credibility of the League of Nations was compromised from the outset.[152]

The fraught legacy and imposed future do not, of course, acquit the Central and Eastern European states of their own responsibility for their domestic and foreign affairs from the early 1920s onwards. Even once the weapons fell silent, and no major conflicts had broken out in the middle of the continent for almost two decades, the atmosphere within, and extending beyond, its new states was tense from the very start. These newly created nation states, ironically, became 'multinational', or 'empires in miniature' that did not possess 'the necessary political experience and skills to secure a certain measure of loyalty from all their subjects'.[153]

Discrimination against minorities in comparison to the treatment of the respective titular nation within the public spheres of the Central and Eastern European states has been eloquently described so many times that there is no need to expand upon it here. Rather, based on the aim of the present volume, under examination here are the cases in which conflicts turned violent or were already violent from the start. And the findings have been surprising: if we look at the

---

152 Mark Mazower, *Dark Continent: Europe's Twentieth Century* (New York: Penguin Books, 1999); Steiner, *The Lights that Failed*; Carole Fink, *Defending the Rights of Others: The Great Powers, the Jews, and International Minority Protection, 1878–1938* (Cambridge: Cambridge University Press, 2004); Ryan Gingeras, 'Nation States, Minorities, and Refugees, 1914–1923', in *The Oxford Handbook of European History, 1914–1945*, ed. Nicholas Doumanis (Oxford: Oxford University Press, 2016), 138–59.
153 Chioveanu, 'A Fragmented World', 84.

year 1923 as a starting point (i.e. if we disregard the violent formation years 1917–1923 outlined in detail above), the examples of violence up until the outbreak of the Second World War are less numerous than one would expect. Ukrainian terrorists in the 1920s and 1930s never managed to win the support of the Orthodox Church, the moderate Ukrainian parties or the Ukrainian-speaking population for their crusade against the Polish state. Although the Second Republic conducted a harsh programme of Polonization and colonialization, 'in 1927, 16.2 per cent of the total number of marriages in Eastern Galicia were between Poles and Ukrainians'.[154] Until 1939, only half a dozen assaults on the lives of Polish politicians or Ukrainian 'collaborators' were actually successful, and the number of casualties in connection with acts of sabotage and armed robberies totalled only around 50.[155] In Macedonia, the IMRO[156] was much more accepted by the population, and until 1934, they acted as a state within a state; but with regard to their popularity and omnipresence, the death toll of 340 non-Macedonians (i.e. Serbians and Bulgarians, amongst others) between 1918 and 1934 is surprisingly low, particularly in comparison to the 4,200 organization members who were killed during that time in the name of 'self-purification', and can therefore neither be listed as victims of ethnic nor political violence.[157] The organization's most prominent coups, however, were launched outside Macedonia and in cooperation with another terrorist organization: in June 1923, in the course of a Bulgarian coup d'état, Prime Minister Aleksandar Stamboliyski was brutally murdered by the IMRO; in October 1934, King Alexander I of Yugoslavia was shot in Marseille by Vlado Chernozemski, an IMRO gunman, who by that time, also worked for the Croatian terrorist movement, the Ustasha. Prominent as they were, these were cases of political rather than ethnic terrorism in interwar Central and Eastern Europe: they were comparable to the assassination of President Gabriel Narutewicz in December 1922 by a lone perpetrator with sympathies for the Polish conservatives; the assassination of the Czech Minister of Finance Alois Rašín by a Czech anarchist two months later; the assassination of the Croatian People's Party leader Stjepan Radić in the Yugoslav Parliament in August 1928 by a member of the Montenegrin People's Radical Party; or, the assassination of the Romanian Prime Minister Ion Duca by members of the fascist Iron Guard in 1933.[158] In April 1925, Bulgarian communists blew up the roof of the St Nedelya Church in Sofia, killing 150 people and injuring around 500.[159] Although two communists, officers of the Polish army, were sentenced to death for the bombing of the Warsaw Citadel in October 1923, which killed 28 and wounded 89 people, the circumstances remain mysterious. These examples are specific and symbolic rather than high-impact forms of violence, which somehow mirrored, but were not immediately linked to the anarchist and nationalist acts of terrorism in Europe

---

154 Tadeusz Piotrowski, *Poland's Holocaust: Ethnic Strife, Collaboration with Occupying Forces and Genocide in the Second Republic, 1918–1947* (Jefferson, NC: McFarland, 1998), 187.
155 Alexander J. Motyl, 'Ukrainian Nationalist Political Violence in Inter-War Poland, 1921–1939', *East European Quarterly* 19, no. 1 (1985): 45–55. Nevertheless, the Ukrainian terrorist milieu would radicalize the biographies of nationalists like Stepan Bandera's, who became a leading figure in the Polish–Ukrainian ethnic struggle at the end of the Second World War, see Grzegorz Rossoliński-Liebe, *Stepan Bandera: Fascism, Genocide, and Cult* (New York: Columbia University Press, 2014).
156 See Part I of the present chapter, 93–4.
157 Troebst, 'Nationalismus und Gewalt im Osteuropa der Zwischenkriegszeit', 290.
158 John P. Newman, *Yugoslavia in the Shadow of War: Veterans and the Limits of State Building, 1903–1945* (Cambridge: Cambridge University Press, 2015), 95–7, 224–5; Paul Brykczynski, *Primed for Violence: Murder, Antisemitism, and Democratic Politics in Interwar Poland* (Madison, WI: The University of Wisconsin Press, 2016).
159 Richard J. Crampton, *Bulgaria* (Oxford: Oxford University Press, 2008), 236–9.

before the First World War. The main purpose of these acts was to spread fear and anxiety in order to destabilize the respective state system, and in this regard, the interwar political radicals certainly succeeded.[160]

So, are the historians wrong who characterize the two decades between the wars as a time of fragile peace, constantly threatened by domestic and foreign enemies of the Central and Eastern European states? Yes and no. To be sure, there was nothing like a permanent state of emergency after 1923, let alone an encompassing civil war shaking the middle of the continent to its very core; if there were, historians could speak of a 'thirty years' war' from 1914 to 1945. But there *were* areas in which post-war violence receded at a slower pace than in others, or in some cases, not at all: for example, political violence – as opposed to ethnic violence – which involved armed robberies and either wounding or killing political adversaries or even local representatives of the government, police or military, never totally ceased in the Balkans. As John Paul Newman has demonstrated, the Serbian veterans (Chetniks) tipped the scales for the stabilization and destabilization of the newly founded democratic 'South Slave State' until the beginning of King Alexander I's dictatorship in 1929 (a point to which I will return). After the king's death, the Chetniks were unleashed, and a wave of paramilitary violence against the non-Serb minorities overshadowed the second half of the 1930s. Like no other state of the region, the Yugoslav state was split between the 'winners' (Serbian soldiers fighting for independence) and the 'losers' (Croat soldiers fighting for the Habsburg Monarchy) of the First World War, a division which was exacerbated in peacetime mainly by the growing influence and state support of the former – this is what Newman calls a 'culture of victory' – and the relative weakness of the latter.[161] Eastern Poland in the 1920s saw Poles on the winning side and Ukrainians on the losing side, featuring state-sponsored projects of colonialization via military settlers, and a level of criminality and contraband which earned it the epithet the 'Wild East'[162] which was colourfully depicted in former smuggler-turned-writer Sergiusz Piasecki's novels.[163] It is surely no coincidence that here of all places, a Polish police officer shot the alleged bombers of the Warsaw Citadel during a prisoner exchange with the Soviet Union in 1925.[164] It cannot be overlooked that the Yugoslav and the Polish case have one thing in common: the described forms of violence were performed remotely from the capital, where state authorities were weak and few and far between, and where ethnic tension and the burdensome legacies of the First World War were more perceptible than in the rest of Central and Eastern Europe.

Given the measure of tension in the air, there were not as many casualties as one would expect. As leading experts on the topic confirm, even ethnic violence (i.e. the boycotts against Jewish-owned businesses, the *numerus clausus* for Jewish students at the universities and the pogroms committed by the interwar right-wing and fascist movements that largely took

---

160 Heinz-Gerhard Haupt and Klaus Weinhauer, 'Terrorism and the State', in *Political Violence in Twentieth-Century Europe*, eds Donald Bloxham and Robert Gerwarth (Cambridge: Cambridge University Press, 2011), 176–209, here 179–92.
161 Newman, *Yugoslavia in the Shadow of War*.
162 Kathryn C. Ciancia, 'Poland's Wild East: Imagined Landscapes and Everyday Life in the Volhynian Borderlands, 1918–1939', PhD diss., Stanford University, 2011. For the published book, please consult the Further Reading section at the end of this chapter.
163 The most famous was even translated into English: Sergiusz Piasecki, *Lover of the Great Bear* (London: Routledge & Sons, 1938).
164 Borodziej, *Geschichte Polens im 20. Jahrhundert*, 123; MAB, 'Zagadkowa śmierć rosyjskich szpiegów pod Stołpcami' [The mysterious death of Russian spies near Stolpce], *Wschodnia Gazeta Codzienna*, 26 March 2014, https://kresy24.pl/zagadkowa-smierc-szpiegow-pod-stolpcami/ (accessed 10 December 2021).

place in Romania, Yugoslavia and Hungary, but also in Poland and Latvia), which surely added to the insecurity that is so characteristic of interwar Europe, did not, in the end, lead to high numbers of casualties on either side. Paul Hanebrink describes the trickling away of the paramilitary White Terror in post-revolutionary Hungary:

> Slowly, the terrorist squads found themselves marginalized, much to the chagrin of the officers on the radical right. The counter-revolution had indeed triumphed, but the officers had been forced to abandon the war they had waged in its name.[165]

According to Constantin Iordachi:

> Romanian authorities were successful in implementing a smooth demobilization, unlike in Italy, for example. It is true that you have fascist mobilization from 1927 on, and especially in 1932–1937, but in Romania the fascists did not engage in mass terror … It is often said that the Legion [the Iron Guard] gave more martyrs than it made victims.[166]

In Latvia, after a bloody reckoning between nationalist, Freikorps and Bolshevik forces in 1919, right-wing paramilitary organizations mushroomed during the 1920s, and in 1933, the fascist *Pērkonkrusts* ('Thunder Cross') was founded, which after 1941 – like the Ustasha in Croatia, the Arrow Cross in Hungary and the Iron Guard in Romania – actively participated in German programmes of ethnic cleansing. Except for a brief showdown with the paramilitary wing of the Social Democratic Party at the turn of 1924–25, Latvian interwar fascist paramilitaries have no record of killing their political or ethnic foes.[167] Bullying state measures of nationalization against minorities notwithstanding, the conflict between the minorities and the states from the early 1920s onwards was usually negotiated without bloodshed, either internally by way of mutual reluctant compromising, or on the international diplomatic circuit in form of petitions to the League of Nations.[168] At the risk of sounding cynical: if we tend to think of Central and Eastern Europe from the mid-1920s to the late 1930s as a hotspot of deadly interethnic violence, it should at least puzzle us that at that time, more people died in car accidents in Great Britain alone.[169]

Certainly, in areas further to the southeast, which do not form part of this concise overview, things looked different. The Greek-Albanian borderlands featured an unravellable mixture of 'brigandage, paramilitarism and nation-building' which took place from the turn of the century far into the post-First World War peace order. It originated in a symbiosis of the state and the different brigand gangs operating in the area, plus a strong antagonism between the local minority population and the state centre. Here, 'while violence was far from absent, it was also not extremely intense as no social group was strong enough to challenge the state. [The 1920s] can thus be characterized as a very low-key civil war during which new cleavages arose and old

---

165 Paul A. Hanebrink, *In Defense of Christian Hungary: Religion, Nationalism, and Antisemitism, 1890–1944* (Ithaca, NY: Cornell University Press, 2006), 83–9, here 89.
166 Email correspondence with Constantin Iordachi from 11 September 2017.
167 Matthew Kott, 'Latvia's Pērkonkrusts: Anti-German National Socialism in a Fascistogenic Milieu', *Fascism: Journal of Comparative Fascist Studies* 4 (2015): 169–93, here 178.
168 For the relation between the states and their minorities in interwar Central and Eastern Europe see also Motta, *Less than Nations*.
169 J. J. Leeming and G. M. Mackay, *Road Accidents: Prevent or Punish?* (London: Cassell, 1969), 22.

ones were intensified'[170]. It was more the new politics of the Venizelos government from 1931 onwards than the novel policing methods of the late 1920s which eased the strained relations with the country's minorities and finally pacified the area.[171]

It also has to be stressed that the impact of terrorist violence in Central and Eastern Europe was greater than that of interethnic violence, the peaks of which reached a broad European audience via newspaper and newsreel (the assassination of the Yugoslav king was the first one in history to be filmed); but terrorist violence in Central and Eastern Europe was by no means greater than in Western European countries like, for example, in Ireland, Germany and Spain, the latter of which witnessed a bloody civil war in the mid-1930s, from where Ernest Hemingway reported:

> [Our chauffeur] made you realize why Franco never took Madrid when he had the chance. Hipolito and the others like him would have fought from street to street and house to house as long as any one of them was left alive, and the last ones left would have burned the town.[172]

The authoritarian turn

As previously mentioned, democracy was generally accepted in Central and Eastern Europe at the start of peacetime, but it was generally replaced by authoritarian rule towards the end. In the years 1920/1921, 'universal, equal, and direct male suffrage was ... the rule. Female suffrage was by now equally on the agenda throughout the region ... In most states, new constitutions were passed that asserted parliamentary control of their respective governments'. However, 'the authoritarian challenge to constitutional government had not vanished'.[173] Beside the consequences of the war and the lack of political experience, two financial crises – hyperinflation immediately following the war, and the Great Depression of 1929 – further destabilized the political systems, accelerating their dissolution. These nexuses are obvious, and the related literature is ample.[174] What is often overlooked is that there were not only ruptures, but also continuities which facilitated the authoritarian turn. In Central and Eastern Europe after 1918, the old elites of the nobility and the army gained influence almost everywhere that parliamentary democracy was in crisis: both institutions had traditionally been in charge of political

---

170 Email correspondence with Spyros Tsoutsoumpis from 31 August 2017.
171 Spyros Tsoutsoumpis, 'Land of the Kapedani: Brigandage, Paramilitarism and Nation-Building in 20th Century Greece', *Balkan Studies* 51 (2016): 35–67; See also Spyros Tsoutsoumpis, '"Political Bandits": Nation-Building, Patronage and the Making of the Greek Deep State', *Balkanistica* 30, no. 1 (2017): 1–27.
172 Ernest Hemingway, 'Spanish Fatalism Typified by Driver', *New York Times*, 23 May 1937, http://www.nytimes.com/books/99/07/04/specials/hemingway-fatalism.html (accessed 10 Decmber 2021).
173 Joachim von Puttkamer, 'Collapse and Restoration: Politics and the Strains of War in Eastern Europe', in *Legacies of Violence: Eastern Europe's First World War*, eds Jochen Böhler, Wlodzimierz Borodziej and Joachim von Puttkamer (München: Oldenbourg, 2014), 9–23, here 20–1.
174 Dirk Berg-Schlosser and Jeremy Mitchell, eds, *Conditions of Democracy in Europe, 1919–39: Systematic Case-Studies* (Basingstoke: Macmillan, 2000); Oberländer et al., *Autoritäre Regime in Ostmittel- und Südosteuropa, 1919–1944*; Hans Lemberg, ed., *Ostmitteleuropa zwischen den beiden Weltkriegen (1918–1939): Stärke und Schwäche der neuen Staaten, nationale Minderheiten* (Marburg: Verl. Herder-Inst., 1997); with a bit too much emphasis on the economic perspective, Iván T. Berend, *Decades of Crisis: Central and Eastern Europe before World War II* (Berkeley, CA: University of California Press, 2001).

leadership and state security, but in their fundamental convictions they were surely no training grounds for staunch democrats.

The most obvious example is Hungary, where admiral Miklós Horthy, a descendant of the squirearchy from the Great Hungarian Plain with a long-standing record in the imperial navy, headed the conservative counter-government against Béla Kun's revolutionary Republic of Councils in 1919. Victorious, he became 'Regent' (i.e. head of state in a 'monarchy without a king') and led the country's fate almost until the end of the Second World War. Hungary thus skipped the phase of parliamentary democracy which all of its neighbouring countries went through.

Other countries later witnessed similar developments: in Poland, Józef Piłsudski and his followers, according to Joseph Rothschild, 'emerged from the war with a profound elitist self-awareness, a conviction that they alone had sired reborn, independent Poland'.[175] Indeed, Rothschild underlines that these *Legionnaires'* self-awareness not only stemmed from their shared war experience, but also from the fact that most of them came from nobility. After half a decade of crises, petty fights in parliament and constantly changing governments, it was these men who Piłsudski relied on when he seized power in a coup d'état in 1926. Whether part of the Polish interwar army or not, these veterans stood side by side and were the unchallenged political force until Piłsudski's death in 1935 and beyond in the now openly anti-democratic 'Colonels' Regime'.[176] Whereas prior to 1926, war veterans and paramilitaries had made up almost 10 per cent of the political elite of Poland, afterwards it was almost 60 per cent.[177] In Romania, 'preservation of the monopoly of power in the hands of the Romanian aristocracy and upper bourgeoisie, of the old Romanian military leaders and the Orthodox hierarchy precluded acceptance of diversity – social, political, ethnic or economic' from the very start.[178] In Bulgaria, the bloody abolition of Stamboliyski's agrarian government in 1923 and the incoming regime of Aleksandar Tsankov was largely backed by the military and the court. A little more than a decade later, in 1935, tsar Boris officially assumed governance.[179]

The military's influence on state affairs was felt most in Yugoslavia. King Alexander had managed to checkmate his military opponents in the first half of the 1920s, and he based his royal dictatorship (from 1929 onwards) on the army and the Serbian veterans. These veterans had served under his supreme command in the First World War, and during parliamentary democracy, 'continually railed against the failures of the state's political parties'. During the 1920s, the Association of Reserve Officers and Warriors held close ties with the army and the royal court. The attitude of the active army officers paralleled that of the veterans. Along with the growing disappointment in the democratic experiment amongst the country's military circles – the 'caste of warriors', as John Paul Newman calls them – came the bitter insight that glorious war victories and the celebration of a 'culture of victory' were not enough to secure such international support and internal stability as featured in the Czechoslovak case.[180]

---

175 Joseph Rothschild, 'Marshal Józef Piłsudski's Concept of State Vis-À-Vis Society in Interwar Poland', in *East Central European War Leaders: Civilian and Military*, eds Béla K. Király and Albert A. Nofi (Boulder, CO: Social Science Monographs, 1988), 290.
176 Ibid., 290; see also Mieczysław B. Biskupski, *Independence Day: Myth, Symbol, and the Creation of Modern Poland* (Oxford: Oxford University Press, 2012), 47.
177 Biskuspki, Independence Day, 47–8.
178 Stephen Fischer-Galati, 'Romania: Crisis without Compromise', in Berg-Schlosser and Mitchell, *Conditions of Democracy in Europe*, 381–95, here 381.
179 Crampton, *Bulgaria*, 236–56.
180 Newman, *Yugoslavia in the Shadow of War*, 53–81, here 60, reference to Czechoslovakia on 79.

Indeed, Czechoslovakia had also emerged from the trenches on the winning side but chose a different path. For nearly the entire interwar period, Tomáš Garrigue Masaryk, a civilian head of state – in a country without any residual gentry to speak of in 1918 – was generally respected by the state military, which might explain the unusual persistence and tranquillity of his reign.[181] The influence of the military circles was generally lessened by the widespread anti-militarist attitude of the population, so that from the 1930s onwards, the government advertised the army 'not as a tool of militarism, but as a democratic peacekeeper'.[182] Additionally, from the outset, the Masaryk government was able to count on the support of the most influential Czech veteran organizations.[183] What outlasted the war here – instead of military and noble cliques – was an imperial bureaucracy trained in administrative, political and legal affairs, all areas which the new constitution of 1920 deliberately left largely untouched.[184] This high level of personal, structural and legal continuity in genuine democratic spheres was probably the underlying reason for the Czechoslovak interwar success story. The most politically stable country in Central and Eastern Europe was the only one which tolerated the existence of a communist party.

Historians have recently cautioned against the lock, stock and barrel condemnation of the more authoritarian regimes (despite their bad reputations) in the Central and Eastern Europe of the late 1920s. Piotr Wróbel explains that in 1926, Piłsudski and his officers were strengthening 'antiliberal and antiparliamentarian trends', but that while doing so, they at least 'believed that they were defending democracy [by] stopp[ing] potential revolutions from the Left and the Right'.[185] The Hungarian government, writes Philip Longworth, 'was not democratic, but it gave Hungary political stability and allowed civil rights to be extended to a higher proportion of the population than in some neighbouring states'.[186] The newest and arguably most astonishing findings are related to Romania, a country notorious for its crude interwar mixture of fascism and religious fanaticism as embodied in the fascist movement of the 'Iron Guard'. General Alexandru Averescu, a charismatic Romanian Armed Forces Commander during the First World War who served three times as Prime Minister (1918, 1920–21 and 1926–27), approached the fascists in the second half of the 1920s and helped install the old monarchy under Prince Carol II in 1930. Nevertheless, his People's Party – supported mainly by war veterans and peasants – was instrumental in the country's demobilization and democratization process in the early 1920s, and the connection between military circles and radical paramilitaries was much looser and less developed as hitherto assumed.[187] Mark Levene subsumes the current trend in historiography by stating that the Central and Eastern European authoritarian regimes,

---

181 Bradley, John F. N, 'Czechoslovakia: External Crisis and Internal Compromise', in Berg-Schlosser and Mitchell, *Conditions of Democracy in Europe*, 85–105.
182 Zückert, 'National Concepts of Freedom', 334.
183 Kocourek, 'In the Spirit of Brotherhood, United We Remain!', 153–4.
184 Zückert, 'National Concepts of Freedom', 334.
185 Piotr Wróbel, 'The Rise and Fall of Parliamentary Democracy in Interwar Poland', in *The Origins of Modern Polish Democracy*, eds Mieczysław B. Biskupski, James S. Pula and Piotr J. Wróbel (Athens: Ohio University Press, 2010), 110–64, here 154.
186 Philip Longworth, *The Making of Eastern Europe* (New York: Saint Martin's Press, 1994), 77, referring also to Andrew C. Janos, *The Politics of Backwardness in Hungary, 1825–1945* (Princeton, NJ: Princeton University Press, 1982).
187 Constantin Iordachi and Blasco Sciarrino, 'War Veterans, Demobilization and Political Activism: Greater Romania in Comparison', *Fascism: Journal of Comparative Fascist Studies* 6, no. 1 (2017): 75–117.

paradoxically ... may actually have acted as a brake on more radical demotic violence against minority groups in these countries, Jews in particular. Dictatorship, thus, even where it clearly spelt internal coercion – and violence – cannot *in itself* be assumed to be more inherently genocidal than liberal democracy.[188]

Speaking of 'internal coercion', it is still impossible to determine how and to what extent state surveillance and persecution affected the everyday lives of the subjects of Central and Eastern European authoritarian regimes. The long-awaited independence after centuries of imperial rule, the horrors of the First World War and the even greater atrocities of the Second World War yet to come, including the ensuing communist rule Moscow installed in the lands between Germany and Russia for almost half a century – all of these factors led to an unreflected glorification of the interwar years in Central and Eastern Europe after 1989. There are almost no systematic, let alone comparative, studies which offer more insight into the subject, and thus future research is badly needed; especially in the light of the deluge of literature dedicated to related questions in the period of state socialism.[189]

The fundamental flaw of interwar Central and Eastern Europe was not so much the act, it was the idea. With the Russian Revolutions and the Central European counter-revolution, the fight for the souls and minds of the population in the lands spanning from Russia to Germany was unleashed, and its political and paramilitary organizations, as I have shown above, took part in the bloody civil war which superseded the First World War.[190] When the ideological battles between the political left and right emerged from the trenches, they were fought out on the streets of interwar Europe, though predominantly outside our region, in Germany, Italy, France and Spain.[191] However, this did not make Central and Eastern Europe immune to the paramilitary fever. Even Czechoslovakia, which is generally treated as the model country for the peaceful transition from war to peace, had its own armada of antagonizing left-wing and right-wing organizations.[192] In the meantime, parliamentary democracy as a new political experiment rooted not in green acres but in blood-red battlefields, lacking credibility and facing crisis from the very start. This was not only the case for the general public, but it was also the case for the elites: 'With its ideological, political and industrial aspects', Erwin Kessler notes of interwar Romania,

> the war had thrown a shadow of distrust over the groundwork of the occidental democracy, on its humanitarian stance, but also on the scientific ideal of the positive modern science, the constant progress to the benefit of humanity. The result ... was an unabashed scepticism and an inclination to forget liberal and democratic individualism in favour of various formulae of collectivism.[193]

What we witness then from the end of the First to the beginning of the Second World War is a permanent radicalization of politics and the growing impact of paramilitary – largely

---

188 Levene, *Devastation*, 243.
189 See Chapter 5, 'State Socialism' in the present volume.
190 Robert Gerwarth, 'Fighting the Red Beast'.
191 Stanley G. Payne, *Civil War in Europe, 1905–1949* (New York: Cambridge University Press, 2011), 96–114. For Germany see Dirk Schumann, *Political Violence in the Weimar Republic, 1918–1933: Battle for the Streets and Fears of Civil War* (New York: Berghahn Books, 2009).
192 Ivo Pejčoch, *Armády českých politiků: české polovojenské jednotky 1918–1945* [Armies of Czech politicians: Czech paramilitary units, 1918–1945] (Cheb: Svět Křídel, 2009).
193 Erwin Kessler, 'Ideas And Ideology In Interwar Romania', *Plural* 29, no. 1 (2007): 7–21, here 15.

right-wing – organizations all over the region. These organizations were all formed as a reaction to the peace settlement which frustrated their hopes – first and foremost – for ethno-nationalist domination and fairer distribution of land; furthermore, what they all had in common was an anti-intellectualist, anti-capitalist and anti-Semitic sentiment.

The parliamentary and financial crises of the early 1920s and 1930s exacerbated the political, social and economic tensions and further filled the ranks of paramilitary organizations which promised a glorious and transcendent future.[194] According to Aristotle Kallis, one of the leading pioneers of the theory of generic fascism, 'political religion' charted 'convincingly a different path out of perceived decay, degeneration, and collapse towards rebirth, regeneration, and salvation'. Although, as we have seen, the destruction of the ethnic or political enemy was not the order of the day, in the troubled interwar era, there was a direct line which led from ethnic nationalism to the practical exclusion and the potential elimination of the perceived 'other' in pursuit of the racially defined 'ideal nation state'.[195] This involved the active participation of intellectuals, the churches and the press, and was sometimes more radical in the provinces than in the capitals.[196] As the examples of Italy and Germany – which always serve as a point of reference for the fascist movements further to the east – show, this was no characteristic Central and Eastern European development, but a result of the global crisis of economy, democracy and liberalism in the interwar period. Like in Germany and Italy, the right-wing organizations' martial demeanour, vociferous slogans, their bullying and intimidating perceived enemies and their readiness to engage in paramilitary violence (although with few casualties) provided an atmosphere of insecurity and thus further destabilized the Central and Eastern European states' fragile architecture to such a degree that the few remaining left-wing paramilitary organizations never reached.[197] With the exception of Czechoslovakia, communist parties were banned all over Central and Eastern Europe. However, since the proto-fascist militias did not form part of any government either, nowhere were their radical views translated par for par into state policy. The authoritarian turn of the late 1920s paved the way towards the radicalization of interwar politics in the region, but simultaneously took the wind out of the fascist vessel's sails.[198]

Picket fences

This chapter began with general contemplations as to why a Central and Eastern European confederation of states failed in the interwar period. I will now conclude this chapter with a brief overview of how, in practice, interstate and intrastate tensions poisoned the atmosphere

---

194 John R. Lampe and Mark Mazower, eds, *Ideologies and National Identities: The Case of Twentieth-Century Southeastern Europe* (Budapest: CEU Press, 2004).
195 Aristotle Kallis, *Genocide and Fascism: The Eliminationist Drive in Fascist Europe* (London: Routledge, 2009), 3.
196 Ionuț Biliuță, 'Sowing the Seeds of Hate: The Antisemitism of the Romanian Orthodox Church in the Interwar Period', *S.I.M.O.N. - Shoah: Intervention, Methods, Documentation* 3, no. 1 (2016): 20–34; Viktoria Pollmann, *Untermieter im christlichen Haus: Die Kirche und die 'jüdische Frage' in Polen anhand der Bistumspresse der Metropolie Krakau 1926–1939* (Wiesbaden: Harrassowitz, 2001); Adriana Sorescu, 'The Watchdog of Nationalism: The Romanian Press in Interwar Transylvania and its Role in the Creation of National Identity', MA Thesis, Carleton University, 2015.
197 For the symbolic meaning of interwar anti-Semitic violence in the Romanian case, see Radu H. Dinu, 'Antisemitismus als soziale Praxis: Gewalt gegen Juden in der Rumänischen Zwischenkriegszeit', in *Inszenierte Gegenmacht von rechts: Die 'Legion Erzengel Michael' in Rumänien 1918–1938*, eds Armin Heinen and Oliver J. Schmitt (München: Oldenbourg, 2013), 113–29.
198 Ian Kershaw, *To Hell and Back: Europe, 1914–1949* (London: Penguin Books, 2016), 241–6.

and led to disruption instead of unity – a story told so often that a few sentences might suffice to sum it up: the Central European Civil War and the new frontiers drawn through the middle of the continent turned neighbours into enemies and rivals. Hungary never overcame the shocking loss of both territory and people (largely) to Romania, Czechoslovakia and Yugoslavia as a result of the Treaty of Trianon (1920). For their part, the trio formed the 'Little Entente', partly to nip Hungarian revisionism in the bud but they were, however, divided on numerous economic and political matters. Due to disputed border regions, Poland was at odds with Czechoslovakia and Lithuania. Economically speaking, in the wake of the Great Depression, the sea was getting rougher and rougher, and no common ground could be found.

The only foreign power which was willing to match the expectations of the Central and Eastern European states was, for geopolitical reasons, a Germany that was gaining strength with Hitler's rise to power. In the course of the 1930s, Central and Eastern Europe (with the exception of Poland which was proudly holding on to its independence) came more and more under German control. Half-hearted French attempts to stem the tide were as fruitless as the British policy of appeasement, both rather an expression of disinterest than interest in the region, which without international support, was doomed: in 1938–39, Hitler smashed Czechoslovakia, simultaneously dealing a death blow to the 'Little Entente'.[199] By that time, the Baltic States, Poland, Hungary, Czechoslovakia, Romania, Yugoslavia and Bulgaria had 1 million soldiers under arms all together; Nazi Germany had 3 million, and the Soviet Union had nearly 6 million, which is not to speak of the technical superiority of both superpowers' armies.[200] That is to say, the lands between did not stand a chance. With the Hitler–Stalin Pact of 1939, the two totalitarian dictators sealed the fate of Central and Eastern Europe, drawing it into the abyss of another world war. This new confrontation deepened the fissures that crossed the region: while up to the summer of 1941 the Czech parts of Czechoslovakia, Poland, the Baltic States and the Serbian part of Yugoslavia fell prey to the German war of conquest, Hungary, Bulgaria and Romania joined the Axis, and Slovakia and Croatia emerged as German puppet states.[201]

Conclusion

To return to the question raised at the outset of this chapter: was the era of the World Wars rather a new 'Thirty Years War' or a 'European Civil War'? From the perspective of interwar Central and Eastern Europe the answer is no. This erroneous notion was mainly influenced by the birth of the two totalitarian ideologies – fascism and bolshevism – out of the revolutionary end-quarrels of the First World War. In the course of the 1920s and 1930s, they materialized as two powerful totalitarian states neighbouring the region under scrutiny here and directed their destructive powers against their own population. With the outbreak of the Second World War, they imported their particular forms of state violence into the states that had emerged between them. And shortly after, they directed their destructive powers against each other.

---

199 Chioveanu, 'A Fragmented World'; Hugh Seton-Watson, *The Sick Heart of Modern Europe: The Problem of the Danubian Lands* (Seattle, WA: University of Washington Press, 1975).
200 Andrzej Rzepniewski, 'Siły zbrojne średnich i małych państw wchodnioeuropejskich 1921–1941' [The armed forces of medium and small Eastern European states, 1921–1941], in *Międzymorze: Polska i kraje Europy Środkowo-Wschodniej; XIX–XX wiek*, ed. Andrzej Ajnenkiel (Warsaw: IH PAN, 1995), 265–74, here 274.
201 See Chapter 4, 'Mass violence and its immediate aftermath in Central and Eastern Europe during the Second World War, 1939–47' in the present volume.

The fact that Central and Eastern Europe twice became the theatre of eschatological battles over the course of three decades, has led to the common assertion that there was a continuum of violence from 1914 (or rather, if we include the Balkan Wars, from 1912) to 1945. Yet, during peacetime, the region had relatively little to do with the totalitarian surge washing its shores. Immediately following the First World War, the region's states were – first and foremost – struggling with material hardships and with establishing functioning institutions. As we have seen, nearly all of them turned towards certain forms of authoritarian, not totalitarian, rule in the 1930s. Paramilitary right- and (to a lesser degree) left-wing organizations, along the lines of the German, Italian and/or Russian models, appeared all over the place, but nowhere were they a part of the ruling elites. To be sure, the democratic edifice of Central and Eastern Europe between Germany and Russia never really solidified before it crumbled on the eve of the Second World War; and after 1939, Romania, Hungary and Bulgaria sided with the Nazis – a story which will be told in the following chapter. But between the wars, the region dozed in doldrums only disturbed by minor disturbances and was thus absolutely not prepared for the storm which devastated it between 1938–39 and 1945. The preceding two decades of relative tranquillity are incommensurable to the presumed continuum of violence which the notions of a 'Thirty Years' War' or a 'European Civil War' – terms which, by the way, have been coined by Western intellectuals – insinuate.

If that is the case, why bother writing a whole chapter on the 1920s and 1930s in a volume devoted to violence in the region? First of all, as I have shown, the very formation of its state systems in the wake of the First World War did indeed include a short but intense period of civil war, which, until recently, has been almost completely ignored by historians, and was therefore treated comprehensively in Part I of this chapter. And although from 1923 onwards, no further war, civil war, revolution or wave of mass persecution and mass destruction hit the region for almost two decades (as Part II of this chapter has shown) violence did not just ebb away. The experience of military and paramilitary violence of the previous decade had an enormous impact on the region and influenced the political culture, the domestic developments and foreign relations of the Central and Eastern European states even in peacetime. Tension was indeed high in the region. Although prior to 1938–39 there was no major outbreak of violence, the potential for it was ever-present and always retrievable – the vehemence with which the ethnic conflicts were fought in the shadow of the imperial assault of 1939–1945 bears ample witness.

Further reading

Bartov, Omer, and Eric D. Weitz, eds. *Shatterzone of Empires: Coexistence and Violence in the German, Habsburg, Russian, and Ottoman Borderlands* (Bloomington, IN: Indiana University Press, 2013).

Bauerkämper, Arnd and Grzegorz Rossoliński-Liebe, eds. *Fascism Without Borders: Transnational Connections and Cooperation Between Movements and Regimes in Europe from 1918 to 1945* (New York: Berghahn, 2017).

Berend, Iván T. *Decades of Crisis: Central and Eastern Europe before World War II* (Berkeley, CA: University of California Press, 2001).

Berger, Stefan, and Alexei Miller, eds. *Nationalizing Empires* (Budapest: Central European University Press, 2015).

Berg-Schlosser, Dirk and Jeremy Mitchell, eds. *Conditions of Democracy in Europe, 1919–39: Systematic Case-Studies* (Basingstoke: Macmillan, 2000).

Biskupski, Mieczysław B., ed. *Ideology, Politics and Diplomacy in East Central Europe* (Rochester, NY: University of Rochester Press, 2003).

Bloxham, Donald, and Robert Gerwarth, eds. *Political Violence in Twentieth-Century Europe* (Cambridge: Cambridge University Press, 2011).

Bodó, Béla. *The White Terror: Antisemitic and Political Violence in Hungary, 1919–1921* (London: Routledge, 2019).
Böhler, Jochen. *Civil War in Central Europe, 1918–1921: The Reconstruction of Poland* (Oxford: Oxford University Press, 2018).
Böhler, Jochen, Włodzimierz Borodziej, and Joachim von Puttkamer, eds. *Legacies of Violence: Eastern Europe's First World War* (München: Oldenbourg, 2014).
Böhler, Jochen, Ota Konrád, and Rudolf Kučera, eds. *In the Shadow of the Great War: Physical Violence in East-Central Europe, 1917–1923* (New York: Berghahn, 2020).
Borzęcki, Jerzy. *The Soviet-Polish Peace of 1921 and the Creation of Interwar Europe* (New Haven, CT: Yale University Press, 2008).
Brown, Kate, *A Biography of No Place: From Ethnic Borderlands to Soviet Heartland* (Cambridge, MA: Harvard University Press, 2003).
Brubaker, Rogers, ed. *Nationalism Reframed: Nationhood and the National Question in the New Europe* (Cambridge: Cambridge University Press, 1996).
Brykczynski, Paul. *Primed for Violence: Murder, Antisemitism, and Democratic Politics in Interwar Poland* (Madison, WI: The University of Wisconsin Press, 2016).
Chernev, Borislav. *Twilight of Empire: The Brest-Litovsk Conference and the Remaking of East-Central Europe, 1917–1918* (Toronto: University of Toronto Press, 2017).
Chu, Winson. *The German Minority in Interwar Poland* (Cambridge: Cambridge University Press, 2012).
Ciancia, Kathryn. *On Civilization's Edge: A Polish Borderland in the Interwar World* (New York: Oxford University Press, 2020).
Clark, Roland. *Holy Legionary Youth: Fascist Activism in Interwar Romania* (Ithaca, NY: Cornell University Press, 2015).
Cornwall, Mark and John P. Newman, eds. *Sacrifice and Rebirth: The Legacy of the Last Habsburg War* (New York: Berghahn Books, 2016).
Diner, Dan. *Cataclysms: A History of the Twentieth Century from Europe's Edge* (Madison, WI: University of Wisconsin Press, 2008).
Djokić, Dejan, *Elusive Compromise: A History of Interwar Yugoslavia* (London: Hurst, 2007).
Doumanis, Nicholas, ed. *The Oxford Handbook of European History, 1914–1945* (Oxford: Oxford University Press, 2016).
Fink, Carole. *Defending the Rights of Others: The Great Powers, the Jews, and International Minority Protection, 1878–1938* (Cambridge: Cambridge University Press, 2004).
Gerwarth, Robert, ed. *Twisted Paths: Europe 1914–1945* (Oxford: Oxford University Press, 2007).
Gerwarth, Robert, and John Horne, eds. *War in Peace: Paramilitary Violence in Europe After the Great War* (Oxford: Oxford University Press, 2012).
Gerwarth, Robert, *The Vanquished: Why the First World War Failed to End, 1917–1923* (London: Allen Lane, 2016).
Gingeras, Ryan. *Sorrowful Shores: Violence, Ethnicity, and the End of the Ottoman Empire, 1912–1923* (Oxford: Oxford University Press, 2009).
Hagen, William W. *Anti-Jewish Violence in Poland, 1914–1920* (Cambridge, MA: Cambridge University Press, 2018).
Hanebrink, Paul. *In Defense of Christian Hungary: Religion, Nationalism, and Antisemitism, 1890–1944* (Ithaca, NY: Cornell University Press, 2006).
Hanebrink, Paul, *A Specter Haunting Europe: The Myth of Judeo-Bolshevism* (Cambridge, MA: Harvard University Press, 2018).
Heimann, Mary. *Czechoslovakia: The State that Failed* (New Haven, CT: Yale University Press, 2011).
Horne, John, ed. *A Companion to World War I* (Chichester: Wiley-Blackwell, 2010).
Jones, Mark. *Founding Weimar: Violence and the German Revolution of 1918–1919* (Cambridge: Cambridge University Press, 2016).
Juszkiewicz, Piotr, Burkhard Olschowsky, Jan Rydel, and Tobias Weger, eds. *Central and Eastern Europe after the First World War* (Berlin: De Gruyter, 2021).
Kalyvas, Stathis N. *The Logic of Violence in Civil War* (Cambridge: Cambridge University Press, 2006).
Kasekamp, Andres. *The Radical Right in Interwar Estonia* (New York: St. Martin's Press, 2000).
Kasekamp, Andres. *A History of the Baltic States*, 2nd ed. (Basingstoke: Palgrave Macmillan, 2018).
Kershaw, Ian. *To Hell and Back: Europe, 1914–1949* (London: Penguin Books, 2016).
Klier, John D., and Shlomo Lambroza, eds. *Pogroms: Anti-Jewish Violence in Modern Russian History* (Cambridge: Cambridge University Press, 2004).

Levene, Mark. *The Rise of the West and the Coming of Genocide* (London: I.B. Tauris, 2005).
Levene, Mark. *Devastation: The European Rimlands 1912–1938* (Oxford: Oxford University Press, 2013).
Levene, Mark. *Annihilation: The European Rimlands 1939–1953* (Oxford: Oxford University Press, 2013).
Longworth, Philip. *The Making of Eastern Europe* (New York: Saint Martin's Press, 1994).
MacMillan, Margaret. *Paris 1919: Six Months that Changed the World* (New York: Random House, 2003).
Mann, Michael. *The Dark Side of Democracy: Explaining Ethnic Cleansing* (Cambridge: Cambridge University Press, 2005).
Mayer, Arno J. *The Furies: Violence and Terror in the French and Russian Revolutions* (Princeton, NJ: Princeton University Press, 2000).
Mazower, Mark. *Dark Continent: Europe's Twentieth Century* (New York: Penguin Books, 1999).
Mazower, Mark. *No Enchanted Palace: The End of Empire and the Ideological Origins of the United Nations* (Princeton, NJ: Princeton University Press, 2009).
Mitrović, Andrej. *Serbia's Great War, 1914–1918* (London: Hurst, 2007).
Moffat, Ian. *The Allied Intervention in Russia, 1918–1920: The Diplomacy of Chaos* (Basingstoke: Palgrave Macmillan, 2015).
Motta, Giuseppe. *Less than Nations: Central-Eastern European Minorities after WWI* (Newcastle Upon Tyne: Cambridge Scholars Publishing, 2014).
Naimark, Norman M. *Fires of Hatred: Ethnic Cleansing in Twentieth-Century Europe* (Cambridge, MA: Harvard University Press, 2001).
Newman, John P. *Yugoslavia in the Shadow of War: Veterans and the Limits of State Building, 1903–1945* (Cambridge: Cambridge University Press, 2015).
Orzoff, Andrea. *Battle for the Castle: The Myth of Czechoslovakia in Europe, 1914–1948* (Oxford: Oxford University Press, 2009).
Panayi, Panikos, ed. *Minorities in Wartime: National and Racial Groupings in Europe, North America, and Australia During the Two World Wars* (Oxford: Berg, 1993).
Payne, Stanley G. *Civil War in Europe, 1905–1949* (New York: Cambridge University Press, 2011).
Piahanau, Aliaksandr, and Bojan Aleksov, eds. *Wars and Betweenness: Big Powers and Middle Europe, 1918–1945* (Budapest: Central European University Press, 2020).
Plakans, Andrejs. *A Concise History of the Baltic States* (Cambridge, Cambridge University Press, 2011).
Polonsky, Antony. *The Jews in Poland and Russia: 1914–2008* (Oxford: The Littman Library of Jewish Civilization, 2012).
Prusin, Alexander V. *Nationalizing a Borderland: War, Ethnicity, and Anti-Jewish Violence in East Galicia, 1914–1920* (Tuscaloosa, AL: University of Alabama Press, 2005).
Prusin, Alexander V. *The Lands Between: Conflict in the East European Borderlands, 1870–1992* (Oxford: Oxford University Press, 2010).
Radkey, Oliver H. *The Unknown Civil War in Soviet Russia: A Study of the Green Movement in the Tambov Region, 1920–1921* (Stanford, CA: Hoover Institution Press, Stanford University, 1976).
Read, Christopher. *War and Revolution in Russia, 1914–22: The Collapse of Tsarism and the Establishment of Soviet Power* (Basingstoke: Palgrave Macmillan, 2013).
Reill, Dominique Kirchner. *The Fiume Crisis: Life in the Wake of the Habsburg Empire* (Cambridge, MA: Harvard University Press, 2020).
Retish, Aaron B. *Russia's Peasants in Revolution and Civil War: Citizenship, Identity, and the Creation of the Soviet State, 1914–1922* (Cambridge: Cambridge University Press, 2008).
Richter, Klaus. *Fragmentation in East Central Europe: Poland and the Baltics, 1915–1929* (Oxford: Oxford University Press, 2020).
Roshwald, Aviel. *Ethnic Nationalism and the Fall of Empires: Central Europe, the Middle East and Russia* (London: Routledge, 2001).
Rothschild, Joseph. *East Central Europe Between the Two World Wars* (Seattle, WA: University of Washington Press, 1992).
Sanborn, Joshua A. *Imperial Apocalypse: The Great War and the Destruction of the Russian Empire* (Oxford: Oxford University Press, 2014).
Schnell, Felix. *Räume des Schreckens: Gewalträume und Gruppenmilitanz in der Ukraine, 1905–1933* (Hamburg: Hamburger Edition, 2012).
Schumann, Dirk. *Political Violence in the Weimar Republic, 1918–1933: Battle for the Streets and Fears of Civil War* (New York: Berghahn Books, 2009).
Segal, Raz. *Genocide in the Carpathians: War, Social Breakdown, and Mass Violence, 1914–1945* (Palo Alto, CA: Stanford University Press, 2016).

Smele, Jonathan D. *The 'Russian' Civil Wars 1916–1926: Ten Years that Shook the World* (Oxford: Oxford University Press, 2015).

Smith, David J., Artis, Pabriks, Thomas Lane, and Aldis Purs, eds. *The Baltic States: Estonia, Latvia and Lithuania* (London: Routledge, 2002).

Snyder, Timothy, *The Reconstruction of Nations: Poland, Ukraine, Lithuania, Belarus, 1569–1999* (New Haven, CT: Yale University Press, 2003).

Steiner, Zara S. *The Lights that Failed: European International History, 1919–1933* (Oxford: Oxford University Press, 2005).

Steiner, Zara. *The Triumph of the Dark: European International History, 1933–1939* (Oxford: Oxford University Press, 2011).

Tasić, Dmitar. *Paramilitarism in the Balkans: The Cases of Yugoslavia, Bulgaria, and Albania, 1917–1924* (Oxford: University Press, 2020).

Tooze, Adam. *The Deluge: The Great War and the Remaking of Global Order 1916–1931* (London: Lane, 2014).

Traverso, Enzo. *Fire and Blood: The European Civil War, 1914–1945* (London: Verso, 2017).

Vago, Bela. *The Shadow of the Swastika: The Rise of Fascism and Anti-Semitism in the Danube Basin, 1936–1939* (Farnborough: Saxon House for the Institute of Jewish Affairs, 1975).

Veidlinger, Jeffrey. *In the Midst of Civilized Europe: The Pogroms of 1918–1921 and the Onset of the Holocaust* (New York: Metropolitan Books, 2021).

Watt, Richard M. *Bitter Glory: Poland and its Fate, 1918 to 1939* (New York: Hippocrene Books, 1998).

Wilson, Tim. *Frontiers of Violence: Conflict and Identity in Ulster and Upper Silesia 1918–1922* (Oxford: Oxford University Press, 2010).

Wynot, Edward D. *Caldron of Conflict: Eastern Europe, 1918–1945* (Wheeling, IL: Harlan Davidson, 1999).

4
MASS VIOLENCE AND ITS IMMEDIATE AFTERMATH IN CENTRAL AND EASTERN EUROPE DURING THE SECOND WORLD WAR, 1939–47

Alexander Korb and Dieter Pohl

Introduction

When discussing the violence that took place during the Second World War in Europe, the Central and Eastern parts of the continent play a particular role for several reasons: first and foremost, both regions were major sites of extra-military violence. Between six and seven million civilians were killed in the region stretching from the Baltic states in the north, Czechoslovakia and Poland in their pre-1938–39 borders in the centre, and – in the south-east – Hungary, Romania and Bulgaria, as well as Yugoslavia, Albania and Greece.[1] Approximately 15 million civilians were deported during the war and in the immediate post-war period. Millions were confined in prisons and camps; large, forced labour programmes were enacted that affected millions. The vast majority of all the victims of the Nazi Regime were Central and Eastern Europeans, and more were transported there from other parts of Europe. Central and Eastern Europe were the sites of some of the heaviest fighting during the Second World War: some regions were conquered and re-conquered up to three times. Every offensive brought destruction, immense suffering and violence against civilians. Moreover, deadly civil wars were fought in the region during the war and its aftermath.

---

1 Of these, there were 4.2 million Jews, approximately 1.2 million non-Jewish Polish citizens, 600,000 Yugoslav citizens, 300,000 inhabitants of the Baltic states, 40–50,000 Czechoslovak citizens, roughly 10 thousand Greek and Romanian citizens, and a number of Bulgarian and Albanian citizens. Due to the thematic composition of *The Routledge History Handbook of Central and Eastern Europe in the Twentieth Century*, of which this volume is a part, this chapter concentrates specifically on the regions from the Baltic North, Poland and Czechoslovakia, to Southeastern Europe. The tremendous loss of millions of civilian lives in the pre-war territories of Ukraine and Belarus are not included.

Central and Eastern Europe were very heterogeneous in terms of their ethno-religious structure, which was partly due to the heritage of the Romanov, the Habsburg and the Ottoman Empires. Both the German and Soviet occupiers, along with local nationalist movements tried to destroy that heterogeneity during the war, to unravel ethnic groups, to relocate minorities and to form ethnically homogeneous and compact territories. Central and Eastern Europe were the cradle of Jewish life in Europe and also home to the Romani. Both groups, including their respective cultures, were, by and large, eradicated by the Germans and their local partners. In the lands between the German *Reich* and Soviet Russia, the Germans and their local collaborators murdered approximately 4.2 million Central and Eastern European Jews (out of the overall 5.6–5.8 million victims of the Holocaust). The 1 million-plus Jews from the Soviet Union that were murdered east of our region are not included in this figure; 400,000 Western and Southern European Jews were deported to occupied Poland to be killed in the German extermination facilities. Locally, other minorities – such as Serbs in Croatia and Bosnia, Poles in Western Ukraine (i.e. the historic regions of Volhynia and Eastern Galicia), but also majority populations like the Slovenes in Northern Yugoslavia – were targeted either by the Germans or by local nationalist movements. Moreover, Central and Eastern Europe constitute the part of Europe where Nazi Germany and the Soviet Union interacted most aggressively.[2] It was in this part of the region that the German and the Soviet armies encountered each other. The first encounter in 1939 was peaceful; and then in 1941 and again in 1944–45, the encounters turned into a total and existential war from which the line between military violence and mass violence against non-combatants is not easy to draw. Hundreds of thousands of Soviet POWs (prisoners of war) died in camps within occupied Poland alone; and partisan warfare in Poland, Lithuania, Slovakia, Yugoslavia, Greece and Albania was fought until the end of the war, and literally everyone who lived in these partisan areas was involved in the fight. Finally, the Central and Eastern European regions were under Germany's grasp for up to six years, and the utopian goals of the German occupation policies were implemented much stronger there than in other regions, especially with regard to genocidal population policies.

In contrast, Southeastern Europe presents a different picture of German occupation, a picture that looks much more indecisive and weaker than in Eastern Europe (but by no means less brutal). In Southeastern Europe, non-German regimes and independent or semi-independent governments played a more important role, as well as Germany's most significant ally (and imperial rival): fascist Italy. In every region, especially those under German occupation, violence affected a large part of the population. Approximately 100 million inhabitants lived in Central and Eastern Europe in 1939, and at least 15 per cent of them were either killed, deported or imprisoned between 1939 and 1945.

Another important aspect of wartime violence is forced labour: German occupation authorities deported millions of people for forced labour into Nazi Germany where they had to work under miserable conditions. Forced labour was also organized within occupied territory, for Jews and criminalized groups in ghettos and camps; Axis states like Hungary, Romania and Bulgaria installed labour service units for minorities. From 1944 on, Soviet authorities deported inhabitants of Central and Eastern Europe for forced labour to the Soviet Union, and the new regimes set up labour camps early on.[3]

During the last seven decades historiography has, by and large, reconstructed the extermination policies and the crimes themselves, identified perpetrators and victims. Traditionally, by

---

2 Timothy Snyder, *Bloodlands: Europe between Hitler and Stalin* (New York: Basic Books, 2010).
3 See the volume *Statehood* in this series.

Map 4.1 Central and Eastern Europe, 1941–42

focussing on the Jewish victims, many historians have treated the Holocaust in isolation. The same applies for the fewer studies on non-Jewish victims. There are numerous publications with national, regional or local foci; but there is a lack of studies with a transnational and comparative perspective. Only the past few years have seen Eastern European societies in a broader sense, their involvement, experiences and discourses relating to violence come into focus.[4] And

---

4 See for example Alexander V. Prusin, *The Lands Between: Conflict in the East European Borderlands, 1870–1992* (Oxford: Oxford University Press, 2010); Snyder, *Bloodlands*; Mark Levene, *Annihilation: The European Rimlands 1939–1953*, vol. 2, *Crisis of Genocide* (Oxford: Oxford University Press, 2013); for Southeastern Europe, see Mark Biondich, *The Balkans: Revolution, War, and Political Violence since 1878*, vol. 3, *Zones of Violence* (Oxford: Oxford University Press, 2011); Arnold Suppan, *Hitler – Beneš – Tito* (Wien: Verlag der Österreichischen Akademie der

Mass violence and its immediate aftermath

Map 4.2 Southeastern Europe, 1941

research has only started to apply a general perspective on all features of violence in Central and Eastern Europe, not exclusively German, but also enacted by other Axis countries, by local militias or by local communities. The spectre has also been broadened with the attempt to combine the histories of Nazism and Stalinism, not only by integrating the Holocaust into Eastern European history, but also by looking at how the Soviet and the German approaches

Wissenschaften, 2013), abridged translation: *Hitler–Beneš–Tito: National Conflicts, World Wars, Genocides, Expulsions, and Divided Remembrance in East-Central and Southeastern Europe, 1848–2018* (Vienna: Austrian Academy of Sciences Press, 2019).

to Central Europe were intertwined, and how they influenced each other.[5] In that respect it became essential to also take into account the violence committed by the Soviet Union, be it the brutal Soviet occupation of annexed territories in 1939–41, the actions of the Soviet partisans during the war, or the violence enacted by the Red Army and the NKVD (People's Commissariat for Internal Affairs) towards the end of the war and the subsequent occupation regimes with their often ruthless policies.

This chapter aims to integrate all major forms of extra-military violence in Central and Eastern Europe between September 1939 and late 1947 into one account, when the last waves of post-war violence, civil wars, Soviet policing campaigns and mass expulsions came to an end (with the exception of Greece, where the civil war ended in 1949), and when the onset of the Cold War changed the geopolitical setting in Europe. In the first part, we analyze the Nazi ideological perspective and the German imperial setting, which set the framework for mass violence in Eastern Europe and the Balkans. The second and main part deals comparatively with the German and the indigenous policies of violence in Eastern Europe and the Balkans, with emphasis on the Holocaust. Stalinist approaches to Eastern Europe are the subject of part three, with Stalinist violence being less connected with German mass crimes between 1939 and 1941 but becoming more interrelated in 1944–45. The fourth part of this chapter takes a closer look at the societies under occupation, and the mechanics of the forms of violence described before, with a focus on ethnic cleansing and civil war. It examines the campaigns of mass violence directed by Nazi Germany, looks at its non-German allies in Southeastern Europe and also considers Soviet policies. Finally, in the chapter's fifth and sixth parts, we examine cases of early post-war violence such as the expulsions of (predominately German-speaking) ethnic minorities, pogroms against Jews, forms of violent 'revenge', civil war patterns and repression during the early communist takeover.

By simultaneously taking into account the affected societies in Central and Eastern Europe, this chapter paints a broad picture of the macro-region between the Baltic and the Black Seas. It looks at both regional and national actors that operated within these countries, many of which had violent agendas of their own. This contribution is guided by the following questions: why was German, and in relation to that Soviet rule in Central and Eastern Europe so violent? What were the levels and forms of mass violence in Eastern and Southeastern Europe, and how can one map it? To what extent did the wartime history in Southeastern Europe differ from the situation in Central Europe? To what extent were the societies in these countries affected by mass violence, and what societal processes were caused by war and occupation? And finally, how did violence ebb away when the Second World War came to an end?

Before we address these crucial questions, we'd like to do away with the widespread prejudice (especially seen in the West) that prior to the Second World War, Eastern and Southeastern European societies were more infested with violence than societies in Western Europe, thus significantly facilitating the German occupants' ensuing violent rule. Indeed, Central and Eastern Europe had experienced a variety of internal and international conflicts before 1939. It is a complicated task to assess the degree of violence prior to 1939, and its impact on mass violence during the war years. But it is clear that there is no causal link: in

---

5 Mark Mazower, *Dark Continent: Europe's Twentieth Century* (New York: Penguin Books, 1999); Dietrich Beyrau, *Schlachtfeld der Diktatoren: Osteuropa im Schatten von Hitler und Stalin* (Göttingen: Vandenhoeck & Ruprecht, 2000); Jörg Baberowski, Anselm Doering-Manteuffel, *Ordnung durch Terror: Gewaltexzesse und Vernichtung im nationalsozialistischen und im stalinistischen Imperium* (Bonn: Dietz, 2006); Snyder, *Bloodlands*; Levene, *Annihilation*; Keith Lowe, *Savage Continent: Europe in the Aftermath of World War II* (New York: Picador, 2013).

some regions, armed groups reignited older conflicts that dated back to the Balkan Wars, the First World War or the Russian Civil War. Other regions had been, up to that point, spared of violent outbreaks. Overall, Poland, Yugoslavia, Czechoslovakia were, by and large, functioning states where the level of everyday violence was not remarkably higher than, say, in Germany or Italy prior to 1933–39. Romania might be seen as the exception to the rule, as the Romanian fascists brought a higher level of violence into the country. What is clear is that after 1939, German, Italian, Hungarian, Bulgarian and Soviet occupiers fuelled pre-existing conflicts and successfully exploited them. Often, these external factors were key and lead to the outbreak of local conflicts or even civil wars. More often than not, the occupiers would lose control over the conflicts they sparked.

Despite authoritarian suppression and nationalist terror in the 1930s, Central and Eastern Europe were not considerably more violent than other parts of Europe in the aftermath of the First World War.[6] Therefore, it was by no means 'a given' that the region would become a site of mass death and that violence would escalate in the 1940s. Major sites of repression and violence could be found elsewhere in Europe, in the Soviet Union, in Nazi Germany, in the European colonies, and from 1936 onwards, in Spain. What was specific for the East was its political drift towards authoritarian rule in combination with its ethnic heterogeneity, including societal political rifts and ethno-religious divisions, the culture of revisionism and the lack of democratic forces capable of countering the attacks on culture and humanity. But these deficits notwithstanding, it is important to note that violence in the region escalated during the Second World War because the region became the target of extreme and imperialist approaches by Germany and the Axis states on the one hand and by the Soviet Union on the other.

The German imperial perspective

There can be no doubt that the major factor for violence in Central and Eastern Europe during and immediately after the war was the practical application of Germany's polices of expansion, occupation and genocide. The majority of mass atrocity crimes arose either from Germany's extermination policies or from their methods of repressing both real and alleged resistance. Not only that, Germany's occupation in the East sparked criminal collaboration and fuelled local conflicts and civil wars; moreover, it was a major precondition for the violence against German-speaking minorities after liberation.

From the day Hitler seized power, Nazi Germany aimed to expand. While Hitler himself envisaged war with Czechoslovakia and France in order to prepare his central campaign – the war for *Lebensraum* against the Soviet Union – the majority of German elites before and after 1933 aimed to revise the Treaty of Versailles and achieve hegemony in continental Europe. There was a broad consensus reaching beyond the Nazi movement that especially the Eastern frontier was to be revised by annexation of Western and Northern Poland and parts of Western Czechoslovakia, territories populated by German-speaking minorities. Nazi aspirations, however, reached well beyond that: they envisaged a German 'racial' and economic hegemony in Central and Southeastern Europe, spearheaded by a dominant 'Germanic Empire' in the centre and the north; they would profit from the prosperous Western European economy,

---

6 For a comparative approach, see Julia Eichenberg and John P. Newman, 'Aftershocks: Violence in Dissolving Empires after the First World War', *Contemporary European History* 19, no. 3 (2010): 183–94, and Jochen Böhler's chapter on the interwar period 'The radicalization of violence and Intermarium's interwar' in the present volume.

and based on race, they would restructure Eastern Europe's demographics and brutally exploit them economically. German conservatives and right-wing extremists not only perceived Eastern Europe as agrarian and backward, but also as an unstable seedbed of bolshevism and 'international Jewry'. The Eastern European agrarian economy was considered weak, the area it covered 'overpopulated', and the cities and towns – especially those in Poland, Hungary and Slovakia – were perceived as being dominated by Jews. As early as 1937, German *Ostforscher* had already forwarded proposals for the 'dejudaization' of the Eastern European economy.[7]

Southeastern Europe, on the other hand, was to serve as the agrarian foundation for the German empire and was to feed the Germans – a strategy that would ultimately fail. Beginning in the mid-1930s, German policy began pursuing a project called '*Großraumwirtschaft*' ('large-scale economy') with economies dependent upon Germany and its currency. The creation of large-scale economic zones was a general tendency in response to the global economic crisis of the early 1930s, and Southeastern European states opted for an economic alliance with the German dictatorship. But the economic crisis was not the only reason why Hungary and Romania issued anti-Jewish laws as early as 1938, and why politicians in the autonomous Slovakian territory even attempted to expel a part of their Jewish minority.[8] The idea of expelling and assimilating ethnic and religious minorities with the goal of building a homogenized and compact state was widespread, and Eastern European nationalists did not need any German influence to dream of a state cleansed of Jews. Germany's success in revising the post-First World War order and rising to the leading power in continental Europe reinforced such tendencies but was not the only reason for home-grown anti-Semitism in Central and Eastern Europe. Moreover, there was a broad alliance between Germany and the Southeastern European states for the creation of a new ethno-political order in Europe, though in different directions.[9]

Nazi imperialism can be interpreted as a continuation of the expansion schemes of the First World War, but can also be viewed within the framework of the Paris post-war order collapse and the rise of a new imperialism in the 1930s. Japan set up its indirect rule in north-eastern China from 1931 onwards; Italy radicalized its colonial expansion first in Libya, then in 1935 by attacking Abyssinia (the Ethiopian Empire), and finally in April 1939 by annexing Albania. The restrictions of international law were under discussion, and the League of Nations was not able to cope with the new imperialism. There was a general discussion during the interwar years about what future wars would look like. Based on the negative experience of the First World War's stalemate, the military sought new ways of leading a short and decisive war, both by new techniques and by totalizing the war societies. International laws, like the Hague Conventions, were often considered an obstacle to successful future campaigns.[10]

---

7 Götz Aly and Susanne Heim, *Architects of Annihilation: Auschwitz and the Logic of Destruction* (Princeton, NJ: Princeton University Press, 2002); Götz Aly, *Final Solution: Nazi Population Policy and the Murder of the European Jews* (London: Arnold; New York: Oxford University Press, 1999); Ingo Haar and Michael Fahlbusch, eds, *German Scholars and Ethnic Cleansing (1920–1945)* (New York: Berghahn Books, 2005).

8 Stephen G. Gross, *Export Empire: German Soft Power in Southeastern Europe* (Cambridge: Cambridge University Press, 2015); for Slovakia, see Jan Láníček, *Czechs, Slovaks and the Jews, 1938–48: Beyond Idealization and Condemnation* (London: Palgrave Macmillan, 2013).

9 See Alexander Korb, Philipp Ther, eds, 'Ethnic Homogenizing in Southeastern Europe', *Journal of Genocide Research Volume* 18, no. 4 (2016).

10 Stig Förster, ed., *An der Schwelle zum Totalen Krieg: Die militärische Debatte über den Krieg der Zukunft 1919–1939* (Paderborn: Ferdinand Schöningh, 2002).

Thus, occupation regimes by dictatorships and authoritarian systems – in contrast to the First World War – tended to ignore international law, especially in Eastern Europe and Asia. This is already obvious during the de facto annexation of what had remained of Bohemia and Moravia in the spring of 1939, but even more so after the German military victory in Poland. Contrary to international law, the German military administration was abolished, and Western Poland was incorporated into the Reich; central Poland was kept as a kind of colony under the civil administration of the 'General Government for the occupied Polish territories'. After Germany's victories in Northern, Western and Southeastern Europe, parts of the conquered territory were put under civil administration (Norway, The Netherlands), some under military rule (Belgium, Northern France, and later, Serbia and parts of Greece) while some remained semi-autonomous (Denmark, Vichy France). But unlike Poland, in all of these countries both international relations and the internal public sphere still played a major role for German policy. Poland, however, which figured in Hitler's earlier plans as an inferior ally in his war against the Soviet Union, was completely wiped off the European map in 1939. However, Germany's political aims for the occupation in Poland were not fully developed before 1939–40. In first place, the Polish territory was of major importance for Hitler's general strategy, his campaign against the West and his prospective war against the Soviet Union. Thus, these areas had to come under full German control, and any potential resistance was to be subdued. The annexed territories were to be integrated into the Reich not only in a legal, but also in a racial sense: this meant implementing a radical policy of 'Germanization', either by deporting certain Polish groups, by suppressing the Poles and their development, or by 'racial selection', that is, integrating a small portion of the Polish population with alleged German origins into the German demographic body.[11] It is unclear, however, what position German-occupied Poland should play in the war economy. The Czech lands, in contrast, had specifically been occupied as an important industrial area. In general, Poland was meant to become a reservoir of grain imports and cheap labour, while industrial development was to be restricted to the annexed territories; the General Government was meant to be plundered and used as the destination for the deported, unwanted parts of the population from the annexed territories and from Germany. Poland only became an object of German industrial interest from 1942 onwards. On the other hand, specific policies were pursued in the Baltics but only after the German attack on the Soviet Union. The Baltic states, which had been destroyed by Stalin, were not re-established by Hitler, but rather only limited collaboration administrations were installed.

A position somewhat similar to the Baltic states was foreseen for Yugoslavia. But as Yugoslavia and Greece were not perceived as vital for the German war effort, Hitler left large parts of both countries for occupation by his allies. Subsequently, the Western Balkans were divided by a 1000-mile demarcation line that ran from Ljubljana in the Alps to Larissa, Thessaly at the Aegean Sea, and which separated the German and Italian empires. Most of Macedonia was occupied by Bulgaria; the northern Yugoslav borderlands were annexed by Hungary; big parts of Dalmatia were annexed by Italy; Kosovo was added to Italian-ruled Albania, and Slovenia was divided up between Germany and Italy. Montenegro became an Italian protectorate, as Albania had already been since 1939. The largest parts formed the NDH (Independent State of Croatia), which became a German-Italian satellite state. All that the Germans left of Serbia was a small rump territory that roughly followed the Serbian borders of 1912. In the Western Banat region north of Belgrade, the ethnic-German minority held the local power.

---

11 Catherine Epstein, *Model Nazi: Arthur Greiser and the Occupation of Western Poland* (Oxford: Oxford University Press, 2010).

Occupied Yugoslavia was particularly prone to violence since the destruction of the state by Germany and Italy caused a series of problems and since annexations and occupations disrupted the complex ethnic fabric. The Croatian Ustasha was an openly fascist regime, and its instalment by the German and Italian regimes would backfire shortly thereafter, as the Ustashe caused fighting and chaos. The fact that the Germans allowed their partners to persecute the Serbs reinforced the civil and partisan war that broke out in 1941 and led to the rise of Josip Broz Tito. In addition, the destruction of Yugoslavia sparked a fierce and sometimes hostile conflict between Germany and Italy.

The other Southeastern European independent states – Hungary, Romania, Bulgaria and semi-independent Slovakia – all partook in brutal ethnic homogenization projects enabled by the new German order, into which the Southeastern European states were to be integrated. The general German policy was to endorse the authoritarian governments rather than fascist grassroots movements. Hitler saw them as more reliable, and it was easy to put them under pressure as there was always a more radical option which the Germans could support in case the respective governments would not collaborate. That principle is particularly obvious in the case of Hungary and Romania.

Germany's sympathies differed from country to country. In Hitler's view, Bulgaria and Hungary were traditional allies, whereas he made Serbia responsible for the First World War and as such disliked the country. Once the Southeastern European borders were put into motion following the Vienna Awards in 1938 and 1940, Hungary was the biggest winner by gaining Southern Slovakia, Northern Transylvania, Carpathian Ruthenia and the Bachka and Prekmurje regions; Bulgaria received the Dobruja region in 1940 and Western and Eastern Macedonia together with Western Thrace in 1941; Romania had to hand over large parts of Transylvania to Hungary but regained Bessarabia and Northern Bukovina (which had been ceded to Stalin in 1940 after the attack on Western Europe) and was allowed to occupy Transnistria, even though the Romanian government never aspired to annex the region. The Germans saw Romania as the most important state due to its oil reserves. Both Yugoslavia and Greece were considered kind of exposed in Southeastern Europe, a potential area of British intervention, which might endanger the projected war in the Soviet Union. Yugoslavia was offered Greek territories and access to the Aegean Sea if it was to join the Axis bloc in 1940; but the country was ultimately destroyed in April 1941.

In the course of the war, the Germans increasingly penetrated their semi-independent Southeastern European allies. They often called upon their system of German embassies, German counsellors installed within local governments, and the local ethnic-German communities to bring allied countries in line. Ethnic-German conscripts, who were drafted by the SS in the thousands, would become Heinrich Himmler's key instrument for expanding and taking over military and police positions in Southeastern Europe. This went hand in hand with pressure on the Southeastern European states to deport their Jewish minorities. By mid-1944, all German partner states with the exception of Romania and Bulgaria were occupied by the German army.

Here, the role of Fascist Italy needs to be taken into consideration. Italy was the sole German ally to develop a major, though unsuccessful, imperial programme that would encompass a *grande spazio* ('greater space') from the Eastern Mediterranean region to Northwest Africa and the Horn of Africa, which would form the outer part of its *spazio vitale* – a concept resembling that of the German concept of *Lebensraum*. The Italian imperial approach was one of concentric circles: the territories closer to the Italian mainland were to be annexed (Slovenia, Dalmatia), the next zone was to be occupied and directly controlled (Southern Croatia, Western Greece), and the adjacent countries were to be influenced and controlled indirectly.[12] Concepts of Italianization played a role in the contested Italian–Slavic borderlands, but to a lesser extent in other annexed territories such as Dalmatia or Slovenia.[13] The overall Italian policy can be described as 'divide and conquer', as the Italian armies and occupation authorities were quite skilful in building alliances with local partners.

Hitler's Germany meanwhile developed general concepts for restructuring Central and Eastern Europe that had originated in their plans for Western Poland in 1939. German minorities that lived or were to come under Soviet or Italian rule were to be resettled to the German sphere; territories with German minorities under the German imperial umbrella should ultimately become 'German'. Beginning in the 1920s, German experts had widened the concept of *Volksboden* (where Germans live or lived) to *Kulturboden* (where German cultural influence was visible, for example in places that had adopted the privileges of the medieval town, Magdeburg). After the attack on the Soviet Union, SS chief Himmler ordered the creation of a new plan for the East, which was compiled at the turn of 1941–42 as *Generalplan Ost* ('Master Plan for the East'), both a scheme for settling Germanic people and for deporting approximately 31 million Slavs who were predominantly from Western and Eastern Poland, but also from parts of Lithuania. There were even discussions to deport 50 million Slavs, which would indeed have been the biggest deportation scheme in history. Due to the course of the war, these projects were abandoned in early 1943, though in some of the target areas deportations did take place.[14]

Like the *Generalplan Ost*, the planning of the Nazi 'Final Solution of the Jewish Question' developed from 1939 until 1942. In contrast to the former, however, it was almost completely put into practice. Before Hitler started the war, the general aim of his anti-Jewish policies was to expel Jews from the 'Greater German Reich'. In late 1939, new schemes for a spatial 'solution' arose, like the so-called 'reservation plan', which envisaged the segregation of Jews and their deportation to certain areas – or reservations – in Poland. With the defeat of France in June 1940, the former anti-Semitic idea of expelling the Jews to the French colonial island of Madagascar was re-actualized albeit in a radical manner, now as the destination for millions of European Jews who would have perished there within one generation. During the preparation for the war against the Soviet Union new destinations were under discussion, like Northern Russia or the Pripyat Marshes in Western Belorussia. In autumn 1941, however, as the German campaign in the East was slowing down, such plans were stopped, and the Nazi leadership, together with the occupation administrations, decided rather to kill the Jews on site, i.e. in mass executions and in newly established extermination camps. Most of the Jews of Central and Eastern Europe were dead by mid-1943.[15]

---

12 Davide Rodogno, *Fascism's European Empire: Italian Occupation during the Second World War* (Cambridge: Cambridge University Press, 2006)
13 Davide Rodogno, 'Italiani brava gente? Fascist Italy's Policy Toward the Jews in the Balkans, April 1941–July 1943', *European History Quarterly* 35, no. 2 (April 2005): 213–40; see also Amedeo Osti Guerrazzi, *The Italian Army in Slovenia: Strategies of Antipartisan Repression, 1941–1943*, trans. Elizabeth Burke (New York: Palgrave Macmillan, 2013).
14 Mark Mazower, *Hitler's Empire: How the Nazis Ruled Europe* (London: Allan Lane, 2008), 204–11; Czesław Madajczyk, ed., *Vom Generalplan Ost zum Generalsiedlungsplan*, (München: Saur, 1994); Mechthild Rössler and Sabine Schleiermacher, eds, *Der 'Generalplan Ost': Hauptlinien der nationalsozialistischen Planungs- und Vernichtungspolitik* (Berlin: Akademie, 1993); Bruno Wasser, *Himmlers Raumplanung im Osten: Der Generalplan Ost in Polen 1940–1944* (Basel: Birkhäuser, 1994).
15 Christopher R. Browning, *The Origins of the Final Solution: The Evolution of Nazi Jewish Policy, September 1939–March 1942* (Lincoln, NE: University of Nebraska Press, 2004).

But the German leadership was not the only one to develop large and often genocidal schemes of resettlement. In Southeastern European countries, ideas of deporting Jews were interwoven with schemes to ethnically engineer and homogenize the nation as such. *Völkisch* scholars advocated the idea that the Balkan nations needed to be transformed into ethnically homogeneous states in order to become productive members of a new European order, as the region's multi-ethnicity was perceived as one of the key obstacles to modernization.[16] The Germans facilitated bi-national agreements on the mutual resettlement of minorities such as the Treaty of Craiova between Romania and Bulgaria (1940), after which Bulgaria and Romania 'exchanged' 200,000 individuals. German minorities were resettled from Dobruja and Bessarabia at the same time, mostly to be shipped to German-annexed Poland where they were meant to increase the German portion of the local population.[17] Of course, during the war, the Romanian leadership and its demographic experts worked out a 'Romanization' project for inner Romania and Bessarabia (the so-called *Regat*), envisaging the deportation not only of Jews, but also of Romani and Ukrainians.[18] The two states Slovakia and Croatia, newly created by Hitler, also pursued ethnic purity and undertook resettlements – and in the Croatian case, on a large scale. Hungary and Bulgaria pursued revisionist policies and had specific plans for their 'regained' borderlands, from which they expelled Jews (from Carpatho-Ukraine) and Greeks (from Thrace) and into which they brought settlers from the mainland.

The German occupation authorities set a framework for the territorial and demographic restructuring of Central, Eastern and Southeastern Europe. The major feature of German occupation was economic and military exploitation, which intensified the longer the war lasted, especially from early 1942 onwards. This not only included plundering, but also the restructuring of the economy to serve Germany's needs, the deportation of a workforce to the Reich, and the drafting of military-age men. The specific concept of 'racial security' was considered the basis of German rule in the East, which manifested as the killing or imprisonment of all groups who were considered *potentially* dangerous to German rule (i.e. communist activists and functionaries, Polish elites), and the characterization of the Jews as alleged global enemies; finally, the strategic – but only partially realized – resettlement of German minorities in certain Eastern frontier territories that constituted a mix of racial, spatial and security policies.

Most of the German (and Axis) occupation regimes were not installed according to international law but rather for the purpose of securing unrestricted rule. Thus, the German military administration was quite restricted for a short period of two months in Poland, and to some regions in Yugoslavia (Serbia) and Greece (Saloniki and the Aegean). Everywhere else civil administrations were installed that were directly subordinate to Hitler and dominated by Nazi Party veterans with extreme political beliefs. Even in the areas annexed to the Reich (Western and Northern Poland, Northern Slovenia), which were officially subject to the traditional civil administration, Nazi *Gauleiter* held autonomous positions and only had to answer to Hitler. In

---

16 See Johannes Dafinger and Dieter Pohl, eds, *A New Nationalist Europe Under Hitler: Concepts of Europe and Transnational Networks in the National Socialist Sphere of Influence, 1933–1945* (London: Routledge, 2018).

17 Philipp Ther, *The Dark Side of Nation-States: Ethnic Cleansing in Modern Europe*, vol. 19, *War and Genocide* (Oxford: Berghahn Books, 2014); see also Marina Cattaruzza, Stefan Dyroff and Dieter Langewiesche, eds, *Territorial Revisionism and the Allies of Germany in the Second World War: Goals, Expectations, Practices* (New York: Berghahn Books, 2013).

18 Viorel Achim, 'Romanian-German Collaboration in Ethnopolitics: The Case of Sabin Manuilă', in *German Scholars and Ethnic Cleansing 1920–1945*, eds Ingo Haar and Michael Fahlbusch (Providence, RI: Berghahn Books, 2005), 139–54.

Eastern and Southeastern Europe, the German Police- and SS-apparatuses were able to achieve a much stronger position than in the Reich or in occupied Western Europe; the occupation regime gave opportunities to unqualified but radical party activist and officials from Germany who sought to advance their careers in the East. The administrators thought of themselves as racially superior *Herrenmenschen* ('master humans') – especially in Poland – and without any administrative or legal restrictions, they installed an arbitrary and highly corrupt regime. Even among professional administrations like the economic and technical branches, a radical discourse prevailed that considered most of the locals inferior.

From ethnic cleansing to the 'final solution'

Germany's unleashing of mass violence, September 1939 – spring 1941

The German war campaigns were accompanied by extremely brutal measures including the mass murder of civilians and POWs right from the outset. Even before the attack on Poland in 1939, Germany's 'peaceful' expansion into Austria and the Czechoslovak borderlands meant the transferring of the Nazi dictatorship to foreign countries. Repression and persecution campaigns, as realized within the Reich, were exported, but such tactics were enacted more radically in the annexed territories, which in turn had a radicalizing effect on the situation in the Reich. Following the annexation of Western Bohemia, the Sudeten region in 1938, suspected political opponents of Nazism were put into concentration camps, while Jews were discriminated against and persecuted. In March 1939, the Germans occupied the Czech parts of former Czechoslovakia and formed the so-called Protectorate of Bohemia and Moravia. The Gestapo (*Geheime Staatspolizei*) began arresting people, but anti-Jewish policy at this point was left to the government of the Protectorate, which of course was dependent on orders from Germany. The Memel (Klaipeda) region of Lithuania was annexed in March 1939: almost 10,000 Lithuanians fled the region, while 1,300 Jews were expelled to what remained of Lithuania.

The decisive step, however, was not made until September 1939, when Germany attacked Poland and made the move towards mass murder. Three complexities of this process deserve closer analysis: 1) the war crimes that were committed; 2) the extermination of the Polish elites and institutionalized psychiatric patients; and 3) the mass deportations that took place from 1939 to 1941. From the first days of the German attack, Wehrmacht and SS units killed POWs and civilians considered to be snipers or saboteurs. The first of these massacres occurred on 4 September 1939 in Częstochowa. In numerous instances, enemy soldiers were killed as alleged guerrilla fighters. Based on a hysteria of alleged *franc-tireurs*, the German military and the SS shot thousands of POWs and civilians. Jews were targeted from the very first days, specifically selected as hostages or terrorized so that they would flee to the Soviet occupation zone in order to escape German massacres.[19]

But the major systematic mass crime of 1939–40 was the killing of the so-called 'Polish intelligentsia', especially in Western and Northern Poland. This mass murder programme has to be interpreted in the context of Germany's 'internal' preparation for war, which started in 1937. The German SS and Police apparatuses were able to monopolize the persecution of alleged enemies of the Reich and applied more radical methods than the justice system, including mass

---

19 Jochen Böhler: *Auftakt zum Vernichtungskrieg: Die Wehrmacht in Polen 1939* (Frankfurt a.M.: Fischer Taschenbuch, 2006); Alexander B. Rossino, *Hitler Strikes Poland: Blitzkrieg, Ideology, and Atrocity* (Lawrence, KS: University Press of Kansas, 2003).

arrests and the implementation of concentration camps with forced labour and high death rates. Most important was the turn to direct murder: Security Police Chief Reinhard Heydrich announced on 3 September 1939 that such a tactic was justified 'since, if necessary, brutal liquidation of such elements will follow on higher order'.[20] What applied to the 'internal enemy' during wartime was considered even more appropriate for the external enemy. Beginning in May 1939, the Security Police prepared the *Sonderfahndungsbuch Polen* ('Special Prosecution Book, Poland'), a proscription list of no less than 61,000 Poles who were allegedly considered dangerous. And the *Einsatzgruppen* of the Security Police received killing orders, 'according to which the police acted, that were extraordinarily radical (for example, liquidation orders for several Polish leadership circles, which numbered in the thousands)', as Heydrich put it retrospectively.[21]

In order to execute these orders, an ethnic-German militia was set up by the SS in Poland, the *Volksdeutsche Selbstschutz*, with German-speaking Poles who were supposed to identify any alleged enemies and assist in their murders. Among the groups targeted for killing were Polish politicians, academic elites, clergy, lawyers, activists who participated in the 1918–1921 uprisings, plebiscites, and finally, leading members of allegedly anti-German organizations like the Polish Western Union (*Polski Związek Zachodni*). The victims were arrested either according to proscription lists or after denunciations, and then they were brought to specific execution sites. Most of these mass killings took place in the annexed territories, especially in the newly created Reichsgau Danzig-Westpreußen, where approximately 1,000 executions with around 40,000 victims were registered. The Soldau SS camp (Działdowo) was a major execution site; around 12,000 Poles were shot in Piaśnica; thousands were executed in Minszek and Szpęgawsk, and at least 2,000 were killed in Palmiry. Similar dimensions are visible in the Reichsgau Wartheland, less in northern Mazovia and Polish Silesia.[22]

In central and southern Poland – in what had become the 'General Government' on 26 October 1939 – the German Security Police conducted spectacular mass arrests, especially among professors of the Cracow and Lublin universities who they deported to German concentration camps. Some of them were released after international protest.[23] At the same time, there were killings all across the General Government. In May 1940, the German Security Police started a new operation called the Extraordinary Pacification Operation (*Außerordentliche Befriedungsaktion*, or the *AB-Aktion*), which cost the lives of approximately 2,000 Poles.[24]

---

20 Timothy W. Mason, *Arbeiterklasse und Volksgemeinschaft* (Köln: Westdeutscher Verlag, 1974), 1061.
21 Helmut Krausnick, 'Hitler und die Morde in Polen: Ein Beitrag zum Konflikt zwischen Heer und SS um die Verwaltung der besetzten Gebiete', *Vierteljahrshefte für Zeitgeschichte* 11, no. 2 (1963): 196–209, here 207.
22 Maria Wardzyńska, *Był rok 1939: Operacja niemieckiej policji bezpieczeństwa w Polsce 'Intelligenzaktion'* [It was 1939: The operation of the German security police in Poland, 'Intelligenzaktion'] (Warsaw: Inst. Pamięci Narodowej Komisja Ścigania Zbrodni Przeciwko Narodowi Polskiemu, 2009); Barbara Bojarska, *Eksterminacja inteligencji polskiej na Pomorzu Gdańskim* [The extermination of the Polish intelligentsia in Gdańsk Pomerania (September–December 1939)], Badania nad okupacją niemiecką w Polsce 12 (Poznań: Inst. Zachodni, 1972).
23 Jochen August, *'Sonderaktion Krakau': Die Verhaftung der Krakauer Wissenschaftler am 6. November 1939* (Hamburg: Hamburger Edition, 1997); Dieter Schenk, *Der Lemberger Professorenmord und der Holocaust in Ostgalizien* (Bonn: Dietz, 2007).
24 Snyder, *Bloodlands*, 147–50; *Ausserordentliche Befriedungsaktion 1940 – akcja AB na ziemiach polskich: materiały z sesji naukowej (6–7 listopada 1986 r.)* [Extraordinary Pacification Operation 1940 – The AB action in Poland: materials from the scientific session (November 6–7, 1986)], ed. Zygmunt

Almost parallel to the murders of the Polish intelligentsia, the mass murder of psychiatric patients and people with physical disabilities began in occupied Poland in September 1939. Such mass murders were not restricted to Poland, but they were part of the larger Nazi programme to murder specific groups of psychiatric patients in Germany. The discussion about whether to kill those lives deemed to be 'unworthy of life' (*lebensunwertes Leben*) began in Germany in the 1920s, but the practice was rejected by the majority of German physicians and lawyers at the time. Only in the immediate pre-war period, in mid-1939, did the Nazi leadership, assisted by psychiatrists, decide to set in motion the mass euthanasia of psychiatric patients. Preparations in Germany were already under way when Germany attacked Poland.

The new health departments of the occupation administration, with the help of the SS and the police, began 'clearing' psychiatric institutions in annexed Poland in order to take over the buildings either for ethnic Germans who had been resettled or for the purposes of the Waffen-SS. The killings were conducted in conjunction with the mass crimes against the Polish intelligentsia. In November 1939 in an old fortress (Fort VII) in the city of Poznań, which was used as a killing site, the first improvised gas chamber was installed for the murder of institutionalized mental patients. By spring 1940, all in all 6,000 people were murdered in the territories annexed to Nazi Germany, some more in the General Government. The *Gauleiter* of Pomerania ordered the deportation of German patients from his realm to the killing sites in occupied Poland.[25]

It is unclear, however, whether the mass murder of those deemed to be mentally ill was extended to other regions in Central, Eastern and Southeastern Europe. There is evidence of transports from German-annexed eastern Slovenia to euthanasia centres,[26] and in the Baltic region patients were either put to death in the psychiatric institutions themselves or in the nearby killing fields.

The mass murder of psychiatric patients continued during the attack on the Soviet Union. From the end of August 1941, at the very moment when the euthanasia programme in Germany was interrupted, German Security Police officers shot the patients of a psychiatric clinic in Choroszcz, Poland, near Białystok. There was, however, no systematic murdering of *all* the patients in the occupied areas. Rather, the health administration and Germany's military physicians decided whether or not the patients should live or die. In the General Government, patients of psychiatric institutions were deliberately starved to death, like in Kulparków district of Lviv. Local medical personnel were involved in some of the killings, though it is unclear whether they were forced to do so or if they participated voluntarily.[27]

Mańkowski (Warsaw: Zakład Historii Najnowszej Uniwersytetu Marii Skłodowskiej-Curie i OKBZpNP-IPN w Lublinie, 1992).

25 Volker Rieß, *Die Anfänge der Vernichtung "lebensunwerten Lebens" in den Reichsgauen Danzig-Westpreußen und Wartheland 1939/40* (Frankfurt a.M.: Peter Lang, 1995).

26 Bojan Himmelreich, 'The Nazi "Euthanasia" in Slovenia in 1941', in *Die nationalsozialistische 'Euthanasie'-Aktion 'T4' und ihre Opfer*, eds Maike Rotzoll et.al. (Paderborn: Ferdinand Schöningh, 2010), 184–8.

27 Tadeusz Nasierowski, *Zagłada osób z zaburzeniami psychicznymi w okupowanej Polsce: Początek ludobójstwa* [The extermination of people with mental disorders in occupied Poland: The beginning of genocide] (Warsaw: Neriton, 2008); Björn Felder, '"Euthanasia", Human Experiments and Psychiatry in Nazi-Occupied Lithuania 1941–1944', *Holocaust and Genocide Studies* 27 (2013): 242–75; Alexander Friedman, Rainer Hudemann, eds, *Diskriminiert – vernichtet – vergessen: Behinderte in der Sowjetunion, unter nationalsozialistischer Besatzung und im Ostblock 1917–1991* (Stuttgart: Steiner, 2016).

After the summer of 1940, the mass arrests and mass murders of the Poles were scaled down for a longer period. Violence against the non-Jewish population of Poland was on the rise again with the beginning of anti-partisan warfare from mid-1942 on. In December 1942, the Security Police staged another mass repression operation, the so-called *Asozialenaktion* in which a large number of arrests took place, especially in Warsaw. All of the arrestees were sent to concentration camps and treated especially bad, the majority of whom were already dead by the end of 1943.[28]

It is astounding how the German policy towards Poland changed from the non-aggression pact of 1934 to the attack on Poland in 1939. For a long time, Poland was considered as an inferior ally for a war against the Soviet Union, as deeply anti-Bolshevik, and as a nation with a Catholic culture not too dissimilar from Germany's. The German perception of Polish people changed drastically in 1939, reaffirming old stereotypes of Slavs and the ethnic war propaganda used during 1918–1921. Plans to murder the Polish elites marked a new element in Nazi policy; such an atmosphere was stirred up by the violence against ethnic Germans in Poland in August 1939 and during the first days of the war. The *Bromberger Blutsonntag* ('Bydgoszcz bloody Sunday') that took place between 3–4 September, in which 365 Germans were killed (many more in other regions), provided a decisive element for German propaganda and their self-perception during the war. Indeed, war propaganda inflated the official number of Germans killed by Poles by at least 10–12 times (from 5,400 to 58,000). Germany's retaliation was merciless: they killed thousands of Poles and Jews in Bydgoszcz and its surrounding areas throughout the following weeks.[29]

Nevertheless, the crimes committed by the police and SS in Poland 1939 did not go undisputed among German elites. Especially after the Polish Campaign, several German generals criticized the SS massacres, arguing that they had not been justified and that Himmler's men had interfered in military matters. There was little dispute, however, about the anti-Jewish violence that accompanied the campaign, and the discussions regarding who was actually in charge – the military or the SS – were finished by spring 1941. During the attack on the Soviet Union, hardly any German officers would complain about the murderous conduct pursued jointly by the police, the SS and the army.

Mass executions as 'reprisal'

Germany's executing of alleged hostages as a form of reprisal occurred both in Eastern and in Southeastern Europe and was a typical response to both real and alleged acts of armed resistance. The origins of Germany's reprisal massacres during the Second World War can be traced back to the ideological way that war was fought in the post-First World War era. The experience of anti-Bolshevik warfare, by and large, shaped the patterns of reaction to resistance: first, only a few of the international laws should apply to a perceived communist enemy; second, Eastern Europe was considered to be a region outside of international law and the international public – here, the populations engaged in archaic forms of warfare and were

---

28 Władysław Bartoszewski, *Warszawski pierścień śmierci 1939–1944* [The Warsaw ring of death, 1939–1944], 3rd revised ed. (Warsaw: Swiat Ksiazki, 2009).
29 Tomasz Chinciński, Paweł Machcewicz, eds, *Bydgoszcz 3 – 4 września 1939* [Bydgoszcz, 3–4 September 1939] (Warsaw: IPN, 2008). It is estimated that in September 1939, roughly 4,500 Germans in Poland either fell victim to German bombardments, to Polish atrocities or were simply accounted for as missing.

considered less civilized than the populations of Western Europe; third, collective responsibility was applied as early as the 1919–20 conflicts in which alleged 'hostages' of specific strata were killed as acts of revenge or deterrence; finally, there was basically no limit to the reprisals for violent acts committed by the enemy – the total extermination of 'the enemy's' population might be the consequence.

These patterns were not limited to the conflicts that took place immediately after the First World War, e.g. the Russian Civil War, but they also applied to colonial warfare and to Japanese rule in China from 1931 onwards. Germany's alleged 'reprisals' began as early as the war against Poland in September 1939, but they played a rather minor role in the period following. Only in the spring of 1941 did the typical German (and Axis) strategy to combat armed resistance evolve.[30]

Since March 1941, the German military leadership discussed the role of international law in the envisaged war against the Soviet Union. Most important in this respect was the *Kriegsgerichtsbarkeitserlass* (Decree on the Jurisdiction of Martial Law), which excluded almost any sanctions for violence enacted by German soldiers against the Soviet civil population.

Outside of Poland, the first mass executions of 'hostages' occurred in May 1941 in Yugoslavia, in response to remnant Yugoslav army units that continued fighting after the cease-fire, and in occupied Crete, where civilians allegedly took part, along with British troops, in military action. Communist partisan warfare began almost at the same time – in July–August 1941 – in occupied Soviet territory and in Yugoslavia. Within the occupied Soviet territory, partisan groups operated, particularly in Belorussia, in northern and north-eastern Ukraine, and in Russia proper (near Leningrad), the Bryansk region and the Crimean Peninsula. The Yugoslav resistance movement in 1941 focused on Serbia, where both the Chetniks and communist groups attacked German troops and facilities. In 1942, most partisan activities moved to Montenegro, Bosnia and Croatia. These were the areas of violent German (and Axis) anti-partisan violence. As early as May 1941, a reprisal ratio was announced for the attacks on German army units that consisted of 100 people executed for every German killed, and 50 people executed for every wounded German soldier. For the campaign against the Soviet Union, ratios of 1:30 were debated. It goes without saying that Germany's ruthless approach and their tendency to shoot all partisan prisoners did not help in their attempt to 'pacify' the partisan regions; further, local resentment against the Germans only grew as there was no incentive to surrender.[31]

Little wonder that in August 1941, Germany's occupation of Serbia was facing collapse. But within two months, Germany regrouped and managed to crush the uprising. The reasons they succeeded lie in their military tactics, their political choices and the mass terror campaign they inflicted on the local population. Whilst the first is evident, the latter two reasons require further discussion. Indeed, Germany responded to the uprising by executing civilians en masse. In October 1941, the Wehrmacht shot 4,000 civilians – most of them Jewish men – in the cities of Kraljevo and Kragujevac alone. Up to 30,000 civilians were shot in the autumn of 1941. The ruthlessness of this murderous approach was to a certain extent successful and led to what Germany dubbed the 'pacification' of Serbia. At the same time, such an approach was faced with local and internal criticism, so the Wehrmacht soon started executing the ethnically

---

30 Oliver von Wrochem, ed., *Repressalien und Terror: 'Vergeltungsaktionen' im deutsch besetzten Europa 1939–1945* (Paderborn: Schoeningh, 2017); Daniel Brewing, *Im Schatten von Auschwitz: Deutsche Massaker an polnischen Zivilisten 1939–1945* (Darmstadt: WBG, 2016).

31 Philip H. Blood, *Hitler's Bandit Hunters: The SS and the Nazi Occupation of Europe* (Washington, DC: Potomac, 2006).

and socially unwanted civilians as 'hostages' (mostly Jews and Romani). Since the first victims were Jewish refugees from Germany and Austria, the Wehrmacht's approach was presented as a concession towards orthodox Serbian society as fewer Serbian citizens were affected. For this reason, the history of the Holocaust in Serbia is unique in its European context: the male Jewish population were largely shot as hostages as early as October 1941; in a second phase between December 1941 and May 1942, Jewish women and children were gassed to death in mobile 'gas vans' near their place of internment, the Sajmište concentration camp (dubbed by the Germans as *Judenlager Semlin*) in a western suburb of Belgrade.[32]

Yugoslavia was co-occupied by Italian troops, and at times the Italians outnumbered the Wehrmacht 10:1 on Yugoslav soil. In 1942, the Italian army started razing entire villages to the ground in partisan territories. The largest massacre occurred on 12 July 1942, when the army shot 108 inhabitants of the village Podhum in retaliation for the murder of four Italians; they deported the remaining 889 villagers before destroying the village.[33]

Occupation and deportation

The defeat of Poland gave the German experts who were concerned with *Lebensraum* the unique opportunity to plan the restructuring of an occupied society. Projects of modernization, 'dejudaization' and even 'depolonization' had already been secretly discussed before the war.[34] During the final months of 1939, various expert groups came forward with concrete deportation schemes. Hitler himself, during his infamous Reichstag speech on 6 October 1939, announced the demographic restructuring of Central Europe. Ethnic-German minorities who came under Soviet rule, according to the Molotov-Ribbentrop Pact, were to be taken 'Home to the Reich', like the Germans residing in the northern Italian borderlands/South Tyrol; 'undesired' inhabitants were to be deported out of the territories of Poland and annexed to the *Reich*. SS chief Himmler was entrusted to conduct both settlement and resettlement as the newly appointed *Reichskommissar für die Festigung deutschen Volkstums* ('Reich Commissioner for the Consolidation of German Nationhood').[35]

Within weeks, Himmler's experts set up the first long-term plan (*Fernplan*), a project to deport one million Poles and Jews from western Poland. A more extreme version suggested the deportation of up to 3.4 million people. Deportations to central Poland began in December 1939 as part of an initial short-term plan (*Nahplan*). Eighty-seven thousand men, women and children, predominately Jews from Lodz, were deported in a chaotic fashion. Criticism even came from other occupation offices. Thus, the second projected *Nahplan* was delayed, the number of people they planned to deport was reduced and they were better prepared for the deportations than in the first instance. Nevertheless, in February and March 1940, another 42,000 Polish citizens (Jewish and non-Jewish) were deported eastward, and many more during the latter part of the year. A third *Nahplan* from January 1941 envisaged restarting a major resettlement programme, including the deportation of 771,000 Poles. Twenty-five thousand Poles

---

32 Ben Shepherd, *Terror in the Balkans: German Armies and Partisan Warfare* (Cambridge, MA: Harvard University Press, 2012).
33 Jozo Tomasevich, *War and Revolution in Yugoslavia, 1941–1945: Occupation and Collaboration* (Stanford, CA: Stanford University Press, 2001), 75.
34 Ingo Haar, *Historiker im Nationalsozialismus: Deutsche Geschichtswissenschaft und der 'Volkstumskampf' im Osten* (Göttingen: Vandenhoeck & Ruprecht, 2000); Aly and Heim, *Architects of Annihilation*, 39–72.
35 Alexa Stiller, *Völkische Politik: Praktiken der Exklusion und Inklusion in polnischen, französischen und slowenischen Annexionsgebieten 1939–1945* (Göttingen: Wallstein, 2021).

and 5,000 Jews from Vienna were forcibly brought to the General Government. However, all resettlement programmes were stopped in March 1941 so as not to interfere with the preparations for Germany's attack on the Soviet Union.

There were, however, many more deportations conducted in Poland, not from one administrative region to the other, but within each district, especially from the west to the east. In East Upper Silesia, a specific area (*Oststreifen*) was created, to which all 'undesirable' Poles and Jews were deported. Later on, entire regions were resettled in order to make space for German military testing grounds.[36]

The attack on the Soviet Union led to the further radicalization of the planning and its implementation. Between summer 1941 and summer 1942, the deportation schemes for the *Generalplan Ost* were developed, and regional occupation authorities worked out details for major resettlements. In July 1942, SS chief Himmler and his subordinate in the Lublin District, SS and Police leader Odilo Globocnik, began the resettlement of Poles who lived south of Lublin. From the end of November 1942, the German Police and SS forces deported nearly 51,000 Poles from the Zamość-Hrubieszów regions. Another 60,000 fled in order to escape the deportations. The victims underwent a political-racial screening, the majority were sent to towns in the Warsaw district, a minority of them were sent to Auschwitz. Thousands died in consequence, especially children. Ultimately, the goals of the violent resettlement failed since Polish resistance attacked German units who then lost control over the area. In August 1943, when Globocnik stopped the operation, only 11,000 of the envisaged 65,000 ethnic-German settlers had arrived in the region. A similar resettlement operation, though on a smaller scale, was undertaken south of Zhytomyr in eastern Volhynia. After Germany's defeat at Stalingrad the general deportation plans in Eastern Europe were abandoned.[37]

Germany's re-arrangement of the Southeastern European borders from 1938 onwards were not underlined by an equally monstrous plan as that of the *Generalplan Ost*. But they set in motion a series of other deportation programmes and forced migration, initiated either by Germany or more frequently, by local governments. In 1938–39, 195,000 Jewish and non-Jewish Czechs fled or left the Sudeten region. As early as the autumn of 1938, the autonomous Slovak administration tried to deport Jews who originated from regions ceded to Hungary; due to Hungarian protests, this project failed. Furthermore, up to 80,000 Czech individuals were expelled from Slovakia to the Czech lands.[38] The Bulgarian case demonstrates how quickly deportations and expulsions could turn violent. In that respect, the Bulgarian occupation regime, especially in Thrace, revived horrible memories of the First World War and of the Balkan Wars. The Bulgarian occupation regime in eastern Macedonia and Western Thrace pursued a Bulgarization policy, putting pressure upon the Greeks and deporting Greek officials and members of the intelligentsia. All in all, approximately 100,000 Greeks were expelled by late 1942. The Bulgarian occupation of northern Greece was violent; when faced with resistance, army units massacred them. After an insurgency broke out in Drama (Thrace) in September 1941, Bulgarian soldiers executed almost the entire male civilian population of the town of Doxato, with at least an additional 200 individuals having been shot during the

---

36 Stiller, *Völkische Politik*.
37 Czeslaw Madajczyk, ed., *Zamojszczyzna – Sonderlaboratorium SS. Zbior dokumentow polskich i niemieckich z okresu hitlerowskiej* [The Zamość region – A *Sonderlaboratorium* of the SS: Collection of Polish and German documents from the Nazi period] (Warsaw: PWN 1977); Wendy Lower, *Nazi Empire-Building and the Holocaust in Ukraine* (Chapel Hill, NC: UNCP, 2005).
38 Ther, *The Dark Side of Nation-States*, 88–9, for Slovakia see 104–95.

night of 28–29 September 1941. More murders occurred at other places in Thrace, with around 1,600 Greeks having been killed in total. Ethnic cleansing, anti-partisan warfare and draconic security measures went hand in hand.[39]

In an even more radical fashion, violent expulsions were pursued by the Romanian government, which killed or expelled Jews and deported Romani and a number of Ukrainians from northern Bukovina and Bessarabia in autumn 1941. As in the Bulgarian and in most other cases, the expulsions took place in territories that were re-conquered and that were seen as an integral part of the homeland. In that perspective, its original demographic status was to be achieved by expelling those who had 'entered'.

One of the most extensive cases of ethnic homogenization, however, took place on Yugoslav soil. On 4 June 1941, German and Croatian representatives in Zagreb agreed on a large-scale resettlement scheme that would affect approximately half a million people: 170,000 Slovenes from the parts of Slovenia that had been annexed by Germany were to be deported into Croatia. In return, Croatia was allowed to deport 250,000 Serbs from Croatia to Serbia. An additional 180,000 Slovenes were to be deported from Slovenia to Serbia directly. Croatian population-planners intended to complete the population exchange by resettling Croats from other parts of Yugoslavia, from Austria and from overseas. Germany, in the meantime, resettled ethnic Germans from the parts of Slovenia annexed by Italy (Gottschee, today Kočevje) and attempted to Germanize the parts of Slovenia they had annexed.

The Croatian government created a national agency that they called the 'State Directory for Renewal' (*Ponova*), which was responsible for all resettlements including calls to Croats to return from the diaspora; they were also responsible for the accommodation of Slovenes deported into Croatia. The expellees were placed in trains to Belgrade or pushed over the green border, during which many drowned in the Drina River.

As in all other countries, population transfers became an enormous effort of social engineering. In Croatia, the State Directory for Renewal managed to get many ordinary Croats involved in the resettlements on a local level, either as experts (i.e. doctors, nurses, veterinarians, agronomists), or as ordinary beneficiaries. Such involvement broadened the regime's popular base, a point which applies to all cases of ethnic cleansing in the Southeastern European states and regions. One did not have to be a party member or an active supporter of a regime in order to benefit from ethnic cleansing.[40]

At the same time, expulsions resulted in chaos and mass violence, undermining any regimes' efforts to create a new order or to engage in social engineering. Attempted resettlements often ended in violent attacks. In Croatia, many Serb villages were too far from the Serbian border for its population to be smoothly resettled; more often than not, villagers did not want to be resettled, so they resisted. The brutal behaviour of the Croatian Ustasha bands, and the arrival of traumatized refugee survivors (some of whom had even been stripped of their shoes), in Serbia, which was under German administration, sparked intense protests by the Orthodox Church, the Serbian government and the German military and civil institutions in Serbia; so

---

39 For the uprising, see R. J. Crampton, *Bulgaria*, Oxford History of Modern Europe (Oxford: Oxford University Press, 2007), 261; for the Bulgarian policies more generally, see Theodora Dragostinova, *Between Two Motherlands: Nationality and Emigration among the Greeks of Bulgaria, 1900–1949* (Ithaca, NY: Cornell University Press, 2011), 251–52.

40 Alexander Korb, *Im Schatten des Weltkriegs Massengewalt der Ustasa gegen Serben, Juden und Roma in Kroatien 1941–1945* (Hamburg: Hamburger Edition, 2013), 171–95. An English translation with Oxford University Press is forthcoming.

much so that resettlements were officially terminated by the autumn of 1941, at least as far as international border crossings were involved.

At the same time, the Chetniks' goal for the war was to achieve a Greater Serbia that was ethnically homogenized. Basically, this Greater Serbia would consist of all of Yugoslavia including some Hungarian, Bulgarian and Albanian territories with the exception of a rump Croatia and a greater Slovenia, which was to expand into the Julian March and Carinthia.[41] A memorandum suggested the resettlement of 2,675,000 non-Serbs from Greater Serbia by the means of population transfers of Croats to Croatia and Muslims to Turkey and Albania.[42] It needs to be added that such population transfers were not a viable option under wartime conditions.

Most demographic plans for the resettlement of minorities were only partially put into practice. They are, however, of key importance in understanding wartime violence for two reasons. First, they built the ideological backbone for many of the non-German right-wing movements in Southeastern Europe that were in charge during the war. Whether it was the Iron Guard in Romania (until 1941), the Ustasha in Croatia, the Hlinka-Guard in Slovakia, the Arrow Cross movement in Hungary (in 1944) or the authoritarian right-wing governments of Romania (from 1941), Bulgaria or Hungary (until 1944), they all perceived the war as an opportunity for ethnic cleansing. They further hoped to make certain that contested territories would stay part of their national territory after the war – regardless of its outcome.

Second, the policies of ethnic homogenization involved an element of violence that escalated in the regions in which population transfers were actually carried out. Those to be deported often resisted resettlement and either rose-up directly against their oppressors or fled their villages and joined the partisans. Those who were actually resettled often ended up in camps, because the initial sites for resettlement were blocked. Concentration camps as well as refugee camps were overcrowded with displaced persons; many fell victim to disease or to the brutal conditions under which they were forced to live during resettlement or while in the camps. Thousands of farmers fell out of the agricultural production process due to their deportation, and many more because it was not safe to cultivate and harvest in certain regions. The consequence of the loss of production was famine which struck city populations, refugees and the inmates held in camps and prisons the hardest. Diplomatic arguments between the powers involved were another consequence.

Finally, population exchanges had a direct and radicalizing impact on the persecution of Jews and other minorities in several countries. Once the discourse of population engineering entered the practical sphere, it did not take long for experts to come up with suggestions regarding the resettlement of Jews and Romani. The structures that had been built for population transfers, like transit camps or enterprises for the management of looted property, accelerated the process and could be quickly reactivated once it came to the deportation of the Jews.[43]

---

41 Jozo Tomasevich, *War and Revolution in Yugoslavia, 1941–1945: The Chetniks* (Stanford, CA: Stanford University Press, 1975), 167.

42 See Michael Schwartz, *Ethnische 'Säuberungen' in der Moderne: Globale Wechselwirkungen nationalistischer Gewaltpolitik im 19. und 20. Jahrhundert*, Quellen und Darstellungen zur Zeitgeschichte 95 (München: Oldenbourg, 2013); for the similar memorandum see Mihailović's headquarters to the commander of the Second Sarajevo četnik Brigade, quoted after Norman L. Cigar, *Genocide in Bosnia: The Policy of 'Ethnic Cleansing'* (College Station, TX: Texas A & M University Press, 1995); for debated continuities since the Balkan Wars, see Ther, *The Dark Side of Nation-States*, 44.

43 On Soviet deportations in Eastern Poland and from the Baltic states in 1940, see the subchapter 'Stalinist Violence – Annexed territories 1939–1941'.

Soviet POWs

The Soviet POWs constituted one of the biggest groups of Germany's occupation victims, second to the European Jews. Approximately 5.3 million people, among them tens of thousands of women, came into German captivity and were treated in an inhuman fashion, without any protection of international law. Tens of thousands were shot while being marched in the western direction, most of them because they were too exhausted to continue walking. Moreover, hundreds of thousands died in the transit camps (*Durchgangslager*) in Russia, Ukraine and Belorussia. Their final destination was to reach the main POW camps (*Stammlager* or *Stalag*) that were situated in Germany, in the Baltics and in Poland. Thus, these countries were the sites of mass crimes against Soviet POWs.[44]

Red Army prisoners were transported to the Baltics and to Poland from the beginning of the war. The German POW administration had set up several larger *Stalag* camps in different regions, among them *Stalags* in Daugavpils, in Rēzekne and in Riga, in Kaunas and in Vilnius.[45] Many more of these camps were located on Polish soil, the worst ones likely being in Siedlce, Dęblin and Chełm.[46]

Most of the Red Army soldiers were already in bad physical shape before they arrived in the camps. Those who fell into captivity during the great cauldron battles of September–October 1941 were especially malnourished but were kept on their westward course. In October 1941, the High Command of the German Army reduced the food rations, especially for those POWs who were considered 'unfit for work'. In all the POW camps that held Red Army soldiers in Nazi Europe, mass death began in October, and the death rates continued to rise until the end of December. For example, in the Dęblin-Irena camp alone, after Christmas 1941, between 1,000 and 2,000 POWs died each day.

Though the order had been given to kill all the political functionaries of the Red Army immediately upon capture (the so-called *Kommissarbefehl*), most of the selections of who was considered a functionary took place within the camps. Alleged commissars, Jews and even Asian-looking POWs – until late 1941 – were sorted out and shot by the German Police or the military. Among the first victims in Poland were the POWs who were deported from the Lamsdorf Stalag to the Auschwitz concentration camp in August 1941. Some of them were among the first prisoners to be murdered with the gas Cyclone-B (*Zyklon-B*) in early September 1941. Few of the 12,000 Soviet POWs who came to Auschwitz survived the spring of 1942.[47]

The Polish population was quite aware of the Red Army POWs' plight: everybody knew about the disastrous conditions within the camps and the inhabitants living nearby were even aware of the mass killings. Nevertheless, the attitude of the Polish population towards the POWs was quite mixed. Many Poles had direct contact with the POWs in the workplace where they could assist them. But the Polish underground often referred to them as 'Bolsheviks'. Hundreds of thousands of POWs managed to escape from the horror in the camps, and often joined

---

44 Christian Streit, *Keine Kameraden: Die Wehrmacht und die sowjetischen Kriegsgefangenen 1941–1945* (Stuttgart: Deutsche Verlagsanstalt, 1978).
45 For an in-depth analysis, see, Dieckmann, *Deutsche Besatzungspolitik in Litauen*, 1328–80.
46 Wiesław Marczyk, *Jeńcy radzieccy w niewoli Wehrmachtu na ziemiach polskich w latach 1941–1945* [Soviet prisoners-of-war in *Wehrmacht* captivity on Polish territory between 1941 and 1945] (Opole: Centr. Muzeum Łambinowice, 1987).
47 Jerzy Brandhuber, 'Die sowjetischen Kriegsgefangenen im Konzentrationslager Auschwitz', *Hefte von Auschwitz* 4 (1961): 5–46.

communist partisans or formed their own groups to look for food. The peasants were quite critical of the POWs; in Eastern Poland, however, the Belorussian and Ukrainian majority considered the POWs to be fellow countrymen.

For the Balts – unlike for the Poles – the fate of the Red Army POWs was in a certain sense their *own* tragedy, since men from the Baltic countries had been drafted into the Red Army in 1940–41. The German military, however, pursued a policy of ethnic segregation among the POWs. Soviet Germans, POWs of Baltic origin and even some of the Ukrainian POWs were released in autumn 1941, either in order to perform auxiliary services for Germany or to return to the collective farms and secure the autumn harvest. It was predominately Russian POWs, including non-Russians, who were starved to death during the winter of 1941–42.[48]

Only from spring 1942 did the situation for the Soviet POWs improve somewhat; the standards of international law, however, were never applied. The Commissar order was revoked in May 1942, and there were no mass starvations during the winters between 1942 and 1944. The killing of Jewish POWs continued. But from 1942 onwards, most captured Red Army soldiers were transferred to Germany to perform forced labour there.

The Holocaust

There is no doubt that the Holocaust, the systematic mass murder of Jews, stood at the centre of Germany's extermination policies, especially in Central Europe. Historiography has investigated these crimes, by and large, as a separate phenomenon by isolating the histories of different countries and regions, but even more so by isolating such crimes from the crimes committed against other groups. Yet, the persecution and murder of Eastern European Jews was closely controlled by Berlin; it followed similar patterns in all regions, and at least until the end of 1941, it was integrated into a general policy of violence against both Jews and non-Jews alike.[49]

Germany's attack on Poland marks a watershed in the Nazi persecution of Jews. Not only did an additional two million people of Jewish origin come under German rule, but persecution from that point on was also accompanied by murder on a mass scale. In Germany, a disparaging take on Eastern European Jews was the norm. The so-called *Ostjuden* were considered inferior both according to Nazi activists and to the more nationalist conservative majority of Germany's personnel system. Moreover, they were much poorer and less integrated in their surrounding societies than the German, Austrian or Czech Jews. Thus, the occupation of Poland was not simply a continuation of anti-Jewish persecution, but it provided an entirely new dimension. Although several hundred thousand Polish Jews escaped to the Soviet Union or to Hungary and Romania, the majority ended up under German rule. They were outlawed completely, discriminated against, stripped of the majority of their property and were wholly segregated from Polish society.[50]

During the German-Polish war, both Wehrmacht and SS/police units committed crimes against the Jews as alleged reprisal for acts against the German military, as a means to stir up anti-Semitic terror at the hands of the locals and for the purposes of random anti-Semitic outbursts. Police Battalion 4 in Ostrów Mazowiecka is responsible for one of the worst massacres. The

---

48 Pohl, *Herrschaft der Wehrmacht*, 210–38.
49 Cf. especially, Christian Gerlach, *The Extermination of the European Jews* (Cambridge: Cambridge University Press, 2016).
50 Dan Michman, *The Emergence of Jewish Ghettos during the Holocaust* (Cambridge/Jerusalem: Cambridge University Press/Yad Vashem, 2011).

German policemen tried to drive the Jewish community over the demarcation line into the Soviet zone, and on 11 November killed all Jews who had stayed in Ostrów, around 350 men, women and children. Similar atrocities were undertaken by the *Einsatzgruppe z.b.V.* (a security police unit for special tasks) in Upper Silesia and Galicia.[51]

All in all, several thousand Jewish civilians were killed during the German–Polish war; however, Germany did not yet have a plan for what would become their systematic killings. At this point, German officials were still developing projects for the deportation of Jews. Indeed, Jews consisted of the majority of the early deportees from the annexed territories in November–December 1939, but not during 1940. Instead, the idea of a separate 'reservation' for Jews somewhere between Cracow and Lublin was discussed. Some transports of Jews from Moravia and Austria were unloaded in Nisko in the south-eastern corner of the Polish territory that was occupied by Germany, but the overall plan was abandoned in spring 1940 due to criticism of the German administration within the General Government: there was no way of employing the deportees, nor could they live off the land. Moreover, Nisko was not far from the Soviet demarcation line. Since deportation schemes failed, administrations in both the annexed territories and the General Government began installing local ghettos as an intermediate means. They started organizing the internal deportation of Jews from the countryside and from smaller towns to the ghettos that were established in the larger cities.

There was no consistent policy of ghettoization in Poland until spring 1941; rather, up to that point, the German occupation administrations had failed at a combination of large-scale deportation projects and local initiatives. Some of the occupation administrations considered the creation of ghettos as a means not only of isolating Jews and stripping them of their belongings, but also as a way of creating the circumstances under which they would die in large numbers. This was actually the case in the Warsaw Ghetto by the end of 1940, when the area was totally overcrowded, particularly with Jews who had been expelled from the regions west of Warsaw. From early 1941 on, thousands of ghetto inmates died each month, predominately children and elderly people, but also the newly arrived who came to the ghetto as 'refugees'.

Generally, the ghettos were set up in quarters with insufficient infrastructure, often those that had been destroyed during the 1939 bombing campaigns. The living space the Jews were allocated was minimal. In most flats, there were several families living together. Some of the ghettos – especially the one in Lodz – were completely isolated from the outside world. The inmates depended on the official supply system of the Jewish Councils, which itself was dependent on the insufficient German deliveries. The lack of medical supplies and heating material in the winter only aggravated the situation. Thus, ghetto society was divided among those who still had resources for participating in the black-market economy or with connections to the outside world, and those who were completely reliant on the supply system. Smuggling from the outside world became more and more dangerous as time went on and was punishable by death – in Lodz starting in 1940, in the General Government starting in late 1941.[52]

---

51 Markus Roth, Annalena Schmidt, *Judenmord in Ostrów Mazowiecka: Tat und Ahndung* (Berlin: Metropol, 2013); Jürgen Matthäus, Jochen Böhler and Klaus-Michael Mallmann, *War, Pacification, and Mass Murder, 1939: The Einsatzgruppen in Poland* (Lanham, MD: Alta Mira Press, 2014); Alexander B. Rossino, 'Nazi Anti-Jewish Policy during the Polish Campaign: The Case of the Einsatzgruppe von Woyrsch', *German Studies Review* 24 (2001): 35–53.

52 Cf. *Die Verfolgung und Ermordung der europäischen Juden durch das nationalsozialistische Deutschland 1933–1945*, vol. 4, Polen: September 1939 – Juli 1941, ed. Klaus-Peter Friedrich (München: Oldenbourg, 2011) (English translation forthcoming).

Violence was even more present in the forced labour camps for Jews in occupied Poland. Adult Jews served as a major resource for forced labour: as early as 1940, hundreds of small camps were set up, some of them with rather bearable conditions, where workers could return home to sleep. Others, like the infamous *Buggraben* ('Bug ditch') camps in the Lublin District, rather resembled concentration camps with unbearable working conditions and random acts of violence perpetrated by the guards. Simultaneously, the governments of other axis states like Hungary and Bulgaria set up forced labour service units for Jews in their respective realms, in order to isolate Jewish men (who were not allowed to join the armies anymore) and to exploit them physically.[53]

The turn to mass extermination

The period between the spring and the end of 1941 was decisive for Germany's turn to the systematic mass murder of the Jews; this period marks the so-called 'fateful months'.[54] Due to a lack of sources, it is not possible to fully reconstruct the origins of the 'Final Solution'. Nevertheless, there was consensus within the German leadership that the projected war against the Soviet Union would include the killing of alleged enemies, which not only included high-ranking Soviet functionaries among the party, the state and the army, but also all of the Jews among them. There is circumstantial evidence that from the outset the German SS and Police units planned to kill all Jewish Red Army soldiers who would fall into German hands, which likely also included all Jewish males between the ages of approximately 17 and 45. Exterminating all potential resistance (as in Poland) was considered an intermediate means of facilitating the attack; it was not, apparently, seen as a systematic extermination of all the Jews inside the Soviet Union. Germany's attack on the Soviet Union was expected to achieve military victory within 8 to 12 weeks (!), thus leaving the 'Final Solution to the Jewish Question' (*Endlösung der Judenfrage*) to an expected 'post-war' period; the idea of sending European Jews to a reservation within the Soviet Union was still on the agenda.

From the early days of the campaign, German invaders began killing Jewish men in western Lithuania and western Ukraine; they further initialized or supported the pogroms of local nationalist militias. Outbursts of local violence had already occurred during the September 1939 war: groups from the OUN (Organization of Ukrainian Nationalists) exploited the power vacuum in Eastern Poland to settle the score with the Poles whom they considered to be their former suppressors; others organized themselves in the newly formed Workers-Peasants' militias under Soviet rule for the same purpose. All in all, several thousand Poles and a number of Jews were killed in September–October 1939. The same patterns reappeared, though more violently, during Germany's attack on the Soviet Union. Even under the Hungarian military administration, OUN cells killed at least 2,000 perceived enemies, including entire Jewish families. The OUN helped set up militias under German rule in June–July 1941, as did the Lithuanian underground organizations further to the north. The LAF (Lithuanian Activist Front) and the Iron Wolf (*Geležinis Vilkas*) had negotiated with German agencies prior to June 1941 to start 'anti-Soviet' action in the case of war. The situation escalated with the mass crimes committed by the Soviets in late June 1941 when the NKVD massacred its political prisoners just before

---

53 Browning, *Origins*, 36–168; Witold W. Mędykowski, *Macht Arbeit frei? German Economic Policy and Forced Labor of Jews in the General Government* (Lanham, MD: Academic Studies Press, 2018).

54 Christopher R. Browning, ed., *Fateful Months: Essays on the Emergence of the Final Solution*, rev. ed. (New York: Holmes & Meier, 1991).

the Red Army retreated. Popular belief, fed by German and local propaganda, held the Jewish minority responsible for these crimes. Both the Germans and local groups were responsible for instigating major pogroms, especially in Eastern Galicia (Western Ukraine) and Lithuania. Some 10,000 Jewish men fell victim to these massacres, often committed at the sites where the NKVD had murdered its prisoners. The infamous photographs taken by German soldiers of local nationalists in Lviv (Lwów/Lemberg) and Kaunas slaughtering Jews in broad day light have become iconic images of the Holocaust. It is difficult to distinguish responsibilities here, whether German military and *Einsatzgruppen* or local nationalist groups were responsible, and to what extent the local population was involved. Similar instances occurred in the countryside, namely in the Białystok and Łomża areas, where local activists killed Jews in several towns including Jedwabne, briefly after German Security Police had been to the places. Another terrible massacre was committed in Tarnopol (Ternopil) by the Waffen-SS 'Wiking' Division in cooperation with local activists. After July 1941, pogroms almost completely ceased, since the German Police took full control and conducted such killing operations on their own.[55]

Parallel to the abovementioned pogroms, the Romanian army and Gendarmerie committed massacres during the first days of the war against the Soviet Union, in which Romania partook as Nazi Germany's ally, targeting the Jewish communities near the new Romanian-Soviet frontier. In Iași, the Romanian police and army units staged a major massacre, somewhat inaptly called the 'Jassy pogrom', which resulted in the mass murder and deportation of thousands of Jews. The victims were not driven towards a specific destination but were deliberately transported around the region in overcrowded wagons so that they would die in transit. At least 13,000 Jews died in the city of Iași proper and inside the 'death trains'.[56] Meanwhile, Romanian army units conducted several other massacres in the area. They were the first to exterminate entire Jewish communities including women and children, as was the case in Mărculești.[57] In re-occupied Bessarabia, the Romanian Secret Service staged pogroms when Romanian troops entered the territory, resulting in at least 10,000 murdered Jews. All others were transported by Romanian troops from Bessarabia and Bukovina in death marches to Romanian-occupied Transnistria (the area around Odessa between the Dniester and the Southern Bug). The Romanian military and police conducted their genocide within the framework of Nazi Germany's war against the Soviet Union, but they acted rather independently in Romania proper, in re-occupied Bessarabia and in occupied Transnistria; most of the Jews from these regions were shot between December 1941 and March 1942.[58]

During the first 10 weeks after the attack on the Soviet Union, Nazi Germany's death squads, the *Einsatzgruppen*, the Order Police battalions, the SS brigades and several Wehrmacht units shot Jewish men who mostly belonged to the local elites or the intelligentsia. These

---

55 Witold Mędykowski, *W cieniu gigantów: Pogromy 1941 roku w byłej sowieckiej strefie okupacyjnej: kontekst historyczny, społeczny i kulturowy* [In the shadow of giants: the pogroms of 1941 in the former Soviet occupation zone – historical, social and cultural contexts] (Warsaw: ISPPAN, 2012). For a detailed analysis for Eastern Galicia, see Kai Struve, *Deutsche Herrschaft, ukrainischer Nationalismus, antijüdische Gewalt: Der Sommer 1941 in der Westukraine* (München: de Gruyter, 2016).
56 Jean Ancel, *Prelude to Mass Murder: The Pogrom in Iași, Romania, June 29, 1941 and Thereafter* (Jerusalem: Yad Vashem, 2013).
57 *International Commission on the Holocaust in Romania: Final Report*, eds Tuvia Friling, Radu Ioanid and Mihail E. Ionescu (Iași: Polirom, 2004), 128–34.
58 Vladimir Solonari, *Purifiyng the Nation: Population Exchange and Ethnic Cleansing in Nazi-Allied Romania* (Baltimore, MD: Johns Hopkins University Press, 2010); Simon Geissbühler, *Blutiger Juli: Rumäniens Vernichtungskrieg und der vergessene Massenmord an den Juden 1941* (Paderborn: Ferdinand Schöningh, 2013).

murders were perceived as 'reprisals' in internal correspondence, in agreement with the higher echelons of the Wehrmacht. However, several factors led to the expansion of victim groups, which first resulted in the inclusion of women, children and the elderly, and then extended to the total extermination of Jewish communities (the most infamous of which was the Babi Yar massacre in Kiev on 29–30 September 1941). Despite the fact that it is difficult to reconstruct the orders that the German death squads received, the first contributing factor is that it is obvious that these special units had a significant amount of leeway to enforce all measures they considered necessary for 'security'; the longer the war lasted, the more widespread and accepted was the perception that mass killings would help to enforce security. Second, during his trips to the east, Himmler urged these task forces to broaden the scope of the massacres. Third, there was a certain element of competition between the various death squads regarding a killing quota. Fourth, after killing off the Jewish men, they realized that most of the Jewish families' breadwinners were dead; thus, both civil and military administrations urged the SS and police to 'get rid' of the remaining Jews – the women, children and elderly – whom the occupation administration had to feed.

The turn to systematic mass murder in Poland and Serbia came almost simultaneously in September/October 1941. It is plausible to argue that there existed central decisions, planning or at least approval of this last decisive step. At the end of July 1941, Security Police chief Heydrich was put in charge of the 'Final Solution to the Jewish Question'. In coordination with Hitler and Himmler, he enforced the most radical version of this crime. Historians are still debating whether there was a general order issued by Hitler to kill all European Jews and, if so, when it was issued. The most convincing argument is to speak of a series of orders which culminated in the systematic killing of all Jews within Nazi Germany's reach. This would have started in March 1941 with the orders to murder all Jewish communists in preparation for the war against the Soviet Union; it was radicalized in summer 1941 when the orders extended to women and children in the occupied Soviet Union, and then further in September–October with the systematic mass murder of Jews in Poland and Serbia; it went further still in December 1941 when the orders extended to all European Jews. But it was probably only in June 1942 that the decision-making and planning was finalized.[59]

For Central Europe, the months of September and October 1941 were crucial. All projects to deport Jews to the newly occupied Soviet (or Eastern Poland) areas were abandoned, and the systematic mass murder of Jews began in Poland, both in the Warthegau region and in Eastern Poland, with large-scale massacres in Stanisławów (Ivano-Frankivsk), Równe (Rivne), and other places, resulting in tens of thousands of victims. In Latvia and Lithuania, Jews in the small towns and in the countryside had been murdered since August; in November, the Germans carried out large-scale murders in Vilnius, Kaunas and in Riga in an attempt to 'empty' the ghettos so as to make space for the Jews who were deported from Germany, Austria and the Protectorate.

The German military had exterminated all Jewish men in Serbia by January 1942. Women and children were imprisoned by the Security Police in the Sajmište concentration camp in Zemun (Semlin), Belgrade's western suburb. In January 1942, the police began murdering them by gassing them with exhaust fumes in the 'gas vans' mentioned above. In March, the Security Police sent a message to Berlin, claiming that 'Serbia is free of Jews'.[60] All the Jews that had remained in Estonia had been killed by the end of 1941.

---

59 See: Browning, *The Origins of the Final Solution*; Gerlach, *The Extermination of the European Jews*.
60 Walter Manoschek, *'Serbien ist judenfrei': Militärbesatzungspolitik und Judenvernichtung in Serbien 1941/42* (München: Oldenbourg, 1993).

The establishment of extermination camps in occupied Poland began after all the deportation plans to the territories further east had proved unfeasible. Obviously, it was the regional administration and SS/police institutions that brought forward the initiative to kill all the Jews considered 'not fit for work', as they claimed. These initiatives stemmed from the Reichsgau Wartheland leadership and the SS and Police leaders in Lublin. Personnel who had served in the murder operations of people with disabilities, served under both commands. The *Sonderkommando Lange* ('Special Command Lange', named after SS-*Sturmbannführer* Herbert Lange) in the Warthegau established the Kulmhof (Chełmno) extermination camp; the Lublin SS staff together with men from the Euthanasia Programme in Germany and Austria constructed three extermination camps in the eastern part of the General Government: Bełzec in November 1941, Sobibór in March 1942 and Treblinka in May 1942. It is unclear, however, when the Auschwitz concentration camp was remodelled into an extermination facility. In early September 1941, the camp staff had already killed hundreds of inmates with the cyanide Cyclone-B. The first mass killings of Jews in Auschwitz took place in March 1942, but the large-scale murder of the Jews in the newly erected camp Auschwitz-Birkenau began in May 1942. From June 1942 on, nearly all deportees coming to Auschwitz were selected either for murder in the gas chambers or as slave labourers in the camp.[61] In August 1942, in Majdanek, which was a major concentration camp near Lublin, a gas chamber was installed. Altogether, four extermination policies were practiced in Poland in 1942: (1) the selection of Jews who were allegedly 'unfit for work' in the ghettos of the Warthegau were sent to the extermination centres at Kulmhof; (2) Operation Reinhard (*Aktion Reinhardt*) was put into practice, which was the plan to exterminate all the Polish Jews in Central and Southern Poland; (3) deportations to Auschwitz and Lublin-Majdanek occurred, where the selections took place within the camps; and (4) mass executions were carried out in Eastern Poland, especially between May and November 1942.

Deportations from the ghettos to extermination camps began in the Warthegau countryside in December 1941 and were extended to Lodz in January 1942. On 16 March 1942, German civil administration and SS/police forces had finished the preparations for mass extermination in the General Government and organized the first deportations from the Lublin and Lviv regions, beginning in the two district capitals. The Cracow region followed in early June 1942. During these three months, the German authorities explicitly envisaged the wholesale murder of all the Jews without a work permit, relying on cooperation with the Jewish councils who were in charge of handing over those to be deported. At the same time, administrations and Wehrmacht armament offices were discussing the extension of Jewish forced labour in Poland.

Both the leadership in Berlin and the SS/police in occupied Poland decided, however, to annihilate the vast majority of the Polish Jewry within a year. The extermination programme was extended in July 1942. The months from July to November 1942 witnessed not only the annihilation of most of the Polish Jewry but they constituted the worst period of genocide in all of the Nazi rule, likely even the worst in world history. SS and police units, assisted by the administration and either Polish or Ukrainian auxiliary forces, raided all the ghettos in Poland, deported the victims to extermination camps – including Auschwitz and Lublin – or

---

61 Andrea Rudorff, *Die Verfolgung und Ermordung der europäischen Juden durch das nationalsozialistische Deutschland 1933–1945*, vol. 16, *Das KZ Auschwitz 1942–1945 und die Zeit der Todesmärsche 1944/45* (München: de Gruyter, 2018), introduction.

shot them at execution sites in Eastern Poland: all in all, approximately two million human beings were murdered.[62]

The Holocaust in all other states in Central and Eastern Europe evolved in the context of various German occupation and Axis policies. The Jews living in the so-called Protectorate of Bohemia and Moravia, by and large, shared the fate of German and Austrian Jewry: they were deported in late 1939 and were transported to extermination centres from autumn 1941 on, with the difference that Bohemian and Moravian Jews were mostly deported through the Theresienstadt (Terezín) ghetto, which served as a kind of transit camp.[63]

From autumn 1941, the Slovak leadership negotiated the deportation of Slovak Jews with its German allies. The transports through transit camps in Poprad, Sered and Žilina went to Poland from March to August 1942, some to Auschwitz, some to the Lublin region and the Majdanek camp. Even though this wave of mass murder was stopped through interventions by Slovak politicians and the Catholic Church, only a small number of Jews were still alive in 1944.[64]

Similarly, the Croatian government asked for Nazi Germany's permission to deport Jews to other countries – even before the Holocaust began as systematic mass murder – as it was part of the Croatian government's utopian idea to create an ethnically homogeneous society. From the summer of 1941 onwards, Croatian Jews were murdered in two different contexts that were not necessarily intertwined. In the summer of 1941 – beginning with the leaders, the Zionist youth and leftist activists – Jewish victims were deported to Croatian concentration camps, many of which were makeshift and involved extremely high death rates so that the inmates had little chance of survival to begin with. Additionally, with the help of the Croatian authorities, the Nazi regime themselves organized two waves of deportations to Auschwitz in 1942 and 1943. It was only the presence of the Italians and the partisans in the country that allowed many Jews to escape so that a quarter of Croatia's Jewish population would ultimately survive.[65]

The Romanian government in 1941–42 fully participated in the Holocaust, or they themselves organized the genocide of the Romanian Jewry, both in the re-occupied regions and in occupied Transnistria. Approximately 250,000 Jews fell victim to the Romanian policy of extermination. The deportation of Jews from inner Romania, the Old Kingdom, to the extermination camps were already in full preparation in the late summer of 1942. But in September 1942, the Romanian leadership suddenly stopped its collaboration and began to cover its tracks. There were several reasons for this turn in Romanian policy: the churches and the political opposition, which to some extent still existed, intervened on behalf of the Jews and pressed for the deportation plans to be halted. Intense debates between the Romanian and German regimes revolved around the supply of Romanian troops to the Soviet Union, but also about the profits received from plundering the Jews; moreover, there was pressure from the US government who warned the Romanian leadership not to participate in Nazi Germany's mass crimes.[66]

---

62 Michael Alberti, *Die Verfolgung und Vernichtung der Juden im Reichsgau Wartheland 1939–1945* (Wiesbaden: Harrassowitz, 2006), 407–57; Stephan Lehnstaedt, *Der Kern des Holocaust: Bełżec, Sobibór, Treblinka und die Aktion Reinhardt* (München: C.H. Beck, 2017).

63 Wolf Gruner, *Die Judenverfolgung im Protektorat Böhmen und Mähren: Lokale Initiativen, zentrale Entscheidungen, jüdische Antworten 1939–1945* (Göttingen: Wallstein Verlag, 2016).

64 Ivan Kamenec, *On the Trial of Tragedy: Holocaust in Slovakia* (Bratislava: Hajko & Hajková, 2007).

65 Ivo Goldstein and Slavko Goldstein, *The Holocaust in Croatia* (Pittsburgh: Univ. of Pittsburgh Press, 2016).

66 Cf. Hildrun Glass, *Deutschland und die Verfolgung der Juden im rumänischen Machtbereich 1940–1944*, Südosteuropäische Arbeiten 152 (München: de Gruyter, 2013); Jean Ancel, *The History of the Holocaust in Romania* (Lincoln, NE: Univ. of Nebraska Press, 2012).

In Bulgaria, Nazi Germany's only ally that did *not* participate in the war against the Soviet Union, things developed in a different way. In March 1943, Bulgaria started deporting the Jewish population from the occupied territories to Nazi death camps. But as there was serious opposition, the deportations were finally halted and the mass murder of 50,000 Bulgarian Jews (who lived in Bulgaria proper) was prevented. Those who resisted the deportations prevailed over the openly anti-Semitic and pro-German fraction. The issue was heatedly debated both inside and outside the parliament. This was a remarkable public conflict, which, after the war, was framed as 'the rescue of the Bulgarian Jews'.[67] The Bulgarian government, however, decided to deport the Jews from the occupied territories – from Vardar Macedonia, Eastern Macedonia and Western Thrace. This was similar to the Romanian case, where the Jews in annexed and contested territories lived in a much more precarious state than those in the heartlands. In March 1943, Bulgarian authorities handed over 12,000 Jews to Nazi Germany who deported them to the Treblinka death camp. Not a single person survived.[68] Historians have rightly argued that a partial deportation can hardly be labelled as a 'rescue'. The revision of the rescue-paradigm in the late 1990s was met with considerable resistance by a coalition of nationalist historians and Jewish survivors who owed their lives to the halting of the deportations by the Bulgarian authorities. Such arguments are a common phenomenon for most of the countries in Southern and Southeastern Europe, which pursued anti-Semitic policies of their own, but did not fully comply with the Nazi genocide. While historiography has largely focused on the fate of the Bulgarian Jews, it should be noted that other groups – like ethnic Turks – were victimized by the Bulgarian State as well.

Parallel to the deportations from Bulgarian-occupied Northern Greece, the German administration in the Salonika-Aegean region deported the Jews from Salonika who were facing persecution since the spring of 1941. Salonika was home to the most important Jewish community in Southeastern Europe. It was the largest assembly of Judaeo-Spanish speakers in the world. The entire community was transported to Auschwitz in 1943 and almost completely annihilated. In autumn 1943, when Italy surrendered, German forces took over the Italian-occupied territories and the Dodecanese islands. In 1944, a number of Jews from those areas were deported to Auschwitz, with the Jewish community of Rhodes being the largest target.[69] Only in Albania, which was also occupied by Nazi Germany in September 1943, was a small Jewish community – including Jewish refugees – able to survive.

The Holocaust was to be intensified once more in the spring of 1944. Facing the advancing Red Army, Hitler decided to occupy Hungary in March 1944. Until then, its 700,000 Jews (incl. those from the annexed territories) and the approximately 100,000 Christians of Jewish descent had lived in relative safety, despite the fact that the Hungarian governments themselves had conducted explicit anti-Semitic policies of discrimination, expropriation and forced labour since 1938. In summer 1941, Hungarian authorities had even deported Jews from

---

67 Hans-Joachim Hoppe, *Bulgarien – Hitlers eigenwilliger Verbündeter: Eine Fallstudie zur nationalsozialistischen Südosteuropapolitik*, Studien zur Zeitgeschichte 15 (Stuttgart: DVA, 1979); Frederick B. Chary, *The Bulgarian Jews and the Final Solution, 1940–1944* (Pittsburgh, PA: Univ. of Pittsburgh Press. 1972).

68 Nadia K. Danova and R. Avramov, *Deportiraneto na evreite ot Vardarska Makedoniĭa, Belomorska Trakiĭa i Pirot, mart 1943 g.: Dokumenti ot bŭlgarskite arkhivi* [The deportation of the Jews from Vardar Macedonia, White Sea Thrace and Pirot, March 1943: Documents from the Bulgarian Archives] (Sofia: Obedineni izdateli, 2013).

69 Steven B. Bowman, *The Agony of Greek Jews, 1940–1945* (Stanford, CA: Stanford University Press, 2009).

Hungarian-annexed Transcarpathia to the part of the Soviet Union occupied by Hungarian troops; SS units murdered 14,000 Jews who were expelled from Hungary on 27–28 August 1941 in Kamianets-Podilskyi. Nevertheless, Miklós Horthy constantly refused to comply with the German requests to deport Hungarian Jews to Poland.[70]

Atrocities occurred mainly in the annexed borderlands and in some Honvéd (the Hungarian army) units into which Jewish males of military age had been pressed and forced to perform often deadly labour service. Typically for any Axis state, the degree of violence was higher in annexed territories than in the mainland. The Honvéd – with the help of the police – committed at least one massacre in the Ukraine in the summer of 1941.[71] On 23 January 1942, Hungarian police and army forces massacred 2,000 Serbs and Jews on the banks of the Danube in Novi Sad (Vojvodina). The city had been annexed in 1941 and bore its Hungarian name Újvidék during the war; the massacre was considered a reprisal against partisan attacks, but actually, it was an attempt to Magyarize the city. Altogether, the Hungarian forces killed roughly 4,000 Serbs and Jews in the Vojvodina. This case, however, also shows the limitations for genocide in Hungary since the massacre sparked considerable remonstration. After international protest, a parliamentary commission was installed, and in 1943 a trial led to the conviction of 15 war criminals (both army and local police), even though the main culprits, Ferenc Feketehalmy-Czeydner and others, escaped to Germany where they found asylum.[72] Secret negotiations with the Western Allies regarding a Hungarian withdrawal led to no immediate results and culminated in Germany's invasion of Hungary in March 1944 and subsequently to the opening of the 'last chapter' of the Holocaust.[73]

During the occupation, German authorities left the Hungarian State apparatus intact, but urged Horthy to replace positions in the administration and the Gendarmerie with German-oriented and extremely anti-Semitic personnel. The newly appointed men in the ministry of the interior – especially, Andor Jaross, László Baky and László Endre – came forth with extensive deportation programmes and organized the ghettoization of the Hungarian Jewry within a very short period of time.[74] In the most brutal fashion, the Hungarian regional administrations and Gendarmerie implements the resettlement of all Jews living outside of Budapest into ghettos. In May 1944, deportations to Auschwitz began, starting with the annexed territories and then proceeding to the other provinces. Altogether, 437,000 Jews were deported to Auschwitz;

---

70 Randolph L. Braham, *The Politics of Genocide: The Holocaust in Hungary* (New York: Columbia University Press, 1994); Thomas Sakmyster, *Hungary's Admiral on Horseback: Miklós Horthy, 1918–1944* (Boulder, CO: East European Monographs, 1994).

71 Krisztián Ungváry, 'Das Beispiel der ungarischen Armee: Ideologischer Vernichtungskrieg oder militärisches Kalkül?' in *Verbrechen der Wehrmacht: Bilanz einer Debatte*, eds Christian Hartmann, Johannes Hürter and Ulrike Jureit (München: C.H. Beck, 2005), 98–106; idem, *A magyar honvédség a második világháborúban* [The Hungarian army in the Second World War] (Budapest: Osiris, 2004).

72 Árpád v. Klimó, *Remembering Cold Days: The 1942 Massacre of Novi Sad and Hungarian Politics and Society, 1942–1989* (Pittsburgh, PA: University of Pittsburgh Press, 2018).

73 Götz Aly and Christian Gerlach, *Das letzte Kapitel: Realpolitik, Ideologie und der Mord an den ungarischen Juden 1944/1945* (Stuttgart: Deutsche Verlags-Anstalt, 2002); Ferenc Laczó, *Hungarian Jews in the Age of Genocide: An Intellectual History, 1929–1948* (Leiden: Brill, 2016).

74 On Hungarian initiatives cf. Gábor Kádár and Zoltán Vági, *A végső döntés: Berlin, Budapest, Birkenau 1944* [The final decision: Berlin, Budapest, Birkenau 1944] (Budapest: Jaffa K, 2013); Krisztián Ungváry, *A Horthy-rendszer mérlege: Diszkrimináció, szociálpolitika és antiszemitizmus Magyarországon, 1919–1944* [The balance of the Horthy regime: discrimination, social policy and anti-Semitism in Hungary, 1919–1944] (Pécs: Jelenkor K, 2012); Holly Case, *Between states: The Transylvanian Question and the European Idea During World War II* (Stanford, CA: Stanford University Press, 2009).

320,000 of them were murdered immediately upon arrival. All the others were either made slave labourers within the Auschwitz camp complex or were transferred to other camps around Germany and occupied Europe.

In July 1944, however, Horthy stopped the deportations. The major motive behind this step was the prospect of the war since the Allies had started offensives both in Northern France and in Belorussia, and Germany's defeat at this point seemed inevitable. The Roosevelt administration explicitly warned Horthy not to participate in the Holocaust, and then the US Army bombed Budapest; moreover, there are indications that Horthy refrained from deporting the Budapest Jews. Later, Horthy was forced to resign, with the fascist Arrow Cross movement taking over in October 1944 and its leader Ferenc Szálasi becoming head of state and prime minister. Though they did not continue deportations to Auschwitz, the Arrow Cross' bloody reign over Budapest and Western Hungary was an ordeal for the remaining Jews, Romani as well as for many other Hungarians. Arrow Cross militias might have executed up to 38,000 individuals (9,000 in the Budapest Ghetto alone) and sent up to 70,000 Jews on death marches and to last-minute labour assignments towards the Hungarian-Austrian border where they were deployed to build fortifications – often with a deadly outcome. The Red Army liberated the city from fascist rule after the battle of Budapest was won in January 1945. It is within this violent context that the Swedish diplomat Raoul Wallenberg and other international diplomats saved the lives of several thousand Jews.

In November 1944, mass extermination was halted in Auschwitz and the crematoria (including adjacent gas chambers) were dismantled. The surviving Jews either came into the turmoil of fatal camp evacuation or continued to suffer in hiding. The Jewry of Central and Eastern Europe was, by and large, annihilated: first, in Poland, Hungary, Lithuania and Czechoslovakia, and then in smaller Jewish minorities in other countries. Only the Jewish communities in Albania, Bulgaria and most of the Jews in Romania proper were spared from the onslaught. The losses were the highest in all of Europe. In Germany and Austria, the majority of Jews were able to emigrate in time; in Western, Northern and Southern Europe, all in all, less than half of the Jews were murdered, and inside the Soviet Union (in its old frontiers) approximately one third was evacuated or able to escape, though nearly all the others who came under German rule were murdered.

The mass murder of the Romani

Alongside the mass murder of the European Jewry, the genocide of the Romani provides a second case of racially motivated mass crimes. Unfortunately, there is much less evidence and research on the Romani genocide, especially for Eastern Europe. Germany's anti-Romani policies originated in their long-time anti-Gypsyism that combined practices of discrimination and administrative persecution. In 1935–36, the German regime intensified their persecution of Romani in their system of racial discrimination and began establishing camps for Romani (*Zigeunerlager*) in several cities. The anti-Romani drive was determined by exponents of 'racial science', the criminal police department and the communal administrations. No consistent policy of extermination was developed although Romani would be killed in great numbers all over Europe once the war started.

The anti-Romani policies were motivated by racism and were based on social prejudice. The Romani, especially vagrant people, were considered to be racially inferior by the Nazi regime, and to the majority of German citizens they were perceived to be a social 'nuisance'. When Germany attacked Poland in 1939, regional administrations and police took the opportunity to deport Romani into the projected 'reservation' around Lublin. More Romani were deported from eastern Prussia to the Brześć (Brest) area. Romani who lived in the occupied territories themselves were often included in the anti-Jewish policies: some were forced to move into ghettos; Romani from Austria were deported to the Lodz ghetto, and along with the Jews, were murdered in the Kulmhof death camp. In 1943-44, Sinti and Romani from Central and Western Europe met their death in Auschwitz.[75]

Parallel to the mass murder of the European Jewry, Germany's occupation administrations and police units, especially in the Baltics and in the General Government, took the initiative to kill local Romani who were often claimed to be spying for the partisans. Though a general regulation on the Romani was under debate in Berlin until the end of the war, local units started murdering them in autumn 1941, with most of the killings taking place during early 1942. It has been incredibly difficult to establish the actual identities of the victims since the perpetrators often categorized vagrant people without Romani-background as 'gypsies'.

Romani were also killed during the German anti-partisan violence in Serbia in 1941. However, there is little knowledge about Germany's anti-Romani policies in occupied Greece and Hungary where killings commenced with the German occupation in 1944.[76] It is, however, obvious that the Axis states themselves independently enforced violent anti-Romani policies. While the Slovak government imprisoned Romani in specific camps, the Romanian leadership deported 25,000 Romani to Romanian-occupied Transnistria where 11,000 of them died under horrible living conditions.[77] Among the German allies, the Ustasha regime conducted the most radical anti-Romani policies without any actual German involvement or even interest in their particular policies. Romani were subject to racial laws quite similar to the anti-Jewish laws, and 25,000 of them were deported to the Jasenovac concentration camp where nearly all of them were murdered in 1942.[78]

Though the Axis regimes did not consider the Romani dangerous enemies like the Jews or the communists, they nevertheless killed them in great numbers: in some cases, the killings were racially-socially motivated and enacted at the behest of German agencies; in other cases, like in Croatia and Romania, they were murdered in the context of ethnic cleansing. Due to the imprecise statistics on the Romani population and to fragmented perpetrator evidence, it is unclear how many Romani were murdered in Central, Eastern and Southeastern Europe during the Second World War. A figure of more than 100,000 victims – approximately half of all European Romani victims – seems to be a reasonable estimate. Their fate has been neglected both by historiography and in public memory for a long time.

---

75 Michael Zimmermann, *Rassenutopie und Genozid: Die nationalsozialistische 'Lösung der Zigeunerfrage'* (Hamburg: Christians, 1996).
76 János Bársony and Ágnes Daróczi, eds, *Pharrajimos: The Fate of the Roma During the Holocaust* (New York: International Debate Education Association, 2008).
77 Viorel Achim, ed., *Documente privind deportarea țiganilor în Transnistria* [Documents on the deportation of gypsies to Transnistria] (București: Editura Enciclopedică, 2004).
78 Narcisa Lengel-Krizman, *Genocid nad Romima: Jasenovac 1942* [The Romani genocide: Jasenovac 1942] (Jasenovac and Zagreb: Biblioteka Kameni Cvijet, 2003); Alexander Korb, 'Ustaša Mass Violence Against Gypsies in Croatia, 1941/42', in *The Nazi Genocide of the Gypsies: Reevaluation and Commemoration*, ed. Anton Weiss-Wendt, War and Genocide (New York: Berghahn, 2011); Danijel Vojak, Bibijana Papo, Alen Tahiri, *Stradanje Roma u Nezavisnoj Državi Hrvatskoj 1941–1945* [The suffering of the Romani in the Independent State of Croatia 1941–1945] (Zagreb: Institut društvenih znanosti Ivo Pilar, 2017).

Violence during the retreat of 1944–45

The next phase of the genocide of the European Jewry occurred during Germany's retreat from the Eastern Front, which began in February 1943 and reached the former Polish borders in March 1944. From the outset, the Germans tried to forcibly evacuate all the able-bodied population and prisoners, which, on several occasions, ended in their deaths. As early as October–November 1943, SS and police units killed the last of the Jewish forced labourers in the Lublin and Galicia areas, especially during the so-called *Erntefest* ('Harvest festival') massacres on 3–4 November in Lublin-Majdanek, Trawniki, Poniatowa and other camps.[79]

Camps in central Poland were evacuated in July 1944 and in northern and western Poland in January 1945 during the Red Army's Vistula–Oder offensive. Some of the prisoners, especially in the summer of 1944, were deported in trains; most of the victims of the January 1945 evacuation were forced to walk on foot in death marches, where weakened prisoners were shot, and several massacres occurred.

From 1943 onwards, German Police began murdering all prison inmates during their retreats from the Red Army. During the Red Army's summer offensive in June/July 1944, the German Security Police shot their prisoners in several places, i.e. in the Lublin castle and in Białystok. More massacres occurred in January 1945, for example, in the Radogoszcz prison in Lodz. Thus, the general dimensions of violence in Central Europe declined for a short while in the summer of 1943 – after the nearly total extermination of the Jews – and then gathered momentum again during the different phases of retreat. In Southeastern Europe, retreating German troops also committed numerous massacres. The Army Group E with its 300,000 soldiers began their retreat from Greece and Romania in August 1944. Their retreat was largely successful because of Germany's determination to crush any resistance and its goal to retreat into Croatia and Austria, which at least partly explains the massacres that German troops committed on their way north. Massacres were also committed on Crete, where the German troops (who could not withdraw) were involved in intense fighting with the partisans that was deadly for both sides. Wehrmacht soldiers committed massacres in the villages of Viannos in September 1943 and those of Kedros on August 22, 1944. There were, however, still 150,000 German soldiers on Yugoslav soil when the European armistice was signed in May 1945.

Systematic research on the late stages of Germany's violence has only recently begun during the last decade. Thus, it is difficult to find a general analytical approach to the period between spring 1944 and January 1945. Nevertheless, it is obvious that during this final period of German occupation, violence was – again – directly connected to the course of the war, and the fates of different victim groups became more intertwined.[80]

Structures and agencies of violence

Can we consider the region of Eastern Europe during the Second World War (and its immediate aftermath) a 'Bloodlands', as Timothy Snyder has called it?[81] Had it already been an area of inherent mass violence since 1914, scattered with mass graves and sites of mass murder?

---

79 Wojciech Lenarczyk, Dariusz Libionka, eds, *Erntefest 3–4 listopada 1943: zapomniany epizod Zagłady* [Erntefest, 3–4 November 1943: a forgotten episode of the Holocaust] (Lublin: Państwowe Muzeum na Majdanku, 2009).
80 Daniel Blatman, *The Death Marches: The Final Phase of Nazi Genocide* (Cambridge, MA: Belknap Press of Harvard University, 2011).
81 Snyder, *Bloodlands*.

The answers depend on how we define certain things. There is no doubt that the majority of the Nazi regime's victims had lived in Central and Eastern Europe. One reason that the borderlands from the Baltics in the north to the Balkans in the south became the sites of extreme mass violence and extermination camps during the war was due to the region's demographic structure, especially when it comes to the Jewish population. The majority of Jews from western and central Poland, from Hungary, Czechoslovakia and Southeastern Europe were deported to the Nazi extermination centres in Poland and killed there; those in the Baltics, Eastern Poland and Bessarabia were shot near their hometowns. Moreover, the ethnic complexity of the region invited 'homogenizers' to use the war for attempts to reshape its demographic constitution by means of ethnic cleansing. That, again, sparked armed resistance and partisan warfare. Finally, the imperial competitions between Germany and the Soviet Union, and Germany and Italy, sparked proxy wars and, again, partisan warfare. Therefore, a number of different phenomena – from the mass shootings in Poland in 1941 to the extermination of Jews in 1942; from the genocide of Serbs in Croatia to the German massacres in occupied Greece and, of course, the ghettoization and deportations in Hungary during the spring of 1944 – are all intricately intertwined and must all, therefore, be taken into account.

But all this does not automatically indicate that these areas can be considered as 'structurally' violent, i.e. containing severe long-term, open or implicit conflict. Structural violence certainly applies to some of the borderlands that were subjects to waves of violence from 1915 to 1921, to a very limited extent during the 1930s, and again from 1939. But most of the other regions were not very different from Western Europe in this respect until the beginning of the Second World War.

During the Second World War, specific regions in Central and Eastern Europe were infested with extreme violence, others were sites of mass deportation while others still did not experience major mass violence at all. That said, ethnic cleansing, anti-partisan warfare, civil war and mass deportations affected the regional societies in a traumatic way. For example, Western Belorussia (i.e. the Polish voivodships Nowogródek and Polesia) not only witnessed the extreme mass murder of the local Jews, but they also witnessed the deaths of Soviet POWs en masse as well as extreme violence during German anti-partisan warfare and the violence perpetrated by the Soviet NKVD in 1939–41 and 1944–45;[82], the ethnic cleansings in Volhynia at the hands of the UPA (Ukrainian Insurgent Army) in 1943–44 can be added to this list. Bosnia was the site of mass murder committed by the Ustasha in 1941–42, followed by relentless Axis anti-partisan warfare and Yugoslav civil war until 1945. For the Jewish population, most regions were extremely dangerous to live in, but there were exceptions, too, such as the mainland of Bulgaria, Romania and Hungary up until 1944, and the Italian-occupied zones in the Balkans (up until 1943) were all relatively safe. In contrast, after the dissolution of nearly all the ghettos in summer 1943, and most of the camps in autumn 1943, it was virtually impossible for Jews to move within the country or even to survive in occupied Poland. Civilians who robbed and murdered Jews in 1943–44 could do so without having to consider the consequences.

According to post-war investigations, in Poland alone (in its post 1944 borders) more than 5,000 camps and sub-camps existed during the German occupation.[83] More such sites were

---

82 Alexander Brakel, *Unter Rotem Stern und Hakenkreuz: Baranowicze 1939 bis 1944: Das westliche Weißrussland unter sowjetischer und deutscher Besatzung* (Paderborn: Ferdinand Schöningh, 2009).
83 Czesław Pilichowski, ed, *Obozy hitlerowskie na ziemiach polskich 1939–1945: Informator encyclopedyczny* [Nazi camps in Poland 1939–1945: Encyclopaedic reference book] (Warsaw: PWN, 1979). The US Holocaust Memorial Museum has established even higher figures.

situated in Eastern Poland, as well as under the Soviet regime. The actual features of these camps differed enormously, for example, as with the rates of survival, which were rather high in labour camps for non-Jews and rather low in camps for Jews, though there were notable exceptions. Though the satellite states also installed camps in their own regions, only the Ustaha regime established a proper camp system of its own which had an extremely high mortality rate.

Also, the living conditions in the approximately 1,100 ghettos differed,[84] with the largest – Warsaw – being one of the worst, and with sometimes somewhat better conditions in the countryside. Only a limited number of actual concentration camps (administered by the Inspection of the Concentration Camps in Oranienburg) were located in Central Europe, most notoriously Auschwitz and Lublin-Majdanek, of course, but also Stutthof, Riga-Kaiserwald, Klooga, Cracow-Plaszow and Warsaw, each with dozens of sub-camps. Approximately 500,000 prisoners died in these camps, and another 700,000–800,000 Jews were killed there without ever being registered as prisoners. Several extermination camps with the sole purpose of mass destruction were built on Polish soil and mostly served for the annihilation of the Jewish communities in the wider vicinity of these camps. During Operation Reinhard, approximately 1.4–1.5 million Jewish individuals were murdered in Bełżec, Sobibór and Treblinka in 1942–43; the Kulmhof site (Chełmno) served for the destruction of the Jews in the Warthegau. The fate of prison inmates in Central, Eastern and Southeastern Europe has been neglected by Western research, though the death rates were comparatively high and the German Security police periodically murdered inmates in order to make room for others. Further, the mass murder of Soviet POWs is still under-researched. Most of Eastern Europe became a universe of imprisonment facilities, especially from 1941–42 on. The German administration was committed to rule over a multi-purpose empire of camps. The public was either shut out, or completely paralyzed, even though there were numerous interactions between the public and the camps, and even the sites of mass destruction.

Over the last few decades, historiographers have gone to extreme efforts to identify the agencies and the actors of German violence in the occupied countries. According to the results, there were many more perpetrators than had been previously assumed. Hundreds of thousands of Germans, including Austrians and ethnic Germans, participated in mass crimes in Eastern Europe, among them also likely thousands of women. This, of course, makes it increasingly difficult to identify specific social or even biographical patterns among the perpetrators.

Nevertheless, most of these people acted within the framework of Germany's official institutions, most importantly within the German occupation administration and the SS/police apparatus. While the occupation administration was responsible for the overall planning of the population policies and the persecutions, the joint SS and Police system served as the executive force for carrying out the mass murder. Officially, the Gestapo, i.e. the German political police, had the task of 'combatting the enemies of the Reich'. But due to its personnel weakness, they had to rely heavily on all the other SS and Police structures, especially the Criminal Police, which together with the Gestapo made up the Security Police. Those who worked for the Security Police along with the SD (Security Service of the SS, or *Sicherheitsdienst*) were expert killers and made up the core of Germany's mass murder perpetrators. More manpower came from the Order Police (*Ordnungspolizei*) and the uniformed police (*Schutzpolizei*) in the cities, and the Order Police battalions and the Gendarmerie – particularly important in the occupied East – in the countryside. The Wehrmacht, the largest

---

84 Martin Dean and Geoffrey P. Megargee, eds, *Encyclopedia of Camps and Ghettos, 1933–1945*, Vol. 2: *Ghettos in German-Occupied Eastern Europe* (Bloomington, IN: Indiana University Press, 2012).

German force, was responsible for violence during the campaigns in Poland, Yugoslavia and the Soviet Union, but also for the violence in the areas of military occupation (i.e. Serbia and the Salonica region in Greece), for the vicious treatment of the Soviet POWs and for the anti-partisan warfare.

All the other German agencies were involved in mass murder to some extent, especially in occupied Poland and the Baltic states. The health departments were pressing to 'cleanse' the psychiatric institutions, while the labour departments organized forced labour, deportations to Germany and the selection of the Jewish workforce during the ghetto round-ups; others looted Jewish and non-Jewish property especially during the ghettoization and after massacres.[85]

Nevertheless, the logic and extent of violence under German hegemony cannot be understood without the phenomenon of collaboration. Of course, one has to distinguish whether one is referring to collaboration on a national, regional, local or individual level – and historians have not always done that. The policies of violence enacted by the non-German Axis governments, especially by Romania and Croatia, but also by Italy, Hungary, Slovakia and Bulgaria, can rather be characterized as cooperation between political partners, though on an asymmetric level. The various collaboration governments that were under German occupation acted from within a different framework. While the Hungarian government, which was under German occupation from March 1944, were still relatively independent, the central administrations of the Protectorate, Greece, Estonia, Latvia and Serbia were more subordinate to German power. The latter three were especially involved in mass crimes through their own local police forces.[86]

Local police organizations were absolutely instrumental for German occupation. Nazi Germany set up auxiliary police structures in all their occupied regions, except in the annexed Polish territories. Aside from the territories annexed by the Soviet Union in 1939–40, portions of the pre-war personnel were taken over by the occupation administration. The local police supplied the occupation forces both with manpower and local knowledge. From 1942, almost every time the Germans committed mass crimes, local policemen were deployed as auxiliaries, particularly during the ghetto raids and deportations, but also during mass shootings. Sometimes local policemen participated in the killings themselves. This was even more the case after the dissolution of the ghettos and the labour camps for Jews, when the German Gendarmerie along with the auxiliary police forces hunted the Jews who were in hiding. Baltic, Ukrainian, Belorussian and Polish policemen apprehended tens of thousands of Jews and either transferred them to the German Police or shot them of their own accord.[87]

Auxiliary police battalions (*Schutzmannschaftsbataillone*) were deployed similarly; the *Schuma-Battalion* 12 partook in mass killings in both Lithuania and Belorussia. Local Security Police consisted of politically selected personnel who were highly integrated into the Nazi system of extermination: they worked directly in the offices of the German Security Police, sometimes on a collegial basis. Most of the Jews in Latvia were murdered by the Arajs command, a unit consisting of Latvian Security policemen. The Estonian Omakaitse Police acted rather

---

85 Cf. Dieter Pohl, *Nationalsozialistische Verbrechen*, Gebhardt Handbuch der deutschen Geschichte 21 (Stuttgart: Klett-Cotta, forthcoming in 2022).
86 Klaus Kellmann, *Dimensionen der Mittäterschaft: Die europäische Kollaboration mit dem Dritten Reich* (Wien: Böhlau, 2018).
87 Leonid Rein, *The King and the Pawns: Collaboration in Byelorussia during World War II* (New York: Berghahn Books, 2011); Jan Grabowski, *Na posterunku: Udział polskiej policji granatowej i kryminalnej w Zagładzie Żydów* [At the police station: the involvement of the Polish Navy-Blue and Criminal Police in the Holocaust of the Jews] (Warsaw: Wydawnictwo Czarne, 2020).

autonomously and killed most of the Estonian Jews themselves. In Serbia, the Special Police organized the major anti-Jewish actions.[88]

It is, however, unclear what role the regional and communal administrations played in the execution of Nazi Germany's extermination policies. No doubt, the local administrations were involved in setting up ghettos, looting Jewish property and recruiting forced labour. However, their participation in the extreme violence that took place remained limited; in many cases, the local administrators had to cover the mass graves after the Germans committed mass executions. Up until today, research has largely focused on the administrations in occupied Western Europe.[89]

Stalinist violence

Annexed territories 1939–41

The Soviet Union entered the Second World War on 17 September 1939 and immediately applied Stalinist violence to its occupied territories, to Eastern Poland, and starting in 1940, to Eastern Finland, the Baltic states, Bessarabia and Northern Bukovina. Hundreds of thousands of locals were deported, imprisoned or shot during that period up until July 1941 when the Red Army had to retreat in the face of Nazi Germany's attack.

Stalin's expansionist goals lay not as in the open as Hitler's. The Soviet Union itself came into being as partial territorial restoration of the Tsarist Empire and by the successful and brutal campaigns of the Red Army in 1919–20. Though the 1920s were marked by a specific policy of cultural support for most nationalities, so-called *korenizatsiia* ('rooting') – the state has even been called an 'affirmative action' empire[90] – the limits of these policies were obvious: every sign of national independence was suppressed, and beginning in the late 1920s, these policies were beginning to be revoked, particularly regarding Ukrainians, but also towards other nationalities. The political famine in the southern USSR in 1932–33 especially hit the Ukraine, Southern Russia and Kazakhstan and was a major catastrophe. During the 1930s, cultural autonomy for non-Russians was reduced, and the policy of *korenizatsiia* more or less came to an end. Russians dominated in most spheres of Soviet life, and Russian culture was preponderant. Thus, it seems reasonable to speak of a Soviet Empire in the late 1930s.

There was a constant of expansionism underlying Soviet policies, openly visible during the period of their efforts to install the 'World Revolution' from 1918 to 1924, and more sublimely after the declaration of 'Socialism in One Country'. The Communist International held up its revolutionary policy in the colonial and Chinese periphery until the early 1930s. The Soviet Union exerted considerable hegemony over Tuva, its first satellite in 1920 (the state would be annexed in 1944), Mongolia beginning in 1924 and intervened in the Chinese province of Xinjiang from 1934 onwards.

It seems that Stalin was driven by several foreign policy motives in the late 1930s: first and foremost was their security from Nazi Germany; second was to exert influence on the

---

88 Martin C. Dean, *Collaboration in the Holocaust: Crimes of the Local Police in Belorussia and Ukraine, 1941–1944* (Basingstoke: Palgrave Macmillan, 2000); Joachim Tauber, ed., *Kollaboration in Nordosteuropa: Erscheinungsformen und Deutungen im 20. Jahrhundert* (Wiesbaden: Harrassowitz, 2006).

89 See also Markus Eikel and Valentina Sivaieva, 'City Mayors, Raion Chiefs and Village Elders in Ukraine, 1941–4: How Local Administrators Co-operated with the German Occupation Authorities', *Contemporary European History* 23, no. 3 (2014): 405–28.

90 Terry Martin, *The Affirmative Action Empire: Nations and Nationalism in the Soviet Union, 1923–1939* (Ithaca, NY: Cornell University Press, 2001).

communist parties; third, was to regain the lost territories of the Russian Empire; and fourth – as a long-term goal – was to achieve a World Revolution. In August 1939, Hitler offered Stalin what he could not get from the Western Allies that he was negotiating with: a sphere of influence nearly the same size as the former western borders of Tsarist Russia. In 1943, however, even the Western Allies finally conceded most of these expansions.

In general, Stalin acted quite carefully: he only occupied Poland when it was about to be defeated, and he moved on towards the Baltics and Bessarabia/Bukovina when Western Europe succumbed to Hitler in May–June 1940. Only the attack on Finland in December 1939 met fierce military and international resistance. The major Soviet goal in all of these areas was to enlarge the Soviet Empire, adapting the newly occupied, often much more developed areas to the Soviet political, social and economic system, and thus, in Stalin's perspective, strengthening the Soviet Union, socialism and his own position.

Each and every step of Bolshevik expansion was accompanied by radical violence, first during the civil war and the war against Poland in 1920, but also in Mongolia and Xinjiang, when NKVD advisers in 1937–38 extended the 'Great Terror' to the foreign world. Inside the Soviet Union, this wave of mass terror firstly affected the Polish minority, approximately 110,000 citizens of Polish nationality were killed under bizarre pretexts. Poles were considered a potential 'fifth column' of the Polish State and were especially vulnerable to mass terror since they lived close to the Soviet–Polish border.[91]

Though the Great Terror was abandoned in late 1938, the anti-Polish propaganda and repression campaign continued, albeit on a smaller scale. It was renewed, however, during the attack in September 1939. Apparently, the Soviet leadership was not fully prepared for the invasion of Poland and the consecutive wave of Secret Police repression that followed.[92] After the NKVD installed its branches in Eastern Poland, and then in 1940, also in the Baltics and Bessarabia/Northern Bukovina, mass arrests began of the alleged opposition, especially pre-war politicians, members of specific organizations and also those who had tried to 'illegally' cross the German-Soviet demarcation line in Poland. According to official Soviet statistics, the NKVD arrested around 107,000 people in Eastern Poland, whilst even more arrests were conducted by other organs. Thirty-nine thousand arrestees received sentences by the OSO (Special Council of the NKVD), among them, 1,200 death penalties were issued. All others remained in the prisons of Eastern Poland, where hundreds died from ill treatment or neglect.[93]

The Red Army invaded the Baltic states on 15–16 June 1940. Since in 1939–40, the Soviet leadership expected their control over these states to last for a very long time, extensive preparations for the NKVD's work there were already being undertaken. As early as January 1940, the NKVD estimated the presence of 320,000 political suspects in Lithuania alone. Immediately after occupation, the NKVD arrested approximately 15,000 people, often entire families. In Lithuania, more than 6,600 locals came into NKVD custody, 15 per cent of whom were Polish,

---

91 Terry Martin, 'The Origins of Soviet Ethnic Cleansing', *The Journal of Modern History* 70 (1998): 813–61; Jerzy Bednarek and Margarita Chilińska, eds, *Wielki Terror: operacja polska 1937–1938* [The Great Terror: Operation Poland 1937–1938] (Warsaw, Kijów: Instytut Pamięci Narodowej, 2010).

92 Cf. Beria's order from 15 September 1939, in Vasyl' M. Danylenko, *Radjans'ki orhany derzhavnoyi bezpeky u 1939 – chervni 1941 r: Dokumenty HDA SB Ukraïny* [Soviet State security agencies in 1939 – June 1941: Documents of the HDA SB of Ukraine], Bilshe ne tayemno 3 (Kiev: Vydavn, Dim 'Kyjevo-Mohyljans'ka Akad', 2009), 46–8.

93 A.E. Gurianov, *Repressii protiv poliakov i polskikh grazhdan* [Repressions against Poles and Polish citizens] (Moscow: Memorial, 1997).

8 per cent of whom were Jewish.⁹⁴ Some of the victims died en route, some while imprisoned in the Gulag. The death rates between 1942 and 1944 are the highest, certain prisoners having been executed according to specific orders by the OSO. In Soviet-occupied Bessarabia, more than 32,000 people received political sentences; of those, 8,360 were executed or died during interrogations.⁹⁵

A similar fate befell the Polish POWs who were in Soviet hands. The Red Army captured approximately 240,000 Polish prisoners, though the Soviet Union had not officially declared war against Poland. The NKVD established a specific camp system for POWs and civilian internees, the GUPVI (Main Administration for Affairs of Prisoners of War and Internees). Around 85,000 POWs were released due to their Belorussian or Ukrainian ethnicity, or they were handed over to the German Wehrmacht because their place of residence was in the German territory. Nearly all other POWs were deported to camps farther to the east. In March 1940, Stalin and NKVD-chief Lavrentiy Beria decided to have specific groups of POWs killed, especially officers, gendarmes and members of the military intelligence. These groups had been kept separately in specific camps in Kozelsk, Starobelsk and Ostashkov. Between 3 April and 19 May, 14,192 POWs were transferred to NKVD compounds in Katyn, Kharkov and Kalinin (today, Tver) and then shot. The same order applied to specific groups of Polish inmates in NKVD prisons. Of those prisoners, 7,300 were murdered during the same time period, the majority, apparently, were killed in Kurapaty near Minsk, and in Bykyvnia near Kiev.⁹⁶ The motives of the Stalinist leadership for these crimes were probably similar to the Nazi's rationale for killing the intelligentsia. Elites were to be killed in order to exterminate all potential for Polish resistance based on national identity. Nevertheless, there were specific differences between the respective killing operations. The Nazi leadership ordered far more extensive killings, often initialized by local police, militias or administrations, but treated the Polish officer POWs – unlike the rank-and-file – more or less according to international law. Moreover, the Nazi leadership made far less effort to hide their crimes. There have been rumours about a Soviet-German coordination of the mass murder of the Polish intelligentsia, even of detailed NKVD-Gestapo cooperation, but no convincing evidence has been found to date.⁹⁷

While direct imprisonment and execution was meant for those whom the NKVD considered dangerous, 'class warfare' was conducted, by and large, through mass deportations. The societies of Eastern Poland were targeted through the implementation of four mass-deportation operations: the first major operation took place on 10 February 1940 in which 139,000 Polish military colonists (*osadniki*) and forest workers (*lesniki*) were deported along with their families; the second deportation of roughly 61,000 people took place on 13 April 1940 and predominately concerned the families of Polish military personnel who had been deported to Katyn and other places and

---

94 Arvydas Anušauskas, *Arrests and other Forms of Coercion: Report* (Vilnius: Commission for the Evaluation of the Crimes of the Soviet and Nazi Occupation Regimes in Lithuania 1940–1941, 2003).

95 Alexandru Usatiuc-Bulgăr, *Cu gîndul la "O lume între două lumi": Eroi, martiri, oameni-legendă* [Thinking about 'a world between two worlds': heroes, martyrs, legendary people] (Chișinău: Lyceum, 1999).

96 Claudia Weber, *Krieg der Täter: Die Massenerschießungen von Katyń* (Hamburg: Hamburger Edition, 2015).

97 O. V. Vishlev, '"Krakovskii protokol" 1940 g. Bylo li "antipol'skoe soglashenie" mezhdu NKVD i Gestapo? Iz germanskich arkhivov' [The 'Cracow Protocol' of 1940: Was there an 'anti-Polish agreement' between the NKVD and the Gestapo? From the German archives], *Novaia i Noveishaia Istoriia*, no. 5 (1995): 104–13; Piotr Kołakowski, *NKWD i GRU na ziemiach polskich 1939–1945* [The NKVD and the GRU in Poland 1939–1945] (Warsaw: Neriton, 2002).

killed onsite; the third wave of deportations happened between June and July 1940 and totalled more than 78,000 refugees from Western Poland who had refused to accept Soviet citizenship, most of them Jewish; the fourth and final wave occurred in May–June 1941, in which around 40,000 'counter-revolutionaries' were deported. Additionally, tens of thousands of inhabitants were deported from the Western frontier to Soviet industrial areas for forced labour.[98]

In the Baltics, deportations began comparatively late and probably were disrupted by Germany's attack in June 1941. But early that month, 11,000 individuals from Estonia, 16,000 from Latvia and 21,000 from Lithuania were deported to Gulag camps and special settlements under NKVD-supervision inside the Soviet Union. Simultaneously, the NKVD transported 30,000 people from Bessarabia and Northern Bukovina eastward. The major targets of this last wave of deportations prior to Germany's attack were the family members of men they had arrested in 1940/41. Thus, the major constituency consisted of women, children and the elderly, which were considered by the NKVD rather 'unfit for work' and were not able to cope with the harsh life in the special settlements. There are estimates that between 30 and 70 per cent of the deportees did not survive imprisonment. For example, among the deportees from Latvia, 34 per cent died while imprisoned; 341 prisoners alone were shot.[99]

While being attacked in June 1941, the Soviet Secret Police decided to partially evacuate its prison inmates, but to kill all political prisoners on the spot. Thus, more than 15,000 people were murdered during the retreat in June 1941, especially in Lviv, Lutsk and other cities in Western Ukraine and Lithuania. Nazi troops became immediately aware of these crimes which were used for propagandistic warfare in the summer of 1941. Thousands of other prisoners died en route during the evacuation or were shot by their guards.[100]

Stalinist violence after 1941

Despite the military defeats of 1941–42, Stalin soon prepared to reconquer the old Soviet and annexed territories, not only militarily, but also in a political and 'security' sense. Between 1941 and 1943 his capabilities were quite limited, but he at least tried to intervene in the German-occupied areas by way of the NKVD and the partisan movement. From March 1944 on, the Soviet forces re-entered Central and Eastern Europe.

The violence of the Soviet communist partisans has hitherto only rarely been discussed in the context of Second World War-crimes. But new research, especially conducted by Polish and Ukrainian scholars, documents the extreme violence of partisan groups not only against the

---

98 Piotr Wróbel, 'Class War or Ethnic Cleansing? Soviet Deportations of Polish Citizens from the Eastern Provinces of Poland 1939–1941', *The Polish Review* 59 (2014): 19–42; Aleksandr Gurianov, 'Masshtaby deportatsii naseleniia v glub SSSR v mae-iiune 1941 g.' [The extent of the deportation of the population into the depths of the USSR in May–June 1941], in idem, *Represii*, 137–75.

99 Among the enormous amount of literature, see, for example: Björn Michael Felder, *Lettland im Zweiten Weltkrieg: Zwischen sowjetischen und deutschen Besatzern 1940–1946* (Paderborn: Schoeningh, 2009), 138–63.

100 Janina Mikoda, ed., *Zbrodnicza ewakuacja więzień i aresztów NKWD na kresach wschodnich II Rzeczypospolitej w czerwcu – lipcu 1941 roku: materiały z sesji naukowej w 55. rocznicę ewakuacji więźniów NKWD w głąb ZSRR: Łódź, 10 czerwca 1996 r.* [The criminal evacuation of NKVD prisons and arrests in the eastern borderlands of the Second Polish Republic, June–July 1941: materials from the scientific session on the 55th anniversary of the evacuation of NKVD prisoners into the USSR: Łódź, June 10, 1996] (Warsaw: Główna Komisja Badania Zbrodni Hitlerowskich w Polsce Instytut Pamięci Narodowej; Okręgowa Komisja Badania Zbrodni Hitlerowskich w Łodzi, 1997); for further detail, see Struve, *Deutsche Herrschaft, ukrainischer Nationalismus, antijüdische Gewalt*.

occupying forces, but also against collaborators and other civilians. It is necessary to underline that the partisan units operated in a framework that was dominated by Nazi Germany: the units were established as a reaction to German occupation, and they were radicalized by Germany's war of extermination.

The Soviet partisan movement was only fully established in 1942, after the first groups that operated in autumn 1941 were destroyed or dissolved. The partisan groups rested on three pillars, the NKVD, the Red Army and the Communist Party. Despite the problems that the partisan staff had in trying to control these organizations, they can still be considered Stalinist groups, with their central task being to destroy Germany's manpower and infrastructure, but also with the aim of upholding Stalinist rule in the German-occupied areas.

Soviet partisan groups were especially active within regions inside the old Soviet borders, like Eastern Belarus, north-eastern Ukraine, Leningrad and the Bryansk areas. Considering Central Europe, Soviet partisans were especially operating in Western Belarus and Southern and Eastern Lithuania, to a limited extent in Northern Volhynia. As these were all regions where the Germans were in the middle of murdering their Jewish populations, many Jews tried to escape from the ghettos and to join the partisans, but they were in an extremely difficult position since they often possessed less resources and were discriminated against within the partisan milieu. And, of course, they had no chance of going over to the German side.

The partisan groups had a rather ambivalent relationship to the populations in their operational areas. After mass recruitment for forced labour in Germany began, more young people decided to join the partisans. On the other hand, the partisan groups often supplied their ranks by coercing the peasants, which in turn endangered the local population who became the targets of Germany's mass murder operations. From the beginning of their activity, the partisans executed any locals who worked for the Germans, like auxiliary policemen, mayors and local *starosta* ('village elders') as well as individuals, often people only suspected or denounced as collaborators who were often killed along with their families. From 1943 on, the partisans also recruited former auxiliary policemen who had participated in the Holocaust before but then went over to the Soviet side in the face of Germany's defeat.[101]

From spring 1943 on, new non-communist underground forces surfaced in Eastern Poland and Lithuania whom the Soviet partisans considered to be enemies. Different, but structurally similar, was the situation in Yugoslavia and Greece. To a certain extent, a civil war was unleashed against the Polish units, particularly in the Vilnius and Nalibaki areas, and against the UPA in Volhynia. During these conflicts, partisans not only killed members of the opposing underground, but in several instances also committed mass murder in villages that were considered strongholds of the Polish underground forces, like the May 1943 Nalibaki massacre or the Koniuchy (Kaniūkai) massacre in January 1944.[102]

There is even less new critical research on the Red Army. The Red Army, which occupied a major portion of Central, Eastern and Southeastern Europe in 1944–45, in itself was part of the Stalinist system, but was also heavily affected by Stalinist violence. Large parts of the officer corps had been killed during the Terror of 1937–38. Within the army, ruthless discipline was enforced, especially during the retreat of 1941–42. Approximately 150,000 soldiers were shot as

---

101 For a captious evaluation of the Soviet partisans, see Bogdan Musial, *Sowjetische Partisanen 1941–1944: Mythos und Wirklichkeit* (Paderborn: Ferdinand Schöningh, 2009). See also, Alexander Gogun, *Stalin's Commandos: Ukrainian Partisan Forces on the Eastern Front* (London: IB Tauris, 2015).
102 Bernhard Chiari, ed., *Die polnische Heimatarmee: Geschichte und Mythos der Armia Krajowa seit dem Zweiten Weltkrieg* (München: Oldenbourg, 2003).

alleged deserters or defeatists during the German-Soviet War; hundreds of thousands were sent to punishment units with little chance for survival.[103]

The first war crimes committed by the Red Army in the Second World War occurred as early as the occupation of Eastern Poland in September 1939. In March 1944, the Soviet military re-entered the old Polish borders of 1939. The most infamous of the Red Army's war crimes are the mass rapes: these crimes were not only committed against German women but occurred in all countries through which the Red Army marched, regardless of whether they were fascist or friendly towards the Soviet Union. The second wave of troops to arrive in the newly occupied countries were especially vicious and assaulted local women and girls all over Central, Eastern and Southeastern Europe. It is almost impossible to define the dimension of these crimes, but it seems that mass rape occurred in a more systematic fashion on German soil as well as in Hungary and Romania than further to the east. In that respect, it seems, that there was a retributory element to those crimes.[104]

Though also integrated within a radical totalitarian system, the Red Army was far less involved in mass crimes when compared to the Wehrmacht who played a central role both in the mass murder of POWs and in the Holocaust. Contrary to the German case, the Red Army did not act within a genocidal framework and had little control of the occupied territories; all 'security matters' were transferred to the NKVD/NKGB Secret Police apparatus within a short period of time. The Soviet occupation apparatus was, by and large, an extension of the structures within the Soviet Union. Thus, matters were highly concentrated in Moscow in Stalin's inner circle. Nevertheless, the party chiefs in the occupied territories and the party representatives within the advancing Red Army organized the vehicles of repression. The NKVD under Beria probably had more influence than they did under his predecessors, nevertheless they remained an executive tool of the party. Historiography up until now has not yet fully investigated the NKVD (and from 1943, the NKGB) structures and personnel in the annexed and occupied countries.[105] The NKVD itself was professionalized in combatting alleged enemies, but was also seriously affected by the purges of 1938–39, and the lack of educated personnel.

The NKVD/NKGB structures had much larger dimensions than their German counterpart, the Gestapo, but the NKVD/NKGB monopolized Stalinist violence, while all armed German units – the SS, the Wehrmacht and the Order Police – were highly integrated into the system of mass crime. The NKVD had its own troops at its disposal, but they also closely cooperated with the party organs on all levels. Though the NKVD largely relied on personnel who lacked higher

---

103 Cf. Alexander Hill, *The Red Army and the Second World War* (Cambridge: Cambridge University Press, 2017).
104 Cf. Andrea Petö, 'Stimmen des Schweigens: Erinnerungen an Vergewaltigungen in den Hauptstädten des "ersten Opfers" (Wien) und des "letzten Verbündeten" Hitlers (Budapest) 1945', *Zeitschrift für Geschichtswissenschaft* 47 (1999): 892–914; James Mark, 'Remembering Rape: Divided Social Memory and the Red Army in Hungary 1944–1945', *Past & Present* 188, no. 1 (2005): 133–61; Constantin Hlihor and Ioan Scurtu, eds, *The Red Army in Romania* (Iaşi: Center for Romanian Studies, 2000).
105 Albin Glowacki, *Sowieci wobec Polaków na ziemiach wschodnich II Rzeczypospolitej 1939–1941* [The Soviets and the Poles in the eastern territories of the Second Polish Republic 1939–1941], 2nd ed. (Lodz: Wydawnictwo Uniwersytetu Łódzkiego, 1998). Most importantly, on the inner Soviet Union: A.G. Tepliakov, *Mashina terrora: OGPU-NKVD v Sibiri v 1929–1941 gg* [The terror machine: OGPU-NKVD in Siberia in 1929–1941] (Moscow: Book on Demand, 2008).

and middle education, they seemed to be rather effective when combatting their 'enemies', especially when compared with the German SS and Police failures in occupied Poland.[106]

Right from the beginning of the 1944 re-occupation, the Soviet forces faced serious armed resistance from underground groups, especially in Latvia, Lithuania and Western Ukraine, but also in parts of Poland and Estonia.[107] The NKVD relied on its experience with combatting 'banditry' and the Soviet partisans' conflicts with anti-communist underground groups. Between 39,000 and 48,000 Poles were arrested and deported to the Soviet Union, thousands were shot during military operations, nearly 600 of whom were shot after being arrested in the infamous 'Augustów Roundup' of August 1945.[108]

Societies at war

Nazi Germany's attack on independent countries like Poland in September 1939, or Yugoslavia 20 months later, was a violent disruption in two ways. On the one hand, and as previously discussed, the Germans imported their violence directly into Eastern European societies by killing POWs and parts of the intelligentsia, and by killing both alleged and real opponents of the occupation. On the other hand, Germany's occupation fuelled internal conflict by supporting extremist groups and by providing them with both power and weapons, and by marginalizing other groups whom they deprived of traditional rights which often drove them into resistance. Thus, Nazi Germany's rule, often unintendedly, sparked civil wars that raged on for many years and were extremely violent. More often than not, the primary targets of the resistance groups were not the Nazi occupiers but rather their local opponents. They knew that Germany's response to attacks on their personnel would be more powerful than if they attacked the Nazi collaborators. More importantly, everybody knew that the war would end at some point and that Germany would withdraw. Thus, the internal civil wars that raged from 1942 on, in the shadow of the Second World War, were also fought over a post-war order.

Until the 1990s, Nazi Germany's occupation apparatus, especially the SS and police forces, were considered almost the only actors of violence in (Eastern) Europe during the Second World War. This perception has been partially reversed, shedding light on the other Axis regimes and the non-German auxiliaries. There were processes of violence that were not solely initiated by Nazi rule, but rather originated in local and regional groups, some of them even acting against Germany's interests. Nevertheless, it is most important to emphasize the role of German hegemony, direct rule and the cultural importance of the 'German example' during the late 1930s and during the war. These were necessary preconditions for the violence that reached beyond Nazi orders, sometimes even contrary to Germany's political aims. Historians have long discussed the concept of collaboration and have acknowledged that it is difficult to unite a plethora of different phenomena – ranging from local actors in villages and neighbourhoods to independent states like Romania – under one umbrella. Moreover, the term 'collaboration' has been criticized for being morally too charged. The term 'collaborator' derives from specific

---

106 Cf. Rafał Wnuk, *'Za pierwszego Sowieta': Polska konspiracja na Kresach Wschodnich II Rzeczypospolitej (wrzesień 1939 – czerwiec 1941)* ['For the First Soviet': Polish conspiracy in the eastern borderlands of the Second Polish Republic (September 1939 – June 1941)] (Warsaw: IPN, 2007).
107 Grzegorz Motyka, Rafał Wnuk, Tomasz Stryjek and Adam F. Baran, *Wojna po wojnie: Antysowieckie podziemie w Europie Środkowo-Wschodniej w latach 1944–1953* [War after the war: the anti-Soviet underground in Central and Eastern Europe, 1944–1953] (Warsaw: Wydawnictwo Scholar, 2012).
108 Grzegorz Motyka, *Na Białych Polaków obława* [A manhunt for White Poles] (Cracow: Wyd. Literackie, 2014).

wartime and post-war contexts, often equating collaboration with morally deviant behaviour and representing collaborators as traitors. German historians have suggested using a less normative concept and have proposed using 'cooperation' instead.[109] This approach, they argue, shifts the focus to the genuine political goals of the non-German perpetrators, and away from the view that perceives them primarily as Germany's henchmen and puppets. After the war, in many societies, collaborators have been portrayed as 'Quislings' named after the Norwegian prime minister; this can also be seen as an attempt to exoticize and to downplay home-grown collaboration. In the following chapter, we will continue to speak of 'collaboration', but we will specify the actual political context of such collaborative behaviour.

But first, there is another important aspect related to collaboration that must be discussed. The divisions within Southeastern European societies were not solely caused by the question of whether to collaborate with one outside power or another; the political divide between the left and the right had a pre-history of political exclusion and violent hostilities. This made it easy to exploit such divisions for any occupying power, and this explains why violence often erupted once a country was occupied. Right-wing forces used the situation to 'settle the score' with their internal enemies and they began arresting and killing communists or others who were seen as adversaries to the right-wing cause. Communists responded by engaging in partisan activities in many of the countries in Eastern Europe. Such resistance was facilitated by the fact that the Nazi regime was so brutal and either aimed at the destruction of entire countries, like Poland, or left the future unclear, like in the case of the Baltics; it was further facilitated by the fact that anti-Communism was deeply entwined with the persecution of ethnic groups in many countries; and it was even further facilitated by the design of the landscapes of Eastern and Southeastern Europe with the region's vast and thick forests of the north and the wide and largely wooded mountain ranges of the Balkans.

All of these social conflicts were fought in a violent manner: in some countries, open civil wars broke out, namely in Yugoslavia (on the Independent State of Croatia's territory), in Greece and in the borderlands between Poland, the Ukraine and Lithuania. In all of these conflicts, several groups were involved: local fascist groups such as the *Ustasha* in Croatia or the SDK (Serbian Volunteer Corps), communist partisans such as Tito's NOV (National Liberation Army) in Yugoslavia or the ELAS (Greek People's Liberation Army) and the EAM (National Liberation Front) in Greece, nationalistic militias such as the UPA in the Ukraine, the Chetniks in Croatia and Serbia, or the *Domobran* ('home guard') in Slovenia, including more centrist groups like the *Armia Krajowa* ('home army') in Poland; all of these groups built violent triangles of civil war in which the constellations and alliances changed quickly and frequently.

Outside powers such as Germany, Italy, the Western Allies and the Soviet Union supported local groups, but their support was far from being static, and as it happened (especially in Yugoslavia) the Germans or the Allies would 'change horses' in the midst of the war, withdrawing support from one group and granting it to another. Consequently, civil wars in Eastern and Southeastern Europe were also proxy wars fought between competing major powers who fuelled these wars and who were also responsible for the immense human losses

---

109 Christoph Dieckmann, Babette Quinkert and Tatjana Tönsmeyer, 'Editorial', in *Kooperation und Verbrechen: Formen der 'Kollaboration' im östlichen Europa 1939–1945*, eds Christoph Dieckmann, Babette Quinkert and Tatjana Tönsmeyer (Göttingen: Wallstein, 2003), 9–21. For general overviews on collaboration during the Second World War in Eastern Europe, see: Dean, *Collaboration in the Holocaust*; Rein, *The Kings and the Pawns*; Jochen Böhler and Jacek Andrzej Młynarczyk, 'Collaboration and Resistance in Wartime Poland (1939–1945): A Case for Differentiated Occupation Studies', *Journal of Modern European History* 16, no. 2 (2018): 225–46.

incurred. For instance, the civil war between the Serbian Chetnik movement and the Croatian Ustasha also represented the geopolitical conflict between the German and Italian empires in the Balkans, as both Germany and Italy each armed belligerent groups respectively. The extent to which these conflicts were fought along ethno-religious lines differed from country to country, but such lines always played a role. The civil war in Eastern Poland was primarily a conflict between Ukrainian groups on the one hand, and Polish groups on the other. In Greece, members of the Slavic minority tended to support the communist movement. Jews were mostly affected by the civil war's violence in a negative way, but they could sometimes benefit from the situation by aligning themselves to one of the parties and thus increasing their room for manoeuvre. Jewish refugees in Eastern Poland could find shelter in villages that were besieged by Ukrainian militias, as the Ukrainian nationalists were a common enemy of both the Poles and the Jews.[110] A final feature that these wars have in common is the fact that violence usually did not stop in 1944–45. As these conflicts were, to a certain extent, fought independently of the Second World War, the warring parties kept on fighting for a total victory over their enemy (or tried to resist total annihilation) even after the armistice.

Societies and violence

It is necessary to distinguish between the two general types of societies under scrutiny here: on the one hand, there were the societies under direct German occupation, like in the Baltics, Poland, the Czech lands, Yugoslavia and Greece. On the other hand, there were the former allies of Germany whose societies were subjected to German rule only at a very late stage of the war, when their governments defected from the Axis. This goes for Hungary and Slovakia in 1944, but it also comprises not only those parts of Italy which the Germans occupied in 1943, but also the societies of those areas which up to that point had been militarily occupied by the Italians – like the Peloponnese, Albania or Dalmatia – and were now taken over by the Wehrmacht.

The extent of wartime violence within the different regions was determined by several factors, the first being the scope of military action which was often accompanied by war crimes. The Czech lands in 1938–39, and Slovakia and Hungary in 1944 were occupied without military conflict, which was nearly the case in Romania and Bulgaria in 1944 when the new governments switched from the German to the Soviet side. In all other areas, military conflict occurred at least twice: during German occupation from 1939 to 1941, and then again during the retreat of the Wehrmacht in 1944–45. Most war crimes committed by the Nazi frontline units were perpetrated during the war against the Soviet Union, which was also fought in the eastern-Polish and Baltic territories in 1941 and in 1944–45.

But the most important factor for mass violence to break out at the hands of the Germans in an area was the presence of Jewish communities. The highest density of Jewish people in Europe (and the world) was situated in Central and Eastern Poland, Southern Lithuania and in Bessarabia. The Jewish population in the cities and towns of these regions often consisted of 30+ per cent, in some places there was even a Jewish majority. In those areas, the Christian population not only witnessed the presence of ghettos and the deportation of its Jewish citizens, but also scenes of the utmost ruthless violence during the Germans' ghetto raids; they also will have witnessed mass executions in Eastern Poland, the Baltics and Bessarabia, which in many cases were open to a public audience, like the pogroms of June–July 1941. In 1944, anti-Jewish

---

110 Jared McBride, 'A Sea of Blood Tears: Ukrainian Volhynia under Nazi Occupation, 1941–1944', PhD diss. University of California, Los Angeles, 2014.

violence extended to Hungary where both rapid ghettoization and deportations to Auschwitz occurred in front of the Hungarian public.

The geography of mass violence was also determined by the activities of armed anti-German resistance. From early on, the occupation forces applied excessive violence as retaliation for armed attacks on German troops and institutions. Aside from the Soviet territories, such excessive violence began in Serbia in the autumn of 1941, then moved to Croatia and Bosnia in early 1942. By the autumn of 1942, the Soviet partisan movement extended its activities to Eastern Poland, especially those parts which had been annexed as Western Belorussia. In central Poland, left-wing partisan warfare also unfolded from the end of 1942 on in the region south of Lublin where the Germans had tried to deport and expel the Polish population for their settlement projects; this was also the case later on in the Kielce region. Partisan warfare and Nazi Germany's genocidal response soon extended to large parts of the Yugoslav territory and to parts of Northern Greece. In all of these regions, Nazi units – both the SS and the Wehrmacht – retaliated by executing civilians en masse for either actual or alleged partisan attacks.

Moreover, the geographical extent of mass violence was determined by ethnic conflicts. The right-wing extremist Croatian Ustasha movement especially turned Bosnia-Herzegovina into a killing field in 1941 by massacring the Serbs, but they also mass-murdered the Jews and Romani in extermination camps. A similar strategy of 'ethnic cleansing' followed in Western Ukraine in 1943, when the anti-communist UPA started killing Poles en masse. And the various underground groups in several regions – like the Chetniks in Bosnia, and in some cases, even the Polish underground groups – did not refrain from killing civilians who had cooperated with competing resistance groups.

All in all, large segments of Central and Eastern European societies were affected in one way or another by extreme mass violence. This was not restricted to the regions occupied by Hitler and Stalin – those that Timothy Snyder calls the 'Bloodlands' – but it also includes all of Yugoslavia, parts of Greece, and in 1944–45, also to Hungary and Slovakia. And the extreme violence was not determined by the two totalitarian dictatorships alone. Of course, Hitler and Stalin – in that order – were responsible for destabilizing the societies of the region, and the Germans committed the overall majority of the crimes. Nevertheless, such destabilization created new, violent environments and forces that occasionally acted independently of the occupation power.

Inside Germany and Austria, Nazi persecution was directed at such specific groups (according to the Nazi definition) as Jews, Sinti and Romani, the mentally ill and any political opponents. The overall majority of the German population felt quite safe under Nazism until the terror extended to the public in 1943–44 when more and more average citizens were criminalized for minor offences, and again, during the final terror of 1945. In occupied Central and Eastern Europe, the situation was different. Of course, the Jewish populations there were also the major targets of occupation violence, and the German authorities were not so hesitant in deciding how to treat so-called '*Mischlinge*' (people of mixed Jewish and Christian descent) or those Jewish men and women with non-Jewish spouses.

The Christian populations of the region were also affected by Nazi violence in various ways, and the violence was applied much more randomly than in the Reich or in occupied Western and Northern Europe. Romani were killed all over Eastern Europe, not only by German forces, but also by the Croatian and Romanian authorities. In Poland, the Baltics and the occupied Soviet territories, the Germans 'emptied' dozens of psychiatric institutions by murdering the patients, although, apparently not in the Czech lands or in occupied Southeastern Europe (probably with the exception of Slovenia). Furthermore, Soviet POWs died en masse in the Soviet Union proper, in the Baltics, in Poland (and in Germany).

The Germans were much more violent when combatting resistance groups in occupied Eastern Europe. In Poland and the Soviet territories, they even tried to exterminate the upper social stratum in order to prevent any potential of resistance. The Polish intelligentsia fell victim to mass murder in 1939–40, and then the Soviet functionaries in 1941. Hundreds of thousands of inhabitants from Poland and the Soviet Union were deported to Germany's concentration camps, where they constituted the majority of prisoners in 1943–44.

While it is not difficult to identify the geographies and the victim groups of Nazi Germany's mass crimes, reconstructing the societal impact of violence remains a complicated task. It is obvious that the occupation violence was much more public in Poland, the Baltics, the Soviet Union and Yugoslavia in comparison to the other parts of Europe under Hitler's domination. Public executions of alleged resisters – and sometimes even hostages after armed attacks – were performed in all of these regions. Even the mass murder of Jews was at times public, though after the summer of 1941 the occupiers tried to avoid public audiences, even German spectators.[111] Two of the extermination centres, Kulmhof near Poznań and Bełżec south of Lublin, were situated *within* small towns, the inhabitants of which could even hear the victims.

Those living in the 'zones of violence' were quite aware of what was going on even if they had not witnessed it first-hand. There was constant private talk about the last *akcja* ('action') in town, and at the very least rumours about the extermination camps circulated within Poland. Polish railwaymen knew best about the fate of the deportees. The underground press reported extensively on crimes against Poles, though less on the Holocaust.[112] In some areas, it was possible to hear Allied radio, either BBC or Radio Moscow, which both reported to a limited extent on the crimes being committed in Eastern Europe. Moreover, the constant transport of people for forced labour and soldiers either allied with Germany or acting as auxiliaries, enhanced the circulation of information of what was happening in the zones of violence. Hungarian soldiers fighting in the war against the Soviet Union reported on crimes when they were on leave. It is important to underline here, that an enormous amount of people were in close contact with the German occupiers, and they sometimes heard news directly from them. Diaries published after 1945 leave no doubt that a large part of the population within Central and Eastern Europe were aware of the mass killings.[113]

There are major methodological obstacles that make it difficult to establish the societal perception of violence during the war. The major problem is the absence of a democratic

---

111 Omer Bartov, *The Anatomy of a Genocide: The Life and Death of a Town Called Buczacz* (New York: Simon & Schuster, 2018).

112 Cf. Joshua D. Zimmerman, *The Polish Underground and the Jews, 1939–1945* (Cambridge: Cambridge University Press, 2015); Adam Puławski, *W obliczu zagłady: Rząd RP na Uchodźstwie, Delegatura Rządu RP na Kraj, ZWZ-AK wobec deportacji Żydow do obozów zagłady (1941–1942)* [In the face of extermination: the government of the Republic of Poland in exile, the delegation of the government of the Republic of Poland at home, and the ZWZ-AK facing the deportation of Jews to death camps (1941–1942)] (Lublin: Instytut Pamięci Narodowej, 2009); idem, *Wobec 'niespotykanego w dziejach mordu': Rząd RP na uchodźstwie, Delegatura Rządu RP na Kraj, AK a eksterminacja ludności żydowskiej od 'wielkiej akcji' do powstania w getcie warszawskiem* [In the face of 'unprecedented murder': The Government of the Republic of Poland in Exile, the Delegation of the Government of the Republic of Poland to the Country, the Home Army and the extermination of the Jewish population from the 'great action' to the Warsaw Ghetto Uprising] (Chelm: Stowarzyszenie Rocznik Chełmski, 2019).

113 Among the most important of the published diaries, see: Zygmunt Klukowski, *Tagebuch aus den Jahren der Okkupation 1939–1944*, eds Christine Glauning and Ewelina Wanke (Berlin: Metropol, 2017) (see also the abridged Polish, French and English versions).

peacetime public sphere in Nazi dominated Eastern Europe. The Baltic, Polish, Czech and Serbian public spheres were completely repressed; in other occupied areas, censorship and propaganda prevailed, as in all the Axis states. Indeed, part of the population was directly confronted with the extreme violence. The ghetto raids in Polish towns and cities were especially known publicly: one could see the manhunts, arrests and shootings take place in the streets, or after the victims were apprehended, one could see them being led to the train stations or to the killing sites outside the city. The gas van that killed the Jewish women and children inmates from the Sajmište camp drove the victims directly through Belgrade city.[114] In many instances, the mass executions were a public spectacle, especially when they were conducted inside the towns, for example, in Jewish or Orthodox cemeteries. The murders of individual Jews who were apprehended in the countryside were often committed in full public view; the railroads the headed towards the extermination camps often were scattered with the corpses of those who had tried to escape the trains and were shot by the guards; the Ustasha frequently threw the corpses of those they killed into the Sava and Drina rivers, from which the bodies floated to Belgrade or even to Romania, which appalled both the locals and the Germans alike. The German Police sometimes organized public executions or hangings of alleged resisters or 'hostages' in front of large audiences; often the corpses of the hanged were left in public for several days. Large (German or Croatian, Italian, etc.) posters gave notice of executions in a multitude of languages.

In a few exceptional cases, the media reported on the 'resettlement of Jews' or the anti-partisan warfare taking place. For example, the *Krakauer Zeitung* announced the 'resettlement' of Lublin Jews, by which they actually meant they were deporting the Jews to a death camp. The *Bukarester Zeitung*, an organ controlled by the Gestapo, frequently informed the public about anti-Jewish operations, though in obscure terms.[115] In Romania, the Union of Jewish communities' request for alleviating the repression of Jews was indirectly published, as Ion Antonescu publicly refused to intervene on their behalf. And in Croatia, there was a very public discourse regarding the resettlement of Serbs, Jews and Romani, as well as regarding partisan warfare.

If the perception of violence in the public sphere poses problems, it is even more difficult to reconstruct the awareness and reception of more than 100 million people across several different countries. It is obvious, however, that in the first place, widespread violence had a socially disruptive effect. Neighbours, friends or colleagues were arrested, deported or killed. Among the Jewish communities, everybody was affected; among the Christians, even family members or relatives could fall victim to Nazi violence.

The persecuted Jews especially experienced a lack of solidarity. Though there was a period of shared experience amongst Poles and Jews right after they were defeated by Germany, such a shared feeling obviously declined during 1940–41. The Poles considered themselves the predominant victims of the occupation, and especially conservative circles came forward with allegations of 'Jewish collaboration' in Soviet-occupied Eastern Europe. Among Germany's allies, Romania and Hungary, a general anti-Jewish mood prevailed with broad public support for anti-Jewish legislation. In some instances, Poles, Ukrainians, Lithuanians and Bessarabians participated in the anti-Jewish pogroms of June–July 1941, but these had largely been organized by the German- and Romanian-occupation forces.[116]

---

114 Christopher R. Browning, *Fateful Months: Essays on the Emergence of the Final Solution* (New York: Holmes and Meier, 1985).
115 Robert Moses Shapiro, ed., *Why Didn't the Press Shout? American and International Journalism during the Holocaust* (New York: Ktav, 2003).
116 Struve, *Deutsche Herrschaft*; Diana Dumitru, *The State, Antisemitism, and Collaboration in the Holocaust: The Borderlands of Romania and the Soviet Union* (Cambridge: Cambridge University Press, 2016).

There is no doubt that some of the locals participated in the occupation violence while others participated in civil war and ethnic conflict. Most important is the institutional framework of cooperation (to avoid the term collaboration in this context) with the occupier. The collaboration governments not only in Romania, Bulgaria and Slovakia, but also in occupied Croatia and 1944-Hungary had their own executive forces upon which they could rely. Tens of thousands of administrators and policemen participated in the mass deportations and in mass murder, including whole units of the Romanian Army in occupied-Soviet Union. Some collaboration administrations, for example in Serbia and Estonia, participated in the persecutions.[117] In general, however, the auxiliary police were directly subordinate to the German officers. Hundreds of thousands of local men worked for the auxiliary police in all of occupied Europe (with the exception of the annexed Polish territories and Bulgarian-occupied Greece). The majority of these men were complicit in the crimes committed by the Germans and in the Holocaust; they also played a role in the persecution of other criminalized segments of the population and the recruitment of people for forced labour. Though most of them performed according to Nazi Germany's rules and orders, only a minority of them were right-wing extremists or organized anti-communists. On the local level, they behaved quite differently. Some fully complied to Nazi orders and ill-treated or even killed their victims on their own accord, while others warned the victims ahead of time that they were going to be arrested. Quite a few of them had contacts to the underground, and in 1943, mass desertions began.[118]

Except with the mobile units, most of the auxiliary policemen worked in a familiar environment and thus often arrested their former neighbours; but they were also influenced by local social relations. There were even families where one brother was serving in the police while the other brother or sister went underground. But the policemen were not the only ones to be involved in occupation violence. The local administrations had to register specific groups like Jews, Romani or communist party members. Local administrators were involved in setting up ghettos in their towns, together with the labour exchanges in recruitment of Jews and Christians for forced labour. As previously stated, it was the local administration which had to take care of the mass graves after German massacres. Even other units like the *Baudienst*, which consisted of young Poles who had been drafted, occasionally participated in the Holocaust.

Over the last two decades, the unorganized participation in the Holocaust and other crimes has come into focus, including denunciations, pogroms and neighbours killing neighbours.[119] The study of denunciation under German occupation is much more difficult than when looking at similar practices in Germany since the files are largely missing. As in Germany, however, there was constant fear of being denounced to the occupation authorities. On the other hand, denunciations were widely considered as treason of national identity, unlike in the Reich. Nevertheless, the German Police could heavily rely on both employed informers and individual denunciations. They lacked, however, the broad web of party functionaries, which were available on the micro level. Obviously, the denunciations first and foremost targeted Jews,

---

117 Branislav Božović, *Specijalna policija u Beogradu 1941–1944* [The special police forces in Belgrade 1941–1944] (Belgrade: Zavod za udžbenike, 2014); Ruth B. Birn, *Die Sicherheitspolizei in Estland 1941–1944: Eine Studie zur Kollaboration im Osten* (Paderborn: Ferdinand Schöningh, 2006).
118 Dean, *Collaboration in the Holocaust*.
119 First was Jan Tomasz Gross, *Neighbors: The Destruction of the Jewish Community in Jedwabne, Poland* (Princeton, NJ: Princeton University Press, 2001); see especially the more recent, Bartov, *The Anatomy of a Genocide*.

especially those in hiding or protecting themselves under false identities.[120] The occupation power even offered rewards for denouncing Jews. However, members of the resistance movement were also denounced and executed, the most famous among them Stefan Rowecki (a.k.a. 'Grot'), the leader of the Polish Home Army.

As new research shows, individual killings were much more frequent than was previously assumed. Jews in hiding were especially endangered not only by the German Police, but in many instances also by underground groups, criminal gangs or other individuals. Even people who first permitted Jews to hide in their houses could kill them later out of fear or greed.[121]

Robbing one's persecuted fellow countrymen was much more common than killing them. Among the Christian population, the myth of 'Jewish wealth' had been circulating for a long time. Most of the valuables and the real estate belonging to the murdered Jews were acquired by the Germans, but clothing and everything else that was left in the emptied flats were robbed on a large scale. After the brutal ghetto raids in Poland, the Baltics and in 1944-Hungary, locals often entered the former housing areas of the Jews in order to plunder them.[122] Jewish enterprises were, by and large, closed or appropriated by Germans or ethnic Germans as the trustees, the majority of whom were incapable of running a business. The Axis governments organized the systematic plundering of Jewish minorities, all of them installed administrations for 'Magyarization', 'Romanization', etc., exploiting the minorities without German interference.[123]

All in all, Germany's hegemony and direct occupation rule unleashed an enormous degree of barbarization among the societies of Central and Eastern Europe, and at times it is difficult to distinguish between the ramifications of Germany's occupation and local societal developments. There were, however, societal restraints on Germany's onslaught. The governments-in-exile of the occupied countries tried to influence their respective societies, but more important were the churches and the underground movements.

In most of Central Europe, the churches remained in an important position under German hegemony.[124] The Polish Catholic Church, however, suffered from the Nazi policy of annihilation, with thousands of priests being murdered or put into concentration camps. Despite these heavy losses, the Church's role in Polish society apparently remained intact. For example, the Church tried to play an active role in the protection of Polish society against German violence

---

120 Barbara Engelking, *'Szanowny panie gistapo': donosy do władz niemieckich w Warszawie i okolicach w latach 1940–1941* ['Dear Mr. Gestapo': denunciations to the German authorities in and around Warsaw in 1940–1941] (Warsaw: IFiS PAN, 2003).

121 For a ground-breaking work, see: Dariusz Libionka, Jan Grabowski and Barbara Engelking, eds, *Dalej jest noc: Losy Żydów w wybranych powiatach okupowanej Polski* [Night without end: the fate of Jews in selected counties in occupied Poland] (Warsaw: Stowarzyszenie Centrum Badań nad Zagładą Żydów, 2018). The publication was heavily attacked by the Polish nationalist press and government.

122 Jan Grabowski, Dariusz Libionka, eds, *Klucze i kasa: O mieniu żydowskim w Polsce pod okupacją niemiecką i we wczesnych latach powojennych, 1939–1950* [Keys and cash: on Jewish property in Poland under German occupation and in the early post-war years, 1939–1950] (Warsaw: Stowarzyszenie Centrum Badań nad Zagładą Żydów, 2014).

123 Jean Ancel, *Economic Destruction of the Romanian Jews* (Jerusalem: INSHR publishing house, Yad Vashem, 2008); Gábor Kádár, Zoltán Vági, *Self-financing Genocide: The Gold Train, the Becher Case and the Wealth of Hungarian Jews* (Budapest: CEU Press, 2004); Ungváry, *A Horthy-rendszer mérlege*.

124 Mordecai Paldiel, *Churches and the Holocaust: Unholy Teaching, Good Samaritans, and Reconciliation* (Jersey City, NJ: KTAV Publishing House, Inc., 2006). For a balanced view, see, Jan Bank and Lieve Gevers, *Churches and Religion in the Second World War* (London: Bloomsbury, 2016).

by reporting to the Vatican and the exiled government. But the Polish Catholic Church's stance vis-a-vis the mass murder of the Jews remains a matter of controversy. The hierarchy spoke out for the Jews only to a limited extent, and assistance was limited to individual cases of priests or monasteries that protected Jewish children.[125]

The same applies to the Catholic churches in other occupied countries. In Croatia, the Church openly supported the radical Ustasha regime, but only at a later point did they begin to criticize the violence. The Muslim hierarchy in Bosnia was apparently the only one in all of Hitler's Europe to intervene on behalf of the Muslim Romani, though without much success.

Much more problematic was the behaviour of the Romanian Orthodox Church. While there were some efforts to save the Jews in inner Romania, the Romanian Church in Transnistria – the region where the Romanian Holocaust occurred – took a rather anti-Semitic stance.[126] On the other hand, the Archbishop of Athens, Damaskinos Papandreou, and the Greek-Catholic Metropolitan of Lviv, Andrey Sheptytsky, were among the few to openly protest the Holocaust.[127]

The underground movements in Central and Eastern Europe represented complex political orientations, and at times even fought each other under occupation. They tended to protect, first and foremost, their milieu and showed rather ambivalent behaviour towards the Holocaust. The Polish Underground State condemned the crimes against the Jews and, at a comparatively late stage, installed structures to assist the Jews (*Rada Pomocy Żydom*, the Council to Assist the Jews). Nevertheless, the Polish underground press was not free of anti-Semitic content. One major issue was whether the surviving Jews should return to Poland, and what should happen to Jewish property after the war. Left-wing groups tended to accept Jews in their ranks, while extreme right-wing organizations like the *Konfederacja Narodu* openly applauded the Holocaust.[128] Apparently, only the Yugoslav partisans under Tito fully accepted the Jewish people and thus had the impetus to save thousands of them. It was, first and foremost, up to individuals to assist the persecuted.

Civil wars in the Balkans

Regardless of the exact definition of 'genocide', it was clear that the Croatian Ustasha government wanted to destroy the culture and the religion of the Serbian community; wanted to eliminate part of the community and expel an even larger one. In that respect, there can be no doubt that it was the goal of the Ustasha government to completely destroy the Serbian entity. Semi-independent paramilitary groups in the countryside often engaged in local onslaughts against the Serbian communities. These attacks might initially have been looked upon favourably by the regime, but the government quickly recognized that such attacks caused more harm than anything else.

---

125 Cf. the special issue of *Zagłada Żydów* 5 (2009) with articles focussing on the Polish Catholic Church and the Holocaust.
126 Ion Popa, *The Romanian Orthodox Church and the Holocaust* (Bloomington, IN: Indiana University Press, 2017); Ionut Florin Biliuta, 'The Archangel's Consecrated Servants: An Inquiry in the Relationship between the Romanian Orthodox Church and the Iron Guard, 1930–1941', PhD diss., Central European University, Budapest, 2013.
127 Paul Robert Magocsi, ed., *Morality and Reality: The Life and Times of Andrei Sheptytsky* (Edmonton: CIUS, 1989); Paldiel, *Churches and the Holocaust*, 311–13.
128 Puławski, *W obliczu zagłady*; Zimmerman, *The Polish underground and the Jews*; Klaus-Peter Friedrich, 'Der nationalsozialistische Judenmord in polnischen Augen: Einstellungen in der polnischen Presse 1942–1946/47' PhD diss., University of Cologne, Köln, 2003.

The Ustasha mass murders led to the outbreak of an uprising by both the communist and Chetnik forces in the summer of 1941. The resistance movements in former Yugoslavia were not limited by the boundaries that the Axis powers had drawn after the dissolution of Yugoslavia in 1941, as they were a transnational phenomenon. Once regional warlords took control over their respective areas, it was almost impossible for the government to oversee them. They made themselves seemingly indispensable by fighting the resistance groups, whose very defiance – more often than not – the warlords themselves caused; moreover, they did not even shy away from conflicts with the German or Italian militaries. In that respect, the Ustasha militias are comparable to any militia that forms part of a civil war, be it Yugoslavia in the 1990s or the Levant in the present day. A warlord economy, a brutalized paramilitary culture, fear of the enemy and the dynamic of violence and counter-violence committed by vigilant enemy groups lead to a perpetuation of a very high level of violence, with no promising exit strategy in sight. By the end of 1941, large parts of former Yugoslavia were torn apart by a bloody and ethnically charged civil war with three or more camps fighting one another.

Yugoslavia

Being pushed out of Serbia during the fall of 1941, Tito's partisan forces escaped to Eastern Bosnia and regrouped there. By that time, a bloodbath had emerged in large parts of Croatia, and Bosnia-Herzegovina in particular. Ustasha militias had begun, by force, to break the Serbian communities and any expressions of Serb nationality, and they expelled as many Serbs as possible to Serbia. Thirty per cent of the country's Serbian population was killed and as such resulted in a violent civil war as Serb peasants rose against the Ustasha. The interaction between genocide on the one hand, and armed resistance on the other, has led to heated debates within Yugoslav historiography, as we are dealing with a highly pro-active victim group that often struck back forcefully, so the lines between the Ustasha genocide and the civil war are sometimes blurred.[129]

The Chetniks were quite a loose partisan movement led by the former Yugoslav general Drazha Mihailovich. Some of their militias acted independently, others were puppets of the German- or Italian-occupation regimes. All of them were at war with the Ustasha, which can be seen as an act of self-protection, but which was accompanied by Chetnik counter-violence; by November 1941, after a short phase of cooperation, Chetnik and communist partisans entered a bloody civil war that lasted until 1946. Their actions differed considerably depending on whether they operated in Serbia, Montenegro, the German or the Italian parts of occupied Croatia, but they always cooperated, to a certain degree, with the occupation force.

The Chetniks soon began an ethnic cleansing campaign of their own in the area that was under their control, and in a number of cases, the expulsion of Muslims and bloody massacres went hand in hand. Many field commanders were involved in carrying out these policies, but the local conditions varied considerably. It is therefore a controversial issue as to whether Serb nationalists committed genocide against Muslims and the Croats during the war. This, of course, depends on the definition of the concept as well as on some reliable figures regarding the total number of human lives lost at the hands of the Chetnik forces. In communist Yugoslavia, historians had already partly acknowledged the Muslim plight during the Second World War.[130] What such Yugoslav historians did not acknowledge, however, was that partisan forces

---

129 Jovan Çulibrk, *Historiography of the Holocaust in Yugoslavia* (Belgrade: University of Belgrade, 2014).
130 Vladimir Dedijer and Antun Miletić, eds, *Genocid nad Muslimanima, 1941–1945: Zbornik dokumenata i svjedočenja* [Genocide against Muslims, 1941–1945: a collection of documents and testimonies] (Sarajevo: Svjetlost Sarajevo, 1990).

also committed anti-Muslim massacres, the worst of which was perpetrated in Kulen Vakuf in north-western Bosnia in September 1941.[131] The largest massacres, however, were committed by Chetnik troops in Eastern Bosnia during the winter of 1941 in Muslim villages that they had captured or that were handed over by the Italians. In 1943, the Chetniks systematically attempted to ethnically 'cleanse' the Sandžak region of Muslims altogether.[132] Tens of thousands of Muslims tried to escape into territories controlled by the Croatian State, namely to Sarajevo, where, throughout the war, thousands of civilians lived in refugee camps.[133] On a much smaller scale, the Chetniks also committed mass crimes against the Croats.[134] The Yugoslav historian Vladimir Žerjavić, estimates that about 65,000 Croat and Muslim civilians were killed by Chetniks in the Independent State of Croatia, but the figures are likely to be somewhat higher. The fact that the Italian army actively supported the četniks, who were responsible for the mass murder of Muslims, is an entirely understudied chapter of the Second World War. It is very likely that tens of thousands of Muslims were shot with weapons provided by the Italians, and that Italian liaison officers were well aware of – if not even present at – the killing sites. At times, Italian officials protested; but their exceptional statements rather demonstrate how little was done to stop the atrocities perpetrated by the Chetniks.[135]

Muslim communities were caught in-between the fronts in a very fragile position. This is the main reason why Muslim elites entered an alliance with Heinrich Himmler's SS, who formed the 13th Waffen Mountain Division of the SS Handschar.[136]

Italy's surrender

The fall of Benito Mussolini in July 1943, and more importantly the Italians' surrender in September that same year, sparked a new round of violence throughout Southeastern Europe that was specific to that event: it was characterized both by Nazi Germany's ruthless rush to occupy the territories abandoned by Fascist Italy, and by the Germans' revenge killings of Italian soldiers. Following these killings, German troops intensified their use of violence against both actual and alleged partisans in Yugoslavia, Greece and Albania (as well as in Italy), as the resistance movements had gained momentum and were effectively opposing the Nazi regime. Partisans, nationalist militias and local warlords and chiefs anticipated an Allied landing and tried to grab as much territory as possible before the expected advance. The Yugoslav Partisans especially greatly benefited from the collapse of Italian Fascism.

---

131 See Marko A. Hoare, *Genocide and Resistance in Hitler's Bosnia: The Partisans and the Chetniks, 1941–1943* (Oxford: Published for the British Academy by Oxford University Press, 2006), 106–8; Max Bergholz, *Violence as a Generative Force: Identity, Nationalism, and Memory in a Balkan Community* (Ithaca, NY: Cornell University Press, 2016).
132 Marko A. Hoare, *The Bosnian Muslims in the Second World War: A History* (New York: Oxford University Press, 2013), 355.
133 Emily Greble, *Sarajevo, 1941–1945: Muslims, Christians, and Jews in Hitler's Europe* (Ithaca, NY: Cornell University Press, 2011).
134 Tomasevich, *Chetniks*, 259.
135 Sabrina P. Ramet, ed., *The Independent State of Croatia 1941–45* (London: Routledge, 2006), see 146 for a discussion of the victim numbers.
136 David Motadel, *Islam and Nazi Germany's War* (Cambridge, MA: Harvard University Press, 2014); Xavier Bougarel, Alexander Korb, Stefan Petke and Franziska Zaugg, 'Muslim SS units in the Balkans and the Soviet Union', *The Waffen-SS: A European History*, eds Jochen Böhler and Robert Gerwarth (Oxford: Oxford University Press, 2017), 265–6.

Germany's revenge was brutal and full of wrath. Some Italian military leaders like General Amico in Dubrovnik, who had the reputation of being particularly anti-German, were killed outright. The Italian units that did not immediately surrender were attacked. The 'Division Acqui' that was stationed on the Greek island of Kephalonia refused to lay down their arms and to subordinate; only after fierce resistance did they surrender on 22 September 1943. Germany's *Gebirgsjäger* ('mountain troops') shot between 2,500 and 5,000 of their former brothers-in-arms.[137] The Italian soldiers who survived were divided into two groups: a smaller portion of them volunteered to keep fighting for the Nazi empire, whilst the majority were deported to Germany as 'military internees' (not POWs) for forced labour. The occupation of the Balkan parts of the Italian Empire also gave way to a renewed wave of deportations of Jews to the death camps of the Holocaust in 1944.[138]

Greece

Greece is yet another country that was torn apart by civil war in the 1940s. The German and Italian militaries, who both terrorized the Greek populations in their own respective ways, soon developed an antagonistic relationship between one another, which partly affected their respective perspectives on the local populations. Under German occupation there were already tendencies towards civil war, as three major armed groups, the German-led security battalions, the nationalist EDES (National Republican Greek League) and the communist ELAS-partisans started coming into confrontation with each other. The ELAS was the fastest growing and largest of the movements, with approximately 30,000 fighters in 1944. Beginning in 1943, they gained control of some northern Greek regions that had been abandoned by the Italians. By 1944, 2.5 million people lived in liberated territories, and the partisans started to transform into a state organization. When the Germans withdrew, the ELAS first began settling the score with the Greek collaborators. For instance, members of the security battalions were overcome in a battle at Meligalas (Peloponnese), which was followed by a massacre of up to 1,000 former collaborators.[139] Yet, as in Yugoslavia and Poland, it became clear that the real conflict was about what the post-war order would look like after the inevitable German withdrawal. Therefore, the real conflict was between the larger ELAS and the EDES, the latter of whom were supported by the British. The first skirmishes between the two parties took place in 1944. In December 1944, after Germany withdrew, a battle for the control of Athens, referred to as *Dekemvriana* ('December events'), ended with an ELAS-retreat after British forces intervened on behalf of the EDES.[140]

Wherever the Wehrmacht met armed resistance, German atrocities from retaliatory executions to full-scale massacres were the consequence. The most severe massacre on Greek soil was committed by the Wehrmacht's 117th Jäger Division in Kalavryta on 10 December 1943. In an attempt to destroy the resistance movement in that part of the Peloponnese and to retaliate for the shooting of German prisoners, German soldiers shot at least 500 male inhabitants of the town above the age of 12 and then massacred some women, children and elderly as well.[141]

---

137 Hermann F. Meyer, *Blutiges Edelweiß: Die 1. Gebirgs-Division im Zweiten Weltkrieg* (Berlin: Ch. Links, 2008).
138 Nathan Shachar, *The Lost Worlds of Rhodes: Greeks, Italians, Jews and Turks between Tradition and Modernity* (Brighton: Sussex Academic Press, 2013).
139 Ibid., 358.
140 S.N. Kalyvas, *The Logic of Violence in Civil War* (Cambridge: Cambridge UP, 2006); Heinz A. Richter, *Griechenland 1940–1950: Die Zeit der Bürgerkriege* (Wiesbaden: Harrassowitz, 2012).
141 On Germany's occupation of Greece, see Mark Mazower, *Inside Hitler's Greece: The Experience of Occupation, 1941–44* (New Haven: Yale University Press, 1993), 191–7.

Ethnic cleansing in Volhynia, 1943–44

After Germany's defeat at Stalingrad and the prospects of an advancing Red Army were at hand, tensions grew in Eastern Poland: while the Polish government wanted to retain the *kresy* ('borderlands') after the war, Soviet partisans and the Ukrainian anti-communist underground prepared for their projects of state-building. The OUN set up a military force, the UPA, partly consisting of Ukrainian auxiliary policemen from Volhynia who had deserted. Apparently, in March–April 1943, the Volhynian UPA leadership decided to launch a violent attack on the Polish settlements in Volhynia. Though there had been mutual violence between Poles and Ukrainians before that, the major reasons for the regional UPA leadership to unleash a campaign of ethnic cleansing and mass violence were strategic: it was meant as a way of preparing for a post-war settlement that would prevent Polish claims for reconstituting the prior Polish border. From April 1943 on, UPA units, together with local Ukrainian peasants, started attacking villages inhabited by Poles. On 11 July 1943, 99 villages were attacked, and large parts of the Polish population were slaughtered, many with axes and knives. From February 1944 on, this violence was extended to Eastern Galicia. Estimates on the number of victims run up to 80,000. Hundreds of thousands of Poles escaped to the areas west of the Bug, where Polish units attacked and killed Ukrainian citizens.[142] Similar massacres, though in a much smaller dimension, occurred during the conflict of Polish Underground and Soviet partisans in Ukraine.

Revenge violence, 1944–47

Though the nightmare of mass murder at the hands of the Germans was over in 1944–45, the advance of the Red Army and its occupation of Eastern and large parts of Southeastern Europe denoted liberation to many, whilst for others, the advance brought repression and sometimes deadly persecution. Violence did not end with the arrival of the Red Army or the Yugoslav partisans. More than elsewhere in Europe the early post-war years in Eastern, Central and Southeastern Europe were characterized by new waves of mass violence, revenge for German occupation and collaboration, civil war and Stalinist terror in order to prepare for communist takeovers. In the Baltics, in several regions of Poland, Yugoslavia, Albania and Greece, political murders occurred almost on a day-to-day basis between 1944 and 1946. The old patterns of enemy propaganda against Jews and communists, were now replaced with new villains: collaborators, counter-revolutionaries and capitalists who had allegedly made a fortune during the war.

Nevertheless, anti-Semitism persisted in this new environment. The new communist agencies were considered 'judeo-bolshevik' by large parts of the population in Central Europe, and the Jewish survivors who returned from camps or came out of hiding blamed their neighbours either for their lack of assistance or even for their denunciations during the occupation; they also tried to recover their lost property.[143] The infamous pogrom in Kielce on 4 July 1946,

---

142 McBride, 'A Sea of Blood Tears'; Jared McBride, 'Peasants into perpetrators: the OUN-UPA and the Ethnic Cleansing of Volhynia, 1943–1944', *Slavic Review* 75 (2016): 630–54; Ihor I. Il'jushyn, *Volyns'ka trahediia 1943–1944 rr.* [The Volhynian tragedy 1943–1944] (Kiev: Natsionalna Akademiia Nauk Ukraïny, 2003); Grzegorz Motyka, *Ukraińska partyzantka 1942–1960* [Ukrainian partisans 1942–1960] (Warsaw: Rytm, 2006); Timothy Snyder, 'The Causes of Ukrainian–Polish Ethnic Cleansing 1943', in *Past and Present* 179 (2003): 197–234. There is abundant Ukrainian apologetic literature on the subject, claiming that this had been a consequence of an alleged 'Second Polish-Ukrainian War'.

143 Paul Hanebrink, *A Specter Haunting Europe: The Myth of Judeo-Bolshevism* (Cambridge, MA: Harvard University Press, 2018).

with more than 40 Jews killed, was not the only instance of post-war anti-Jewish violence. Jewish survivors were attacked in several Polish cities and towns. In Slovakia, anti-Jewish outbursts occurred in 1945–46 in at least 14 towns; on 29 September 1945 in Topol'čany, 49 Jews were injured, some heavily.[144]

On the other side, criminal violence was on the rise. In a situation of extreme material shortage and social disruption, with abundant weapons available, criminal gangs terrorized shopkeepers and the common citizen. It was only by 1947 that the police were able to reduce the open violence, though mass arrests and other Stalinist crimes continued until the mid-1950s. In all the countries of the region, camps for political enemies of the communists, for collaborators, and for Axis minorities were set up; in Greece, thousands of communists were incarcerated.[145]

Violence against collaborators

After the collapse of the collaborationist regimes, purges and revenge were the norm; the extent of those, however, differed from country to country. Most communist governments of Southeastern Europe were quite harsh on the leadership of their right-wing predecessors and competitors, but considerably less harsh on the rank-and-file supporters of fascism. In Bulgaria, the communist-led resistance staged a *coup d'état* against the government (that had already withdrawn from the alliance with Germany and the war) on 9 September 1944, which was later transformed into a myth of partisan resistance and a tale of a heroic communist victory.[146] The partisans descended from the mountains and seized power in most of the towns and villages, which caused reprisals in many locations. It is odd that the end of the war in Bulgaria was particularly bloodthirsty as there was no proper German occupation since wartime-Bulgaria had maintained some democratic elements; the country further withdrew from the Axis relatively peacefully and the Soviet advance was not particularly brutal. Yet, the minimum number of executions carried out in 1944–45 is 3,000. That number includes massacres in September 1944 during and in the immediate aftermath of the putsch, as well later executions. More than one hundred public officials including former Prime Minister Filov were sentenced to death by a 'People's Tribunal' on the afternoon of 1 February 1945 and executed by firing squad that night in a Sofia cemetery.[147] In Romania, a smaller number of people were sentenced to death. On 1 June 1946, Ion Antonescu was shot in Jilava – the very same prison where the Legionaries massacred 46 prisoners 6 years before.[148] Trials against collaborators were staged in all countries, the most famous against Slovakia's head of state Josef Tiso, in Hungary against several prime ministers, and tens of thousands more from the Baltics down to Yugoslavia. Greece dealt with it in a much more lenient way, as no member of the wartime-establishment was sentenced to death.

---

144 Anna Cichopek, *Beyond Violence: Jewish Survivors in Poland and Slovakia, 1944–48* (Cambridge: Cambridge University Press. 2014); Joanna Tokarska-Bakir, *Pod klątwą: Społeczny portret pogromu kieleckiego* [Under the curse: a social portrait of the Kielce pogrom] (Warsaw: Wydawnictwo Czarna Owca, 2018).
145 Marcin Zaremba, *Wielka trwoga: Polska 1944–1947; ludowa reakcja na kryzys* [Great terror: Poland 1944–1947; popular responses to the crisis] (Cracow: Wydawn. Znak, 2012).
146 Crampton, *Bulgaria*, 280.
147 Aleksandăr Vezenkov, *9 septemvri 1944 g* [9 September 1944] (Sofia: Siela Norma AD, 2014).
148 Dennis Deletant, *Hitler's Forgotten Ally: Ion Antonescu and his Regime, Romania 1940–44* (Basingstoke: Palgrave Macmillan, 2006), 2.

Countries that went through brutal civil wars had a more extreme way of purging their societies of the enemy. This is not surprising, as it is the nature of civil wars that the internal enemy in the war is simultaneously a competitor for the post-war order, and that fear and panic are elements that fuel violence.[149] Whilst in a war between countries, a captured soldier tends to become a prisoner of war, a captured soldier in a civil war continues to be the enemy. Paranoia, emotional intensity and the urge to take revenge for previous wartime atrocities to a great deal explain the atrocities that occurred between 1944 and 1946: violence did not end immediately after Germany's capitulation, but rather only once the enemy was destroyed and the victory was thus total. Aside from that, the atrocities, ethnic cleansing and genocide committed by civil war parties always also served a purpose: the strategy was to destroy the enemy and to transform society and prepare it for the new post-war order. Such a communist new order in Eastern and Southeastern Europe was a politically mono-cultural state and, when compared prior to 1939, was ethnically homogeneous.

By 1944, it became apparent that the communists were to become the victors of the civil war in Yugoslavia. At least the leaders of the nationalist belligerents had no illusions that they were unlikely to survive a Partisan victory. As the Ustasha had launched a genocidal war against the partisans, they did not expect any mercy. On the other hand, thousands of Ustashe, Chetniks and Muslim fighters deserted to the partisans in the last months of the war, as the partisans proactively called for desertion. The promised amnesty especially triggered mass desertions. Many Chetniks particularly changed sides as they found it easy to merge with the predominantly Serb partisans. That was, by the way, one of the reasons why Greater Serb nationalism managed to survive in communist Yugoslavia.[150]

An Ustasha army defeated the remaining Chetnik forces in early April 1945 on the Lijevče Field near Banja Luka. A number of Chetnik leaders were captured and subsequently executed.[151] Mihailović retreated into Serbia instead, but his force was beaten and dispersed in early May 1945.

Axis forces successfully held the Yugoslav People's Liberation Army at bay, but on 6 May 1945, the last defence line collapsed, and Zagreb and Slovenia lay open to their advance. What followed was the chaotic exodus of more than 100,000 soldiers, militia-men and their families, government officials and civilians. Under heavy fighting, a transnational army consisting of Wehrmacht units, Croat Ustash and Domobran, Slovenian militias, Serbian Home Guard and Chetniks, Montenegrin and Bosnian Muslim Militias as well as Russian Cossacks who were operating in the Balkans tried to rush into Austria in order to avoid being captured by the partisans. Tens of thousands of people fled, most of whom reached the Austrian province of Carinthia where they were stopped by advancing British forces. From the largest group, consisting of approximately 40,000 individuals, many surrendered at the town of Bleiburg to British units on 15 May, i.e. after they had fought for more than a week following the official capitulation of all Axis forces. British and Yugoslav authorities had agreed that all Yugoslav nationals would be handed over to the Yugoslav forces, but individual groups – including Ante Pavelić and the bulk of his entourage – managed to escape.

Though it was not actually the site of a massacre, 'Bleiburg' is the symbol for a string of massacres and has turned into one of the most important and most contested *lieu de mémoire*

---

149 Randall Collins, *Violence: A Micro-sociological Theory* (Princeton, NJ: Princeton University Press, 2008); Kalyvas, *The Logic of Violence*.
150 Hoare, *Genocide and Resistance*.
151 Tomasevich, *Chetniks*, 447.

in modern Croatia since the 1970s. It is being portrayed as the Croatian Via Dolorosa (*križni put*), exploited by right-wing activists and sometimes downplayed by their left-wing opponents.

One needs to distinguish between the outright massacres of prisoners in Slovenia and Croatia, and the mass violence that occurred in regions like Istria or Vojvodina where the situation remained more dynamic and chaotic and where the violent onslaught of the enemy was intertwined with ethnic cleansing. Hundreds of prisoners seem to have been killed when they were still on Austrian soil.[152] Once the prisoners were marched into Slovenia, some kind of selection took place, in which a great number of them were executed at former mines or anti-tank trenches. Excavations have revealed that men and women of various national and military backgrounds were shot, indicating that the victim group did not consist of fascists and collaborators alone. The largest massacres took place in the Macelj Forest, at the Teza trench near Maribor and at the Barbara-mine in Northern Slovenia where the victims were apparently locked in alive and left to die.[153] The survivors were marched deep into Yugoslavia. The question is to what extent the mass killings were ordered by the Yugoslav leadership. For one, Tito had repeatedly warned those soldiers who would not capitulate, merciless consequences.[154] Throughout the war, prisoners in the Yugoslav civil war were hardly ever taken alive, and that practice continued in the post-war period. At the same time, Tito ordered an end to unauthorized executions and commanded military courts to rule over suspect prisoners. Regardless of Tito's specific knowledge of all the immediate post-war massacres – he might not have been involved in the detailed decision-making – it is clear that it was the prime goal of the People's Liberation Army to destroy the enemy and to set the stage for the rebuilding of Yugoslavia unharmed by political competitors. A particular form of revenge-driven violence developed in Northwestern Yugoslavia, namely in Istria where the victorious Partisans violently purged the brutal legacy of fascism and Italianization by throwing their enemies – dead or alive – into the deep Karst caves and ravines that are so typical for that region. The victims were primarily, but not solely, Italian prisoners and civilians. This killing culture is called *foibe* in Italian and is one of the most important *lieu de mémoire* for the right-wing political spectre.[155] Historians now estimate that the partisans might have killed up to 100,000 of their enemies towards and after the end of the war, including Croatians, Bosnians, Slovenians and Albanians.[156]

---

152 Florian T. Rulitz, *Die Tragödie von Bleiburg und Viktring: Partisanengewalt in Kärnten am Beispiel der antikommunistischen Flüchtlinge im Mai 1945* (Klagenfurt: Hermagoras; Mohorjeva, 2011).
153 Seja, Mateja Jančar and Jernej Letnar černič, eds, *Poročilo o pobojih: Vmesno poročilo o raziskovanju povojnih množičnih pobojev Preiskovalne komisije Državnega zbora Republike Slovenije o raziskovanju povojnih množičnih pobojev, pravno dvomljivih procesov in drugih tovrstnih nepravilnosti* [Report on the killings: Interim report on the investigation of post-war mass killings conducted by the Parliamentary Commission of inquiry of the Republic of Slovenia for the investigation of post-war mass killings, legally dubious trials and other similar irregularities] (Ljubljana: Inštitut dr. Jožeta Pučnika, 2010).
154 Zdravko Dizdar, 'Prilog istraživanju problema Bleiburga i križnih putova (u povodu 60. obljetnice)' [Contribution to the investigation of the Bleiburg problem and the Crusaders (on the occasion of the 60th anniversary)], *Senjski zbornik* 32 (2005): 135.
155 For a balanced discussion of the *foibe*, see Rolf Wörsdörfer, *Krisenherd Adria 1915–1955: Konstruktion und Artikulation des Nationalen im italienisch-jugoslawischen Grenzraum* (Paderborn: Schoeningh, 2004).
156 Tomasevich, *War and Occupation*; realistic estimates by Vladimir Geiger; Martina Grahek Ravančić, *Bleiburg i križni put 1945: Historiografija, publicistika i memoarska literatura* [Bleiburg and the crusaders, 1945: historiography, journalism and memoirs] (Zagreb: Hrvatski Institut za Povijest, 2009).

The expulsion of Germans and other minorities

So-called 'expulsion' represents the largest forced mass migration of people in Europe, and not only after the Second World War, but people also were expelled immediately after the First World War from, among other places, the Balkans. In the 'Convention between Greece and Bulgaria Respecting Reciprocal Emigration' that happened on the fringes of the Neuilly Peace Treaty (in which Bulgaria had to concede in 1919 as a defeated ally of the Central Powers), Bulgaria and Greece committed themselves to an exchange of minorities with their respective neighbouring countries. It was to follow the principle of interstate reciprocity and be based on the willingness of those concerned to volunteer.[157] In Lausanne in 1923, however, the British Foreign Minister Lord Georges Curzon enforced the principle of a 'population exchange' between Greece and Turkey that was no longer voluntary: roughly 1.6 million people (about ten times as many as the number resulting from the Neuilly Convention) were forced to leave their former homeland. At the same time, there were hundreds of thousands of people migrating from Alsace or Western Poland, where Germans refused to become citizens of France or the Second Polish Republic. But these were all merely preludes to the expulsions in the wake of the Second World War, which are the subject of this section.

The process began with the expulsion of Jews from the German, and later also the Austrian, civic communities from 1933 onwards and continued after the occupation of the Czech Republic in 1938–39. As has been shown above, with the Nazi occupation of several countries between 1939 and 1941, the German and Soviet expulsions reached a dimension nobody in Lausanne would have imagined: here, millions of people were forcibly resettled. In the case of the Germans who were living in the western parts of the Soviet Union in 1939–1940, we are dealing with a slightly different phenomenon: this was so-called 'situational coercion'. In theory, they were allowed to stay in Riga or Volhynia, but most of them could not imagine living under the new Stalinist regime.

At the war's end, governments in Eastern and Southeastern Europe, for their part, saw the Second World War as proof that their nations could not thrive with minorities in them. Minorities were punished for the nationalist aspirations of wartime leaders of Europe. Of course, that was especially the case with German minorities in Eastern Europe. The anti-German sentiment was obvious, as most Eastern European societies had suffered enormously under Nazism, under the participation of ethnic Germans in the German occupation system as well as their participation in mass crimes. Yet, it would be too simplistic to blame the German occupation and the behaviour of the ethnic-German minorities living in the region for the expulsion of ethnic Germans from Eastern and Southeastern Europe, namely, because they were expelled from most countries indiscriminately, regardless of how they had behaved during the war. Revenge was not the sole motive. Rather, the end of the war provided a good opportunity for Eastern European societies and their governments to expel the ethnic-German minorities for a multitude of reasons. Ethnic homogenization and expulsion were the order of the day in post-war Europe, especially in those regions that were contested between states and that changed hands during the war. At the same time, there were huge differences among the scope and the violence of post-war ethnic cleansings, with more violence having been committed in

---

157 This section often follows the considerations of Philipp Ther, *The Dark Side of Nation-States*, here 72.

those regions where demographic changes were intertwined with ongoing fighting and civil war.[158]

In October 1944, with the mass exodus of ethnic Germans from East Prussia, the final and numerically largest chapter of migration began, although against the background outlined above it is by no means exceptional. In January 1945, flight and evacuation merged. Frost, hunger and bombs now truly affected everyone. It is one of the little-known paradoxes that the 6,000 to 7,000 people who died on the Wilhelm Gustloff, a military transport ship that was also carrying civilian refugees, which was sunk by a Soviet submarine at the end of January 1945, was the exception, not the rule. The chances of survival for East and West Prussians who made it to Danzig or Gdingen and boarded a ship there were considerably higher than those of their compatriots in Lower Silesia, for example, who were heading west; and their chances were incomparably higher than those of concentration camp prisoners who were sent on death marches from Auschwitz to Buchenwald at the same time. On the ships in the Baltic Sea, less than 2 per cent of those being transported died; for those on the death marches, it was likely up to 30 per cent.

In spring 1945, a new phase of reckoning set in, with so-called 'wild expulsions', i.e. arbitrary 'deportations', especially in Poland and Czechoslovakia. The Germans fared no better than the Polish or Slovene deportees a few years prior. In Hungary, tainted by state collaboration with the Nazi regime, everyday life seems to have been less violent. The same goes for Romania, where 600,000 Hungarians and Germans fled from the advancing Red Army and their Romanian allies, fearing revenge for the annexation of Northern Transylvania in 1940. The 345,000 Germans who stayed were subject to internment and confiscation of their property. Up to 80,000 able-bodied Germans were deported into the Soviet Union for forced labour in the heavy industry and the mining sectors; the death rates here reached up to 15 per cent. Further, the Romanian government deported 40,000 citizens of various backgrounds including Germans, Slavs, wealthy peasants, Nazi collaborators and 'Titoists' mainly from the borderlands into Southern Wallachia for land reclamation in the steppe—a practice that was clearly reminiscent of the fascist population policies prior to 1945. But in summary, Romanian ethnic cleansing was far from 'total', and the country remained multi-ethnic. This was partly a consequence of Soviet intervention. The Austrian historian Philipp Ther calls it one of the few cases of aborted ethnic cleansing and argues that by keeping Transylvania populated with many Hungarians and Germans, Stalin had a tool in hand to threaten Romanian territorial integrity and to force the Romanian communists to stay in line.[159] In Hungary, the Soviet administration deported ethnic Germans into the Soviet Union for forced labour, whilst the government expelled up to 200,000 Germans to the US- and Soviet zones of occupied Germany. Ultimately, the anti-German measures were less violent and less total, as about 50 per cent of ethnic Germans remained in Hungary.

Yugoslavia was a multi-ethnic state before the war and would remain one thereafter. The best example of the internal political constraints is Josip Broz Tito's outburst of anger at the Politburo meeting of the Yugoslav Communist Party in December 1945: 'No one is afraid of capital punishment any longer!' In 1946 he added, 'We extend our hand to all mislead. We

---

158 Detlef Brandes, *Der Weg zur Vertreibung 1938–1945: Pläne und Entscheidungen zum 'Transfer'der Deutschen aus der Tschechoslowakei und aus Polen* (München: Oldenbourg, 2001).
159 Ther, *The Dark Side of Nation-States*, 167.

extend our hand over the innumerable graves, over these ruins, we forgive them!'[160] As stated, Tito wanted to hold together a multi-ethnic state. Ethnically motivated violence against his own citizens was therefore significantly reduced from above.

Nevertheless, some multi-ethnic regions like Istria, the Vojvodina or the Kosovo underwent dramatic demographic changes. Many Italians fled Istria in 1945, and the remainder was resettled in the immediate post-war years as well as in the context of the Trieste-settlement in 1954. When Yugoslav troops liberated the Vojvodina from the German-Hungarian occupation in 1944, reprisals of Hungarian and German civilians occurred, who were held responsible for the atrocities committed by Hungarian troops in the previous years. Up to 90 per cent of the Germans who had stayed were interned by Yugoslav authorities, most of them in the Knićanin camp in the Banat, where approximately one-third of the 33,000 inmates died in the years between 1945 and 1948. Most starved to death or died because of the poor health conditions, but a small number of inmates were shot, too.[161] The ethnic cleansing of Germans and Italians from Yugoslavia was fairly total, the expulsion of other groups like Hungarians were largely selective. As for the Germans, the Yugoslav government asked the Western Allies for permission to resettle the German minority in its entirety, which was, however, rejected. Subsequently, Yugoslavia expelled the Germans in small groups, and later in larger groups once the Federal Republic of Germany agreed to receive them. Neighbouring countries used the end of the war as well to expel their minorities. Expulsions and population transfers were always accompanied by killings, whether intentionally or not. Greek troops under EDES-leader Napoleon Zervas expelled up to 20,000 Muslim Çhams to Albania.

The Prague Castle was faced with a theoretically different case than in Yugoslavia. The main targets for expulsion were the German minorities in Czechoslovakia – here called the 'Sudeten Germans'.[162] Most of the German-speaking inhabitants of the Baltics, Eastern Poland and Bulgaria had been evacuated in the context of the German-Soviet exchange treaties of 1939–40 to German-occupied Western Poland, and many of them were overrun there by the Red Army in 1945. Additionally, a large number of German citizens living in the areas east of the Oder-Neisse rivers, fled from Soviet occupation in January 1945. After the loss of Transcarpathia and the mass exodus of Hungarians from Southern Slovakia, significantly fewer minorities remained. The Romani did not have an internationally recognized lobby that would allow them to claim, let alone establish, minority status. Furthermore, there were statistically insignificant Polish and Hungarian minorities in Czechoslovakia who could not be deported, because Poland, Hungary and Czechoslovakia were now, as neighbours in the emerging Eastern bloc, allies and not enemies.

The only solvable obstacle on the road to a theoretically Czech-Slovakian national state was the problem of the 'Sudeten Germans'. In the First Czechoslovak Republic they had counted over 3 million citizens. Hundreds of thousands of them had fled in the spring of 1945, either as Wehrmacht soldiers or as POWs. But still, 2.5 million people remained and were now considered collectively responsible for the Munich Agreement of November 1938, the

---

160 Quotes taken from Marie-Janine Calic, *A History of Yugoslavia* (West Lafayette, IN: Purdue University Press, 2019), 161, 165.

161 For repressions against Germans see Zoran Janjetovic, *Between Hitler and Tito: The Disappearance of the Vojvodina Germans* (Belgrade: n.i., 2005); Vladimir Geiger, 'Prisoners and Victims of the Communist Internment Camp "Krndija", 1945–1946', *Review of Croatian History*, no. 1 (2007): 175–99.

162 This common term is misleading because ethnic Germans lived in several regions of the Czech Republic, including South Moravia, which was far from the Sudeten Mountains.

total dismantling of what was left of Czechoslovakia in March 1939 and the ensuing German occupation. Only the most prominent or obvious perpetrators were brought to justice, all in all hardly more than 20,000 people. The *odsun* ('forced deportation') of an entire ethnic group, proved to be a practical solution in Czechoslovakia. On 18 July 1946, the Prague Parliament passed a law according to which 'Sudeten Germans' would not be prosecuted unless there were reasonable grounds for suspicion. All others were simply expelled.[163]

In Poland the situation was quite complicated, since not only Germans from the Reich, but also Germans with Polish citizenship and evacuated ethnic Germans from other regions had lived there under the German occupation. Approximately 120,000 came under Soviet occupation, some of them were interned in camps but the majority were deported to occupied Germany in 1946.[164] In the years following, the western parts of Poland were systematically 'Polonized'.[165]

In general, there were four patterns of the forced movement of Germans towards the West, and three of them we have already encountered: flight, wild expulsions (mostly by local police and military) and targeted expulsion policies implemented by the new state authorities. Whereas a large group of Germans managed to escape with the retreating Wehrmacht troops, hundreds of thousands were targets of wild expulsions especially by the end of the war, while the majority were systematically evacuated from the summer of 1945 onwards. Hundreds of thousands were arrested by Allied troops or underground movements; those captured by the Red Army were sent as forced labourers to camps inside the Soviet Union. The German-speaking minority in Czechoslovakia were largely expelled in 1945–46. Approximately 800,000 of them fled to the West or they were expelled by local Czech organizations during May/June 1945, often under brutal circumstances. During the 'Brno death march', approximately 5,000 people lost their lives. In 1946, another 2.2 million inhabitants were deported to the zones of occupied Germany, including former members of the anti-Nazi resistance.[166]

The Western Allies, by allowing the governments of Eastern and Southeastern Europe to systematically expel their German and, in some instances, other minorities, opened Pandora's box, as they set in motion a powerful drive that promised ethnic homogeneity and allowed governments to push for social engineering and thus to consolidate their power. It was the Allies who, in some cases, tried to turn back the wheel when they banned countries like Hungary and Romania from further expulsions.

---

163 See Piotr Majewski, *'Niemcy sudeccy' 1848–1948: Historia pewnego nacjonalizmu* ['Sudeten Germans' 1848–1948: the story of a certain nationalism] (Warsaw: Wydawnictwo Uniwersytetu Warszawskiego, 2007), 446–9. More literature on the subject can be found in Ther, *Dark Side* and Eva Hahn and Hans Henning Hahn, *Die Vertreibung im deutschen Erinnern: Legenden, Mythos, Geschichte* (Paderborn: Schoeningh, 2010).

164 Włodzimierz Borodziej and Hans Lemberg, eds, *'Unsere Heimat ist uns ein fremdes Land geworden...' Die Deutschen östlich von Oder und Neiße 1945–1950; Dokumente aus polnischen Archiven, vol. 2: Zentralpolen: Wojewodschaft Schlesien (Oberschlesien)* (Marburg: Herder-Institut Verlag, 2003), 3–76. This is not the place to discuss the fate of the nearly 7 million citizens of Eastern Germany who were transferred to Poland and the Soviet Union (such as the Kaliningrad Oblast, i.e. the former East Prussian city of Königsberg and its surrounding areas).

165 Beata Halicka, *Polens Wilder Westen: Erzwungene Migration und die kulturelle Aneignung des Oderraums 1945–1948* (Paderborn: Ferdinand Schöningh, 2013); Peter Polak-Springer, *Recovered Territory: A German-Polish Conflict Over Land and Culture, 1919–1989* (New York: Berghahn Books, 2015), 183–231.

166 Ray Douglas, *Orderly and Humane: The Expulsion of the Germans after the Second World War* (New Haven, CT: Yale University Press, 2012).

Thus, the fourth pattern that framed the expulsion of Germans from the East was a large number of memoranda and negotiation protocols resulting from the power-political logic of 1945 and also applied in 1946 and 1947. After flight, wild and systematic expulsion had set millions in motion, the Western Allies came to the conclusion that further millions of displaced persons would only destabilize their occupation zones in Germany which were already difficult to administer. For example, in the summer of 1945, there was simply no housing and no jobs to offer them, neither was there a sufficient amount of food or coal for the coming winter. For similar reasons, the Kremlin interrupted the forced resettlement of Hungarians and Germans from Transylvania, and the same happened in Yugoslav Vojvodina.

The most important Allied regulation for the expulsion of the Germans was Point XIII from the conclusions of the Potsdam Conference of 2 August 1945, according to which 'any transfers that take place should be effected in an orderly and humane manner'.[167] Poland, Czechoslovakia and Hungary were called upon to suspend the forced resettlement that was in progress. After this reprieve, the Allied Control Council adopted a resettlement (and de facto settlement) plan on 20 November that regulated the division of the deportees into the British, US and Soviet occupation zones.[168] It was implemented in the Czechoslovak case in 1946 and in the Polish case in 1946 and 1947.

The gradually more ordered 'transfers' that took place between 1946 and 1947 to the three occupation zones brought at least six million Germans 'home to the Reich' (*heim ins Reich*), which no longer existed. Their integration into the later Federal Republic of Germany and the German Democratic Republic (where they were called '*Umsiedler*', i.e. 'resettlers') went reasonably well when measured against the initial conditions. At the same time, millions more were displaced, mainly on the East–West axis, especially in Central and Eastern Europe and the Soviet Union. Many had already fled, in alphabetical order, because the list of the mass movements of people can be read elsewhere: mainly Croats, Finns,[169] Germans, Hungarians, Italians, Poles, Slovaks and Ukrainians, a total of around 15 million people, with Germans accounting for about two-thirds of those affected. A mixture of physical and situational coercion, voluntariness and coincidence, crime and the relief of those affected to finally be allowed to leave what had once been their homeland and now seemed a foreign land to them, indecisiveness and the desire of the state power to keep the workforce within the country resulted in the strangest combinations. Millions more voluntarily migrated back to their homeland: among them were former forced labourers, concentration camp prisoners, exiles and POWs, all of whom now fell under the collective term 'displaced persons'.[170]

More than three million Germans were deported from the new Polish territory, about 2.5 million from Czechoslovakia, and millions more, who would have preferred to emigrate, were not allowed to – with exceptions such as the reunification of families or the semi-legal emigration of Jews, which was often quietly promoted by the state.

---

167 Berlin (Potsdam) Conference, 17 July–2 August 1945, Protocol of the Proceedings (Press Release), in *Germany 1947–1949: The Story in Documents*, ed. US Department of State (Washington, DC: US Government Printing Office, 1950), 47–57, here 55.
168 The context of this decision is outlined in, among others, Borodziej, Lemberg, '*Unsere Heimat ist uns ein fremdes Land geworden…*', here, the introduction to vol. I, 50–76. Further information can be found in Ther, *The Dark Side of Nation-States*, and – often interpreted differently – Hahn and Hahn, *Die Vertreibung im deutschen Erinnern*.
169 Their forced mass migrations ended around 1944 and are therefore not discussed here.
170 For 'displaced persons', see also the volume *Statehood* in this series.

With regard to the question posed in our volume, several posthumous stories of the expulsions at the end of the war seem important. Firstly, the connection between Nazi crimes and brutality against strangers and enemies in the immediate post-war period is crucial. After the ordinary Polish 'neighbours' – workers and policemen, petty bourgeoisie and military – had murdered more than 40 Jews in Kielce on 4 July 1946, the sociologist Stanisław Ossowski wrote a remarkable piece in which he expressed his concern about the state of society: several National Socialist thought patterns, above all nationalism based on racism, were discernible in post-war public opinion; the poison of the occupation continued its work.[171] What Ossowski could not foresee, however, was the brutality, contempt for humanity and humiliation of both alleged and actual opponents as a matter of course, and not least of all the awareness of one's own impunity, that were reflected in the terror against one's own compatriots in the following years. Whether they were party members or not, did not actually play a role in their marriage with Stalinism.

Secondly, the unmixing of peoples between 1938 and 1948 eliminated most of the historically developed ethnic-cultural neighbourhood relations, but by no means all of them. In the suburbs of Vilnius, the Poles remained a conspicuous minority; in Southern Slovakia, it was the Hungarians, in Transylvania, it was the Germans, in Carinthia the Slovenes and in Bulgaria the Turks. The Romani lived everywhere and in very different densities. Thus, in every country there were people who fit into the imposed official statistics, but in reality – and this differed from country to country – were allowed to vote with their feet against foreign rule in post-Stalinism from the mid-1950s to the 1980s. Several migratory flows, mainly on the East–West axis, were set in motion, not as a result of physical violence, but as a result of situational compulsion – or simply because of the economic attractiveness of the so-called 'West'. The topic of migration is touched upon several times in Volume I of our series, *Challenges of Modernity*, and it hardly has anything to do with 'expulsion', just like the Polish–West German and Czech–West German post-histories in the context of the Cold War.

Thirdly, it was only during the so-called 'Yugoslav Wars' at the turn of the millennium that a comparable percentage of the people in our region of interest were uprooted. They were murdered en masse, fled ethnic cleansing or were forced by armed men – who were often former neighbours – to leave their homes. The new solutions for Bosnia-Herzegovina and Kosovo, this time mainly imposed by the US, were in a sense linked to the era before Lausanne. New state formations were possible or, as a lesser evil, even desired, but forced resettlement according to ethnic criteria was unacceptable.

Let us return, however, to the four decades or so that will be discussed in the following sub-chapter. Gradually, the experience of war, occupation and expulsion faded. Without the memory of the degradation caused by foreign occupation regimes, the memory of one's own involvement in crimes, which was forced by the state and which was just as often suppressed, violence in Central and Eastern Europe after 1948 might have played a different role as a means of seizing power. One can polemicize against this thesis with the justified argument that the Soviet Union was already persecuting its own citizens, including the systemic carriers, years before 1939 with simply incomprehensible brutality and consistency.

There will never be a completely convincing answer in this argument, since the rapid Stalinization of Central and Eastern Europe took place precisely after the experiences of the

---

171 Borodziej, *Geschichte Polens im 20. Jahrhundert*, 269. Today, Ossowski's essay is forgotten outside the sphere of Holocaust research. His core statement, however, is likely to apply to several countries in our region of interest.

decade 1938–1948 – not during the Great Purge that took place prior to that decade, the time when all the instruments employed after 1948 were developed. In any case, the pattern of violence was pre-determined. It is possible – and this too will never be proven – that this pattern was given a kind of moral legitimation by the experience of war, occupation and expulsion that did not exist before 1938. How had Curzon formulated it during the Lausanne Conference after his dictation had been incorporated into the draft treaty? 'He deeply regretted that the solution now being worked out should be the compulsory exchange of populations – a thoroughly bad and vicious solution, for which the world will pay a heavy penalty for a hundred years to come'.[172]

After the end of the Second World War, the great powers, like the states of our region, followed Curzon's argumentation without moral reservations about a 'bad and vicious solution': nobody had put a better alternative on the negotiating table.

The Sovietization of Central and Eastern Europe

On their march westward, the Red Army and the NKVD units broke the last of the German resistance and expelled the civil population. Their task was not only to end Nazi rule in Eastern Europe, but also to replace it with Soviet rule. This means that the superpower that came to 'liberate' the country, at the same time subjected it to a new occupation regime – an occupation which, by the way, many Poles and Balts regarded as only abolished once there was the peaceful regime change in 1989, half a century after the Second World War had begun.

The fact that the Soviet Union mutated from ally to enemy – at least in the eyes of the non-communist population of Central Europe – had a strong formative impact on the relation between local resistance groups and the Soviet armed forces – partisan and Red Army units. In Poland, the Home Army had fought side by side with them in a joint effort to throw the Germans out of the country. But the Warsaw Uprising in 1944 already featured the fissures between Polish nationalists and the Soviet authorities: Operation Storm (*Akcja 'Burza'*), ordered by the Polish government-in-exile, was meant to put important Polish cities under the control of the Home Army *before* the Red Army's arrival, thus ensuring that the Poles would have a say in their country's post-war fate. On the other hand, the plan to capture Warsaw from a superior German garrison – in armament, not in manpower – without Allied support was especially suicidal. What the Home Army counted on was Allied air support and that the Red Army, which on 1 August 1944 was in eyesight of the eastern outskirts of Warsaw, would come to their aid.[173]

Neither the one, nor the other, materialized. The fighting, which started in the afternoon of 1 August, took place exclusively in the main part of the city on the western bank of the Vistula, and the Red Army hesitated to cross the river, whether for military or political reasons (to let the Germans finish off the Polish national resistance in the city) is still discussed today. A clearer language speaks of the fact that the Russians only allowed one Allied-supply plane take off from their airbases – the western airbases being too remote from Warsaw.[174] For almost two months, the Home Army fought a desperate fight, but being cut off from supplies and

---

172 Ther, *The Dark Side of Nation-States*, 77.
173 For a comprehensive description of the Uprising, see Norman Davies, *Rising '44: The Battle for Warsaw* (New York: Macmillan, 2004).
174 Włodzimierz Borodziej, *Der Warschauer Aufstand 1944* (Frankfurt: S. Fischer, 2001), 127–8, 169–70, 175.

reinforcements, they were doomed. The lives of thousands of Home Army fighters were saved due to the fact that the German command – in hindsight of the treatment of German soldiers in Allied captivity – granted them combatant status. The death toll was nevertheless enormous: between 150,000 and 180,000 people – 90 per cent of them civilians – not only fell victim to the fighting, but to the Nazi-led atrocities, the most horrendous of which were perpetrated by the German Police and the SS-Division *Dirlewanger* in the Wola district.[175]

The Warsaw Uprising set the course for future events. Cooperation between the Polish non-communist underground and the Soviet forces became more and more rare as former allies turned enemies. The Soviet side regarded them as representatives of the bourgeois Second Polish Republic and secret agents of the West at best, or – absurdly – as collaborators with Nazi Germany. Starting in late 1944, Polish units were tricked into ambushes, forced to surrender and sent to the interior as prisoners, often to forced labour camps or Gulags. Some of their commanders were even tried in 1945 in a show trial, known as the 'Trial of the Sixteen' (*Proces szesnastu*) in Moscow.[176] Both sides now had knives to each other's throats. The Polish resistance movement shifted from anti-German to anti-Soviet and organized itself to combat the new invader. But with the Soviets gaining a foothold in Poland, they did not stand a chance, and most of them followed the call of their commanders to disband before being hunted down by the NKVD and its Polish communist auxiliaries. After two years in the woods, the majority of the remaining 'cursed soldiers' (*żołnierze wyklęcy*) gave up their hopeless resistance. But armed resistance against the Soviet occupation forces would only actually cease in 1953.[177]

The development in the Baltic states was comparable, but not similar. There, in contrast to the Polish case, the Germans managed to mobilize a significant portion of the resistance in the fight against the Soviets. One reason for this is that the Polish resistance movement was already in full bloom when the Germans were facing defeat and a Soviet counterattack at the Eastern Front. In the Baltic states, local partisan units were often trained by the Germans and enhanced in order to establish a national anti-communist resistance. Thus, a transitional phase from ally to enemy was not observed here – the bulk of Baltic partisans were first and foremost anti-Bolsheviks from the first moment of their activity. Although, like the Polish case, they were soon outnumbered and fled to the woods, giving them their name the 'wood brothers' (in Estonian, *metsavennad*, in Latvian, *meža brāļi*, in Lithuanian, *miško broliai*) who fought against the Sovietization of their homeland until the early 1950s.[178]

Apart from the Polish Home Army, towards the end of the war, the largest anti-Soviet partisan force in the area was the Ukrainian one. By that time, Ukrainian armed units were divided over the issue of whom to fight. Many had joined the Waffen-SS in the ranks of the so-called 'Galicia Division', but the largest influx of fighters joined the UPA who, in Volhynia in 1943–44, massacred the Polish population through their campaign of ethnic cleansing (see the sub-chapter *Ethnic cleansing in Volhynia, 1943–1944* above). As long as there was a faint hope that the Third Reich would not only win the war, but also grant the Ukraine some form of

---

175 Daniel Brewing, *Im Schatten von Auschwitz: Deutsche Massaker an polnischen Zivilisten 1939–1945* (Darmstadt: WBG 2016), 282–9; Snyder, *Bloodlands*, 302–05.
176 Anne Applebaum, *Iron Curtain: The Crushing of Eastern Europe, 1944–1956* (New York: Doubleday, 2012), 90–104.
177 Rafał Wnuk, 'Antysowieckie podziemie estońskie, łotewskie, litewskie, ukraińskie, białoruskie i polskie. Zarys dziejów i próba porównania' [The Estonian, Latvian, Lithuanian, Ukrainian, Belarusian and Polish Anti-Soviet Underground: an outline of the history and an attempt to compare], in Motyka et al., *Wojna po wojnie*, 132–69.
178 Wnuk, 'Antysowieckie podziemie', 34–95.

independent statehood, they sided with Germany; once such hope was gone, however, the UPA turned its weapons not only on the German Police and SS (and sometimes even on their fellow countrymen who were in the ranks of the Waffen-SS), but also on the Red Army who were on the march. Like the resistance in Poland and the Baltics, the UPA's struggle against their new masters abated in 1945–46 but was nevertheless not completely over until the early 1950s.[179]

Unlike the ethnic strife between Ukrainians and Poles in Volhynia, the diverse Baltic, Polish and Ukrainian resistance groups' struggle against their Soviet invader was nothing akin to civil war. Therefore, the title of Anita J. Prażmowska's meritorious 2004 monograph on the Polish case, *Civil War in Poland, 1942–1948: Challenges to Communist Rule* – one of the rare studies on the topic published in a Western language – is a bit misleading.[180] The Red Army and NKVD units were the regular and secret forces of an empire that was invading Central Europe from the east and either incorporating the pre-war countries of the area into its 'Soviet Union' or bullying them into alliance and sealing them off from the western part of the continent with an Iron Curtain. The Western Allies, for their part, although soon facing the Soviet Union in the Cold War, gave their then-associate Stalin major concessions.

The countries further to the south and the southeast – Hungary, Romania, Bulgaria and later, Czechoslovakia – also faced Sovietization, but in these countries as a rule, the struggle between nationalist/anti-communist circles and the new communist rulers did not result in bloody skirmishes but were rather a matter of Secret Police operations against individuals or smaller resistance cells, both actual and alleged. The methods applied were nevertheless brutal, with beatings and torture being daily routine in commissariats and prisons.[181] Only Yugoslavia (and Albania) provides a different case: here, the communist partisan movement under Tito had won the civil war with their nationalist and fascist rivals, and his post-war government was able to count on extensive support from the local population. This secured a privileged position within the Eastern bloc for the legendary former-partisan leader who then became a charismatic politician. As the following chapter, 'State Socialism', will show, all the other countries within our region of interest featured far less support for the Soviet cause, with their respective communist nomenklatura representing only a tiny portion of the population. One major reason for this is situated in the violent waves of Sovietization they experienced – the German interregnum between 1941 and 1944, notwithstanding – from 1941 onwards.

Conclusion

Central and Eastern Europe was not the only region affected by extreme violence during the 1930s and 1940s. Comparable losses occurred in the western and southern regions of the Soviet Union by way of crimes committed during mass collectivization, the politically induced famines from Ukraine to Kazakhstan in the early 1930s, the Stalinist mass terror of 1937–38 and those

---

179 Ibid., 95–115. On Ukrainians in the Waffen-SS, see Jacek Andrzej Młynarczyk, Leonid Rein, Andrii Bolianovskyi, and Oleg Romanko, 'Eastern Europe: Belarusian auxiliaries, Ukrainian Waffen-SS soldiers and the special case of the Polish "Blue Police"', in Böhler and Gerwarth, *The Waffen-SS*, 165–208, here 198–206.
180 Anita J. Prażmowska, *Civil War in Poland, 1942–1948: Challenges to Communist Rule* (Basingstoke: Palgrave Macmillan, 2004).
181 A comprehensive overview of the Sovietization of Central and Southeastern Europe between 1944 and 1956, including economic and political aspects as well as various nuances and local differences, can be found in Applebaum, *Iron Curtain*, 1–246. The political dimension of this process is also dealt with in the volume *Statehood* of this series.

areas occupied by the Wehrmacht in 1941–44. Similar mass violence was visible during the civil war in China, especially in the early 1930s, and during the Japanese occupation of 1931–37, not only in central, but also northern China. This raises the question to what extent totalitarian regimes are a necessary precondition for the murder of millions. The Japanese case shows that imperialism could escalate to genocidal dimensions if implemented by a non-totalitarian state.

Why was there such an enormous amount of violence enacted on civilians and POWs in Central Eastern Europe between 1939 and 1947, resulting in the murder of around 7 million people? By far the most important factor was Germany's new imperialism in the region, which not only aimed at German hegemony and rule in these areas, but also in the political and demographic restructuring of the continent, realized by the killing of Polish and Soviet elites, and the deportation of 'undesirables' in parts of the East. The belief that 'world Jewry' was an imminent danger not only to Germany but to the world as a whole, resulted in the murder of Jewish people all across Europe. These schemes were radicalized both by the German patterns of warfare – especially in Poland, the Soviet Union and parts of Yugoslavia – and by the ongoing war against the Soviet Union and the Western powers. From autumn 1941, Germany's counter-insurgency strategies were accompanied by massacres of the civil population. And the deliberate starvation of Soviet POWs, who were considered racial and political enemies, largely took place in Central and Eastern Europe (as well as within the German Reich).

The second major factor, closely related to Nazi-German imperialism, was constituted by the violence enacted by Germany's allies. This relates to Italy's ruthless occupation of the Western Balkans, but more importantly to the active participation of the Croatian, Romanian and – in 1944 – Hungarian states. Inside the occupied Soviet Union, in Yugoslavia, Bulgaria and Greece, other Axis powers imitated forms of anti-resistance violence applied by the Germans, though on a much smaller scale. In Croatia and the Ukraine, the Germans only instigated 'ethnic cleansings' as far as Jews were concerned; local groups would follow in their footsteps rather independently by persecuting Serbs in Croatia and Bosnia, and Poles in Western Ukraine. Further, Germany set the stage for the outbreak of civil wars in Yugoslavia in 1941 and in Greece in 1943 but were only indirectly responsible for the atrocities committed. However, German hegemony in these areas was a necessary precondition for unleashing this kind of mass violence. The Germans outlawed large parts of the population, encouraged right-wing regimes and extremist groups and provided an example of how to deal with alleged enemies.

Relating to the number of victims killed in Central and Eastern Europe during the Second World War, Stalinist imperialism can be interpreted as the third major force of mass violence: first, during the violent integration and transformation of societies in the Baltics, Eastern Poland and Bessarabia/Northern Bukovina; and from 1944 on, by destroying the anti-communist resistance in all liberated territories and countries occupied by the Red Army in 1944–45.

Stalinist violence is closely intertwined with the fourth major factor, i.e. the efforts of new regimes to establish their power from 1944 onwards, to seek revenge for Axis occupation, and to create ethnically homogenous nation states. The communist groups supported by the Soviet Union were especially ruthless when combatting their political enemies, collaborators and the ethnic-German and other minorities. However, the democratic government of the Beneš administration in Czechoslovakia also urged for the complete expulsion of the German and Hungarian populations.

Thus, there were different major forces of violence over time, beginning in 1939 with Hitler and – to a limited extent – Stalin, followed by the Axis allies and nationalist groups and finally, non-Soviet communist groups and regimes. All of them considered violence an appropriate means of pursuing their ideological and political aims, especially under wartime conditions. And all of them perceived any resistance to their aims as illegitimate and thus did not hesitate to kill people they considered to be the opposition; and not only the resisters, but also *their* alleged supporters and even people believed to be part of their social milieu.

Nevertheless, the overall projects of these forces were quite different. The Nazi projects for Eastern Europe included – from late 1941 on – not only the extermination of all Jews, but also other 'pernicious' groups like the Romani and the institutionalized psychiatric patients in Poland and the Baltics. And the Germans' grand design for Eastern Europe that was eclipsed in the *Generalplan Ost* envisaged the deportation of 31 million Slavs. The allies of Nazi Germany rather aimed at territorial revisions and the ethnic homogenization of their enlarged countries. This included the deportation and sometimes mass murder of Jews, though both the Romanian and the Hungarian governments reversed their policies of genocide at a later point. The Soviet design first and foremost meant the 'Sovietization' of all new territories under Stalinist rule: in other words, it meant adapting to structures within the old Soviet Union, including the installation of communist governments, the atomizing of pre-Soviet societal structures, the deportation of specific social strata of the population, and the killing of resisters and particular portions of the social elite, like in Poland. All major actors resorted to extreme forms of propaganda against their enemies and did not hesitate to kill their victims in public.

The years of violence had a major impact on the societies of Central and Eastern Europe. First and foremost, the annihilation of the European Jews, which was almost completely ignored in how the war was remembered from the 1950s to the 1980s, is crucial. In Poland, 10 per cent of the population were killed in a most brutal way; in the towns and cities of Central and Eastern Poland, Jews had constituted up to 50 per cent of the population. In regions with major Jewish communities, hundreds of thousands of locals not only witnessed these mass crimes, but many of them participated by denouncing, robbing and sometimes even killing their 'neighbours'. The portions of Jewish property that had not been confiscated by the Germans, were acquired by non-Jewish administrations and locals. This was especially the case among Germany's allies. Moreover, the societies of the region suffered an enormous loss with the total annihilation of their Jewish communities in the spheres of culture, knowledge and economy. Poland and Lithuania are especially scattered with the mass graves of Jewish victims in each and every region.

During the war, among the majority of the population in the region, the Holocaust was considered to be a separate phenomenon of violence, which, in the beginning, seemed to have little effect on non-Jewish people. These Christian majorities considered their own ethnicities as the major targets of violence, as was underlined by the governments-in-exile of the occupied countries. The murder of Polish elites that occurred early on by both the Nazi and the Stalinist regimes were especially considered the major crime of the occupiers, culminating in the discovery of the Katyn massacre in 1943, which became an iconic mass crime against the Polish people.

The extreme violence in Central and Eastern Europe was one of the leading causes for the success of the communist takeovers between 1945 and 1948. Of course, the major factor behind the Sovietization of the region lies in strong Soviet leadership, with use of the Red Army, the Secret Police and local communists as instruments on the ground. But wartime violence facilitated the political transformation after the war: in Poland – a country of vital importance for Soviet strategy – a large part of the political and cultural leadership had been executed, first by the Germans, followed by the Soviets; in Yugoslavia, the communist partisans won the civil war and took power, not least which was due to the fact that they destroyed their political enemies. Everywhere the legitimacy of pre-war elites suffered – they who had not been able to protect their citizens from invasions and extreme violence – even after Germany's defeat. Thus, the conditions for establishing a new political order were fertile. In a certain sense, it is a paradox of history that another violent regime could earn legitimacy by defeating the wartime proponents of violence.

The war left large parts of Central and Eastern European societies traumatized. First and foremost, were the groups targeted by the Nazi regime and its Axis Allies. Their survival was often followed by new forms of oppression under communist rule. New groups came under pressure after the communist takeovers between 1944 and 1948. Social relations were, by and large, deteriorating especially in those areas where violence occurred on a day-to-day basis. Greece remained the site of an ongoing civil war. Both alleged and actual collaborators were severely punished, much more forcibly than their former German superiors. German, Hungarian and Italian minorities had to pay the price for Axis rule, sometimes for their active role in it. Nevertheless, there were also profiteers from wartime violence, especially those who joined communism.

Further reading

Aly, Götz, and Susanne Heim. *Architects of Annihilation: Auschwitz and the Logic of Destruction* (Princeton, NJ: Princeton University Press, 2002).

Aly, Götz. *Final Solution: Nazi Population Policy and the Murder of the European Jews* (London: Arnold; New York: Oxford University Press, 1999).

Ancel, Jean. *Economic Destruction of the Romanian Jews* (Jerusalem: INSHR publishing house, Yad Vashem, 2008).

Ancel, Jean. *Prelude to Mass Murder: The Pogrom in Iași, Romania, June 29, 1941 and Thereafter* (Jerusalem: Yad Vashem, 2013).

Anušauskas, Arvydas. *Arrests and other Forms of Coercion: Report* (Vilnius: Commission for the Evaluation of the Crimes of the Soviet and Nazi Occupation Regimes in Lithuania 1940–1941, 2003).

Applebaum, Anne. *Iron Curtain: The Crushing of Eastern Europe, 1944–1956* (New York: Doubleday, 2012).

Bank, Jan, and Lieve Gevers. *Churches and Religion in the Second World War* (London: Bloomsbury, 2016).

Bársony, János, and Ágnes Daróczi, eds. *Pharrajimos: The Fate of the Roma During the Holocaust* (New York: International Debate Education Association, 2008).

Bartov, Omer. *The Anatomy of a Genocide: The Life and Death of a Town Called Buczacz* (New York: Simon & Schuster, 2018).

Bergholz, Max. *Violence as a Generative Force: Identity, Nationalism, and Memory in a Balkan Community* (Ithaca, NY: Cornell University Press, 2016).

Biondich, Mark. *The Balkans: Revolution, War, and Political Violence since 1878*, vol. 3, *Zones of Violence* (Oxford: Oxford University Press, 2011).

Blatman, Daniel. *The Death Marches: The Final Phase of Nazi Genocide* (Cambridge, MA: Belknap Press of Harvard University, 2011).

Blood, Philip H. *Hitler's Bandit Hunters: The SS and the Nazi Occupation of Europe* (Washington, DC: Potomac, 2006).

Böhler, Jochen, and Robert Gerwarth, eds. *The Waffen-SS: A European History* (Oxford: Oxford University Press, 2017).

Borodziej, Włodzimierz. *Der Warschauer Aufstand 1944* (Frankfurt: S. Fischer, 2001).

Bowman, Steven B. *The Agony of Greek Jews, 1940–1945* (Stanford, CA: Stanford University Press, 2009).

Braham, Randolph L. *The Politics of Genocide: The Holocaust in Hungary* (New York: Columbia University Press, 1994).

Browning, Christopher R. *The Origins of the Final Solution: The Evolution of Nazi Jewish Policy, September 1939–March 1942* (Lincoln, NE: University of Nebraska Press, 2004).

Browning, Christopher R., ed. *Fateful Months: Essays on the Emergence of the Final Solution*, revised edition (New York: Holmes & Meier, 1991).

Calic, Marie-Janine. *A History of Yugoslavia* (West Lafayette, IN: Purdue University Press, 2019).

Case, Holly. *Between States: The Transylvanian Question and the European Idea During World War II* (Stanford, CA: Stanford University Press, 2009).

Cattaruzza, Marina, Stefan Dyroffm and Dieter Langewiesche, eds. *Territorial Revisionism and the Allies of Germany in the Second World War: Goals, Expectations, Practices* (New York: Berghahn Books, 2013).

Chary, Frederick B. *The Bulgarian Jews and the Final Solution, 1940–1944* (Pittsburgh, PA: University of Pittsburgh Press, 1972).

Cichopek, Anna. *Beyond Violence: Jewish Survivors in Poland and Slovakia, 1944–48* (Cambridge: Cambridge University Press, 2014).

Cigar, Norman L. *Genocide in Bosnia: The Policy of 'Ethnic Cleansing'* (College Station, TX: Texas A & M University Press, 1995).
Collins, Randall. *Violence: A Micro-sociological Theory* (Princeton, NJ: Princeton University Press, 2008).
Crampton, R. J. *Bulgaria, Oxford History of Modern Europe* (Oxford: Oxford University Press, 2007).
Čulibrk, Jovan. *Historiography of the Holocaust in Yugoslavia* (Belgrade: University of Belgrade, 2014).
Dafinger, Johannes, and Dieter Pohl, eds. *A New Nationalist Europe Under Hitler: Concepts of Europe and Transnational Networks in the National Socialist Sphere of Influence, 1933–1945* (London: Routledge, 2018).
Davies, Norman. *Rising '44: The Battle for Warsaw* (New York: Macmillan, 2004).
Dean, Martin C. *Collaboration in the Holocaust: Crimes of the Local Police in Belorussia and Ukraine, 1941–1944* (Basingstoke: Palgrave Macmillan, 2000).
Dean, Martin, and Geoffrey P. Megargee, eds. *Encyclopedia of Camps and Ghettos, 1933–1945*, vol. 2: *Ghettos in German-Occupied Eastern Europe* (Bloomington, IN: Indiana University Press, 2012).
Deletant, Dennis. *Hitler's Forgotten Ally: Ion Antonescu and his Regime, Romania 1940–44* (Basingstoke: Palgrave Macmillan, 2006).
Douglas, Ray. *Orderly and Humane: The Expulsion of the Germans after the Second World War* (New Haven, CT: Yale University Press, 2012).
Dragostinova, Theodora. *Between Two Motherlands: Nationality and Emigration among the Greeks of Bulgaria, 1900–1949* (Ithaca, NY: Cornell University Press, 2011).
Dumitru, Diana. *The State, Antisemitism, and Collaboration in the Holocaust: The Borderlands of Romania and the Soviet Union* (Cambridge: Cambridge University Press, 2016).
Epstein, Catherine. *Model Nazi: Arthur Greiser and the Occupation of Western Poland* (Oxford: Oxford University Press, 2010).
Friling, Tuvia, Radu Ioanid, and Mihail E. Ionescu, eds. *International Commission on the Holocaust in Romania: Final Report* (Iași: Polirom, 2004).
Gerlach, Christian. *The Extermination of the European Jews* (Cambridge: Cambridge University Press, 2016).
Gogun, Alexander. *Stalin's Commandos: Ukrainian Partisan Forces on the Eastern Front* (London: IB Tauris, 2015).
Goldstein, Ivo, and Slavko Goldstein. *The Holocaust in Croatia* (Pittsburgh: University of Pittsburgh Press, 2016).
Greble, Emily. *Sarajevo, 1941–1945: Muslims, Christians, and Jews in Hitler's Europe* (Ithaca, NY: Cornell University Press, 2011).
Gross, Jan Tomasz. *Neighbors: The Destruction of the Jewish Community in Jedwabne, Poland* (Princeton, NJ: Princeton University Press, 2001).
Gross, Stephen G. *Export Empire: German Soft Power in Southeastern Europe* (Cambridge: Cambridge University Press, 2015).
Hanebrink, Paul. *A Specter Haunting Europe: The Myth of Judeo-Bolshevism* (Cambridge, MA: Harvard University Press, 2018).
Hill, Alexander. *The Red Army and the Second World War* (Cambridge: Cambridge University Press, 2017).
Hoare, Marko A. *Genocide and Resistance in Hitler's Bosnia: The Partisans and the Chetniks, 1941–1943* (Oxford: Published for the British Academy by Oxford University Press, 2006).
Hoare, Marko A. *The Bosnian Muslims in the Second World War: A History* (New York: Oxford University Press, 2013).
Janjetovic, Zoran. *Between Hitler and Tito: The Disappearance of the Vojvodina Germans* (Belgrade: n.i., 2005).
Kalyvas, S.N. *The Logic of Violence in Civil War* (Cambridge: Cambridge UP, 2006).
Kamenec, Ivan. *On the Trial of Tragedy: Holocaust in Slovakia* (Bratislava: Hajko & Hajková, 2007).
Klimó, Árpád v. *Remembering Cold Days: The 1942 Massacre of Novi Sad and Hungarian Politics and Society, 1942–1989* (Pittsburgh, PA: University of Pittsburgh Press, 2018).
Korb, Alexander. *Im Schatten des Weltkriegs Massengewalt der Ustasa gegen Serben, Juden und Roma in Kroatien 1941–1945* (Hamburg: Hamburger Edition, 2013). An English translation with Oxford University Press is forthcoming.
Laczó, Ferenc. *Hungarian Jews in the Age of Genocide: An Intellectual History, 1929–1948* (Leiden: Brill, 2016).
Láníček, Jan. *Czechs, Slovaks and the Jews, 1938–48: Beyond Idealization and Condemnation* (London: Palgrave Macmillan, 2013).
Levene, Mark. *Annihilation: The European Rimlands 1939–1953*, vol. 2, *Crisis of Genocide* (Oxford: Oxford University Press, 2013).
Lowe, Keith. *Savage Continent: Europe in the Aftermath of World War II* (New York: Picador, 2013).

Martin, Terry. *The Affirmative Action Empire: Nations and Nationalism in the Soviet Union, 1923–1939* (Ithaca, NY: Cornell University Press, 2001).
Matthäus, Jürgen, Jochen Böhler, and Klaus-Michael Mallmann. *War, Pacification, and Mass Murder, 1939: The Einsatzgruppen in Poland* (Lanham, MD: Alta Mira Press, 2014).
Mazower, Mark. *Hitler's Empire: How the Nazis Ruled Europe* (London: Allan Lane, 2008).
Mazower, Mark. *Inside Hitler's Greece: The Experience of Occupation, 1941–44* (New Haven, CT: Yale University Press, 1993).
Mędykowski, Witold W. *Macht Arbeit frei? German Economic Policy and Forced Labor of Jews in the General Government* (Lanham, MD: Academic Studies Press, 2018).
Michman, Dan. *The Emergence of Jewish Ghettos during the Holocaust* (Cambridge/Jerusalem: Cambridge University Press/Yad Vashem, 2011).
Motadel, David. *Islam and Nazi Germany's War* (Cambridge, MA: Harvard University Press, 2014).
Osti Guerrazzi, Amedeo. *The Italian Army in Slovenia: Strategies of Antipartisan Repression, 1941–1943*, trans. Elizabeth Burke (New York: Palgrave Macmillan, 2013).
Paldiel, Mordecai. *Churches and the Holocaust: Unholy Teaching, Good Samaritans, and Reconciliation* (Jersey City, NJ: KTAV Publishing House, Inc., 2006).
Polak-Springer, Peter. *Recovered Territory: A German-Polish Conflict Over Land and Culture, 1919–1989* (New York: Berghahn Books, 2015).
Popa, Ion. *The Romanian Orthodox Church and the Holocaust* (Bloomington, IN: Indiana University Press, 2017).
Prażmowska, Anita J. *Civil War in Poland, 1942–1948: Challenges to Communist Rule* (Basingstoke: Palgrave Macmillan, 2004).
Prusin, Alexander V. *The Lands Between: Conflict in the East European Borderlands, 1870–1992* (Oxford: Oxford University Press, 2010).
Ramet, Sabrina P., ed. *The Independent State of Croatia 1941–45* (London: Routledge, 2006).
Rein, Leonid. *The King and the Pawns: Collaboration in Byelorussia during World War II* (New York: Berghahn Books, 2011).
Rodogno, Davide. *Fascism's European Empire: Italian Occupation during the Second World War* (Cambridge: Cambridge University Press, 2006).
Rossino, Alexander B. *Hitler Strikes Poland: Blitzkrieg, Ideology, and Atrocity* (Lawrence, KS: University Press of Kansas, 2003).
Sakmyster, Thomas. *Hungary's Admiral on Horseback: Miklós Horthy, 1918–1944* (Boulder, CO: East European Monographs, 1994).
Shachar, Nathan. *The Lost Worlds of Rhodes: Greeks, Italians, Jews and Turks between Tradition and Modernity* (Brighton: Sussex Academic Press, 2013).
Shapiro, Robert Moses, ed. *Why Didn't the Press Shout? American and International Journalism during the Holocaust* (New York: Ktav, 2003).
Shepherd, Ben. *Terror in the Balkans: German Armies and Partisan Warfare* (Cambridge, MA: Harvard University Press, 2012).
Snyder, Timothy. *Bloodlands: Europe between Hitler and Stalin* (New York: Basic Books, 2010).
Solonari, Vladimir. *Purifiyng the Nation: Population Exchange and Ethnic Cleansing in Nazi-Allied Romania* (Baltimore, MD: Johns Hopkins University Press, 2010).
Suppan, Arnold. *Hitler – Beneš – Tito (Wien: Verlag der Österreichischen Akademie der Wissenschaften, 2013)*, abridged translation: *Hitler–Beneš–Tito: National Conflicts, World Wars, Genocides, Expulsions, and Divided Remembrance in East-Central and Southeastern Europe, 1848–2018* (Vienna: Austrian Academy of Sciences Press, 2019).
Ther, Philipp. *The Dark Side of Nation-States: Ethnic Cleansing in Modern Europe*, vol. 19, *War and Genocide* (Oxford: Berghahn Books, 2014).
Tomasevich, Jozo. *War and Revolution in Yugoslavia, 1941–1945: Occupation and Collaboration* (Stanford, CA: Stanford University Press, 2001).
Tomasevich, Jozo. *War and Revolution in Yugoslavia, 1941–1945: The Chetniks* (Stanford, CA: Stanford University Press, 1975).
Weiss-Wendt, Anton, ed. *The Nazi Genocide of the Gypsies: Reevaluation and Commemoration*, War and Genocide Series (New York: Berghahn, 2011).
Zimmerman, Joshua D. *The Polish Underground and the Jews, 1939–1945* (Cambridge: Cambridge University Press, 2015).

5
STATE SOCIALISM
Violence, oppression and surveillance

Włodzimierz Borodziej and Dragoș Petrescu

Introduction

'Fate placed us within the realm of totalitarianism', a small group of committed anti-communist Polish students programmatically declared in 1969. In their definition, totalitarianism entailed a centralized state, which controlled all spheres of society and suppressed all opposition by means of police truncheons, machine guns and interrogation chambers. Political power ultimately rested with the Soviet imperial patron, which denied Poland and its neighbours their national independence and jeopardized their spiritual and moral development.[1] The following years proved the students both painfully right and wrong. In June 1970, the authorities thwarted the group's attempt to blow up the Lenin Museum in provincial Poronin. Of the group, the seven instigators would eventually serve long prison sentences. They had not sufficiently taken into account the omnipresent secret police, which had infiltrated their group months prior to their attempt. Once released from prison, the conspirators would join the most powerful opposition movement ever to be observed in Eastern Europe and they would openly defy the secret police state.

We understand the magnitude: over the course of roughly 45 years, millions of citizens – mostly men – worked for the political police between the Baltic Sea, the Black Sea and the Adriatic Sea; they decisively helped to enforce the socialist dictatorship and, once the system was established, was supposed to protect it from its perceived or actual enemies. Millions more supported the repressive apparatus by secretly reporting as informants on their colleagues, acquaintances and sometimes even their own families. We know little about the motives of the full-time employees: it seems that adaptation and the will to shape things, patriotism and conformism entered into peculiar alliances. Ideology – i.e. the belief in the superiority of state socialism over capitalism – probably played only a minor role. In the case of the informers, similar motivations are at play, but one must also take fear and blackmail into account. In some cases that seem all too obvious to us, we find another motive: outwitting the system.

---

1 Andrzej Czuma, 'Deklaracja programowa "Mijają lata..." RUCHU niepodległościowego' [Programme declaration, 'the years are passing...' of the Independence Movement], http://ruchniepodleglosciowy.pl/program-mijaja-lata/ (accessed 5 July 2021).

By betraying their private sphere, work colleagues, subordinates as well as superiors, some informants seem to have believed that they were achieving historical accomplishments, i.e. they believed they were civilizing the system by explaining the real situation to the decision-makers so that the latter could come to reasonable solutions on their own.

After 1989 – with the exception of those who appeared in criminal court or in press headlines, which is a minuscule fraction of the total number – nearly all informants disappeared: the zealous customs officer who gleefully rummaged through the traveller's luggage, and depending on his mood would sometimes confiscate less, sometimes more – sometimes he would make a distinction between compatriots and foreigners, sometimes not; the border guard soldier who caught a fugitive and escorted him to the local security service; the clerk at the passport office who refused to issue a travel document, or only offered one on the condition that the applicant agreed in writing to cooperate with the apparatus; or, others who threatened suspects that they would be fired from their jobs or that their family members would be persecuted; the informer – a receptionist at a hotel or in the office of a campsite – who reported on guests; the policeman who beat someone during an interrogation, or his colleagues from the riot units who beat down workers who were on strike; the technician who installed a wiretaps; the professor who told his student that he had no chance of receiving a position at the university unless he became a member of the party – all, or nearly all of them, disappeared.

The files, however, remain, and the situation varies in each country. In some instances, the files are relatively well preserved, others less so. In any case, a considerable number of the total of hundreds of kilometres of shelf space produced by the national 'security' agencies has been available for research for several years. Researching the secret police documents is necessary in order to understand the role and scale of state repression in Sovietized CEE (Central and Eastern Europe). A comprehensive analysis of the activity of the secret police agencies in the communist countries in CEE are far beyond the scope of this chapter. One should note, however, that after 1989, the archives of the secret police agencies in seven European countries – that is, Germany, Bulgaria, Czech Republic, Hungary, Poland, Romania and Slovakia – were opened for research and administered by public bodies created after the model of the German *Bundesbehörde für die Stasi-Unterlagen* ('Stasi Records Agency'). One can speak of an intra-regional diffusion of the German model of dealing with the files of the former communist Ministry for State Security (*Stasi*) to the six countries mentioned above, which consists of the spreading of a specific legal and institutional model from Germany to these countries. These institutions, established to administer the files of the former secret police agencies in their respective countries, jointly founded the *European Network of Official Authorities in Charge of the Secret Police Files* in December 2008 in Berlin.[2]

Some notes on historiography

Research on repression in socialist states has gone through various stages. Institutional sources were made available only after the fall of communism, but even before that, there had been

---

2 For details regarding the legal framework, structure and mission of these institutions, see Bundesbeauftragter für die Stasi-Unterlagen (BStU), *The European Network of Official Authorities in Charge of the Secret Police Files: A Reader on their Legal Foundations, Structures and* Activities, 2nd revised edition (Berlin: BStU, 2013). For more on the formation and content of, as well as access to, the archives administered by the above-mentioned institutions, see Rafał Leśkiewicz and Pavel Žáček, eds., *Handbook of the European Network of Official Authorities in Charge of the Secret-Police Files* (Prague: ÚSTR & IPN, 2013).

a common sense agreement that in the case of countries of the European 'outer empire' (i.e. the Eastern European satellites of the Soviet Union), there was an enormous intensification of repression and control (as part of what we call 'revolution from abroad') in the period from the end of the war to the end of Stalinism. The demise of this Soviet-emulating model came about at various times in different countries. Only in Poland and Hungary did it come along with the symbolic watershed of 1956. In other countries, repression usually decreased gradually, the classical model of Stalinism being replaced by various types of national state security systems. Later episodes of increased institutional violence, directed at local unrest, reform movements considered dangerous and 'revolutions from below' (i.e. 1968, 1970 and 1976 in Poland, 1968–71 in Czechoslovakia, 1981–82 in Poland and the 1980s in Romania) were national matters; and, in spite of Moscow's determination to have trustworthy comrades in power, these matters generally did not result from Moscow's efforts to enforce a uniform Soviet model as was the case in the first post-war decade.

Hence our periodization follows the classical narrative of political history. The first part covers the period of Stalinization and nationalization of CEE. We start with 1948, when Stalinist regimes came into existence. Depending on the country, Stalinism lasted for different lengths of time: in Czechoslovakia, it only ended in the early sixties; in Poland, more than five years earlier. The 1960s are consistently characterized by a 'nationalization' of oppression and violence, the relevance of which – for the practice of rule – decreases almost everywhere.

Parts two (1968–81) and three (1981–89) concentrate on patterns of state repression between the Prague Spring and the demise of state socialism. They address the means and methods employed by the communist regimes in order to contain and suppress protest actions. Without a shadow of a doubt, the suppression of the Prague Spring in August 1968 by the Soviet-led military intervention of the WTO (Warsaw Treaty Organization) was an event of major importance for the Soviet bloc countries; the imposition of martial law in Poland in December 1981, then, constitutes the chronological landmark between parts two and three. 'Solidarity' (*Solidarność*) exercised an influx possibly stronger than the Hungarian Revolution of 1956: even after crushing the enemy with martial law the pivotal satellite of the Soviet Union remained different from its neighbours and 'Solidarity' a point of reference for any dissident movement within the European outer empire. In part three, we also stress the peculiarities of national state security systems during the 1980s and ask to what extent their shape preconditioned national ways out of state socialism in 1989–90. It ends in December 1989, when the revolutionary wave initiated early that year in Poland finally reached Romania, where the communist dictatorship was brought down by a bloody revolution in which over 1,100 people were killed and over 3,300 were wounded.

Predominant interpretive patterns and questions

Let us start with some widely held certainties that document the dubiousness of stereotypes. As the experience of the GDR (German Democratic Republic), Poland and Hungary show, state socialism in CEE would have been inconceivable without the presence of Soviet troops in the country. But even this basic assumption is called into question by counterexamples: Soviet units were withdrawn from Romania as early as 1958, they were stationed in Czechoslovakia only starting from 1968, and they were never in Yugoslavia or Albania. The other basic assumption is similarly dubious: without the latent danger of a Soviet military intervention, the dependent state authorities could neither have been installed nor maintained. The first assumption actually applies to all countries except Yugoslavia and Albania; the second one applies to all except Yugoslavia, Albania and Romania. Bulgaria does not fit into this pattern at all: who – from the secretary general to the average citizen – ever felt threatened by a possible Soviet intervention in a country that does not only *not* share a border with the Soviet Union, but also had no significant opposition?

Similarly, there appears to be no correlation between Soviet presence and the local regime's willingness to use violence or their claim to control. From the beginning to the end of state socialism, Albania remained a totalitarian dictatorship whose citizens could only dream of the liberties that were the norm in several countries after de-Stalinization. Yugoslavia – Joseph Stalin's archenemy after 1948 – suppressed opponents and suspects until the mid-1950s entirely according to classic Stalinist patterns, including the physical destruction of part of the party apparatus. In the Romania of the 1970s and 1980s, where national communism with a distinctly anti-Soviet undertone had already become state doctrine in the 1960s, deviance – let alone disobedience – was also punished with a striking brutality that accompanied the truly Stalinist personality cult around Nicolae Ceaușescu. In contrast to his megalomaniacal projects, however, it remained a kind of public secret. Everyone knew that the Securitate was dangerous, but nobody was allowed to talk about it publicly.

From the early 1950s to the present day, research on state socialist repression has been dominated by two interpretive approaches.[3] One refers explicitly or implicitly to Hannah Arendt's theory of totalitarianism. According to her, totalitarian violence 'is expressed much more frighteningly in the organization of its followers than in the physical liquidation of its opponents'.[4] Arendt knew little about our region and it was not the focus of her study of Stalinism. She perceived totalitarianism as a deadly threat to humanity because of its capacity to destroy the fundamental characteristic of human beings, that is, perceiving the world rationally and with reference to facts. According to Arendt, in totalitarianism, this perception gives way to individuals 'acting according to the rules of a fictitious world, and thereby actively denying themselves'.[5]

Arendt warned against the Soviet model of Stalinism, which she watched from afar. The Moscow show trials of the 1930s seemed to her to be its essence: the self-accusations of prominent communists were as absurd as they were in line with investigation results; the men on trial publicly negated their own biographies and seemed to accept death if that was the will of the Party. Of course, Arendt knew that through torture one can force people to confess anything. She did not know, however, that the show trials in different states within the Soviet sphere of influence, which were beginning as she was writing *The Origins of Totalitarianism*, would not be on the same scale of the Moscow Trials, and further, that the purges would not lead to the elimination of (the majority of) the party leaders as it did in the Soviet Union in the 1930s. The accusations against members of the inner circles that took place between 1949 and 1954 were of prime importance to top party functionaries, who feared they would be forced to suffer the same fate as their comrades. Admittedly, a member of the party elite in Stalinism was probably more exposed to danger than any other professional, but still, the numbers tell a different story. In Poland, around 800 communists were taken into custody or sent to prison; few died or were murdered. In other countries, the number of death sentences ranged from less than 20 to several dozen, and dozens of accused were sentenced to long imprisonment.

---

3 Grzegorz Ekiert, *The State Against Society: Political Crises and their Aftermath in East Central Europe* (Princeton, NJ: Princeton University Press, 1996); Mark Pittaway, *Eastern Europe 1939–2000* (London: Arnold, 2004).
4 Hannah Arendt, *The Origins of Totalitarianism* (Orlando, FL: Harcourt, 1979), 364.
5 Anne-Marie Roviello, 'The Hidden Violence of Totalitarianism: The Loss of the Groundwork of the World', *Social Research* 74, no. 3 (Fall 2007): 923–30, here 924.

At the same time, hundreds of thousands of common people, not affiliated with the party in any way, experienced repression and were the targets of the hundreds of thousands of who worked for the regular and secret police forces. Western diplomats and journalists knew about it, but extensive repression against an anonymous mass of peasants was as uninteresting as the *holodomor* – the deliberate starving to death of millions of Ukrainian peasants – had been 20 years earlier; at that time, they had also preferred to write about sudden and mysterious earthquakes within the Moscow centre. This lack of attention, in turn, would leave a trace in the minds of historians and Sovietologists.

Although a relatively small part of it deals with Stalinism, *The Origins of Totalitarianism* (published in 1951 and later supplemented and rewritten several times) is probably the most influential book on our subject to date: since explicit terror, accompanied by the extensive use of propaganda as the essence of Stalinism/State Socialism, still provides a useful, almost practical basis for describing – even in the twenty-first century – the violence and oppression that occurred in CEE from 1944 to 1989. Still there are at least three general reasons for serious reservations towards Arendt's interpretation of the system. First, as already mentioned, regimes in European communist countries began to evolve, gradually moving away from Stalinism. Second, the fear of a 'New Man' being bred, a fear that clearly motivated Arendt, eventually gave way to a sense of surprise that so little had changed. The 'greengrocer' created by Václav Havel a quarter of a century later was the pillar of the system not because he had believed in the New Man; neither did he believe in the superiority of socialism; nor was he brainwashed. He simply preferred to adapt – like under any preceding regime. Third – and this is the insight brought about by the access to previously secret police sources after 1989 – we now know infinitely more about glitches in the mechanisms of the repression apparatus, its permanent difficulty with ensuring the level of control demanded by the party, and finally, the adaptation strategies of citizens. In other words, we know how little remained after 40 years of the original ambitions to create a new state based on perfect surveillance and – more importantly – a New Man.

Nevertheless, at the end of the twentieth century, the authors of the definitive work *The Black Book of Communism* pretty much followed in Arendt's footsteps by emphasizing – despite some nuances and differentiations – mass terror as the main feature of the system.[6] In the subsequent French (turned international) discussion, the matrix of 'state socialism equals terror' was vehemently discussed,[7] among others by those researchers who had long been working on a different interpretation of the relationship between state and society in post-war CEE.

Here we come to the second line of interpretation. In Germany, it was Alf Lüdtke's classic formula of the *Eigensinn* (or: *Eigen-Sinn*),[8] which is still only partially translatable into other languages (it is close to 'willfulness' in English), that shaped this approach. In Poland, sociologists had already discovered in the 1980s that violence was by no means the key element in the practice of dictatorship. Rather, it was the particular, active adaptation strategies developed within the framework provided by the dictatorship that domesticated the system, in a sense sanding its hardest edges and thus creating a relatively stable order in which physical violence

---

6 Stéphane Courtois, ed., *The Black Book of Communism: Crimes, Terror, Repression* (Cambridge, MA: Harvard University Press, 1999).

7 The controversy is documented in, among others, the special issue, 'Unterdrückung, Gewalt und Terror im Sowjetsystem: Diskussionbeiträge zum "Schwarzbuch des Kommunismus"', *Osteuropa* 50 (June 2000).

8 Thomas Lindenberger, ed., *Herrschaft und Eigen-Sinn in der Diktatur: Studien zur Gesellschaftsgeschichte der DDR* (Köln: Böhlau, 1999).

became largely superfluous.[9] Thus, this chapter should be read in conjunction with the corresponding chapter in the *Statehood* volume of this series: therein, Ulf Brunnbauer and Claudia Kraft describe state socialism as a kind of modernizing dictatorship, which, in the context of the nation state, treads different paths in order to adapt the system to local conditions.[10] What we are attempting to show here is when, why and how coercion and violence were used in the course of implementing this project.

This said, a basic requirement must – even if generally known – be emphasized here again. Violence that was specifically political represented an inherent feature of the communist regimes brought to power throughout CEE. They made use of force – very often disproportionately and/or deadly – against individuals or groups within the territorial jurisdiction of the respective states.[11] State repression, i.e. the use of state power against all those perceived as 'enemies of the people', was a specific form of political violence widely applied. Random terror was arguably a key characteristic of the 'revolutions from above' unleashed in the countries in CEE under Soviet control in the aftermath of the communist takeovers. In his analysis of the 'second' Soviet revolution of 1928–41, Robert C. Tucker observes:

> The revolution from above was a state-initiated, state-directed, and state-enforced process … State power was the driving force of economic, political, social and cultural change that was revolutionary in rapidity of accomplishment, forcible methods and transformative effect.[12]

The 'revolutions from above' in post-1945 CEE closely followed the model of the 'second' Soviet revolution. Over the period 1945–53, the communist parties in CEE consolidated their monopoly of power and domesticated their populations.

After the death of Stalin in March 1953, the same communist parties increasingly made use of selective terror instead of random terror. In fact, the death of Stalin marked the end of the period of indiscriminate emulation of the Soviet model by the power elites in CEE. His death further initiated a process of 'nationalization' of the Soviet model, which accelerated at different speeds in the communist countries in CEE over the period 1953–56 and culminated with the Polish October of 1956. The emergence of national communism in Sovietized CEE also implied a more nuanced recourse to state repression and a gradual recourse to selective terror. Thus, the wave of state repression which followed the defeat of the Hungarian Revolution of

---

9 In addition, see Andrzej Rychard, 'Konflikt i przystosowanie: dwie koncepcje ładu społecznego w Polsce' [Conflict and adaptation: two concepts of social order in Poland], in *Rzeczywistość polska i sposoby radzenia sobie z nią*, eds Mirosława Marody and Antoni Sułek (Warsaw, 1987), 89–108; Mirosława Marody, *Warunki trwania i zmiany ładu społecznego w relacji do stanu świadomości społecznej* [Conditions for the duration and changes of the social order in relations to the state of social awareness] (Warsaw, 1986).
10 Ulf Brunnbauer and Claudia Kraft, 'Statehood in Socialism', in *The Routledge History Handbook of Central and Eastern Europe in the Twentieth Century, Volume 2: Statehood*, eds Włodzimierz Borodziej, Sabina Ferhadbegović and Joachim von Puttkamer (New York: Routledge, 2020), 215–90.
11 On the theoretical and methodological problems concerning the study of violence committed by political actors, see Donald Bloxham and Robert Gerwarth, 'Introduction' to idem, eds, *Political Violence in Twentieth-Century Europe* (Cambridge: Cambridge University Press, 2011), 1–10. See also Perry Mars, 'The Nature of Political Violence', *Social and Economic Studies* 24, no. 2 (June 1975): 221–38.
12 Robert C. Tucker, 'Preface' to idem, *Stalin in Power: The Revolution from Above, 1928–1941* (New York: W. W. Norton & Co., 1990), xiv–xv.

1956 confirms this assertion. After coming to power, the regime of János Kádár made use of selective terror — by no means random — in order to repress the 1956 revolutionaries.

In the post-1968 context, the communist regimes in CEE increasingly made use of surveillance and prevention in order to ensure societal quiescence. As past events in CEE indicated, urban mass mobilization proved to be a major threat to communist power. Consequently, when public protest did emerge, despite constant surveillance and preventive actions by the secret police, targeted state repression was swiftly applied.

When such protests turned violent, repression was neither predictable nor consistent, let alone well thought out. The decision-making process was often emotional: helplessness paired with the conviction of one's own superiority or even infallibility, dilettantism (where should decision-makers have gained experience in dealing with public controversy?), fear and hatred of 'the masses' who so obviously contradicted the illusions of the system.[13] There were also other options that were probably only used by a minority of the functionaries, although they were open to all. Kazimierz Barcikowski, who was promoted to the office of First Party Secretary in 1968 in Poznań, hardly knew 'his' new, economically powerful voivodeship, but he certainly knew that the Poznań 'events' outlined below (today often stylized as the 'workers' uprising' of June 1956) were caused by, among other things, the inability of his predecessors to negotiate with angry workers of the large (20,000 workers strong) and traditional Cegielski Works (renamed in 1949 as ZISPO, or 'Joseph Stalin Metal Works in Poznań' — *Zakłady Metalowe im. Józefa Stalina w Poznaniu*).

In 1968, placed on his desk, Barcikowski had the top-secret files on the June uprisings of 12 years prior. There he found 'warnings about what not to do, what to watch out for in order to avoid extreme situations'.[14] When the news from the coastal towns (see the subchapter *Working-class protests* in Part Two, 1968–81) reached Poznań in December 1970, he resorted to hitherto unresolved demands from the workers at Cegielski for the payment of a bonus. The Minister of Finance rejected his telephone request to pay the disputed premium immediately — at the start of the next day's shift — due to a 'lack of legal basis'. Only the responsible deputy prime minister arranged for the immediate transfer, so that the workers received the bonus in hand before their morning shift began. As a result, the strike at the largest industrial plant in the region did not take place.

In Barcikowski's memoirs, we find another indication of the incompetence of the authorities when under pressure. During the turbulent days of December 1970, Barcikowski received an urgent call from the local police headquarters one evening: a group of young people were planning to gather near the monument of the 1918–19 Poznań Uprising against the Germans, who had occupied the region a century earlier. It soon became clear, however, that this was not the beginning of a political demonstration, but a completely legal event organized by the boy scouts on the occasion of the upcoming anniversary of the uprising. 'The officer [i.e. the caller from police headquarters] who was psychologically attuned to illegal gatherings did not anticipate the possibility of a "patriotic event",' Barcikowski commented later, 'Good thing he did not have it broken up'.[15] After Stalinism, it was probably not only the Polish party elite that was aware of the devastating consequences of a 'crackdown' on workers in particular — especially the psychological consequences, which

---

13 Polish 'świat wyobrażony'.
14 Kazimierz Barcikowski, *Z mazowieckiej wsi na szczyty władzy* [From the Mazovian countryside to the peak of power] (Warsaw: Wydawnictwo Projekt, 1998), 268.
15 Barcikowski, *Z mazowieckiej wsi*, 296–8.

were basically essential to the dictatorship. This was rarely addressed directly or written down. We do know, however, that in 1976 the Polish Politburo apparently controversially discussed the question of to what extent the use of violence against the workers' protest in Radom was justified?[16]

One way to avoid 'extreme situations', i.e. the issuing of a firing order, was to use the riot police units. Depending on the circumstances, such units that specialized in crowd control and were established in the communist countries of CEE from the mid-1950s onwards, were sent in. According to the situation, such operations involved various institutions from the system of state repression, such as the secret police, army, militia, firefighters or border guards. Controlling people's minds rather than their actions proved far more ambiguous, particularly where emerging dissent movements relied on legalistic strategies. But here as well, repressive violence remained the last resort.

The communist secret police agencies were ordered to devise complex action plans that focused on widespread surveillance of their populations, active prevention of anti-regime activities, as well as targeted repression aimed at isolating, containing and silencing open criticism or protests by individuals or groups. Moreover, the West's limited access to the communist states of CEE, which was initiated during the 1960s, led to an increased permeability of the borders of these states. The number of Western citizens who visited the communist countries of CEE, as well as the number of citizens of these states who travelled to the West, increased significantly. In order to cope with this new situation and keep their populations under surveillance, the communist regimes of CEE had to reform their secret police agencies. For instance, the increased contact between the local populations and Western citizens imposed an expansion of the networks of informers with a special emphasis on the tertiary sector of the economy. A significant number of people working in the tourism industry, such as national and international tour guides, receptionists, waiters and waitresses, national and international coach drivers and hotel phone operators were included among the collaborators with the secret police. At the same time, more and more university graduates – some of them able to master foreign languages and more capable of using electronic surveillance equipment – joined the secret police apparatuses throughout CEE. In order to enhance the efficiency of their networks of collaborators or to engage in specific activities such as the thorough vetting of passport applicants, the secret police agencies' use of electronic data processing equipment gained momentum. An analysis of the secret police agencies in CEE – from their establishment in the aftermath of the Second World War to their dissolution after the 1989 regime changes – would extend beyond the scope of this chapter.[17]

A fundamental aspect related to the activity of the secret police agencies in the Soviet bloc countries must be stressed once again. These agencies always obeyed the orders of the communist parties in power. With very rare exceptions, the acts of repression were carried out by the secret police on direct orders from the communist power elite.

---

16 See also, Kazimierz Barcikowski, *U szczytów władzy* [At the peak of power] (Warsaw: Wydawnictwo Projekt, 1998), 83–6.
17 Apart from the large amount of information available on the institutional websites of the member institutions, the European Network released two relevant publications, which allow for a comparative view on the scope, organization, evolution and archives of the secret police agencies in the above-mentioned former communist countries (see footnote 2 above).

Political violence and state repression in Sovietized CEE: Part One, 1948–68 (by Włodzimierz Borodziej)

1948: point of departure

With the exception of Czechoslovakia, in the countries where legal opposition to communism had managed to survive for about two years, such opposition was a thing of the past by the end of 1947. Anti-communist resistance movements also became a thing of the past, setting aside local exceptions, which did not pose a threat to the authorities. In many ways, the situation in 1948 was unique. First, most of the countries in the region had experienced shattering events in the previous decade: the dismantling of the state and the emergence of a new regime subject to Germany (the Czech Second Republic, the Slovak state and Hungary), military defeat and occupation (Poland), the annihilation of the state and double occupation (Baltic republics and Poland; here simultaneously, 1939–41), territorial losses (Czechoslovakia, Poland, Romania). Second, from Latvia to Yugoslavia, people had witnessed the extermination of Jews. In the case of Poland, bystanders saw not only deportations, pogroms, mass executions and slow death in the ghettos, but also trains full of people sent straight to the gas chambers. Third, violence in everyday life, as one can read in the previous chapter to this volume, by no means ended on 8 May 1945: the revenge of the victors was directed both at the Germans (in Yugoslavia, also at the Italians) as well as at their own compatriots who were either rightly or wrongly labelled as collaborators during the occupation and opponents of the new regime.[18] These experiences were bound to influence the reception of the new system – the price of human life was low, violence an everyday experience and previous norms had almost ceased to exist.

The moral void was filled by state socialism, which, by definition, did not intend to respect traditional boundaries between citizens' private lives and state interference. While in other areas of life one can find connections between social democratic or generally leftist visions of society and state socialist policies, in the area of control there are no links: the system of discipline and repression for potentially or actually stubborn citizens was imported in its entirety from the Soviet Union – with Felix Dzerzhinsky as its patron saint – and lacked any local traditions. Another novel aspect was the fact that the norms in force since 1948 were set by people from nowhere. With the exception of a tiny number of functionaries (usually quickly climbing up the ladder) they were not trained in the USSR. Yet they firmly implemented the Stalinist model, though – or perhaps: because – most of them had no first-hand knowledge of it. Though the origins of state security services during the immediate post-war years varied considerably, these were largely streamlined between 1948 and 1952.[19]

On principle, legally and institutionally, socialism rejected national state security systems from before 1938–39. In many pre-war dictatorships, for instance in Poland or Romania, the Second Department (in Bulgaria – Military Intelligence or *Razuznavatelen Otdel*) of the General Staff played a significant role. After 1945, military intelligence quickly found itself pushed to the side. In 1946, a purge took place among the Bulgarian military, and in May 1947,

---

18 One of the most influential books on the Stalinization of Central and Eastern Europe is Anne Applebaum, *Iron Curtain: The Crushing of Eastern Europe, 1944–1956* (New York: Doubleday, 2012).

19 Molly Pucci, *Security Empire: The Secret Police in Communist Eastern Europe* (New Haven, CT: Yale University Press, 2020).

Bulgarian political police started to take over intelligence and counter-intelligence.[20] In Poland things took a little bit longer. Until 1948, the Second Department of the General Staff had some role to play – though judging against pre-1939 standards, it performed rather poorly – after the new (communist) leaders were arrested, the department did not rebuild its position.

The character of counter-intelligence fundamentally changed. To simplify matters, prior to 1939 it usually dealt with spies and communists, while in the new reality its focus was on all who did not fit the new norm, namely, members of national minorities, 'fallen' and 'unnecessary' classes, churches and all the other 'anomalies' from the point of view of the Stalinist system. Thus, the system of repression was taken over by civilians, usually employees of the national Ministry of Public Security. The names varied slightly, but the USSR People's Commissariat for Internal Affairs remained the model.

Another important feature was the difference in size. Pre-war political police forces were usually small. The Bulgarian secret police employed about 450 people during the war. The Polish political police under parliamentary democracy consisted of fewer than 1,000 positions and under authoritarian dictatorship (when it officially no longer existed) about 2,500. At the beginning of the period under study, Bulgaria employed eight times as many people (more than 3,600 in 1949) and by the mid-1950s, that number had doubled. In 1953, the Polish security service employed approximately 13 times as many people as before the war. In Czechoslovakia, the size of the StB (State Security) tripled between 1949 and Stalin's death.

Nearly everywhere, the building of the apparatus, the increase in the number of employees and their tasks and responsibilities were carried out by trial and error. Because of a lack of suitable candidates, all applicants were accepted in the beginning; soon, most of them turned out to be totally unqualified, useless and redundant. In Poland, where in 1947 there were 28,000 members of the apparatus, 25,000 people had been discharged in the previous years, so the rotation was as high as 90 per cent.[21]

The building-up of the security apparatus

The Ministries of State Security entered the new era without having solved their internal problems. One such problem was a lack of education. In the Stalinist period, most of the employees did not have an elementary education. As a result, the Czechoslovakian StB at the peak of its power, in 1952, had only 470 officers instead of the 8,700 planned, yet, they had 8,600 employed as NCOs instead of their intended 4,600. This did not differ substantially from the situation in the party and state administrations. It was not until the following decade that the situation improved significantly, in part, as a result of intensive courses and internal training.

The other problem of the early 1950s was the principle of permanent purge. In Czechoslovakia, the founders of StB became victims of a purge as early as the first year of the separate ministry's existence. In Bulgaria, the purge lasted throughout the period of Stalinism – up to 1956, when the apparatus consisted of 7,000 employees, over 5,100 people had been dismissed.

---

20 Later, reconnaissance (RUMNO – *Razuznavatelno upravlenie kym Ministerstvoto na narodnata otbrana*) was returned to the General Staff, with greatly reduced tasks. Military intelligence and counter-intelligence were also rebuilt in other countries.
21 Antoni Dudek and Andrzej Paczkowski, 'Poland', in *A Handbook of the Communist Security Apparatus in East Central Europe*, eds Krzysztof Persak and Łukasz Kamiński (Warsaw: Institute of National Remembrance, 2005), 221–83, here 242–3. Along with *The Black Book of Communism* by Courteois et al., this handbook is the most valuable comprehensive source on Communist Security Apparatuses.

Membership in the party was a concern everywhere, and apparently it was considered a guarantee for both loyalty to the 'leading force' and a deep commitment to the cause of socialism. Usually, nearly 100 per cent of high-ranking officers belonged to the party; the percentage was lower or even significantly lower among the rest of the population. Management positions were reserved for members of the nomenklatura. Promotion to a position outside of the capital required a recommendation from a local party unit. Positions in the central headquarters of the security service were assigned by the appropriate bodies of the CC (Central Committee), and the top positions were appointed by the Political Bureau/Praesidium.

Tasks

The task of the apparatus of violence was to support Stalinization, mainly by creating the sense of omnipresent control and constant danger and, to a lesser extent, by physical violence. Symbolic violence was the task of the party, which monopolized the press, radio and film-making industries, set new norms for public language, appropriated city space (in the villages, there was usually nothing to appropriate) and created a new canon of national culture. The ministries of 'homeland security' carried out tactics of repression and prevention that were certainly not symbolic. Such a calibre had been previously unknown outside of the USSR: the all-encompassing definition of the enemy, the size of the apparatus, the fusion of repression and prevention into one ubiquitous threat to life and personal security (such at least was often the impression of the citizens) were greater than ever before.

The definition of 'the enemy', by and large, was the same in all Stalinist regimes. In many countries, churches were an important, structural enemy (see John Connelly's contribution in the *Intellectual Horizons* volume of this series). After the legal opposition was defeated, the remainder of anti-communist resistance movements were a lesser enemy than the *byvshie lyudi* ('people from the past'). This USSR's definition of the enemy is known today only to specialists. It seems that the term was coined by Maksim Gorky in 1897 as he wrote about people with no trade and no future under capitalism.[22] In the USSR, it became a synonym for other groups: proprietors, in the broadest sense of the word, and those who did not fit into the new system because of their birth and/or status in the previous system, and they were thus considered at least suspicious. On the whole, these basic features were adapted in the outer empire, though no one really implemented a system that resembled the Soviet one of the 1930s.

For a few years from the start of collectivization, peasants were the most numerous enemy in all countries. They were forced into collective farming (a point which we will describe in more detail below); then there was the salt of the third sector: namely, traders, private, state and local officials, teachers, scientists, often former police officers and professional soldiers. Clergymen were directly targeted, as were national minorities (with notable exceptions like Hungarians in Transylvania) and immigrants.

The scope of the definition of the enemy differed only slightly from country to country. It is probable that to some extent, it reflected the social structure and distribution of property prior to 1939. There is no Polish equivalent for *byvshikh lyudei*, perhaps because after the hecatomb of the war and occupation, only enclaves of the pre-war world remained. The term exists in Czech, however, as given the Czech war losses and emigration, the situation can hardly be compared to that of Poland. In Czechoslovakia in 1956, state security estimated that there were

---

22 Maksim Gorky, *Creatures That Once Were Men* (London: Alston Rivers, 1905) (first published in Russian in 1897).

a million *byvali lidé* in a population of 16 million. In one way or another, 10 per cent of them were monitored. In Poland, a few actions against pre-war proprietors and public persons also took place, but in comparison with other countries, the scale of repression was significantly lower: even under Stalinism, situations that would be difficult to imagine in neighbouring countries were possible. Tadeusz Manteuffel, a descendant of Courland barons did not have to join the party or denounce his biography (which included, for instance, volunteering in the war of 1920 against Bolshevik Russia) to become the founder of one of the most prestigious scholarly institutes in the country.[23] The picture of Polish uniqueness was perhaps best painted by Czesław Miłosz in his *Seizure of Power*, published in exile in 1953. One of the characters in the novel, a pre-war professor of Classical Studies, is forced to leave the university. The official reason is due to ill health after surviving Auschwitz. He is able to keep his flat, however, and is given the task of translating Thucydides's *Peloponnesian War* into Polish:

> The professor could remember the face of the director of the state publishing house as they signed the contract. He was looking down, his eyes hidden by their lids: his benevolent, almost cordial smile an indefinable mixture of indulgence, bitterness and irony.[24]

A Czech, Romanian or Hungarian professor of Classical Studies who distanced himself from the new system could only dream of such lenient treatment.

Show trials

The highest members did not feel the difference. As early as 1936–38, Stalin had had the majority of the Soviet elite destroyed in the Moscow show trials.[25] The patterns of public 'court' hearings were always the same: members of the highest authorities of the Bolshevik Party, including Lenin's old associates from the pre-1917 illegality era, were arrested, blackmailed and tortured. Gradually, the resulting confessions gave rise to the image of a cross-border conspiracy against the Soviet Union, at the centre of which were the former leaders of the Bolshevik (or Communist) Party on the one hand, and the Western intelligence services or the Japanese secret service on the other. Hardly any detail, and no alleged fact withstood objective scrutiny; the prosecutor's charges offended common sense. Nevertheless, the leaders of the alleged conspiracies were sentenced to death. Western observers were left with the image of a horrifying, monstrously fallacious parody of a criminal trial by the state against its own leadership. What

---

23 Other examples: Feliks Młynarski, renowned finance expert and president of the *Emissionsbank* established by the Germans during the occupation had to move from a semi-palace to a big, 4-room flat, but continued to be employed by the same university (though he had no chance of becoming a full professor). And the former deputy prime minister of the *Sanacja* government Eugeniusz Kwiatkowski – though released into uneasy obscurity – remained a retired senior citizen.

24 Czesław Miłosz, *The Seizure of Power*, trans. by Celina Wieniewska (New York: Criterion, 1955), 4. John Connelly's masterly study remains the crucial point of reference: *Captive University: The Sovietization of East German, Czech, and Polish Higher Education, 1945–1956* (Chapel Hill, NC: The University of North Carolina Press, 2000).

25 This denotes only the three public trials which took place between 1936 and 1938. A fourth trial against the Red Army leadership ended in 1937 with the execution of most of the accused, but it remained a secret trial – like the thousands of others that took place after 1945 in the triangle between Berlin, Tirana and Sofia.

remained was the impression of bewilderment, which Arthur Koestler tried to counteract with his book *Darkness at Noon*.[26]

Moscow experienced its last show trial in June 1945, when the 16 leaders of the 'Polish underground state', i.e. the anti-German resistance, stood trial. They had voluntarily appeared in March, equipped with Soviet security guarantees, for negotiations with the Soviet military in the part of Poland that had just been liberated/occupied, to discuss the formation of the transitional government envisaged in Yalta, but were instead arrested and taken to Moscow. The chairman of the court was Vasiliy Ulrich, who had already made a name for himself in the great trials of the 1930s. Since the sentences appeared mild by Soviet standards,[27] the West silently accepted this posthumous humiliation of the underground state and the breach of the Yalta agreements.

The 'Trial of the 16' was about the enemy. In the 'Show Trials in the Eastern Bloc' of 1949–52, the party indicted its own leaders, and this adoption of the Moscow pattern of 1936–38 will be dealt with in what follows.

After the Soviet Union had conquered the countries between the Elbe and the Black Sea in 1944–45 and eliminated both opposition and resistance between 1945 and 1948, the question arose as to how this European extension, with its thoroughly separate cultures and traditions, should be administered. In retrospect, everything that constituted the political (lack of) culture of the countries west and southwest of the Soviet borders until after Stalin's death in 1953 seems to have been thoroughly thought out and planned. However, if we pose this question differently, in the sense of possible alternatives, we could presumably support Dietrich Geyer's 1985 thesis (which was formulated without knowledge of the Moscow archives):

> For a task of such enormous dimensions[28] there were no precedents in the history of the Soviet Union and Soviet-impregnated communism. There is little to suggest that Moscow had to use other methods outside the Soviet empire's borders to secure its rule and loyalty than those that had been practiced when the Stalinist system was established in the USSR itself. As far as the practice of rule was concerned, Stalinism could not be any different in Eastern Europe and Germany than at home.[29]

---

26 First published by Macmillan in London, 1940. When it was first published, the European, non-Communist elites had other concerns. The book's career began with the French translation *Le Zéro et l'Infini* in 1945, when the novel became part of the internal French Cold War. The French Communist Party vehemently attacked the anti-Stalinist novel as well as its author, thus prompting its considerable circulation.

27 The maximum sentence was 10 years imprisonment. Three of the 16 accused were acquitted. A total of 13 returned to Poland and three died in prison. For the most detailed English-language presentation and documentation, see: Andrzej Chmielarz, Andrzej K. Kunert, Eugeniusz Piontek, *Proces moskiewski przywódców polskiego państwa podziemnego* [The Moscow Trial of the leaders of the Polish Underground State] (Warsaw: Światowy Związek Żołnierzy Armii Krajowej/Oficyna Wydawnicza RYTM, 2000).

28 Geyer is referring both to the administration of the informal empire and the role of the communists in the Western zones, as well as to the setting of the communist parties in Western Europe 'on a course ... that would be conducive to the imperial interests of the USSR'. Dietrich Geyer, 'Germany as a Problem of Soviet European Policy at the End of the Second World War', in *Kalter Krieg und Deutsche Frage: Deutschland im Widerstreit der Mächte 1945–1952*, ed. Josef Foschepoth (Göttingen: Vandenhoeck & Ruprecht, 1985), 50–65, here 61.

29 Ibid., 61. British diplomats considered it pure cynicism when their Soviet 'colleagues' on an inter-allied control committee in a country of the nascent Eastern bloc declared that they would only use the same methods in the Red Army-controlled country as they did at home. Victor Rothwell, *Britain and the Cold War 1941–1947* (London: Jonathan Cape Ltd., 1982), 364.

A strange copy of the Moscow show trial was staged in Sofia in December 1949. Trajcho Kostov, leader of the communist resistance during the war and prime minister until June of that year, stood before 'the court' with 10 co-defendants. He was accused of forming an anti-Bulgarian conspiracy supported by Western and Yugoslav intelligence services. Kostov – like all the others mentioned below, of course, a loyal communist and one of the most important founders of Stalinist Bulgaria – did not admit to the main charge. He was nevertheless sentenced to death and executed in December 1949. His trial, however, was only a partial success: the Moscow script did not provide for the main defendant not to confess.

The case of Ana Pauker was even more difficult. Born into a poor, orthodox Jewish family, she made a career in the weak Communist Party of Romania. Arrested and sentenced several times by the pre-war regime, she spent the war in exile in Moscow. In 1947, she became Romania's – and thus Europe's – first female foreign minister. Pauker was deposed as early as May 1952. Arrested in February 1953, she was released after two months and placed under house arrest. The show trial did not take place. Biographers find it difficult to relate the life story of a Stalinist with Pauker's views.[30] One need not necessarily follow Norman Naimark, who suggests several similarities between Pauker and Gomułka (see below); it is rather about political actions and omissions that may be true for her, but not for him.[31] The difference not addressed in this comparison is essential: Gomułka stood for right-wing nationalist dissent, Pauker for Jewish 'cosmopolitanism'. And this seemed more dangerous to the Moscow centre than all other signs of dissidence (with the exception of 'Titoism') compared to the agenda of Stalinization of the European area of operation set in 1948–53.

The motif of Jewish roots – as a basis for conspiracy theories, sometimes addressed directly, often indirectly – had a code that transcended its boundaries in the form of the 'struggle against cosmopolitanism' just mentioned: 'the Jews' would use their worldwide relations to harm the cause of socialism; the parallel to the 'Wise Men of Zion' was palpable. Elsewhere 'Titoism' was the main accusation,[32] or 'right-wing deviation', which in turn was associated with 'nationalism'. Useful for the prosecution was the supposedly unclear and thus suspicious past of the Spanish fighters, yet exile in Moscow during the war did not help much either. The activity in the anti-German, communist resistance could also provide a possible starting point. In the planned show trial against leading communist functionaries in the GDR, even a sentence of several years in Nazi prisons became an indication of treason. In every version, subversive secret meetings and collusion with Tito's representatives, the United States' OSS (Office of Strategic Services) – later, the CIA (Central Intelligence Committee) established in 1947 – or other Western intelligence agencies were necessary in order to elevate the indictment to a component of the anti-socialist policy of imperialism. Hence the importance of the 'Field affair' (see the

---

30 Robert Levy, *Ana Pauker: The Rise and Fall of a Jewish Communist* (Berkeley, CA: University of California Press, 2001).
31 '[Pauker's] politics and agricultural policies in the period 1945–1948 are remarkably similar to those of the Polish leader Władysław Gomułka. She encouraged coalitions with the 'historical' parties, urged compromises with 'bourgeois' politicians, and sought to deflect the persecution of social democrats and liberals'. Norman Naimark, 'Review', *Slavic Review* 61, no. 2 (Summer 2002): 389–90, here 389.
32 In this section we will ignore the private trials of former members of the closest elite, such as the Albanian trial of Koçi Xoxe (1949) or the East German trial of Paul Merker (1955), where similar 'arguments' were used. They had to do with the public to the extent that press releases about death sentences or long prison terms were intended to trigger the same insecurity and fear within the 'apparatus'. Torture and the invention of a multi-headed conspiracy against the socialist state were common to both public and secret trials.

subchapter *Ministry of Internal Affairs – Party* on page 216), where a bona fide US-American, Noel Field, was held in Hungarian custody whose contacts with future CIA chief Allan Dulles were among the few facts that did not have to be fabricated. However, Field and Dulles helped victims of Nazi persecution from Switzerland during the war; they did not plan a conspiracy against state socialism.

The Budapest show trial of László Rajk in 1949 (member of the Politburo, Minister of the Interior from 1946 to 1948, and Foreign Minister at the time of his arrest in 1949) took place almost at the same time as that of Kostov. Nevertheless, the difference was considerable: while in Bulgaria the trials were about 'Titoism', in Hungary the selection of the accused pointed to the 'cosmopolitan' motive. According to the Nuremberg Laws, six of the seven defendants (i.e. all except Rajk) were of Jewish origin. The death sentences mainly concerned high Communist Party functionaries. The staging worked perfectly. The communists, hitherto regarded as pioneers of Stalinism, were executed, the quasi-public in Hungary as in the socialist sister countries, but mainly the Hungarian *nomenklatura*, were intimidated: not even at the top was one safe from persecution, loss of privileges, torture and death; on the contrary. A mathematician would certainly be able to calculate that the danger of being murdered by one's own comrades increased with each ascent and was far greater than the danger the average citizen was exposed to.

In the 1952 Prague trial of Rudolf Slánský, former First Secretary of the Communist Party of Czechoslovakia, the anti-Semitic aspect came to the fore even more powerfully. Out of the 14 defendants, 10 (including Slánský) were 'Jews' according to the Nuremberg Laws. In 11 cases, the court sentenced the death penalty. According to the court proceedings, the conspiracy was nearly worldwide. Top politicians of the United States and Israel were supposed to have developed a new 'Morgenthau Plan' in April 1947. The Czech-Jewish members of the conspiracy were to provide an advance for US aid to Israel through espionage for the CIA.

Parallel to these show trials, preparations for others were underway, but they did not materialize in the end. In Poland, Władysław Gomułka (the de facto party leader, 1944–48) and his supporters had no Jewish roots and therefore were deemed 'right-wing nationalist dissenters'. Gomułka was gradually ousted from power in 1948–49 and arrested in 1951. He made no confession until his release in 1954. He and a large number of his supporters were not tortured. We do not know why the show trial against Gomułka and his followers, which was obviously considered several times, did not take place. Perhaps in Stalinist Poland a simple confession of the New Faith, made in time, as the former communist partisan leader Mieczysław Moczar (who became a 'National Communist' in the 1960s) made in 1948, was sufficient: 'The Soviet Union is not only our ally, it is success for the nation; for us, for party members. The Soviet Union is our fatherland, and I am incapable of defining our borders, which are today beyond Berlin and tomorrow at Gibraltar.'[33]

The last of the trials which never materialized was that of Kurt Müller. He was a member of the West German parliament (*Bundestag*) for the KPD (Communist Party of Germany), expelled from the party in 1950, lured to the GDR and then brutally interrogated there for five years by the NKVD (Ministry for State Security and the People's Commissariat for Internal Affairs). Like Gomułka, he refused to become a 'German Rajk'.

---

33 Krystyna Kersten, *The Establishment of Communist Rule in Poland, 1943–1948* (Berkeley, CA: University of California Press, 1991), 451.

Let us try to summarize this insertion. The show trials concerned a statistically almost inconceivable minority. The hundreds of thousands of persecuted, expropriated, imprisoned, condemned and forcibly resettled people often play a comparatively minor role, among other reasons, because the persecution of alleged or actual opponents is part of the essence of every dictatorship. In the case of the show trials in the 'Eastern bloc', the focus was on paranoid inventions whose contexts are hardly comprehensible and which were directed against hitherto ardent advocates of the system.

An explanatory pattern is likely to apply to all countries in our region. The local/national leader wanted – against a backdrop that may have been different in each state and is of little interest to us – to eliminate his most important rivals. According to the Moscow models (others were not available, as mentioned above), the show trial seemed an effective means of eliminating a potential adversary. The process was coordinated with the 'Centre' until the deaths of Stalin and Lavrentiy Beria in 1953; afterwards, in the shadow of the Moscow power struggles, the secret police in the 'socialist sister countries' lost a reliable supervisor. What remained was an intimidated *nomenklatura*, who for years had been shown how unpredictable, and personally dangerous (especially for them), the state they had built was.

The spectre must have left mental traces whose depth and breadth elude measurement. Khrushchev's famous secret speech at the 20th Congress of the CPSU (Communist Party of the Soviet Union) in 1956 – a speech that shocked the communist parties all over our region – has to be read in this context. By enumerating Stalin's crimes of against the ruling class for hours in his speech, he offered the *nomenklatura* a kind of collective security treaty: the new party leadership would never take action against its own loyal party and state cadres in the manner of Stalin.

Yet, another question arises: why did only three of the planned six show trials in the Eastern bloc come to pass (of which only 2.5 were successful)? With the exception of the Field case, a transnational history of local circumstances and their interconnectedness has yet to be written. Its explanatory potential is likely to be limited, since the crimes were irrational: apart from the mechanism of the struggle between the local party boss and his internal rivals described above, for which a suitable foil in the form of the Moscow example of 1936–38 offered itself, it will hardly be possible to find a common denominator.

The Western provinces of the Soviet Union: a cursory comparison

The situation in the Soviet 'outer empire' should be compared with the fate of countries incorporated into the USSR. The latter had neither a period of legal opposition nor a transition stage between 1944 and 1947. They were a problem for the empire mainly because their separateness – or so-called nationalism – intertwined with the structure of property-holding, especially in the case of peasant's property. Early in 1948, Soviet officials in the Baltic republics complained that collectivization 'was hindered by bourgeois nationalists and their armed gangs' with their counter-activities, as well as the farming system in general.[34]

---

34 Meelis Saueauk, 'Eestimaa Kommunistliku Partei rollist märtsiküüditamise läbiviimisel 1949. aastal' [On the role of the Estonian Communist Party in the March deportations of 1949], as quoted in Aigi Rahi-Tamm and Andres Kahar, 'Deportation Operation "Priboi" in 1949', in *Estonia since 1944: Reports of the Estonian International Commission for the Investigation of Crimes Against Humanity*, eds Peeter Kaasik, et al. (Tallinn: Tallinna Raamatutrükikoda / Estonian Foundation for the Investigation of Crimes Against Humanity, 2009), 429–60, here 430.

A year later, on 29 January 1949, the USSR Council of Ministers passed the decree on carrying out the decision No 390–139 on,

> The deportation of kulaks and their families, families of bandits and nationalists residing illegally, convicted or killed in armed conflicts, legalized bandits continuing resistance and their families, as well as helpers of the families of repressed bandits, from the territory of Lithuania, Latvia and Estonia.

Over the course of the secret operation code-named *Priboi* ('coastal surf'), 87,000 people in total were to be deported from the Baltic republics: 25,500 from Lithuania, 39,000 from Latvia and 22,500 from Estonia. Approximately 40 per cent of the names on the lists of Estonian deportees were so-called *kulaks* ('rich peasants'), and 60 per cent were enemies of the people. Armed anti-communists were a marginal enemy at the time; they had scattered over the previous years. The 1949 deportations brought about surprising results. In Estonia, after the deportation of over 20,000 potential opponents of collectivization (i.e. two per cent of the population, which took place the night of March 25–26), the number of underground armed attacks in 1949 was higher than in the previous two years put together, almost as high as in 1946. More than half of them were assaults on emerging kolkhozes. Only in the following three years did the MVD (Ministry of the Interior) eliminate the underground. In Latvia, the deportation of two per cent of the population (more than 44,000 people) – which took place on the same night as it did in Estonia – brought about an opposing result: the anti-communist underground resistance, defeated in 1946, did not rise again. Similarly, in the Socialist Republic of Moldova, the deportation in July 1949 of about 36,000 people, the majority being *kulaks*, crushed the resistance against collectivization. Between the beginning and end of 1949, membership in cooperatives rose from 20 to 80 per cent. In Lithuania, underground movement had been controlled by the MGB (Soviet Ministry of State Security) since 1946. Over the course of 1948–49, nearly 100,000 people were deported. Half of the underground soldiers fighting in 1947 had lost their lives by 1949. However, there were still some soldiers 'in the forest'. In 1953, their last commander was shot.[35]

The most terrifying numbers come from Ukraine: over 30,000 casualties on the side of the authorities, over 150,000 from the UPA (Ukrainian Insurgent Army), more than 200,000 people deported and 130,000 arrested and sentenced. Considering that the UPA was almost only active on the territory referred to today as Western Ukraine, where the pre-war population was about eight million, the numbers are not only higher than the sum of all the victims in the incorporated countries and those in the outer empire, but they clearly demonstrate that nowhere was resistance as strong as in Ukraine. Nevertheless, the underground units, which were gradually demobilized after the Soviet's 'great blockade' in the first quarter of 1946, had long ceased being a threat to the state by 1949. With the exception of the Ivano-Frankivsk Oblast, the activity was coming to an end. In 1949, the commander of the Western Ukrainian UPA was killed, and the commander in chief fell in the following year.[36]

---

35 Rahi-Tamm and Kahar, 'The Deportation Operation 'Priboi' in 1949', 361–89.
36 Figures according to Rafał Wnuk. 'Antysowieckie podziemie estońskie, łotewskie, litewskie, ukraińskie, białoruskie i polskie. Zarys dziejów i próba porównania' [The anti-Soviet, Estonian, Latvian, Lithuanian, Ukrainian, Belarusian and Polish underground: an outline of history and an attempt to compare], in *Wojna po wojnie: Antysowieckie podziemie w Europie Środkowo-Wschodniej w latach 1944–1953*, eds Grzegorz Motyka, Rafał Wnuk, Tomasz Stryjek and Adam F. Baran (Gdańsk-Warsaw: Wydawnictwo Naukowe Scholar/ISP PAN/Muzeum II Wojny Światowej, 2012), 14–177, here 95–115.

Armed anti-communist movements in countries under Soviet influence were incomparably weaker. In Poland, the core of resistance had been controlled by the political police since 1948; in Czechoslovakia and Hungary, there was no armed resistance at all. In Bulgaria, like in Estonia, the underground suddenly became more active as a result of the collectivization at the end of 1950 and the beginning of 1951. *Goriani*, or the 'wood people', supported by specialists trained in Greece and Turkey, formed units of 50 to 70 people. This rather numerous armed resistance was soon defeated.

Forced collectivization

Almost everywhere in the region, farmers were by far the largest group of professionals. Moreover, as individual producers, they were largely autonomous, i.e. relatively resistant to state control and regulation. The idea to move the farm into the collective assets, i.e. to de facto nationalize private property and to seize the former owners as state-dependent agricultural workers in so-called production cooperatives, came from the Soviet Union. There, collectivization in the early 1930s met considerable resistance and was broken with brute force. The supply situation worsened almost immediately and soon led to catastrophe: in the cities of Ukraine, millions of people were starving, and in the countryside, they starved to death. The transfer of this now obviously economically counterproductive model to the countries of the European outer empire can only be understood as an ideologically rooted project. From the outset, decision-makers must have been aware that it could not be enforced without coercion or violence directed at the (by far) largest part of the population.

Collectivization, which almost everywhere immediately turned into forced collectivization, took place successively with considerable regional and temporal differences.[37] The corresponding resolution of the Cominform,[38] printed in the Moscow *Pravda* on 29 June 1948 (i.e. one day after the exclusion of Yugoslavia from the community of socialist states), may be regarded as a symbolic break here. In fact, as a rule, it actually began in 1948 or the following year (earlier in Albania and Bulgaria, later in the GDR). Almost everywhere, Stalin's death in 1953 brought about a disruption or a slowdown of this enormous project. The nationalization of agriculture was completed only around 1960.

Poland and Yugoslavia, where the agricultural cooperatives referred to as 'kolkhozes' were particularly hated, had abandoned forced collectivization in 1956 and 1953, respectively. In both cases, for various reasons, widespread violence against hundreds of thousands of people made no sense: in Poland, because de-Stalinization was eager not to put more people into defensive

---

37 See the ground-breaking text: Arnd Bauerkämper and Constantin Iordachi, eds., *The Collectivization of Agriculture in Communist Eastern Europe: Comparison and Entanglements* (Budapest: CEU Press, 2014); Dariusz Jarosz and Grzegorz Miernik, *'Zhańbiona' wieś Okół: opowieść o buncie* [The 'disgraced' village of Okół: Tales of rebellion] (Warsaw: Instytut Historii PAN, Wydawnictwo Uniwersytetu Jana Kochanowskiego w Kielcach, 2016). Unless stated otherwise, this subchapter follows the information in these two books, where further references to the respective countries can be found.
38 The 'Information Bureau of the Communist and Workers' Parties', founded in September 1947, was intended to theoretically provide a platform for the 'exchange of views' between the Soviet Union and its 'allies' as the successor to the 1946 dissolved Comintern. In practice, it soon proved superfluous, as at the height of Stalinism, the Moscow guidelines were announced in bilateral communication.

positions than was absolutely necessary; in Yugoslavia, 'because the open militancy in the rural areas threatened to seriously damage the credibility of socialist Yugoslavia'.[39]

We can assume that the overwhelming majority of peasants between the Baltic, the Adriatic and the Black Seas were passive, and in a few cases active, opponents of expropriation. In response to the easily foreseeable, usually passive resistance, the respective nation state party developed a range of measures that, despite all local peculiarities, certainly bore similar traits. On the first, 'positive', i.e. non-violent level, it was the propaganda – carried into the village in the form of films, posters, promotional events and brigades of young urban activists – that tried to convince the supposedly backward peasants of the superiority of the collective mode of working. On a second level, fiscal pressure was exerted in the form of compulsory deliveries at prices fixed by the state. The principle was very simple: the proportional burden on the farm increased with its size. This measure was flanked by enemy-related propaganda. The – typically few – wealthy peasants, preferably also mill owners and other intermediaries between town and country, were attacked as bloodsuckers and exploiters, enemies of the village community of the poor; the local priest was also a welcome target.

Then came the harassment: the only shop in town was ordered to sell certain goods only to members of the emerging collective farm. Then there were the farm searches that were supposed to prove that the farmer was claiming to be unable to deliver anything but was actually hoarding goods in order to sell them to so-called speculators for prices that were in line with the black market. His children, deemed co-responsible for the anti-progressive behaviour of their father, could not attend high school in the district town, let alone study. The sons were the first to be drafted into military service, and their younger siblings were forced to sign the transfer of the farm to the 'cooperative' on behalf of their father.

With criminal charges, tax repayment notices and finally arrests, repression escalated to an even higher level. If the victim did not comply, he could be beaten while in custody, then transferred to a prison camp; or the prosecutor filed a petition to open criminal proceedings. In the worst case, they ended with the economic bankruptcy of the 'kulak', a legally binding conviction, stigmatization, resettlement and the destruction of an entire transgenerational family. At the top of this macabre pyramid, we find death sentences.

The number of indirect victims of forced collectivization will never be calculated. Only the direct victims – convicted, murdered and deported – are known. In Bulgaria alone there were more than 43,000 court cases between 1948 and 1955, with 250–280 death sentences per year; and more than 18,000 people were deported. In 1951, a spectacular show trial took place in Czechoslovakia – resistance to collectivization was said to have resulted in the shooting of three party officials in a South Moravian village – in which seven death sentences were passed (including two against priests); in the subsequent trials, the courts sentenced another 11 people to death and about 100 to long prison sentences; roughly 10,000 people were deported.[40]

These exemplary 'tips of the iceberg' should not give the impression that forced collectivization in CEE had similar class-murdering consequences as in the Soviet Union in the 1930s.

---

39 Marie-Janine Calic, *A History of Yugoslavia* (West Lafayette, IN: Purdue University Press, 2019), 186.
40 Mihail Gruev, 'Collectivization and Social Change in Bulgaria, 1940s–1950s', in Iordachi and Bauerkämper, *The Collectivization of Agriculture*, 329–68, here 352–6; Gregory R. Witkowski, 'Collectivization at the Grass Roots Level: State Planning and Popular Reactions in Bulgaria, Romania, Poland, and the GDR, 1948–1960', in ibid., 467–96, here 475–81; Jan Rychlík, 'Collectivization in Czechoslovakia in Comparative Perspective, 1949–1960', in ibid., 181–210, here 196.

Firstly – and this would be most comparable to the attitude of the peasants in the 'motherland of the revolution' – there was occasional resistance. In the Soviet Union, however, resistance gave rise to an even stronger attack, but in the dependent countries, it was much more often a reason to make collectivization slower and thus somehow more bearable for the peasants as a whole – regardless of the draconian punishment for the 'ringleaders'; the local peasant uprisings from Poland (through Romania) to Yugoslavia certainly played a role as an explanation for the suspension of forced collectivization after Stalin's death. Secondly, on the one hand, the protest actions remind us of the systemic, to some extent universal interaction between coercion, resistance and repression in the state socialist countryside; on the other hand, they document regional and local differences.

Let us begin with the 'Cazin rebellion' (*cazinska buna*) in the border area between the Yugoslav Federal States Bosnia-Herzegovina and Croatia. After the drought of 1949, the (mainly) Muslim peasants supplied only a fraction of the imposed compulsory deliveries. The administration searched the farms and confiscated the supplies. Two Serbs and a Muslim, all former partisans, began to prepare an uprising in March; they were hoping for foreign Anglo-American help. The insurgents, about 90 per cent of them Muslims, were only poorly armed when in the night of 5–6 May[41] they attacked local police stations, archives, storerooms and seats of the cooperatives. Police and military retaliated on 6 May. Soon there were hundreds of arrests and convictions; about 30 participants were sentenced to death by the autumn of 1950 or shot during the clashes and subsequent hunt for the ring leaders.[42]

In Romania, the peasant protests spread across several years and districts. They began in May 1949, reached a temporary peak in the summer of the following year and lasted until the summer of 1952. After the slowdown in forced collectivization in 1953 and resumption of the project in 1957, it turned out that the authorities did not want to abandon any of the means tried under Stalinism: propaganda, fiscal pressure, intimidation and extortion against individual recusants were the order of the day. The situation exploded in Vadu Roşca in the Galaţi district at the end of 1957. In some villages in the region, the peasants seized the official offices and burned their forced declarations of membership in the 'cooperatives'. In Vadu Roşca, they thwarted the invasion of the municipal agitation brigade and arrested its members as hostages. In return for their release, the authorities promised negotiations. On 4 December, the Securitate surrounded the village and fired into the crowd of assembled peasants. Nine were killed, and about 60 were injured. A then unknown 'special representative' from Bucharest made himself conspicuous during this operation. His name was Nicolae Ceauşescu.

Similar but numerically different clashes have been reported in Bulgaria, especially in July 1950 and in the spring of 1951. Czechoslovakia has already been mentioned. In Hungary, forced collectivization progressed slowly, and by 1958 about three-quarters of farmers remained private economic subjects. Their resistance was again violently broken in 1961, but without peasant revolts and death; the horror of the recent years had gripped them to the bone. Ultimately, the rural subjects acquiesced and thus later became a part of the new social contract à la Kádár. It is in this context that József Kovács speaks of the 'rationalization of subjection'.[43]

---

41 In the local Muslim tradition, 5 May is St. George's Day which marks the anniversary of the uprisings against the Ottoman rule; this day is highly symbolic as a reminder of the struggle against the authorities.
42 See the groundbreaking text, Vera Kržic-Bukić, *Cazinska buna 1950* [Cazin Rebellion, 1950] (Sarajevo: Svetlost, 1993).
43 Bauerkämper and Iordachi, *The Collectivization of Agriculture*, 232–4.

Coercion, resistance and terror also existed on a massive scale in Poland until 1956. The most impressive example is the large, somewhat untypical village Okół about 150 kilometres south of Warsaw. Not only had the communists in this area been relatively strong before 1945; nearly two-thirds of the villagers also belonged to the national church, which was Catholic, but nonetheless dissident to the Roman Catholic hierarchy.

In March 1950, the women of Okół, equipped with sticks and stakes, attacked the surveyors and prevented any drawing of new borders for the planned kolkhoz. Eight arrests and 60 sentences later, internal investigations revealed that, on the one hand, the party had not done enough to convince people (of the 60 party members in Okół, only 17 belonged to the cooperative), and on the other hand, the security police had been as indiscriminate as they were excessive; as in all the cases described above, the authorities saw the 'enemy' and the 'reaction', not angry peasants at work. The conflict was smouldering. On 28 August 1953, three tractors were to plough the field of collective farms. They came upon an angry crowd, which first threw sand at them and then stones. The tractors had to stop. The drivers as well as accompanying surveyors, officials and agitators were beaten, the machines demolished. Among the protesters, women played a prominent role.

In the following days, the security police arrested up to 20 people. Only four of them were sentenced to 1–4 years in the first instance, and in the second, they were sentenced to 1–2 years in prison; death sentences or deportations were out of the question. In the first half of 1953, the number of administrative penalties had reached a national high, and in the autumn of 1953, the party was already in retreat and was more interested in de-escalating tension in the countryside.[44]

To summarize, resistance to forced collectivization was typically counteracted by brutal repression that, after several years in most countries, led to the implementation of the project, i.e. among other things, the elimination of the peasantry as a large, autonomous stratum of citizens. The forms and means of resistance varied greatly. In Yugoslavia, those affected tried to fall back on the partisan tradition. In Bulgaria, Poland, Romania and Hungary, women played a surprisingly prominent role in terms of their historical position on the farm. Everywhere, the revolt against state socialism combined national and local characteristics with a protest against modernity, whose most important symbols included the loudspeaker, the surveyor and the tractor. Thus, the physical conflicts were part of a long tradition of peasant resistance against the authorities, in this case, in the form of the state and not the landowner. In the history of the long twentieth century, the usually brutal, often widespread reaction of the state socialist apparatus of violence – during peacetime – can only be compared to the repression of peasants in the Russian Empire in 1905–07 and in Romania in 1907. However, the number of fatalities of forced collectivization is incomparably lower than that of these revolutions, because after 1948, even local centres of resistance (regional, let alone national ones, never materialized) had a negligible share in the rebellions; by far the most of them took place within the village

---

44 See specifically, Jarosz and Miernik, *'Zhańbiona' wieś Okół*, 140–76, especially 175; Grzegorz Miernik, 'Strategie przystowawcze chłopów polskich do systemu władzy w latach 1948–1956 (na przykładzie województwa kieleckiego)' [Attachment strategies of Polish peasants to the government system in the years 1948–56 (based on the example of the Kielce Province)], in *Polacy wobec PRL: Strategie przystosowawcze*, ed. Grzegorz Miernik (Kielce: Kieleckie Towarzystwo Naukowe/Akademia Świętokrzyska, 2003), 117–45, here, one finds, inter alia, numerous hints that in the Polish People's Republic only a fraction of the recalcitrant peasants were punished in the form originally intended by the police (only a small minority of the ads came on the desk of prosecutors and only a few of those ended up in court).

community and were spontaneous reactions. The state tried different approaches in different places – none was reminiscent in its dimension of the mass deportations in the Baltic republics of the Soviet Union at the end of the 1940s – repeatedly faltered in the face of threateningly frequent clashes, but gradually prevailed. As early as the 1960s, the village no longer played a role as a potential opponent, and it was to remain that way until 1989.

Informers

The foundation of the system was constituted not only by political police, but also by a hitherto unknown network of informers and secret collaborators, usually much more numerous than the employees of state security. Every country had its own classification of informers. It would not be an oversimplification to say that three groups of people were recruited: 1) supporters of the system, who collaborated convinced that in this way they would be making the world and their homeland a better place; 2) opportunists, who, for one reason or another, decided that informing was good for their career or their welfare; and 3) people who succumbed to blackmail, felt themselves in danger, wanted to clear a trespass against the system and to regain their former status. In practice, an informer could find himself in all of those situations simultaneously. Let us imagine a staunch communist whose career had slowed down, who was earning less and less; imagine he was caught smuggling by the border guards, and that the regular police know him to be a homosexual. There were an infinite number of possible combinations for becoming an informer: work-related issues intertwined with personal matters, conformism with various degrees of fear for oneself and one's family. The Bulgarian instruction for recruiting informers rather laconically synthetized their targets: recruitment was to be based on ideological-party loyalty, on 'dependency, material or other interest'.[45]

Every country had its own customs in the field of recruitment. In Bulgaria, members of the party could be enlisted as 'regular' informants only under exceptional circumstances, while it was the norm in Czechoslovakia that only party officials could *not* be regular informers. Nevertheless, the so-called residents, who sometimes coordinated an entire network of regular agents, were preferably selected from among the first group, usually from prominent party members: 'the ideologically persuaded and loyal to the Party and the People's Republic, predominantly members of the BCP [Bulgarian Communist Party]'. The other criteria were 'prestige in society, high general culture, political and special training'.[46]

In the mid-1950s in Bulgaria, there were about 55,000 informers and the number, though it fluctuated, remained roughly the same until the end of Bulgarian People's Republic.[47] This means that the ratio of informers to citizens was about 1:1,400. In Poland, the fluctuations were extreme: from 1:3,000 under Stalinism, to 1:25,000 in 1957 and 1:4,500 in the 1980s. In Hungary, at the peak of Stalinism (1953), it was 1:2,000 – more than in East Germany at the time – and then the numbers gradually decreased. Under Kádár, the system operated in a totally different and – in certain aspects like in churches – surprisingly efficient way. The number of functionaries did not go beyond 25 per cent of the pre-1956 figure; the number of informers after 1956, never exceeded 10,000 (roughly 1:10,000). Most information was based on willing cooperation of supporters. Collaboration of blackmailed or threatened people apparently played

---

45 Jordan Baev and Kostadin Grozev, 'Bulgaria', in Kamiński and Persak, *A Handbook of the Communist Security Apparatus*, 37–86, here 56.
46 Ibid., 55.
47 Baev and Grozev, 'Bulgaria', 41 and 52.

a less significant role.⁴⁸ Quite the opposite happened in Romania: whereas in 1956 the Ministry of the Interior supervised 12–13,000 informants, their number at the start of Ceaușescu era 11 years later reached 110,000.⁴⁹ By way of comparison with countries incorporated into the USSR, one might add that in the 1960s in the Socialist Republic of Lithuania, the ratio of informers was 1:1,000 citizens.⁵⁰

All these statistical data point at presumable national differences. They might be misleading as well: there is no research on the yearly or monthly number of reports (not to speak of their quality in terms of reliability) submitted by informers. If in Lithuania the informers filed a report once a year and in Hungary once a month, the density of control would reach more or less a comparable level.

Ministry of Internal Affairs – Party

In the subchapter on 'show trials' we have outlined the basic features of Stalinist terror against its previous protagonists. At this point, we return to the more practical aspects of the harassment and to the lesser-known consequences that extended beyond 1956 and shaped the relationship between the party and the political police until 1989.

Starting in 1948, prompted by First Secretary Mátyás Rákosi, the Hungarian security apparatus began investigating an alleged multinational spy network (the Field affair mentioned above), which was suspected to have spread to the top leadership of the communist parties in Hungary, Czechoslovakia, East Germany and Poland. Rákosi's comrades in the other capitals seemed less convinced, but they finally agreed to help with 'uncovering the conspiracy'. One of the chief investigators in Budapest was Ernő Szűcs, recruited by the NKVD in 1942, who had been regularly informing Moscow employers about his comrades. The chief of the Hungarian security apparatus gave him a free hand. Dozens of prominent party officials, including the Hungarian Foreign Affairs Minister László Rajk, were arrested, mainly in Budapest and Prague. They were beaten until they testified to whatever the investigators wished. Accordingly, a problem arose: the tortured men signed anything, fabricated information and incriminated all their comrades, while at the same time, the investigators did not know where the investigation was supposed to be headed. As a provision, they kept beating the accused and creating new files in which one could find ever more fantastical accusations. As early as two months after the arrest of Noel Field – the key actor in the alleged conspiracy – a vicious circle was created:

> By the middle of June, the unmanageable volume of confessions had already led to a complete confusion of the matter: admissions and retractions, real and false

---

48 They were also given the right to quit (or to continue on a voluntary basis) after having served as informers for a certain period of time (which was identical to the highest sentence of the offence committed). Krisztián Ungváry, 'Repressionen und "lustigste Baracke" – Der Funktionswandel des Terrors im ungarischen Parteistaat' (unpublished paper delivered at Imre Kertész Kolleg's annual conference in Warsaw, 13 June 2014).

49 Stefano Bottoni, 'Nation-building through Judiciary Repression: The Impact of the 1956 Revolution on Romanian Minority Policy,' In *State and Minority in Transylvania, 1918–1989: Studies on the History of the Hungarian Community*, ed. Attila Hunyadi (New York: Columbia University Press, 2012), 403–27, here 406.

50 Saulius Grybkauskas, 'Sowjetlitauen', in *Das Baltikum: Geschichte einer europäischen Region*, vol. 3: *Die Staaten Estland, Lettland und Litauen*, eds Karsten Brüggemann, Ralph Tuchtenhagen and Anja Wilhelmi (Stuttgart: Hiersemann, 2020), 421–65, here 454.

confessions, verified and artificially coordinated statements, contradictory confessions made the whole affair inscrutable … our difficulties and problems were not revealed to the party by Péter [the chief of the Hungarian security apparatus] … As a result, we systematically misinformed and misled the party.[51]

Rákosi called in KGB (the Committee for State Security) 'advisers' for help (their leader was arrested in Moscow three years later as a member of another Jewish conspiracy, this time in the very centre of power, which also belongs to the history of party-political police relations), but it did not solve the problem. The accusations made by tortured people began to pose a threat to all; the initiator was losing control over the matter. The culmination of the conflict, for which there is no logical explanation has been described by Krisztián Ungváry:

> Rákosi was in charge of arranging these measures; during the interrogation of State Security (*Államvédelmi Hatóság*, ÁVH) chief Ernő Szűcs (deputy head of the ÁVH and himself a proven sadist) he said:'You shall beat him for two days so that his bones rattle' – Szűcs and his innocent brother were then beaten to death in an orgy of violence that lasted a few hours.[52]

Party officials from Tallinn to Sofia hardly knew the violent details of the Field affair or the show trials, but they probably surmised them. Furthermore, the political police officials, familiar with the fate of Beria – the chief of the Soviet security apparatus who was executed after Stalin's death – and his partners (very few likely knew about the last hours of Szűcs's life), doubtless saw no reason to share the fate of their predecessors. The new relationship between political police and party was thus based on the principle of the superiority of the latter.

There were exceptions. In 1968 in Poland, the political police manipulated the information delivered to the First Secretary. After the political crisis (caused in part by this practice) had been solved according to the plans of the Ministry of the Interior, the reaction was swift: Mieczysław Moczar was given the theoretically higher post of the Secretary of the CC but was in fact removed from direct power over the apparatus. When he likely tried to start a conspiracy against the new leader of the party in 1971 – details remain incomprehensible or unknown to this today – he was demoted to a secondary position, and one of his prominent subordinates was sentenced to a long prison term. Similar elements can be found in Bulgaria in 1965[53] but the attempt to topple the dictator was not connected with the security apparatus. What was left from it was a special, small department (25 members) set up in 1968 to monitor factional activity in the party and state administration.[54] Still, generally speaking, the political police remained a – powerful, self-confident and largely autonomous – instrument of the party after 1956. This also belonged to the process of nationalization and rationalization of the system which we address below.

---

51 See Bernd-Rainer Barth and Werner Schweizer, eds, *Der Fall Noel Field: Schlüsselfigur der Schauprozesse in Osteuropa* (Berlin: BasisDruck Verlag, 2005), 82, 89.
52 Quoted in Ungváry, 'Repressionen und "lustigste Baracke"' (unpublished paper).
53 Baev and Grozev, 'Bulgaria', 61.
54 Ibid., 44–5.

From workers' revolts to national upheavals: 1953–56

Forced collectivization and rapid industrialization changed the structures of everyday life and the patterns of communication everywhere. Jobs in industry, once highly valued, became easily accessible as never before. It was now the (state) companies searching for workers, not people begging for jobs – opening a space of choice and liberty despite all regulations aiming at social and administrative control. In regions with industrial traditions, workers quickly learned how to deal with thus far unknown circumstances, maybe most successfully in the Czech lands; it was here that in 1952, Stakhanovism (i.e. the propagation of heroic 'shock workers' who boasted extreme productivity during regular shifts) attracted nearly half of industry workers on paper – only to die the following year largely unnoticed.[55]

Surprisingly, the first to revolt came from the Bulgarian tobacco industry employees. The reason for this was higher work norms. On 3 May 1953, the workers in factories near Plovdiv and a few other places went on strike. The Bulgarian party reacted surprisingly promptly, sending a special envoy to negotiate the demands, and soon promising to consider some of them – which they did so in part. Strike leaders were prosecuted only afterwards, silently. A major crisis was avoided, workers and police ultimately did not clash.

Things developed differently in the Czech town of Plzeň. The Škoda industrial complex was perhaps the most renowned example of high-tech industry in CEE, delivering military equipment, industrial tools and all kinds of vehicles since the late nineteenth century. Here, authorities had to deal with 27,000 workers and a workers' council, which in some ways, during high Stalinism, had already silently departed from most of the nonsensical Prague guidelines. On 30 May 1953, a 'currency reform', which was repeatedly denounced in previous months that would practically reduce savings to nil, was announced to take effect two days later, on 1 June.

When 1 June arrived, party officials tried to calm the angry Škoda workers down, albeit in vain; they had no arguments. The employees went on strike and formed a demonstration heading for the city centre. Thousands of workers from other Plzeň factories joined them. Within a few hours, the protesters took city hall, attacked one of the local prisons and occupied the city court. Barricades were built, busts of Soviet and Czechoslovak communist leaders were thrown out of the windows (symbolically reminiscent of the deadly defenestration of foreign minister Jan Masaryk, a representative of the old elites, which took place five years prior), Soviet flags were burned and communist propaganda material destroyed. In the court building, the occupiers burned files and destroyed equipment. Several functionaries of StB were beaten; private property, however, was not looted. Shortly thereafter, anti-communist posters appeared, demanding free elections und the return of US troops to Plzeň.[56] The city quickly filled with symbols of pre-war Czechoslovakia. In most encounters with demonstrators, the regular police

---

55 Peter Heumos, 'Arbeitswelt, Lebenswelt, industrielle Machtverhältnisse: Zum Konzept des sozialwissenschaftlichen Funktionalismus am Beispiel der Tschechoslowakei 1945–1968' *Zeitschrift für Ostmitteleuropaforschung* 63 (2014): 341–73; idem, 'Stalinismus in der Tschechoslowakei. Forschungslage und sozialgeschichtliche Anmerkungen am Beispiel der Industriearbeiterschaft', *Journal of Modern European History* 2, no. 1 (2004): 82–109, here 103. On Poland: Padraic Kenney, *Rebuilding Poland, Workers and Communists, 1945–1950* (Ithaca, NY: Cornell University Press, 1996).

56 Masaryk was commonly believed to have been murdered by the secret police (the official version spoke of suicide); Plzeň had been liberated by US-American troops in May 1945.

(i.e. the People's Militia) withdrew and refrained from 'restoring order'; some policemen (and party members) even joined the rebels.

The fighting began when a considerable number of police and army units with machine guns and armoured personnel carriers, supported by tanks, entered the rebellious city the following day. They prevailed, forcing the last protesters to surrender within hours. Martial law was imposed on the city and an estimated 2,000 suspects were immediately arrested. In roughly 20 other Czech and Moravian cities, the protests – a few thousand workers strong – were limited to strikes and street demonstrations that never came to violence.

Under the umbrella of martial law, participants who were suspected of being leaders of the revolt in Plzeň (the roughly 30 hours that the rebellion lasted turned out to be too short for a centralized leadership to arise) were tried and sentenced to long prison terms; one of the participants was even executed. The propaganda depicted these supposed leaders as tools of imperialist agents and accused the West of having instigated a failed 'counter-revolution'. Some regulations like higher prices for consumer goods imposed in Spring 1953 were soon suspended, although the 'currency reform' remained in force.

Two weeks later, on 17 June, Soviet tanks rattled along the streets of East Berlin. The day before, workers on Stalinallee, the regimes most prestigious building project, had protested against a rise in work norms. With the help of West Berlin radio, news of the strike quickly spread throughout the country. The following day, people were out on the streets across the GDR. In several cities, demonstrators occupied local administration and party buildings and police stations. Within hours, demonstrations exploded into a national uprising. The SED regime seemed to crumble away. Calling out Soviet troops from their garrisons was their only resort. At the end of the day, some 40 people lay dead, including 5 members of the East German security forces. Court martials issued more than 20 death sentences in the days following the uprising. Their reliance on Soviet troops exposed the fragility and the true nature of the East German regime to the rest of the world. The GDR rested on Soviet power, and even if most of the population would come to terms with the communist party state in the following decades, it was clear that socialism would not take root. The regime mistrusted its people like nowhere else in the Soviet bloc, and it had felt the impact of West German media. Repression intensified; the regime expanded the security apparatus and imposed a taboo on the experience.[57]

Three years later, the workers' uprising in Poznań followed a similar scenario. On 28 June 1956, workers from the local ZISPO metalworking plant marched into the city centre, calling for higher wages and better working conditions. They first stormed the city hall, then local party headquarters and erected barricades. From there, they moved on to the city jail and freed the inmates. Police forces remained passive as they were being overwhelmed. When demonstrators attacked the local state security office, security forces opened fire. Some demonstrators had captured weapons in a police station and fired back. Within hours, the peaceful demonstration had developed into a full-blown insurrection. It took regular army units working in combination with special forces to put down the uprising. More than 60 workers and 9 security personnel were killed that day.[58]

---

57 Ilko-Sascha Kowalczuk, *17. Juni 1953* (München: C.H. Beck, 2013); Christian F. Ostermann and Malcolm Byrne, eds, *Uprising in East Germany 1953: The Cold War, the German Question, and the First Major Upheaval behind the Iron Curtain* (Budapest: CEU Press, 2001); Richard Millington, *State, Society and Memories of the Uprising of 17 June 1953 in the GDR* (Basingstoke: Palgrave Macmillan, 2014).
58 Paweł Machcewicz, *Rebellious Satellite: Poland 1956* (Washington, DC: Woodrow Wilson Center Press, 2009), 78–124.

During the following months, minor upheavals occurred in several Polish cities. Unlike East Germany, the Poznań uprising did not immediately engulf the entire country. Yet it had enormous political repercussions. Anti-communist slogans had been prominent early on, and anti-Soviet feelings further built up during the summer. Soviet leader Nikita Khrushchev's secret speech had coincided with the death of Polish First Secretary Bolesław Bierut, and the Polish party leadership was divided. Party rule was consolidated when the reformist group prevailed and the designated new leader, Władysław Gomułka, dramatically confronted Khrushchev in October, and Khrushchev actually backed down. Soviet hegemony was slightly tuned down, Catholic primate Stefan Wyszyński was released from confinement, and the regime finally acknowledged previous crimes as well as the legitimacy of the Poznań Uprising. Within Poland, the prospect of peaceful socialist rule based on popular support briefly seemed realistic;[59] to Western observers, the cracks in the Soviet bloc had widened substantially – both prospects were equally exciting.

The crisis in Poland spilled over into Hungary. On 23 October, people were out in the streets of Budapest to demonstrate their solidarity with their Polish brethren. As in Warsaw, the disclosure of regime crimes against both opponents and against leading communist regime figures had resulted in an unresolved leadership crisis. Reformist hopes were vested in former prime minister Imre Nagy, who had lost the power struggle with Stalinist party leader Mátyás Rákosi the year before. In the evening hours of 23 October, the situation in Budapest spun out of control. Snipers fired into the crowd, which then stormed the national television building and, later in the evening, toppled the Stalin statue on Hősök tere. The party leadership hastily restored Imre Nagy to the position of prime minister. Soviet tanks from garrisons surrounding Budapest were already on their way to the city centre. They met with the dogged resistance of highly motivated street fighters. Cases of lynching allowed the communist authorities to speak of a counter-revolutionary attempt and to play on Hungary's fascist recent past. The fighters saw themselves involved in a national uprising to liberate the country and to restore its full independence. Parallels to the revolution of 1848–49 saw them in the most uplifting national traditions. Within days, the fighting had engulfed almost all major cities.

The newly appointed prime minister Imre Nagy faced an impossible situation. In order to stop the fighting, he had to concede to revolutionary demands, while at the same time struggle to maintain Soviet trust. The reports that Soviet emissaries Mikhail Suslov and Anastas Mikoyan sent to Moscow did not alleviate his task. After days of manoeuvring and hesitation, Nagy chose to take the bull by the horns, so to speak. On 30 October, he formed a coalition government and announced the return to restricted forms of pluralism. Soviet forces returned to their garrisons outside the city. After a week of fighting, the crisis seemed to have been resolved.

Minutes of a Politburo meeting in Moscow the same day indicate that at first Khrushchev chose to acquiesce with this outcome and to negotiate the withdrawal of Soviet troops from Hungary. The crucial question remained whether Imre Nagy could be trusted and whether he would keep Hungary within the Soviet camp. The following day, the Soviet party leader had changed his mind. Chinese advice may have played a role, as much as the ongoing Suez crisis. Khrushchev then explained to the Politburo that a troop withdrawal would be perceived as weakness by the imperial camp. János Kádár, the newly elected communist party leader, was secretly ordered to Moscow. The movement of Soviet troops on Hungary's eastern border alarmed Imre Nagy. In the face of an imminent military intervention, he declared Hungary's

---

59 Andrzej Paczkowski, *The Spring will be Ours: Poland and the Poles from Occupation to Freedom* (University Park, PA: The Pennsylvania State University Press, 2003), 262–78.

neutrality in a dramatic rally for public support. Western help failed to materialize. After another week of stubborn and futile resistance, martial law was declared. During the three weeks of fighting, 2,200 people lost their lives. More than 200,000 Hungarians crossed the Austrian border and went into exile. The feeling of abandonment was further solidified when Imre Nagy, who had fled to the Yugoslav embassy, was arrested. He was tried in Romania and executed in June 1958.[60] For the Soviet ambassador, Yuri Andropov, his crucial role in the crushing of the Hungarian revolution, however, was the start of his stunning career: in 1967, the 'Butcher of Budapest' became head of the KGB; in 1982, he became secretary general of the CPSU.[61]

Whereas de-Stalinization proceeded slowly or very slowly in the case of the ČSSR (Czechoslovak Socialist Republic) or Bulgaria, Poland and Hungary went their own, clearly contradicting ways. Under Władysław Gomułka, First Secretary of the Polish United Workers' Party from 1956 onwards, state security was reduced to one-quarter and the number of informers to one-eighth of its former capacity It was only about 10 years later that it regained its breadth within state and party structures, however, their means and goals differed fundamentally from Stalinist times. The first aim of the security apparatus, headed by Moczar and by and large consistent with the party line, was to integrate combatants from anti-German resistance into official structures and 'nationalizing' communist anti-German resistance as one of the mainstream organizations of the nation's heroic efforts 1939–45. The second tool consisted in the production of a new, quite popular enemy, the 'Zionists', including many prominent party leaders during Stalinism and their children, often students. The success story soon came to an end after its climax in 1968, since in the eyes of party leadership it posed a threat similar to Stalinism, i.e. political police would again decide on the fate of members of the inner circle.

Hungary went another way between 1957 and 1962. János Kádár's regime needed a few months for inner consolidation and the invention of a coherent picture of the enemy within. Instead of Marxism-Leninism-Stalinism (as it was up to 1956), it resorted to contemporary Hungarian history, presented as a dialectical chain, or rather, a fight between reaction and progress: the Soviet Republic of 1919 was defeated by counter-revolution in 1920. The reactionary dictatorship of Horthy had been strengthened in 1933 by the national socialist takeover in Germany and finally gave way to the arrow-cross fascist regime of 1944, which was overthrown by the Red Army and progressive forces in 1945. In 1956, the seminal counter-revolutionaries, heirs and remnants of Hungarian fascism, launched a final assault against history, lynching innocent peasants and workers. This paradigm served as moral justification for the 341 death sentences and executions of 'enemies of progress' and the roughly 35,000 people who were imprisoned between 1957 and 1962. In the years following, Kádár reversed his policy: 'only' about 1,000 people per year were sentenced on political grounds and only one – a political terrorist – was executed in 1967.[62]

The impact of Hungary on Romania was immense: after November 1956, authorities – apparently afraid of similar protests in their own countries – relaunched a truly Stalinist campaign

---

60 Csaba Békés, Malcolm Byrne and M. János Rainer, eds, *The 1956 Hungarian Revolution: A History in Documents* (Budapest: CEU Press, 2002); M. János Rainer, *Imre Nagy: A biography* (London: I.B. Tauris, 2009).

61 Richard John Crampton, *Eastern Europe in the Twentieth Century* (London: Routledge, 1994), 295, 300.

62 Krisztián Ungváry and Gábor Tabajdi, 'Ungarn', in *Handbuch der kommunistischen Geheimdienste in Osteuropa 1944–1991*, eds Lukas Kaminski, Krzysztof Persak and Jens Gieseke (Göttingen: Vandenhoek & Ruprecht, 2008), 481–554 [This chapter is not included in the original English edition]; Krisztián Ungváry, 'Repressionen und "lustigste Baracke"' (unpublished paper).

against presumed enemies of socialism. The numbers of those arrested again reached the tens of thousands; roughly 10,000 were sentenced; and up until 1959, at least 45 people were executed for political offences. Still, the campaign lacked two elements that were typical for Stalinist-Romanian repression prior to 1956: neither were show trials of fallen communist leaders organized, nor were mass deportations used as a means of pacification. Nevertheless, it was only in the early 1960s (about the same time as in Hungary) that general amnesties were granted and most of political prisoners were set free.[63]

Czechoslovakia and Bulgaria went a different way than Hungary and Romania after the national parties felt safe enough to stop punishing fellow citizens on a large scale. Finally, political police in post-Stalinist times abandoned general, indiscriminate terror and switched to selective measures and specialized tools instead everywhere. This also involved the creation of a new type of police unit. In Poznań, members of regular police had proved totally unprepared for combatting crowds of protesters. Therefore, in 1957, ZOMO (Motorized Reserves of the Citizens' Militia; in fact, riot police) were created, a paramilitary force stationed in major Polish cities. They were equipped with, among other things, batons and helmets, water cannons, tear gas grenade launchers, and later with shields, and they were deployed to fight mass protests in 1968, 1970, 1976 and several times in the 1980s.[64] Comparable units were formed within the police forces in other socialist countries, but on a smaller scale.

The most important change to have taken place in the aftermath of the uprisings might be the attitudes towards peasants, who, up to this point, had been the most numerous enemy of socialism. In some countries, they were now left alone, though their living conditions and places in society fundamentally differed. In Poland, they remained relatively independent producers – at least, they were theoretically alien to the system – but with a few exceptions, like in 1981, peasants were considered so politically unimportant that state security did not even bother to run a separate department for peasant affairs. The department for 'rural areas and farming' ('pork intel' as colleagues from other departments called it), was only created in 1984.

In Lithuania, where in the beginning, peasants formed the bulk of anti-Soviet resistance, the picture fundamentally changed within one generation. Among the yearly 1,000–2,000 suspects, young urban dwellers – both students/pupils and workers – clearly dominated. In 1982, only 18 kolkhoz workers were under KGB scrutiny.[65]

Nationalization and rationalization

Nationalization meant limiting Moscow's direct influence. Political police in the countries of the outer empire had their own local enemies. Often, they were the same as in neighbouring states – churches, peasants (in some countries), the opposition – but the fight was carried out in accordance with the current policy of the national party, and not according to instructions from Moscow.

---

63 Bottoni, 'Nation-building through Judiciary Repression', 404–07.
64 On ZOMO, see Tom Junes, 'From Army Bullets and Police Batons to Cobblestones and Petrol Bombs: State Violence in Socialist Poland as a Generational Experience', in *Physical Violence in Late Socialism: Institutions, Practices and Everyday Life in the Soviet Union and Eastern Europe after Stalinism*, eds Jan Claas Behrends, Pavel Kolář and Thomas Lindenberger (Forthcoming).
65 Saulius Grybkauskas, 'All-Union Patterns and Peculiarities of Soviet Lithuania KGB in Dealing with Anti-Soviet Manifestations and Nationalism' (unpublished paper delivered at Imre Kertész Kolleg's annual conference in Warsaw, 12 June 2014).

The party enforced its supervision of the security apparatus. Quite often party officials were delegated to work there. On the other hand, it was a very rare occurrence for security-apparatus workers to pursue a political career outside of their sector. With the above-mentioned exception of Andropov, a member of the political police never became head of the party or prime minister.

Rationalization was supported by the post-Stalinist model of power: the goal was no longer to create a New Man, but to have conformist coexistence of the party (dominant in all areas) and the citizens (leading their lives the way they wanted as long as they did not break the rules in force). The police respected the unwritten social contract for which the party was the sole notary. If – as in the case of Bulgaria and Romania in the 1980s – the party decided to confront the citizens, it could be sure of the loyalty of the security apparatus.

Nationalization and rationalization also shaped the relations between the political police and the regular police, usually under the Ministry of Internal Affairs. In the Stalinist era, there was a clear tendency to maintain separate ministries for the political and regular police forces. In Czechoslovakia, the StB gradually separated from the SNB (National Security Corps) after February 1948; until in May 1950, it formed the MNB (Ministry of National Security). After three years, the independence of the political police was curtailed as it was incorporated into the MV (Ministry of Internal Affairs).[66] The outcome of an analogous experiment in Poland took place at the same time and with similar results: as part of the silent de-Stalinization, the MBP (Ministry of Public Security) *Ministerstwo Bezpieczeństwa Publicznego*) was dissolved in 1954 and turned into the Committee for Public Security responsible to the Council of Ministers. Two years later, at the end of 1956, security was incorporated into the MSW (Ministry of Internal Affairs), and it remained so until the end of communism. In Bulgaria, security was set apart a decade later. In 1965, the KDS (Committee for State Security) was temporarily separated from the Ministry of Internal Affairs and made responsible to the Council of Ministers, but three years later, the experiment ended in the same way it did in Czechoslovakia and Poland, and security became once again a part of the MV.[67]

In most countries (the GDR's Ministry for State Security was an exception as it mirrored the Soviet Union's KGB), this structure – political police as an autonomous part of the Ministry of Internal Affairs – remained in place until the end of communism; therefore, the Minister of Internal Affairs and his de facto superior, the respective secretary of the CC, usually belonged to the top decision-makers. They typically became members (or deputy members) of the Political Bureau – the institution which ruled the state in practice – because they oversaw the security service, but – at least formally – they did not have more power than other members/deputy members of the Political Bureau or CC-secretaries responsible for agriculture, industry or culture.

Rationalization also meant placing limits on the autonomy of the security service in everyday life. This, of course, had nothing to do with a return to 'local features' in the sense of the interwar period. Some Stalinist inventions – such as the Ministry's internal network of hair salons, bakeries, cobblers' and tailors' shops – were no longer part of the empire of state security, yet larger and more important institutions, such as housing cooperatives, the healthcare system (hospitals and sanatoriums), holiday resorts and their internal sports clubs remained. It cannot be taken to mean, however, that in post-Stalinist countries the repression apparatus enjoyed special

---

66 Petr Blažek and Pavel Žáček, 'Czechoslovakia', in Persak and Kamiński, *A Handbook of the Communist Security Apparatus*, 87–161, here 89.
67 Baev and Grozev, 'Bulgaria', 41.

treatment. All of the more important sectors of the state like army and miners, for instance, had this kind of infrastructure. In other words, in most post-Stalinist regimes, the security apparatus lost its unconditionally privileged position but remained one of the key elements of the post-totalitarian state.

Rationalization did not mean an utter rejection of Stalinist practices. Some of the clearly pointless cases were closed, but by way of inertia, observation of certain groups that were considered oppositional during the Stalinist era went on for decades. The classic – and probably transnational – example is Freemasonry, but the situation was similar in other cases. In Romania in the late 1950s, out of 290,000 suspects (2 per cent of the population) roughly two-thirds were listed because of their memberships in long-since dissolved organizations such as the Iron Guard movement, the National Peasant's Party or the National Liberal Party, and an additional 15,000 were listed for being 'former policemen, gendarmes and officials of the bourgeois spy organizations'.[68] In Poland, former functionaries of the pre-war Polish Border Protection Corps and the Polish Border Guard were under surveillance. There were thousands of them, and Stalinist and post-Stalinist services' interest in them lasted for decades. When in 1969 the case files started to be closed, it turned out that the police observed over 260 former members of the pre-war Second Department of the General Staff and the Border Protection Corps, as well as over 500 of the agents' wives and children. The police stated rather laconically that the group of people suspected on the basis of their work prior to 1939 did not stand out for anything suspicious 30 years later. Only one per cent of those investigated were considered hostile towards the People's Republic of Poland. 'The vast majority of them have a positive or loyal attitude towards People's Poland', concluded the authors of the final report,

> and during the period of political tension (Israel's aggression in the Middle East, the March incidents, events in Czechoslovakia), they fully supported the party and government stance … The vast majority of the children of those examined have a positive attitude towards the current reality and actively participate in building socialism in their stretches of work.[69]

'Rule by law'

Nationalization and rationalization were expressed by way of the law. Immediately after the war, special legislation was passed everywhere, which usually established more severe punishments than those of the pre-war Criminal Codes of Law. The decrees and bills turned out to be such useful instruments of repression that some of them remained in force even after 1956 – in Poland, it was called the 'Little Criminal Code of Law' until 1969 – offering socialist justice a convenient tool to punish political disobedience.

Yet, in the post-Stalinist period, 'class struggle' ceased to intensify as socialism 'developed'. What was left of the revolutionary state was a bureaucracy of daily control but of a limited scope – something akin to the German film *The Lives of Others* (2006) or its Czech equivalent *Pouta* (2010), minus the chief characters (i.e. the investigators). Their partners – in *The Lives of Others*, a dopey sergeant, in *Pouta* a joyful Slovak – would symbolize the system much

---

68 Bottoni, 'Nation-building through Judiciary Repression', 406.
69 Agnieszka Chrzanowska, ed., *Aparat bezpieczeństwa wobec żołnierzy Korpusu Ochrony Pogranicza i funkcjonariuszy Straży Granicznej* [The security apparatus and the soldiers of the Border Protection Corps and Border Guard officers] (Warsaw: IPN, 2013), doc. 53, 39.

better. Repressive monitoring included deliberate harassment and forceful demoralization. But 'enemies of the people' were no longer created.

In a system in which everything is political, and every opinion that differs from the official one can be considered a sign of an anti-state or anti-system attitude, occasional clashes between the authorities and elite intellectual circles were also systemic. In such clashes, use of administrative repression – in extreme cases, arrests; and even more rarely, the filing of a political lawsuit in some countries – one could say, occurred only when the rebels 'asked' for it. They purposely broke post-Stalinist rules that were designed by the authorities to defeat the dissident without taking away his freedom. One of the few political prisoners, Karol Modzelewski, recently wrote about being imprisoned in 1965, along with Jacek Kuroń, for their highly revisionist 'Open Letter': 'This time the authorities did not hesitate to use penal repression. We left them no choice'.[70] In most of the countries, the repression apparatus was equally hesitant to jail citizens unless they became as dangerous as so-called dissidents. As such, in Hungary, the political police after 1972 definitely preferred to silence dissenters by way of suppression, compromise and manipulation, rather than submit files to the prosecutor's office. The Polish counterpart behaved very much the same, with a growing (still statistically not very impressive) number of exceptions in the late 1970s.

Another fundamental difference between pre- and post-1956 attitudes towards the law became obvious for those few who were actually sentenced and jailed. To again quote Modzelewski about the late 1960s:

> A miraculous aura had hung over that place since the early fifties. Our block, built back then on the initiative of the director of the Investigative Department of the Ministry of Public Security, was linked by an underground corridor with a parallel building where, during the Stalinist era, the state security interrogated and tortured its prisoners. There, they extracted false confessions and constructed false accusations. The place used to be called the 'palace of miracles'. Their methods have since changed, and the miracle workers now act slowly and more subtly, without using physical violence …[71]

To sum up: if we compare the number of citizens prosecuted around 1950 and around 1980, the difference is striking. With notable exceptions like the Turkish minority in Bulgaria or the 1980s in Romania, the national regimes rather refrained from persecuting the 'greengrocer', who dared to disobey – as long as he did not join the 'dissidents'.

Joachim von Puttkamer and Dariusz Stola have examined this phenomenon, referring to Ernst Fraenkel's classic differentiation between a prerogative and a normative state. Von Puttkamer claims that the theory, based on the National Socialist regime, cannot be applied to real socialism in a meaningful way.[72] Stola, on the other hand, describes the bureaucratic machine – after de-Stalinization – that was created to rationalize the system of issuing (or refusing) passports:

---

70 Karol Modzelewski, *Zajeździmy kobyłę historii. Wyznania poobijanego jeźdźca* [Riding the mare of history: Confessions of a bruised rider] (Warsaw: Wydawnictwo Iskry, 2013), 110, English translation quoted in Junes, 'From Army Bullets' (forthcoming).
71 Ibid., 156–7.
72 Joachim von Puttkamer: 'Sozialistische Staatlichkeit: Eine historische Annäherung', in *Sozialistische Staatlichkeit*, eds Jana Osterkamp and Joachim von Puttkamer (München: Oldenbourg, 2012), 1–18, here 12–13.

In the early 1960s, the Passport Bureau established a special division for reviewing complaints and appeals, of which there were more than ten thousand per year, and a few years later – tens of thousands per year. Summaries and conclusions were presented at ministry meetings, and to some extent, they were taken into account – as long as they did not counter the guidelines of party leadership and the Ministry of Internal Affairs.

Based on this example of 'socialist rule of law', Stola reaches a different conclusion:

> The (collective) dictator himself introduced limitations on the prerogative state. He did it in a way that allowed for an easy change (shifting or suspending) of the limitations, should the need arise. The key aspect of the self-limiting dictatorship is giving party leaders the power to determine the boundaries of the prerogative state.[73]

Michal Kopeček follows a similar path in describing the differences between the 1950s and the following decades:

> In contrast to Stalinist times, the gap between reality and the statutory law effectively lessened and the traditional choice between *zakonnosť* and *partiinosť* in Soviet-type societies became much less relevant because the political repression and terror, such as that in Poland after 1981 martial law, had been realized through *zakonnosť* – legal regulation ....[74]

Kopeček – for lack of a better category – calls the post-Stalinist system 'repressive legalism' and – coming from this different angle – arrives at a similar conclusion to Stola's: high bureaucracy aimed at curbing the potential arbitrary power by way of a relatively transparent legal system.

From Moscow's domination to a system of relative distrust

During the transition period of 1945–48, control of the emerging national repression apparatuses was based on the so-called advisers from Moscow, who were permanently placed in appropriate ministries and committees. Being ever-present, they enjoyed a monopoly on information – no important news could be transmitted between Warsaw and Prague or between Budapest and Sofia without their knowledge.

In addition, there were special missions: in Poland an operational unit of the Soviet MGB made a significant contribution to the falsification of referendum results in 1946 and election results in 1947. In Bulgaria, between 1947 and 1949, special KGB missions prepared the purge among top party members and the previously mentioned trial of Traicho Kostov. Special units appeared in all countries where there were purges.

In Poland, the 'advisers' in the security apparatus and the military continued to play their part after Stalin's death, until 1955. The composition of the units varied depending on the pecking

---

73 Dariusz Stola, *Kraj bez wyjścia? Migracje z Polski 1949–1989* [A country without exit? Migrations from Poland 1949–1989] (Warsaw: ISP PAN, 2012), 158–9.
74 Michal Kopeček 'Was there a Socialist Rechtsstaat in Late Communist East Central Europe? The Czechoslovak Case in a Regional Context', *Journal of Modern European History* 18 (2020): 281–96, here 288.

order both in Moscow and in the local capital. Bulgarian party leader Vulko Chervenkov was so outraged at one of the KGB advisers' high-handed intrigues that he protested officially to Stalin. As a result, the adviser was called back to Moscow and subsequently sentenced.[75] Everywhere the number of advisers was inversely proportional to their impact. For instance, in Czechoslovakia there were only 50 advisers at the time of greatest terror.

Under Khrushchev, groups of advisers were gradually transformed into KGB liaison missions at USSR embassies. In Czechoslovakia in the early 1960s, it turned out that 10 Soviet functionaries were enough.[76] A similar number of people – usually less than 20 –were in the operational groups from one country and permanently stationed in the capitals of 'brother states'. Their mission was of the most delicate character. The matter of the autonomy of national repression apparatuses against the dominating 'Big Brother' and competing (though officially allied) police bureaucracies, could never be directly referred to; Romania after 1968 being the exception. Here, a special 'anti-KGB' military unit, the UM (*Unitate Militară*), was set up, whose main targets were the Soviet Union and Hungary.[77]

In other countries, we do not find this kind of clear evidence; minutes were not taken so that there would be no record of the special units being created. Nevertheless, historian Tytus Jaskułowski, who studies the cooperation of the political police (including intelligence and counter-intelligence) between Poland and East Germany, documents permanent hypocrisy, distrust and suspicion. He shows that one of the reasons Poland tried to give as little important information as possible to East Berlin was the (not entirely unfounded) fear that such information would pass from the Stasi and find its way to the KGB.[78] Of course, such fears could neither be officially verbalized nor transcribed in the minutes. Plans for cooperation were being realized (especially in the last decades of the communist regimes) and an inordinate number of reports were exchanged, effectively cluttering up the desks, cabinets and archives of the recipients. It was only the Romanian Securitate which apparently did not conform to the rules of the game, openly refusing to cooperate with the socialist security community more intensely than Ceaușescu did with his foreign comrades.[79]

Even less is known about fluid loyalties within the apparatus. The data of the Bulgarian political police – considered very obedient to Moscow – show that during a period of more than 20 years, over 1,000 Bulgarians studied in KGB and MVD schools.[80] It is likely that USSR training was a cause for suspecting that the alumni of Moscow schools would be more loyal towards the KGB than towards their own superiors. In this case, there is a lack of sources: no Czechoslovakian, Polish or Hungarian colonel could formulate in writing his fear that a graduate of an 'elite' course in Moscow should not be trusted because of his curriculum vitae.

---

75 Baev and Grozev, 'Bulgaria', 47.
76 Blažek and Žáček, 'Czechoslovakia', 105.
77 Stefano Bottoni, 'Integration, Collaboration, Resistance: The Hungarian Minority in Transylvania and the Romanian State Security', in *Die Securitate in Siebenbürgen*, eds Joachim von Puttkamer, Stefan Sienerth and Ulrich A. Wien (Köln: Böhlau Verlag, 2014), 187–211, here 205.
78 Tytus Jaskułowski, *Przyjaźń, której nie było. Ministerstwo Bezpieczeństwa Państwowego NRD wobec MSW* [A friendship that never existed: The GDR Ministry of State Security vis-à-vis the Interior Ministry] (Warsaw: Wydawnictwa Uniwersytetu Warszawskiego, 2014), 451.
79 Stefano Bottoni, '"Freundschaftliche Zusammenarbeit": Die Beziehungen der Staatssicherheit Ungarns und Rumäniens 1945 bis 1982', *Halbjahresschrift für Südosteuropäische Geschichte, Literatur und Politik* 24, nos. 1–2 (2012): 5–27.
80 Baev and Grozev, 'Bulgaria', 41.

Political prisoners

In the aftermath of the war, political incarceration and forced labour were rife throughout the Red Army-occupied territory, and depending on the situation, they took on different forms. Poland was a unique case. Its situation was the result of a great number of citizenship changes, numerous cases of individual (i.e. *not* legitimized by state) indirect and direct collaboration with the Nazis, and other wartime actions that were penalized after the war. Between 1945 and 1948, the most important detention places were the camps inherited from the Germans. All suspects against whom an indictment could not be drawn up – in today's terms, they would probably be called 'internees' – were sent to the camps. In most cases, it was a matter of settling accounts from the period of occupation – not resistance to communism. In likewise overcrowded prisons, there were those accused of specific actions and regular convicts. In December 1946, there were over 53,000 people in camps and more than 63,000 in prisons; by mid-1947, there were 75,000 and 46,000, respectively; in February 1948 (at the beginning of the period under scrutiny), the numbers were 47,000 and 62,000, respectively. Paradoxically, under Stalinism the role of the camps became less significant, and the number of people imprisoned there decreased. They were instead turned into forced labour camps. They might have resembled pre-war concentration camps, but the death rate remained far from the rate in the two years after the war, when it often reached 20 per cent or more.

In other countries, camps became very important under Stalinism. In Bulgaria, the number of political prisoners during the worst period of Stalinist terror was about 6,000–7,000.[81] Until it was closed down in 1962, 1,235 prisoners had been in the terrifying forced labour camp in Lovech; 147 people, including 30 political prisoners, died in the camp. Until 1962, in all the Bulgarian forced labour camps combined, there were 23,500 inmates, over 60 per cent of whom were political prisoners.[82]

The cruellest camps were the Yugoslav Goli Otok (1949–58)[83] and the Romanian Pitești. The former mainly held opponents of Josip Broz Tito who were suspected of loyalty to Moscow (the *ibeovci*, presumed supporters of the communist Information Bureau). In the first few years following 1948, more than 55,000 people in Yugoslavia were suspected of being Cominformists including many former communist partisans. Goli Otok, with altogether roughly 16,000 inmates, became a threatening symbol of violence against presumed Stalinists, not only because of the torture and unbearable living conditions, but also because of the yet unknown system of humiliation developed there: upon arrival, inmates ran the gauntlet – they were heavily beaten by the other prisoners who had no choice but to abuse their former comrades as thoroughly as the guards behind them demanded. It was only in 1953 that the regime in Goli Otok eased up on such practices, and thus turned into a kind of 'normal' forced labour camp.[84]

It will always be difficult to explain the Pitești experiment, because on the one hand it was based on systematic torture that was practiced over the course of many years, and on the other, it very much reflected Hannah Arendt's fear of Stalinism as an incubator of the 'new man'.

---

81 Ibid., 74.
82 Ibid., 76–7.
83 Venko Markovski, *Goli Otok: The Island of Death – A Diary in Letters* (Boulder, CO: Social Science Monographs, 1984).
84 Ivo Banac, *With Stalin Against Tito: Cominformist Splits in Yugoslav Communism* (Ithaca, NY: Cornell University Press, 1988), 243–54; Sabrina Ramet, *The Three Yugoslavias: State-building and Legitimation, 1918–2005* (Bloomington, IN: Indiana University Press, 2006), 176–9.

Until 1949, Pitești prison was a relatively small prison with about 1,000 inmates. In that year, one of the inmates came up with an idea for the former 'Centre for the Re-education of Students', which was tempting for the Securitate and appealed to the ambitions of all Stalinists. The 'experiment' consisted of transforming the prison into a torture facility, in which some inmates tormented and humiliated others (the Pitești experiment was hardly surpassed in sadistic ingenuity) until they became willing enforcers of the orders of their previous tormentors. The fourth and final stage of the programme was considered proof of successful 're-education': the previous victim had to become the perpetrator and use the same torture to which he had previously been subjected on one of his fellow prisoners. The 'experiment' was extended in various forms to some Romanian camps. In Pitești itself, it was discontinued in 1952.[85]

The torture regimes in both places are very similar to Hanna Arendt's vision: the real goal was not only to physically annihilate – as most prisoners survived – but also to break the person's spirit.

The Romanian Sighet prison provides a separate case. Beginning in May 1950, the authorities imprisoned over 200 *byvshikh lyudei* – ministers and other politicians, generals, bishops, journalists, in short, the Romanian elite from before 1944 – in Sighet. It appears that no one was physically tortured. It was enough to create conditions fit only for death. Over the course of 5 years, more than 50 prisoners died. In the course of de-Stalinization, which did not occur simultaneously, but rather varied chronologically from country to country, camps such as Sighet or Goli Otok lost their raison d'être. In post-Stalinism, obedience could be enforced by means other than through death camps.

Methods of coercion

The methods of extracting testimony and exacting further cooperation were so varied that it is impossible to even briefly describe them. Physical beatings and torture were common under Stalinism (and much later, also in Romania). Another method was to psychologically threaten the person being interrogated and his or her loved ones. The basic methods, not connected with the code of criminal law, were demotion or dismissal from work of the person and the members of his/her family, seizure of all or part of the person's property, the loss of privileges tied to the person's place in the social hierarchy, informing either a husband or wife of their spouse's marital infidelity, refusal of passport issuance, prohibiting one's child from entering university, committing one to a psychiatric ward, etc. The options were endless and varied according to external circumstances – in most countries, people were rarely threatened with the refusal of passport issuance as most citizens had no right to apply for one anyway.

One innovative element, which remained until the system's end, was intergenerational responsibility. For example, children bore responsibility for their parents because of their 'inappropriate' backgrounds (i.e. noble, bourgeois or equally alien), and as such they were either not accepted into universities or had restricted access to university education. On the other hand, parents were deprived of their social standing (including their loss of position or work) if their children engaged in oppositional activity, demonstrated other non-conformist stances or declared their wish to emigrate to the West. In the practice of repression and forming social attitudes, the rule of intergenerational responsibility seems more significant than Hannah

---

85 Monica Ciobanu, 'Pitești: A Project in Reeducation and its Post-1989 Interpretation in Romania', *Nationalities Papers* 43 (2015): 615–33.

Arendt's fear of a 'new man' who lacked all traditional moral norms; the system of intergenerational responsibility was built upon reckless misuse of traditional moral norms.

Lastly, there were sophisticated methods, based not on threat or fear, but on the natural human tendency to believe basic impressions from the outside world. For years, the Czechoslovak StB led the operation *Kameny* ('Stones'):

> False border stones with a pseudo-German border guard station were placed at a certain distance from the actual state border. Fake smugglers then took their 'victims' there and made them give an account of their anti-communist activities to fake American officers.[86]

Similarly sophisticated methods were used by the Polish political police against university students who were arrested in March 1968; the police passed around false secret messages throughout the cells that were allegedly signed by other students who had been arrested. From the messages it was clear that the others were 'spilling their guts' and the police knew everything. Few did not fall for that trick. We do not know if this was the case in all countries of the Eastern bloc, but in systematically led investigations after the Stalinist period – when the police considered the matter important – the percentage of people refusing to give testimony (often false ones and not in line with the expectations of the police) was very low. The situation in Czechoslovakia, Poland and Hungary changed in the 1970s when the opposition became professional. Many prominent suspects suddenly refused to testify. Caught by the police by chance, the occasional supporter of the dissidents often turned out to be helpless. Without a point of reference or a role model, this helplessness would have been difficult to overcome. It was enough to threaten him that he would lose his job, be dismissed from the university and sent to the military; threats against the family were equally effective.

The methods used against those that remained at liberty were essentially the same. Additionally, telephones were tapped, mail was controlled, neighbours, acquaintances and co-workers were interrogated, some were prohibited from working in their chosen profession, and for some men, their military service was either to begin earlier or last longer. These methods were more important in the case of those who were at liberty because the suspects were not necessarily aware of them. During the 'normalization' period after 1968, the fate and status of 300,000–350,000 people in Czechoslovakia was made worse in one way or another.[87] Whether repressions of this kind, not usually connected with revoking freedoms, were used against a greater number of victims of degradation in Yugoslavia after 1948, Hungary after 1956 or Romania in the 1980s, we do not know. And we will likely never know as the criteria of lowering status can be very different and the numbers can only be roughly estimated. However, in Poland, where the population was the largest, after the crises – even during martial law (1981–83) – the number of people whose status was lowered was likely not even close to that of the level of Czechoslovak 'normalization'.

As an example of other systematic operations, let us take the case of churches, which were infiltrated everywhere for decades (as described in John Connelly's contribution in the *Intellectual Horizons* volume of this series). In Bulgaria, between 1948 and 1952, persecution (including death sentences issued to bishops of various denominations) was carried

---

86 Blažek and Žáček, 'Czechoslovakia', 117.
87 Ibid., 141.

out against all religions.⁸⁸ On the other hand, the term 'double-decker' illustrates another, equally important, characteristic of the system: while political police tried ardently to persecute clergymen of all ranks, it was particularly successful in demoralizing the bishops. For reasons unknown the most successful were the Hungarians. Ninety per cent of Catholic and Reformed bishops were listed as informers; by the mid-1960s, the Christian churches were fully under control. But, by 1971, clergymen were no longer arrested, because their superiors took care of any disobedience against the state.⁸⁹

There is no evidence (thus far) of any widespread prosecution of homosexuality during state socialism. The exception seems to be the above-mentioned 1964 trial in Bulgaria and in 1950s Budapest (but not elsewhere in Hungary) where police compiled '"homosexual inventories" of potential blackmail victims who could be coerced into becoming police informers'.⁹⁰ The extent to which the police actually used the inventories remains unknown. In Yugoslavia, oral histories of gay men illustrate a hassle-free life:

> I didn't like the previous political system [communism], but it was quite open in this regard. It is true they have punished the political dissidents, but they did allow people to live as they wish and to love whom they wanted. They didn't interfere with one's private life.⁹¹

In Warsaw, it was different. The new penal code of 1932 already decriminalized homosexuality, so that it did not provide grounds for investigation or prosecution in the period we are interested in. The social stigma, however, weighed more heavily. Homosexuals were at least observed and blackmailed.

The most prominent case was the young, already internationally renowned humanities scholar Michel Foucault, founding director of the Centre de civilization française at the University of Warsaw in 1958–59. He was quickly called back to Paris because his homosexual contacts were known to the security service and could be used as a means of blackmail. Nearly three decades later (1985), the political police launched 'Operation Hyacynt', which registered some 11,000 Warsaw homosexuals. The extortion material was enormous. Whether and how it was used, we do not know.⁹²

Political violence and state repression in Sovietized CEE: Part Two, 1968–81 (by Dragoș Petrescu)

Between 1968 and 1981, the communist authorities applied deadly force only when they felt threatened by individuals or groups. As illustrated below, when insurgent violence occurred, especially in the case of working-class protests supported by city dwellers, which unfolded

---

88 Baev and Grozev, 'Bulgaria', 73.
89 Ungváry, 'Repressionen und "lustigste Baracke"' (unpublished paper).
90 Judit Takács, Roman Kuhar and Tomás P. Tóth, '"Unnatural Fornication" Cases under State-Socialism: A Hungarian-Slovenian Comparative Social-Historical Approach', *Journal of Homosexuality* 64, no. 14 (2017): 1–18, here 4, https://core.ac.uk/download/pdf/95354492.pdf (accessed 2 July 2021).
91 An unnamed Slovenian film director quoted in Kuhar, 'Ljubljana: The Tales from the Queer Margins of the City', 138.
92 In the Foucault case, neither the files of the Quai d'Orsay nor those of the French secret services are cited. In the case of 'Operation Hyacynt', we also have to rely on experiential accounts.

violently and thus offered a pretext for bloody retaliation, the respective regime reacted swiftly and resolutely to put down the protest, and they did not hesitate to open fire on the demonstrators (e.g. the Baltic Coast cities of Poland, 1970). When student unrest or working-class protests did not turn violent, the communist regimes employed non-violent means of controlling and subsequently pacifying the respective actions, such as sealing off the areas or regions where the protests occurred and negotiating with the protesters.[93] In the aftermath of non-violent student protests, administrative measures were preferred. In such cases, the usual measures taken against protesters included: expulsion from university, demotion or even loss of job. In the case of non-violent working-class protests, punishment was selectively applied only after the protest was quelled. Usually, the protesters received warnings from the secret police, while the ringleaders and their close collaborators were moved to workplaces located outside the respective region (e.g. Jiu Valley, Romania, 1977). In the aftermath of the 1975 Helsinki Accords, when more voices of dissent started to be heard across CEE, the communist regimes engaged in harassment of dissidents, which also implied selective use of individual violence against the most vocal or influential opponents. Once labelled as enemies of socialism, party and statehood, dissidents became the subject of harassment and humiliation. In some cases, the regime's opponents died after mistreatment during their interrogation or detention (e.g. Czechoslovakia, 1977).

In order to provide factual information about the way the communist regimes in power actually acted and applied repression throughout the period under scrutiny, Part Two addresses, in chronological order, the most relevant forms of state repression employed during the period 1968–81 against workers, students, ethnic minorities and dissidents, who were active inside their respective country or from abroad. Such forms of repression are relevant for all Sovietized countries in CEE, all the more that at some point all the regimes under discussion were confronted with more or less similar forms of contestation and were compelled to apply similar forms of repression. The purpose of Part Two is to present the way the communist regimes in CEE responded to major forms of contestation 'from below' and not to provide an exhaustive treatment of the subject. Therefore, the analysis focuses on the forms of state repression employed in response to the most representative instances of contestation from below. Analogously, Part Three will analyze and present the period 1981–89.

It is also worth noting that the major events that marked the beginning and the end of the period discussed in this section, that is, the suppression of the Czechoslovak Prague Spring and the imposition of martial law in Poland were both atypical. The suppression of the Prague Spring was conducted from 'abroad and above' through a Soviet-led military intervention of the WTO and thus had a supra-statal dimension as well. Since 1948, Czechoslovakia was a quiescent satellite of the Soviet Union. In the late 1960s, however, under the leadership of a newly elected First Secretary, Alexander Dubček, the CPCz (Communist Party of Czechoslovakia) launched a bold programme of reforms, known since as the 'Prague Spring'. The project was originally aimed at reforming the system 'from above', but the societal reaction to the reform plan was beyond any expectation. Intellectuals and students, especially, started to formulate demands for

---

93 For forms of 'soft' – in contrast to 'hard' – repressions, see Myra Marx Ferree, 'Soft Repression: Ridicule, Stigma, and Silencing in Gender-Based Movements', in *Repression and Mobilization*, eds Christian Davenport, Hank Johnston and Carol Mueller (Minneapolis, MN: University of Minnesota Press, 2005), 138–56. While 'soft' repression can be seen as involving 'the mobilization of non-violent means to silence or eradicate oppositional ideas', 'hard' repression can be seen as involving 'the mobilization of force to control or crush oppositional action through the use or threat of violence', ibid., 141–2.

real democratization. Such a situation worried the Soviets, who feared that the CPCz would lose its control over society. Eventually, in August 1968, WTO troops under Soviet command invaded Czechoslovakia and brutally put an end to this experiment in reform communism.

The imposition of martial law in Poland represented a departure from the existing pattern of state repression in CEE that was established in 1953, 1956 und 1968. In 1981, Poland did not witness a Soviet-led military intervention, but the coming to the fore of the military arm of the communist party in power with the mission of defeating Solidarity (*Solidarność*), the independent trade union born in August 1980. General Wojciech Jaruzelski, who had been appointed prime minister in February 1981, became First Secretary of the PUWP (Polish United Workers' Party) in October 1981. For the first time ever in the history of PUWP, as well as that of the entire Soviet bloc, a 'communist in uniform' had taken over the leadership of the party. On 13 December 1981, General Jaruzelski carried out the coup that brought the 'military party' to power.

Repression, statal and supra-statal: Czechoslovakia, August 1968

The reform communism movement in Czechoslovakia, generally known as the Prague Spring, triggered the first major wave of state repression during the period analyzed. Ironically enough, the Prague Spring did not represent a form of contestation of the communist rule in Czechoslovakia from below, but an attempt at introducing a set of reforms from above by the very elite of the communist party in power. Once the 1953 wave of working-class unrest had been suppressed, Czechoslovakia became a silent and subservient satellite of the Soviet Union.

As H. Gordon Skilling once noted: 'Ever since the Prague coup in 1948, indeed, Czechoslovakia has been regarded in the West as the "loyal" or "stable" satellite, offering no spark of resistance to the general line of the USSR'.[94] In the late 1960s, however, the CPCz went through a peaceful transfer of power and a new leadership took over. Headed in January 1968 by First Secretary Dubček, it devised a set of reforms that were aimed at reforming the 'socialist system' and did not envisage the renunciation to the leading role of the communist party and the introduction of a multiparty system. The Soviets, however, were definitely not pleased with the situation in Czechoslovakia. Among other reasons, the Kremlin was worried about the increasing demands for real democratization, pressed forward by intellectuals and students. A key moment in this respect was the publication, on 27 June 1968, of a highly influential text by Ludvík Vaculík titled, 'Two Thousand Words that Belong to Workers, Farmers, Officials, Scientists, Artists, and Everybody', which was considered 'counter-revolutionary' by the Soviets.[95] Eventually, the Soviet leadership decided to put an end to the Czechoslovak experiment in 'socialism with a human face', although the CPCz leadership remained faithful to Moscow over the entire duration of the Prague Spring. An armed suppression of the reform movement, which emerged from the party leadership and was strongly supported by parts of

---

94 H. Gordon Skilling, *Communism National and International: Eastern Europe after Stalin* (Toronto: University of Toronto Press, 1974), 84; originally published in 1964.
95 See 'Two Thousand Words that Belong to Workers, Farmers, Officials, Scientists, Artists, and Everybody', in *The Prague Spring 1968: A National Security Archive Documents Reader*, eds Jaromír Navrátil et al. (Budapest: CEU Press, 1998), 177–81. It is worth noting the impact of the 'Two Thousand Words' manifesto on other communist regimes in the region. For the reaction of the Kádár regime, for instance, see Csaba Békés, 'Hungary and the Prague Spring', in Günther Bischof, Stefan Karner and Peter Ruggenthaler, eds, *The Prague Spring and the Warsaw Pact Invasion of Czechoslovakia in 1968* (Lanham, MD: Lexington Books, 2010), 386–7.

the ruling elite, demanded a great deal of persuasion. Gomułka and Ulbricht were in favour of a violent solution from the outset. Others had to be 'brought in line' in negotiations that lasted for hours, with the exception of Kádár whose support was secured at a later stage. Only after Gomułka had presented a new definition of the Leninist-Stalinist view of counter-revolution – in a highly developed socialist society, they would try to cover/disguise a return to the past as a 'peaceful evolution' – that the aggression against Czechoslovakia was ideologically secured and became feasible.[96] The WTO military intervention began on 20 August 1968, at 11:00 p.m., under the code name 'Operation Danube'. Czechoslovakia was invaded by 27 divisions comprising over 500,000 troops, supported by 6,300 tanks, 2,000 pieces of artillery, 550 combat aircraft and 250 transport aircraft.[97] The intervention force comprised Soviet, Hungarian, Polish and Bulgarian military personnel. Although Erich Honecker, soon to be General Secretary of the Socialist Unity Party of Germany, was quite keen on being part of the operation and on deploying GDR troops in Czechoslovakia, the troops remained operational and were not deployed. Thirty years after the Munich Agreement, the Moscow leadership did not want to undertake such a suicidal association. The Soviet-led military intervention and the brutal interference in the domestic affairs of a 'fraternal' country was legitimized in the Brezhnev Doctrine, which – as an immediate reaction to the Prague Spring – defined any inner or outer thread to one socialist state as a menace to all. It initiated the so-called 'normalization', which in fact was a return to political orthodoxy, as it was understood in Moscow.

On the morning of 21 August, the leadership of the CPCz was arrested and interned at the Soviet military base in Legnica (Lower Silesia, Poland).[98] Following the military intervention, a new leadership – whose subservience to the Kremlin was as unquestionable as it had always been since 1929 – was established in Prague. The change of the CPCz leadership, however, did not occur overnight. The ice hockey world championship in March 1969 provided the welcome pretext for the definitive implementation of 'normalization'. The Czechoslovak team had a good chance of winning the title. In the preliminary round, they beat the Russian team (*sbornaja*) 2–0. That same evening, there were celebrations of joy in Prague's Wenceslas Square, which paralyzed the public transport system.

A week later, on 28 March, Czechoslovakia beat the USSR 4–3 in another dramatic match. In the centre of Prague, tens of thousands gathered; according to some estimates, there were over 100,000 people. When the display windows of the local Aeroflot office were destroyed, the anti-Soviet character of the demonstration was unmistakable. The police remained passive for a long time. Similar scenes took place in several Czech and Moravian towns. The Soviets took advantage of this welcome opportunity. On 31 March, a high-ranking Moscow delegation led by the Minister of Defence left for Prague. Negotiations on Dubček's dismissal was then made concrete, and on 17 April 1969, Dubček

---

96 For the Polish protocols of the summits between February and September 1968, see Andrzej Garlicki and Andrzej Paczkowski, eds, *Zaciskanie pętli: Tajne dokumenty dotyczące Czechosłowacji 1968 r.* [Tightening the noose: secret documents on Czechoslovakia, 1968] (Warsaw: Wydawnictwo Sejmowe, 1995); Navrátil, *Prague Spring*.
97 Figures provided in Slavomír Michálek and Stanislav Sikora, 'August 1968 as Seen from Bratislava', in *The Prague Spring and the Warsaw Pact Invasion of Czechoslovakia, 1968: Forty Years Later*, ed. M. Mark Stolarik (Mundelein, IL: Bolchazy-Carducci Publishers, 2010), 82.
98 Jan Rychlík, 'The "Prague Spring" and the Warsaw Pact Invasion as Seen from Prague', in Stolarik, *The Prague Spring and the Warsaw Pact Invasion of Czechoslovakia*, 49.

was replaced by Gustáv Husák as First Secretary of the CPCz. This date can be considered to mark the official initiation of 'normalization'.[99]

The supra-statal intervention was accompanied by statal measures, which took the form of a wave of repression carried out within the legal framework of the Czechoslovak state. This type of repression accompanied the process of 'normalization' and consisted primarily of administrative measures, which affected those actively involved in the reform programme. Dubček's reformers represented the prime target of Husák's 'normalizers'. Around half a million party members were expelled from the ranks of the CPCz, and thus the 'socialist' opposition in Czechoslovakia was gradually silenced during the 1970s. As Jacques Rupnik observes: 'It was necessary to normalize the Party in order to normalize the society'.[100] Prominent figures of the Prague Spring, such as Zdeněk Mlynář and Ota Šik, were forced into exile,[101] while many other reform communists, who chose not to leave their country, were marginalized and pushed into internal exile. Some scholars have emphasized the difference between the Czech and Slovak lands in terms of 'normalization' processes, and have argued that after 21 August 1968, the purges were carried out according to a double standard. While in the Czech lands the purges took the form of a 'cold civil war', in Slovakia they were carried out more cautiously and had less serious consequences. As Petr Pithart aptly states:

> The Czech part of the federal republic suffered from a much greater shock than did the Slovak part during the normalization period. In the Czech Republic, hundreds of thousands of people had become politically active in favour of a democracy which ended up being spectacularly defeated, and the vanquished had to be commensurately punished. In the Slovak Republic, people became politically active towards the national cause, Slovak statehood and the federation which had apparently triumphed.[102]

As for the scale of repression, Mlynář recalls: 'Thousands of highly qualified people could not find work in their profession in any kind of responsible position, not to speak of the total ban on such people working in science, in higher education, or in the press'.[103]

In 1969 alone, some 40,000 individuals identified as close to the Dubček regime were vetted, and as many as half of them lost their positions. Furthermore, by January 1970, roughly 136,000 functionaries, of whom around 80 per cent were Czech, had been dismissed or forced

---

99 Jörg Ganzenmüller, 'Bruderzwist im Kalten Krieg: Sowjetisch-tschechoslowakische Länderspiele im Umfeld des "Prager Frühlings"', in *Sport zwischen Ost und West: Beiträge zur Sportgeschichte Osteuropas im 19. und 20 Jh.*, eds Arié Malz, Stefan Rohdewald and Stefan Wiederkehr (Osnabrück: fibre Verlag, 2007), 113–30. For a standard monograph on 'normalization' in English, see Kieran Williams, *The Prague Spring and its Aftermath: Czechoslovak Politics, 1968–1970* (Cambridge: Cambridge University Press, 1997). In the end, Czechoslovakia finished third in the Ice Hockey World Championships due to goal difference.
100 Jacques Rupnik, '1968 et les paradoxes du communisme tchécoslovaque', in *Le Printemps tchécoslovaque 1968*, eds François Fejtö and Jacques Rupnik (Brussels: Éditions Complexe, 1999), 38.
101 Mlynář emigrated to Austria in 1977 after signing Charter 77. Šik, who was on vacation in Yugoslavia at the time of the WTO invasion, moved to Switzerland in October 1968.
102 Petr Pithart, 'Towards a Shared Freedom, 1968–89', in *The End of Czechoslovakia*, ed. Jiří Musil (Budapest: CEU Press, 1995), 210.
103 For Mlynář's recollections regarding the suppression of the Prague Spring and the wave of repression which accompanied 'normalization', see Mikhail Gorbachev and Zdeněk Mlynář, *Conversations with Gorbachev: On Perestroika, the Prague Spring, and the Crossroads of Socialism*, trans. George Shriver (New York: Columbia University Press, 2002), 39–45, here 44.

to quit their positions.[104] The purges also affected the officer corps of the Czechoslovak armed forces. Thus, during the 'normalization' period, around 10,000 military personnel were purged for alleged right-wing convictions.[105] But in spite of the large-scale military operation carried out by the WTO in Czechoslovakia, in August 1968, the application of deadly force proved to be rather accidental. At the same time, the military intervention had a major psychological impact on the population. There were nevertheless more than 100 fatalities in the course of eventual blockades, traffic and other accidents.

An extreme gesture of protest against the invasion of Czechoslovakia was that of a history student from the Charles University in Prague, Jan Palach, who set himself on fire on 16 January 1969 and died of his injuries three days later.[106] It was the most famous, but by no means the only self-immolation in the so-called Eastern bloc at the time.[107] The police had nothing to oppose this form of resistance, which was as individual as it was rare. The damage control – the similarity to the simultaneous protests against the US intervention in Vietnam was obvious, making the self-immolations even more embarrassing for state socialism – could only consist of cover-ups and secrecy.

Working-class protests

Although – before and after 1968 – strikes rarely transgressed the factory walls and in most cases ended in compromise, they were still the most common form of working-class protest in the socialist countries of the 1970s and 1980s. Workers usually engaged in defensive strikes, protesting against food shortages, food price increases, living and working conditions, stiff work norms, reduction of pay or loss of social benefits. Violent strikes rather constituted an exception. Nevertheless, when strikes turned violent and the rebellious workers attacked official buildings or blocked road and railway traffic, the intervention forces were sent in and the protests were ruthlessly repressed. It was therefore a major achievement of the Jiu Valley miners in 1977, and of the Polish strike leaders at the Gdańsk Lenin shipyard in August 1980, that they managed to avoid police intervention.

Working-class unrest was a major issue of concern for the power elites in the Soviet bloc. When workers living in a 'workers' state' rebelled against the ruling elite, the matter was serious and received the outmost attention from both the party and the secret police. During the 1970s, the Polish working class proved to be the most rebellious. This argument is supported by the very fact that during said period, Poland witnessed three waves of working-class unrest. The first wave of working-class insurgent violence, which resulted in many victims from among the rebellious workers, occurred in 1970 in response to the Gomułka regime's announcement that the prices of a series of basic foodstuffs would be raised significantly.[108] Workers from the Lenin

---

104 Vít Šimral, 'Czechoslovakia 1989 and Rational Choice Theory: A General Model of Regime Change', *Politologický časopis: Czech Journal of Political Science* 3 (2009): 227–54, here 240.
105 Navrátil, *Prague Spring*, 441.
106 For more on the significance of Jan Palach's extreme form of protest, see Jan Palach, 'Charles University Multimedia Project', https://cuni.cz/UKEN-113.html (accessed 12 March 2021).
107 See several articles by Sabine Stach, most recently, 'An Ordinary Man, a National Hero, a Polish Palach? Some Thoughts on the Memorialization of Ryszard Siwiec in the Czech-Polish Context', *Acta Poloniae Historica* 112 (2016): 295–313.
108 The following examples of price increases are telling: the price of meat rose by 17.5%; fish by 11.7%; lard by 33.4%; jams and marmalade by 36.8%. The fact that the new food prices were introduced just before Christmas aggravated the anxiety of the workers. See Roman Laba, *The Roots of Solidarity: A Political Sociology of Poland's Working-Class Democratization* (Princeton, NJ: Princeton University Press, 1991), 16 and 19.

Shipyard in Gdańsk went on strike on 14 December 1970 and demanded the cancellation of the planned food price increase. Strikes occurred also in the neighbouring town of Gdynia, at the Paris Commune Shipyard, as well as in the other major shipbuilding town of the Baltic Coast, Szczecin, at the Warski Shipyard. The way the Gdańsk protest unfolded was quite similar to the Poznań uprising of 1956: the workers went on strike and marched into the town, where the protest turned violent. The authorities intervened with force and the protest was ruthlessly suppressed. In Gdynia, on 17 December, the troops fired at the demonstrators. The overall number of victims of the violent protests in the Baltic Coast cities of Poland is estimated at 42 workers killed and over 1,000 wounded.[109] As Grzegorz Ekiert and Jan Kubik perceptively argue, the 1970 coastal workers revolt had a particular significance to the Polish working class:

> The December 1970 revolt was a turning point in the tradition of workers' protest. … For an entire generation of workers, especially those living in coastal cities who participated in strikes and demonstrations, the brutal and repressive nature of the regime was revealed.[110]

On the other hand, it remains obvious that the ratio of fatalities to wounded is four per cent; in street fighting, which normally resembles a public execution – on one side soldiers and policemen with orders to shoot and live ammunition, on the other more or less unarmed demonstrators – the relatively low number of fatalities suggests the question whether the state officials, although (or precisely because?) it had given the order to shoot, did not want to keep human losses as low as possible?[111]

The waves of protest of 1956 and 1970 indicated that under extreme conditions in working-class milieus, social discontent was likely to result in violent protests. Furthermore, the two waves of violent protests showed that industrial workers from relatively large enterprises were capable of engaging in large-scale revolts, which were repressed with difficulty, all the more that city dwellers did join the protesting workers. In fact, the angered crowds in Poznań in 1956, or in the shipbuilding cities of the Baltic Coast in 1970, were silenced only after the army was brought in and fired at the protesters. At the same time, the very way in which protests were carried out allowed for an immediate and violent solution of suppressing them from the part of the communist authorities. As long as the protesting workers left their workplace and marched into the downtown area where they attacked and ransacked official buildings, the regime was offered the best pretext for applying deadly force in order to re-establish order and authority.

---

109 Radio Poland, Polish Radio English Section, '1970 Gdynia massacre of 42 workers remembered' (17 December 2012), http://www.thenews.pl/1/9/Artykul/121690,1970-Gdynia-massacre-of-42-workers-remembered (accessed 12 March 2021).
110 Grzegorz Ekiert and Jan Kubik, *Rebellious Civil Society: Popular Protest and Democratic Consolidation in Poland, 1989–1993* (Ann Arbor, MI: The University of Michigan Press, 2001), 36.
111 One of the authors owes this reference to Andrzej Wajda, who reported several times and publicly about a conversation he had with Wojciech Jaruzelski, in which the latter emphasized that the officers had received a verbal order to aim at the pavement in front of the demonstrators. The ricochets caused enough damage and terror. Contemporary historians have never addressed this explanatory approach but have recorded evidence pointing in this direction. See Jerzy Eisler, *Grudzień 1970* [December 1970] (Warsaw: Instytut Pamięci Narodowej, 2012), 183–4, 237, 240, 270, 337, where the most diverse constellations are reconstructed: officers – even in the rank of a colonel – demanding to get the firing order in writing, soldiers shooting with practice ammunition, an unrealistic triple warning system for demonstrators, finally the ricochets witnessed by the latter.

Simply put, violent actions by protesters always triggered swift and violent retaliation from the part of the regime.

Communist regimes were always faced with a chronic imbalance between the purchasing power of the population and the quantity of consumer goods available on the market. True, the communist authorities did have a simple and effective measure at their disposal to reduce this imbalance, that is, the increase in the prices of consumer goods. Workers, however, were always extremely sensitive to such price increases and the authorities were therefore fully aware that such a measure had to be used only as a last resort. The scenario of the Polish working-class revolts of 1956 and 1970 were partially repeated in 1976.

Confronted with such a situation, the authorities were compelled to raise the prices of basic foodstuffs in June 1976. They believed they had learned from the 1970 disaster. This time, the price increase was presented to the Sejm and passed, a unique process, which showed only the lack of orientation of the party apparatus: the belief that the pseudo-parliament had a higher authority than the party or government proved to be a pure fallacy.

As a reaction to the price increases, on 25 June 1976 workers from the Ursus Tractor Factory, located in the vicinity of Warsaw, and General Walter Mechanical Works in Radom went on strike. The Ursus protesters occupied the nearby railway lines and stopped traffic. The protest in Radom, however, took a violent turn. Following an already established pattern of protest, the strikers marched into the town where they were joined by workers from other factories as well as city dwellers. Estimates put the total number of individuals involved in the protest at around 6,000. Whereas the Ursus protest was suppressed more easily, the Radom events degenerated into violent clashes between riot police and protesters. Here, however, the authorities really had learned something: The army remained in the barracks, while the police received no firing orders. Nevertheless, two protesters died over the course of the riot, and dozens were injured on both sides.

On that same evening of 25 June 1976, the price reform was withdrawn. It was not the only night in which the station houses would witness acts of extensive police brutality, however. As compared to similar situations in the past, the post-strike pattern of repression took a more serious turn with regard to the number of protesters sentenced with misdemeanours. The estimates vary from 10,000 to 20,000 dismissed.[112] Numerous workers were sentenced to various terms in prison or were given heavy fines. In response, intellectual groups and other nuclei of civil society mobilized themselves and joined forces in order to provide support for the families of the imprisoned workers. Adam Michnik has recalled how he decided to support the workers put on trial because of their participation to the 1976 riots:

> I remember attending a trial in 1976 that implicated some Ursus workers; I heard the condemnations, I saw the wives crying, and I shook with rage. I felt that it would be inadmissible to drop these people. And I started writing a protest letter on the part of the intellectuals right after.[113]

---

112 Michael H. Bernhard, *The Origins of Democratization in Poland: Workers, Intellectuals, and Oppositional Politics, 1976–1980* (New York: Columbia University Press, 1993), 64; Pawel Sasanka, *Czerwiec 1976: Geneza, przebieg, konsekwencje* [June 1976: origins, events, consequences] (Warsaw: IPN, 2006).

113 Adam Michnik, *Letters from Freedom: Post-Cold War Realities and Perspectives*, ed. Irena Grudzińska Gross (Berkeley, CA: University of California Press, 1998), 53.

State socialism

The year 1976 is significant because, for the first time in Poland's post-war history, a cross-class alliance between the most active workers and dissident intellectuals was established that year through the creation of the KOR (Workers' Defence Committee). The KOR was founded on 23 September 1976 in order to assist the repressed victims and their families of the June 1976 riots, and its activity was structured on two levels: (1) to provide legal and financial aid to the victims and their families and (2) to provide information about the victims of repression through open letters and illegal press. The birth of a cross-class alliance in Poland also led to a change of the pattern of working-class protests. As discussed below, non-violent occupation strikes were soon to replace violent demonstrations. This change had its roots in the experiences of 1956, 1970 and 1976, when the workers had left the factories and were shot at or bludgeoned in the streets by the police and the military. Now, in the years between 1976 and 1980, the formula elaborated by KOR and coined by Jacek Kuroń applied: 'Instead of burning committees, set up your own'; such protests proved much more difficult to contain and subsequently to suppress.[114]

In terms of working-class unrest, during the time period addressed in this section, there was a major difference between the recurrent protests by the Polish workers and the relative quiescence of their fellows in the rest of Sovietized Europe, with the exception of the isolated strike by the Jiu Valley miners in Romania. In this respect, Detlef Pollack and Jan Wielgohs aptly observe: 'With the exception of the Polish workers' protests of 1970 and notwithstanding the support for the reformers of the Prague Spring from segments of the Czech skilled workers, large protest mobilizations were absent outside of the intellectual milieu'.[115]

While in Poland the most notable working-class protests unfolded violently until 1976, in Romania the first major working-class protest took the form of a non-violent, around-the-clock occupation strike. The strike organized by Jiu Valley miners on 1–3 August 1977 represents one of the most significant workers' protests carried out in Romania under communist rule. The Jiu Valley protest was sparked by the new legislation (Law 3/1977) regarding pensions. With regard to the mining sector, the law introduced some new provisions, such as: a rise in the retirement age from 50 to 55; an extension of the workday in mines from 6 to 8 hours; and the cancellation or limitation of various categories of sickness benefits and entitlements to one's disability pension.[116] The strike began on 1 August in the morning, at the Lupeni mine and reached its

---

114 English translation of the famous Kuroń quote in Lorenzo Marsili and Niccolò Milanese, *Citizens of Nowhere: How Europe Can be Saved from Itself* (London: Zed Books 2018), 159. This is not a contribution on the learning capacity or evolution of latent or active oppositional milieus, so this change can only be hinted at, not illuminated. From the extensive literature, for the Polish case see above all, Andrzej Friszke, *Czas KOR-u: Jacek Kuroń a geneza Solidarności* [The time of the KOR: Jacek Kuroń and the origins of Solidarity] (Cracow: Wydawnictwo Znak/Instytut Studiów Politycznych PAN, 2011).
115 See Jan Wielgohs and Detlef Pollack, 'Comparative Perspectives on Dissent and Opposition to Communist Rule', in *Dissent and Opposition in Communist Eastern Europe: Origins of Civil Society and Democratic Transition*, eds Detlef Pollack and Jan Wielgohs (Aldershot: Ashgate, 2004), 231–66, here 239. For more on working-class unrest, see Peter Heumos, 'Workers under Communist Rule: Research in the Former Socialist Countries of Eastern-Central and South-Eastern Europe and in the Federal Republic of Germany', *International Review of Social History* 55, no. 1 (2010): 83–115; and Peter Hübner, Christoph Kleßmann and Klaus Tenfelde, eds, *Arbeiter im Staatssozialismus: Ideologischer Anspruch und soziale Wirklichkeit* (Köln: Böhlau, 2005).
116 See 'Legea 3 din 30 iunie 1977 privind pensiile de asigurări sociale de stat şi asistenţă socială' [Law 3 of 30 June 1977 on state social insurance pensions and social assistance], in Ioan Velica and Dragoş Ştefan Velica, *Lupeni '77: Laboratorul puterii* (Deva: Editura Polidava, 2002), 39–71.

climax on 3 August.[117] One can summarize the main aspects of the strike as follows: (1) there was the emergence of a strike leadership and the establishment of a strike command-post inside the Lupeni mine; (2) the protest was organized to take the form of a non-violent, round-the-clock sit-down strike; and (3) the strikers requested to negotiate their list of demands with the supreme party leader, Ceaușescu, face to face.[118]

Given its non-violent nature, the suppression of the Jiu Valley strike took on a different form when compared with the Polish workers' protests of 1956, 1970 or 1976. The first measure taken by the authorities was to send an official delegation to negotiate with the protesters. On 2 August 1977, the delegation of high party officials was sent in to open a discussion with the miners, but the strikers made it clear that they were not going to talk to anyone except for the supreme party leader. Ceaușescu, who finally agreed to speak to the strikers, arrived at Lupeni on 3 August. Faced with a determined, but non-violent crowd, the supreme party leader basically agreed to the miners' demands. As one of the leaders of the strike remembers, when Ceaușescu arrived, the miners shouted rhythmically, 'We don't enter the mine!', and they continued to shout until it was announced that their demands would be met. At that moment, the crowd started to shout 'Ceaușescu and the miners!' This was the end of the strike, which ceased on 3 August 1977 at around 3:20 p.m.[119] Ceaușescu and the Securitate did not use force to suppress the strike. Repression followed only gradually, during the winter of 1977–78. In spite of rumours, the Securitate did not assassinate the ringleaders. They were forcefully moved to other regions, where they remained under strict surveillance.

The 1977 Jiu Valley strike did not lead to the establishment of a free trade union or other independent working-class association. Such an initiative emerged however in 1979, when RFE (Radio Free Europe) spread the news about the founding of a free trade union in communist Romania, named SLOMR (Free Trade Union of the Working People in Romania). RFE broadcast the founding declaration of SLOMR on 4 March 1979. The authorities reacted promptly and arrested the three main initiators of the project, that is, Ionel Cană, Gheorghe Brașoveanu and Nicolae Dascălu. Although the initiative was short-lived – the SLOMR existed from January to June 1979 – it represented a courageous attempt at creating a cross-class alliance between workers, technical intelligentsia and other professional groups in Romania.[120]

---

117 A detailed witness account of the unfolding of the strike is provided in Mihai Barbu and Marian Boboc, *Lupeni '77: Sfânta Varvara versus Tanti Varvara* [Lupeni '77: Saint Varvara versus Tanti Varvara] (Cluj-Napoca: Editura Fundației pentru Studii Europene, 2005), 180–270.
118 For the list of strikers' demands, see Barbu and Boboc, *Lupeni '77*, 215–16. An analysis of the patterns of working-class protest in communist Romania is provided in Dragoș Petrescu, 'Workers and Peasant-Workers in a Working-Class' "Paradise": Patterns of Working-Class Protest in Communist Romania', in *Arbeiter im Staatssozialismus: Ideologischer Anspruch und Soziale Wirklichkeit*, eds Peter Hübner, Christoph Kleßmann and Klaus Tenfelde (Köln: Böhlau Verlag, 2005), 119–40; and idem, 'Commuting Villagers and Social Protest: Peasant-Workers and Working-Class Unrest in Romania, 1965–1989', in *Countryside and Communism in Eastern Europe: Perceptions, Attitudes, Propaganda*, eds Sorin Radu and Cosmin Budeancă (Vienna: LIT Verlag, 2016), 497–524.
119 Testimony of Constantin Dobre in Barbu and Boboc, *Lupeni '77*, 204–35 and 238.
120 For more on the SLOMR, see Oana Ionel and Dragoș Marcu, 'Vasile Paraschiv și "Securitatea lui"' [Vasile Paraschiv and 'His Securitate'], in Vasile Paraschiv, *Lupta mea pentru sindicate libere în România: Terorismul politic organizat de statul comunist*, eds Oana Ionel and Dragoș Marcu (Iași: Editura Polirom, 2005), 367–71.

Student unrest

Students were naturally rebellious and tended to disobey the officially imposed values and norms. Especially from the mid-1960s onwards, when the communist regimes of CEE gradually opened towards the West and exposure to Western culture increased, student conflicts with the authorities were on the rise. Students protested in general against the cultural and educational policies of the regime or against the studying conditions in universities and the living conditions in the dormitories. Such protests were mostly spontaneous and non-violent, and the measures taken by the authorities were usually administrative. In some cases, students organized large-scale protests, in which they put forward more general economic and social demands, related to difficulties in finding employment after graduation or to regional inequalities. Nationalism and identity politics also led to student mobilization and protests against the regime. Throughout CEE, students also joined, individually, various dissident groups. There were also cases in which students who were known for their dissident activity died in dubious circumstances, their deaths were later blamed on the secret police agencies.

When ideological orthodoxy was rigidly imposed, or the emulation of Western trends in popular culture was brutally punished, the natural rebelliousness of the young generation evolved into anti-regime stances. Beginning in the mid-1960s, the Gomułka regime in Poland had to face growing activism by young scholars and intellectuals. In January 1968, the authorities decided to terminate the performance of the play *Dziady* ('The Forefathers'), by Adam Mickiewicz (1798–1855), staged at the National Theatre in Warsaw. The pretext was that the play of the great Polish Romantic poet stirred anti-Russian – now perceived as anti-Soviet – sentiment among audiences. Indeed, lines that expressed criticism towards Russia, such as: 'Moscow sends only rogues to Poland', were vividly applauded as hints of hostility towards the Soviet Union.[121]

Students in Warsaw organized a protest on the occasion of the last performance of the play. The authorities responded swiftly, and arrests were carried out. This opened a period of student unrest (as well as of other young people, first and foremost that of workers and schoolchildren) and intellectual criticism against the regime, culminating in protests and clashes with the police on 8 March on the campus of Warsaw University. During the following weeks, students and professors at Warsaw University – some of them of Jewish origin – were harassed or even ousted from the university. Instead of easing the tense situation, the authorities escalated the conflict into another round of the previous year's campaign against so-called 'Zionist elements', which culminated with purges of communists of Jewish descent from prominent positions in the party and other institutions. The 'anti-Zionist' campaign also served the purpose of marginalizing Gomułka's enemies within the Politburo and helped purge the 'revisionists' who allegedly advocated for system reform.[122] The University of Warsaw, where several ex-Marxists were

---

121 Quoted in Gale Stokes, *The Walls Came Tumbling Down: The Collapse of Communism in Eastern Europe* (New York: Oxford University Press, 1993), 15.
122 On Poland in March 1968, see Jerzy Eisler, 'March 1968 in Poland', in *1968: The world transformed*, eds Carole Fink, Phillip Gassert and Detlef Junker (Cambridge: Cambridge University Press, 1998), 237–52. On the scope and meaning of the 1968 'anti-Zionist' campaign, see Dariusz Stola, 'Anti-Zionism as a Multipurpose Policy Instrument: The Anti-Zionist Campaign in Poland, 1967–1968', *The Journal of Israeli History* 25, no. 1 (March 2006): 180–96. See also Bożena Szaynok, *Poland–Israel, 1944–1968: In the Shadow of the Past and of the Soviet Union*, trans. Dominika Ferens (Warsaw: Institute of National Remembrance, 2012), 445–57. On the Polish youth in 1968, see Piotr Osęka, *My, ludzie z Marca: Autoportret pokolenia '68* [We, the March people: a self-portrait of the 1968 generation] (Warsaw: ISP PAN, 2015), and on the Polish student movement under State Socialism in general, see Tom Junes, *Student Politics in Communist Poland: Generations of Consent and Dissent* (London: Lexington Books, 2015).

dismissed – who were meanwhile internationally recognized figures in the human sciences – suffered the biggest losses. Even the most prominent among them, the philosopher Leszek Kołakowski, went to the West. Norman Davies commented on it over 30 years ago as succinctly as aptly: 'Oxford's gain is Warsaw's loss'.[123]

All this was almost petty compared with the cleansing in Czechoslovakia, which a few months later would hit the entire scientific and artistic world. Here, oppression was laid out on a large scale, and from the very beginning was more profound. In addition to affecting well-known and lesser-known reformers and artists who were regarded as supporters of the Prague Spring, the policies of oppression also affected leftists and alternatives.[124]

Student protests emerged in Czechoslovakia immediately after the suppression of the Prague Spring. A radical left-wing group named RYM (Revolutionary Youth Movement), established by students in Prague, engaged in open protest in November 1968, when they organized a student strike against the Soviet occupation.[125] In December 1969, the secret police arrested all the members of the group, who were subsequently put on trial in the spring of 1971.[126] Other similar initiatives were suppressed by the authorities with the help of the secret police. Throughout the Soviet bloc, the communist regimes were determined to discourage the emulation of new Western popular culture trends by youngsters living under state socialism. Non-conformist people, who chose to withdraw into private niches, posed no threat for the regime. Underground culture, however, was considered a serious threat for the communist regime. The younger generations living under state socialism found refuge from conformism and ideological orthodoxy in rock music and Western popular culture. For their part, the communists in power were determined to repress the cultural currents which were likely to undermine the 'socialist culture' and nurture dissident action. The plight of the experimental rock group named the 'Plastic People of the Universe' under the Husák regime is highly relevant in this respect.

The Plastic People of the Universe (PPU) was a rock band that rose to prominence not only because of the kind of music they played, but also because of the repressive measures taken against them by the communist authorities in Czechoslovakia. The band, which began performing publicly in 1971, was banned from doing so in 1973. The Husák regime spent a lot of effort marginalizing the PPU, but the band nevertheless had its followers who obstinately attended private concerts. The band also managed to produce unofficial recordings, which were distributed through underground networks.[127]

---

123 Norman Davies, *God's Playground*, vol. II: *1795 to the Present* (Oxford: Oxford University Press, 1981), 552.
124 Witness accounts abound in this respect. See, for instance, Mlynář's recollections in Gorbachev and Mlynář, *Conversations with Gorbachev*, 44–5.
125 For more on the RYM members' ideas and ideals, including recollections by two of the group members, Jaroslav Suk and Petruška Šustrová, who were both students at the Prague Philosophical Faculty at the time, see Marie Černá, John Davis, Robert Gildea and Piotr Osęka, 'Revolutions', in *Europe's 1968: Voices of Revolt*, eds Robert Gildea, James Mark and Anette Warring (Oxford: Oxford University Press, 2013), 121–3.
126 Oldrich Tůma, 'Czechoslovakia', in Pollack and Wielgohs, *Dissent and Opposition*, 36–37.
127 With regard to the kind of music PPU played at the time see, for instance, The Plastic People Of The Universe, *Egon Bondy's Happy Hearts Club Banned*, PPU III./1974–75, Globus Music, 2001, CD. On rock music in Central and Eastern Europe in general, Timothy W. Ryback, *Rock around the Bloc: A History of Rock Music in Eastern Europe and the Soviet Union* (New York: Oxford University Press, 1990).

Ultimately, the regime decided to take more resolute measures. In September 1976, several members of the band were arrested and put on trial on charges of alcoholism, drug use and indecent behaviour – the official Soviet terms for such accusations were *chuliganstvo* ('public indecency') and *tunejadstvo* ('criminal unemployment', used to morally condemn free leisure). Among those put on trial was Ivan Jirous, a major figure of the underground music scene in Prague, who was also the artistic director and manager of the PPU band. Apparently apolitical, this trial nonetheless represented a watershed in the structuring of anti-communist dissent. Milan 'Mejla' Hlavsa, founding member, chief songwriter and original bassist of the band, has not overstated the political influence of PPU. For Hlavsa, the trial of several PPU band members was an event that brought together likeminded individuals determined to engage in open protest against the violation of a basic human right, that is, the freedom of expression:

> Historians see the Plastics' arrest and sentence in direct relation to the origins of Charter 77. Of course, I also see the relations, but only in that the trial brought together people concerned about the fate of our country. Václav Havel was the engine of the efforts. The band itself had no political ambition and we did not intend to destroy communism by our music, but if we helped we are only glad.[128]

Havel, who was a friend of Jirous, mobilized critical intellectuals in Czechoslovakia and in the West, including the German Nobel laureate writer Heinrich Böll, in support of the underground musicians. However, Jirous and several other musicians were convicted and sent to jail.[129]

The decision of the communist authorities to stage a trial against PPU had a perverse effect, since the trial offered an unexpected opportunity for a number of critical intellectuals to join their efforts in support of a group of underground musicians unjustly persecuted by the communist regime. In his essay, 'The Trial', written in October 1976 and widely circulated in Czechoslovakia and abroad, Havel mentioned the 'challenge of example' as one of the major lessons he learned from the PPU trial. Havel also confessed that he was impressed by the special sense of community felt by those who openly supported the underground musicians on trial:

> Only the exalting awareness of an important, shared experience, and only the urgency of the challenge that everyone felt in it, could have explained the rapid genesis of that very special, improvised community that came into being here for the duration of the trial.[130]

Obviously, the Husák regime wanted to make an example of PPU and make others afraid to follow in their footsteps. Contrary to the regime's wishes, the trial of the PPU band members

---

128 Hlavsa's statement is cited in Richie Unterberger, 'The Plastic People of the Universe', http://www.richieunterberger.com/ppu.html (accessed 15 March 2021).
129 On 'normalization' and the subsequent structuring of dissent, see Kevin McDermott, *Communist Czechoslovakia, 1945–89: A Political and Social History* (London: Palgrave, 2015), 152–81. On the Prague underground musical scene, see Barbara J. Falk, *The Dilemmas of Dissidence in East-Central Europe: Citizen Intellectuals and Philosopher Kings* (Budapest: CEU Press, 2003), 84–7. Regarding the trial of the PPU band, see also Sabrina P. Ramet, *Social Currents in Eastern Europe: The Sources and Meaning of the Great Transformation* (Durham, NC: Duke University Press, 1991), 102.
130 Václav Havel, 'The Trial', in idem, *Open Letters: Selected Writings 1965–1990*, selected and edited by Paul Wilson (New York: Vintage Books, 1992), 106–7.

contributed to the emergence of the most prominent movement for human rights in communist Czechoslovakia; that is, Charter 77.

Another major student protest in communist CEE emerged in June 1968, this time in the Yugoslav capital, Belgrade. The protest was sparked on 2 June by a quarrel concerning the right to attend a performance by a troupe of actors, which the authorities organized in a small theatre in New Belgrade, a suburb of the capital city. The performance was intended for an audience of Youth Action workers (volunteer youth brigade members). However, students from the nearby complex of dormitories also wanted to attend the free performance, but they were expelled from the theatre. Subsequently, a crowd of over a thousand students gathered in front of the theatre and engaged in violent clashes with the police. Students were forced to withdraw to their dormitories, but they took to the streets the following day.[131]

On 3 June, a large student crowd left the dormitories in New Belgrade and marched towards downtown. Riot police intervened in force and dispersed the crowd using batons and tear gas. Estimates put the number of students injured in the events of 2–3 June to 169, of whom as many as 12 were hospitalized.[132] The Faculty of Philosophy building became the centre of the Belgrade student strike, which all in all lasted from 3 to 9 June. According to eyewitness accounts, around 60,000 students participated in the strike. The strikers issued a proclamation, in which they addressed a number of problems, ranging from difficulties in finding a job after graduation to the significant inequalities in Yugoslavia and the need to increase the level of self-management. Tito, the supreme leader of the Yugoslav communists, did not intervene until 9 June, when he delivered a televised speech in which he supported, in principle, the students' demands and asked for their help in order to solve their problems. As some authors pointed out, although Tito's speech was not the only factor, it was probably the deciding one in ending the student strike.[133] Repression followed shortly in the form of criminal trials staged against the ringleaders, and non-criminal investigations were carried out against other prominent participants. Eight professors from the Faculty of Philosophy in Belgrade were eventually expelled after a procedure that lasted until January 1975.[134] Student protest in Croatia fared no better in 1971.

As already mentioned, there were cases of students who individually associated themselves with dissident groups and who died in unclear conditions. A prominent case in this respect is that of Stanisław Pyjas, a student at the Jagiellonian University in Cracow who belonged to a group of students who were actively cooperating with KOR. The circumstances of Pyjas'

---

131 For a detailed account of the June 1968 events in Belgrade, see D. Plamenić, 'The Belgrade Student Insurrection', *New Left Review* I/54 (March–April 1969): 61–78; https://newleftreview.org/I/54/d-plamenic-the-belgrade-student-insurrection (accessed 15 March 2021). See also Boris Kanzleiter, '"Nieder mit der roten Bourgeoisie!" Die Studentenproteste von 1968 in Jugoslawien', in *Mythos Partizan. (Dis-)Kontinuitäten der jugoslawischen Linken: Geschichte, Erinnerungen und Perspektiven*, eds Dorde Tomić, Roland Zschächner, Mara Puškarević and Allegra Schneider, (Hamburg: Unrast Verlag, 2013), 268–85.
132 Goran Musić, '1968 Movements in Belgrade and Mexico City: A Comparative Analysis', Master Thesis, University of Vienna (August 2008), 47, http://othes.univie.ac.at/1108/1/2008-08-28_0450183.pdf (accessed 15 March 2021).
133 Hrvoje Klasić, 'Tito's 1968 Reinforcing Position', in *Revolutionary Totalitarianism, Pragmatic Socialism, Transition*, vol. 1: *Tito's Yugoslavia, Stories Untold*, eds Gorana Ognjenović and Jasna Jozelić (London: Palgrave Macmillan, 2016), 175.
134 For details regarding the scale of repression, see Nebojša Popov, 'The University in an Ideological Shell', in idem, ed., *The Road to War in Serbia: Trauma and Catharsis* (Budapest: CEU Press, 2000), 312.

death – he was found dead having suffered severe head injuries in a passageway in Cracow's old town on 7 May 1977 – have remained unclear to this day.[135]

Acts of dissent

Beginning in the mid-1970s, dissent became a major concern for the communist regimes in CEE. Throughout the Soviet bloc, those who opted to 'live in truth' were the subjects of constant harassment by the secret police, public humiliation, administrative measures (demotion, or loss of job) or imprisonment. In a number of cases, accidental death occurred during interrogation or detention.

Dissent that centred on observing fundamental human rights spread across Sovietized Europe in the aftermath of the signing of the Helsinki Accords in 1975. The case of communist Czechoslovakia is very telling in this respect. After the suppression of the Prague Spring, one could talk of a 'dispersed opposition in a demobilized society' – to use Oldřich Tůma's inspired words – rather than of a structured opposition with clearly defined goals. The communist regime was thus faced with the rather easy task of preventing a structured societal opposition by making use of extended surveillance. In his book-length dialogue with Gorbachev, Mlynář speaks of the reaction of the regime in response to a document he wrote in early 1975 on the theoretical and practical significance of the Prague Spring. Mlynář sent the respective document to the CCs of the communist parties that were supposed to participate in Berlin the following year, 1976, in a conference of representatives of European communist parties. To this, the Husák regime reacted swiftly:

> The response came very quickly in the form of a group of state security agents who broke into my apartment at 5:00 in the morning and carried out a search. The big 'find' that they carried away was the manuscript that the CC of the CPCz had already received by mail.

Furthermore, Mlynář emphasizes an important aspect of the regime's strategy of dealing with alternative thinking or dissident ideas prior to the founding of Charter 77: 'The official communist party refused to engage my criticism in any way other than by police methods'.[136]

The establishment of Charter 77 represented a major breakthrough in the structuring of dissent in Czechoslovakia. The founding document of Charter 77 was a declaration issued on 1 January 1977. The document, which was also an indictment of acts of non-observance of basic human rights by the Husák regime, opened with the following statement:

> On 13 October 1976, there were published in the Codex of Laws of the čSSR, no. 120, an 'International Pact on Civil and Political Rights' and an 'International Pact on Economic, Social and Cultural Rights', which had been signed on behalf of Czechoslovakia in 1968, confirmed at Helsinki in 1975 and which came into force in

---

135 For more on the Pyjas affair, see Jan Józef Lipski, *KOR: A History of the Workers' Defense Committee in Poland, 1976–1981*, trans. Olga Amsterdamska and Gene M. Moore (Berkeley, CA: University of California Press, 1985), 142–50; and Cardinal Stanisław Dziwisz, *A Life with Karol: My Forty-Year Friendship with the Man Who Became Pope* (New York: Doubleday, 2008), 52–4.
136 Gorbachev and Mlynář, *Conversations with Gorbachev*, 44–45, here 45.

our country on 23 March 1976. Since that time our citizens have had the right and our state the duty to be guided by them.[137]

Throughout the text, the signatories put forward numerous examples of human rights violations by the communist regime in Czechoslovakia, thus illustrating that the regime's domestic political actions were in direct contradiction with the international pacts it had signed. The document also referred to the famous trial of the members of the PPU rock band:

> The implementation of the right 'to seek, receive and spread information and ideas of all kinds, regardless of frontiers, either orally, in writing or in print, or by means of art' (pt. 2, art. 13 of the first pact) is subject to persecution, not only outside the courts but judicially too, often under the guise of criminal charges (as is borne out, among others, by the trials of young musicians now going on).[138]

In accordance with its founding document, Charter 77 was represented by three spokespersons who were elected annually. The first three spokespersons were philosopher *Jan Patočka*, playwright Václav Havel and politician and diplomat *Jiří* Hájek.[139] The Charter 77 declaration initially bore some 240 signatures, but the number of signatories rose gradually to around 2,000. A majority of the Chartists were intellectuals, among whom writers featured prominently. Among the signatories of Charter 77, one could find Rudolf Slánský, the son of the former general secretary of the CPC who was executed in 1952 after a famous show trial.[140] Like other reform communists who supported the Prague Spring and were purged after its suppression, Slánský openly dissented once the Charter was launched.[141] Slánský's political biography is vividly reminiscent of László Rajk Jr.'s. The number of children of the now disempowered *nomenklatura* who have revolted since 1968 has been pointed out many times. Indeed, the role of children whose Stalinist fathers ultimately went down in history as victims, would be worthy of cross-national investigation.

The Chartists' main avenue for action was the publication of documents, such as declarations, petitions or open letters. For instance, Skilling calculated that during its first decade of its existence, Charter 77 issued around 340 documents.[142] Equally important, Charter 77 was devised in such a way as to permit the emergence of a radical critique of the communist system from the perspective of human rights protections. The issue of protecting human rights was meant to unite the Czechs and Slovaks in their critique of the Husák regime irrespective

---

137 For a comprehensive collection of documents from different sources related to the establishment and activity of Charter 77, see National Security Archive, 'Charter 77 After 30 Years', http://nsarchive.gwu.edu/NSAEBB/NSAEBB213/ (accessed 15 March 2021).
138 For an English version of the Declaration of Charter 77, see Roy Rosenzweig Center for History and New Media (CHNM), George Mason University, *Making the History of 1989*; https://chnm.gmu.edu/1989/archive/files/declaration-of-charter-77_4346bae392.pdf (accessed 15 March 2021).
139 Ramet, *Social Currents in Eastern Europe*, 102–03.
140 See the subchapter *Show trials*, 205–09.
141 National Security Archive, *Charter 77 After 30 Years*; Document 4, original signature cards: Václav Havel, Jiří Hájek, Pavel Kohout, Zdeněk Mlynář, Jan Patočka, Rudolf Slánský, Ludvík Vaculík, and Prokop Drtina; http://nsarchive.gwu.edu/NSAEBB/NSAEBB213/czdocs/cz04.pdf (accessed 15 March 2021); H. Gordon Skilling, *Charter 77 and Human Rights in Czechoslovakia* (London: Allen & Unwin, 1981).
142 Quoted in Falk, *The Dilemmas of Dissidence in East-Central Europe*, 91.

of their ideological conviction or religious faith, as well as to offer a common, transnational platform to dissident groups in Sovietized CEE. The emergence of Charter 77 prompted similar initiatives by other civic groups, of which the most important was the establishment of VONS (the Committee for the Defense of the Unjustly Persecuted) in April 1978. While Charter 77 had a broader scope of action, VONS concentrated on specific citizen's cases of persecution by the communist authorities. In this respect, VONS was similar to the Polish KOR.

The Husák regime was very harsh on Charter 77 from the beginning. The Chartists, the founding members and the spokespersons in particular, were subject to various forms of repression, ranging from 'soft' to 'hard' repression. Repression, therefore, took various forms, from public humiliation, social exclusion, stigmatization and marginalization to harassment, arrests and court trials, which resulted in convictions of prison terms to varying degrees. One of the tragic consequences of the wave of repression unleashed upon Charter 77 was the death of *Patočka*. The philosopher, who had to endure intimidation and long hours of interrogation by the secret police, died in a Prague hospital on 13 March 1977.[143]

The Czechoslovak authorities launched a sustained campaign of denigration against the Chartists. As mentioned above, Charter 77 made public its declaration on 1 January 1977. To this, the regime responded with an unremitting anti-Charter propaganda, which included several official anti-Charter documents. Thus, on 12 January the official press – starting with the main party daily, *Rudé právo* – published an extensive article entitled 'Losers and Usurpers' in which Charter 77 was characterized as a 'subversive, anti-socialist, demagogic pamphlet'.[144] Another anti-Charter document, entitled 'For New Creative Deeds in the Name of Socialism and Peace', and signed on behalf of the official unions representing writers, visual artists, composers, dramatic artists and architects, was widely circulated on 29 January.[145] Through such actions as constant harassment by the secret police or public denigration campaigns, the communist authorities managed to obtain the perverse effect of attracting domestic as well as international public attention to the plight of the Chartists. Moreover, Havel, who was already known for his literary talent as playwright and essayist, rose to prominence as the most representative Czech dissident.[146]

In Hungary, the founding of Charter 77 prompted an act of dissent by 34 Hungarian intellectuals, who signed a letter in support of the Charter on 9 January 1977. The essence of Kádár's 'goulash communism' was a policy of 'live and let live', to quote Rudolf L. Tőkés,[147] or of 'repressive tolerance', to use the term coined by Herbert Marcuse.[148] As János Kis observes, beginning in the early 1960s, Hungarian society was offered an 'unwritten social contract', that is, a 'deal of leaving politics and social control to the nomenklatura in exchange for receiving

---

143 Aviezer Tucker, *The Philosophy and Politics of Czech Dissidence from Patočka to Havel* (Pittsburgh, PA: University of Pittsburgh Press, 2000), 86–8.
144 See Ian Willoughby, interview with Martin Palouš, *Radio Prague* (6 January 2017); http://www.radio.cz/en/section/special/charter-77-an-original-signatory-on-communist-czechoslovakias-most-important-protest-movement (accessed 15 February 2021).
145 For an English version of the text, see CHNM, George Mason University, *Making the History of 1989*, 'Czechoslovak Anti-Charter 1977', https://chnm.gmu.edu/1989/archive/files/Anticharter_translation_3947df7081.pdf (accessed 15 March 2021).
146 For a biography of Havel, see John Keane, *Václav Havel: A Political Tragedy in Six Acts* (New York: Basic Books, 2000).
147 Rudolf L. Tőkés, 'Introduction' to idem, ed., *Opposition in Eastern Europe* (London: Macmillan, 1979), xv.
148 Herbert Marcuse, 'Repressive Tolerance', in *A Critique of Pure Tolerance,* Robert Paul Wolff, Barrington Moore, Jr. and Herbert Marcuse (Boston, MA: Beacon Press, 1969), 81–117.

a tolerable margin experiment in the private sphere'.[149] This situation led to the emergence of two main currents of opposition politics, which George Schöpflin identifies as the New Left and the 'para-opposition'.[150]

The New Left, or the reform socialist current, included followers of the Marxist philosopher György Lukács, most of them associated with the so-called 'Budapest School of Marxism', of whom one can mention András Hegedüs, Ágnes Heller, Ferenc Fehér and Mihály Vajda. One of the public gestures of leftist political opposition was the protest letter signed by five Hungarian philosophers in response to the WTO military intervention in Czechoslovakia.[151] In addition, out of the Budapest School's circle, originated many lucid sociological analyses of contemporary Hungarian society, which revealed the flaws of 'really existing socialism'.

'Para-opposition' comprised politicized intellectuals of different convictions, but one can identify two dissident subcultures within, that is, national-populist and urban-liberal. These subcultures originated in two main currents of political thought in modern Hungary, populist and urbanist. The populists, on the one hand, advocated a national 'third way' between East and West, that would develop Hungary on its own terms, to preserve traditional values and foster the development of national culture. The urbanists, on the other hand, advocated the adoption of the Western model of parliamentary democracy, market economy and liberal values.[152] As Máté Szabó points out, the regime was fully aware of the differences between these dissident subcultures:

> The cleavage between the urbanists and the populists from the 1960s onward formed the dominant principle structuring the Hungarian opposition. The communist party leadership likewise differentiated its political strategy towards the opposition along the lines of the two currents, identifying the former as 'the bourgeois' (*polgári*) and the latter as the 'radical nationalists' (*nemzeti radikális*).[153]

The national-populist dissident subculture was represented by populist writers and poets belonging to different generations, such as Gyula Illyés, László Németh, Sándor Csoóri, István Csurka and Zoltán Bíró.[154] The urban-liberal dissident subculture, which led to the emergence of what would be named 'democratic opposition' in the late 1980s, gathered individuals with different ideas, ranging from radical civic activism, focusing on liberal values and issues of human rights, to the *samizdat* culture which emerged in reaction to the communist regime's

---

149 János Kis, 'Between Reform and Revolution: Three Hypotheses About the Nature of the Regime Change', in *Lawful Revolution in Hungary, 1989–94*, eds Béla K. Király and András Bozóki (Boulder, CO: Social Science Monographs, 1995), 44.
150 George Schöpflin, 'Opposition and Para-Opposition: Critical Currents in Hungary, 1968–78', in Tőkés, *Opposition in Eastern Europe*, 142–86.
151 For more on this, see Aleksandar Pavlović and Mark Losoncz, 'Belgrade 1968 Protests and the Post-Eventual Fidelity: Intellectual and Political Legacy of the 1968 Student Protests in Serbia', *Filozofija i društvo* 30, no. 1 (2019): 149–64, http://www.doiserbia.nb.rs/img/doi/0353-5738/2019/0353-57381901149P.pdf (accessed 22 June 2021).
152 Schöpflin warns against an oversimplification of this 'extremely complex debate', Schöpflin, 'Opposition and Para-Opposition', 155.
153 Szabó, 'Hungary', in Pollack and Wielgohs, *Dissent and Opposition in Communist Eastern Europe*, 58.
154 László Kontler, *A History of Hungary: Millennium in Central Europe* (Budapest: Atlantisz, 1999), 462–3; Tőkés, *Hungary's Negotiated Revolution*, 196–7.

monopoly of information. Among the prominent figures of this dissident subculture, one can mention: János Kis, György Bence, György Konrád and Gáspár Miklós Tamás,[155] as well as Gábor Demszky (who became a central figure of *samizdat* culture) and László Rajk Jr.

One should stress that the regime saw in national-populist intellectuals and groups potential fellow-travellers and therefore treated them more leniently, while individuals and groups belonging to the democratic opposition were subject to harassment. Thus, an important moment in the structuring of the urban-liberal dissent was the trial of Miklós Haraszti. As a student, Haraszti held ultra-leftist views, and because of his political activism, he was eventually expelled from university in 1970. Subsequently, he worked for about a year as a worker at the 'Red Star' Tractor Factory in Budapest. In 1972, Haraszti submitted for publication the manuscript of a book titled *Piece-Rate*, which was based on his experience as a worker and addressed, among other things, the issue of dehumanization of industrial workers under state socialism.[156] The authorities found Haraszti's reflections on the situation of industrial workers in Hungary extremely offensive and arrested him in May 1973. The trial attracted unexpected attention both in Hungary and abroad, and many prominent public figures spoke in Haraszti's favour. In 1974, he finally received an eight-month suspended sentence.[157]

In Romania, the most significant collective act of dissent – the so-called 'Goma movement for human rights' – also emerged in response to the establishment of Charter 77. The context in Romania was different from other countries, because here the shift from random terror to targeted repression was accompanied by a cautious distancing from Moscow of the ruling elite. Under Gheorghe Gheorghiu-Dej, the Romanian communists managed to avoid de-Stalinization by adopting a policy based on industrialization and independence. Ceauşescu only adapted the strategy of his predecessor to the post-1968 context and focused on nation-building and modernization. After 1968, the regime was also able to instrumentalize nationalism, which allowed the creation of a relatively enduring focus of identification with the regime and hampered to a certain extent the development of intellectual dissidence. As Cristina Petrescu observes, after August 1968 a major part of the population perceived Ceauşescu as a most prominent 'dissident' because of his alleged anti-Soviet stance.[158]

The movement for human rights was inaugurated in January 1977, when Goma sent a letter of solidarity to the Czech writer Pavel Kohout. Goma also wrote an appeal to the 1977 Helsinki follow-up conference, which was held in Belgrade. This appeal, which became the fundamental document of the movement, demanded that the Ceauşescu regime comply with the provisions of the 1975 Helsinki Accords concerning the observance of human rights. However, apart from writer Ion Negoiţescu and psychiatrist Ion Vianu, no other prominent intellectual supported Goma's actions. Looking back at the movement he initiated, Goma stresses the lack of solidarity displayed by the Romanian writers back in 1977:

> In February–March 1977, of all very good poets, excellent novelists, not to speak of the outstanding Romanian literati, only Ion Negoiţescu understood that 'human

---

155 Falk, *The Dilemmas of Dissidence in East-Central Europe*, 281.
156 Miklós Haraszti, *A Worker in a Workers' State: Piece-Rates in Hungary* (Harmondsworth: Penguin Books, 1977).
157 See Note 82 in Richard Porton, *Film and the Anarchist Imagination* (London: Verso, 1999), 262.
158 Cristina Petrescu, 'Ar mai fi ceva de spus: Despre disidenţa din România lui Ceauşescu' [There would be more to say: On dissidence in Ceauşescu's Romania], afterword to Dan Petrescu and Liviu Cangeopol, *Ce-ar mai fi de spus: Convorbiri libere într-o ţară ocupată*, new and rev. ed. (Bucharest: Editura Nemira, 2000), 319.

rights' ... referred also to writer's rights and ... that exactly the writers should have been the first in a community compelled to defend them.[159]

In a similar vein, Vianu reflects upon the lack of support for the Goma movement:

> Nobody wanted to talk, to expose themselves. Yet, it was not a time of such a violent terror like in the 1950s. One could speak up. True, by taking certain risks. But people must be capable of taking risks. It was not the case.[160]

Approximately 200 individuals eventually signed the appeal authored by Goma. Many of the signatories, however, actually wanted to obtain a passport, the so-called 'Goma passport', in order to emigrate to the West. Such a constellation existed for years in the GDR; there, open and repeated dissent was initially punished by way of disadvantage (i.e. having one fired from their job and/or denying one's children admission to higher education), later by arrest – often with a conviction – and later still, quasi-recognized with a one-way passport to the West.

In Romania, the communist authorities first attempted to persuade Goma to renounce his radical stance. Fellow writers close to the party tried in vain to convince him to abandon his demands. When Goma adamantly refused, an 'outraged citizen', who turned out to be a former boxer on the payroll of the Securitate, attacked him in the street. Goma was eventually imprisoned on 1 April 1977. His arrest, however, caused an uproar in the West. An unrelenting international campaign for Goma's liberation, in which the RFE and the Romanian exiles in Paris played a major role, was launched immediately.

Under mounting international pressure, the communist authorities in Romania released Goma from prison on 6 May 1977. When Goma was liberated, the Securitate had already managed to suppress the movement for human rights that he had initiated. Marginalized by his fellow writers and harassed by the Securitate, Goma left Romania definitively in November 1977 and settled in Paris.[161] Twenty years later, Goma wrote that he had left Romania with his wife, his child, two suitcases and two typewriters.[162]

The Polish oppositionists did not allow themselves to be forced into emigration. Like Goma and Havel, they often encountered conformism, fear or otherwise motivated restraint on the part of the intellectual elites.[163] The contrast between the urban world of the big cities and the provinces was similarly as strong as it was in Hungary, but it did not produce any essential differences – there was no Polish Csurka. On the other hand, the very Polish tradition of 'to fight or not to fight' ('*bić się czy nie bić*') soon led to division and polarization. The KOR, which had already been formed in 1976, focused on an evolutionary transformation of the state in which

---

159 Paul Goma, *Jurnalul unui jurnal, 1997* [A diary's diary, 1997] (Cluj-Napoca: Editura Dacia, 1998), 269.
160 Ion Vianu, *Exercițiu de sinceritate* [An exercise in sincerity] (Iași: Editura Polirom, 2009), 127.
161 Goma wrote extensively on the events of January–April 1977. See Paul Goma, *Culoarea curcubeului '77: Cutremurul oamenilor. Cod "Bărbosul:" Din dosarele Securității, 1957–1977* [The colour of the rainbow '77: People's earthquake – Codename 'bearded man': From the Securitate files, 1957–77] (Iași: Editura Polirom, 2005).
162 Goma, *Jurnalul unui jurnal*, 269.
163 The discussion about the extremely diverse behaviour of the mandarins ('authorities') did not get off the ground in the Polish counter-public until the 1980s. The trigger was the vitriolic comments made by the eternal outsider Piotr Wierzbicki, collected and supplemented in the pamphlet 'Traktat o gnidach' (Wrocław: Oficyna Niepokornych, 1987).

the opposition would use social pressure to reform the regime and take away its monopoly on power in the unforeseeable future. By contrast, KOR's right-wing rival – ROPCiO (Movement for Defence of Human and Civic Rights) – favoured a faster path towards sovereignty and adjective-free (i.e. non-socialist) democracy. In the summer of 1980, it became clear that KOR had chosen the safer path to this future. It benefited from the fact that the initiative to found free trade unions had largely (except in Gdańsk) run aground, but the voluntary willingness of students to take risks, especially in Wrocław, Gdańsk, Cracow, Lublin and Warsaw – estimated at only a few hundred people – had opened up a stream of information and communication that could hardly be surpassed in effectiveness.[164]

Ethnic mobilization

As already shown in Part One, nationalism did not 'freeze' under communist rule. On the contrary, nationalism, understood as a political principle having to do with the control of the state, was instrumentalized – to varying degrees of success – by both the communist regimes in power and by the opposition.[165] In several cases, the forced assimilation of minority groups or ethnic mobilization and conflict were phenomena that triggered various forms of state repression.

Nationalism and ethnic mobilization also triggered state repression, and former Yugoslavia features prominently in this respect, although the nationalist legitimation of political authority was already on the agenda of the communist regimes in neighbouring Romania and Bulgaria. In 1970–71, the Croatian population supported the Croatian party leadership in its demands for greater political and economic autonomy. Beginning in the early 1960s, heated debates were sparked in Yugoslavia concerning the introduction of economic, social and political reforms. From 1965 onwards, the leadership of the LCC (League of Communists of Croatia) became the most vocal in its demands for de-centralization and increased autonomy, as well as for a radical reform of the foreign currency system.[166] Croatia, which produced some 40 per cent of Yugoslavia's earnings from the tourism industry and from revenue by individuals working abroad, wanted to retain a larger share of its foreign currency earnings.[167] In July 1966,

---

164 See, among others, Włodzimierz Borodziej, *Geschichte Polens im 20. Jahrhundert* (München: C.H. Beck, 2010), 360–8; Friszke, *Czas KOR-u*; Andrzej Paczkowski, *Revolution and Counterrevolution in Poland 1980–1989: Solidarity, Martial Law, and the End of Communism in Europe*, trans. Christina Manetti (Rochester, NY: University of Rochester Press, 2015).

165 As John Breuilly notes: 'Nationalism is, above and beyond all else, about politics and that politics is about power. Power, in the modern world, is principally about control of the state. The central task is to relate nationalism to the objectives of obtaining and using state power'. John Breuilly, *Nationalism and the State*, 2nd ed. (Chicago, IL: The University of Chicago Press, 1994), 1. With regard to the relation between ethnic mobilization and political violence, Daniel Chirot and Clark McCauley observe: 'When there are concentrated ethnic minorities within a state who are actually majorities within their own region, and where they have some serious grievances against the dominant state, violent civil war is likely as soon as state control weakens'. Daniel Chirot and Clark McCauley, *Why Not Kill Them All? The Logic and Prevention of Mass Political Murder* (Princeton, NJ: Princeton University Press, 2006), 212; see also, Marcin Zaremba, *Communism – Legitimacy – Nationalism: Nationalist Legitimization of the Communist Regime in Poland* (Berlin: Peter Lang, 2019).

166 Vesna Pešić, 'The War for Ethnic States', in Popov, *The Road to War in Serbia*, 19–23.

167 Ante Batović, *The Balkans in Turmoil: Croatian Spring and the Yugoslav Position Between the Cold War Blocs 1965–1971* (London: LSE IDEAS/LSE Cold War Studies Programme, 2009), 16, https://wikileaks.org/gifiles/attach/128/128054_Croatian%20Spring.pdf (accessed 23 June 2021).

Aleksandar Ranković – the Yugoslav vice-president and head of the secret police (UDBA)[168] – and his key supporters were ousted from their positions in the party and state apparatus. The fall of Ranković, who was perceived as a symbol of centralism and conservatism, was also seen as a victory against the conservative centre and Serbian domination.

National fervour in Croatia reached new heights in 1971 when the population openly supported the demands for greater political and economic autonomy put forward by the Croatian party leaders. The series of events which unfolded in Croatia throughout 1971 have generally been known since as the Croatian Spring. Croatian students also supported the Croatian party leadership: they became increasingly active beginning in April and they took political action by organizing a strike on 23 November, which was observed by students at all the Croatian universities and attended by some 30,000 individuals.[169] The central power under the charge of Tito took resolute action against the Croatian Spring: in December 1971, during the Twenty-First Session of the Presidium of the LCY (League of Communists of Yugoslavia), the leadership of the LCC was accused of promoting dangerous forms of nationalism and liberalism. The suppression of the Croatian Spring was followed by several trials and numerous purges, demotions and forced resignations. In response, mass demonstrations took place in Zagreb in mid-December 1971, during which some 550 individuals, mostly university students, were arrested.[170]

With regard to ethnic mobilization and conflict, a particular situation developed in the Yugoslav province of Kosovo. In this case, particular constitutional arrangements permitted an ethnic minority, which constituted a majority in the region, to repress other ethnic groups while the local authorities turned a blind eye to the matter. From a historical perspective, from the mid-nineteenth century onwards, the relations between Serbs and Albanians were described as a 'pendulum of domination', in which the role of victim switched periodically from one community to another.[171] The provinces of Kosovo and Vojvodina gained increased autonomy due to the amendments to the Yugoslav constitution introduced in 1969 and 1971. The new constitution, adopted in 1974, further enhanced the autonomy of the provinces towards the federal government. In the case of Kosovo, some authors argue, this conducted an 'Albanization' of the province, which also led to discrimination against Serbs and Montenegrins. According to estimates, from 1966 to 1991 roughly 100,000 ethnic Serbians left Kosovo, of whom 75 to 85 per cent decided to move because of pressure and ethnic prejudice.[172] Further research is needed in order to clarify the extent to which the emigration of ethnic Serbs from Kosovo was

---

168 The Yugoslav secret police was generally known by its acronym, which indicated that it originated in the military intelligence, that is, the UDBA (*Uprava Državne Bezbednosti Armije* / State Security Administration of the Army). On Ranković's fall from power, see for instance, Dennison Rusinow, *Yugoslavia: Oblique Insights and Observations*, ed. Gale Stokes (Pittsburgh, PA: University of Pittsburgh Press, 2008), 56–7. See also Central Intelligence Agency, 'Yugoslavia: The Fall of Ranković', *Current Intelligence Weekly – Special Report* (5 August 1966), https://repositories.lib.utexas.edu/handle/2152/79145 (accessed 23 June 2021).

169 Steven L. Burg, *Conflict and Cohesion in Socialist Yugoslavia: Political Decision Making Since 1966* (Princeton, NJ: Princeton University Press, 1983), 149–51. See also Batović, *The Balkans in Turmoil*, 17.

170 Following the repression of the Croatian national movement, 741 individuals were expelled from the party, 131 lost their positions and 280 were forced to resign. See Burg, *Conflict and Cohesion in Socialist Yugoslavia*, 157–8.

171 Lazar Nikolić, 'Ethnic Prejudices and Discrimination: The Case of Kosovo', in *Understanding the War in Kosovo*, eds Florian Bieber and Židas Daskalovski (London: Frank Cass, 2003), 57.

172 Nikolić, 'Ethnic Prejudices and Discrimination', 62–3.

prompted by economic reasons – as the Albanian argument claims,[173] or to what extent it was due to ethnic prejudice – as other authors argue.[174]

Suppression of exile criticism

Political exiles who settled in the West often expressed radical criticism of the communist power in CEE and thus became targets of the respective regimes. Foreign intelligence branches of the communist secret police agencies thoroughly plotted and carried out assassinations against such exiles. The studios of RFE in Munich, Germany, as well as the editors and speakers working for the national desks of RFE, were preferred targets of infiltration and – in a few cases – of assassination attempts and bombings.

Propaganda warfare was a constant feature of the Cold War. Even the spirit of détente did not alleviate much of the fierce struggle fought by the two global superpowers, the United States and Soviet Union, via radio waves. Cold War propaganda warfare also influenced, and in some instances determined, the development of critical stances against the communist regimes in CEE. The message broadcast by the national desks of RFE symbolized truth contradicting communist lies; or, the message of freedom, to put it differently. The authorities were fully aware of the impact the RFE programmes had on the populations living under state socialism. Consequently, the communist regimes strove to contain the spread of the information broadcast by RFE and to suppress the critical voices that spoke from the RFE studios in Munich. One should note that the RFE programmes were broadcast in the languages of Sovietized Europe and were meant to counteract the Soviet propaganda. Apart from being an ideological weapon during Cold War propaganda warfare, RFE managed to keep the hope of liberation and self-determination alive.[175] In the cases of Bulgaria or Romania, because of the lack of a reformist faction within the party or of a structured anti-communist opposition, RFE played a more prominent role in fuelling the population's discontent with the respective regimes. As a consequence, the secret police agencies of these countries organized assassination attempts against the most critical voices in exile.[176]

The assassination of the Bulgarian author and anti-communist dissident Georgi Markov in September 1978 in the centre of London represents one of the most spectacular spy stories of the Cold War. Markov left Bulgaria in 1969, settled in London and worked for different international broadcasting agencies. During the period 1975–78, Markov authored a series of reports on communist Bulgaria, which were critical of the personal rule of Todor Zhivkov. On

---

173 Valon Murati, Blerim Ahmeti, Selatin Kllokoqi and Glauk Konjufca, 'Actors and Processes of Ethno-National Mobilization in Kosovo', Report compiled in the framework of the FP6 project 'Human and Minority Rights in the Life Cycle of Ethnic Conflicts – MIRICO' (Bolzano: European Academy, 2007), 16, http://www.eurac.edu/en/research/autonomies/minrig/Documents/Mirico/Kosovo%20report.pdf (accessed 18 March 2021).

174 On the role of Serbian *ressentiment* in the development of the Kosovo crisis, see Vesna Pešić, 'Serbian Nationalism and the Origins of the Yugoslav Crisis', *Peaceworks*, no. 8 (Washington, DC: United States Institute of Peace, 1996): 14–17, https://www.files.ethz.ch/isn/30963/1996_april_pwks8.pdf (accessed 18 March 2021).

175 As George R. Urban aptly put it, RFE's role was to speak to 'Poles *as* Poles, Czechs *as* Czechs'. George R. Urban, *Radio Free Europe and the Pursuit of Democracy: My War Within the Cold War* (New Haven, CT: Yale University Press, 1997), 2. See also (though more on the 1950s) Melissa Feinberg, *Curtain of Lies: The Battle over Truth in Stalinist Eastern Europe* (New York: Oxford University Press, 2017).

176 Paweł Machcewicz demonstrates subtler ways of fighting the Polish section of RFE in *Poland's War on Radio Free Europe: 1950–1989* (Stanford, CA: Stanford University Press, 2015).

the morning of 7 September 1978, while he was waiting for a bus in central London, he was injected with a miniature metal pellet containing a powerful poison (ricin). The assassination was blamed on the Bulgarian communist secret police, the DS (*Darzhavna Sigurnost*), which was known to be working closely with the KGB. It was believed that the pellet was fired on Markov by an umbrella-gun of special design and thus the case went down in the history of the Cold War as the 'poisoned umbrella case'.[177] The Markov case fuelled heated debates, all the more that a similar assassination attempt was carried out a few days earlier in Paris against another Bulgarian exile, Vladimir Kostov, who nevertheless survived the attempt.[178]

In neighbouring Romania, beginning in the early 1970s, the Securitate was requested to silence the critical voices of the Romanian exiles and the activities of the RFE's Romanian desk.[179] A Securitate document, dated 8 September 1971, shows that the secret police was ordered to find the most appropriate ways to 'annihilate the Romanian desk of RFE'.[180] A vicious attack against an RFE editor was carried out on 18 November 1977 in Paris, when two mercenaries, allegedly hired by the Securitate, assaulted and severely injured Monica Lovinescu. A reputed literary critic and RFE editor, Lovinescu was one of the most powerful voices for Romanians in exile and one of the most prominent personalities involved earlier that year in the international campaign for the liberation of Paul Goma.[181]

Confronting a cross-class alliance

Part Two ends with an analysis of the events of 1980–81 in Poland, which inaugurated a period of great turmoil and which eventually triggered a wave of state repression that was unmatched in the Soviet bloc. After the 1976 working-class protests, the Gierek regime was faced with growing economic problems. Aware of the fact that raising prices would provoke a new wave of social protest, the regime tried hard to avoid any new price increases. However, towards the late 1970s, the state of affairs proved to be increasingly difficult to maintain in the same way. A campaign for 'austerity and unity', which was meant to prepare the population for – in fact modest – food price increases, was initiated in the aftermath of the Eighth Congress of the PUWP (in February 1980).[182]

---

177 Kelly Hignett, 'The Curious Case of the Poisoned Umbrella: The Murder of Georgi Markov', https://thevieweast.wordpress.com/2011/09/09/the-curious-case-of-the-poisoned-umbrella-the-murder-of-georgi-markov (accessed 18 March 2021).

178 On both the Markov and Kostov cases, see R. J. Crampton, *A Concise History of Bulgaria*, 2nd ed. (Cambridge: Cambridge University Press, 2005), 198; and Anthony J. Bertino and Patricia Nolan Bertino, *Forensic Science: Fundamentals and Investigations*, 2nd ed. (Boston: Cengage Learning, 2015), 295.

179 Mihai Pelin, foreword to idem, *Operaţiunile "Meliţa" şi "Eterul:" Istoria Europei Libere prin documente de Securitate* [Operations 'Meliţa' and 'Eterul': The history of Radio Free Europe through Securitate documents] (Bucharest: Editura Albatros, 1999), 8–9.

180 Document 154 (8 September 1971): 'Scrisoarea nr. 34/A-124 din 8 septembrie 1971 privind obiectivul "Meliţa"' [Letter nr 34/A-124 from 8 September 1971 concerning the objective 'Meliţa'], in *Securitatea: Structuri-cadre, obiective şi metode*, vol. II, 1967–1989 [The Securitate: Structures-cadres, objectives and methods], eds Florica Dobre, Elis Neagoe-Pleşa and Liviu Pleşa (Bucharest: Editura Enciclopedică & CNSAS, 2006), 409.

181 It seems that the Securitate had orders to incapacitate her physically, but not to kill her. For Lovinescu's own recollections of the assault, see Monica Lovinescu, *La apa vavilonului, 1960–1980* [By the waters of Babylon] (Bucharest: Editura Humanitas, 2001), 247–52.

182 David S. Mason, *Public Opinion and Political Change in Poland, 1980–1982* (Cambridge: Cambridge University Press, 1985), 57.

Edward Gierek dismissed the former prime minister. In July, the new government tried to raise the prices of some meats and sausages. Strikes broke out almost immediately in various parts of the country – the largest in Lublin – which lasted the whole month. Time and again, the authorities managed to persuade the individual workforces to return to work with wage increases, but the wave of protests did not abate. Even before an agreement was signed in one plant, a strike broke out in the next. The economically suicidal approach of the state-owned subcontractors to get away with chequebook crisis management in individual cases proved to be simply unbelievable naivety in the view of the meanwhile lively flow of information via the illegal press and RFE.

After a few weeks of unrest, the Gdańsk Lenin shipyard went on strike in mid-August.[183] This time, the pattern of working-class protest was different. The workers at the shipyard engaged in a non-violent, around-the-clock sit-in, to which almost 500 companies from Gdańsk, Gdynia and the surrounding region joined within days. Together they formed the MKS (Inter-Factory Strike Committee), which was intended to enable communication among, and ultimately unite, the workplaces where strikes were declared.[184]

Given the non-violent nature of the strike, the communist authorities had to employ a different strategy to allay the protest. In spite of regime's efforts of sealing off the protest area, the strike spread to other workplaces on the Polish Baltic Coast; soon the Szczecin MKS represented 100 enterprises. On 18 August 1980, the representatives of the Gdańsk strikers issued a list of 21 demands. An essential point on the list of demands was the request to establish 'free unions, independent from the party and from employers, according to the 87th Convention of the International Organization of Labour, ratified by the Polish People's Republic'.[185] As Jadwiga Staniszkis notes, by 28 August 1980, there were already four MKSs established in Poland, representing over 800 workplaces in Gdańsk (with more than 600 enterprises), Szczecin (over 200 enterprises), Wrocław and Elbląg.[186]

A situation that had no precedent whatsoever in the Soviet bloc developed in Poland: the working-class rebelled against the power elite of the workers' state without attempting to change – at least formally and legally – the 'socialist order' in the country. The authorities had no pretext for an intervention in force. Eventually, on 31 August 1980, the government was compelled to subscribe to the workers' demands and a formal agreement was signed in Gdańsk. In Szczecin, a similar agreement had already been signed the previous day, but this scene – unlike the signing in the Lenin shipyard – was not broadcast live on television. Lech Wałęsa, the electrician who emerged as the leader of the Gdańsk strikers, became the national leader of Solidarity, the first independent trade union established under a communist regime. The following month, on 17 September, the nucleus of determined strikers from the Lenin Shipyards in Gdańsk saw themselves transformed into a large independent trade union with approximately 3 million members in some 3,500 workplaces. By the end of 1980, Solidarity had up to 9 million members in a country in which the total active population amounted to around 17 million people.[187] The situation in Poland had no precedent in the Soviet bloc. An independent free trade union was born and was about to create a sort of alternative society.

---

183 Borodziej, *Geschichte Polens*, 359–60.
184 Mason, *Public Opinion and Political Change*, 90.
185 See the complete list of demands in Jadwiga Staniszkis, *Poland's Self-Limiting Revolution* (Princeton, NJ: Princeton University Press, 1984), 43–5.
186 Ibid., 6.
187 Laba, *The Roots of Solidarity*, 99.

Solidarity used exclusively peaceful means: in the 16 months of their legal existence, no windowpane was broken for political reasons. Rather, they put pressure on the authorities by creating a counter-public sphere in which the grievances of 'real existing socialism' were discussed and denounced.

The party could not tolerate this practice, which was incompatible with the unwritten laws of state socialism. Under pressure from the Soviet Union to preserve the 'socialist order' in their country, the communists in military uniform seized power and proclaimed martial law on 13 December 1981. Martial law defused some of the tensions that had emerged from the 'self-limiting revolution', as Staniszkis called it. It also demonstrated that the communists had ultimately given up on their claim to lead society to a brighter future, and that repression was their last resort.

Political violence and state repression in Sovietized CEE: Part Three, 1981–89 (Dragoş Petrescu)

The second part of this chapter (1968–81) was inaugurated by a particular event of the utmost significance at the Soviet bloc level, that is, the Soviet-led military intervention in Czechoslovakia. Interestingly enough, the third part of this chapter (1981–89) will be inaugurated by an event of similar importance, that is, the imposition of martial law in Poland on 13 December 1981. The year 1989 is the other chronological milestone of this part, and marks not only the end of the time interval addressed in this section, but also the end of the communist rule in Central and Eastern Europe. Thus, part three of this chapter will put a special emphasis on the crucial events mentioned above, that is, martial law in Poland and its aftermath, and the regime changes of 1989. In terms of state repression, the 1989 events in Romania deserve particular attention as it was only here that the collapse of the communist regime was accompanied by violence and bloodshed, and thus contradicted the non-violent character of the 1989 regime changes in Poland, Hungary, East Germany, Czechoslovakia and Bulgaria.

Moreover, one should note that the actions by individuals or groups which triggered state repression after 1981 were quite similar to those before. There were, however, some exceptions to this general trend. For instance, in Romania, the Ceauşescu regime adopted a strict anti-abortion stance that led to an increase in the number of illegal and unsafe abortions. The number of women who died or suffered long-term health complications because of unsafe abortion is yet to be established.[188] Another aspect relates to the number of deaths that resulted from attempts to illegally cross the national border. East Germany and Romania seem the most notorious cases in this respect, although for the time being, the East German case is better researched.[189]

---

188 For more on this, see Gail Kligman, *The Politics of Duplicity: Controlling Reproduction in Ceausescu's Romania* (Berkeley, CA: University of California Press, 1998).

189 See Table 1 in Hans-Hermann Hertie and Maria Nooke, *The Victims at the Berlin Wall, 1961– 1989: Findings of a Research Project by the Center for Research on Contemporary History Potsdam and the Berlin Wall Memorial Site and Documentation Center* (Potsdam/Berlin, November 2013), 4. On the Romanian case see William Totok, '"Fenomenul frontierist" – Un capitol uitat din istoria comunismului românesc' ['The border crossing phenomenon': a forgotten chapter in the history of Romanian communism] (16 March 2009), *Deutsche Welle*, http://www.dw.com/ro/fenomenul-frontierist-un-capitol-uitat-din-istoria-comunismului-rom%C3%A2nesc/a-4100952 (accessed 19 March 2021).

State socialism

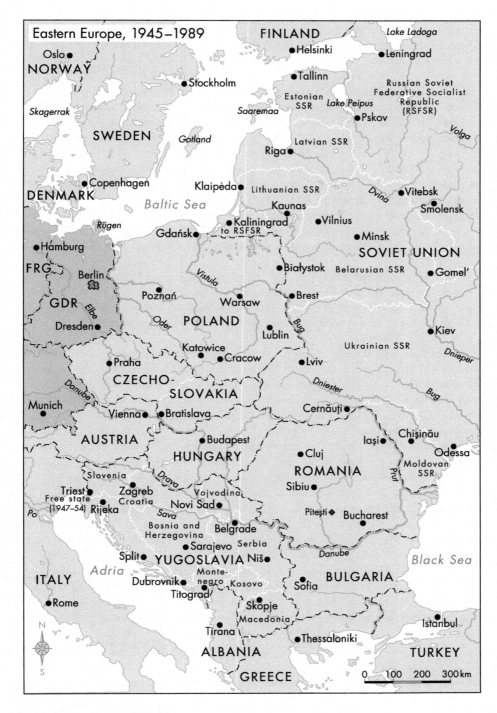

Map 5.1 Eastern Europe, 1945–89

Martial law in Poland

Solidarity has been approached and analyzed primarily as a social movement that transformed Polish society. As Michael D. Kennedy observes:

> It was the 'innovations' of occupation strikes, solidarity strikes, inter-enterprise strike committees, independent trade unions and national solidarity that enabled the movement Solidarity to be born and cause a major, if temporary, transformation of Soviet type society.[190]

According to Alain Touraine et al., Solidarity's initial success was due to the self-imposition of three strategic limits to its action: (1) the leading role of the party in the state was explicitly guaranteed by the Gdańsk agreement; (2) Poland remained within the socialist camp; and (3) trade union demands were to be moderated because of the economic crisis.[191] Others saw the newly born free trade union as 'an association of state workers' who rebelled against their sole employer, that is, the communist state. As a Solidarity leader observes:

> Poland was as homogeneous ethnically and religiously as never before; and homogeneous materially as well from the point of life aims: 'Workers of a state-owned enterprise.' Solidarity emerged out of this homogeneity of human experience. It was an association of state workers who rose up against their state employer.[192]

The time of Solidarity as a sort of alternative society came to an end on 13 December 1981. Nearly all members of the leadership of Solidarity were already arrested on the night of 13 December so that the movement that seemed so powerful in the prior few months suddenly appeared to be headless, so to speak. Since the regional structures had also been shattered that night, only the cells on the lowest level, i.e. the factory level, were able to react to the declaration of martial law. On 14 December, 200 to 260 of the many thousands of businesses decided in favour of the strike. The strike proved to be an utterly inefficient weapon in the face of the military machine of the state. The military was well prepared in advance and repression was carried out swiftly and with precision. Several thousand more Solidarity leaders were arrested in the days following, and communication lines (telephone and telex) had been interrupted since the previous day. On 16 December, only 58 factories were still on strike; on 19 December, only 29; and by 21 December, only 3 remained. These last bastions were all located in the Silesian coal mines. Ultimately, the authorities made use of deadly force in order to suppress the protesters. In the Silesian coalmining basin, the final strike lasted until 28 December 1981 (the Piast coalmine). A tragic episode, known as the Wujek massacre, took place on 17 December 1981 at the Wujek coalmine where troops intervened and fired at the miners, killing nine of them. With regard to the significance of the Wujek massacre, Andrzej Paczkowski observes: 'The Wujek mine massacre was a watershed, it can be argued, because not

---

190 Michael D. Kennedy, *Professionals, Power and Solidarity in Poland: A Critical Sociology of Soviet-Type Society* (Cambridge: Cambridge University Press, 1991), 56.
191 Alain Touraine, François Dubet, Michel Wieviorka and Jan Strzelecki, *Solidarity: The Analysis of a Social Movement: Poland 1980–1981* (Cambridge: Cambridge University Press, 1983), 179.
192 Conversation with Jacek Merkel in Michael Szporer, *Solidarity: The Great Workers Strike of 1980* (Lanham, MD: Lexington Books, 2012), 114.

a single new strike broke out after the tragedy – no one rose up in protest against the crime committed against these workers'.[193]

With regard to the forms of state repression employed by the Jaruzelski regime, one can divide the period December 1981–January 1989 into four major time intervals: (1) the martial law period, 13 December 1981–21 July 1983 (from the declaration of martial law up to its lifting); (2) July 1983–July 1984 (from the partial amnesty of 1983 to the general amnesty of 1984); (3) July 1984–September 1986 (a period of increased control of society by the regime, during which the number of political prisoners rose again); and (4) September 1986–January 1989 (starting with a genuine general amnesty for political prisoners for the first time: a period of increased social mobilization, culminating in the wave of strikes in the summer of 1988 which contributed to the historic decision of the PUWP to initiate talks with Solidarity).

During the period of martial law (13 December 1981 to 21 July 1983), some 7,400 people were sentenced for 'crimes related to resisting martial law', of whom around 5,700 were sentenced by military courts. Under martial law, the Polish authorities made extensive use of the instrument of internment in isolation centres, solely on the basis of 'legitimate grounds for suspicion'. All in all, there were 50 or 60 isolation centres in which, by December 1982, a total of 9,736 individuals had been interned.[194] The term 'internment' came close to this kind of deprivation of liberty: building complexes that were still used as holiday homes in the summer served as isolation centres. There was no beating or other physical abuse. There was no forced labour, but there was a separate, almost luxurious isolation centre for some 400 women.[195]

The inmates received packages of clothing and food, which were apparently insufficient and simply abominable, at least in the first weeks. Above all, however, an institution that had been taken for granted in the interwar period and was based on customary law returned: the community of the inmates. Since there were plenty of prominent intellectuals among the internees, there were seminar-like events held in some isolation centres on various questions of human and social sciences.

This remarkably civil treatment of the de facto prisoners, in comparison with Stalinism, also served the former party leader and some of his closest collaborators who were interned on 13 December. The public prosecutor never filed a bill of indictment against the scapegoats that could be tried in court. The state socialist military dictatorship also refrained from show trials. In this respect, too, the Stalinist patterns of repression had had their day.[196]

Solidarity was interdicted and subsequently outlawed in October 1982. Some of the most prominent leaders of Solidarity and the KOR were arrested, and after a period of internment, were declared 'suspects under arrest'. The authorities wanted to prove that both the KOR and Solidarity were in fact subversive organizations aiming to overthrow the existing political order

---

193 Paczkowski, *Revolution and Counterrevolution*, 90.
194 Andrzej Swidlicki, *Political Trials in Poland 1981–1986* (Beckenham: Croom Helm, 1988), 27. Regarding the number of people interned or sentenced for resisting martial law, see Paczkowski, *Revolution and Counterrevolution*, 99 and 104.
195 A total of 1,008 women were interned on 23 December 1981, i.e. more than 10% of the total number of those detained without a court order. The isolation centre at Gołdap mentioned here was previously owned by the state television network. This tele-station is said to have often referred to the allegedly luxurious internment conditions in Gołdap. An investigation of this campaign, which on the one hand emphasized a particularly humane image of those in power, and on the other hand was intended to arouse the envy of millions of working women, is still pending.
196 Although many personal stories are recorded, research – strangely enough – has been less interested in this episode. Even in the voluminous *Encyklopedia Solidarności* (the fourth volume is scheduled for publication in 2020), there is a remarkably short article devoted to internment.

in Poland. After being delayed for nearly two and a half years, the trial of the most prominent 11 'suspects' – advisers und members of the National Commission of Solidarity – was terminated through the amnesty granted by the regime in July 1984.

At the beginning, KOR was not much larger than *Charta 77*. As already mentioned, drawing from a broad network of student circles and intellectuals, it developed into a mass movement within just a few months and spawned further affiliate organizations like the Flying University (*Towarzystwo Kursów Naukowych*) and the Helsinki commission as well as competing oppositionist circles on the right; these would form the organizational backbone of Solidarity. In Poland in 1982, the authorities were confronted with the serious problem of the approximately 10,000 internees during the initial phase of martial law, from whom it was generally difficult to expect a conversion to state socialism. Jaruzelski found the Cuban example worthy of emulation even before 13 December 1981: Fidel Castro had allowed around 125,000 people to legally leave the country (to the USA) in 1980 (so-called *marielitos*); as part of this operation, the regime had released thousands of criminals from prison to get them out of the country. Jaruzelski followed suit. In March 1982, the Polish government announced that internees would be allowed to leave the country. Internally, a fast-track procedure was introduced to process applications from this group of people. Like in Cuba, criminals also benefited from the campaign which was politically motivated: 'It was sufficient', a former policeman recalled,

> to express the will to permanently leave the country and state that you were a criminal. The passport department checked with the criminal department whether the person in question actually appeared on the register. If this was the case, he was given the passport.[197]

The 'export of criminals' probably proceeded more smoothly than the export of opponents of the regime. Only slightly over 2,200, i.e. just over 20 per cent of the internees (until 1988) filled out the relevant form. Without exception, the most prominent rejected the 'offer', which was supposed to isolate them from underground Solidarity and stigmatize them as quasi-deserters. As eloquent as ever, Adam Michnik, who had been in custody for two years, came forward. On 10 December 1983, he wrote an 'open' letter to the Minister of the Interior, which was soon made public by RFE and the underground press.

According to Michnik, he had learned in November that the recipient of the letter had publicly confronted him 'with a rather curious choice':

> either I shall be given the chance to spend Christmas on the Côte d'Azur as a free man, or I would have to face trial and many years in prison. You assured me that after the trial, once 'the authorities will have swallowed this frog', my leaving the country will be out of the question.[198]

With this 'offer', the Minister of the Interior had proved that the defendant Adam Michnik had no chance of a fair trial: the verdict was already established, despite the lack of credible evidence:

---

197 Stola, *Kraj bez wyjścia?* 317.
198 The English translation quoted here appeared in January 1984 in Information Centre for Polish Affairs, London, ed., *Uncensored Poland News Bulletin* 2, no. 84 (26.01.1984): 14–18, here 14–15. The authors thank Eugeniusz Smolar, one of the editors of the bulletin, for providing the typescript.

You admit that the purpose of the punitive procedure is not to see that justice is done, but to get rid of embarrassing political opponents.
I am of the same opinion.
From here onwards, however, we begin to differ. I think namely that:

- To admit to such open disregard of the law, one has to be an idiot;
- To offer a man, held in prison for two years, the Côte d'Azur in exchange for his moral suicide, one has to be a swine;
- To believe that I could accept such a proposal is to consider every man to be a police henchman.[199]

Michnik continued by referring to the collective personality of the police henchmen. It is clear that the regime needed the images of oppositionists in the West, where they taste capitalist luxuries, in order to present themselves as noble liberals and to make Poles realize that even the leaders of Solidarity have

> lost faith in a democratic Poland. You need it, above everything else, to improve your opinion of yourselves, to be able to say with relief 'After all they are not better than I am'. For you are worried by the fact that there are people for whom the thought of Poland brings to mind not a ministerial chair, but a prison cell, who prefer Christmas in investigative detention to a holiday on the Côte d'Azur.
> You do not really believe that such people exist.[200]

And that was precisely why the Minister of the Interior publicly designated the imprisoned members of the opposition as 'idiots', and 'fanatics' since, as Michnik claims, 'we prefer to stay in prison to rambling along Paris boulevards'. Michnik continues:

> After all, not one of you would hesitate, given such a choice! You cannot think of us otherwise, for that would make you face – if only for a brief moment – the truth about yourselves. The truth that you are a vindictive, dishonourable swine. The truth that if there even was a spark of decency in your hearts – you have long buried it in that brutal and dirty struggle for power which you wage among yourselves. And, being knaves, you want to drag us down to your level. Well – I am going to deny you that pleasure.[201]

Not all of them were as eloquent as Michnik. Nevertheless, the vast majority remained in the country. The ambitious campaign thus ultimately failed to meet its goal: by 1988, only 2,119 former internees, 613 other oppositionists and 319 criminals were to leave the country.[202]

A comprehensive investigation of the complex issues related to repression and resistance in Poland during the period December 1981–January 1989 would go beyond the scope of this section. The above figures include tens of thousands of persecutees who were never arrested but suffered nonetheless through deprivation and humiliation.

---

199 Ibid., 16.
200 Ibid.
201 Ibid., 17.
202 The rest of the nearly 4,400 emigrants were family members. Stola, *Kraj bez wyjścia?* 315–17, 321–2.

Curiously enough, under martial law, Poles enjoyed much more freedom than their neighbours: travel to the West soon reached numbers comparable to the late 1970s. In 1979, the party state allowed nearly 409,000 private trips to Western countries. After the decline in the number of such journeys during martial law (less than 169,000 in 1982), 417,000 journeys to the West were permitted as early as 1984. The corresponding numbers increased in the following years.[203] The state was not concerned with private conversations and allowed official festivals of alternative music to take place, which was not the case in the neighbouring states; samizdat flourished like never before and the same applied for the valuta with respect to the black and grey markets.

The official statements announcing the number of illegal activities suppressed by the regime can give an idea about the extent of the opposition networks in Poland. In 1986, for instance, the Minister of Internal Affairs, General Czesław Kiszczak, announced that the authorities had dissolved some 1,600 illegal groups, discovered around 1,200 printing locations and confiscated approximately 700 printing machines.[204] The minister knew, of course, that his apparatus had only crushed part of the opposition. The most important milieu, grouped around Lech Wałęsa, represented an alternative option and an alternative public sphere which continued to pose a challenge to state power, even more so after the general amnesty in that same year.

Apart from the special case of Poland under martial law, some of the major forms of state repression analyzed for the period 1960–81 were also employed during the period 1981–89. Let us examine these in the order of their enumeration.

Working-class protests

With the exception of Poland, during the last decade of communist rule, violent working-class revolts occurred only in Romania, where the economic crisis forced many categories of workers to think in terms of biological survival. The working-class uprisings in Motru (October 1981) and Brașov (November 1987) were reminiscent of the 1953 uprising in East Berlin or the Polish working-class revolts of 1956, 1970 and 1976. The October 1981 uprising occurred in the Motru basin in Gorj county and was provoked by the food rationing measures introduced by Decree 313 of 17 October 1981.[205] Bread, a staple food for miners and their families, was rationed at 400 grams per person in the decree. The news that each worker would receive such a small daily ration sparked the uprising on 19 October 1981. The miners preparing to enter their second shift refused to go to work; they waited outside for their co-workers from the first shift to finish work and join them. After a while, the strikers started shouting slogans such as: 'We want bread!' or 'Ceaușescu – RCP [Romanian Communist Party], our bread, where is it?'[206] In spite of efforts to appease them, the protest turned violent: miners marched to the town of Motru, the administrative centre of the area, and stormed official buildings. One of the witnesses, a Militia officer at the time, remembers that the protesters brought a blackboard from a nearby grammar school, on which they wrote different slogans. One of the slogans was 'Down with communism!' which the witness had never encountered before during a protest action.[207] Repression was quick and resolute. The violent confrontation between the riot

---

203 Stola, *Kraj bez wyjścia?* 486–7.
204 Ibid., 13–14.
205 Gheorghe Gorun, *Rezistența la comunism: Motru '981* [Resistance to communism: Motru 1981] (Cluj-Napoca: Editura Clusium, 2005), 51–101.
206 Gorun, *Rezistența la comunism*, 58.
207 Liviu Bălănescu's testimony in Gorun, *Rezistența la comunism*, 61.

police supported by militia and Securitate agents and the angry crowds lasted the whole night. Numerous arrests were made but, in spite of the violence and destruction of 'socialist property', only nine workers were sentenced to jail. During the 1981 Motru uprising, the rebellious miners shouted, 'Down with Ceaușescu!' which marked a change in attitude regarding the secretary general of the RCP.[208] While back in 1977 the miners in the Jiu Valley believed that Ceaușescu would comply with their requests and consequently demanded to negotiate with him directly, those in Motru considered him responsible for the food crisis in Romania.

A similar pattern of protest action, including the way it was quelled by the communist authorities, can be observed in the case of the Brașov workers protest of 15 November 1987. This working-class protest also turned into a violent anti-Ceaușescu revolt. Workers of the tractor plant, joined by a significant number of city dwellers, marched to the county party headquarters, shouting 'Down with Ceaușescu!'[209] Protesters entered the building, threw furniture and office equipment outside and set fire to them; a similar scenario was repeated at the People's Council building. The repression was quick and ruthless. The crowd was dispersed by special intervention troops (i.e. riot police). Subsequently, the Securitate arrested many workers of whom eventually 61 received varying terms in prison ranging from 6 months to 3 years.[210] Although the suppression of protest was brutal, no protester was killed.

Student unrest

The main sources of student unrest in the 1980s originated in problems concerning both the living and studying conditions in universities, as well as such major concerns as minority rights. In the midst of a deep economic crisis unmatched within the Soviet bloc (with the possible exception of Albania), protests against the living and studying conditions in universities took place in communist Romania during the 1980s. On 17 February 1987, in the city of Iași, a few hundred students marched from the university campus towards the downtown area shouting, 'We want [electric] lighting to learn, and water to wash ourselves!' The non-violent demonstration, which was somewhat reminiscent of the student protests of 1968, lasted for several hours. Because the demonstration was non-violent, the students who took part received only administrative warnings.[211] Nevertheless, the student protest in Iași revealed that the population was deeply affected by the poor economic policies of the Ceaușescu regime.

In Kosovo, students emerged as major actors in the process of ethnic mobilization in the early 1980s.[212] As mentioned in the previous section, after the amendments to the Yugoslav constitution were introduced in 1969 and 1971, a new constitution was adopted in 1974, which further enhanced the autonomy of the provinces towards the federal government. In

---

208 Gorun, *Rezistența la comunism*, 89–90.
209 Dennis Deletant, *Ceaușescu and the Securitate: Coercion and Dissent in Romania, 1965–1989* (London: Hurst, 1995), 250.
210 On the prison sentences, see Romulus Rusan, ed., *O zi de toamnă, cândva … 15 Noiembrie 1987, Brașov* [A day in autumn, once … 15 November 1987, Brașov] (Bucharest: Fundația Academia Civică, 2004), 101–21.
211 See Cătălin Hopulele, 'Revolta studenților din 1987 putea să aducă revoluția cu doi ani mai devreme' [The student revolt of 1987 could have brought about the revolution two years earlier], *Opinia studențească* (Iași), 23 February 2014, http://www.opiniastudenteasca.ro/informare/honoris-fara-causa/revolta-studentilor-din-1987-putea-sa-aduca-revolutia-cu-doi-ani-mai-devreme.html (accessed 24 March 2021).
212 Murati, Ahmeti, Kllokoqi and Konjufca, 'Actors and Processes of Ethno-National Mobilization', 7 and 12.

the case of Kosovo, the adoption of the new constitution led to an acceleration of the process of national awakening. In the spring of 1981, students at the University of Pristina engaged in a series of protests against the studying conditions at the university, in particular, regarding the quality of food and the accommodation in dormitories. The protest, which lasted from 11 March until 3 April, degenerated into rioting and clashes with police. Moreover, towards the end of March, the initial protest evolved into an ethno-political one, during which some of the protesters asked that Kosovo be granted the status of republic, while others went even further and requested unification with Albania. Estimates put the number of victims to 11 people killed and 57 injured, while 22 individuals were arrested. The 1981 revolt in Kosovo prompted the Yugoslav authorities to declare a state of emergency in the province for the first time in the post-war period, which opened a period of severe crisis between the Serbs and Albanians.[213]

Polish student protest remained rife, particularly in Cracow throughout the 1980s, which regularly resulted in almost ritual clashes with the riot police. Another, more artistic kind of dissent arose in Wrocław in 1985. The Orange Alternative started to organize street happenings, against which the police could hardly intervene without making a fool of themselves; the slogans were sometimes political, but more often, they were absurd. They often parodied official rituals. For example, on the 60th anniversary of the October Revolution in 1987, the Orange Revolution (signed in this instance as the 'Council of People's Commissars') invited people to a happening under the title 'Pravda [written in Cyrillic] will liberate us'. Trotsky was honoured with Lenin in one sentence and participants were asked to bring dogs with a red ribbon on a leash, because the subsequent dog show would be under the motto 'Dogs for the Revolution'.[214]

Acts of dissent

During the period 1981–89 – very much like in the previous period – dissidents were the subjects of public humiliation, harassment by the secret police or long periods of detention without receiving proper trials. In some cases, individuals identified as particularly dangerous opponents of the regime were assassinated or died under suspicious circumstances while in detention. A telling example in this respect is the gruesome murder of the pro-Solidarity priest Jerzy Popiełuszko. The curate of the Church of St. Stanisław Kostka in Warsaw had been a target of the secret police for years because of the pro-Solidarity messages that he included in his sermons. For instance, in a sermon delivered in May 1984 he stated: 'Solidarity remains a glorious word to which millions of Poles attach their hopes and desires'. In August that same year, speaking about the significance of the birth of Solidarity he said, 'Solidarity, born in August 1980, was not only a union … it was the striving of the whole nation for truth, justice and

---

213 Patrick F. R. Artisien and R. A. Howells, 'Yugoslavia, Albania and the Kosovo Riots', *The World Today* 37, no. 11 (November 1981): 419. See also Zachariah Henry Claybaugh, 'The 1981 Kosovar Uprising: Nation and Facework', MA Thesis, University of Illinois at Urbana-Champaign (2013), https://www.ideals.illinois.edu/bitstream/handle/2142/44144/Zachariah_Claybaugh.pdf?sequence=1 (accessed 24 March 2021). On the rapid population growth among the Albanian minority, see Central Intelligence Agency, Directorate of Intelligence, 'Yugoslavia: A Growing Albanian Minority', 9 August 1985, https://www.cia.gov/readingroom/print/1550693 (accessed 22 June 2021).
214 See the trilingual, lavishly illustrated volume, Waldemar Fydrych and Bronisław Misztal, eds, *Pomarańczowa Alternatywa – Orange Alternative – Die Orange Alternative: Rewolucja Krasnoludków – Revolution of Dwarves – Revolution der Zwerge* (Wrocław: Wydawnictwo Pomarańczowa Alternatywa, 2008).

State socialism

freedom'.[215] On 19 October 1984, Father Popiełuszko was kidnapped; he was beaten half to death and then drowned by three secret police officers later that day.

At that time, he was probably the most famous opposition cleric in Poland next to Pope John Paul II. Nevertheless, the murderers, strangely enough, had made no effort to cover their tracks and they were arrested on 23 October by their colleagues in the secret police. Four days later, the Minister of the Interior publicly admitted that Father Popiełuszko had been kidnapped by officers of the secret police. What followed was unique in several respects. On 3 November more than 100,000 people (according to other figures, much more) participated in the funeral. The priest's grave, which lie on the grounds of the St. Stanisław Kostka Church, immediately became a freely accessible site of pilgrimage, where a state socialist crime was almost publicly commemorated. As early as 27 December, the trial against the three officers of the Security Service and their immediate superiors was opened. The pressure from the public was so strong that the negotiations were broadcast live on the state radio broadcasting – a process unimaginable in the history of the so-called Eastern bloc. The prosecutor unsuccessfully tried to turn the trial into an indictment of the Roman Catholic priesthood, which was alleged to be deeply involved in illegal activities of the opposition, as well as in customs and tax evasions, thereby ridiculing the Party State. The defendants were found guilty and sentenced to between 14 and 25 years of imprisonment.

Those who commissioned the murderers were never found, and the distrust of the Jaruzelski regime against its own political police (whose representatives had disavowed his cooperative line towards the church) led to the dismissal of about 600 employees – including several of the generalship – from the state security ranks. This resulted in uncertainty within the apparatus, which was hardly measurable in figures and reports. Such uncertainty was fostered with the creation of an internal anti-corruption department (*Zarząd Ochrony Funkcjonariuszy*), which supervised the conduct of state security and police officers.

As a general remark, opponents of the communist regimes benefited from some protection against the repressive measures employed by the authorities if their cases were known in the West, and organizations such as RFE or Amnesty International organized campaigns to support them. Many courageous acts of opposition simply passed unnoticed in the West because their authors were unable to make their actions known abroad. In a number of cases, the fact that information about various gestures of defiance against the communist regimes did not reach the West had dire consequences for their authors. The tragic fate of Gheorghe Ursu, a construction engineer from Romania, illustrates this aspect. Ursu was a critical intellectual who kept a private diary in which he also recorded critical remarks on the political situation in Romania and the ruling Ceaușescu couple. His diary was accidentally discovered by some colleagues, who read it and informed the Securitate about its content. Eventually, Ursu was imprisoned in September 1985. While in custody, he was beaten to death and died in November 1985. Unfortunately, Ursu's family and friends did not transmit information about his arrest to the West and therefore international organizations could not intervene for his release.[216]

---

215 Swidlicki, *Political Trials in Poland*, 304–5.
216 Cristina Petrescu, *From Robin Hood to Don Quixote: Resistance and Dissent in Communist Romania* (Bucharest: Editura Enciclopedică, 2013), 348; on gender and dissent, see idem, 'A Genderless Protest: Women Confronting Romanian Communism', *Analele Universității București – Științe Politice* XVI, no. 2 (2014): 79–102.

Ethnic mobilization

Repressive actions against minorities (ethnic, religious or sexual) did take place under communist rule throughout CEE. Nevertheless, the violent campaign of forced assimilation of the Turkish minority in communist Bulgaria, launched by the Zhivkov regime in the mid-1980s, rather came as a surprise. By that time, Western democracies were more concerned with the policies aimed at slowly and quietly assimilating the Hungarian minority in Romania – devised by the Ceaușescu regime beginning in the late 1960s – or they were concerned with the growing ethnic tensions in the Yugoslav province of Kosovo. In Bulgaria, on the backdrop of a structural regime crisis, the leadership of the BCP devised a set of nationalizing policies and practices in the mid-1980s aimed at assimilating the largest historic national minority in Bulgaria, the Turks. At the time, the Turkish minority comprised between 830,000 and 960,000 individuals, and thus amounted to over 10 per cent of the country's total population.

The most radical nationalizing measure taken by the Zhivkov regime, initiated during the winter of 1984–85, was the campaign of changing ethnic Turkish names into Bulgarian, or Slavic names.[217] The 'renaming campaign' was part of the so-called 'revival process', which also sought to limit Islamic rituals and restrict the use of the Turkish language. A key element of the campaign was ethno-politically motivated violence: those who opposed it were imprisoned or sent to labour camps. According to an estimate by Amnesty International, more than 100 ethnic Turks were killed during the campaign.[218] Internationally, the 'revival process' stirred widespread outrage – especially among Muslim countries – and considerably damaged relations with neighbouring Turkey.

The 1984–85 campaign of forced assimilation of the ethnic Turks in Bulgaria led to organized, non-violent resistance by members of the Turkish minority. Thus, in the summer of 1985, philosopher Ahmed Dogan established an organization for the defence of human rights called the Turkish National Liberation Movement, which numbered at the moment of its founding some 200 members. Dogan's initiative was rooted in the Bulgarian Turkish community's pressing need to organize itself in order to resist the process of forced assimilation. The Zhivkov regime, however, reacted in force and Dogan was sentenced to 12 years in prison in 1986.[219]

In March–April 1989, unrest grew among ethnic Turks, who demanded to be able to use their Muslim names, and to be allowed to leave the country and settle in Turkey. Towards the end of May, violent protests occurred in several Bulgarian districts, such as Shumen, Varna and Razgrad, and resulted in several people killed and many others wounded. In the aftermath of the violent events of May 1989, some 10,000 members of the Turkish minority were expelled from Bulgaria. Subsequently, the communist regime in Sofia decided to allow the emigration of the ethnic Turks from Bulgaria.[220] As a matter of fact, the Zhivkov regime had earlier, on the basis of an agreement it signed with Turkey in 1968, allowed the emigration of ethnic Turks for the purpose of reunifying families. Consequently, over the 10-year period of the agreement, some 130,000 ethnic Turks left Bulgaria and settled in Turkey.[221] In contrast, the emigration

---

217 Maria N. Todorova, 'Improbable Maverick or Typical Conformist? Seven Thoughts on the New Bulgaria', in *Eastern Europe in Revolution*, ed. Ivo Banac (Ithaca, NY: Cornell University Press, 1992), 154–5.
218 Todorova, 'Improbable Maverick', 155.
219 Ibid., 166–7.
220 Dimitrina Petrova, 'Bulgaria', in Pollack and Wielgohs, *Dissent and Opposition in Communist Eastern Europe*, 161–84, here 170.
221 Crampton, *A Concise History of Bulgaria*, 199.

in the aftermath of the violent events in the spring of 1989 exceeded all calculations by both Bulgarian and Turkish governments. During the period May–August 1989, some 350,000 people left the country for neighbouring Turkey. It is also true that because of the treatment emigrants received in Turkey, the flow of migration was reversed during the period August–December 1989, when approximately 155,000 ethnic Turks returned to Bulgaria.[222]

Widespread concern with environmental issues grew rapidly in Bulgaria due to the Chernobyl nuclear disaster of April 1986, even more so since the Zhivkov regime had developed a nuclear power plant at Kozloduy on the river Danube in 1970 that was based on a similar Soviet design.[223] Moreover, during the 1980s, the Bulgarian city of Russe was severely affected by pollution that was caused by a chemical plant located across the Danube in the Romanian town of Giurgiu, a situation that led to widespread mobilization.[224]

Environmental issues triggered mass protests in Central Europe as well, and Hungary featured prominently in this respect. In the mid-1980s, the project of the Gabčikovo-Nagymaros dam on the Danube became a focal point for contestation. Sanctioned by the Budapest Treaty of 16 September 1977, the project envisaged the construction of a hydroelectric power plant on the Danube as a joint project between Hungary and Czechoslovakia. The project prompted open protests by Hungarian environmentalists from the early 1980s onwards, when it became clear that the construction of the dam would endanger the ecosystem in the dam area in northwest Hungary. A very active civic organization against the project was the Danube Circle (*Duna Kör*), which received the Alternative Nobel Prize in 1985. On 2 September 1988, some 35,000 people demonstrated in Budapest against the Gabčikovo-Nagymaros dam project.[225]

The protest over the environmental threat posed by the dam signalled that the population was prone to engage in mass protests on issues of public interest, and the protection of minority rights was definitely such an issue. Protection of the cultural identity of Hungarian minorities in neighbouring countries, particularly in Romania and Slovakia, proved to be an issue with a high potential for open protest, which, however, was not met with violent repressive measures from the part of the communist power in Hungary. In particular, the systematization of the territory and settlements launched by the Ceaușescu regime envisaged a significant reduction of the

---

222 With regard to the number of ethnic Turks who emigrated by August 1989, figures vary from 344,000 (provided in Petrova, 'Bulgaria', 170) and 369,000 (provided in Kyril Drezov, 'Bulgaria and Macedonia: Voluntary Dependence on External Actors', in *Democratic Consolidation in Eastern Europe: International and Transnational Factors*, vol. 2, eds Jan Zielonka and Alex Pravda [Oxford: Oxford University Press, 2001], 426).

223 The Kozloduy Nuclear Power Plant (NPP) was equipped with pressurized water reactors of Soviet design and was developed over the period 1970–91. Units 1 and 2 were built during the period 1970–75 and were equipped with standard first-generation reactors (WWER–440); units 3 and 4 were built during the period 1973–82 and were equipped with enhanced first-generation reactors (WWER–440); finally, units 5 and 6 were built during the period 1982–91 and were equipped with standard second-generation reactors (WWER–1000). For details, see World Nuclear Association, 'Early Soviet Reactors and EU Accession: Appendix to Safety of Nuclear Power Reactors', updated June 2019, http://www.world-nuclear.org/info/Safety-and-Security/Safety-of-Plants/Appendices/Early-Soviet-Reactors-and-EU-Accession/ (accessed 24 March 2021).

224 Petrova, 'Bulgaria', 172 and 173.

225 For more on the Gabčikovo-Nagymaros case, see Miklós Sükösd, 'The Gabčikovo-Nagymaros Dam: Social, Political and Cultural Conflicts', in *Biopolitics: The Bio-Environment*, vol. VI: *Danube River Bonds*, eds. Agni Vlavianos-Arvanitis and Jan Morovic (Athens: Biopolitics International Organization, 1998), https://biopolitics.gr/biowp/wp-content/uploads/2013/04/VOL-VI-sukosd.pdf (accessed on 24 March 2021); See also Szabó, 'Hungary', in Pollack and Wielgohs, *Dissent and Opposition in Communist Eastern Europe*, 61–2.

number of villages in Romania. Ceaușescu's unreasonable project, once completed, would have first and foremost affected Romanian villages.[226] Nevertheless, in Hungary, the systematization plan was perceived as having the aim of liquidating the Hungarian villages in Transylvania. Protests in Hungary intensified from the mid-1980s onwards and reached their peak in 1988. On 27 June 1988, several independent groups organized a large demonstration in Budapest, protesting against the Romanian plans of rural resettlement. At the time, Radio Free Europe reported that between 30,000 and 100,000 individuals took part in the event and stated that it was 'the biggest independent demonstration since the 1956 revolution'.[227]

Suppression of exile criticism

Communist regimes were always irritated by sharp criticism coming from Western broadcasting agencies, especially from RFE/RL (Radio Free Europe/Radio Liberty), which could reach the populations living under state socialism with relative ease via radio waves. The most daring attempt at silencing RFE/RL was the February 1981 bombing of the RFE/RL headquarters in Munich, carried out by a terrorist group headed by Ilich Ramírez Sánchez (also known as 'Carlos the Jackal'). In preparing and carrying out the attack, Carlos benefited from the joint support of secret police agencies from several communist states (East Germany, Hungary, Czechoslovakia, Bulgaria and Romania). Declassified archival documents indicate that the Securitate played a prominent role in organizing this attack.[228] On 21 February 1981, a bomb made of roughly 20 kilograms of plastic explosives was mounted on the ground wall of the RFE/RL building and detonated. The huge explosion caused extensive damage to the building (evaluated at the time at over 2 million USD) and injured six individuals, of whom four were employees of RFE/RL. Although spectacular, the bomb attack did not reach its goal of silencing the broadcasting agency.[229]

As one of the most ideologically orthodox regimes in CEE, the Ceaușescu regime was particularly irritated by the RFE programmes. After Ronald Reagan was elected President of the United States, the Romanian communists became even more worried about the anti-communist propaganda disseminated through RFE. A Securitate synthesis of 14 October 1981 evaluated the situation in the following terms: 'The Reagan administration pays special attention to the offensive actions in its relations with the socialist states indicating the expansion

---

226 For more on this, see Cristina Petrescu, 'Peasants into Agro-Industrial Workers: The Communist Modernization of Romanian Villages, 1974–1989', in Radu and Budeancă, *Countryside and Communism in Eastern Europe*, 594–618.

227 Dan Ionescu, 'Chronology of Hungarian Protests at Romanian Rural Resettlement Plans', Radio Free Europe Research, *RAD Background Report/129 (Eastern Europe)*, (9 July 1988): 6, OSA/ Digital Archive/ Background Reports, https://catalog.osaarchivum.org/catalog/osa:4d81c039-65c9-41ea-81ff-128a47be937a (accessed 24 March 2021).

228 See 'Minutes of Meeting between Czechoslovak and Hungarian Interior Ministry Officials on the Carlos Terrorist Group and Radio Free Europe Bomb Attack', 25 April 1981, Wilson Center, History and Public Policy Program Digital Archive, AMV C., H-720/svazek c.4, listy 281–85; obtained by Prokop Tomek, translated by Blanka Pasternak, http://digitalarchive.wilsoncenter.org/document/121525 (accessed 3 March 2017).

229 For more details on the attack, see Richard Cummings, 'Special Feature: The 1981 Bombing of RFE/RL', Radio Free Europe/Radio Liberty, http://www.rferl.org/content/article/1080043.html (accessed 24 March 2021).

of the "Polish experience" to other socialist states, as an obvious "proof" of the failure of the socialist system'.[230] In order to reach its goals, the same document stated:

> the CIA indicated to '[Radio] Free Europe' to formulate its programmes with émigré persons who have recently left the country due to their rebellious-dissident activities and who know 'the Romanian realities' in order to ensure that the programmes receive greater credibility and a larger audience.[231]

The Ceaușescu regime wanted to silence the acerbic criticism coming from RFE. Still, there is no hard evidence that the Securitate was involved in the deaths of three directors from the Romanian desk, which occurred during the 1981–88 period: Noel Bernard (1981), Mihai Cismărescu (1983), and Vlad Georgescu (1988). However, all three premature deaths were highly suspicious. General Ion Mihai Pacepa, one of the most prominent Securitate defectors to the West, affirmed that the Romanian secret police used to assassinate the regime's opponents with the help of a portable radioactive device, code-named 'Radu'.[232] Such a hypothesis, however, should be taken with great caution, as some authors argue.[233]

In the 1980s, the Securitate had a realistic overview of the proportions of the audience that the RFE programmes had in Romania. As the Securitate files show, the act of listening and disseminating information broadcast by RFE was considered a serious offence and was met with maximum severity. Reports by Securitate officers abound in such statements as: 'the subject listens at home to the RFE and circulates the news to his workplace – we propose the subject be placed under informative surveillance' or 'the subject listens to the programmes of reactionary foreign radio stations, especially RFE, and she is an adept of the hostile ideas transmitted by this radio'. The party and the Securitate feared that the young public who listened to the musical programmes of RFE would gradually develop a dissident mindset. Harsh measures were therefore taken to identify and punish those who dared to write to RFE. A report dated 16 February 1985 informed on three adolescents from Bucharest schools who had sent messages to the RFE musical programme. In spite of the risks incurred, scores of youngsters were writing to the RFE under funny pseudonyms and their identity was difficult to establish.[234] The very act of listening to RFE programmes was considered a dissident gesture. Individuals who wrote letters

---

230 See Document 180 (14 octombrie 1981): 'Notă a U.M. 0544 privind acțiunile de încurajare a activității disidente în România de către 'Europa Liberă' și CIA' [Informative note by military unit 0544 regarding actions of encouraging dissident activity in Romania by Radio Free Europe and CIA], in Dobre, Neagoe-Pleșa and Pleșa, *The Securitate, 1967–1989*, 545.
231 Ibid., 546–7.
232 Ion Mihai Pacepa, *Red Horizons* (London: Heinemann, 1988), 416. On the impact of Pacepa's defection to the West on the communist regime in Bucharest, see Document 13 (1 October 1978): 'Raport cu privire la rezultatul cercetărilor efectuate asupra cauzelor care au determinat și a condițiilor care au favorizat actul de trădare săvârșit de Ion Mihai Pacepa' [Report regarding the outcome of the inquiry regarding the causes which determined, and conditions which favoured, the act of betrayal committed by Ion Mihai Pacepa], in Mihai Pelin, *Culisele spionajului românesc: DIE, 1955–1980* [Behind the scenes of Romanian espionage: DIE, 1955–1980] (Bucharest: Editura Evenimentul Românesc, 1997), 288–303.
233 René Al. de Flers, *Radio « Europa Liberă » și exilul românesc: O istorie încă nescrisă* [Radio 'Free Europe' and the Romanian exile: A history still unwritten] (Bucharest: Editura Vestala, 2005), 474–6.
234 Pelin, *History of Radio Free Europe*, 278–80.

to RFE became the subjects of strict surveillance, while the exiles working for or collaborating with RFE were prime targets of the Securitate.[235]

Patterns of state repression during the 1989 regime changes in CEE

The regime changes in Poland and Hungary, which were based on the roundtable principle, were certainly non-violent and they paved the way for regime change throughout the collapsing Soviet bloc. In the cases of East Germany, Czechoslovakia and Bulgaria, the communist authorities allowed the limited use of violence against the demonstrators who poured into the streets in the autumn of 1989. It may be argued that in the cases of Poland and Hungary, the factionalism of the power elite, which provoked major splits at the top of the communist hierarchy, in the light of previous revolutionary experiences that had lasting society-wide effects – 'self-limiting' as in Poland (August 1980–December 1981) or genuine as in Hungary (23 October–4 November 1956) – led to 'negotiated revolutions'.

The monolithism of the power elite and the more or less structured societal opposition, coupled with the lack of emancipation from Moscow, led to 'peaceful revolutions', i.e. non-negotiated and non-violent revolutions (East Germany and Czechoslovakia), or, in the case of Bulgaria, to a palace coup, followed by unprecedented widespread mobilization in support of the opposition. Nevertheless, in these three countries, the regime changes, although non-negotiated (with the exception of the GDR), were non-violent. As already noted, the only case in which the shoot-to-kill order was given to the repressive apparatus was that of communist Romania. In this case, the monolithism of the power elite and a poorly structured societal opposition, coupled with the emancipation of the power elite from Moscow, led to a non-negotiated and violent revolution. In Romania, in December 1989 the ruling elite ignored the recent developments within the Soviet bloc, ordered the repressive apparatus to use deadly force against demonstrators; its orders were obeyed from the first instance. In the following, the cases of East Germany, Czechoslovakia, Bulgaria and Romania are briefly addressed in order to illustrate these claims.[236]

In the fall of 1989, Leipzig emerged as the most rebellious city in East Germany. There, on 25 September 1989, a series of 13 consecutive demonstrations took place, organized every Monday until 18 December. These Monday demonstrations in Leipzig significantly contributed to the demise of the East German dictatorship and the subsequent unification of Germany. On 9 October 1989, many feared that the authorities would use deadly force against the demonstrators in Leipzig. Internment camps for more than 80,000 people had already been prepared.[237] Fortunately, this did not happen. During the month of October, as many as 330 demonstrations and mass rallies were organized in different places around the country. By November, the

---

235 Document 195 (26 September 1986): "Documentar realizat de U.M. 0544 din Departamentul Securității Statului privind postul de radio "Europa Liberă"" [Compilation devised by military unit 0544 from the Department of State Security regarding Radio Free Europe], in Dobre, Neagoe-Pleșa and Pleșa, *The Securitate, 1967–1989*, 654.

236 An analysis of the fall of the communist regimes in these four CEE countries is provided in Dragoș Petrescu, *Entangled Revolutions: The Breakdown of the Communist Regimes in East-Central Europe* (Bucharest: Editura Enciclopedică, 2014), 155–332. For the GDR, see Martin Sabrow, ed., *1989 und die Rolle der Gewalt* (Göttingen: Wallstein, 2012).

237 See Ulrich Herbert, *Geschichte Deutschlands im 20. Jahrhundert* (München: C. H. Beck, 2014), 1103–4.

number of such protests rose to 871.[238] According to the Stasi figures, between 16 October and 5 November, some 400 demonstrations and mass rallies – gathering over two million people in total – took place in East Germany and contributed decisively to the collapse of the communist rule in that country.[239]

In Czechoslovakia, the breakdown of the communist regime was precipitated by the violent intervention of the repressive forces in order to disperse a student demonstration in Prague, in November 1989. As Timothy Garton Ash has noted, student anti-regime activism was at the core of the 10-day demonstration that ultimately brought down the communist regime in that country.[240] On Friday, 17 November, a student public gathering aimed at commemorating the death of Jan Opletal, the student killed by the Nazis in November 1939, was followed by a peaceful march towards downtown Prague. The riot police intervened in force to disperse the non-violent crowd. The use of disproportionate police force to disperse the peaceful demonstrators sparked a wave of criticism against the regime. Civic initiatives, petitions, public protests, strikes and demonstrations multiplied. On Sunday, 19 November, the opposition established the Civic Forum (*Občanské Fórum*) in order to coordinate the anti-regime protests, while Havel emerged as the undisputed leader of the opposition. In Slovakia, the Civic Forum's corollary aptly named itself 'The Public against Violence' (*Verejnosť proti násiliu*). Civic initiatives – demonstrations, petitions, strikes by students and actors – multiplied and finally led to the regime change in Czechoslovakia.[241]

In Bulgaria, protests from below multiplied in the summer of 1989 in the context of the mass migration of the ethnic Turks to neighbouring Turkey. During this time, civic groups and human rights activists became more active. Such actions were taking place at a moment when communist rule was already collapsing in Poland and Hungary. Ultimately, environmental activism proved to be the platform that permitted the mobilization of large crowds. On 3 November 1989, the civic group Ecoglasnost initiated a march in Sofia in order to present a petition to the Bulgarian authorities on environmental issues, which was signed by some 12,000 people. Quite unexpectedly, around 10,000 people joined the march. A palace coup organized by a Gorbachevite faction of the Bulgarian Communist Party provoked the fall of Todor Zhivkov one week after the above-mentioned march through the capital city. The political transformation in Bulgaria took an irreversible course in early December 1989, when the non-communist political opposition decided to join forces. On 7 December 1989, several emerging political parties and civic organizations formed the UDF (Union of Democratic Forces).[242] The UDF was particularly successful in mobilizing the educated urban strata and in

---

238 See Table 4 in Uwe Schwabe, 'Der Herbst '89 in Zahlen – Demonstrationen und Kundgebungen vom August 1989 bis zum April 1990', in *Opposition in der DDR von den 70er Jahren bis zum Zusammenbruch der SED-Herrschaft*, eds. Eberhard Kuhrt, Hannsjörg F. Buck and Gunter Holzweißig (Wiesbaden: VS Verlag für Sozialwissenschaften, 1999), 719–35, here 726.
239 Christian Joppke, *East German Dissidents and the Revolution of 1989: Social Movement in a Leninist Regime* (New York: New York University Press, 1995), 155.
240 Timothy Garton Ash, *The Magic Lantern: The Revolution of '89 Witnessed in Warsaw, Budapest, Berlin and Prague* (New York: Vintage Books, 1993), 79–80, originally published in 1990.
241 For an analysis of the regime change in Czechoslovakia focusing on non-elite actors and the 'collective effervescence' that prompted the fall of communism in that country, see James Krapfl, *Revolution with a Human Face: Politics, Culture, and Community in Czechoslovakia, 1989–1992* (Ithaca, NY: Cornell University Press, 2013).
242 Duncan M. Perry, 'From Opposition to Government: Bulgaria's 'Union of Democratic Forces' and its Antecedents', in *Revolution auf Raten: Bulgariens Weg zur Demokratie*, ed. Wolfgang Höpken (München: Oldenbourg, 1996), 34.

organizing large demonstrations in favour of the continuation of the democratization process. Thus, the UDF organized a massive popular demonstration on 14 December in the capital city of Sofia, which clearly demonstrated that the political opposition had become a serious contender for power. From mid-December 1989 onwards, the political changes in Bulgaria were accelerated, also under the impact of the bloody events in neighbouring Romania. On 29 December, it was announced that the 'revival process' was officially revoked. The decisive step towards a new political order was taken when the BCP conceded to open 'roundtable negotiations' with the UDF in order to ensure an effective transition to a democratic system.[243]

The Romanian revolution lasted from 16 to 22 December 1989 and was the only violent revolution among those of 1989. The revolution was sparked in the city of Timișoara and spread to the rest of the country. It started with an apparently minor incident. On Friday, 15 December, a small group of believers – the majority were of Hungarian ethnicity – demonstrated peacefully in support of Reverend László Tőkés, a rebellious minister of the Reformed church, who had developed a conflict with both his superiors and the communist authorities.[244] On Saturday, 16 December, the demonstration in support of Tőkés turned into a demonstration against the Ceaușescu regime, which was increasingly joined by the population of Timișoara. Although the night of 17 December, the forces of repression opened fire on the demonstrators, the protest gained momentum and the city was virtually in the hands of the protesters by 20 December. The same day, Wednesday, 20 December, Ceaușescu, who had just returned from an official visit to Iran, delivered a televised speech at 7:00 pm in which he announced that a state of emergency had been declared in Timiș county. In the meantime, protests by the local population had already broken out at around 6:00 pm in the small town of Lugoj, situated some 60km east of Timișoara.[245]

One day later, on 21 December 1989, unrest was sparked in major cities throughout Romania. In Bucharest, Ceaușescu organized a mass rally that day at 12:00 pm. While he was delivering his speech from the balcony of the CC party building, people from the crowd began yelling. Among the yells from the crowd, one could hear shouts of 'Timișoara!' Confused, Ceaușescu tried to calm the crowd but nobody listened. Intended to reinforce Ceaușescu's rule, the mass rally turned into an anti-communist demonstration. In response, Ceaușescu convoked the Minister of National Defence, the head of the Securitate, and the Minister of Internal Affairs. Meanwhile, gathered in the university square, demonstrators shouted anti-Ceaușescu slogans such as: 'Yesterday in Timișoara, tomorrow in the whole country!', 'Down with communism!', 'Freedom!' and 'Death to the tyrant!'[246] In total, 50 individuals were killed, 462 wounded and 1,245 arrested in Bucharest that day. On 22 December, starting at 09:00 am, large crowds poured into the streets and made their way towards the centre of the city. Once they

---

243 On the Bulgarian roundtable talks, see Rumyana Kolarova and Dimitr Dimitrov, 'The Roundtable Talks in Bulgaria', in *The Roundtable Talks and the Breakdown of Communism*, ed. Jon Elster (Chicago, IL: The University of Chicago Press, 1996), 178–205.
244 Marius Mioc, ed., *Revoluția, fără mistere: Cazul László Tőkés. Documente din arhiva Judecătoriei Timișora; Documente din arhiva parohiei reformate Timișoara; Mărturii* [The Revolution, void of mysteries: the László Tőkés case; documents from the archive of the reformed parish Timișoara – witness accounts] (Timișoara: Editura "Almanahul Banatului," 2002), 144–5.
245 Costache Codrescu, ed., *Armata Română în revoluția din decembrie 1989* [The Romanian Army in the revolution of December 1989], 2nd rev. ed. (Bucharest: Editura Militară, 1998), 82.
246 Ion Pitulescu, ed., *Șase zile care au zguduit România: Ministerul de interne în decembrie 1989* [Six days that shook Romania: the Ministry of the Interior in December 1989] (Bucharest: n.p., 1995), 169; Stelian Tănase, 'Solstițiu însângerat la București' [Bloody solstice in Bucharest], in idem, *Șocuri și crize* (Bucharest: Editura Staff, 1993), 14–15.

reached the palace square, the crowds began attacking the CC party building. However, not a single shot was fired at the protesters. The general secretary of the RCP, who had spent the night inside the building with his wife and the summoned ministers, escaped by helicopter from the upper platform of the building.[247] The moment Ceaușescu and his wife, Elena, flew away, was the moment that the communist regime in Romania collapsed.[248] What remains unclear to this day, however, is why the consolidation of the newly established regime claimed more victims than the repression carried out by the Ceaușescu regime. One should note that out of the total number of victims officially registered in the 1989 events, namely, 1,104 dead and 3,321 wounded, 944 died and 2,214 were wounded after 22 December.[249] It is no wonder why many have claimed that in 1989, Romania witnessed an anti-communist revolution during the period 16–22 December, and a counter-revolution in the days following, from 22–25 December.

The Soviet policy of non-intervention during the revolutionary year of 1989 played a key role in the non-violent character of the regime changes in CEE, with the exception of Romania. As Archie Brown aptly points out:

> The key to change in Eastern Europe was Gorbachev's decision in principle to abandon Soviet foreign military interventions and his refusal to contemplate resort to them, even when the Soviet Union was faced with an utterly changed relationship with the area it had controlled since the end of the Second World War.[250]

The Brezhnev Doctrine of 1968 was gradually replaced by Gorbachev in 1989 with other policies. The most famous – though not necessarily binding anyone in the Soviet leadership – was coined by the Soviet Foreign Ministry spokesman, Gennady Gerasimov, on 25 October 1989. In a highly quoted assertion, Gerasimov said that in accordance with the new political vision of the Kremlin, every country must decide for itself the path to be pursued, referring to Frank Sinatra's song 'My Way'.[251]

---

247 When history accelerates itself, as was the case in Romania in December 1989, a thorough event-centred analysis helps one make sense of the sequence of events and understand the complexity of the situation. An event-centred reconstruction of the 1989 events in Timișoara and Bucharest is provided in Dragoș Petrescu, *Explaining the Romanian Revolution of 1989: Culture, Structure, and Contingency* (Bucharest: Editura Enciclopedică, 2010), 87–108.

248 The Ceaușescu couple were arrested on 22 December. On 25 December, after a staged trial, Nicolae and Elena Ceaușescu were executed by a firing squad in the city of Târgoviște, 74 km north of Bucharest. See Grigore Cartianu, *Sfârșitul Ceaușeștilor: Să mori împușcat ca un animal sălbatic* [The end of the Ceausescus: to die shot like a wild animal] (Bucharest: Editura Adevărul Holding, 2010).

249 On the official number of victims registered in the 1989 events in Romania, see Emil Constantinescu, *Adevărul despre România* [The truth about Romania] (Bucharest: Editura Universalia, 2004), 113; and Codrescu, *Armata Română în revoluția din decembrie 1989*, 462. See also Stan Stoica, *România, 1989–2005: O istorie cronologică* [Romania, 1989–2005: A chronological history] (Bucharest: Editura Meronia, 2005), 19.

250 Archie Brown, *The Gorbachev Factor* (Oxford: Oxford University Press, 1996), 249. For more on the new political line adopted under Gorbachev, see Moshe Lewin, *The Gorbachev Phenomenon: A Historical Interpretation* (Berkeley, CA: University of California Press, 1991).

251 Timothy Garton Ash, *In Europe's Name: Germany and the Divided Continent* (New York: Vintage Books, 1994), 4.

Conclusion

Political violence and state repression under communist rule is a fascinating topic of research. The communist takeovers in CEE were accompanied by the use of illegitimate violence, and thus the element of violence became intrinsically linked with communist rule. In a majority of the situations, the 'revolutionary struggle' of the local communists neither encompassed a 'first revolution' on the model of the Bolshevik Revolution, nor a mixture of a revolution and a war for independence on the model of Tito's partisan war in Yugoslavia. Consequently, with few exceptions, the communist elites in power carried out solely a 'revolution from above'. As Cyril E. Black has noted, when those who are newly in power represent a minority viewpoint, they face a serious problem:

> They may find themselves in control of formal political power, but lacking in any of the informal attributes of tradition and loyalty that hold together the fabric of society. This they can achieve only after they have educated a generation or two of citizens to an acceptance of their policies.[252]

This section has concentrated on the main actions undertaken by individuals or groups that triggered state repression over the period 1968–89, that is, more than two decades after the communist takeovers. When examining the patterns of public protest, as well as the means and methods employed by the communist regimes to suppress such actions, one quickly observes that during the period 1968–89, the level of state repression decreased sharply when compared with the previous period, 1948–68. Over the time interval under discussion, the types of actions perceived as posing a major threat to the communist regimes in CEE were the working-class protests, student unrest, acts of dissent, ethnic mobilization and exile criticism. In some cases, attempts to illegally cross the national border often ended in tragedy, because the border guards were ordered to use deadly force in order to prevent such actions. In other instances, the regime's strict anti-abortion laws prompted a rise in the number of unsafe abortions and claimed the lives of many women.

Nevertheless, political violence alone cannot explain why the communist regimes of CEE remained in power until 1989–91. Notable achievements were made in terms of industrialization, urbanization, education and public health, although these were modest in comparison with developed Western societies. True, perceptions from below differed from country to country. Large segments of the population living under 'really existing socialism' perceived the communist regimes as having something to offer to those societies. At the same time, relative deprivation (i.e. the constant comparison between the standard of living under state socialism and the standard of living in Western societies) did contribute to the growing dissatisfaction with those regimes. 'Socialist modernization' allowed people to own radios and television sets, but this allowed them access to what was happening in the outside world. In some cases, apart from economic improvement and social benefits, the communist regimes managed to legitimize themselves through the instrumentalization of anti-fascism or ethnic nationalism. As one scholar of the region endeavours to answer in his book, *Communist Czechoslovakia, 1945–89*, is

---

252 Cyril E. Black, 'Revolution, Modernization, and Communism', in *Communism and Revolution: The Strategic Uses of Political Violence*, eds. Cyril E. Black and Thomas P. Thornton (Princeton, NJ: Princeton University Press, 1964), 7.

why communism in Czechoslovakia attracted at times substantial levels of support, lasted with relatively scant overt opposition for over 40 years, and how Czech and Slovak citizens adapted to the regime and lived their everyday lives under 'state socialism'.[253]

And these questions hold true for all the communist countries of CEE. Last, but by no means least, it may be argued that the issue of legitimation of communist rule in the region represents another fascinating topic, which could be addressed separately as an equally rewarding intellectual enterprise.

The use of selective terror and targeted state repression became a major feature of the communist regimes in Central and Eastern Europe during the period discussed in this section, namely, 1968–89. In spite of the policy changes regarding the recourse to state repression, the use of immediate and deadly force by the power elites in Sovietized CEE remained, at the least, a possibility throughout the entire communist period. In order to better understand why the potential for the use of immediate and deadly force by the communist regimes in the region remained high, one has to examine one fundamental aspect concerning the relationship between the Soviet Union and the countries in the Soviet bloc during the period 1953–85: whenever the power elite in a communist country proved unable to contain and suppress widespread unrest or to control political processes that endangered the very existence of the communist system in that country, the Soviet Union intervened militarily in order to restore the 'socialist order', as was the case in June 1953 in East Berlin, in November 1956 in Hungary and in 1968 in Czechoslovakia.

This fundamental aspect became official doctrine only in the aftermath of the Soviet-led military intervention of August 1968 in Czechoslovakia, and has been known since as the Brezhnev Doctrine, or the Soviet doctrine of 'limited sovereignty'.[254] It may be argued, therefore, that a triangular relational nexus characterized the relations between the communist regimes in Sovietized CEE, the populations of the respective countries and the Soviet Union during the period 1953–85; that is, from the popular uprising in East Berlin until a new secretary general of the Communist Party of the Soviet Union, Mikhail S. Gorbachev, came to power in March 1985, which had an immense impact on the Soviet outer empire in Europe. As already discussed, after 1968 the relations between the USSR and its satellites remained under the control of the Brezhnev Doctrine, which asserted that the USSR had the right to intervene in any country in which the communist government was threatened. After Gorbachev's coming to power, this situation gradually changed and finally culminated with Moscow's renunciation of the Brezhnev Doctrine.

Ideological orthodoxy and subservience to Moscow were thus necessary but not sufficient conditions for ensuring the survival of the power elite in a Sovietized country. In order to remain in power, the communist elite had to ensure social quiescence through surveillance and prevention; and, when open protests occurred, they had to be prepared to act resolutely to contain and suppress them. The aim being to avoid Soviet intervention that could lead to the leadership's removal from power for having failed to control their respective society.

---

253 McDermott, *Communist Czechoslovakia, 1945–89*, 2.
254 For more on the origins and significance of the Brezhnev Doctrine see Matthew J. Ouimet, *The Rise and Fall of the Brezhnev Doctrine in Soviet Foreign Policy* (Chapel Hill, NC: The University of North Carolina Press, 2003) and Robert A. Jones, *The Soviet Concept of 'Limited Sovereignty' from Lenin to Gorbachev: The Brezhnev Doctrine* (New York: St. Martin's Press, 1990).

Nevertheless, the use of firearms remained the last alternative even in times of crisis. Even surveillance in the narrower sense of the term (the network of informers, letter and border controls, incitement to denunciation, etc. outlined above) was probably not necessarily decisive. It was more about the fear of attracting the attention of the 'organs' than about the personal experience of repression that stabilized the system.

The shadow of the unpredictable – in this case inherited from Stalinism and reinforced in 1956, 1968, 1970 and 1981 – is sometimes much longer than the memory of one's own individual experiences. In his drama *Fortinbras Gets Drunk* from 1982, the Polish–American writer Janusz Glowacki masterly captures this ambivalence:

> 1st GUARD: [paranoia setting in] Do you think someone's listening in on our conversation?
> 2nd GUARD: Definitely. No doubt about it.
> 1st GUARD: That's good. I don't like talking if they're not listening in. My thoughts get all confused.[255]

Further reading

Applebaum, Anne. *Iron Curtain: The Crushing of Eastern Europe, 1944–1956* (New York: Doubleday, 2012).
Arendt, Hannah. *The Origins of Totalitarianism* (Orlando, FL: Harcourt, 1979).
Ash, Timothy Garton. *In Europe's Name: Germany and the Divided Continent* (New York: Vintage Books, 1994).
Ash, Timothy Garton. *The Magic Lantern: The Revolution of '89 Witnessed in Warsaw, Budapest, Berlin and Prague* (New York: Vintage Books, 1993).
Banac, Ivo, ed. *Eastern Europe in Revolution* (Ithaca, NY: Cornell University Press, 1992).
Banac, Ivo. *With Stalin Against Tito: Cominformist Splits in Yugoslav Communism* (Ithaca, NY: Cornell University Press, 1988).
Batović, Ante. *The Balkans in Turmoil: Croatian Spring and the Yugoslav Position Between the Cold War Blocs 1965–1971* (London: LSE IDEAS/LSE Cold War Studies Programme, 2009).
Bauerkämper, Arnd and Constantin Iordachi, eds. *The Collectivization of Agriculture in Communist Eastern Europe: Comparison and Entanglements* (Budapest: CEU Press, 2014).
Békés, Csaba, Malcolm Byrne and M. János Rainer, eds. *The 1956 Hungarian Revolution: A History in Documents* (Budapest: CEU Press, 2002).
Bernhard, Michael H. *The Origins of Democratization in Poland: Workers, Intellectuals, and Oppositional Politics, 1976–1980* (New York: Columbia University Press, 1993).
Bertino, Anthony J. and Patricia Nolan Bertino. *Forensic Science: Fundamentals and Investigations*, 2nd ed. (Boston: Cengage Learning, 2015).
Bieber, Florian and Židas Daskalovski, eds. *Understanding the War in Kosovo* (London: Frank Cass, 2003).
Bischof, Günther, Stefan Karner and Peter Ruggenthaler, eds. *The Prague Spring and the Warsaw Pact Invasion of Czechoslovakia in 1968* (Lanham, MD: Lexington Books, 2010).
Black, Cyril E. and Thomas P. Thornton, eds. *Communism and Revolution: The Strategic Uses of Political Violence* (Princeton, NJ: Princeton University Press, 1964).
Bloxham, Donald and Robert Gerwarth, eds. *Political Violence in Twentieth-Century Europe* (Cambridge: Cambridge University Press, 2011).
Borodziej, Włodzimierz. *Geschichte Polens im 20. Jahrhundert* (München: C.H. Beck, 2010).
Borodziej, Włodzimierz, Sabina Ferhadbegović and Joachim von Puttkamer, eds. *The Routledge History Handbook of Central and Eastern Europe in the Twentieth Century, Volume 2: Statehood* (New York: Routledge, 2020).
Breuilly, John. *Nationalism and the State*, 2nd ed. (Chicago, IL: The University of Chicago Press, 1994).
Brown, Archie. *The Gorbachev Factor* (Oxford: Oxford University Press, 1996).

---

255 Janusz Głowacki, *Fortynbras się upił* [Fortinbras Gets drunk], in Dialog 1 (1990), 24–55. English translation by courtesy of Konrad Brodzinski. Thanks also to Artur Koczara for helping us trace the translation history of the play.

Bundesbehörde für die Stasi-Unterlagen (BStU), *The European Network of Official Authorities in Charge of the Secret Police Files: A Reader on their Legal Foundations, Structures and Activities*, 2nd revised edition (Berlin: BStU, 2013).
Burg, Steven L. *Conflict and Cohesion in Socialist Yugoslavia: Political Decision Making Since 1966* (Princeton, NJ: Princeton University Press, 1983).
Calic, Marie-Janine. *A History of Yugoslavia* (West Lafayette, IN: Purdue University Press, 2019).
Chirot, Daniel and Clark McCauley. *Why Not Kill Them All? The Logic and Prevention of Mass Political Murder* (Princeton, NJ: Princeton University Press, 2006).
Connelly, John. *Captive University: The Sovietization of East German, Czech, and Polish Higher Education, 1945–1956* (Chapel Hill, NC: The University of North Carolina Press, 2000).
Courtois, Stéphane, ed. *The Black Book of Communism: Crimes, Terror, Repression* (Cambridge, MA: Harvard University Press, 1999).
Crampton, R. J. *A Concise History of Bulgaria*, 2nd ed. (Cambridge: Cambridge University Press, 2005).
Crampton, R. J. *Eastern Europe in the Twentieth Century* (London: Routledge, 1994).
Davenport, Christian, Hank Johnston and Carol Mueller, eds. *Repression and Mobilization* (Minneapolis, MN: University of Minnesota Press, 2005).
Davies, Norman. *God's Playground, Vol. II: 1795 to the Present* (Oxford: Oxford University Press, 1981).
Deletant, Dennis. *Ceaușescu and the Securitate: Coercion and Dissent in Romania, 1965–1989* (London: Hurst, 1995).
Dziwisz, Cardinal Stanisław. *A Life with Karol: My Forty-Year Friendship with the Man Who Became Pope* (New York: Doubleday, 2008).
Ekiert, Grzegorz and Jan Kubik. *Rebellious Civil Society: Popular Protest and Democratic Consolidation in Poland, 1989–1993* (Ann Arbor, MI: The University of Michigan Press, 2001).
Ekiert, Grzegorz. *The State Against Society: Political Crises and their Aftermath in East Central Europe* (Princeton, NJ: Princeton University Press, 1996).
Elster, Jon, ed. *The Roundtable Talks and the Breakdown of Communism* (Chicago, IL: The University of Chicago Press, 1996).
Falk, Barbara J. *The Dilemmas of Dissidence in East-Central Europe: Citizen Intellectuals and Philosopher Kings* (Budapest: CEU Press, 2003).
Feinberg, Melissa. *Curtain of Lies: The Battle over Truth in Stalinist Eastern Europe* (New York: Oxford University Press, 2017).
Fink, Carole, Phillip Gassert and Detlef Junker, eds. *1968: The world transformed* (Cambridge: Cambridge University Press, 1998).
Gildea, Robert, James Mark and Anette Warring, eds. *Europe's 1968: Voices of Revolt* (Oxford: Oxford University Press, 2013).
Gorbachev, Mikhail and Zdeněk Mlynář. *Conversations with Gorbachev: On Perestroika, the Prague Spring, and the Crossroads of Socialism*, trans. George Shriver (New York: Columbia University Press, 2002).
Gorky, Maksim. *Creatures That Once Were Men* (London: Alston Rivers, 1905).
Haraszti, Miklós. *A Worker in a Workers' State: Piece-Rates in Hungary* (Harmondsworth: Penguin Books, 1977).
Havel, Václav. *Open Letters: Selected Writings 1965–1990*, selected and edited by Paul Wilson (New York: Vintage Books, 1992).
Hertie, Hans-Hermann and Maria Nooke. *The Victims at the Berlin Wall, 1961–1989: Findings of a Research Project by the Center for Research on Contemporary History Potsdam and the Berlin Wall Memorial Site and Documentation Center* (Potsdam/Berlin, November 2013).
Hiio, Toomas, Meelis Maripuu and Indrek Paavle, eds. *Estonia since 1944: Reports of the Estonian International Commission for the Investigation of Crimes Against Humanity* (Talinn: Tallinna Raamatutrükikoda / Estonian Foundation for the Investigation of Crimes Against Humanity, 2009).
Hunyadi, Attila, ed. *State and Minority in Transylvania, 1918–1989: Studies on the History of the Hungarian Community* (New York: Columbia University Press, 2012).
Jones, Robert A. *The Soviet Concept of 'Limited Sovereignty' from Lenin to Gorbachev: The Brezhnev Doctrine* (New York: St. Martin's Press, 1990).
Joppke, Christian. *East German Dissidents and the Revolution of 1989: Social Movement in a Leninist Regime* (New York: New York University Press, 1995).
Junes, Tom. *Student Politics in Communist Poland: Generations of Consent and Dissent* (London: Lexington Books, 2015).
Keane, John. *Václav Havel: A Political Tragedy in Six Acts* (New York: Basic Books, 2000).

Kennedy, Michael D. *Professionals, Power and Solidarity in Poland: A Critical Sociology of Soviet-Type Society* (Cambridge: Cambridge University Press, 1991).

Kenney, Padraic. *Rebuilding Poland, Workers and Communists, 1945–1950* (Ithaca, NY: Cornell University Press, 1996).

Kersten, Krystyna. *The Establishment of Communist Rule in Poland, 1943–1948* (Berkeley, CA: University of California Press, 1991).

Király, Béla K. and András Bozóki, eds. *Lawful Revolution in Hungary, 1989–94* (Boulder, CO: Social Science Monographs, 1995).

Kligman, Gail. *The Politics of Duplicity: Controlling Reproduction in Ceausescu's Romania* (Berkeley, CA: University of California Press, 1998).

Kontler, László. *A History of Hungary: Millennium in Central Europe* (Budapest: Atlantisz, 1999).

Krapfl, James. *Revolution with a Human Face: Politics, Culture, and Community in Czechoslovakia, 1989–1992* (Ithaca, NY: Cornell University Press, 2013).

Laba, Roman. *The Roots of Solidarity: A Political Sociology of Poland's Working-Class Democratization* (Princeton, NJ: Princeton University Press, 1991).

Leśkiewicz, Rafał and Pavel Žáček, eds. *Handbook of the European Network of Official Authorities in Charge of the Secret-Police Files* (Prague: ÚSTR & IPN, 2013).

Levy, Robert. *Ana Pauker: The Rise and Fall of a Jewish Communist* (Berkeley, CA: University of California Press, 2001).

Lewin, Moshe. *The Gorbachev Phenomenon: A Historical Interpretation* (Berkeley, CA: University of California Press, 1991).

Lipski, Jan Józef. *KOR: A History of the Workers' Defense Committee in Poland, 1976–1981*, trans. Olga Amsterdamska and Gene M. Moore (Berkeley, CA: University of California Press, 1985).

Machcewicz, Paweł. *Poland's War on Radio Free Europe: 1950–1989* (Stanford, CA: Stanford University Press, 2015).

Machcewicz, Paweł. *Rebellious Satellite: Poland 1956* (Washington, DC: Woodrow Wilson Center Press, 2009).

Markovski, Venko. *Goli Otok: The Island of Death – A Diary in Letters* (Boulder, CO: Social Science Monographs, 1984).

Marsili, Lorenzo and Niccolò Milanese. *Citizens of Nowhere: How Europe Can be Saved from Itself* (London: Zed Books 2018).

Mason, David S. *Public Opinion and Political Change in Poland, 1980–1982* (Cambridge: Cambridge University Press, 1985).

McDermott, Kevin. *Communist Czechoslovakia, 1945–89: A Political and Social History* (London: Palgrave, 2015).

Michnik, Adam. *Letters from Freedom: Post-Cold War Realities and Perspectives*, ed. Irena Grudzińska Gross (Berkeley, CA: University of California Press, 1998).

Millington, Richard. *State, Society and Memories of the Uprising of 17 June 1953 in the GDR* (Basingstoke: Palgrave Macmillan, 2014).

Miłosz, Czesław. *The Seizure of Power*, trans. Celina Wieniewska (New York: Criterion, 1955).

Musil, Jiří, ed. *The End of Czechoslovakia* (Budapest: CEU Press, 1995).

Navrátil, Jaromír, et al., eds. *The Prague Spring 1968: A National Security Archive Documents Reader* (Budapest: CEU Press, 1998).

Ognjenović, Gorana and Jasna Jozelić, eds. *Revolutionary Totalitarianism, Pragmatic Socialism, Transition, Vol. 1: Tito's Yugoslavia, Stories Untold* (London: Palgrave Macmillan, 2016).

Ostermann, Christian F. and Malcolm Byrne, eds. *Uprising in East Germany 1953: The Cold War, the German Question, and the First Major Upheaval behind the Iron Curtain* (Budapest: CEU Press, 2001).

Ouimet, Matthew J. *The Rise and Fall of the Brezhnev Doctrine in Soviet Foreign Policy* (Chapel Hill, NC: The University of North Carolina Press, 2003).

Pacepa, Ion Mihai. *Red Horizons* (London: Heinemann, 1988).

Paczkowski, Andrzej. *Revolution and Counterrevolution in Poland 1980–1989: Solidarity, Martial Law, and the End of Communism in Europe*, trans. Christina Manetti (Rochester, NY: University of Rochester Press, 2015).

Paczkowski, Andrzej. *The Spring will be Ours: Poland and the Poles from Occupation to Freedom* (University Park, PA: The Pennsylvania State University Press, 2003).

Persak, Krzysztof and Łukasz Kamiński, eds. *A Handbook of the Communist Security Apparatus in East Central Europe* (Warsaw: Institute of National Remembrance, 2005).

Petrescu, Cristina. *From Robin Hood to Don Quixote: Resistance and Dissent in Communist Romania* (Bucharest: Editura Enciclopedică, 2013).
Petrescu, Dragoș. *Entangled Revolutions: The Breakdown of the Communist Regimes in East-Central Europe* (Bucharest: Editura Enciclopedică, 2014).
Petrescu, Dragoș. *Explaining the Romanian Revolution of 1989: Culture, Structure, and Contingency* (Bucharest: Editura Enciclopedică, 2010).
Pittaway, Mark. *Eastern Europe 1939–2000* (London: Arnold, 2004).
Pollack, Detlef and Jan Wielgohs, eds. *Dissent and Opposition in Communist Eastern Europe: Origins of Civil Society and Democratic Transition* (Aldershot: Ashgate, 2004).
Popov, Nebojša, ed. *The Road to War in Serbia: Trauma and Catharsis* (Budapest: CEU Press, 2000).
Porton, Richard. *Film and the Anarchist Imagination* (London: Verso, 1999).
Pucci, Molly. *Security Empire: The Secret Police in Communist Eastern Europe* (New Haven, CT: Yale University Press, 2020).
Radu, Sorin and Cosmin Budeancă, eds. *Countryside and Communism in Eastern Europe: Perceptions, Attitudes, Propaganda* (Vienna: LIT Verlag, 2016).
Rainer, M. János. *Imre Nagy: A biography* (London: I.B. Tauris, 2009).
Ramet, Sabrina P. *Social Currents in Eastern Europe: The Sources and Meaning of the Great Transformation* (Durham, NC: Duke University Press, 1991).
Ramet, Sabrina P. *The Three Yugoslavias: State-building and Legitimation, 1918–2005* (Bloomington, IN: Indiana University Press, 2006).
Rothwell, Victor. *Britain and the Cold War 1941–1947* (London: Jonathan Cape Ltd., 1982).
Rusinow, Dennison. *Yugoslavia: Oblique Insights and Observations*, ed. Gale Stokes (Pittsburgh, PA: University of Pittsburgh Press, 2008).
Ryback, Timothy W. *Rock around the Bloc: A History of Rock Music in Eastern Europe and the Soviet Union* (New York: Oxford University Press, 1990).
Skilling, H. Gordon. *Charter 77 and Human Rights in Czechoslovakia* (London: Allen & Unwin, 1981).
Skilling, H. Gordon. *Communism National and International: Eastern Europe after Stalin* (Toronto: University of Toronto Press, 1974).
Staniszkis, Jadwiga. *Poland's Self-Limiting Revolution* (Princeton, NJ: Princeton University Press, 1984).
Stokes, Gale. *The Walls Came Tumbling Down: The Collapse of Communism in Eastern Europe* (New York: Oxford University Press, 1993).
Stolarik, M. Mark, ed. *The Prague Spring and the Warsaw Pact Invasion of Czechoslovakia, 1968: Forty Years Later* (Mundelein, IL: Bolchazy-Carducci Publishers, 2010).
Swidlicki, Andrzej. *Political trials in Poland 1981–1986* (Beckenham: Croom Helm, 1988).
Szaynok, Bożena. *Poland–Israel, 1944–1968: In the Shadow of the Past and of the Soviet Union*, trans. Dominika Ferens (Warsaw: Institute of National Remembrance, 2012).
Szporer, Michael. *Solidarity: The Great Workers Strike of 1980* (Lanham, MD: Lexington Books, 2012).
Tőkés, Rudolf L., ed. *Opposition in Eastern Europe* (London: Macmillan, 1979).
Touraine, Alain, François Dubet, Michel Wieviorka and Jan Strzelecki. *Solidarity: The Analysis of a Social Movement: Poland 1980–1981* (Cambridge: Cambridge University Press, 1983).
Tucker, Aviezer. *The Philosophy and Politics of Czech Dissidence from Patočka to Havel* (Pittsburgh, PA: University of Pittsburgh Press, 2000).
Tucker, Robert C. *Stalin in Power: The Revolution from Above, 1928–1941* (New York: W.W. Norton & Co., 1990).
Urban, George R. *Radio Free Europe and the Pursuit of Democracy: My War Within the Cold War* (New Haven, CT: Yale University Press, 1997).
Vlavianos-Arvanitis, Agni and Jan Morovic, eds. *Biopolitics: The Bio-Environment, Vol. VI: Danube River Bonds* (Athens: Biopolitics International Organization, 1998).
Williams, Kieran. *The Prague Spring and its Aftermath: Czechoslovak Politics, 1968–1970* (Cambridge: Cambridge University Press, 1997).
Wolff, Robert Paul, Barrington Moore. and Herbert Marcuse. *A Critique of Pure Tolerance* (Boston, MA: Beacon Press, 1969).
Zaremba, Marcin. *Communism – Legitimacy – Nationalism: Nationalist Legitimization of the Communist Regime in Poland* (Berlin: Peter Lang, 2019).
Zielonka, Jan and Alex Pravda, eds. *Democratic Consolidation in Eastern Europe: International and Transnational Factors*, vol. 2 (Oxford: Oxford University Press, 2001).

6
THE VIOLENT DISSOLUTION OF YUGOSLAVIA, 1989–2001

Mark Biondich

Deliberations surrounding Yugoslavia's failure and the reasons for its particularly violent demise are likely to continue into the foreseeable future.[1] Even pinpointing the beginnings of Yugoslavia's demise is no simple matter and has generated considerable controversy, although for the purposes of this chapter, the demise of communist regimes in 1989 will serve as a logical starting point. The result in the Socialist Federal Republic of Yugoslavia was not the creation of liberal democratic, Western-oriented regimes, but rather the revitalization of nationalist political regimes, often led by former communists. Their nationalist agendas were not necessarily undemocratic, but more often than not, liberal democratic principles were suppressed in practice in pursuit of the realization of nationalist projects. Old debates about state organization and the nature of federalism had not been resolved in socialist Yugoslavia; there were tensions based on cultural factors, and there was economic decline and concomitant competition for resources. Tito's passing in May 1980 emphasized the departure from leadership of a Partisan generation united by resistance in the Second World War, whose belief in the benefits of a unified socialist endeavour was not shared by their successors, or at the very least, was conceived of differently under changing circumstances. By the 1980s, communist leadership was already subject to public scrutiny in Yugoslavia. After 1989, as the international status quo had been drastically altered, political elites turned increasingly to nationalist discourse, as nationalism undeniably had strong psychological appeal in a time of political uncertainty, social transformation and economic decline.

---

1 The war in Yugoslavia has already produced a massive amount of literature, only some of which will be cited here. A useful starting point can be found in the following surveys: Andrew Wachtel and Christopher Bennett, 'The Dissolution of Yugoslavia', in *Confronting the Yugoslav Controversies: A Scholars' Initiative*, 2nd ed., eds Charles Ingrao and Thomas A. Emmert (West Lafayette, IN: Purdue University Press, 2012), 13–43; and Jasna Dragović-Soso, 'Why Did Yugoslavia Disintegrate? An Overview of Contending Explanations', in Cohen and Dragović-Soso, *State Collapse in South-Eastern Europe: New Perspectives on Yugoslavia's Disintegration*, eds Lenard J. Cohen and Jasna Dragović-Soso (West Lafayette, IN: Purdue University Press, 2007), 1–39. For an excellent account of the origins of the war written by two journalists who conducted extensive interviews with the key figures in the drama, see Laura Silber and Allan Little, *The Death of Yugoslavia*, rev. ed. (New York: Penguin, 1997). See also Dejan Djokić, ed., *Yugoslavism: Histories of a Failed Idea, 1918–1992* (Madison, WI: University of Wisconsin Press, 2003).

The descent into war was conditioned by the confluence of several factors, influenced dramatically by what Stuart Kaufman has labelled 'symbolic politics', the process by which existing myths and stereotypes are employed to legitimize violence against other groups.[2] Several conditions had to be met in the Yugoslav context before the country could descend into war: myths justifying ethnic hostility were required; the presence of fears about the survival of an ethnic group (or groups); and, the availability of an opportunity for these groups to mobilize. Violence resulted from these preconditions as a result of mounting mass hostilities, chauvinist mobilization by elites invoking symbolic appeals, and a security dilemma between groups. In the Yugoslav context, political elites were willing to exploit existing popular stereotypes and nationalist myths to mobilize public opinion, while in many republics, the public believed that it faced real threats to its security, whether in terms of political status, national rights, socio-economic wellbeing, or even its right to exist. The protracted nature of Yugoslavia's demise afforded elites sufficient time and opportunity to mobilize. Had these conditions not been met, conflict might have been avoided and the Yugoslav state, even if it had not survived the transition from communism, may have dissolved peaceably along the Czechoslovak lines. While this model explains how populations were mobilized and conditioned to resort to or simply accept the necessity of violence, there is a risk of conflating the causes of hatred and the causes of violence. Symbolic politics were instrumental to the former, but only determined political elites, backed by functioning state bureaucracies, standing armies and a security apparatus, could mobilize the necessary resources to initiate and sustain violent conflict. In the absence of these elites and the requisite supporting infrastructure, the outcome in former Yugoslavia may have been quite different. This chapter draws heavily on the judicial proceedings at the ICTY (International Criminal Tribunal for the former Yugoslavia) between 1993 and 2017 in The Hague and its successor, the IRMCT (International Residual Mechanism for Criminal Tribunals); these proceedings have shed important light on the drama of state collapse and the role of elite actors in instigating and directing the mass violence that accompanied Yugoslavia's dissolution.

Communist Yugoslavia's complicated constitutional arrangements have often been cited as a principal factor leading to systemic crisis. Between 1945 and the mid-1960s, the country was run as a centralized state through the League of Communists under the charismatic leadership of Josip Broz Tito. Decentralization prevailed as policy because of the League of Communists' ideological need to distinguish itself from both the Soviet Union and its interwar 'bourgeois' progenitor. This tendency was formally institutionalized in Yugoslavia's last Constitution (1974), which also addressed political grievances raised by regional elites over the previous decade.[3] However, after 1974 the Yugoslav state progressively gave way to its constituent parts – the six republics and two autonomous provinces – which were dominated by local party elites whose interests rested in their respective republics and provinces rather than the federation. After 1980, the Yugoslav state was no longer able effectively to challenge republican governments, the primary locus of national identity for the country's six dominant nations. Indeed, after 1974 the republics behaved as de facto independent states,

---

2 Stuart J. Kaufman, *Modern Hatreds: The Symbolic Politics of Ethnic War* (Ithaca, NY: Cornell University Press, 2001), 15–48, 165–202.
3 Dejan Jović, 'Yugoslavism and Yugoslav Communism: From Tito to Kardelj', in Djokić, *Yugoslavism*, 173–5.

with their own political and institutional priorities, including in the critical area of internal affairs.[4] In this setting of institutional drift and waning faith in the state idea, the re-emergence of an overtly nationalist discourse invariably proved problematic.[5]

In Yugoslavia's final days, nationalism undeniably posed the most potent challenge to the prevailing ideology of state socialism.[6] Such nationalism took two forms, either hegemonic or separatist: hegemonism was associated with Serb nationalists, led by Slobodan Milošević after 1987; while the other nationalisms, chiefly the Slovene and Croat manifestations, were either confederalist or separatist. These nationalisms, and the leaders who were their exponents, nurtured one another. Serb nationalists, with their dreams of re-centralization as a prelude to safeguarding Serb national interests within Yugoslavia, further fuelled separatist forces which universally rejected centralizing tendencies. In the same way, manifestations of separatism were regarded in Belgrade and among Serb leaders in Bosnia-Herzegovina and Croatia, as necessitating greater power at the centre.

Long-standing discontent with decentralization was voiced in Serb intellectual circles, beginning with the 'Memorandum' of the Serbian Academy of Arts and Sciences (1986) through to the Congress of Serb Intellectuals (1992) – held in Sarajevo on the eve of the Bosnian war – and beyond. The nationalist narrative focused exclusively on the sacrifices and sufferings of the Serb nation since 1918.[7] This discourse contained an underlying theme of treachery, namely, that Serbs had paid dearly for Yugoslavia's creation but were repeatedly betrayed by their fellow South Slavs. It found its most provocative expression in discussions about the fate of Serbs – and in particular the number of Serbs killed[8] – at the hands of the Croatian Ustasha in the Second World War. But in the mid-1980s, Serb intellectual and political dissidence centred primarily on the status of Kosovo, long regarded as an integral component of Serb national territory and historical patrimony, which had inexplicably been removed from Serbian jurisdiction. Serb nationalists were of the opinion that the Albanian demographic ascendancy in Kosovo threatened their own nation, and further, that the discrimination they were allegedly receiving from the Kosovo Albanians was tantamount to 'genocide'; as such, they believed there were various secret plots being mounted against them. The 'Memorandum', which soon emerged as one of the most controversial texts in modern Serbian history, spoke of Serb victimization and their decline under communism, claiming that Tito's Yugoslavia had discriminated against Serbs; Kosovo was emblematic of this institutional discrimination. The importance of the Memorandum as a Serb nationalist text lay in the extreme language it used

---

4 On the economic dimension of decentralization, see Michael Palairet, 'The Inter-Regional Struggle for Resources and the Fall of Yugoslavia', in Cohen and Dragović-Soso, *State Collapse in South-Eastern Europe*, 222; and, Audrey Helfant Budding, 'Nation/People/Republic: Self-Determination in Socialist Yugoslavia', in ibid., 98.

5 For a discussion of culture and education in Yugoslavia, see Andrew Wachtel, *Making a Nation, Breaking a Nation: Literature and Cultural Politics in Yugoslavia* (Stanford, CA: Stanford UP, 1998), 179–81.

6 Raif Dizdarević, *Od smrti Tita do smrti Jugoslavije: Svjedočenja* [From the death of Tito to the death of Yugoslavia: testimonies] (Sarajevo: Biblioteka Svjedok, 1999), 295.

7 See Jasna Dragović-Soso, *'Saviours of the Nation': Serbia's Intellectual Opposition and the Revival of Nationalism* (London: Hurst and Montreal: McGill-Queen's University Press, 2002).

8 Estimates of the number of Yugoslav citizens killed in the Second World War have been used for political ends ever since 1945. See Bogoljub Kočović, *Žrtve Drugog svjetskog rata u Jugoslaviji* [Victims of the Second World War in Yugoslavia] (London: Naše delo, 1985); and Vladimir Žerjavić, *Gubici stanovništva Jugoslavije u drugom svjetskom ratu* [Population losses in Yugoslavia in the Second World War] (Zagreb: Jugoslavensko viktimološko društvo, 1989).

to depict the situation of Serbs and in the conspiracy theory it relied on to explain it. Its claims made it difficult to envisage how a common state was possible with peoples who were allegedly perpetrating 'genocide' against Serbs. The document openly challenged some of the basic tenets of Yugoslavia's political system and called into question the ability of Serbs to cohabit with others in anything other than a centralized, Serbian-run state.

On the other hand, most non-Serb nationalities believed that they were handicapped by a system in which Serbs were proportionally overrepresented in federal institutions, whether in the JNA (Yugoslav People's Army), the security apparatus or in some republican Leagues of Communists, as in Croatia and Bosnia-Herzegovina. Croat nationalism in particular, suppressed at the end of the Croatian Spring (1971), was nurtured on the belief that Yugoslavia, whether royalist or socialist, was merely a chimera for Serbian hegemony. Where Serbs obsessed over their wartime sufferings, claiming that their anguish was officially downplayed for the sake of 'brotherhood and unity', Croat nationalists alleged that Ustasha crimes were deliberately exaggerated to denigrate Croat national aspirations, while Serb Chetnik and Partisan atrocities were either minimized or denied.[9] For Croat nationalists, the May 1945 repatriation of Croatian (and other) troops and civilians by Allied forces to the Yugoslav Partisans, near Bleiburg on the Austrian-Yugoslav frontier, and the subsequent massacre of tens of thousands of both real and alleged collaborators,[10] became the symbolic counterpoint to the Jasenovac atrocities, proof of a conspiracy of silence about Croat victimization in socialist Yugoslavia. Additionally, they claimed that Croats were economically exploited by Belgrade and exposed to cultural policies designed to undermine Croat individuality.[11] The other constituent nations – Slovenes, Bosnian Muslims, Macedonians and Montenegrins – all possessed their own narratives, but their grievances were generally less pronounced and not nearly as potent a threat to the stability of Yugoslavia as Serb and Croat nationalisms.

Political elites and the mobilization of nationalism

On 24 April 1987, Slobodan Milošević, then head of the League of Communists of the Socialist Republic of Serbia, visited the Autonomous Province of Kosovo at the behest of his mentor, the President of the Socialist Republic of Serbia, Ivan Stambolić, in an attempt to restrain tensions between the Serb minority and Albanian majority.[12] His brief sojourn proved to be a decisive event in the history of Yugoslavia's demise. During the visit, and despite his assigned mission of calming local Serb feelings, Milošević declared his support for local Serbs who rallied during the visit to demand that Serbian authorities intervene in the province to rescue them from alleged discrimination at the hands of the local Albanian communist leadership. In one of his

---

9 On the course and discourses of Croat nationalism after 1945, see Mark Biondich, '"We Were Defending the State": Nationalism, Myth, and Memory in Twentieth-Century Croatia', in *Ideologies and National Identities: The Case of Twentieth-Century Southeastern Europe*, eds John R Lampe and Mark Mazower (Budapest: CEU Press, 2004).

10 These massacres are discussed in the chapter by Alexander Korb and Dieter Pohl, 'Mass violence and its immediate aftermath in Central and Eastern Europe during the Second World War, 1939–47', in this volume.

11 Thousands were arrested while many emigrated. An orthodox Communist leadership was installed in Croatia in 1972 and remained relatively conformist until 1989. See Jill Irvine, 'The Croatian Spring and the Dissolution of Yugoslavia', in Cohen and Dragović-Soso, *State Collapse in South-Eastern Europe*, 149–78.

12 Duško Doder and Louise Branson, *Milošević: Portrait of a Tyrant* (New York: The Free Press, 1999), 43; and, Adam LeBor, *Milosevic: A Biography* (New Haven, CT: Yale University Press, 2004).

most memorable moments, Milošević told a group of Serb protesters that no one had a right to beat them.[13] What lent his words their revolutionary significance was that Milošević had sided with protesters against legitimate authority and, in the process and probably also inadvertently, stirred up nationalist sentiment. Milošević had challenged the Albanian party leadership's right to govern Serbs in Kosovo. This de facto endorsement of the Kosovo Serb position transformed Milošević into a Serb national champion.[14]

In September 1987, Milošević solidified his position within the League of Communists of Serbia and as Serbia's most important political figure.[15] The following year, Milošević loyalists orchestrated mass protests to subvert existing party institutions and elites in Vojvodina (October 1988), Montenegro (January 1989) and Kosovo (March 1989). By early 1989, Milošević had deposed orthodox party elites and installed nationalist allies in Montenegro and Serbia's two autonomous provinces, in what came to be known as the 'anti-bureaucratic revolution'.[16] In June 1989, Serbia commemorated the 600th anniversary of the Battle of Kosovo, in what became one of the most carefully choreographed and largest manifestations of Serb nationalism in Yugoslavia's history. Delivering the defining address, Milošević told a crowd numbering in the several hundreds of thousands that while the Serbs' contemporary struggles were not armed battles, 'such things should not be excluded yet'.[17] Serb nationalism had by now prevailed in the official governing bodies of the republics of Serbia (and its two 'autonomous' provinces) and Montenegro, while the nationalist message was already being carried to Serbs in Bosnia-Herzegovina and Croatia.[18]

By the time the League of Communists of Yugoslavia collapsed in January 1990 and the individual republics began transitioning to new administrations, the Serb nationalist narrative and symbolic politics had raised the public spectre of renewed threats. Following the elections in Croatia (April 1990) and Bosnia-Herzegovina (November 1990), and the rise of nationalist parties in those republics, the Serb nationalist discourse was instrumentalized by political elites.

---

13 Cited in Lenard J. Cohen, *Serpent in the Bosom: The Rise and Fall of Slobodan Milošević* (Boulder, CO: Westview, 2001), 62–4. See also LeBor, *Milosevic*, 79–84.
14 Slavoljub Djukić, *Milošević and Marković: A Lust for Power*, trans. Alex Dubinsky (Montreal: McGill-Queen's University Press, 2001), 17; David Rieff, 'Milošević in retrospect', *The Virginia Quarterly Review* 82, no. 3 (Summer 2006): 3–16.
15 Mihajlo Crnobrnja, *The Yugoslav Drama* (Montreal: McGill-Queen's University Press, 1996), 101; Silber and Little, *The Death of Yugoslavia*, 41–7.
16 Silber and Little, *The Death of Yugoslavia*, 36–41; Emil Kerenji, 'Vojvodina since 1988', in *Serbia since 1989: Politics and Society under Milošević and After*, eds Sabrina P. Ramet and Vjeran Pavlaković (Seattle, WA: University of Washington Press, 2005), 350–5; Louis Sell, *Slobodan Milosevic and the Destruction of Yugoslavia* (Durham, NC: Duke University Press, 2002), 56–7.
17 Cited in Silber and Little, *The Death of Yugoslavia*, 77. See also Cohen, *Serpent in the Bosom*, 78–80, 96–8.
18 Tim Judah, *The Serbs: History, Myth and the Destruction of Yugoslavia* (New Haven, CT: Yale University Press, 1997), 39; and Sabrina P. Ramet, *Balkan Babel: The Disintegration of Yugoslavia from the Death of Tito to Ethnic War*, 2nd ed. (Boulder, CO: Westview, 1996), 30. Serb nationalists reburied thousands of anonymous corpses – victims of the wartime Ustasha regime – that they removed from pits in Herzegovina. The reburial took place in the summer of 1991 in which the corpses were placed in a common grave in Belgrade; a ceremony was held, attended by the Patriarch of the Serbian Orthodox Church, Serbian politicians and Serb nationalists from Bosnia. Robert M. Hayden, 'Recounting the Dead: The Rediscovery and Redefinition of Wartime Massacres in Late- and Post-Communist Yugoslavia', in *Memory, History, and Opposition under State Socialism*, ed. Rubie S. Watson (Santa Fe, NM: School of American Research Press, 1994), 179.

Serbs were allegedly confronted with a repeat of 1941 and an imminent genocide at the hands of neo-fascism in Croatia and Islamist fundamentalism in Bosnia.[19] This rhetoric was later employed as justification for JNA–Serbian military operations in Croatia (1991) and Bosnia (1992), which Serbian propaganda claimed were there to protect the Serb people and their rightful lands.

This was the intellectual and political milieu within which the League of Communists of Yugoslavia convened the Fourteenth Extraordinary Congress in Belgrade in January 1990. The Congress assembled on the heels of the dramatic collapse of the communist regimes in Central and Eastern Europe and the violent demise of Nicolae Ceaușescu in Romania, and it was supposed to address the question of Yugoslav transition. It immediately became apparent that there was no consensus. On 23 January 1990, the Slovenian delegation withdrew – followed shortly thereafter by their Croatian counterparts – marking the effective demise of the League of Communists of Yugoslavia, the country's leading political institution since 1945. Thereafter, each of the socialist republics moved forward with plans for multiparty elections, which occurred between April and December 1990. The first of these occurred in April 1990 in Slovenia and Croatia. The Slovenian elections resulted in the victory of a united democratic coalition. The new Slovenian authorities favoured autonomy, and in July 1990, the Slovenian Assembly declared the republic's sovereignty.[20] In Croatia, the nationalist HDZ (Croatian Democratic Union) led by former Partisan general and nationalist dissident Franjo Tuđman received a majority of seats in the legislature.[21] In February 1990, Serb nationalists in Croatia formed the SDS (Serbian Democratic Party) under Jovan Rašković; the SDS became the undisputed leader of Croatia's Serbian population.[22] Fearing marginalization in the new Croatian legislature, however, on 20 May 1990 the SDS declared a boycott of that institution.

In heterogeneous Bosnia-Herzegovina, which according to the March 1991 census had 4.3 million citizens, of whom 44 per cent were Bosnian Muslim, 31 per cent were Serb and 17 per cent were Croat, three nationalist parties emerged as successors to the local League of Communists.[23] The SDA (Party for Democratic Action), formed in May 1990 by former Bosnian Muslim dissident Alija Izetbegović, supported a unitary Bosnian state in which Muslims, Serbs and Croats would remain the three constituent state peoples. In July 1990, the SDS was formed on the model of its Croatian Serb counterpart, headed by

---

19 One of the academic participants at the Congress of Serb Intellectuals in March 1992 was Radomir Bulatović, an SDS activist in Sarajevo and member of the party's Political Council. He gave a presentation at the Congress on the Jasenovac camp system, based on his earlier research. Bulatović concluded in his 1990 work on Jasenovac that as many as 1.1 million people, the majority of them Serbs, were killed at Jasenovac alone. See the daily newspaper *Oslobođenje*, 30 March 1992, 6; and Radomir Bulatović, *Koncentracioni logor Jasenovac s posebnim osvrtom na Donju Gradinu: Istorijsko-sociološka i antropološka studija* [The Jasenovac Concentration Camp with an overview of Donja Gradina: An historical-sociological and anthropological study] (Sarajevo: Svjetlost, 1990).
20 Susan Woodward, *Balkan Tragedy: Chaos and Dissolution after the Cold War* (Washington, DC: Brookings Institution, 1995), 119–20.
21 Marcus Tanner, *Croatia: A Nation Forged at War* (New Haven, CT: Yale University Press, 1997), 227–8.
22 See Srđan Radulović, *Sudbina Krajine* [The fate of the Krajina] (Belgrade: Dan graf, 1996), 16.
23 See Suad Arnautović, *Izbori u Bosni i Hercegovini '90: Analiza izbornog procesa* [Elections in Bosnia-Herzegovina 1990: an analysis of the electoral process] (Sarajevo: Promocult, 1996), 179–95.

Radovan Karadžić.²⁴ The HDZ BiH (Croatian Democratic Union of Bosnia-Herzegovina), first led by Stjepan Kljuić and then Mate Boban, was founded in August 1990 as an offshoot of Tuđman's party. On the question of Bosnia's status within Yugoslavia, the HDZ BiH favoured the confederal model espoused by Croatia and Slovenia, while the SDS supported a strong federal Yugoslavia. The SDA, SDS and HDZ won decisive victories in the 18 November 1990 elections, with 86, 72 and 44 seats, respectively, of the 240 seats in the bicameral legislature. The three parties dominated the new Presidency, with the SDA controlling three positions and the SDS and HDZ each controlling two. Izetbegović became President of the Presidency of Bosnia-Herzegovina.

In Serbia and Montenegro, Milošević and Momir Bulatović swept to victory in December 1990 as leaders of their republics' new Socialist parties. Reform communists retained their dominant role, buttressed by the fact that they had co-opted the nationalist discourse in advance of the non-communist opposition. In Macedonia, which went to the polls in November 1990, reform communists, known as the Social Democratic League of Macedonia, also retained a major role by forming a coalition government with Macedonian liberals and the largest Albanian party.²⁵

The prelude to war: Croatia and Bosnia, 1990–92

In Croatia, Tuđman's HDZ came to power riding a nationalist wave. Although an ideologically diverse polity, its programme was premised on an affirmation of Croat national rights. However, Croatia's new leaders were confronted by the escalating claims of the Serb minority, which in 1991 accounted for 12 per cent of the population. In July 1990, the HDZ government proposed constitutional amendments which would have relegated Serbs from their earlier status of a constituent nation in Croatia to that of a minority. Similarly, socialist symbols were replaced by traditional Croat nationalist symbols. In the process, the Croatian authorities displayed a good deal of insensitivity to Croatian Serb concerns and failed to appreciate the powerful character of their collective fears. The 'revival of memory' gradually assumed more negative traits when a general remodelling of history commenced, one in which Croat victimization was the central theme.²⁶ The HDZ's symbolic politics reflected the suppressed frustrations that had simmered in the aftermath of the Croatian Spring, but they were also undoubtedly a response to the revival of Serb nationalism under Milošević and certainly played directly into the hands of Serbian propagandists who alleged that a neo-Ustasha regime had been installed in Zagreb.

The SDS boycott of Croatian parliamentary institutions and the nationalist rhetoric of the Croatian authorities made compromise difficult from the outset. The abortive negotiations between the Croatian authorities and Serb minority in July 1990 occurred in a climate of

---

24 Ibid., 41. The SDS had three vice presidents between 1990 and 1992: Momčilo Krajišnik, Nikola Koljević and Biljana Plavšić. During the election campaign, the leaders of the three nationalist parties refrained from direct public attacks and cooperated on the division of post-election spoils. This approach was deliberately intended to forestall victory by the two socialist parties. See Mirko Pejanović, *Bosansko pitanje i Srbi u Bosni i Hercegovini* [The Bosnian question and Serbs in Bosnia-Herzegovina] (Sarajevo: Bosanska knjiga, 1999), 19; Mirko Pejanović, *Through Bosnian Eyes: The Political Memoir of a Bosnian Serb* (West Lafayette, IN: Purdue University Press, 2004), 33–52.

25 Viktor Meier, *Yugoslavia: A History of its Demise* (London: Routledge, 1999) 193–4.

26 See Vjeran Pavlakovic, *Red Stars, Black Shirts: Symbols, Commemorations, and Contested Histories of World War Two in Croatia* (Seattle, WA: National Council for Eurasian and East European Research, 2008).

escalating polemics between the Serbian and Croatian state media.[27] The new Croatian Serb leadership, under Milan Babić, advocated a more assertive Serb policy including a campaign for a separate Serb territory in Croatia.[28] In July 1990, the SDS formed a 'Serb National Council' ostensibly as the supreme coordinating authority of Serb autonomous institutions in Croatia.[29] Babić visited Belgrade on 13 August 1990 and met with Borisav Jović, the Yugoslav President, from whom he seemed to win support for his territorial initiative and assurances of aid.[30] Babić and his supporters proceeded to build their 'Community of Municipalities' by gaining control of local institutions of administration and in particular the police in predominantly Serb-populated areas.[31] Within months of Croatia's first multiparty elections, Croat-Serb relations deteriorated rapidly.[32] On 30 September 1990, the Serb National Council at Knin proclaimed Serb autonomy 'on the ethnic and historical territory on which they live',[33] without defining the extent of that territory. Beginning on 21 December 1990, the SDS announced the creation of the first of three 'Serb Autonomous Districts'.[34] The implementation of Croatian Serb territorial autonomy – establishing control of local government and police – was accompanied by the first instances of violence. Babić would later acknowledge that his goal at the time was to precipitate a state of emergency that would enable the Yugoslav authorities and JNA to suspend Croatian authority in those municipalities inhabited predominantly by Serbs.[35] By this stage, the JNA had appropriated the arms depots of Territorial Defence units in Slovenia and Croatia, a measure intended to deprive these governments of materiel for their own armed forces.[36] As Croatia staged its 19 May 1991 sovereignty referendum, its authorities were hurriedly purchasing arms from former Eastern bloc states. In spring 1991, the JNA was distributing infantry weapons, mortars and ammunition to Serb separatists in Croatia.[37]

---

27 See Gale Stokes, 'From Nation to Minority: Serbs in Croatia and Bosnia at the Outbreak of the Yugoslav Wars', *Problems of Post-Communism* 52, no. 6 (November–December 2005): 3–20.
28 Meier, *Yugoslavia*, 154.
29 Ibid., 146; and Cohen, *Broken Bonds*, 131. Babić was indicted by the ICTY in November 2003 on several counts of crimes against humanity. He pleaded guilty in January 2004 and was sentenced on 29 June 2004 by the Trial Chamber to thirteen years' imprisonment. As part of his plea bargain with the Office of the Prosecutor, Babić testified against several Serb leaders from Serbia, Croatia and Bosnia. He testified in the Milošević trial that, in part because of propaganda from Belgrade, which claimed that the new Croatian authorities were preparing to commit genocide against Serbs, the SDS leadership shifted from its autonomist position to a more radical line. The result was acceptance of Milošević's concept of Serb unification. Babić committed suicide in March 2006, while in an ICTY detention facility. See Mirko Klarin, 'Milošević Trial: Protected Witness Goes Public', *IWPR's Tribunal Update*, no. 292 (2–6 December 2002).
30 Silber and Little, *The Death of Yugoslavia*, 110–11.
31 Ibid., 105–6.
32 For a more detailed discussion, see Tanner, *Croatia*, 221–49.
33 Radulović, *Sudbina Krajine*, 22.
34 On the formation of these three areas, see Radulović, *Sudbina Krajine*, 22–5. These autonomous regions were 'Krajina', followed by 'Western Slavonia' and 'Slavonia, Baranja and Western Srem'.
35 Mirko Klarin, 'Milošević's Greater Serbia Project', *IWPR Tribunal Update*, no. 290, 18–22 November 2002. On the armed clashes in Croatia, see Silber and Little, *The Death of Yugoslavia*, 154–6.
36 Borisav Jović, *Poslednji dani SFRJ; Izvodi iz dnevnika*, [The last days of the Socialist Federal Republic of Yugoslavia: excerpts from a diary], 2nd ed. (Kragujevac: Prizm, 1996), 146.
37 The KOS (Counterintelligence Service of the JNA) and SDB (Serbian State Security Service) allegedly collaborated in the distribution of arms to Croatian Serb security services. This information is derived from the testimony of former Major Mustafa Čandić. See Mirko Klarin, 'Milošević suffers "exhaustion"', *IWPR Tribunal Update*, No. 287, 28 October–1 November 2002, https://iwpr.net/global-voices/milosevic-suffers-exhaustion (accessed 16 June 2021).

Bosnia followed a similar trajectory, as divisions emerged over the contentious issue of internal organization and Bosnian Serb plans for 'regionalization'. The SDS's regionalization campaign was an attempt to secure Serb control in those municipalities with a Serb plurality. It entailed the formation of parallel institutions of authority as a prologue to the removal of territory from the jurisdiction of the Bosnian authorities. Modelled on the Serb experience in Croatia, the Bosnian Serb campaign was multifaceted and began with the configuration of regional 'Communities of Municipalities', followed by attempts to carve out Serb-dominated territories from municipalities where Serbs lacked a clear majority, and the establishment of parallel Serb governing bodies. The SDS was certainly not the only political party in Bosnia to pursue single-party domination of select territory under the rubric of 'regionalization' – on 18 November 1991, the HDZ formed the 'Croat Community of Herzeg-Bosnia' – but it initiated the process and pursued it consistently.[38] In April and May 1991, the SDS proclaimed the formation of three 'Communities of Municipalities', which in September 1991, after war had already begun in neighbouring Croatia, were renamed 'Serb Autonomous Regions', with three additional regions.[39] By the spring of 1991, SDS leaders in both Croatia and Bosnia had codified autonomous local institutions.

War in Slovenia and Croatia, 1991–92

As the political and constitutional crisis in Yugoslavia became ever more intense, with armed clashes in Croatia and regionalization in Bosnia-Herzegovina, the six elected republican presidents held a series of meetings in early 1991 to discuss Yugoslavia's constitutional crisis. These talks occurred in the context of federal paralysis. In May 1991, the representatives of Serbia, Vojvodina, Kosovo and Montenegro, who constituted four of the eight members of the Yugoslav Federal Presidency, refused to accept the Croatian candidate as the new President. At this point federal constitutional mechanisms ceased functioning. The ensuing negotiations among republican leaders failed to reach a consensus.[40] With negotiations stalled, on 25 June 1991 Slovenia and Croatia declared their independence. Two days later, the JNA moved to assert federal control over Slovenia's international border-crossings and airports, triggering a 10-day armed conflict in Slovenia. Under the 'Brioni Accord', mediated by EC (European Community) officials on 18 July 1991, the JNA withdrew from Slovenia, while Slovenia and

---

38 The 'Croat Community of Herzeg-Bosnia' was formed in November 1991 as a rudimentary political authority in predominantly Croat-populated areas and was composed of thirty municipalities in western Herzegovina, central Bosnia and the Posavina (the Sava River basin, northern Bosnia). In those territories adjacent to Croatia, the 'Croat Community' essentially served as an extension of Croatian authority. In August 1993, during the Croat-Bosniak conflict, this entity was proclaimed a republic. Meier, *Yugoslavia*, 206–7.
39 Silber and Little, *The Death of Yugoslavia*, 234–6.
40 On the presidential talks and the Gligorov-Izetbegović proposal, see ibid., 161–7. On the Slovenian and Croatian proposals, see Dejan Jović, 'The Slovenian-Croatian Confederal Proposal: A Tactical Move or Ultimate Solution?' in Cohen and Dragović-Soso, *State Collapse in South-Eastern Europe*, 249–80. In the midst of these discussions, Tuđman and Milošević met at Karađorđevo, Serbia. Since then, the meeting has become a source of much speculation, with allegations that the two presidents secretly agreed to an informal plan to divide Bosnia between them. No evidence has emerged indicating an agreement on territorial division was struck, but it appears that the topic was broached at that time and in later discussions. See Miloš Milić, *Dogovori u Karađorđevu o podeli Bosne i Hercegovine* [The Karađorđevo talks about the partition of Bosnia-Herzegovina] (Sarajevo: Rabić, 1998).

Croatia agreed to defer independence by three months, until 8 October 1991. The EC deployed unarmed military observers to Croatia, but the Brioni Accord did not address the future role of the JNA in Croatia, where the conflict now escalated into open warfare.[41]

The war that was waged from July to December 1991 in Croatia proved remarkably brutal and foreshadowed the Bosnian conflict. The fighting was initially concentrated in ethnically mixed parts of central and southern Croatia, but from late August 1991 spread to eastern Croatia. Several towns endured repeated shelling and significant damage.[42] The case of Ilok in eastern Croatia was symptomatic of the nature of the unfolding conflict. In mid-September 1991, the town, defended by a small detachment of the recently formed Croatian National Guard and local police, was besieged by the JNA. After sustained shelling, on 14 October 1991 the town council formally surrendered to the JNA in the presence of the EC observer mission. Three days later, more than 5,000 non-Serbs were 'evacuated' from Ilok under the eyes of EC observers. But the most devastating example of wilful destruction and ethnic cleansing was the multi-ethnic town of Vukovar, which was besieged by JNA forces from 24 August until 18 November 1991.[43] Repeated heavy shelling razed the town and inflicted more than 1,000 civilian deaths. When JNA troops, supported by Serbian Territorial Defence units and paramilitaries, entered the town they detained several hundred prisoners of war and rounded up non-Serb civilians. In one well-documented incident, more than two hundred wounded Croat soldiers were handed over by JNA officers to a Serbian Territorial Defence unit and executed at a farm in nearby Ovčara. At the same time, more than 20,000 non-Serbs were ethnically cleansed from Vukovar and its environs.[44] The same pattern was discernible elsewhere.[45] The

---

41 The most detailed study to date of the JNA's actions in Croatia and Bosnia in 1991–92, combined with Serbian police and paramilitary operations, is the expert witness report of Reynaud Theunens, 'The SFRY Armed Forces and the Conflict in Croatia – JNA Activity in BiH and JNA (VJ) Support to Bosnian Serb Forces', Military Analysis Team Expert Report Case IT-02-54-T, 16 December 2003, 25–120. More broadly, see Florian Bieber, 'The Role of the Yugoslav People's Army in the Dissolution of Yugoslavia: The Army without a State?' in Cohen and Dragović-Soso, *State Collapse in South-Eastern Europe*, 301–32.

42 For a discussion of the Croatian war, see Tanner, *Croatia*, 249–74.

43 According to the 1991 census, the municipality of Vukovar had 84,024 people, of whom 43.2% were Croats, 37.4% were Serbs and 7.3% were 'Yugoslavs', while Magyars, Slovaks and others made up the remaining 12.1%. See 'Popis stanovništva: Nema više Jugoslavena' [The census: there are no more Yugoslavs], *Danas* (Zagreb), 6 August 1991; and PROSECUTOR v. MILE MRKŠIĆ, MIROSLAV RADIĆ, VESELIN ŠLJIVANČANIN, Judgement, 27 September 2007, https://www.icty.org/x/cases/mrksic/tjug/en/070927.pdf (accessed 7 July 2021), 8.

44 The Office of the Prosecutor of the ICTY indicted three JNA officers for crimes perpetrated at Vukovar: the Commander of the JNA 'Guards Brigade', Colonel (later General) Mile Mrkšić, and his subordinates Major Veselin Šljivančanin and Captain Miroslav Radić. In September 2007, the ICTY Trial Chamber acquitted Radić but found Mrkšić and Šljivančanin guilty of aiding and abetting murder and torture, and for inhumane conditions of detention. Mrkšić and Šljivančanin were sentenced to 20 and 5 years' imprisonment, respectively. On 5 May 2009, the ICTY Appeals Chamber upheld the Mrkšić verdict but increased Šljivančanin's sentence to 17 years. In December 2010, Šljivančanin's sentence was reduced to 10 years. See 'Case No. IT-95-13/1-R.1' at www.icty.org for a case summary.

45 In Dalmatia, the JNA Knin Corps under Deputy Commander Colonel Ratko Mladić – later General and Commander of the Bosnian Serb Army – conducted artillery attacks against several Croat villages which were subsequently ethnically cleansed by Milan Martić's local police detachments, as at Kijevo (August) and Lovinac (September 1991). See Silber and Little, *Yugoslavia*, 171–2; and Goran Jungvirth, 'Martic "Provoked" Croatian Conflict', *IWPR Tribunal Update*, no. 440, 17 February 2006, https://iwpr.net/global-voices/martic-provoked-croatian-conflict (accessed 16 June 2021).

JNA had become, in the words of JNA General Veljko Kadijević, the Federal Secretary of Defence in 1991, a defender 'of the Serb people in Croatia so as to liberate, in every respect, all areas with a majority Serb population from the presence of the Croatian military and Croatian authority'.[46] By December 1991, the JNA and Serb forces had ethnically cleansed more than 80,000 non-Serbs from eastern Croatia and caused the flight of an equal number in other parts of the country.[47]

On 2 January 1992, Croatia and the JNA concluded a ceasefire agreement which provided for the JNA's withdrawal from Croatia and the deployment of a peacekeeping force known as the UNPROFOR (United Nations Protection Force), headquartered at Sarajevo. The UNPROFOR mission 'froze' the territorial status quo and deferred a political solution. On 15 January 1992, the EC extended diplomatic recognition to Slovenia and Croatia.[48] In the meantime, on 19 December 1991 the Croatian Serb leadership under Milan Babić had proclaimed the existence of the RSK (Republic of the Serb Krajina). For opposing the deployment of UNPROFOR troops to Serb-held areas of Croatia, Babić earned a public denunciation from Milošević, who accused him in an open letter published on 10 January 1992 in the Serbian media of endangering the most basic interests of the Serb people. Babić was ousted in early February 1992 and replaced by Goran Hadžić as President of the RSK.[49] In early 1992, the RSK stood at its apogee but remained a dependency of

---

46 Veljko Kadijević, *Moje Viđenje Raspada: Vojska bez države* [My view of the collapse: an army without a state] (Belgrade: Politika, 1993), 134.
47 The figure of 80,000 is derived from Human Rights Watch through a combination of Croatian government statistics and other sources. See Human Rights Watch, *Human Rights in Eastern Slavonia: During and After the Transition of Authority* (New York: HRW, 1997). During his testimony in the Milošević trial, former KOS officer Major General Aleksander Vasiljević claimed that as the JNA ran short of men in 1991 as a result of desertion, it turned increasingly to Serbian Territorial Defence units and paramilitaries. Beginning in October 1991, these units participated in the siege of Vukovar while several paramilitary commanders, including Dragan Vasiljković ('Captain Dragan') and Željko Ražnatović 'Arkan', worked closely with the Serbian Interior Ministry's State Security Service. A former member of the 'Red Berets', a special anti-terrorist unit of the State Security Service, testified at the same trial as protected witness 'K-2', alleging that weapons were transported on a regular basis from Serbia to bases in eastern Croatia and distributed to Arkan's 'Tigers' and other paramilitary formations. During cross-examination, K-2 admitted culpability in the January 2000 assassination of Arkan, widely believed to have been ordered by Milošević. See Mirko Klarin, 'Milošević and the Red Berets', *IWPR Tribunal Update*, no. 295, 6–10 January 2003, https://iwpr.net/global-voices/comment-milosevic-and-red-berets (published online 22 February 2005, accessed 16 June 2021); Chris Stephen, 'Courtside: The Milošević Trial', *IWPR Tribunal Update*, no. 299, 3–7 February 2003, https://iwpr.net/global-voices/courtside-milosevic-trial-19 (accessed 5 July 2021).
48 Steven L. Burg and Paul S. Shoup, *The War in Bosnia-Herzegovina: Ethnic Conflict and International Intervention* (Armonk, NY: M.E. Sharpe, 1999), 84–7, 108–17; Silber and Little, *The Death of Yugoslavia*, 209–25; James Gow, *The Triumph of the Lack of Will: International Diplomacy and the Yugoslav War* (New York: Columbia University Press, 1997), 53.
49 Milan Martić was indicted by the ICTY (2002) and stood trial between December 2005 and January 2007. He was convicted by the Trial Chamber on 12 June 2007. On 8 October 2008, the Appeals Chamber upheld the judgement while reducing his sentence from 38 to 35 years' imprisonment. In July 2011, Goran Hadžić was arrested in Serbia and extradited to The Hague. His trial began in October 2012 but was suspended due to his cancer diagnosis in November 2014; Hadžić died of cancer in July 2016.

Map 6.1 Yugoslavia, 1989–2001

the Serbian regime, which bankrolled the local authorities and even dictated political and military appointments in its structures.[50]

The Bosnian War, 1992–95

The war in Croatia fundamentally altered the situation in Bosnia. In early 1991, the Bosnian Muslim leader, Izetbegović, had raised the possibility of introducing a declaration on Bosnian

---

50 This assessment is drawn in large part on Babić's testimony at the Milošević trial. See Mirko Klarin, 'Milošević Trial: The Disposable Collaborator', *IWPR Tribunal Update*, no. 291, 25–29 November 2002, see https://iwpr.net/global-voices/comment-milosevic-trial-disposable-collaborator (published online 29 April 2005, accessed 16 June 2021); and Mirko Klarin, 'Milošević's Greater Serbia Project', *IWPR Tribunal Update*, no. 290, 18–22 November 2002, see https://iwpr.net/global-voices/comment-milosevics-greater-serbia-project (published online 29 April 2005, accessed 16 June 2021).

sovereignty in the Bosnian Assembly.[51] The SDS leadership, however, rejected the idea outright. A decisive moment came on 14–15 October 1991, during a heated session of the Bosnian Assembly. At the contentious 14 October session, Radovan Karadžić delivered an animated speech, raising the possibility that Bosnian Muslims would 'disappear' as a group if they dared declare Bosnia's independence.[52] Once the session had been adjourned and the Serb delegates had withdrawn, the Bosnian Muslim and Croat deputies reconvened and passed a 'Declaration of Sovereignty'. On 24 October 1991, the SDS responded by forming its own legislature, the 'Assembly of the Serb People of Bosnia-Herzegovina', and calling for a plebiscite to determine whether Bosnian Serbs wished to remain in Yugoslavia. The 9–10 November 1991 Bosnian Serb referendum resulted in an overwhelming endorsement for Yugoslavia's preservation.[53]

By fall 1991, the Bosnian Serbs on the one hand, and Bosnian Muslims and Croats on the other, were on two opposing trajectories. On 17 December 1991, EC foreign ministers adopted a mechanism whereby each Yugoslav republic could 'apply' for independence, which would be assessed by the EC's Badinter Arbitration Commission.[54] Three days later, on 20 December, the Bosnian Presidency voted to submit an application to the Badinter Commission. The move was condemned by the SDS. Three weeks later, on 9 January 1992, the Bosnian Serbs proclaimed the 'Serb Republic of Bosnia-Herzegovina'. On 15 January 1992, the Badinter Commission issued a written opinion recommending that Bosnia-Herzegovina hold a referendum to determine the extent of popular support for independence. Held on 29 February and 1 March 1992 in the presence of international monitors, the referendum provided a strong endorsement for independence but was boycotted by Serbs.[55] On the eve of the vote, the Bosnian Serb Assembly promulgated a 'Constitution of the Serb Republic of Bosnia and Herzegovina'. On 6 April 1992, the government of Bosnia-Herzegovina declared independence and was recognized by the EC. The United States accorded diplomatic recognition the following day as did much of the international community in the following weeks.[56]

As the crisis veered towards armed conflict in early 1992, all three parties created their own armed formations and paramilitary organizations. The Bosnian authorities relied initially on several informal, SDA-affiliated but poorly equipped militias, such as the 'Green Berets' and the 'Patriotic League', formed in late 1991. Following Bosnia's declaration of independence, in April 1992, the authorities formed the ABiH (Army of Bosnia-Herzegovina) from the existing Bosnian Territorial Defence units and by incorporating paramilitary groups. Bosnian Croats began forming local militias in 1991 during the war in Croatia, with the direct assistance of the Croatian authorities. In April 1992, they formed the HVO (Croatian Defence Council).[57]

---

51 'Alija Izetbegović: Bosna će opstati' [Alija Izetbegović: Bosnia will survive], *Danas* (Zagreb), 9 April 1991.
52 Cited in *The Death of Yugoslavia*, 237.
53 Ibid., 237–9.
54 Woodward, *Balkan Tragedy*, 276, and Gow, *Triumph*, 63.
55 Of the two million ballots cast, representing 64.3% of eligible voters, the official count showed 99.4% support for sovereignty. Omer Ibrahimagić, *Državno-pravni razvitak Bosne i Hercegovine* [The State and legal development of Bosnia-Herzegovina] (Sarajevo: OKO, 1998), 45.
56 On 27 April 1992, Serbia and Montenegro formed the 'Federal Republic of Yugoslavia' as the successor state to the Socialist Federal Republic of Yugoslavia (1945–1992).
57 On the formation specifically of the Bosnian military, see Marko Attila Hoare, *How Bosnia Armed* (London: Saqi Books and The Bosnian Institute, 2004); idem, 'Civilian-Military Relations in Bosnia-Herzegovina, 1992–1995', in *The War in Croatia and Bosnia-Herzegovina, 1991–1995*, eds Branka Magaš and Ivo Žanić (London: Taylor & Francis, 2001), 178–99; Jovan Divjak, 'The First

The existence of the system of TO (Territorial Defence) forces, which the Yugoslav authorities had instituted in 1969 following the Soviet invasion of Czechoslovakia, facilitated the formation of national armies in the successor states. The TO had functioned as a decentralized military reserve force, based in and funded by each of the six constituent republics, but ultimately under JNA command and control, which was exercised through a Council for Territorial Defence subordinate to the Federal Secretary for National Defence. TO units were organized around lightly armed infantry whose primary purpose was to serve as an auxiliary force to the JNA in the event of war. Arms depots were placed throughout the republics, in or near municipal buildings, state factories, industrial enterprises and elsewhere, and were to be distributed by local authorities in coordination with the JNA. In principle, the TO could draw on all male citizen-soldiers, who already possessed basic military training, for service either in the reserve militia, the reserve police or in the civilian defence agency.[58] Although JNA managed to seize several arms depots in Bosnia-Herzegovina, Croatia and Slovenia on the eve of the war, the TO system enabled the rapid mobilization of reservists and the escalation of violence in 1991–92.

The Bosnian Serbs relied largely on the JNA. While Milošević resorted to plausible deniability, his collusion in arming the Bosnian Serbs was extensive.[59] By early 1992, the JNA had been transformed in all but name into a Serbian body, an institutional instrument of Serb nationalist objectives.[60] In September 1991, when the JNA mobilized reservists in Bosnia, only the Serb population responded in significant number.[61] That same month JNA reservists from the Užice Corps (Serbia) were deployed to Mostar (Herzegovina), supposedly to calm local tensions. Within weeks they had engaged local non-Serb police and paramilitaries in shootouts. In early December 1991, the Yugoslav authorities ordered all JNA recruits who hailed from Bosnia but were stationed in other republics to be transferred back to Bosnia, while non-Bosnian recruits were to be withdrawn from the republic. The Yugoslav authorities evidently concluded that, with the international recognition of several republics imminent, the JNA in Bosnia should appear to resemble a native force rather than an 'occupying' army.[62] By Christmas 1991 – only days after the Bosnian Presidency had applied to the Badinter Commission for recognition – these transfers had nearly been completed.[63] Indeed, Serbia's representative on the Yugoslav Presidency, Jović, informed the foreign media that by April

---

Phase: Struggle for Survival and Genesis of the Army of Bosnia-Herzegovina', in Magaš and Žanić, *The War in Croatia and Bosnia-Herzegovina*, 133–51; and Helsinki Watch, *War Crimes in Bosnia-Hercegovina*, vol. 1 (New York: Human Rights Watch, 1992), 32–5.

58 On the TO and its importance in the events of 1990–1992, see Dejan Jović, *Yugoslavia: A State that Withered Away* (West Lafayette, IN: Purdue University Press, 2009), 91–2, n. 70; Helsinki Watch, *War Crimes in Bosnia-Hercegovina*, vol. 2, (New York: Helsinki Watch, 1993), 116, n. 158.

59 Mark Mazower, *The War in Bosnia: An Analysis* (London: UK Citizens' Committee for Bosnia-Herzegovina, 1992), 4. In November 2002, during the proceedings against Milošević at the ICTY, prosecutors played more than 50 intercepted phone conversations, many of them involving Milošević and Karadžić. One of these intercepts, from summer 1991, revealed the two leaders discussing where Serb units should be stationed in advance of their deployment to Croatia. 'Prosecutors Play Tape of an Intercepted Call at Milošević's Trial', *The New York Times*, 23 November 2002.

60 Meier, *Yugoslavia*, 207–8. See also *War Crimes in Bosnia-Hercegovina*, vol. 1, 35–8.

61 Kadijević, *Moje viđenje raspada*, 147.

62 Jović, *Poslednji dani SFRJ*, 420.

63 Ibid., 421.

1992 nearly 90 per cent of JNA troops in Bosnia were native to the republic.[64] Bosnian Serb police and paramilitary groups had been equipped with light arms from TO stockpiles. When the JNA withdrew from Bosnia in May 1992, much of its personnel and heavy weaponry was transferred to the newly constituted VRS (Army of the Serb Republic) under General Ratko Mladić.[65] As war began in Bosnia, the Bosnian Serbs possessed a vital advantage in firepower if not in manpower.

Mass violence and ethnic cleansing: the unmixing of peoples

From the beginning of the war in Bosnia-Herzegovina in April 1992, the Bosnian Serb leadership pursued the creation of a nationally homogeneous state.[66] In eastern Bosnia, in ethnically mixed municipalities with a large Bosnian Muslim population, such as Zvornik, Bijeljina and Foča, the JNA (and later the VRS), Bosnian Serb police detachments and Serbian paramilitary forces pursued a policy of ethnic cleansing which involved the use of violence to intimidate non-Serbs into submission and 'voluntary' flight. This was replicated in the Bosnian Krajina of northwest Bosnia and in Posavina, which served as a corridor linking the Bosnian Krajina and eastern Bosnia. Between April and June 1992, the territories 'liberated' by Bosnian Serb forces were incorporated in the 'Serb Republic of Bosnia-Herzegovina'. The policy of ethnic cleansing took variegated form, including deliberate killings, deportation and forced flight. The primary targets were men of military age, who were killed or deported to makeshift detention facilities and concentration camps, the most infamous of which were Manjača, Keraterm, Omarska and Trnopolje in the Bosnian Krajina.[67] Women were particularly vulnerable. Police, paramilitary and regular armed forces perpetrated indiscriminate attacks and mass rape. In some instances, as in the infamous 'rape camps' at Foča, rape was used as a systematic tool of ethnic cleansing.[68] Cultural and religious monuments were systematically

---

64 Silber and Little, *The Death of Yugoslavia*, 240–41.
65 James Gow, *Legitimacy and the Military: The Yugoslav Crisis* (London: Pinter, 1992), 46–7.
66 On the controversies surrounding ethnic cleansing in Bosnia, see Marie-Janine Calic, 'Ethnic Cleansing and War Crimes, 1991–1995', in Ingrao and Emmert *Confronting the Yugoslav Controversies*, 115–46.
67 Public revelation of the existence of these camps and the widespread and systematic nature of the atrocities perpetrated against non-combatants as part of the policy of ethnic cleansing, led to the establishment of a UN commission of experts to investigate serious violations of international humanitarian law in the former Yugoslavia. The commission's final report laid the basis for the creation of the UN ad hoc court, the ICTY. On war crimes and crimes against humanity perpetrated in 1992–93, see Helsinki Watch, *War Crimes in Bosnia-Hercegovina*, vol. 1, and idem, *War Crimes in Bosnia-Hercegovina*, vol. 2 (New York: Human Rights Watch, 1993). Since its inception, the ICTY has indicted 161 persons for war crimes committed on the territory of the former Yugoslavia between 1991 and 2001. As of June 2021, 93 persons were sentenced. The ICTY closed in 2017 and the remaining appeals cases were handed to the IRMCT. On 30 June 2021, the former leaders of the Serbian state security service, Franko Simatović and Jovica Stanišić were convicted by the IRMCT for their role in aiding and abetting crimes committed in Bosnia in 1992. It is the ICTY/IRMCT's last case. See https://www.icty.org/en/cases/key-figures-cases and https://www.irmct.org/en/news/21-08-06-judgement-delivered-case-prosecutor-v-jovica-stanisic-and-franko-simatovic (accessed 5 July 2021).
68 On rape warfare and its use as part of ethnic cleansing, see Alexandra Stiglmayer, ed., *Mass Rape: The War Against Women in Bosnia-Herzegovina* (Lincoln, NE: University of Nebraska Press, 1994); and Caroline Kennedy-Pipe and Penny Stanley, 'Rape in War: Lessons of the Balkan Conflicts in the 1990s', *The Kosovo Tragedy: The Human Rights Dimensions*, ed. Ken Booth (London: Frank Cass, 2001).

destroyed.[69] In some areas, such as Sarajevo, Bihać, Tuzla, Goražde, Žepa and Srebrenica, the Bosnian Serbs were unable in 1992 to expel the non-Serb population, resulting in besieged enclaves whose civilian populations were exposed to repeated shelling.[70] The following year, these enclaves became UN protected 'safe areas'.

At the 16th Session of the Bosnian Serb Assembly of 12 May 1992, both the Bosnian Serb leader Karadžić and the speaker of the Bosnian Serb Assembly Krajišnik declared the 'separation of communities' to be one of the most important strategic objectives of the Bosnian Serb leadership. Within weeks of this session, the VRS and the RS MUP (Bosnian Serb Ministry of the Interior) began reporting on the implementation of the policy of ethnic resettlement. Some of the worst violence was experienced in the ethnically heterogeneous Bosnian Krajina of northwest Bosnia, centred on the town of Banja Luka and consisting of more than 20 municipalities. No single nationality possessed a majority; Serbs, Bosnian Muslims and Croats accounted for approximately 43, 40 and 10 per cent of the population, respectively. The events of 1992 in this region are discussed here to exemplify some of the dynamics of ethnic cleansing and mass violence in Bosnia.

During the initial phase of population expulsions it became apparent that those non-Serbs who were expelled would not be permitted to return, which suggests that their exodus was the principal aim of the conflict.[71] Several VRS military reports attempted to portray this as a peaceful operation and that non-Serbs were leaving 'voluntarily' or were simply fleeing the military conflict.[72] The RS MUP chief of police in Ključ reported to his superiors in Banja Luka that extensive pressure had been applied against Muslims to emigrate.[73] This operation was remarkably brutal from the outset. According to a mid-June 1992 report from the VRS 1st Krajina Corps,

> the attempt to expel them [Muslims and Croats] to Central Bosnia failed because of transportation difficulties and their resistance to leaving their places [of residence]. This is giving rise to vindictiveness and revenge and is resulting in the enemy closing its ranks.[74]

The fact that non-Serbs did not wish to leave and that the VRS and RS MUP were assisting in their removal, unmistakably demonstrates the violent nature of the removal process and that the violence escalated as resistance was encountered. There is little in the way of critical commentary

---

69 On the destruction of cultural monuments as part of ethnic cleansing, see Roy Gutman, *A Witness to Genocide* (New York: Macmillan, 1993), 77–83; and András Riedlmayer, *Killing Memory: Bosnia's Cultural Heritage and Its Destruction* (Philadelphia, PA: Community of Bosnia, 1994).
70 In 1993, the United Nations Security Council declared these besieged areas 'safe havens' under the protection of the UNPROFOR mission in Bosnia-Herzegovina. See William J. Durch and James A. Schear, 'Faultlines: UN Operations in the former Yugoslavia', in *UN Peacekeeping, American politics, and the Uncivil Wars of the 1990s*, ed. William J. Durch (London: Palgrave Macmillan, 1996), 193–274.
71 Ewan Brown, Military Analyst, ICTY, 'Military Developments in the Bosanska Krajina – 1992: A Background Study', 27 November 2002, 111–12. The report is accessible via the ICTY Court Records (registration required): www.icr.icty.org.
72 Ibid., 113–14.
73 Christian A. Nielsen, 'The Bosnian Serb Ministry of Internal Affairs: Genesis, Performance and Command and Control, 1990–1992', Research report prepared for the case of Momčilo Krajišnik (IT-00-39), 13 August 2004, 83.
74 Cited in Brown, 'Military Developments in the Bosanska Krajina', 115.

in VRS or RS MUP documentation on the merits of the policy of ethnic cleansing; when criticisms were raised, for the most part they dealt with logistical matters and non-Serb resistance.[75]

In light of the scale of this operation, considerable planning and coordination were necessary between the Bosnian Serb civilian authorities (central and local), the VRS and RS MUP. Non-Serbs were permitted to leave only if they agreed to depart permanently and 'voluntarily' from their places of domicile. If they agreed, the RS MUP would 'certify' that they were not suspected of committing any crimes. Non-Serbs were required to submit requests to 'unregister' from their municipalities and transfer ownership of their moveable and immoveable properties; they could take with them only DM 300. In this fashion, thousands of non-Serbs were 'evacuated' by the RS MUP and the military police.[76] Warehouses were established to store non-Serb moveable property, while abandoned homes and apartments were duly registered by the police authorities.[77] The ethnic cleansing of entire municipalities was often recorded in great detail. For example, the VRS brigade in the town of Ključ recorded the departure of 16,806 non-Serbs from several local municipalities, which before the war had Muslim pluralities.[78] In the town of Bosanski Novi, the Territorial Defence reserve force and military police units assembled a train consisting of 22 cattle wagons that were used to deport roughly 4,000 inhabitants of Blagaj Japra and environs to Bosnian government territory.[79]

The RS MUP centre in Banja Luka in August 1992 reported of the vast scale and systematic nature of the ethnic cleansing that had occurred in several ethnically mixed municipalities in the Bosnian Krajina. It estimated that nearly 5,000 non-Serbs had departed from the Prijedor municipality on the eve of the conflict, but between May and August 1992 another 20,000 non-Serbs had simply 'left' without following 'the legally prescribed procedure for unregistering citizens' legal places of residence'. Another 13,180 persons, mainly Muslims, had submitted applications to 'unregister' their place of residence, and were awaiting approval to depart as of August 1992.[80] In the Sanski Most municipality, about 3,000 non-Serbs had 'moved out' since May 1992, without prior registration with the Serb police authorities. Between May and mid-August 1992, another 12,000 Muslims and Croats applied to the local police to 'unregister their place of residence'.[81] In the Bosanski Novi municipality, about 500 Muslims had fled the region in May 1992, while 3,500 left the municipality in early June 1992 with the 'agreement' of the local Serb authorities. Another 5,680 persons 'unregistered' their residency in Bosanski Novi and departed on 23 July 1992. Before leaving, according to an RS MUP report, 'these citizens gave statements before the competent municipal organs that their resettlement was voluntary'.[82] Some non-Serbs declared their loyalty to the Bosnian Serb regime in an attempt to avoid 'resettlement'. An RS MUP report of 21 July 1992 from Sokolac noted that the last remaining Muslim family in the town had been murdered by 'unknown perpetrators', despite its declaration of loyalty, and that all Muslim houses had been plundered.[83]

---

75 Ibid.
76 Nielsen, 'The Bosnian Serb Ministry of Internal Affairs', 82.
77 Brown, 'Military Developments in the Bosanska Krajina', 116.
78 Ibid., 119–20.
79 Ibid., 97–8.
80 The Prijedor police station reported, on 29 September 1992, that it had officially processed 15,280 applications for non-Serb emigration from the municipality. Nielsen, 'The Bosnian Serb Ministry of Internal Affairs', 83.
81 Brown, 'Military Developments in the Bosanska Krajina', 120–21.
82 Ibid., 121.
83 Nielsen, 'The Bosnian Serb Ministry of Internal Affairs', 82.

The violent dissolution of Yugoslavia

Mass violence and ethnic cleansing: the detention centres

The VRS, RS MUP and various paramilitaries participated in the mass detention of the non-Serb civilian population. Most of the non-Serb civilians detained during VRS military operations were processed through local police stations or 'investigative and collection centres' for interrogation by the RS MUP. The formation of detention centres was linked closely to the Bosnian Serb capture of several ethnically mixed municipalities. The seizure of Prijedor serves as a case in point. Once the Bosnian Serbs had asserted control, most non-Serbs were removed from positions of responsibility. The local Muslims and Croats attempted to retake the town on 30 May 1992, which led to the roundup of the entire non-Serb population and to harsh VRS attacks against several local Muslim villages, such as Hambarine and Kozarac. Several atrocities were perpetrated during these operations. The mass detention of non-Serb civilians led to the creation of the Omarska, Keraterm and Trnopolje camps, all three of which were formed by order of Simo Drljača, the Serb police chief of Prijedor. Planned initially to function only for a few weeks, the Omarska camp remained in operation until late August 1992.[84]

In the Sanski Most municipality, at least three detention centres existed, one at a sports hall and two at commercial facilities. The guards were typically local police and military reservists. In the Bosanski Novi municipality, many non-Serbs were held at a football stadium, while in the town of Bosanski Šamac a school served as the primary detention facility.[85] In the Prijedor municipality, the Omarska, Keraterm and Trnopolje camps were the main detention facilities. Prisoners of war were sent to the Manjača camp, which was under VRS jurisdiction.[86] The Omarska camp was established at the end of May 1992, but quickly reached its capacity; as a result, the Keraterm and Trnopolje camps were opened the following month. After prisoners had been 'criminally processed' at Omarska, they were dispatched either to Trnopolje and Keraterm or to Manjača. The Omarska and Keraterm camps were under police administration and the guards were under strict orders not to disclose any information about the camps. Some of the guards at the Trnopolje camp were military personnel.[87] An RS MUP police report from August 1992 noted that, between 27 May and 16 August 1992, 3,334 persons underwent 'criminal processing' at the Omarska camp.[88] According to the same source, nearly 6,000 non-Serbs were officially 'processed' through Omarska, Keraterm and Trnopolje, which were guarded by just under 200 RS MUP regular and reserve police.[89] A total of 1,655 non-Serbs were officially 'processed' through the Sanski Most camps.[90] Omarska and Keraterm were dismantled on 21 August 1992, Trnopolje in November 1992 and Manjača in December 1992.[91]

After arriving at the camps and other detention centres, prisoners were placed in priority groups. In Sanski Most, they were categorized either as 'politicians', 'nationalist extremists' or as 'people unwelcome in Sanski Most municipality'.[92] A Bosnian Serb police report on the Omarska camp similarly referred to three categories of detainees who were sorted 'according to

---

84 See the ICTY case summary of *Mejakić et al* ('Omarska and Keraterm Camps') at https://www.icty.org/x/cases/mejakic/cis/en/cis_mejakic_al_en.pdf (accessed 5 July 2021).
85 Nielsen, 'The Bosnian Serb Ministry of Internal Affairs', 78.
86 Brown, 'Military Developments in the Bosanska Krajina', 98–100, 103.
87 Nielsen, 'The Bosnian Serb Ministry of Internal Affairs', 78.
88 Brown, 'Military Developments in the Bosanska Krajina', 100–02.
89 Nielsen, 'The Bosnian Serb Ministry of Internal Affairs', 74–5.
90 Ibid., 79.
91 Ibid., 75.
92 Cited in Brown, 'Military Developments in the Bosanska Krajina', 99.

the degree of their personal responsibility in the armed conflict'.[93] The available documentation demonstrates that both the VRS Main Staff and the RS MUP were aware of the atrocious conditions in the camps.[94] In late July 1992, the international community became aware of the existence of these camps and, as a result of escalating international opprobrium, the Bosnian Serb authorities took steps to close them.[95] According to its own records, the VRS understood that most civilian detainees in the camps had not participated in armed conflict. These camps were thus not merely 'processing' centres, where prisoners were vetted to determine their criminal culpability in the war or, as was the stated purpose of the Trnopolje camp, to protect civilians who had found themselves trapped in a combat zone.[96] The high degree of coordination between the Bosnian Serb civilian authorities, the RS MUP and VRS in establishing and overseeing these camps, in addition to the fact that a significant number of prisoners were regularly transferred between camps, demonstrates a considerable degree of planning and coordination. The fact that prisoners were forced to endure horrendous conditions and not permitted to return to their homes, reveals that the camps were part of a policy of planned expulsion.[97] The abuse of camp detainees began immediately upon their arrival, and thereafter was both constant and widespread. Scores of detainees, probably several hundred, were killed. Detainees were held in crowded conditions, with little food or water and with no real toilets. The sick and wounded received little or no medical treatment. Some women were molested and raped. There was a pervasive climate of violence and fear. The ICTY Trial Chamber concluded, in a case against several former camp personnel, that the crimes of persecution, murder, torture and cruel treatment were widespread. While none of the perpetrators subsequently prosecuted at the ICTY were 'architects' of the camp system, they were fully aware of the system of persecution and participated in the commission of various cruelties. None of the defendants contested the facts surrounding the camps or the abuses perpetrated there, only the degree of their own individual responsibility.[98]

Mass violence and ethnic cleansing: the killing

As the Bosnian Serb military campaign and ethnic cleansing commenced after April 1992, both the VRS and RS MUP documented a number of killings and retaliatory actions against non-Serb civilians and prisoners. The scale of the violence clearly went far beyond what was reported, but those cases that were documented shed light on the killing process. The Korićanske stijene (Korićani Cliffs) massacre involved the murder of more than 200 Bosniak and Croat men on 21 August 1992 by members of a special detachment of Bosnian Serb police

---

93 Ibid.
94 Ibid., 104–07; and Nielsen, 'The Bosnian Serb Ministry of Internal Affairs', 76.
95 Nielsen, 'The Bosnian Serb Ministry of Internal Affairs', 78; and Brown, 'Military Developments in the Bosanska Krajina', 108.
96 Some Bosnian Serb documents refer to the inmates of the Trnopolje camp, which consisted of an elementary school, local community centre, a warehouse and some private homes, as persons who simply sought protection from the fighting or because they wished to emigrate from the region, although it was clear that those interned there were not to be permitted to return to their homes. Brown, 'Military Developments in the Bosanska Krajina', 114–15.
97 Ibid., 109–10.
98 See the ICTY case summary, with review of the facts and evidence, in *Mejakić et al*, available at https://www.icty.org/x/cases/mejakic/cis/en/cis_mejakic_al_en.pdf (accessed 5 July 2021). The case summary contains links to related cases.

from Prijedor, known as the 'Intervention Squad'.⁹⁹ On that day, a group of about 1,200 civilian detainees, including men, women and children, were released from the Trnopolje camp and transported in a convoy of 16 buses, tractors and trailers under Bosnian Serb police escort towards Travnik in Bosnian government-controlled territory. When the convoy approached Mount Vlašić, at least 200 male prisoners, many of them infirm because of the abuses they had suffered at Trnopolje, were diverted from the convoy by the Intervention Squad. The convoy continued to Travnik, but the male prisoners were robbed of their few remaining personal possessions, separated into smaller groups and taken to the Korićani Cliffs, where they were shot at close range with automatic weapons, their bodies dumped over the cliffs into the deep ravine. Before leaving, the perpetrators threw grenades down the ravine to ensure there were no survivors. According to one of the survivors, during the killing one of the policemen had shouted: 'You Turks got what you deserved!'¹⁰⁰ Twelve prisoners survived by jumping into the ravine when the shooting started. Seven were later found by a unit of the VRS. In October 1992, they were handed to the International Committee of the Red Cross.

When the local VRS military commander learned of the massacre, he compiled a special report to the 1st Krajina Corps. He observed that several 'refugees were taken out and genocide [sic] against the civilians was committed by killing them in various ways and throwing them into the [illegible] river canyon'.¹⁰¹ The report made clear that the perpetrators were Bosnian Serb police and that the victims were civilians. The VRS military command later criticized the local Serb civilian authorities for failing to notify them of the convoy, presumably because the VRS presence might have helped to avert the atrocity, but it did not criticize them for their lack of action in prosecuting the perpetrators. Another VRS report from early September 1992 about the Korićani Cliffs massacre simply noted that 'it is very fortunate that the international community did not find out about it in more detail'.¹⁰² The VRS report prompted the Interior Minister Mićo Stanišić to order an investigation. However, the Prijedor police chief, Drljača, whose men had committed the killings probably on his orders, dragged the matter out into October, claiming that his men were deployed in combat operations and that an investigation could not be carried out at the time. The Bosnian Serb authorities never took disciplinary action against any of the perpetrators.¹⁰³

The perpetrators of the Korićani Cliffs massacre were archetypal 'ordinary men', not unlike the Omarska, Keraterm and Trnopolje camp personnel.¹⁰⁴ They were all regular or reserve

---

99 In 2002 and 2009, several of the perpetrators of the massacre were detained in Bosnia-Herzegovina. One of the ringleaders, Darko Mrđa, was arrested in 2002 and transferred to the ICTY, where he plead guilty to two counts of crimes against humanity and one count of violations of the laws of war; he was sentenced to 17 years of imprisonment. Mrđa is believed to have been ordered to commit the massacre by Simo Drljača, the Prijedor chief of police, who was shot and killed by NATO soldiers while resisting arrest in 1997. In May 2009, eight former members of the Prijedor police and Intervention Squad were arrested and charged with perpetrating the Korićani Cliffs massacre before the State Court of Bosnia and Herzegovina.
100 Taken from the Judgement in the Darko Mrđa case, IT-02-59-S, 31 March 2004 at www.icty.org.
101 Cited in Brown, 'Military Developments in the Bosanska Krajina', 94.
102 Ibid.
103 Nielsen, 'The Bosnian Serb Ministry of Internal Affairs', 84.
104 The term is derived from Christopher R. Browning's seminal work, *Ordinary Men: Reserve Police Battalion 101 and the Final Solution in Poland* (New York: Harper Collins Publishers, 1992), which examined the motives of ordinary conscripts and reserve policemen as perpetrators in the Holocaust.

policemen. For the most part they were young, mostly in their twenties and of seemingly unremarkable backgrounds. The Intervention Squad's deputy commander, Petar Čivčić, was only 22 years old at the time of the massacre, while another ringleader, Darko Mrđa, was 25. Mrđa, a local man who had been employed as a worker at the Omarska mines before the war turned him into a low-ranking reserve policeman, had personally participated in the selection and killing of the prisoners, even if the order to commit the killings had been issued by his superiors. The de facto commander of the Omarska camp was Željko Mejakić, a 28-year-old professional police officer, who was found guilty by the ICTY Trial Chamber of several counts of crimes against humanity, including murder, torture, sexual violence and other inhumane acts. Two of the camp shift commanders at Omarska, both young regular policemen, also participated in the murder and torture of detainees. The commander of Keraterm security, Duško Sikirica (28), and the deputy commander of the guard service, Miroslav Kvočka (35), were also regular policeman who actively engaged in a variety of abuses. Many of these men raped female detainees.[105]

At his trial in The Hague, where he plead guilty, Mrđa claimed that he had acted under the duress of his superiors' orders and that, had he not carried them out, he would have suffered 'serious consequences' and possibly death.[106] Furthermore, he alleged that as a young, low-ranking member of the Intervention Squad he had been subjected to the steady anti-Muslim indoctrination and hate propaganda of his superiors.[107] The ICTY Trial Chamber, while not ruling out that circumstance may have had some influence on his behaviour, was not persuaded by the argument that Mrđa had acted under duress. It noted the lack of evidence of any meaningful attempt by Mrđa to dissociate himself from the killings.[108] In subsequent cases against other perpetrators of the Korićani Cliffs massacre, it emerged that at least one policeman did not want to participate in the massacre and became visibly ill during the killing; he was ordered instead to guard the location during the executions, but avoided direct participation.[109] He was never punished by his superiors for refusing to participate in the killings. Other alleged perpetrators reportedly had little difficulty killing, however, and continued to do so for the remainder of the war.[110]

A second large scale massacre, in Kotor Varoš in November 1992, involved the troops of the 1st Krajina Corps, which had earlier labelled the Korićani Cliffs massacre as an act of 'genocide'. The only area of the Kotor Varoš municipality which remained until November 1992 outside VRS control was the hamlet of Večići. The VRS had enveloped Večići and initiated negotiations for the surrender and removal of the non-Serb population. On the night of 2–3 November 1992, the village's defenders, about 400 to 500 Bosnian Muslims and Croats, attempted to fight their way through VRS lines to Bosnian government territory, while the

---

105 Nielsen, 'The Bosnian Serb Ministry of Internal Affairs', 84.
106 See 'Darko Mrdja Guilty Pleas Statement', 22 October 2003, at www.icty.org/sid/216.
107 Ibid.
108 Taken from the Judgment in the Mrđa case, IT-02-59-S, 31 March 2004 at www.icty.org.
109 See 'Korićanske stijene: Gordan Djurić Admits Guilt', *BIRN*, 6 July 2009, https://detektor.ba/2009/07/06/koricanske-stijene-gordan-djuric-admits-guilt/?lang=en (accessed 9 July 2021); and 'Korićanske stijene: Sick Because of Crime', *BIRN*, 17 December 2009, http://www.bim.ba/en/197/10/24494/.
110 'Korićanske stijene: Jednomjesečni pritvor za Sašu Zećeviča', *BIRN BiH*, 3 July 2009, see https://detektor.ba/2009/07/03/koricanske-stijene-jednomjesecni-pritvor-za-sasu-zecevica/(accessed 5 July 2021). Additional information about the massacre and subsequent criminal proceedings are available at the website of the Court of Bosnia-Herzegovina, see http://www.sudbih.gov.ba/.

women and children surrendered. The VRS stopped the advance and captured, according to the 1st Krajina Corps' combat report of 4 November 1992, a large number of 'Ustasha-Muslim soldiers'. The 1st Krajina Corps further noted that 'a brutal massacre of the [roughly 200] captured members of the Green Berets started because of the wounding of four and killing of one soldier of the [1st Krajina Corps'] Kotor Varoš Light Infantry Brigade'.[111] The report claimed that unspecified measures had been taken to prevent such actions in the future, and that the women and children had been 'evacuated' to Bosnian government territory. Within days, however, VRS documents no longer referred to a massacre, but only to combat deaths.[112] In both the Korićani Cliffs and Večići massacres, a variety of motives may have been at play. In the Večići incident, retaliation for the death and wounding of fellow soldiers, who had fought for months to take the hamlet, was the declared cause. At the Korićani Cliffs, the police perpetrators were evidently ordered to carry out the massacre, although revenge and theft may have played a part. In both cases, however, the nationalist component and hatred were clearly contributing factors.

Another incident, from the war in Croatia, serves to further illustrate the nature of wartime violence and the perpetrator phenomenon. The town of Gospić and its environs in the Lika region of Croatia witnessed two well-documented massacres, the first in October 1991 and the other in September 1993. The Lika region had, until 1991, a mixed population of Croats and Serbs, while one-third of Gospić's 9,000 inhabitants were Serbs. Most of eastern and southern Lika were occupied in 1991 by the JNA and Croatian Serb forces, which expelled virtually the entire Croat population. The other areas of Lika, including Gospić, remained under Croatian control. Many Serbs had fled or were forced out, while some, mainly those in mixed marriages, stayed behind. In the summer of 1991, Gospić became a frontline town which sustained considerable damage. It had several JNA garrisons, which were seized by the local Croatian forces in mid-September 1991. On 6 October 1991, a meeting was convened of the Gospić Crisis Staff, an ad hoc provisional administration which had been formed earlier in the war to coordinate the town's defence against the JNA and Croatian Serb forces. The nominal head of the Crisis Staff was Ante Karić, a former communist who gradually lost influence to Tihomir Orešković, the Crisis Staff's Secretary and real authority. Orešković had called the 6 October meeting, the purpose of which was to compile a list of the remaining Serbs of Gospić who were to be arrested and killed, presumably because they formed a fifth column. The ostensible pretext for the 6 October meeting was the recent expulsion and killing of several Croat civilians by Serb forces and the destruction by shelling of the town's church. Orešković emerged as the key architect of the 1991 operations, although the local commander of Croatian forces, Mirko Norac, directed the actual executions.[113]

Within days of the 6 October meeting, dozens of Serbs and some Croats were rounded up by the police in Gospić and the surrounding localities. They were taken by military vehicles to a forest near Pazarište and other sites where between 16 and 18 October, they were executed by members of a police unit of the MUP RH (Croatian Ministry of the Interior) under Norac's command. Norac directed the executions, personally killing one woman in order to incite his

---

111 Cited in Brown, 'Military Developments in the Bosanska Krajina', 96.
112 Ibid., 96–7.
113 See the summary of the evidence and an account of the trial of Norac *et al* in 'View from The Hague: Trial Against Mirko Norac', 2 June 2004, at www.icty.org/x/file/Outreach/view_from_hague/balkan_040602_en.pdf (accessed 16 June 2021). The Gospić killings and the subsequent trials are discussed in Slavenka Drakulić, *They Would Never Hurt a Fly: War Criminals on Trial in The Hague* (London: Abacus, 2004), 2–450.

men to kill. The number of civilians who were killed has not been established conclusively, but more than 100 Serbs and about 40 'unpatriotic' Croats, who had Serb spouses and were thus deemed 'unreliable', may have been murdered.[114] The perpetrators also went to great lengths to conceal all evidence of the crime.[115] Although they had not ordered the killings, the Croatian authorities at Zagreb, including the Defence and Interior Ministers and the president Franjo Tuđman, were soon made aware of the massacre. The head of the Gospić Crisis Staff, Ante Karić, who had not participated in the 6 October meeting, wrote directly to Tuđman claiming that, although the town had been successfully defended, 'various groups' of nationalists and volunteers had appeared in the town and rallied around Orešković, who had emerged as the boss of an unsavoury local regime. Tuđman evidently believed that there was some truth to these claims and ordered an investigation.[116] Orešković was briefly detained, but neither he nor the other perpetrators were punished for their crimes.[117]

Several of these local actors subsequently participated in the Medak Pocket operation between 9 and 17 September 1993, when the Croatian Army attempted to breach a large Serb salient just south of Gospić. After several days of fighting, the Croatian Army routed the local Serb force but also perpetrated crimes against Serb civilians and prisoners of war and looted more than 300 properties. When the UN forces secured the area, they uncovered unambiguous signs of a massacre and of a hasty attempt to conceal the evidence. ICTY investigators later determined the identity of 29 Serb civilian victims but estimated that more than 100 had been killed. The two most senior Croatian military commanders in Gospić, Brigadier Rahim Ademi and General Mirko Norac, were indicted in 2001 and 2004, respectively, by the ICTY for these killings.[118] At the time, however, Norac continued his steady rise through the ranks and was later even promoted in the Croatian Army.

As in the case of the Korićani Cliffs massacre, the perpetrators of the Gospić and Medak Pocket massacres were in many respects 'ordinary' men. At the time of the 1991 killings, the two young ringleaders, Orešković (34) and Norac (24), headed the local civilian and military administrations, respectively. Orešković was an obscure émigré who had returned to Croatia to

---

114 Anonymous, 'Suočavanje Hrvatske sa ratnim zločinima' [Croatia faces up to war crimes], *Vreme*, no. 485, 22 April 2000, at http://www.vreme.com/arhiva_html/485/20.html (accessed 16 June 2021).
115 In March 2001, a Croatian court indicted Norac, Orešković and three others for their role in perpetrating war crimes against Serb and some Croat civilians in October 1991; the indictment listed at least 50 Serb civilian victims. The court later determined that Norac had personally killed at least one woman, while Orešković had ordered the execution of several civilians. The fourteen-month trial of the 'Gospić Group' concluded on 24 March 2003. A Croatian court found Orešković, Norac and one other individual guilty of war crimes, while two others were acquitted of all charges due to lack of evidence. See the summary of the evidence and the trial of Norac, et al. in 'View from The Hague: Trial against Mirko Norac', 2 June 2004, at www.icty.org/x/file/Outreach/view_from_hague/balkan_040602_en.pdf (accessed 16 June 2021).
116 Marko Marković, 'Orešković i Norac zaslužni što Gospić danas nije Teslingrad!' [Because of Orešković and Norac, Gospić today is not called Teslingrad], *Slobodna Dalmacija*, 15 September 2000.
117 Drakulić, *They Would Never Hurt a Fly*, 30–1; and 'Suočavanje Hrvatske sa ratnim zločinima'.
118 On the crimes in question, see the Norac and Ademi case summary at http://www.icty.org/x/cases/ademi/cis/en/cis_ademi_norac.pdf (accessed 16 June 2021). In 2005, the ICTY referred the case of the two generals to the Croatian courts. Their trial began in 2007 and on 30 May 2008, Norac was found guilty by the Zagreb District Court for his role in the killings of more than 30 civilians and prisoners of war in the Medak Pocket and sentenced to 7 years' imprisonment. Ademi was acquitted. Norac was separately convicted for his role in the Gospić killings of September 1991.

participate in the country's defence, while Norac had been a waiter before the war. Both rose quite rapidly through the ranks of the nascent Croatian police/military and civil administrations in 1991. They appear to have understood the conflict as a war of independence and, given their actions at Gospić, as an opportunity to rid the country of Serbs.[119] A nationalist component was certainly at work, although personal gain may also have played a role, given the fact that they and their men participated in extensive looting of abandoned Serb properties. While many local citizens were appalled by the nature of the Orešković-Norac regime in Gospić, no one in the provincial frontline town dared publicly to protest what had happened. Only after the war did some, like the former soldier Milan Levar, speak out against the violence, only to be killed in August 2000 by unknown assailants for providing statements to the press and ICTY investigators against his former commanders. Levar recalled how at the time of the war, given the pervasive atmosphere of fear and insecurity, 'you could do whatever you wanted with the few remaining people'.[120]

Whether in the Balkans or elsewhere, perpetrators typically possess variegated motives, such as commitment to the nationalist cause, obedience to orders, peer pressure, fear or even the opportunity for material gain. Circumstances are important, as individuals, who normally might never consider committing such acts or have the opportunity to commit them, are given the means, permission and encouragement to do so. Prolonged involvement in killing desensitizes perpetrators and does away with any sense of pity for the anguish of the victims. In the context of war and the increasing dehumanization of the 'other', the restraints on the use of violence are few or absent and killing may become routine. In the cases cited above, local actors took it upon themselves to perpetrate killings which, while not directly condoned by their respective ministries, were understood to be permissible in light of the security threat, prevailing nationalist discourse and systematic discrimination against the 'other'. They had licence to operate with impunity.

Mass violence and ethnic cleansing: the role of paramilitaries

The impunity with which many local actors behaved is perhaps best exemplified by the role of paramilitary groups, many of which worked closely or in parallel with the JNA (later the VRS) and RS MUP from the first months of the Bosnian war. On 28 July 1992, the Bosnian Serb VRS reported the existence of at least 60 active paramilitary groups on Bosnian Serb territory at that time.[121] These paramilitaries operated under a range of names but were instrumental in the campaign of ethnic cleansing. Many of the Serb paramilitary groups originated as party militias. For example, the 'White Eagles' were likely formed in early 1991 by Dragoslav Bokan and Mirko Jović, but were linked politically to Vojislav Šešelj's Serbian Radical Party (SRS). Jović split from the group to form the 'Dušan the Mighty' militia, which recruited volunteers in Serbia. Other groups included the 'Serb Volunteer Guard' (aka 'Tigers') of Željko 'Arkan' Ražnatović, the 'Serb Guard' of Đorđe 'Giška' Božović and Đorđe 'Beli' Matić, Dušan Vučković-Repić's 'Yellow Wasps', and Siniša Vučinić's 'Serb Falcons', among others. Virtually all these groups, but especially the larger ones like the White Eagles and Tigers, operated with the assistance of the Yugoslav military intelligence and the SDB (Serbian State Security

---

119 Drakulić, *They Would Never Hurt a Fly*, 29.
120 Cited in ibid., 30.
121 Ibid., 94; Brown, 'Military Developments in the Bosanska Krajina', 81–2.

Service).[122] The former head of Serbia's SDB, Jovica Stanišić, and his deputy commander of special operations, Franko 'Frenki' Simatović, provided material support to these groups through the SDB's special unit, the Red Berets. On 30 June 2021, Stanišić and Simatović were convicted by the IRMCT, the ICTY's successor, for their role in aiding and abetting the crimes of murder, deportation, forcible transfer and persecution in Bosnia in 1992, primarily because of their role in financing and equipping Serb paramilitaries.[123]

Although some senior JNA officers had misgivings in 1991–92 about the use of irregular units, which often appeared to be motivated by the desire to plunder, their presence was deemed expedient to the war effort.[124] This policy carried numerous risks, however. By late May 1992, both the RS MUP and Bosnian Serb civilian authorities were gravely concerned about the striking increase in criminal activity since the regular police was deployed to combat operations.[125] Several RS MUP stations ascribed looting and other criminality largely to the presence of paramilitaries.[126] In October 1992, the RS MUP Banja Luka centre submitted a revealing report, which cited the presence of several paramilitary groups, which had 'stolen everything that they could get'. These groups had 'a halo of untouchability', given their role in the war, leaving the regular police 'in a very delicate situation'.[127] This was perhaps best demonstrated in the Bosnian Serb consolidation of power in eastern Bosnia. According to the testimony of a former Bosnian Serb political official, the April 1992 attack on Zvornik in eastern Bosnia was conducted by paramilitaries drawn from the Tigers and other groups. However, the local Serb civil authorities in Zvornik and neighbouring Bijeljina lost control of the situation and were unable to cope with the paramilitaries.[128] A former Serb official from Zvornik later testified that the local Serb 'Crisis Staff' welcomed Arkan's Tigers, ostensibly to defend the local Serb population against Muslim separatists, but were unable to halt the ensuing 'regime of terror'.[129] Although the Bosnian Serb MUP and senior government officials were aware of the paramilitary violence, they did not intervene until July 1992 to restore a semblance

---

122 Rénéo Lukic, *Europe from the Balkans to the Urals: The Disintegration of Yugoslavia and the Soviet Union* (Oxford: Oxford University Press, 1996), 190; and Iva Martinović and Miloš Teodorović, 'Paravojne formacije – Dušan silni, Beli orlovi, Srpski sokolovi' [Paramilitary formations: Dušan the Mighty, the White Eagles, and Serbian Falcons], *Radio Slobodna Evropa*, 11 April 2010.

123 Sammy Westfall, 'U.N. War Crimes Tribunal Convicts Two Former Serbian Officials Over Crimes in Bosnia', *The Washington Post*, 30 June 2021, https://www.washingtonpost.com/world/2021/06/30/un-war-crimes-tribunal-convicts-two-former-serbian-officials-over-crimes-bosnia/ (accessed 5 July 2021). See also 'Judgement Delivered in the Case of Prosecutor v. Jovica Stanišić and Franko Simatović', https://www.irmct.org/en/news/21-06-30-judgement-delivered-case-prosecutor-v-jovica-stanisic-and-franko-simatovic (accessed 5 July 2021).

124 Velma Šarić, 'Yugoslav Army Units "Commended" Serb Paramilitaries', *IWPR Tribunal Update*, 10 May 2013, https://iwpr.net/global-voices/yugoslav-army-units-commended-serb-paramilitaries (accessed 16 June 2021).

125 Nielsen, 'The Bosnian Serb Ministry of Internal Affairs', 70.

126 Ibid., 71–2.

127 Cited in ibid., 74.

128 Velma Šarić, 'Zvornik Authorities "Unable to Cope" with Paramilitaries', *Institute for War and Peace Reporting*, no. 705, 19 August 2011, see https://iwpr.net/global-voices/zvornik-authorities-unable-cope-paramilitaries (accessed 5 July 2021). Several paramilitary groups were active in and around Zvornik, besides Arkan's Tigers. Some of these groups were simply named after their commanders, such as Vojan Vučković-Žućo's men ('Žućo's group'), Milorad Gogić's men ('Gogić's Group'), etc.

129 Velma Šarić, 'Paramilitary "Terror" in Zvornik', *Institute for War and Peace Reporting*, no. 796, 11 July 2013, see https://iwpr.net/global-voices/paramilitary-terror-zvornik (accessed 5 July 2021).

of public order.¹³⁰ A former VRS colonel, who commanded the VRS's 6th Krajina Brigade in north-western Bosnia, testified that Serb paramilitaries were known to have murdered Muslim civilians in Sanski Most; after the massacres, the Serb civil authorities 'sanitized and cleaned up' the terrain, but the Serb police authorities were seemingly powerless to arrest the paramilitaries.¹³¹ For several months, from April to July 1992, paramilitaries roamed the streets and did as they pleased. Paramilitaries had not simply materialized of their own volition, however. In light of their ties to Serbian state security, particularly during the first months of the Bosnian war, the fact remains that they arrived in contested towns and municipalities at the behest of local Serb authorities and worked collaboratively with them to help consolidate control.¹³² That local authorities could not constrain paramilitary violence did not obfuscate the fact that these armed groups still assisted in the realization of Bosnian Serb war objectives.

The Bosnian Serb central authorities eventually concluded that most paramilitaries had a negative impact on operations and, in mid-June 1992, ordered their dissolution. This was an attempt to impose institutional structures over informal violence as part of the consolidation of the Bosnian Serb state and its assertion of a monopoly of violence. Henceforth, all paramilitaries were to be incorporated either into the reserve police or regular military, although this was a slow process. On 28 July 1992, the VRS still reported the existence of at least 60 active paramilitary groups on Bosnian Serb territory. The same report claimed that these paramilitaries were composed of criminal and 'pathological' elements, were of poor combat quality, devoted most of their efforts to criminal activity and often exhibited extreme hatred of non-Serbs. The VRS report recommended that every armed Serb should 'be placed under the exclusive command of the army'.¹³³ Some of these paramilitary units were in fact subsequently incorporated into the VRS and their commanders given ranks.¹³⁴ In late July 1992, the VRS military police and RS MUP forces were deployed to Zvornik to eliminate the Yellow Wasps. Sixty-five paramilitaries were detained, criminal investigations were initiated against eleven and the others were mobilized into the VRS. An RS MUP investigation uncovered that the Yellow Wasps, who had perpetrated killings of Muslims in the Zvornik area, had cooperated extensively with the local Serb police. It should not be surprising, therefore, that none of the Zvornik paramilitaries were ever prosecuted by Bosnian Serb authorities for their crimes.¹³⁵ Indeed, despite belated attempts by the RS MUP leadership to co-opt paramilitary groups and rein in informal violence, in several localities the police continued to cooperate with these groups. The Serb police chief of Ilidža insisted, in an early August 1992 report to the Interior Minister, that local circumstances necessitated cooperation with Serb 'volunteers', to whom he had distributed arms. Another Bosnian Serb police chief in the Sarajevo region claimed that many reserve policemen had in actual fact joined paramilitary groups.¹³⁶ This same official summed up the problem

---

130 Idem, '"Complete Chaos" in Zvornik', *Institute for War and Peace Reporting*, no. 663, 1 October 2010, see https://iwpr.net/global-voices/complete-chaos-zvornik (accessed 5 July 2021).
131 Idem, 'Serb Paramilitaries Blamed for Murders in Sanski Most', *Institute for War and Peace Reporting*, no. 620, 16 October 2009, see https://iwpr.net/global-voices/serb-paramilitaries-blamed-murders-sanski-most (accessed 5 July 2021).
132 IWPR staff writer, 'Karadzic Condemned by Evidence – Prosecutors', *Institute for War and Peace Reporting Global Voices*, no. 845, 3 October 2014.
133 Nielsen, 'The Bosnian Serb Ministry of Internal Affairs', 94; and Brown, 'Military Developments in the Bosanska Krajina', 81–2.
134 Brown, 'Military Developments in the Bosanska Krajina', 83–4.
135 Nielsen, 'The Bosnian Serb Ministry of Internal Affairs', 95–6.
136 Ibid., 97.

in November 1992 when he observed that at the beginning of the war these paramilitary formations had gained 'informal legitimacy'. Over time they became 'strong and independent and presented a hindrance and a real object of derision in the overall front of the organization of Serbian forces'.[137]

What this official failed to note was that many of the most powerful paramilitary groups had been armed and financed in part by the Serbian state and thus enjoyed tacit endorsement. However, the paramilitary phenomenon in general was yet further testament to the fact that, once political elites (in this case, the Bosnian Serb leadership) initiated the conflict, wartime violence (killing, looting, plunder) frequently acquired a dynamic of its own and was shaped by local actors who, while operating in support of the strategic goals articulated by nationalist elites, frequently pursued their own agendas, interests and vendettas. Of course, these local agendas were not necessarily inimical to elite objectives. On the contrary, especially in instances involving the killing of civilians, none of the local actors, be they paramilitaries, reserve policemen or active duty police and military, were punished by the authorities for crimes ostensibly committed in pursuit of the state-building project. The emergence of the paramilitary phenomenon exemplifies how the disintegration of Yugoslavia, and its monopoly of violence, was attended by various lower-level initiatives which contributed significantly to the decentralization of physical force and shaped the dynamics of local violence.

In the end, however, the proliferation of paramilitary groups should not obscure the centrality of the state's role in endorsing and guiding violence in the former Yugoslavia. The case of the Serb paramilitary unit known as the Scorpions is particularly instructive. Originating in Croatia in 1991, the Scorpions were co-opted into the Croatian Serb military and then deployed in July 1995 to Srebrenica to assist the VRS and Serb police detachments in operations against the enclave. After the town had been taken, the Scorpions perpetrated several killings of unarmed Bosnian Muslim males at Trnovo. In 1996, the unit was transferred to Serbia and functioned as a reserve detachment of the Serbian police's JSO (Special Operations Unit). It was reactivated again in March 1999 and deployed to Kosovo, where on 28 March 1999 the unit perpetrated a massacre of 14 women and children in the town of Podujevo.[138] Much the same might be said of Arkan's Tigers, who saw action in Croatia and then Bosnia in 1991–92 and again in the later stages of those conflicts. Many of the unit's men also saw combat in Kosovo, in 1998–99, not as members of Arkan's 'Serb Volunteer Guard', however, but mostly as members of various state security units, particularly the JSO.[139] The Scorpions and Tigers are in several respects emblematic of the paramilitary phenomenon, which was co-opted by state

---

137 Cited in Nielsen, 'The Bosnian Serb Ministry of Internal Affairs', 98.
138 On 2 June 2005, the Scorpion video was aired on Serbian Television without commentary and led to the arrest of 8 former Scorpions. In March 2004, one of the unit's men, Saša Cvjetan, was convicted by the Serbian War Crimes Court of the Belgrade Regional Court for his participation in the Podujevo massacre and sentenced to 20 years' imprisonment. In April 2007, the same court sentenced four members of the Scorpions, including the unit commander, Slobodan Medić, to a total of 58 years in prison for the execution of 6 Bosnian Muslim males in the village of Trnovo on 16–17 July 1995. 'Škorpionima 58 godina zatvora' [The Scorpions get 58 years in prison], *Politika* (Belgrade), 11 April 2007, 1; Daniel Williams, 'Srebrenica Video Vindicates Long Pursuit by Serb Activist', *The Washington Post*, 25 June 2005, A15; Danial Sunter and Ana Uzelac, 'Serbia: Mladic "Recruited" Infamous Scorpions', *IWPR Tribunal Update*, no. 559, 9 June 2005, see https://iwpr.net/global-voices/serbia-mladic-recruited-infamous-scorpions (accessed 16 June 2021).
139 Denis Dzidic, et al., 'Arkan's Paramilitaries: Tigers Who Escaped Justice', *Balkan Insight*, 8 December 2014, https://balkaninsight.com/2014/12/08/arkan-s-paramilitaries-tigers-who-escaped-justice/ (accessed 18 September 2015).

machineries to become an instrument of state-sponsored programmes of conquest, pacification and ethnic cleansing.

From ethnic cleansing to Dayton

If the first year of the Bosnian war was principally a territorial conflict – originally between Serb forces on the one hand and the ABiH and the HVO on the other – where ethnic cleansing was employed in support of nationalist territorial objectives, thereafter it became increasingly complex as all three parties sought to consolidate their positions at the expense of the others. In April 1993, the ever-more frail coalition between Bosnian Croats and Muslims collapsed. The two sides had supported independence and were united in opposition to the JNA and Bosnian Serb forces throughout 1992. In some areas, as in Herzegovina, the HVO even had separate Muslim detachments. A decisive turn came in January 1993, during the peace talks chaired by Cyrus Vance and Lord Robert Owen. The proposed Vance-Owen Peace Plan called for the creation of ten provinces in Bosnia-Herzegovina, with three assigned to each of three constituent peoples and the tenth with special status. The Bosnian Croat leader Mate Boban signed the plan in January 1993, while a reluctant Izetbegović signed on behalf of the Bosnian government in late March 1993. The Bosnian Serbs rejected the agreement. The Bosnian Croat leadership decided to implement the proposed territorial provisions of the Vance-Owen Plan unilaterally; this entailed enforcing HVO authority over ABiH units and the Muslim population in the designated 'Croat' provinces. By mid-April 1993, a full-scale armed conflict was initiated by the HVO, with the tacit support of the Croatian authorities, in central Bosnia and parts of Herzegovina.[140] In August 1993, the 'Croat Community of Herzeg-Bosnia' was renamed the 'Croat Republic of Herzeg-Bosnia'. In the context of this armed conflict, HVO units perpetrated several atrocities against Muslim civilians, notably in several villages in the Jablanica, Mostar, Vareš and Vitez municipalities.[141] In the process, the Bosnian Croats also established detention camps in which non-Croats were abused. Only in February 1994, following US mediation, was a ceasefire established and a framework adopted for a nominal Muslim-Croat coalition as the future basis of the Bosniak-Croat Federation.

---

140 The architect of Croatia's nascent military in 1991, Martin Špegelj, subsequently had a falling out with Tuđman, whom he accused of supporting the Bosnian Croats and being primarily responsible for the 1993–94 conflict between the Bosnian Croats and Bosniaks. This support was intended to create a Bosnian Croat controlled area of Bosnia that would, through diplomatic negotiations, eventually become part of Croatia. See Martin Špegelj, *Sjećanja vojnika* [Memoirs of a soldier], ed. by Ivo Žanić (Zagreb: Znanje, 2001).

141 On the Croat-Muslim conflict, see Michael Anthony Sells, *The Bridge Betrayed: Religion and Genocide in Bosnia*, 2nd ed. (Los Angeles, CA: University of California Press, 1998), 93–114; and Tone Bringa, *Being Muslim the Bosnian Way: Identity and Community in a Central Bosnian Village* (Princeton, NJ: Princeton University Press, 1995). Several crimes are documented in *War Crimes in Bosnia-Hercegovina*, vol. 2, 228–34, 297–353. More than a dozen leading figures in the Bosnian Croat political and military leadership were indicted by the ICTY for war crimes and crimes against humanity in April 2004 and went on trial in 2006. The most senior HVO commander to be convicted is General Tihomir Blaškić, commander of HVO forces in central Bosnia, who was sentenced in March 2000 to 45 years' imprisonment for committing, ordering or otherwise aiding and abetting various crimes against the Muslim population. In April 2004, the Appeals Chamber acquitted him on several counts and reduced his sentence to nine years' imprisonment. For details on Jadranko Prlić et al., and Tihomir Blaškić et al., see www.icty.org (accessed on 15 June 2021).

While Serb and Croat forces were the main protagonists of ethnic cleansing in Bosnia-Herzegovina, Bosnian government forces also engaged in ethnic cleansing albeit to a lesser degree. This included the establishment of detention camps for and the expulsion of non-Muslims from selected areas, particularly in Sarajevo and central Bosnia. However, unlike the Bosnian Serb and Croat states, the Bosnian persecution of non-Muslims did not assume the character of official policy and was often shaped by local commanders.[142]

The two most brutal years of the Bosnian war were its first and last, when major military offensives were conducted. In an attempt to eliminate the remaining Muslim enclaves and thus secure their grip on eastern Bosnia, in spring and summer 1995, the Bosnian Serbs commenced a series of coordinated attacks on these territories. In the most violent of these assaults, the VRS, supported by special police units of the Bosnian Serb MUP and Serbian SDB, overran the Srebrenica enclave on 10–11 July 1995. Almost immediately upon taking Srebrenica, and lasting from roughly 10 to 19 July, Bosnian Serb forces massacred all teenage and adult males, estimated at 7,000 to 8,000 victims. In multiple prosecutions at the ICTY stemming from the Srebrenica massacre, the Court ruled that the massacre constituted an act of genocide.[143] The Dutch UN battalion in Srebrenica, responsible for its safety, failed to intervene. Muslim females and young boys were deported to territories under the control of the Bosnian authorities. The Srebrenica massacre provoked worldwide opprobrium and helped to galvanize the international community into military intervention. It also provided an opportunity for the Croatian authorities to commence an offensive against the Croatian Serb forces, which at the end of July 1995 participated in a joint operation with the Bosnian Serb VRS against the Bihać enclave in north-western Bosnia, which had a larger Muslim population than Srebrenica. On 4 August 1995, the Croatian military launched 'Operation Storm', the single largest military operation in the Yugoslav war that involved more than 130,000 Croatian troops and police supported by Bosnian Croat HVO and ABiH units. Over the course of four days, Croatian forces completely overran Serb-held territory in Croatia. It is believed that between 120,000 and 150,000 Serb refugees fled or were expelled from Croatia to Serb-controlled Bosnia and Serbia during the operation.[144] Private dwellings and Orthodox churches were deliberately vandalized or

---

142 See *War Crimes in Bosnia-Hercegovina*, vol. 2, 271–4, 354–81. In April 2008, Enver Hadžihasanović and Amir Kubura of the ABiH were sentenced to three and a half years and two years' imprisonment, respectively, the former of failure to prevent or punish cruel treatment in Zenica in 1993 by his subordinates, and the latter of failure to take necessary and reasonable measures to punish plundering by his subordinate troops in several villages between June and November 1993. In September 2008, General Rasim Delić, the former Commander of the Main Staff of the ABiH, was sentenced to three years' imprisonment for cruel treatment by the ABiH's 'El Mujahed Detachment', a unit of foreign Muslim fighters, against captured Bosnian Serb soldiers. Delić was acquitted of three counts of murder and cruel treatment. The Deputy Commander of the Supreme Command Staff of the ABiH and Chief of the Supreme Command Staff of the ABiH, General Sefer Halilović, was acquitted of murder in November 2005 by the Trial Chamber, a ruling upheld in October 2007 by the Appeals Chamber. Although both chambers ruled that ABiH units had perpetrated crimes against civilians in central Bosnia, they found him not guilty of command responsibility. See www.icty.org.

143 For example, General Radislav Krstić of the VRS was convicted of aiding and abetting genocide, among other counts, and sentenced to 35 years' imprisonment. The case was officially referred to as 'Srebrenica-Drina Corps' (IT-98-33). Other Srebrenica cases include IT-05-88, IT-02-60, IT-96-22, IT-02-60/1, IT-02-60/2, IT-05-88/2, and IT-05-88/1, all involving VRS and Bosnian Serb Interior Ministry officers. For case information, see www.icty.org.

144 On Operation Storm and the controversies surrounding the war in Croatia, see Mile Bjelajac and Ozren Žunec, 'The War in Croatia, 1991–1995', in *Confronting the Yugoslav Controversies*, 233–66.

destroyed, while at least 700 Serbs were killed and twice that number disappeared.[145] Tudman allegedly remarked at the end of August that the Serbs had 'disappeared ignominiously, as if they had never populated this land'.[146]

The foreign factor, especially the role of the US, in the events of 1995 and the conclusion of the war proved decisive. European Community efforts at conflict resolution had failed in 1991–92, and thereafter the international community's attempts at mediation evolved through several stages and involved a number of peace proposals. In 1993, both the Vance-Owen Peace Plan and later the Owen-Stoltenberg Plan involved preserving Bosnia-Herzegovina as a state while dividing it internally along ethnic lines. The territorial and other provisions of both proved contentious, however, with the Bosnian Serbs rejecting the former plan and the Bosnian government the latter. In spring 1994 the newly constituted 'Contact Group', consisting of the US, UK, France, Russia and Germany, assumed the lead. From that point, both the US and Russia were actively engaged for the first time in diplomatic discussions to end the war. In spring 1994, the US negotiated a ceasefire between the Bosnian Croats and Muslims in addition to a federation between the two parties. The 1994 Contact Group peace proposal called for a single state with two 'entities', with the newly constituted Bosniak-Croat Federation controlling 51 per cent and the Bosnian Serb entity 49 per cent of the territory. This proposal provided the basic outlines of the settlement that was eventually adopted at Dayton in November 1995.[147] However, the Contact Group's 1994 peace plan was rejected by the Bosnian Serb leadership and thereafter the Contact Group was unable to agree on measures to bring the Bosnian Serbs to the peace table. The US advocated a policy of 'lift-and-strike', that is, lifting the UN arms embargo against the Bosnian government and using NATO (North Atlantic Treaty Organization) airpower against the Bosnian Serbs. The UK and France threatened to withdraw their UNPROFOR contingents from Bosnia if the US adopted this strategy, while Russia was similarly opposed to the policy.[148]

---

145 According to Žarko Puhovski, the former president of the Croatian Helsinki Committee, which conducted an investigation of abuses by Croatian forces during Operation Storm, ethnic cleansing occurred both during and after the operation. Puhovski concluded that between 120,000 and 150,000 Serbs fled Croatia in August 1995. The Croatian Helsinki Committee, which provided its findings to the ICTY, has documented the identities of more than 700 Serbs killed by Croatian forces, although this list is hardly a final tally. 'Puhovski: Etničko čišćenje u Oluji' [Puhovski: Ethnic cleansing in Operation 'Oluja'], *B92*, 24 January 2009. The Office of the Prosecutor of the ICTY, in its case 'Operation Storm' (IT-06-90), Gotovina et al., indicted two senior Croatian Army officers, Ante Gotovina and Ivan Čermak, and the former Assistant Interior Minister, Mladen Markač, for their role in 'Operation Storm'. The ICTY Trial Chamber convicted the accused in 2011, but in one its most controversial rulings, the Appeals Chamber reversed the convictions on appeal in November 2012. For case information, see www.icty.org.
146 Cited in Judah, *The Serbs*, 309.
147 On the role of the international community, the Dayton Accords and the various plans which preceded them, see Ivo H. Daalder, *Getting to Dayton: The Making of America's Bosnia Policy* (Washington, DC: Brookings Institution Press, 2000); Burg and Shoup, *The War in Bosnia-Herzegovina*, 317–418; Leo Tindemans et al., *Unfinished Peace: Report of the International Commission on the Balkans* (Berlin and Washington, DC: Aspen Institute and Carnegie Endowment for International Peace, 1996), 37–76; Susan L. Woodward, 'International Aspects of the Wars in Former Yugoslavia: 1990–1996', in *Burn This House: The Making and Unmaking of Yugoslavia*, eds Jasminka Udovički and James Ridgeway (Durham, NC: Duke University Press, 2000), 217–37; and Richard H. Ullman, 'The Wars in Yugoslavia and the International System after the Cold War', in *The World and Yugoslavia's Wars*, ed. Richard H. Ullman (New York: Council on Foreign Relations, 1996), 9–37.
148 Christoph Schwegmann, *The Contact Group and its Impact on the European Institutional Structure*, Occasional Papers no. 16 (Paris: The Institute for Security Studies, Western European Union, 2000), 5–6.

In the event, in addition to mediating an end to the Bosniak-Croat war, in 1994 the US signed a military cooperation agreement with Croatia, providing for increased contacts between the US and Croatian armed forces, including access to US Defence Department training programmes. Shortly thereafter, retired US-military personnel began providing training to the Croatian military in preparation for its August 1995 'Operation Storm' against Croatian Serb forces.[149] As the violence and brutality of the Bosnian war escalated in 1995 – as a result of the Bosnian Serb attack against UN 'safe areas' in eastern Bosnia (July 1995) and the Sarajevo market massacre (August 1995) – Western policy moved towards direct military intervention. NATO deployed 10,000 troops to Bosnia as part of a Rapid Reaction Force, ostensibly to protect UNPROFOR personnel, and at the end of August 1995 launched 'Operation Deliberate Force', a massive air bombing campaign against Bosnian Serb positions and the first offensive mission in NATO history. In August and September 1995, the Bosnian Serb Army suffered its first serious military reversals since April 1992. Direct foreign intervention, driven primarily by the US, radically altered the military balance of power in Bosnia and Croatia and paved the way to Dayton.

In light of the new military balance on the ground and vigorous NATO involvement, Milošević compelled the Bosnian Serb leadership to accept a ceasefire. This set the stage for a peace deal. On 1 November 1995, the United States convened an international conference on the Bosnian war at Dayton, Ohio, attended by the presidents of Bosnia, Croatia and Serbia; the latter two served as representatives of their Bosnian Croat and Serb proxies, respectively. The Dayton Accords (21 November), or General Framework Agreement for Peace, were formalized in Paris on 14 December and officially ended the 43-month long war in Bosnia-Herzegovina. The country was divided into two 'entities': the 'Republika Srpska', with 49 per cent of the territory of Bosnia-Herzegovina; and the Bosniak-Croat Federation. Despite repeated pronouncements by the international community that policies of ethnic cleansing would not be rewarded, the Dayton Accords codified ethnic segregation even though they contained provisions for the return of refugees and displaced persons. A NATO peacekeeping mission, known initially as IFOR (Implementation Force), was deployed to enforce the Accords. As part of the Dayton negotiations, the Croatian and Serbian governments concluded the Erdut Agreement (12 November) whereby the last remaining area of Croatia under Serb control was demilitarized under UN administration. The region reverted to Croatian jurisdiction in 1998.

The most extensive examination of war casualties to date, published by the Bosnian IDC (Research and Documentation Centre) in Sarajevo, suggests that at least 97,207 combatants and non-combatants were killed, and 1.8 million persons displaced in Bosnia-Herzegovina between April 1992 and November 1995. The majority of the victims were Bosnian Muslims (65 per cent), followed by Serbs (25 per cent) and Croats (8 per cent). The IDC research suggests that the highest rates of civilian victimization occurred in besieged towns, in addition to the Podrinje (Drina River basin), the region of eastern Bosnia with the ethnically mixed towns of Foča, Višegrad and Zvornik, and in the Bosnian Krajina, both of which were ethnically cleansed by Bosnian Serb forces in 1992.[150] The number of deaths in Croatia, where the war was fought

---

149 Human Rights Watch, *Croatia: Impunity for Abuses Committed During Operation Storm and the Denial of the Right of Refugees to Return to the Krajina* (New York: Helsinki Watch, 1996), 4. On US private military contractors, notably MPRI, see Esther Schrader, 'US Companies Hired to Train Foreign Armies', *Los Angeles Times*, 14 April 2002, https://archive.globalpolicy.org/security/peacekpg/training/pmc.htm (accessed 15 June 2021).

150 For a discussion of the data, see Nidzara Ahmetasević, 'Bosnia's Book of the Dead', *BIRN*, 19 June 2007, https://balkaninsight.com/2007/06/19/justice-report-bosnia-s-book-of-the-dead/ (accessed 16 June 2021). These figures do not account for Serbian and Croatian citizens killed while fighting

mainly in 1991–92 and 1995, is probably around 20,000. These figures do not include the tens of thousands of wounded, nor do they convey the extent of destruction of cultural monuments and heritage sites, which was a deliberate component of ethnic cleansing.

The Albanian question: Kosovo and Macedonia

The Dayton Accords did little to ease the strained relations between Kosovo's Serbs and Albanians, who by 1995 lived largely segregated lives. Following the 1989 constitutional amendments, which were subsequently enshrined in the new Serbian constitution (1990), the Kosovo Albanian political elite boycotted Belgrade and local institutions of government.[151] They participated in the elections of the 1990s in the Federal Republic of Yugoslavia, but under the pacifist intellectual Ibrahim Rugova and his LDK (Democratic League of Kosovo) they adopted a policy of passive resistance and established parallel institutions.[152] To a significant degree, this reflected the fact that neither the Serbian authorities nor the Serbian democratic opposition made any serious effort to bring Albanians into the political process. In the eyes of Serbian political society, the Kosovo Albanians remained dangerous separatists. Dayton disillusioned Kosovo Albanians and the Serbian opposition equally; for the former, it failed to recognize their autonomist demands and treated Milošević as a peacemaker, and for the latter, disheartened by Serb losses in Croatia and Bosnia, it served to focus resistance against the Milošević regime. For some Kosovo Albanians, impatient with Rugova's pacifism, Dayton appeared to legitimize the use of violence.

The creation of the KLA (Kosovo Liberation Army) marked an ominous phase in the evolution of Kosovo's political history.[153] The KLA resorted to political violence, entering into a terrorist campaign by assassinating Serbian officials. Harsh Serbian countermeasures ensued, often out of all proportion to the initial attacks. A crucial moment came in March 1997, when civil government in Albania collapsed as a result of failed financial pyramid schemes. Military barracks and depots were plundered and many of these weapons invariably made their way to Kosovo, where in 1998 the nascent KLA engaged the Serbian authorities in a full-fledged war for independence.

The international community's response to the crisis, formulated initially through the Contact Group, was to assign much of the responsibility for the violence to Milošević and the Serbian authorities. The Račak massacre (January 1999), in which Serbian security forces killed at least 40 Albanians, many of them civilians, galvanized international opinion. The UNSC

---

in Bosnia. Both the Serbian and Croatian authorities have been reluctant to provide statistics on the number of their citizens killed while fighting in Bosnia (and, in the Serbian case, in Croatia). On the Serbian side, a widely circulated figure of 2,300 remains speculative, but includes JNA recruits and members of special police units and various paramilitary groups. Half of them are believed to have died on the Vukovar front in 1991. The Croatian figure is likely far lower, but there was certainly Croatian involvement in informal militias in 1991–92, followed by the direct participation of Croatian Army troops, who fought alongside the HVO in 1995. See Marija Vidić and Jasmina Lazić, 'Mrtvi po potrebi' [Dead if necessary], *Vreme* (Belgrade), no. 766, 8 September 2005.

151 Frances Trix, 'Kosovar Albanians between a Rock and a Hard Place', in *Serbia since 1989*, 309–27; and Jasminka Udovički, 'Kosovo', in Udovički and Ridgeway, *Burn This House*, 314–66.

152 See Trix, 'Kosovar Albanians', 327; and Robert Thomas, *The Politics of Serbia in the 1990s* (New York: Columbia University Press, 1999), 423.

153 On the KLA, see James Pettifer, *The Kosova Liberation Army: Underground War to Balkan Insurgency, 1948–2001* (New York: Columbia University Press, 2012); and Henry H. Perritt, *Kosovo Liberation Army: The Inside Story of an Insurgency* (Chicago, IL: University of Illinois Press, 2008).

(United Nations Security Council), US, EU (European Union) and several foreign governments condemned the violence, pressed for renewed negotiations and the deployment of an observer mission. In February 1999, the OSCE (Organization for Security and Cooperation in Europe) deployed unarmed observers to Kosovo as part of the 'Kosovo Verification Mission'. They were withdrawn before the end of the following month.[154] In February 1999, the Contact Group staged peace talks at Rambouillet near Paris, attended by Yugoslav officials and Albanian insurgents, where it presented what was in effect a non-negotiable peace proposal for Kosovo.[155] It was accepted by the Albanians but only under considerable US pressure. In the end, the purpose of Rambouillet was not so much to conclude an agreement as it was to build consensus within NATO that diplomacy without the use of force would fail to bring lasting peace.[156] The Yugoslav rejection of the plan, in particular its military annex, and the escalation of the fighting in Kosovo led to direct NATO intervention.

Initiated on 24 March 1999, the NATO campaign was intended to compel the Serbian authorities to end their security operations in Kosovo and make political concessions. Serbian forces responded by stepping up their assault on the KLA, in the context of which they brutalized broader segments of civilian society.[157] The pattern seen in Bosnia – that of planned and coordinated assaults by military, police and paramilitary units against civilians – was repeated in Kosovo. In the most detailed study to date, Human Rights Watch has estimated that Serbian forces expelled 862,979 Albanians from Kosovo into Macedonia and Albania. Several atrocities, including the killing of civilians and mass rape, perpetrated predominantly by Serbian special police units like the Scorpions, were documented.[158] The final death toll among civilians

---

154 For a thoroughgoing retelling and analysis of the events leading to and including the Kosovo war, including the controversies and debates surrounding the conflict, see James Gow, 'The War in Kosovo, 1998–1999', in *Confronting the Yugoslav Controversies*, 305–36; Dušan Janjić et al., 'Kosovo under the Milošević regime', in *Confronting the Yugoslav Controversies*, 275–97; Tim Judah, *Kosovo: War and Revenge* (New Haven, CT: Yale University Press, 2000); and Julie A. Mertus, *Kosovo: How Myths and Truths Started a War* (Berkeley, CA: University of California Press, 1999).

155 On the Rambouillet talks, see Judah, *Kosovo*, 197–226; Mark Wheeler, 'The Rambouillet conference on Kosovo', *International Affairs* 75, no. 2 (1999): 211–51; and Ivo Daalder and Michael E. O'Hanlon, *Winning Ugly: NATO's War to Save Kosovo* (Washington, DC: The Brookings Institution, 2000).

156 Daalder and O'Hanlon, *Winning Ugly*, 85.

157 See the expert reports of András J. Riedlmayer and Andrew Herscher, 'The Destruction of Cultural Heritage in Kosovo, 1998–1999: A Post-war survey', Case No. IT-02-54-T, 28 February 2002; Phillip Coo, 'OTP Military Analysis Report: Forces of the FRY and Serbia in Kosovo', Case No. IT-02-54-T, 29 May 2002; and Patrick Ball et al., 'Killings and Refugee Flow in Kosovo March – June 1999: A Report to the International Criminal Tribunal for the former Yugoslavia', 15 February 2002, and 'Addendum to Expert Report of Patrick Ball', Case No. IT-02-54-T, 6 March 2002, commissioned by the OTP (Office of the Prosecutor) and submitted at the Milošević trial in the Trial Chamber of the ICTY.

158 In March 2005, the ICTY indicted KLA commander Ramush Haradinaj and two subordinates, Idriz Balaj and Lahi Brahimaj. On 3 April 2008, the Trial Chamber acquitted Haradinaj and Balaj, while Brahimaj was found guilty on two counts for torture. On 21 July 2010, the Appeals Chamber partially quashed the acquittals and ordered the re-trial of all three accused on six counts of the indictment relating to the cruel treatment, torture and murder of prisoners in a KLA-run camp. In November 2012, the three were acquitted. Despite the acquittals, the ICTY Trial Chamber found evidence that KLA soldiers committed acts of cruel treatment, torture, rape and murder. On 26 February 2009, in the first judgement handed down against Serbian officials for alleged crimes committed in Kosovo, five former high-ranking Yugoslav and Serbian political, military and police officials were convicted for their role in a broad campaign of violence directed at the Albanian civilian population in 1999. Former Yugoslav Deputy Prime Minister, Nikola

in Kosovo, either as a result of Serbian policy or KLA actions, remains unknown. The ICTY has exhumed the bodies of more than 4,300 victims, most of whom are presumed to be Kosovo Albanians. More than 3,500 people remain missing.[159]

The Serbian authorities relented on 5 June 1999, at which time the Federal Republic of Yugoslavia and NATO signed an agreement, according to which Yugoslavia withdrew its forces from Kosovo. The agreement allowed for the deployment of a NATO-led peacekeeping mission under the auspices of the UNMIK (United Nations Mission in Kosovo). The agreement between NATO and Belgrade was formalized by the UNSCR (UN Security Council Resolution) 1244, which was adopted on 10 June 1999; it established the right of refugee return and committed member states to uphold the territorial integrity of the Federal Republic of Yugoslavia, of which Kosovo de jure remained a part. UNSCR 1244 also called for a 'political process' providing for 'substantial' self-government for Kosovo. It was recognized by all sides in 1999 that this was not a permanent solution to the Kosovo crisis.

Developments in Kosovo had an immediate impact on neighbouring Macedonia.[160] Although Macedonian-Albanian relations did not suffer from a legacy of recent political violence, comparable to that of Albanians and Serbs in Kosovo or Croats and Serbs in Bosnia and Croatia, the Kosovo conflict fundamentally altered political dynamics in Macedonia. The brief armed conflict in 2001 between the Macedonian authorities and the Albanian NLA (National Liberation Army) is incomprehensible without reference to the Kosovo conflict.[161] When the Republic of Macedonia seceded in September 1991 from the Yugoslav federation, the 'Macedonian Question' was reborn. Without the protection of the Yugoslav federation, Macedonian elites believed their republic's security had been weakened considerably. In response both to Bulgarian and Greek nationalist attitudes and the policies of the latter, a more aggressive strain of Macedonian nationalism soon asserted itself. This was reflected in the new Macedonian Constitution (1991) which declared the republic to be the state of the Macedonian nation. After 1991, the Macedonian political leadership laboured to preserve the exclusive link between the Macedonian nation and the Macedonian state, both from outside threats and

---

Šainović, the Commander of the Yugoslav Army's Third Army, General Nebojša Pavković, and Commander of Serbian Interior Ministry police detachments in Kosovo, General Sreten Lukić, were convicted for crimes against humanity and for violating the laws or customs of war. Yugoslav Army General Vladimir Lazarević and Chief of the General Staff Dragoljub Ojdanić were found guilty of aiding and abetting the deportation and forcible transfer of Albanians. Milan Milutinović, the former President of Serbia, was acquitted of all charges. For further information, see www.icty.org for the rulings and supporting material (accessed 14 June 2021).

159 The figures are derived from Human Rights Watch, *Under Orders: War Crimes in Kosovo* (New York: Human Rights Watch, 2001), 4, 7–8. Patrick Ball et al. have estimated that at least 4,000 civilians were killed in Kosovo between late March and June 1999. Helge Brunborg has concluded that in 1998–99, Kosovo had an estimated population of 2.1 million, of whom 83% (or more than 1.6 million) were Albanian. See her expert report, 'Report on Size and Ethnic Composition of the Population of Kosovo', Case No. IT-02-54-T, 14 August 2002, 1–2, commissioned by the OTP and submitted at the Milošević trial in the Trial Chamber of the ICTY.

160 On the contemporary Macedonian Question, see Andrew Rossos, 'The Macedonian Question and Instability in the Balkans', in *Yugoslavia and its Historians: Understanding the Balkan Wars of the 1990s*, eds Norman M. Naimark and Holly Case (Stanford, CA: Stanford University Press, 2003), 140–59; and Jenny Engström, 'The Power of Perception: The Impact of the Macedonian Question on Inter-ethnic Relations in the Republic of Macedonia', *Global Review of Ethnopolitics* 1, no. 3 (March 2002): 3–17.

161 On the conflict in Macedonia, see John Phillips, *Macedonia: Warlords and Rebels in the Balkans* (New Haven, CT: Bloomsbury, 2004).

from within the republic, where the Albanian minority posed the greatest challenge to the consolidation of the nation-state. Albanian political elites in Macedonia continued to demand the status of a constituent nation – as had their Albanian and Serb counterparts in Kosovo and Croatia, respectively – on an equal footing with the Macedonian nation. These demands only fuelled Macedonian fears that their state would disintegrate. What kept tensions in check after 1991 was both the absence of a history of Albanian-Macedonian communal violence and the perceived threat posed by Milošević's regime in Belgrade.[162] Following the Kosovo crisis and Milošević's ouster (October 2000), the dynamics of political conflict in Macedonia were suddenly altered.

The relatively brief Macedonian conflict did not witness the widespread and systematic abuses seen in Bosnia, Croatia and Kosovo. Although it took fewer than 250 lives, in a relatively small country like Macedonia, the violence was in fact shattering. There were several incidents of violence against civilians. The single worst occurrence was the Macedonian police assault on the Albanian village of Ljuboten on 12 August 2001. Under the command of Johan Tarčulovski, at least 60 to 70 well-armed reserve policemen, including several men from a private security company, entered Ljuboten and indiscriminately attacked its residents. Fourteen Albanian males were killed; dozens were detained and abused, while property was destroyed indiscriminately. The primary objective of the operation appears to have been retaliation against Albanians in the village for the NLA's actions, which the village was thought to have harboured. Two days before the police assault, eight Macedonian soldiers were killed and several wounded by landmines near Ljuboten. But the police operation was also intended as a warning to all local Albanians of the consequences of supporting the NLA.[163] The Ljuboten incident, despite its brutality, was not part of an official policy of ethnic cleansing. In the absence of deeply ingrained historical myths, resentments and political elites determined to resolve disputes by violence and ethnic cleansing, and in light of early and concerted Western engagement and mediation, the outcome in Macedonia was considerably better than elsewhere in former Yugoslavia. In August 2001, the leaders of what were then Macedonia's four governing parties, two of which were Macedonian and two Albanian, signed the Ohrid Framework Agreement.[164]

---

162 See Kevin Adamson and Dejan Jović, 'The Macedonian-Albanian Political Frontier: The Re-articulation of Post-Yugoslav Political Identities', *Nations and Nationalism* 10, no. 3 (2004): 293–311.

163 See Human Rights Watch, *Crimes against Civilians: Abuses by Macedonian Forces in Ljuboten, August 10–12, 2001* (New York: Human Rights Watch, 2001). In March 2005, the ICTY indicted the Macedonian Interior Minister Ljube Boškoski and Johan Tarčulovski for violations of the laws or customs of war. On 10 July 2008, the Trial Chamber convicted Tarčulovski and sentenced him to 12 years in prison, while Boškoski was acquitted of all charges. In May 2010, the Appeals Chamber upheld Tarčulovski's sentence and Boškoski's acquittal. For case information, see www.icty.org.

164 The Ohrid Peace Accord granted the Albanian minority several concessions, including an amnesty for NLA recruits; the use of Albanian as a second official language in administrative districts where Albanians comprised more than 20% of the population; equal opportunity in higher education; and proportional representation in the state administration and security forces. The Ohrid Peace Accord also envisioned a series of laws designed to decentralize the Macedonian administration. On the negotiation of inter-ethnic tensions in daily life and in Macedonian society, see Vasiliki Neofotistos, 'Beyond Stereotypes: Violence and the Porousness of Ethnic Boundaries in the Republic of Macedonia', *History and Anthropology* 15, no. 1 (2004): 1–36.

Assessing the Yugoslav Wars

The war in former Yugoslavia originated in the policies of political elites who sought to realize nationalist projects by invoking symbolic politics to mobilize their populations in a time of momentous systemic crisis. These elites made calculated decisions that exacerbated the existing political crisis and led to war. The Serbian leadership under Milošević brought into play the dynamics of symbolic politics and mass protest after 1987 to solidify their institutional power and to sustain their popular support. Following the collapse of the Yugoslav League of Communists and multiparty elections in 1990, the Serbian leadership forged an alliance with democratically elected Serb nationalists in Croatia and Bosnia and intervened repeatedly to support them if not to guide their every action between 1991 and 1995. The ultimate objective of this alliance was the consolidation of Serb polities in Bosnia and Croatia and their eventual affiliation in a confederal arrangement with Serbia and Montenegro. The Serb national revolution of 1987 to 1992 was inspired from above but advanced from below by popular, indigenous Serb nationalist movements.

Several leading figures in the Yugoslav drama have provided important testimony against former allies, while some have acknowledged their complicity and offered statements of contrition. The former Croatian Serb leader Milan Babić, who committed suicide while in ICTY custody, testified against several former colleagues whom he accused of stoking insurrection and provoking armed conflict. Babić emphasized the role of elites, claiming that the campaign in which he was a participant originated with Milošević, who ultimately 'orchestrated' the rebellion from Belgrade, which deliberately played on real fears within the Serb community.[165] Indeed, in November 1992, Croatian Serb leaders travelled to Belgrade to meet with Milošević, who agreed to a draft plan on the RSK's defence.[166] According to a former JNA Counterintelligence Service officer, who served from February 1992 to August 1995 as a liaison officer with the SVK (Serb Army of the Krajina, i.e. the Army of the RSK), the RSK's most important structures were under Belgrade's control.[167]

The role of political elites was decisive in the Yugoslav war. Far more than hatred, financial resources and materiel are essential for the successful conduct of wars. From the beginning of the war in Croatia and Bosnia, the Belgrade authorities financed local Serb political elites, their incipient states, officialdom and in particular their militaries. Evidence introduced in the Milošević and other trials indicates that a 'single financial plan' existed whereby all three armies – the Army of Yugoslavia (VJ, after April 1992), the VRS and the SVK – were centrally funded. The flow of funds began to slow only after Belgrade began curtailing its profligate printing of money from January 1994, which had fuelled hyperinflation in Serbia.[168] Radovan Karadžić

---

165 Jungvirth, 'Martic "Provoked" Croatian Conflict'.
166 Emir Suljagić, 'Milošević Trial: Puppet States Financed from Belgrade', *IWPR Tribunal Update*, no. 308, 7–11 April 2003, see https://iwpr.net/global-voices/milosevic-trial-puppet-states-financed-belgrade (accessed 16 June 2021).
167 Klarin, 'Milošević suffers "exhaustion"'.
168 The Norwegian forensic accountant Morten Torkildsen was commissioned by the Office of the Prosecutor of the ICTY to review thousands of pages of correspondence and official documents concerning financial transactions between Serbia and the RS and RSK. Torkildsen testified that, based on his review of the documentation and financial records, he had not 'seen any other external source of finance for the RS and RSK'. Milošević agreed with his assessment insofar as the Bosnian and Croatian Serbs had nowhere else to turn but Serbia, denying responsibility for the ways in which they spent the money. See Emir Suljagić, 'Milošević Trial: Puppet States 'Financed from Belgrade'. The report is available as Morten Torkildsen, 'Amended Expert Report of Morten Torkildsen', Case No. IT-02-54-T, 7 June 2002, at www.icr.icty.org.

admitted Belgrade's crucial significance to the Bosnian Serb war effort in early May 1994, when he remarked that 'without Serbia, nothing would have happened, we don't have the resources and we would not have been able to make war'.[169] Similarly, the Bosnian Croat assault in April 1993 against their erstwhile Muslim allies would have been unsustainable without the logistical, financial and political support of the Croatian authorities, which condoned HVO actions in 1993–94.

The policies of ethnic cleansing pursued during the Yugoslav Wars were therefore not merely a by-product of the war. In multi-ethnic Bosnia and Croatia, the only means of attaining nationally homogeneous polities was through policies of ethnic cleansing. This was by necessity a violent process. In a country where 1.2 million citizens declared themselves to be 'Yugoslavs' in 1981 – of whom more than 700,000 were in Bosnia and Croatia, representing nearly eight per cent of the population of the two republics – it could not be otherwise.[170] The wartime circumstances afforded political elites, whether at the state or local level, an opportunity to impose violent solutions on civilian populations, often beyond the scrutiny of their own public and international opinion, while simultaneously habituating perpetrators to follow orders and participate in killings. In some localities, neighbours undeniably perpetrated violence against their neighbours. Quite apart from the wider ideological motives at play, war is a transformative phenomenon and civil conflict 'often transforms local and personal grievances into lethal violence'.[171] Elsewhere, it was 'outsiders' – army recruits, reservists or paramilitary thugs – who swept through towns and villages terrorizing the civilian population and prompting its flight. Multiple and variegated motives were often at play, including ideology, necessity and fear (the perceived sense of threat, and belief that extreme solutions were required), in addition to local vendettas and opportunities to settle grievances, among others.[172] As the cases cited in this chapter indicate, the 'ordinary men' phenomenon was important. But the worst occurrences of mass violence in the Yugoslav war – Vukovar, Srebrenica, Operation Storm and Kosovo – involved modern armies with professional officers who were prepared to implement policies of ethnic cleansing and, at Srebrenica, even genocide when directed by their political masters.

This chapter has suggested that the question of who controlled the state – in addition to their ruling ideology, the relative strength of the political regime, and the international climate – is critically important in determining the likelihood as well as the timing, nature and scale of political violence. In the case of the Yugoslav War, the violence may have been initiated by ideologically motivated and illiberal political elites in support of their nationalist political projects, but in the circumstances of state collapse, irregular warfare and rising nationalist sentiment in a multi-ethnic setting, the violence invariably tended to be highly brutal and even deeply personal. As in the period before and during the Balkan Wars (1912–13), so too during the Yugoslav War, the successor states directed or co-opted irregular paramilitary forms of violence and eventually institutionalized them within their own military and police structures. In doing so, these states effectively condoned earlier instances of irregular violence since it ultimately contributed to the realization of their nationalist projects. What should also be clear when thumbing through the pages of other chapters of this volume, however, is that there was nothing inevitable or peculiarly Balkan about the violence witnessed in this context.

---

169 Cited in Sara Darehshori, *Weighing the Evidence: Lessons from the Slobodan Milosevic Trial* (New York: Human Rights Watch, 2006), 16.
170 On the Yugoslav census data, see Judah, *The Serbs*, 311–15.
171 Kalyvas, *The Logic of Violence in Civil War*, 389.
172 See Drakulić, *They Would Never Hurt a Fly*.

Homogenous nation states are now generally the norm in the Yugoslav successor states and this is perhaps the most significant consequence of the Yugoslav Wars. In four of the seven Yugoslav successor states today, the dominant nation comprises more than 80 per cent of the population. Only Bosnia-Herzegovina, Macedonia and Montenegro are exceptions, but even in the Bosnian case, the Dayton-imposed political division cannot conceal the fact that the country's two entities are now largely ethnically homogeneous. And yet, the region has stabilized since the 1990s, notwithstanding the fact that many of its states continue to suffer from a serious democratic deficit and remain either semi-consolidated democracies or transitional/hybrid regimes.[173] Slovenia and Croatia have joined both the EU and NATO. Political elites in the other successor states remain committed in principle to reform and EU accession, even if this process has stalled. While public opinion about NATO remains deeply divided in Serbia, where many remain bitter about the 1999 intervention and subsequent loss of Kosovo, which declared unilateral independence in February 2008,[174] the political establishment is committed to EU accession. Noteworthy problems persist, however. Among the major regional deficiencies are the relatively weak pace of reconciliation and the slow process of coming to terms with the past. Despite the conviction of the Bosnian Serb leaders Radovan Karadžić and Ratko Mladić in March 2019 and June 2021, respectively, of genocide, war crimes and crimes against humanity,[175] the causes and meaning of the Bosnian war remain highly contested. Although 2020 marked the twenty-fifth anniversary of the Dayton Agreement, it also highlighted the comparatively poor state of relations among several of the region's states. This was demonstrated in a number of competing commemorative events centred on Operation Storm and the Srebrenica genocide in Bosnia-Herzegovina, Croatia and Serbia. There has been progress over the last 25 years, but the Yugoslav Wars continue to cast a long shadow.

---

173 This is an assessment shared by Bertelsmann Stiftung's international Transformation Index (BTI) and Freedom House, among other international observers. See the BTI 2020 report for East-Central and Southeast Europe at https://www.bti-project.org/en/reports/regional-dashboard-ESE.html?&cb=00000 (accessed 5 July 2021) and Freedom House's *Freedom in the World 2021* report at https://freedomhouse.org/report/freedom-world/2021/democracy-under-siege (accessed 5 July 2021). On recent 'democratic backsliding' in the region, see Damir Kapidžić, 'The Rise of Illiberal Politics in Southeast Europe', *Southeast European and Black Sea Studies* 20, no. 1 (2020): 1–17; and Miran Lavrič and Florian Bieber, 'Shifts in Support for Authoritarianism and Democracy in the Western Balkans', *Problems of Post-Communism* 68, no. 1 (2021): 17–26.
174 Opposition to NATO is less pronounced in Montenegro, but several opposition groups continue to oppose the country's membership in the alliance. For example, see Sasa Dragojlo, 'Anti-NATO Protesters Demand Referendum in Serbia', *Balkan Insight*, 4 March 2016, https://balkaninsight.com/2016/03/04/serbian-rightists-protest-demanding-referendum-on-nato-membership-03-04-2016/ (accessed 16 June 2021); and, 'Montenegrin Government Facing Confidence Motion', *Radio Free Europe Radio Liberty*, 25 January 2016, https://www.rferl.org/a/montenegro-nato-confidence-vote/27509711.html (accessed 16 June 2021).
175 In November 2017, the ICTY's Trial Chamber convicted Mladić and sentenced him to life imprisonment. In June 2021, the Appeals Chamber of the IRMCT upheld the original verdict. See https://www.irmct.org/en/news/21-06-08-appeals-chamber-international-residual-mechanism-criminal-tribunals-delivers (accessed 5 July 2021). In March 2016, the ICTY's Trial Chamber convicted Karadžić of genocide, crimes against humanity and violations of the laws or customs of war and sentenced him to 40 years' imprisonment. In March 2019, the IRMCT's Appeals Chamber upheld the original sentence and imposed a sentence of life imprisonment. For the IRMCT judgment, see https://www.irmct.org/sites/default/files/casedocuments/mict-13-55/appeals-chamber-judgements/en/190320-judgement-karadzic-13-55.pdf (accessed 5 July 2021).

Further reading

Booth, Ken, ed. *The Kosovo Tragedy: The Human Rights Dimensions* (London: Frank Cass, 2001).
Bringa, Tone. *Being Muslim the Bosnian Way: Identity and Community in a Central Bosnian Village* (Princeton, NJ: Princeton University Press, 1995).
Browning, Christopher R. *Ordinary Men: Reserve Police Battalion 101 and the Final Solution in Poland* (New York: Harper Collins Publishers, 1992).
Burg, Steven L., and Paul S. Shoup. *The War in Bosnia-Herzegovina: Ethnic Conflict and International Intervention* (Armonk, NY: M.E. Sharpe, 1999).
Cohen, Lenard J., and Jasna Dragović-Soso, eds. *State Collapse in South-Eastern Europe: New Perspectives on Yugoslavia's Disintegration* (West Lafayette, IN: Purdue University Press, 2007).
Cohen, Lenard J. *Serpent in the Bosom: The Rise and Fall of Slobodan Milošević* (Boulder, CO: Westview, 2001).
Crnobrnja, Mihajlo. *The Yugoslav Drama* (Montreal: McGill-Queen's University Press, 1996).
Daalder, Ivo H. *Getting to Dayton: The Making of America's Bosnia Policy* (Washington, DC: Brookings Institution Press, 2000).
Daalder, Ivo, and Michael E. O'Hanlon. *Winning Ugly: NATO's War to Save Kosovo* (Washington, DC: The Brookings Institution, 2000).
Darehshori, Sara. *Weighing the Evidence: Lessons From the Slobodan Milosevic Trial* (New York: Human Rights Watch, 2006).
Djokić, Dejan, ed. *Yugoslavism: Histories of a Failed Idea, 1918–1992* (Madison, WI: University of Wisconsin Press, 2003).
Djukić, Slavoljub. *Milošević and Marković: A Lust for Power*, trans. Alex Dubinsky (Montreal: McGill-Queen's University Press, 2001).
Doder, Duško, and Louise Branson. *Milošević: Portrait of a Tyrant* (New York: The Free Press, 1999).
Dragović-Soso, Jasna. *'Saviours of the Nation': Serbia's Intellectual Opposition and the Revival of Nationalism* (London: Hurst and Montreal; McGill-Queen's University Press, 2002).
Drakulić, Slavenka. *They Would Never Hurt a Fly: War Criminals on Trial in The Hague* (London: Abacus, 2004).
Durch, William J., ed. *UN Peacekeeping, American Politics, and the Uncivil Wars of the 1990s* (London: Palgrave Macmillan, 1996).
Gow, James. *Legitimacy and the Military: The Yugoslav Crisis* (London: Pinter, 1992).
Gow, James. *The Triumph of the Lack of Will: International Diplomacy and the Yugoslav War* (New York: Columbia University Press, 1997).
Gutman, Roy. *A Witness to Genocide* (New York: Macmillan, 1993).
Helsinki Watch, *War Crimes in Bosnia-Hercegovina*, vol. 1 (New York: Human Rights Watch, 1992).
Helsinki Watch, *War Crimes in Bosnia-Hercegovina*, vol. 2 (New York: Helsinki Watch, 1993).
Human Rights Watch, *Crimes against Civilians: Abuses by Macedonian Forces in Ljuboten, August 10–12, 2001* (New York: Human Rights Watch, 2001a).
Human Rights Watch, *Croatia: Impunity for Abuses Committed During Operation Storm and the Denial of the Right of Refugees to Return to the Krajina* (New York: Helsinki Watch, 1996).
Human Rights Watch, *Under Orders: War Crimes in Kosovo* (New York: Human Rights Watch, 2001b).
Human Rights Watch. *Human Rights in Eastern Slavonia: During and After the Transition of Authority* (New York: HRW, 1997).
Ingrao, Charles, and Thomas A. Emmert, eds. *Confronting the Yugoslav Controversies: A Scholars' Initiative*, 2nd ed. (West Lafayette, IN: Purdue University Press, 2012).
Jović, Dejan. *Yugoslavia: A State that Withered Away* (West Lafayette, IN: Purdue University Press, 2009).
Judah, Tim. *Kosovo: War and Revenge* (New Haven, CT: Yale University Press, 2000).
Judah, Tim. *The Serbs: History, Myth and the Destruction of Yugoslavia* (New Haven, CT: Yale University Press, 1997).
Kaufman, Stuart J. *Modern Hatreds: The Symbolic Politics of Ethnic War* (Ithaca, NY: Cornell University Press, 2001).
Lampe, John R., and Mark Mazower, eds. *Ideologies and National Identities: The Case of Twentieth-Century Southeastern Europe* (Budapest: CEU Press, 2004).
LeBor, Adam. *Milosevic: A Biography* (New Haven, CT: Yale University Press, 2004).
Lukic, Rénéo. *Europe from the Balkans to the Urals: The Disintegration of Yugoslavia and the Soviet Union* (Oxford: Oxford University Press, 1996).

Magaš, Branka, and Ivo Žanić, eds. *The war in Croatia and Bosnia-Herzegovina, 1991–1995* (London: Taylor & Francis, 2001).
Mazower, Mark. *The War in Bosnia: An Analysis* (London: UK Citizens' Committee for Bosnia-Herzegovina, 1992).
Meier, Viktor. *Yugoslavia: A History of its Demise* (London: Routledge, 1999).
Mertus, Julie A. *Kosovo: How Myths and Truths Started a War* (Berkeley, CA: University of California Press, 1999).
Naimark, Norman M., and Holly Case, eds *Yugoslavia and its Historians: Understanding the Balkan Wars of the 1990s* (Stanford, CA: Stanford University Press, 2003).
Pavlakovic, Vjeran. *Red Stars, Black Shirts: Symbols, Commemorations, and Contested Histories of World War Two in Croatia* (Seattle, WA: National Council for Eurasian and East European Research, 2008).
Pejanović, Mirko. *Through Bosnian Eyes: The Political Memoir of a Bosnian Serb* (West Lafayette, IN: Purdue University Press, 2004).
Perritt, Henry H. *Kosovo Liberation Army: The Inside Story of an Insurgency* (Chicago, IL: University of Illinois Press, 2008).
Pettifer, James. *The Kosova Liberation Army: Underground War to Balkan Insurgency, 1948–2001* (New York: Columbia University Press, 2012).
Phillips, John. *Macedonia: Warlords and Rebels in the Balkans* (New Haven, CT: Bloomsbury, 2004).
Ramet, Sabrina P. *Balkan Babel: The Disintegration of Yugoslavia from the Death of Tito to Ethnic War*, 2nd ed. (Boulder, CO: Westview, 1996).
Ramet, Sabrina P., and Vjeran Pavlaković, eds *Serbia since 1989: Politics and Society under Milošević and After* (Seattle, WA: University of Washington Press, 2005).
Riedlmayer, András. *Killing Memory: Bosnia's Cultural Heritage and Its Destruction* (Philadelphia, PA: Community of Bosnia, 1994).
Schwegmann, Christoph. *The Contact Group and its Impact on the European Institutional Structure*, Occasional Papers, no. 16 (Paris: The Institute for Security Studies, Western European Union, 2000).
Sell, Louis. *Slobodan Milosevic and the Destruction of Yugoslavia* (Durham, NC: Duke University Press, 2002).
Sells, Michael Anthony. *The Bridge Betrayed: Religion and Genocide in Bosnia*, 2nd ed. (Los Angeles, CA: University of California Press, 1998).
Silber, Laura, and Allan Little. *The Death of Yugoslavia*, rev. ed. (New York: Penguin, 1997).
Stiglmayer, Alexandra, ed. *Mass Rape: The War Against Women in Bosnia-Herzegovina* (Lincoln, NE: University of Nebraska Press, 1994).
Tanner, Marcus. *Croatia: A Nation Forged at War* (New Haven, CT: Yale University Press, 1997).
Thomas, Robert. *The Politics of Serbia in the 1990s* (New York: Columbia University Press, 1999).
Tindemans, Leo, et al. *Unfinished Peace: Report of the International Commission on the Balkans* (Berlin and Washington, DC: Aspen Institute and Carnegie Endowment for International Peace, 1996).
Udovički, Jasminka, and James Ridgeway, eds. *Burn This House: The Making and Unmaking of Yugoslavia* (Durham, NC: Duke University Press, 2000).
Ullman, Richard H., ed. *The World and Yugoslavia's Wars* (New York: Council on Foreign Relations, 1996).
Wachtel, Andrew. *Making a Nation, Breaking a Nation: Literature and Cultural Politics in Yugoslavia* (Stanford, CA: Stanford University Press, 1998).
Watson, Rubie S., ed. *Memory, History, and Opposition under State Socialism* (Santa Fe, NM: School of American Research Press, 1994).
Woodward, Susan. *Balkan Tragedy: Chaos and Dissolution after the Cold War* (Washington, DC: Brookings Institution, 1995).

INDEX

Abyssinia *see* Ethiopia
Ada 15
Adrianople 15, 19, 125
Agram *see* Zagreb
Albania 4–5, 11, 14, 20, 24–6, 36, 49, 64, 111, 122–3, 125, 128–9, 141, 150, 152, 166, 174, 176, 179, 182, 188, 196–7, 207, 211, 252–3, 263–4, 282–4, 286, 311–14
Alsace 180
Anatolia 4, 24, 26
Ankara 24, 124
Archangelsk 97, 98
Armenia 15, 24
Asinara Island 49
Athens 15, 18–20, 34, 125, 172, 175
Augustów 164
Auschwitz (death camp) 124, 128, 137, 139, 142, 148–53, 156, 167, 181, 187, 205
Austria 9, 30, 32, 36, 41–2, 44, 48, 50, 53–5, 60, 66, 75–6, 83, 86, 92, 94, 96, 105–6, 125, 133, 138, 140, 143–4, 147–9, 152–4, 156, 167, 178–81, 221, 235, 283; *see also* Austria-Hungary
Austria-Hungary 3–4, 6, 9, 11, 22–3, 30, 34–5, 37–8, 43–4, 46, 48–52, 54, 59, 64, 73, 83, 91, 92–3, 101, 105–6, 110, 118, 123

Babi Yar (execution site) 124, 147
Bachka 130
Balkans 1–23, 25–7, 34–7, 51–2, 54, 61–2, 65, 67, 75, 78, 80, 82, 88, 92–6, 98–9, 101, 110, 112, 124, 126–7, 129, 131–2, 138–9, 141, 155, 165–6, 172, 174–5, 178, 180, 189, 251–2, 284–5, 292, 294, 303–4, 306, 309, 311, 313, 316–17
Baltic States 30, 38, 40, 47, 56, 58, 64, 70, 72, 78, 80–2, 84, 89, 91, 93, 95–6, 99, 101, 105, 117, 122, 124, 126, 129, 135, 141–3, 153, 155, 157–9, 161, 165–9, 171, 176–7, 181–2, 187–90, 194, 202, 209–10, 212, 215, 232, 237, 255, 257
Banja Luka 125, 178, 291, 295–6, 304
Baranja 287
Barbara (coal mine) 179
Belarus 30, 58, 60, 65, 82, 90, 97, 122, 162, 187–8, 210, 257
Belgium 91, 129
Belgrade 19, 35, 46, 54, 56–7, 66–7, 105, 125, 129, 138, 140, 147, 169, 244, 248–9, 257, 282–5, 287, 290–1, 306, 311, 313–16
Belzec (death camp) 124, 148–9, 156, 168
Berlin 1, 5, 7, 11, 34, 51, 62, 78, 94, 105, 108, 124, 143, 147–8, 151, 153, 184, 195, 205, 208, 219, 227, 245, 256–7, 262, 271, 275, 309
Bessarabia 26, 92–3, 125, 130, 132, 140, 146, 155, 158–61, 166, 169, 189; *see also* Socialist Republic of Moldova
Białowieża 59
Białystok 40, 79, 105, 124, 135, 146, 154
Bihać 291, 295, 308
Bijeljina 294, 304
Bitola *see* Monastir
Bizerte 44
Blagaj Japra 296
Bleiburg 178–9, 283
Bohemia 33–4, 37, 46, 48, 71, 124, 129, 133, 149
Bosanski Novi 296–7
Bosanski Šamac 297
Bosnia 3, 9, 19, 26, 54, 94, 107, 123, 137, 141, 155, 167, 172–4, 178–9, 185, 189, 213, 257, 282–301, 303–17
Bosnia-Herzegovina 3, 19, 26, 107, 213, 282–6, 288, 290, 292–5, 299–300, 307–10, 317–19
Bosniak-Croat Federation 307, 309–10
Braşov 240, 262–3

Index

Brest 40, 77, 81, 89, 105, 124, 153, 257
Brioni 288–9
Brno 105, 183
Bryansk 124, 137, 162
Bucharest 12, 19, 35, 44, 46, 57, 59, 61–2, 67, 105, 124–5, 213, 257, 269, 272
Buchenwald (concentration camp) 181
Budapest 19, 34, 48, 91, 105, 108, 124–5, 151–2, 163, 172, 208, 216, 220–1, 226, 231, 248–9, 257, 267–8, 271
Budapest (ghetto) 152
Bukovina 37–9, 54–5, 57, 65, 92–3, 130, 140, 146, 158–9, 161, 189
Bulgaria 1–3, 5–10, 12–23, 25–6, 35–7, 41, 43, 49, 52, 54, 56–7, 62, 64, 70, 81, 91, 93–4, 104, 107, 109, 113, 117–18, 122–3, 125, 127, 129–30, 132, 139–41, 145, 150, 152, 155, 157, 166, 170, 177, 180, 182, 185, 188–9, 195–6, 202–3, 207–8, 211–15, 217–18, 221–3, 225–8, 230–1, 234, 251, 253–4, 256, 266–8, 270–2, 313
Bulgarian People's Republic *see* Bulgaria
Bydgoszcz 40, 136
Bykyvnia 160

Cameroon 91
Canada 97
Carinthia 141, 178, 185
Carpathians 41–3, 99
Carpatho-Ukraine 130, 132
Cazin 213
Cernăuți 40, 46, 54, 64, 67, 105, 125, 257
Chełm 142
Chełmno *see* Kulmhof (death camp)
Chernobyl 267
China 128, 137, 189
Choroszcz 135
Chyrów 76
Cieszyn Silesia 72, 91
Cisleithania 37, 48, 55, 59
Compiègne 67
Constanța 19, 56
Constantinople *see* Istanbul
Corfu 44
Côte d'Azur 260–1
Courland 40, 56, 59, 205
Cracow 40, 45–6, 105, 124, 134, 144, 148, 156, 160, 244–5, 251, 257, 264
Cracow-Plaszow (concentration camp) 156
Crete 5, 10, 137, 154
Crimean Peninsula 137
Croatia 3–4, 23, 82, 85, 94, 96, 109, 111, 117, 123, 129–30, 132, 137, 140–1, 149, 153–5, 157, 165–7, 169–70, 172–4, 179, 182, 189, 213, 244, 251–2, 257, 282–93, 301–3, 306–11, 313–17
Croatia-Slavonia 23

Cuba 260
Czechoslovakia 70, 82, 85, 91–2, 113–17, 122, 127, 133, 152, 155, 181–4, 188–9, 196, 202–4, 208, 211–13, 215–16, 218, 222–4, 227, 230, 232–6, 242–6, 248, 256, 267–8, 270–1, 274–5, 293
Czech Republic 80, 180, 182, 195, 235; *see also* Czechoslovakia; Protectorate of Bohemia and Moravia
Częstochowa 133

Dąbrowa Basin 59
Dalmatia 94, 129, 131, 166
Danzig 134–5, 181, 210, 236–7, 251, 255, 257–8
Daugavpils 142
Dayton 307, 309–11, 317
Dęblin 142
Dęblin-Irena (POW camp) 142
Denmark 105, 124, 129, 257
Dilessi 5
Dobro Pole 23
Dobruja 56–7, 130, 132
Dodecanese Islands 150
Doxato 139
Drama 21, 75, 139, 284
Dubrovnik 105, 125, 175, 257, 291

East Prussia 37, 39, 41, 51, 64, 153, 181, 183
Edirne *see* Adrianople
Elbląg 255
Epirus 5
Estonia 30–1, 48, 56, 58, 70, 89, 99, 147, 157–8, 161, 164, 170, 187, 209, 210–11, 257
Ethiopia 128
Europe 2–3, 5–6, 8–13, 16, 20, 27, 31, 36, 38, 46, 54, 67, 71, 73–9, 80, 83, 85–7, 90, 92–3, 97–8, 101, 111–12, 115, 122–3, 126–9, 131–2, 138, 142, 145, 147, 152–4, 166, 168, 170, 172, 176, 180, 189–90, 195, 207, 245, 275, 288, 309, 312

Federal Republic of Germany 182, 184, 239
Finland 70, 158–9
Fiume 19, 27, 93, 105, 125, 257
Flanders 43
Foča 294, 310
France 24, 43, 81, 98, 106, 108, 115, 127, 129, 131, 152, 180, 309, 311

Galați District 213
Galicia 33, 37–9, 48, 52–5, 57, 65–6, 73, 90, 96, 109, 123, 144, 146, 154, 176, 187
Gdingen 181, 237, 255
General Government 129, 134–5, 139, 144–5, 148, 153
General Governorate of Lublin 40, 60
General Governorate of Warsaw 55, 60, 62

German Democratic Republic 183–4, 196, 207–8, 211–12, 215–16, 219–20, 223, 227, 234, 250, 256, 268, 270–1
Germany 23, 30, 36, 38, 42, 50–1, 58–60, 63, 70–1, 75–6, 79, 83, 91, 95–8, 105, 108, 112, 115–18, 123–33, 135–40, 142–58, 160–71, 174–8, 181–4, 187–90, 195, 198, 202, 206, 208, 215–16, 219–21, 227, 234, 239, 253, 256, 268, 270–1, 273, 309; *see also* Federal Republic of Germany; German Democratic Republic; Weimar Republic
Gibraltar 208
Giurgiu 267
Gołdap 259
Goli Otok 228–9
Goražde 291, 295
Gorj county 262
Gorlice 41–2, 67
Gospić 301–3
Gottschee 140
Graz 52, 291
Great Britain 38, 98, 108, 111, 124, 206, 236, 293, 309
Greece 2–3, 5–7, 9–13, 16–22, 24–7, 34, 70, 86, 91, 93–4, 99, 112, 122–3, 125–6, 129–30, 132, 139, 150, 153–5, 157, 162, 165–7, 170, 174–7, 180, 189, 191, 211
Grodno 40, 64

Habsburg Empire *see* Austria-Hungary
The Hague 31, 50, 128, 281, 290, 300–2
Hambarine 297
Helsinki 105, 124, 232, 245, 249, 257, 260, 293–4, 309–10
Herzegovina 284, 288, 293, 307; *see also* Bosnia-Herzegovina
Horn of Africa 130
Hungary 9, 23, 30, 36, 42, 44, 46, 48, 50, 53, 60, 70, 76, 79, 80, 81, 83, 91–2, 94–6, 104–5, 107–8, 111, 113–14, 117–18, 122–3, 125, 128–30, 132, 139, 141, 143, 145, 150–3, 155, 157, 163, 166–7, 169–71, 177, 181–4, 188, 195–6, 202, 208, 211, 213–16, 220–22, 225, 227, 230–1, 233, 247–50, 256, 267–8, 270–1, 275

Iași 19, 35, 146, 163, 240, 250, 257, 263
Ilidža 305
Ilok 289
Ioannina *see* Yenya
Iran 272
Iraq 24
Ireland 68, 90, 112
Irkutsk 78
İşkodra 11, 14
Israel 208, 224, 241
Istanbul 19, 24, 78, 105, 257
Istria 26, 179, 182

Italy 11, 24, 41, 78, 93, 96, 106, 111, 115–16, 123–4, 127–31, 140, 150, 155, 157, 165–6, 174–5, 189
Ivano-Frankivsk 147
Ivano-Frankivsk Oblast 210

Jablanica 307
Janina *see* Yenya
Japan 30, 128, 137, 189, 205
Jasenovac (concentration camp) 125, 153, 283, 285
Jedwabne 124, 146, 170
Jilava 177
Jiu Valley 232, 236, 239–40, 263
Julian March 141

Kalavryta 175
Kalinin 160, 183, 257
Kaliningrad Oblast 183; *see also* Königsberg
Kalisz 51
Kamianets-Podilskyi 124, 151
Karađorđevo 288
Katyn 160, 190
Kaunas 40, 63, 105, 124, 142, 146–7, 257
Kavala 15, 21
Kazakhstan 158, 188
Kedros 154
Kephalonia 175
Keraterm (concentration camp) 294, 297, 299–300
Kharkov 124, 160
Kielce 167, 176–7, 185
Kiev 40, 90, 105, 124, 147, 160, 257
Kijevo 289
Kingdom of Poland 30, 37, 39, 58, 65
Kingdom of Serbia 22, 54; *see also* Serbia
Kirghizia 61
Kirov 50
Ključ 295–6
Klooga 156
Knićanin (internment camp) 182
Knin 287, 289
Kočevje *see* Gottschee
Königsberg 40, 45–6, 105, 124, 183
Koniuchy 162
Korićani Cliffs 298–302
Kosovo 2, 11, 13–4, 16–7, 26, 93, 125, 129, 182, 185, 252–3, 257, 263–4, 266, 282–4, 288, 291, 294, 306, 311–14, 316–17
Kozarac 297
Kozelsk 160
Kozloduy 267
Kragujevac 137, 287
Krajina 285, 287, 290, 294–301, 303, 305, 310, 315
Kraljevo 137
Kresy 1–2, 15, 33, 82, 88, 90, 92, 95–7, 106, 110–11, 129, 131–3, 138, 151, 155, 161, 164–5, 176, 181

Index

Kulen Vakuf 174
Kulmhof (death camp) 124, 148, 153, 156, 168
Kumanovo 14
Kurapaty 160

Lamsdorf (StaLag) 142
Larissa 129
Latvia 30–1, 34, 37–8, 48, 55–6, 70, 79, 84, 88, 99, 111, 147, 157, 161, 164, 187, 202, 210, 257
Lausanne 24, 180, 186
Legnica 234
Leipzig 270
Leningrad 105, 124, 137, 162, 257; see also St. Petersburg
Levant 24, 173
Libya 11, 128
Lijevče Field 178
Lika 301
Lithuania 30, 40, 48, 55–6, 58, 60–1, 63, 70, 76, 79–80, 83–5, 88–90, 99, 117, 123, 131, 133, 135, 145–7, 152, 157, 159–62, 164–6, 169, 187, 190, 210, 216, 222, 257
Livonia 34, 47
Ljubljana 125, 129, 291
Ljuboten 314
Lodz 46, 54, 57, 62–3, 65–6, 80, 138, 144, 148, 154
Lodz (ghetto) 144, 153
Łomża 146
London 16, 34, 253–4
Louvain 51
Lovech (forced labor camp) 228
Lovinac 289
Lower Austria 48, 55
Lower Silesia 181, 234; see also Silesia
Lublin 40, 60, 105, 124, 134–5, 139, 144–5, 148–9, 153–4, 156, 167–9, 251, 255, 257
Lublin Castle (prison) 154
Lublin district 139, 145
Luck 161
Lugoj 272
Lupeni 239–40
Lviv 33, 38, 40, 52, 57, 105, 112, 124, 134–5, 146, 148, 161, 172, 183–4, 257
Lviv Kulparków (psychiatric hospital) 135
Lwów see Lviv

Macedonia 1–2, 5, 7–19, 21–4, 26, 43, 52, 57, 62, 93–4, 109, 129–30, 139, 150, 257, 267, 283, 286, 311–14, 317
Macelj Forest 179
Madagascar 131
Madrid 112
Magdeburg 131
Majdanek (concentration camp) 124, 148–9, 154, 156
Manjača (concentration camp) 294, 297

Mărculeşti 146
Mariampol 61
Maribor 125, 179
Marseille 109
Mazovia 134
Meligalas 175
Memel 40, 105, 133, 257
Minsk 40, 105, 124, 160, 257
Minszek 134
Moldova see Bessarabia
Monastir 11, 16, 19
Mongolia 158–9
Montenegro 2–4, 12–3, 20–3, 51, 64, 107, 125, 129, 137, 173, 257, 284, 286, 288, 292, 315, 317
Moravia 37, 48, 124, 129, 133, 144, 149, 182, 212, 219, 234; see also Czech Republic; Czechoslovakia; Protectorate of Bohemia and Moravia
Moscow 52, 65, 78–9, 86, 115, 124, 163, 168, 187, 196–8, 205–7, 209, 211, 216–17, 220, 222, 226–8, 233–4, 241, 249, 270, 275
Mostar 19, 125, 291, 293, 307
Motru 262–3
Mount Vlašić 299
Munich 105, 124, 182, 234, 253, 257, 268

Nalibaki 162
Netherlands 129
Nisko 144
Northern Europe 167
Northern Transylvania 130, 181
Norway 105, 129, 257
Novi Sad 105, 125, 151, 257, 291
Nowogródek 155

Ober Ost 40, 58–9, 63, 65, 89
Odessa 19, 105, 124, 146, 257
Ohio 310
Okół 214
Omarska (concentration camp) 294, 297, 299–300
Oranienburg 156
Ostashkov 160
Ostrów Mazowiecka 143–4
Ottoman Empire 4–9, 11–3, 15, 17–8, 24, 41, 49, 65, 123; see also Turkey
Ovčara 289

Palestine 24
Palmiry 134
Paris 34, 68, 71, 74, 78, 80, 86, 93, 98–100, 108, 128, 231, 237, 250, 254, 261, 310, 312
Pazarište 301
Peloponnese 166, 175
Piaśnica 134
Piast (coal mine) 258

Index

Pilsen region 66, 218, 219
Pitești 228–9
Plovdiv 218
Plzeň 218–19
Podgorica 23
Podhum 138
Podrinje 310
Podujevo 306
Poland 30, 37, 39–40, 55, 57–60, 65, 70, 72, 77, 79–80, 82, 85–6, 88–91, 94, 96–9, 102, 107, 109–11, 113–14, 117, 122–3, 127–9, 131–9, 141–5, 147–9, 151–2, 154–68, 170–2, 175–7, 180–4, 186–90, 194–9, 202–6, 208, 211–24, 226–8, 230, 232–4, 236–9, 241, 245, 251, 253–6, 258–62, 265, 270–1, 299; *see also* Kingdom of Poland; Polish People's Republic; Polish Republic, Second
Polesia 155
Polish People's Republic 214, 224, 255
Polish Republic, Second 72, 74, 91, 100, 109, 161, 163–4, 180, 187, 202
Pomerania 134–5
Poniatowa (SS camp) 154
Poprad 149
Poronin 194
Posavina 288, 294
Posen 33, 40, 105, 124, 134–5, 168, 200, 219–20, 222, 237, 257
Potsdam 184, 256
Prague 32–3, 37–8, 93, 105, 124, 182–3, 196, 208, 216, 218, 226, 232–6, 239, 242–3, 245–7, 271
Prekmurje region 130
Prijedor 296–7, 299
Pripyat Marshes 131
Pristina 11, 26, 125, 264, 291
Prizren 11, 14, 19, 125
Protectorate of Bohemia and Moravia 133, 147, 149, 157
Prussia 37, 39, 41, 51, 64, 106, 153, 181, 183
Przasnysz 41
Przemyśl 52

Račak 311
Radogoszcz (prison) 154
Radom 23, 40, 201, 238, 285
Radomir 23, 285
Rambouillet 312
Razgrad 266
Reichsgau Danzig-Westpreußen 134
Reichsgau Wartheland 148–9
Republic of the Serb Krajina 290
Republika Srpska 290–1, 295–8, 303–5, 310, 315; *see also* Bosnia
Rēzekne 142
Rhodes 150, 175

Riga 34, 38, 40, 46–8, 54, 56–8, 63–5, 89–90, 105, 124, 142, 147, 156, 180, 257
Riga-Kaiserwald (concentration camp) 156
Rijeka *see* Fiume
Rivne 147
Romania 1–4, 12, 20, 25–7, 33, 35–7, 39, 41, 44, 49, 52, 54, 56, 58–61, 63–8, 70, 81, 91–2, 96, 104, 107, 109, 111, 113–18, 122–3, 127–8, 130, 132, 140–1, 143, 146, 149–50, 152–5, 157, 163–4, 166–7, 169–72, 177, 181, 183, 188–90, 195–7, 202, 205, 207, 212–14, 216, 221–5, 227–30, 232, 239–40, 249–51, 253–4, 256, 262–3, 265–70, 272–3, 285
Rostov-on-Don 58, 124
Równe *see* Rivne
Russe 267
Russia 6, 9, 22–3, 30–1, 33–5, 37–53, 55–8, 60–1, 63–5, 67–8, 70–1, 73–90, 91–2, 96–101, 103–8, 110, 115, 118, 123, 127, 131, 137, 142–3, 158–9, 178, 186, 204–5, 214, 234, 241, 257, 309; *see also* USSR
Šabac 51
Sajmište (concentration camp) 138, 147, 169
Sakarya 24
Salonika 12, 15, 19–20, 105, 125, 132, 150, 157, 257
Sandžak 174
Sanski Most (concentration camp) 296–7, 305
Sarajevo 19, 105, 125, 141, 173–4, 213, 257, 282, 285–6, 288, 290–2, 295, 305, 308, 310
Savenay 106
Serbia 3–7, 9, 12–3, 16–7, 20–3, 25, 33, 35, 41, 45, 49–51, 54, 58–60, 65, 68, 75, 81, 86, 107, 129–30, 137–8, 140–1, 147, 153, 157, 167, 170, 173, 178, 284, 286–7, 290–2, 294, 303, 305–6, 308, 311–12, 315; *see also* Kingdom of Serbia; Republic of the Serb Krajina; Republika Srpska
Sered 149
Sérres 15, 21
Sèvres 24
Shumen 266
Siberia 81, 88, 97, 163
Siedlce 142
Sighet 229
Silesia 72, 91, 134, 139, 144, 181, 234, 258
Silesia (coal mines) 258
Skopje 11, 14, 19, 21, 105, 125, 257, 291
Slavonia 23, 94, 287, 290
Slovakia 48, 64, 79, 91, 99, 117, 123, 128, 130, 132, 139, 141, 149, 157, 166–7, 170, 177, 182, 185, 195, 202, 235, 267, 271
Slovenia 41, 53, 64, 129–32, 135, 140–1, 165, 167, 178–9, 231, 257, 285–8, 290, 293, 317
Smolensk 79, 124, 257
Smyrna 19, 24
Sobibor (death camp) 124, 148–9, 156

Socialist Republic of Moldova 210; *see also* Bessarabia
Sofia 19, 105, 124–5, 257, 291
Sokolac 296
Soldau (SS camp) 134
South Moravia 182, 212
South Tyrol 138
Soviet Union *see* USSR
Spain 112, 115, 127
Srebrenica 291, 295, 306, 308, 316–17
Stalingrad 139, 176
Stanisławów *see* Ivano-Frankivsk
Starobelsk 160
Štip 21
St. Petersburg 31, 34, 58, 65; *see also* Leningrad
Stutthof (concentration camp) 124, 156
Styria 53
Sudeten region 133, 139, 182
Suez 220
Switzerland 208, 235
Szczecin 237, 255
Szpęgawsk 134

Tallinn 40, 105, 124, 209, 217, 257
Tannenberg 67
Târgovişte 273
Tarnopol 146
Tarnów 41
Tartu 89
Thalerhof (concentration camp) 52
Theresienstadt (ghetto) 149
Thessaloniki *see* Salonika
Thessaly 5, 18, 129
Thrace 5, 13, 15–9, 57, 130, 132, 139–40, 150
Thuringia 58–9
Timiş county 272
Timişoara 125, 272, 291
Tirana 205
Toplica 22, 54
Topol'čany 177
Transcarpathia 151, 182
Transdanubia 92
Transleithania 64
Transnistria 125, 130, 146, 149, 153, 172
Transylvania 26, 35, 41, 44, 92, 116, 125, 130, 151, 181, 184–5, 204, 216, 227, 268
Travnik 299
Trawniki (SS camp) 154
Treblinka (death camp) 124, 148–50, 156
Trieste 182
Trnopolje (concentration camp) 294, 297–9
Trnovo 306
Turkey 4, 7, 9, 17, 24, 34, 141, 180, 211, 266–7, 271; *see also* Ottoman Empire
Tuva 158
Tuzla 291, 295

Ukraine 58, 60, 77, 81–2, 86, 88, 90, 95–6, 99, 101–2, 122–3, 132, 137, 139, 142, 145–6, 151, 158–9, 161–2, 164–5, 167, 176, 187–9, 210–11
Ulster 91
Upper Silesia 91, 139, 144
Ural 86, 104, 304
USA 97–9, 108, 207–8, 218, 253, 260, 268, 292, 310
USSR 22, 32, 64, 67, 73, 77, 86–8, 98–100, 110, 117, 122–3, 126–7, 129–31, 135–7, 139, 143, 145–7, 149–52, 155, 157–61, 163–70, 174, 180–1, 183–6, 188–90, 196–7, 202–6, 208–13, 215–16, 222–3, 227, 230, 232–4, 241–2, 253, 256, 273, 275, 281, 284, 295, 304, 309

Vadu Roşca 213
Vardar Macedonia 26, 62, 150
Vareš 307
Varna 266
Vasiliada *see* Zagorichani
Večići 300
Vendée 88, 106
Verdun 41
Versailles 67, 127
Viannos 154
Vienna 19, 34, 37–9, 46–8, 51, 53, 55, 60, 62, 78–9, 105, 124–5, 130, 139, 244, 257
Vietnam 236
Vilnius 63, 84, 162
Višegrad 310
Vistula Land 34
Vitez 307
Vojvodina 151, 179, 182, 184, 252, 257, 284, 288
Volhynia 110, 123, 139, 155, 162, 166, 176, 180, 187–8
Vukovar 289–90, 311, 316

Warsaw 31, 33–4, 40–1, 46, 55, 57–8, 60, 62–7, 79–80, 90, 99, 105, 107, 109–10, 124, 136, 156, 159, 168, 177, 186–7, 196, 199, 214, 216, 220, 222, 226, 231, 233, 238, 241–2, 251, 257, 264, 271
Warsaw (ghetto) 144, 168
Warsaw-Wola (city district) 187
Warthegau 147–8, 156
Washington 78
Weimar 91, 115
Weimar Republic 115; *see also* Germany
Western Europe 104, 112, 126–7, 133, 137, 153, 155, 158–9, 206
Westphalia 61–2
White Russia *see* Belarus
Wrocław 250–1, 255, 264
Wujek (coal mine) 258
Wyszków 79

Xanthi 15
Xinjiang 158–9

Yalta 206
Yenya 11, 161
Yugoslavia 4, 23–7, 70, 85, 91, 93–4, 98–9, 109–11, 113, 117, 122–3, 127, 129–30, 132, 137–8, 140–1, 154, 157, 162, 164–8, 173–9, 181–2, 188–90, 196–7, 202, 211–14, 228, 230–1, 235, 244, 251–2, 264, 274, 280–95, 304, 306, 309, 311–15

Zagorichani 10
Zagreb 19, 23, 105, 125, 140, 178, 252, 257, 286, 289, 291–2, 302
Zamość-Hrubieszów region 139
Zemun 138, 147
Zenica 308
Žepa 295
Zhytomyr 40, 124, 139
Žilina 149
Zvornik 294, 304–5, 310